Educational Organization
and Administration

Prentice-Hall Education Series

DAN H. COOPER, *Editor*

second edition

Educational Organization

and Administration

Concepts, Practices, and Issues

EDGAR L. MORPHET

Professor of Education Emeritus
University of California, Berkeley

ROE L. JOHNS

Head, Department of Educational Administration
University of Florida

THEODORE L. RELLER

Dean, School of Education
University of California, Berkeley

Prentice-Hall, Inc., Englewoods Cliffs, New Jersey

In its first edition this book was called:

Educational Administration
Concepts, Practices, and Issues

Library of Congress Catalog Card Number: 67-12197

Printed in the United States of America C-23670

current printing (last digit):

10 9 8 7 6 5

PRENTICE-HALL INTERNATIONAL, INC., London
PRENTICE-HALL OF AUSTRALIA, PTY. LTD., Sydney
PRENTICE-HALL OF CANADA, LTD., Toronto
PRENTICE-HALL OF INDIA (PRIVATE) LTD., New Delhi
PRENTICE-HALL OF JAPAN, INC., Tokyo

to our wives

Camilla

Gladys

and Marjorie

Preface

During the eight years since the first edition of this book was published, many changes have occurred in education and in educational organization and administration. Because these changes have been so significant and far-reaching, it became apparent to the authors that mere updating and minor revisions in the book would not suffice to meet present and future needs. Consequently for this edition, the original materials have been almost completely rewritten and many new concepts introduced.

In the first part of the present edition we have drawn on the behavioral sciences and on the findings from important research studies to provide a sound theoretical basis for many of the concepts, practices, and issues discussed and analyzed in later sections of the book. While educational administration has not yet become a science based on rational and defensible theory, much progress has been made. Most of the significant research in educational administration during recent years has been cast in a theoretical framework. There are now many defensible guidelines that can and should be used by school boards and administrators throughout the country in planning changes and making adjustments in educational programs. This book, therefore, should be of interest and value to school-board members and administrators, as well as to college and university students who are preparing to become administrators or researchers and to the increasing number of teachers who are interested in or concerned about the organization and administration of education.

In this edition theories pertinent to educational organization and administration are presented and applied to practice. Both theory and managerial "know how" are emphasized. All practice is based on some kind of theory, and the modern administrator as well as the researcher should understand the theoretical assumptions underlying educational organization and administration.

As stated in the preface to the original edition, the authors believe that:

> The kind and quality of leadership provided in educational administration is particularly important in the democratic society in which we live, because education is so basic to the satisfactory functioning of that society and superior leadership is essential for the development of an adequate program of education. The educational leader of the future ... must be a highly competent person who believes in democracy, in the potentialities inherent in people, and in the significance of the educational process; a person who has the knowledge, insights, ability, and skills needed to function successfully as a recognized educational leader in helping people identify, analyze, and solve satisfactorily the problems with which they and their society are confronted.

One of the distinctive features of this book is the selection and rather extensive discussion of pertinent problems and emerging issues relating to the topics considered in each chapter. Part 1 is concerned primarily with basic principles, concepts, and issues relating to the organization and administration of education in America; Part 2, with the implications of these theories and concepts for the organization of public education; Part 3, with the implications for the administration of the educational program.

EDGAR L. MORPHET
ROE L. JOHNS
THEODORE L. RELLER

Contents

Educational Organization and Administration

part one

Basic Principles, Concepts,
and Issues

1

The System of Education

The leaders of most countries now recognize that education, or the lack of it, may represent the difference between orderly progress and chaos; however, their assumptions in developing and implementing programs of education vary greatly. Such assumptions have a direct bearing on the purposes that will be recognized, on the plan for the organization and administration that will be developed, and on the procedures that will be used to implement the program of education. They may not only affect the progress of a nation, but also may help to promote understanding or serve to create international tensions.

SOME INTERNATIONAL CONCERNS

The purposes of education that are accepted and the procedures used by a nation's leaders in implementing the program may promote enlightenment and progress for all citizens or may perpetuate ignorance and misery or generate dangerous biases for many. Education has tremendous potential for good or for evil. Among the problems faced by nations that attempt to develop an adequate plan and program for education are one or more of the following:[1]

[1]Adapted from Theodore L. Reller and Edgar L. Morphet, eds., *Comparative Educational Administration* (Englewood Cliffs, N.J.: Prentice-Hall, Inc., 1962), Chap. 1; and Roe L. Johns and Edgar L. Morphet, *Financing the Public Schools* (Englewood Cliffs, N.J.: Prentice-Hall, Inc., 1960), pp. 1–7.

1. The leaders or the group in power may not want the masses to be educated or even recognize the importance of an adequate program of education for all citizens, including minorities against whom there may be strong biases.
2. The members of the controlling group may be so interested in promoting some ideology or fostering some form of nationalism that they fail to recognize the dangers inherent in such a policy and ignore the importance of attempting to provide a sound basis for encouraging better understanding among the peoples of the world.
3. A country's resources may be so limited that little progress can be made, even though the people and their leaders recognize the importance of a good program of education for all and desire to create one.
4. Although a nation may have the resources needed to provide an excellent program of education, the people or their leaders may become complacent because their material needs have been satisfied and may fail to devote a sufficient proportion of their resources to education to assure good schools and institutions of higher learning.

Recent Developments and Needed Studies

During recent years, most nations have become increasingly interested in providing better and more defensible systems and programs of education. This interest has been stimulated by many developments, including the establishment and contributions of the United Nations Educational, Scientific, and Cultural Organization (UNESCO). The UNESCO constitution succinctly states some basic objectives for all member nations and, hopefully, for all nations. However, these trends do not suggest that nations will or should adopt identical systems of education. Some differences, growing out of the diverse cultures, are to be expected and may, in fact, be stimulating and challenging to others. At this stage, most national plans have some weaknesses as well as some strengths. Continuing study is needed to provide background and information that will enable the people of each country to gain better insights into some of their own problems and possibilities.

Improved communication and transportation, provisions for exchange of educational personnel, programs of international cooperation, the establishment of international professional societies and organizations, and many other recent trends have contributed to a growing interest in educational policies, problems, and procedures in other countries. Such trends have also led to an awareness of the need for and value of various kinds of comparative and analytical studies and to more widespread recognition of the fact that much can be learned from studies of certain major developments and problem areas that transcend national boundaries. Systematic analytical and comparative studies in such areas as the following, in which present "solutions" or ways of dealing with problems often differ significantly, should be of interest and benefit to people in many nations:

1. The major educational problems, needs, and ways of meeting them in the rapidly growing cities and metropolitan areas in many countries;
2. The problems for students and the profession arising from increasing specialization in education and ways of maximizing the advantages and minimizing the disadvantages of such specialization;
3. Ways of making the curriculum more functional and meaningful for students at all levels, and of placing in proper perspective the traditional "classical" emphasis, especially in underdeveloped countries;
4. The most appropriate uses of newer media of instruction (such as educational television, programmed learning and audio-visual materials) and the role of the teacher in connection with each;
5. The role, use, and misuse of tests and examinations in the learning situation;
6. The role of educators and of laymen in developing and implementing policies relating to various aspects of the educational program in the schools;
7. The contributions, advantages, and disadvantages of the various kinds of professional organizations for education that have been developed in various countries;
8. The extent to which theory relating to instruction and to the organization and administration of education is culturally oriented, and the possibility of developing culture-free theories;
9. The provisions for, the role and the use of research in education, and ways of increasing its contributions;
10. The extent of control of education by political, religious and other groups and the implications for organization, administration, teaching and learning;
11. The extent of centralization and decentralization for various aspects of education and the implications;
12. The preparation, selection, and role of administrators in relation to teaching and learning and to the operation of the instructional staff;
13. The procedures used and the people involved in the development of national educational policies as related to the kinds of policies developed and to the appropriateness of the program;

14. The procedures used in developing long-range plans for organizing, administering, and financing education and in adjusting them to meet emerging needs, and their implications for the program and its functioning.

The Purposes of Education

Every society and nation has been and will continue to be confronted with the same basic problem: How can its members, especially the children and youth, best learn what they must know and what they should do to survive and to contribute to the preservation, welfare, and improvement of the group to which they belong?

Each society or nation has not only established procedures for educating the young but has also come to accept purposes of education such as one or more of the following: to provide for security, to assure conformity, to preserve stability, to prepare for the hereafter, to develop the potentialities of each individual, or to provide for the continuous improvement of society. The purposes of education that grow out of the ideas, beliefs, values, and ways of looking at things developed by members of a particular group, society, or nation tend to change somewhat over a period of years but, in the absence of some catastrophic or unusual circumstances, generally evolve slowly.

Issues Relating to Educational Organization and Administration

In developing a system of education, the leaders—or the people—of each nation have been confronted at one time or another with the four basic issues listed below, each of which has implications for the others. The manner in which each of these issues was resolved had direct implications for the educational structure as well as for the program.

What should be the relation of education to organized religion?

What should be the relation of education to the political state?

What should be the relation of education to the individual citizen?

What should be the relation of the state to the individual and his development?

RELATION TO RELIGION.   In many countries in which the leaders and a majority of the people belong to one church or religious organization, that organization has either been given control of education or has had a decisive voice in determining how the schools should be organized and operated. For example, the Concordat at Rome signed by Spain in 1857 provided that "Public instruction in the universities, colleges, and seminaries, public and private schools of every description must be at all points in harmony with the teaching of the Catholic Church."[2] In the Concordat of 1953, the right of the Church to control education was again affirmed. At the other extreme is the Soviet Union, which has sought to prevent religious groups from having any active role in education. The United States has attempted to avoid both extremes, providing for the separation of church and state but recognizing the right of religious groups to organize and operate schools of their own.

RELATION TO STATE. Education may be either partly or entirely an instrument of the group in control of the national government or political state, or may have a more autonomous position. Communist Russia and other totalitarian countries have made education a definite arm of the group controlling the political state for the purpose of perpetuating and promoting communist or fascist ideologies. On the other hand, the people of America have gone to great lengths to ensure that education is not dominated by any partisan political organization or controlled by any agency of the federal government. However, this does not imply that education has been isolated from political considerations, or that it should be.

EDUCATION AND THE INDIVIDUAL. The relation of education to the individual citizen has also varied greatly from country to country. The medieval concept of preparing leaders with a strong religious background constituted the basis for the class systems of education developed in many countries. The emphasis in those countries was on the organization of a system of higher education for the leaders, often the most wealthy, with only schools of lower grade for the others. In the United States, the emphasis to some extent has been reversed. Elementary schools were developed for everyone and only gradually were provisions made for secondary schools and colleges. Thus schools in America have been organized to provide opportunities for all, rather than primarily for selected leaders.

THE STATE AND THE INDIVIDUAL. One of the key issues to be resolved in the various countries concerns the relationship of the central government to each individual citizen and his development.[3] In totalitarian countries, chief emphasis has been placed on preserving and perpetuating the state by molding and using individuals for state purposes. In the democratic nations of the world, on the other hand, emphasis generally has been placed on the development of the individual citizen as a con-

[2]Nicholas A. Hans, *Comparative Education* (London: Routledge and Kegan Paul, Ltd., 1950), p. 111.

[3]I. L. Kandel, *Comparative Education* (Boston: Houghton Mifflin Company, 1933), Chap. 3.

tributing member of the group. It is believed that if each citizen is helped to develop in accordance with his capacity and is encouraged to learn to think and evaluate for himself, he will contribute more to the welfare of the state than a citizen who is molded in some predetermined pattern. As stated in the 1956 report of the White House Conference on Education: "This policy of encouraging each child to develop his individual talents will be of greatest use to the nation, for in the long run, if no talent is wasted in our land, no skill will be lacking."[4]

Organization and Administration Related to Purposes

Not only the different purposes of education, as recognized and accepted by the nations existing today, but also the different decisions regarding the basic issues discussed previously, have tended to determine the plan for organization, control, and administration of schools that each country has developed. The countries that believe education should serve the interests of the controlling group, whether that group be political or religious or a political-religious partnership, have generally developed a highly centralized system of education. In such countries, the policies are developed primarily by the leaders and must be observed by all schools and by the groups interested in operating the schools. The entire educational program must be operated within the pattern established for the purpose of developing citizens who will contribute directly to the objectives and welfare of the group that controls the government. Any thinking that is encouraged must be within the framework of the ideologies accepted by the controlling group.

In the democratically organized countries, however, especially in the United States and England, most people have been seriously concerned about avoiding centralized partisan control of education by any group, especially in matters relating to what is taught and how it is taught. In most of these nations the chief objective has been to develop a government that promotes national welfare by educating citizens to think through problems and reach sound conclusions. The control of schools has generally been primarily in the hands of the citizens instead of being vested in religious or political leaders.

Thus in any society the establishment of an educational program calls for some kind of a plan and an organization for carrying it out. In primitive groups the organization was usually relatively simple. As society became more complex and formal educational institutions were developed, the need for an appropriate organization to facilitate achievement of the accepted purposes of education became apparent. As modern nations began to develop, they came to accept different purposes for

[4]*A Report to the President* (Washington, D.C.: Government Printing Office, 1956), p. 10.

education, consistent with what seemed to be their national interests. Each attempted to create a system of education and an organization that seemed appropriate to carry out its purposes. As would be expected, these systems and organizations differed considerably in both structure and functions.

SIGNIFICANCE OF CHANGE

Changes that affect people in one way or another have occurred throughout the history of man. Some of these resulted from natural events; others were brought about by man himself. Thus, the fact of change is not new. What is new is the sharply increasing rate at which changes have occurred during recent years, the variety and kinds of changes that have been taking place, and the role of man in the process of effecting changes.

This challenging and, to many people, disturbing new situation has come about largely because (1) a far larger proportion of the people in many countries are much better educated and informed than ever before and, consequently, are more able to understand problems, recognize inconsistencies, and contribute to solutions; (2) the great increase in new knowledge and understanding tends to stimulate and facilitate the development of further knowledge, discoveries, and inventions, and (3) in several countries an ever increasing share of the resources is being devoted to many kinds of research that result in new knowledge, new theories and, in some cases, in discrediting traditionally accepted assumptions.

All available information points to the conclusion that the rate of discovery, change, and the addition of new knowledge will continue to increase. In the immediate future, however, the rate of increase will be much greater in some parts of the world and perhaps in certain areas of knowledge and action than in others. The resulting imbalances are almost certain to create major tensions and problems that will need to be resolved.

This rapid expansion of knowledge and insights carries tremendous —probably even some unanticipated—implications for the future of mankind. It could and should lead to the further liberation of man and to marked improvements in civilization, but it will also bring new dangers and problems. Many of the assumptions and myths to which substantial numbers of people presently subscribe will be so completely discredited they will have to be abandoned. Even some of the values and value systems held by individuals and groups in various parts of the world will have to be modified. There will probably be difficult periods of confusion and uncertainty for many, but new possibilities and hope for almost everyone should emerge if mankind can learn how to manage and utilize new knowledge and change for the improvement of civilization.

Implications for Education

Not only new knowledge and insights but many innovations and changes have implications for education. Perhaps the most obvious are the curriculum implications of new theories, information, and discoveries in the sciences and mathematics that have already resulted in some major adjustments. Curriculum changes require not only new instructional materials but modifications in teaching-learning procedures, perhaps even in classrooms and in certain aspects of organization or administration. But even more far-reaching changes involving many aspects of the entire educational system are already in prospect as a result of developments during the past few years.

In most organizations there are some people who might well be classified as perennial advocates of change. They seem to view change as something that is highly desirable, regardless of the evidence pertinent to a particular situation. At the other extreme are some—often many—who resist change. Their reaction to any proposal for change tends to be negative, perhaps because it is viewed as a threat to their established habits and patterns of thought. Between these two extremes are those who view change as something that may be either beneficial or harmful, depending on the factors involved, and who support the kinds of change that should enhance their own potential, or enrich and improve the society in which they live.

The above statements are apparently as applicable to people serving in educational organizations as to people generally. At any rate, there is considerable evidence that many school systems and institutions of higher learning have been quite slow in adopting important innovations in education.[5] Such evidence indicates that many educators, for some reason, have failed to adopt a number of changes found to be beneficial. In view of the rapidly increasing rate at which change is taking place in society and the wide variety of changes that are occurring, any serious lag in making needed adaptations should become a major concern, and vigorous steps should be taken to remedy the situation. Some of these should be concerned with the organization, and others with the perceptions and points of view of the personnel involved.

As Gardner has so appropriately pointed out, "It is necessary to discuss not only the vitality of societies but the vitality of institutions

[5]See D. H. Ross, ed., *Administration for Adaptability* (New York: Metropolitan School Study Council, Teachers College, Columbia University, 1958).

and individuals. They are the same subject. A society decays when its institutions and individuals lose their vitality."[6]

The vitality of an organization, an institution, or a society is basically determined by the vitality of its personnel. In the field of education, this means that the vitality of administrators, of the facilitating staff, of the teachers and other employees, and of the students is directly related to the vitality of schools and institutions of higher learning.

The attitude of teachers toward change and innovation, as it is reflected in the teaching and learning process, is important in any society. If teachers encourage their students to court change indiscriminately, they may help to establish the climate for chaos. If, on the other hand, they assist their students to develop a sound basis for appraising the implications of change and to bring the results into line with the evolving purposes of society, they are contributing to orderly progress.

These observations, supplemented by evidence already available concerning the teaching and learning process, point to the conclusion that all teachers must clearly recognize and accept their responsibility for helping to prepare every student to do the following:

1. Look forward to a future that will bring many changes and to accept the responsibility for helping to shape that future;
2. Recognize his special aptitudes and abilities, and thus facilitate the development of his individuality;
3. Develop a sound basis for accepting a defensible and evolving system of moral and ethical values for guidance in exercising his responsibilities as a citizen;
4. Recognize that happiness comes primarily from progress in achieving and helping others to achieve worthwhile goals and objectives;
5. Seek and utilize learning and knowledge as a basis for understanding meanings in relationship to his life and to society;
6. Learn to use the scientific method as a basis for studying and resolving the problems he encounters.

Implications for Organization and Administration

If teachers and other educators are to contribute significantly to the vitality and progress of students and of society, the organization (school system or institution) with which they are associated must provide a favorable climate. Among other things, this means that the purposes, policies, and regulations must facilitate the employment and

[6]John W. Gardner, *Self Renewal: The Individual and the Innovative Society* (New York: Harper & Row, Publishers, 1964), p. 2.

effective functioning of competent personnel who are interested in preparing students to contribute to constructive, orderly change. This climate is least likely to be found in communities in which substantial numbers are fearful of any change and suspicious of those who believe in preparing for change. It is unlikely to be favorable in situations in which administrators are primarily concerned with stability based on traditional concepts, as contrasted with the "stability in motion" that should be associated with progress.

In every community and state, there are pressures for and against change that come from individuals and groups. These pressures create problems that, unless resolved, can result in confusion and chaos for students as well as for staff. One important step is for administrators, teachers, and all other members of the staff to find ways of helping people realize that many of the changes that are occurring require adjustments to be made in the educational program and process, if the needs are to be met. Another is for everyone, especially administrators, to understand better the process—the dynamics—of constructive change. This is a matter concerning which many people in education have been poorly informed, and about which greater understanding is urgently needed.

First, it is essential that some of the barriers to change be recognized. Gardner has listed several under the heading, "Obstacles to Renewal."[7] He points out that most of these are to be found in the minds of people, rather than in external arrangements. Thus, major obstacles include the habits, attitudes, precedents, and belief systems of people. He also notes the tendency of people to become nostalgic about the "good old days" and often to defend present practices by relating them to "high moral principles." Among the obstacles are vested interests, detailed and stultifying rules and regulations, an overconcern with how to do things the "approved" way, and a tendency to be suspicious of innovators and to discredit them.

Carlson, after expressing concern "about the ability of the public schools to make rapid and adequate adaptation to our fast changing times,"[8] listed three barriers to change: (1) The absence of an institutional "change agent" position, such as the county agent for agriculture, who has as his major function the advocacy and introduction of innovations into practice; (2) a weak knowledge base about new educational practices (evidenced by the limited research, experiment, and development practices), as contrasted with that available to the county agent;

[7]*Ibid.*, Chap. 5.
[8]Richard O. Carlson, "Barriers to Change in Public Schools," in *Change Processes in the Public Schools* (Eugene, Ore.: Institute for the Advanced Study of Educational Administration, University of Oregon, 1965), pp. 3–8.

and (3) the establishment of the public school system as a "domesticated" organization which cannot select its clients and whose clients must accept its services. He notes that when important elements of the environment are stable, the necessity for changes is reduced. He might have added that, as important changes occur in certain aspects of the environment of the schools, the situation becomes less stable and change may be facilitated.

In most school systems the administrators are in a position to play a key role in facilitating or in retarding changes and innovations. Those who seek to play the latter role can hardly claim to be "educators" in the modern sense. Those who serve as facilitators can attempt to serve directly as "change agents" or advocates of particular changes, or as what has been called "process initiators." When the evidence regarding the need for a change is strong or reasonably conclusive, the administrator might be justified in assuming the role of "advocate." When the evidence is weak or controversial, the administrator might better assume the role of process initiator—that is, of appointing or arranging for the appointment of a committee or taking other steps to assure that all aspects and implications of the proposal are carefully studied and discussed as a basis for recommendations. A third role, which would be appropriate under certain conditions, might be that of a mediator or catalyst, whose purpose is to facilitate agreement so decisions can be made.

Miles has noted that ". . . successful efforts at planned change must take as a primary target the improvement of *organization health* —the school system's ability not only to function effectively, but to grow and develop into a more fully functioning system."[9] He listed six interventions aimed at improving organizational health: (1) team training, (2) survey feedback of information about attitudes, opinions, and beliefs of members of the system, (3) role workshop or conference of all people in a particular role, (4) target setting and supporting activities, (5) organizational diagnosis and problem solving, and (6) organizational experiment.

It seems apparent that every state and local school system and educational organization must develop defensible plans for effecting appropriate changes, if it is to be prepared to meet future needs. (Consult Chapters 3 to 6 for discussion of basic theory and research.) These plans should be based on considerations such as the following:

1. Appropriate steps should be taken to attempt to ensure that the organizational health is good and that the climate is conducive to the introduction and implementation of defensible innovations.

[9]Matthew B. Miles, "Planned Change and Organizational Health," in *Change Processes in the Public Schools*, pp. 11–32.

2. There should be a conscious effort to include as members of the organization people who are interested in new ideas and procedures and are sufficiently mature that they are not likely to be seeking change for the sake of change.
3. There should be a continuing search within the system, in other school systems and universities and even in other countries and other disciplines, for ideas that seem worthy of consideration and that can be used to develop an inventory and categorization of promising concepts.
4. Appropriate procedures should be developed for analyzing and evaluating the ideas and concepts that seem most promising. The findings of pertinent research studies, analyses of experiences elsewhere, and value judgments should be sought as a basis for distinguishing between defensible concepts and ideas that have little merit.
5. From time to time, the most promising concepts should be selected, with the concurrence of the people who would be involved, for introduction in some school or aspect of the educational program. There should be assurance that all conditions are as favorable as possible for the successful introduction and implementation of these concepts.

EDUCATIONAL ADMINISTRATION AND THE BEHAVORIAL SCIENCES

While educational administration undoubtedly differs in a number of respects from other types of administration, there apparently are some common elements. Lazarsfeld commented as follows on four major tasks faced by all administrators which vary chiefly in relative emphasis:[10]

1. The administrator must fulfill the *goals* of the organization.
2. The administrator must make use of *other people* in fulfilling these goals, not as if they were machines, but rather in such a way as to release their initiative and creativity.
3. The administrator must also face the humanitarian aspects of the job. He wants people who work for him to be happy. This is *morale*—the idea that under suitable conditions people will do better work than they will under unsuitable conditions.
4. The administrator must try to build into his organization *provisions for innovations,* for change and for development. In a changing world, people must adapt to changing conditions.

Administration has been discussed as a common-sense approach to and method of dealing with problems, as an art and as a series of techniques that can best be transmitted from one administrator to another.

[10]Paul F. Lazarsfeld, "The Social Sciences and Administration: A Rationale," in *The Social Sciences and Educational Administration,* eds. Lorne Downey and Frederick Enns (Edmonton: University of Alberta, 1963), pp. 3 and 4.

While some of these elements will undoubtedly persist, the evidence shows that the study and practice of administration is becoming more scientific from year to year. But, as Gross has pointed out, ". . . although administrative thought has made tremendous advances the greatest advances still lie ahead."[11]

The practice of educational administration, as well as of administration in general, is becoming more scientific because the body of pertinent knowledge is being increased by scientific study. Progress in the development of a theory or theories of administration, increases in the volume and quality of research, and other developments have brought new knowledge and understanding that provide sounder bases for improvements in various aspects of administrative operation.

Both education (including teaching and learning) and educational administration are much more complex and have many more facets than were formerly recognized by most people. Through research by psychologists, social psychologists, anthropologists, sociologists, political scientists, and economists, as well as by professional educational researchers, many of the dimensions of the educational and administrative process have been discovered. These findings have resulted in many significant improvements in the curriculum and in methods, materials, organization, and administration. It is important to recognize that many of these advances would not have been possible without the contributions made by the behavioral sciences (often referred to as the social sciences). All of these sciences are concerned with the behavior of man, as are people in the field of education. However, each is concerned with different aspects of man's behavior, or with analyzing the same item of behavior in terms of different concepts.[12]

All these sciences hold that the behavior and products of men can best be understood on the basis of three concepts: (1) *goals* (end states or conditions), (2) *functions* (activities by which men achieve goals), and (3) *arrangements* (structures and mechanisms for arranging activities). Psychology has been primarily interested in the study of individualistic attributes of people and other organisms; the other disciplines, with collective attributes that grow out of group interaction.

Many studies made by behavioral scientists have not been directly concerned with education or educational administration. Nevertheless, these studies have provided significant information and insights that have led to a better understanding of individual behavior, group processes,

[11]Bertram M. Gross, "The Scientific Approach to Administration," in *Behavioral Science and Educational Administration,* ed. Daniel E. Griffiths, The Sixty-third Yearbook of the National Society for the Study of Education, Part II (Chicago: University of Chicago Press, 1964), p. 33.

[12]This discussion is based largely on statements by Fred Fosmire and Richard A. Littman, "The Behavior Sciences—an Overview" in *Social Sciences View School Administration* (Englewood Cliffs, N.J.: Prentice-Hall, Inc., 1964), pp. 36–53.

and organizational problems. Fortunately, during recent years a number of behavioral scientists have become interested in various aspects of education ranging from board-superintendent relations, communication, and decision making, to the economics of school finance, and have made studies that provide much-needed insights and knowledge. Several of these studies are discussed at appropriate places in later chapters in this book. The major point to be emphasized here is that not only students of educational administration but practicing administrators need to be familiar with and make use of these contributions as a basis for effecting improvement in education and in educational administration.

SOME UNIQUE FEATURES OF AMERICAN EDUCATION

The policies and plans that have been developed for the organization and administration of education in the United States have a number of unique features. These features were not designed in an effort to be different; they grew out of the beliefs, attitudes, and experiences of the people who evolved the nation and its institutions.

Neither the schools nor other institutions of a nation can be understood merely by studying them as they are at present. Back of any institution is a long and complex history involving many conflicting ideas, struggles among and within various groups, a variety of experiences, and many other factors.[13] Thus, origins of the American system of education are found in European culture, but the schools were not transplanted in the form in which they had developed in any country. Concepts and practices that seemed to have value were tried out, and either modified or discarded. New ideas that were developed in this country went through a similar process. As pointed out by the Educational Policies Commission some years ago, "Every system of thought and practice in education is formulated with some reference to the ideas and interests dominant or widely cherished in society at the time of its formulation."[14] In every case the crucial but often unrecognized test applied was: *Was the practice or proposal consistent with, and did it contribute to the attainment of, the ideals and value systems that were developing in America?*[15]

[13]For a thorough discussion and analysis of the forces and factors that influenced the development of schools and other educational institutions and the provisions for the organization, administration and control, see R. Freeman Butts and Lawrence A. Cremin, *A History of Education in American Culture* (New York: Holt, Rinehart & Winston, Inc., 1953), especially Chaps. 7, 8, and 16.

[14]Educational Policies Commission, *The Unique Function of Education in American Democracy* (Washington, D.C.: National Education Association, 1937), p. 6.

[15]For discussion of sociological background and meanings, see George S. Counts, *The Social Foundations of Education* (New York: Charles Scribner's Sons, 1934); also Emile Durkheim, *Education and Sociology* (New York: Free Press of Glencoe, Inc., 1956).

Some of the unique features of the organization and administration of education found in the United States are discussed briefly below:

1. *The system of education is relatively decentralized.* The people in the respective states (not in the federal government) have the basic responsibility for the organization and control of education. In most states, much of the responsibility for the actual organization and administration of public schools has been delegated to local school districts. However, the increasing concern of the federal government about education has been indicated by provisions for financial assistance, Supreme Court decisions about the implications of Constitutional provisions, and in other ways. The extent of decentralization in the United States contrasts sharply with the marked centralization of control found in many other countries.

2. *The people, rather than educators or government officials, are ultimately responsible for all basic policies relating to education.* Though in practice many policies are cooperatively developed, the decision as to what policies are to be adopted and followed is usually delegated to the legislature and state board of education (for state policies) and to local lay boards of education selected by the people (for local policies) or, in some cases, the decision is made by the people themselves. The recommendations of educators are usually considered and often followed. In many countries, most operating policies are determined chiefly by educators.

3. *A single-track system of education open freely to all has been established.* This system, contrasting sharply with the dual systems found in many countries, is one logical outgrowth of the concept of equal opportunity in and through education for all citizens. Thus, every person, regardless of his social, economic, political, or racial background, presumably has equal opportunities to develop his talents fully so he may become a socially and economically productive citizen. These opportunities are provided through a system of public education extending from nursery school or kindergarten through comprehensive secondary schools and higher education.

4. *Although primary emphasis is placed on public schools, provision is also made for private and parochial schools.* The American people generally believe that public schools have a special and necessary contribution to make to the development and unity of the American way of life. Provision is made for such schools supported by public tax funds to be available to all, and special effort is made to assure that they are organized and operated in the interest and for the benefit of all people. Parents may, however, send their children either to public or to nonpublic schools. Private and religious agencies have been given considerable freedom to establish, control, operate, and support schools and

other educational institutions in accordance with their own concepts.

5. *The public schools and educational institutions are safeguarded insofar as possible from partisan political control.* Control of the schools or other public educational institutions by any partisan political group is considered not only undesirable but potentially dangerous. Therefore, provision is generally made for the schools to have a comparatively independent status, so there is an opportunity to resolve educational issues separately from other issues and so school boards and educators can be relatively free from domination or control by partisan agencies or groups, and even by other governmental agencies.

6. *Education in the public schools and educational institutions is nonsectarian.* No religious creed or doctrine may be taught in the public schools. Special provisions are made to assure that these schools on all levels are safeguarded against domination or control by any religious organization. Such provisions make it possible for the public schools to teach about religion and to instruct in moral and ethical values but not to present these matters from the point of view of any sect or religious organization.

7. *Americans believe that those who are responsible for the administration of their schools, as well as those who teach in the schools, should be especially prepared to meet their responsibilities.* The idea that educational administrators should have special preparation has developed slowly but is now accepted in practically all states. Outside of this country and a few others, the concept of special preparation for administrators has had comparatively little recognition or acceptance.

Purposes, Policies, and Values

As the nation developed, despite many sharp disagreements and bitter battles along the way, most people began to recognize the need for certain purposes to be achieved and to agree upon some of the basic policies and characteristics of a program of education suitable for America. These agreements grew out of the beliefs, judgments, and experiences of the people.

Statements of purposes and policies that are acceptable must reflect the values and aspirations of the people and should be based on consideration of such concepts as the following:

1. *They should be consistent with the concept that education should help the people of the nation approach the democratic ideal.* Although this ideal has never been defined to the satisfaction of all, practically everyone believes in the democratic way of life as the one most suitable for America and agrees that the schools should help to assure that it is achieved.

2. *They should make clear that the schools must provide for the education of all as a basis for national stability and progress.* It is generally recognized that democracy cannot function satisfactorily unless all members are sufficiently well educated to participate intelligently and constructively in the democratic processes and their improvement.

3. *They should assure that provisions will be made for each individual to have the opportunity to realize fully his own potentialities and, thus, be prepared to contribute to the improvement of his community, state, and nation.* When the potentialities of each individual are fully and properly developed, he should become the type of citizen needed to contribute to the improvement of the nation and, indirectly at least, of the world in which he lives.

4. *They should recognize that education constitutes one essential key to a better life for all.* Although some people are concerned primarily with abundance in a material sense, most recognize that the lives of people will be most meaningful and the improvement of civilization will proceed most satisfactorily when the "abundant" life is interpreted to include cultural, spiritual, and ethical values, as well as material qualities.

5. *They should be developed through intelligent participation, discussion, and understanding by the people.* In matters pertaining to education, Americans are not willing to leave vital decisions such as those involving purposes and policies for education to their leaders or to any one segment of the population. They believe that education is so basic and potentially so significant for the future of the nation and of the world that everyone should be encouraged to attempt to understand the problems, think through the issues, and cooperate in arriving at sound conclusions.

Purposes and Social Policy

The generally accepted statements of purposes of education in the United States constitute the guidelines for one major aspect of social policy that must be fully implemented if the democratic way of life is to function satisfactorily. Such statements have become the basis for a program of action in establishing, organizing, and operating educational institutions designed to serve as the means of satisfying the imperatives for socialization and individualization in modern society. Whether these purposes are classified under self-realization, human relationships, economic efficiency, and civic responsibility, as suggested by the Educational Policies Commission,[16] or under other defensible headings, may not be

[16]Educational Policies Commission, *The Purposes of Education in American Democracy* (Washington, D.C.: National Education Association, 1938), pp. 45 ff.

important as long as the objectives are sound and can be agreed upon.

One of the problems at present confronting the people of each state and of the nation arises from the fact that there are substantial minorities who either do not agree with some of these purposes or objectives, or are not willing to make the effort to provide the kind and quality of schools needed to attain them. At times, differences of opinion may serve to stimulate further thinking and discussion, but long-continued and emotionally supported differences may result only in confusion and uncertainty. Unless some way can be found to resolve major differences, they are likely to interfere with desirable developments. The problem has been complicated during recent years by the organization of vigorous groups of extremists who seem to be more interested in attempting to mold the educational institutions to suit their own narrow purposes than in seeking to understand the educational problems and needs of the nation.[17] The process of serious discussion—attempting to understand, taking into consideration the pertinent evidence and the points of view of others, and striving to find common ground as the basis for agreement —which has been so significant in the past, must be pursued vigorously in the future if the schools and other educational institutions are to continue as a vital force in American life.

In considering purposes of education, four important observations should be kept in mind,

1. Any program of education, including the stated or implied purposes, tends to be continued or perpetuated even after changes have occurred in the society that established the purposes, or after evidence from research has shown the need for modification.

2. Because education is so important and because of its inherent potentialities, a constant struggle may be expected between those who would use education for the improvement of mankind and those who would use it to enhance their own power and position or that of their group.

3. Continuing studies and discussions are necessary to ensure that there is agreement on purposes of education consistent with the desires and needs of the people and that schools are dynamic rather than static institutions.

4. Constant vigilance is essential to ensure that the educational program is developed for the benefit of all and not controlled by or in the interest of any one group or class.[18]

[17]See Roald F. Campbell, Luvern L. Cunningham, and Roderick F. McPhee, *The Organization and Control of American Schools* (Columbus, Ohio: Charles E. Merrill Books, Inc., 1965), Chap. 13.

[18]Adapted from statements in Malcolm MacLean and Edwin H. Lee, *Change and Process in Education* (New York: Dryden Press, 1956), Chap. 1.

ORGANIZATION AND ADMINISTRATION OF AMERICAN SCHOOLS

The general plan for organizing schools in America had to be evolved by the American people somewhat as they evolved purposes. In the early days, a relatively simple organization sufficed. However, as communities became larger and the nation developed, more thought had to be given to problems of organization. Since the educational program that was being developed had some unique features, it is not surprising that the plan for organization and control of education that eventually emerged should also be unique in certain respects. The major features of this plan are:

1. The people in each state are responsible for developing and establishing plans and making provisions for the organization and operation of public schools and institutions of higher learning designed to meet the needs of the state. (See Chapters 2 and 9.)
2. The people in each community during the early days, and now the people in each school district created as a political unit of the state, are responsible for establishing and operating schools designed to meet needs in accordance with standards established by the state. (See Chapters 10 and 11.)
3. The federal government constitutionally has no direct responsibility for controlling, organizing, or operating schools or institutions of higher learning in a state but is expected to encourage and assist the states in developing adequate and effective programs. However, the interest of the federal government in education has increased sharply and its role seems to be changing.

The plans and provisions for the organization and administration of education in this country vary considerably from state to state and, to some extent, among school districts within the same state. But there are more basic similarities than differences. These similarities have grown out of the commonly accepted purposes of education, of experiences with various types of organization, and of studies relating to the subject. As a result, there has been a gradual elimination of some of the least satisfactory developments and an increasing similarity in basic provisions that are considered desirable on the basis of purposes, experiences, and the conclusions from numerous studies. For example, the small school districts established in the early days have generally been found to be inefficient and unsatisfactory and have gradually been replaced in many parts of the country by larger districts.

There was no provision for professional educational administration of the schools in any state for many years after the nation was established. As communities and schools increased in size, more schools were established, and provision was made for financial support through taxation, it became apparent that it was necessary for some competent person to devote his attention to the problems of organization and administration. This was first considered largely a matter of management that could be carried out by a member of the board or a lay citizen. Gradually, however, it became apparent that all aspects of the program should be coordinated and improved as needed and that this was largely a professional job to be assumed by a qualified person.

As the American people have learned from various types of experiences and have had an opportunity to develop realistic concepts regarding educational administration, they seem to have reached general agreement on the following characteristics of a sound plan for the administration and operation of local school systems: (1) the policies for education should be established by a lay board of education representing the people of the area; (2) the educational program and the schools should be administered by professional personnel prepared for that specific purpose; (3) the professionally prepared administrator of the district, with the assistance of his staff, should be expected to recommend policies for consideration and approval by the board, and to execute those that are approved; (4) the schools should be adequately staffed by professionally prepared teachers and other educational specialists, whose work is facilitated by competent operation and maintenance personnel.

Many of the concepts relating to organization and to the administration of education have been considerably modified during the past few years as a result of changes in society, of governmental functions, and of insights based on research studies and findings. Further modifications seem inevitable, because the evidence, some of which is discussed in subsequent chapters, points clearly to the need for such changes.

The system (or systems) of education in this country should be viewed as constituting a (presumably) coordinated unit or part of the system of government. The organization comprises the staff that is organized for the purpose of achieving the purposes and objectives of education. The development and modification of the organization is a function of administration that attempts to relate and fuse the purposes of the schools, the staff, and of society. "It is the continuously developing plan which defines the job and shows how it can be efficiently and effectively accomplished by the people functioning in a certain social environment."[19]

[19]Daniel E. Griffiths, David L. Clark, D. Richard Winn, and Laurence Innaccone,

All organizations are affected to some extent by the prevailing forces and factors in the society and culture in which they operate. Most large organizations in particular tend to develop some of the characteristics of what has come to be called a bureaucracy.

Four fundamental concepts have commonly been used as a basis for studying, attempting to understand, and proposing improvements in organization: the task (or job), the position (relates to a grouping of tasks), the authority (who may initiate action for whom), and the administrative unit or department. For educational organizations, Charters has proposed an analysis of the *work flow* (sequence in which work operations are performed and techniques used in order to effect results) and of the *division of labor* (manner in which tasks in the school's work flow are broken up and distributed among instructional and noninstructional personnel).[20] He considered "organizational maintenance" as comprising input-output functions and work-coordinating functions. Lonsdale explained organizational maintenance as ". . . sustaining the organization in dynamic equilibrium through a developing integration of task-achievement and needs-satisfaction."[21] He noted this is a complex process which involves achieving the tasks of the organization and meeting the needs of the individual.

During recent years, the concepts of administration have moved far from the old idea of "scientific management" and "efficiency" as primary concerns, to a much greater emphasis on consideration of factors involved in human relations. In some respects, an interpretation given fifty years ago is still appropriate: "Administration is the capacity of coordinating many, often conflicting, social energies in a single organization so adroitly that they shall operate as a unity."[22]

Griffiths, after emphasizing and explaining the value of the tri-dimensional concept (the job, the man, and the social setting) for educational administration, analyzed the human-relations aspects of the motives of man, perception, communication, power, authority, morale, group dynamics techniques, decision making, and the human-relations approach to leadership.[23] Simon also gave considerable attention to the

---

Organizing Schools for Effective Education (Danville, Ill.: Interstate Printers and Publishers, Inc., 1962), p. 10.

[20]W. W. Charters, Jr., "An Approach to the Formal Organization of the School," in *Behavioral Science and Educational Administration*, Chap. 11.

[21]Richard C. Lonsdale, "Maintaining the Organization in Dynamic Equilibrium," in *Behavioral Science and Educational Administration*, Chap. 7.

[22]Brooks Adams, *The Theory of Social Revolutions* (New York: The Macmillan Company, 1914), p. 207.

[23]Daniel E. Griffiths, *Human Relations in School Administration* (New York: Appleton-Century & Appleton-Century-Crofts, 1956).

use of fact and value in decision making (both are usually involved), as well as to rationality in behavior.[24]

Present authorities are concerned with the development of a unifying theory as a way of looking at organization and administration, procedures for examining these areas, and the implications of findings from research studies. These and other basic concepts and principles of organization and administration and some of their implications for education are considered in detail in Chapter 3.

PUBLIC AND NONPUBLIC EDUCATION

Because of their belief in democracy and their conviction that all citizens must be educated as a means of assuring that democracy will function satisfactorily, most Americans have become convinced that a good system of public schools and institutions of higher learning is essential. They have depended upon the public schools to help citizens develop the knowledge and understanding necessary to resolve differences and agree upon policies and courses of action to serve the common good —that is, to create national unity out of diversity. The public schools have become the people's schools, and in general the people have been proud of their schools. Nearly eight out of every nine citizens have attended the public schools.

The American people have also recognized that, for one reason or another, some parents may not want their children to attend the public schools. The right of people to provide nonpublic schools and of their children to attend them has been established by the courts.

Theoretically, all schools are subject to control by the state, but in practice in most states there has been little control or supervision of nonpublic schools. The public schools, by the nature of their organization, are publicly controlled. Nonpublic schools are generally privately controlled. They operate under the direction of the owner or the manager, of a specially established board of trustees or, in the case of the denominational schools, under the auspices of church authorities. In this sense they are private schools, and the term "private" is frequently used to refer to all schools other than the public schools.

This book is concerned primarily with the organization and administration of public education. However, many of the basic theories of organization, administration, and leadership discussed in subsequent chapters are equally applicable to nonpublic schools.

[24]See Herbert A. Simon, *Administrative Behavior: A Study of Decision-Making Processes in Administration,* 2nd ed. (New York: Free Press of Glencoe, Inc., 1957).

SOME IMPORTANT PROBLEMS AND ISSUES

As indicated by the previous discussion, there are many unresolved issues relating to the systems of education developed in various countries. A few of the most important are discussed briefly on the following pages, and others are considered in subsequent chapters.

How Should Education Contribute to Community, State, and National Development?

Two major problems that should be of concern to educators as well as all other citizens are: (1) How can the educational program best be adapted to the needs of a rapidly changing civilization? and (2) How can and should education contribute to community, state, and national development (improvement) and help to assure that the direction and results of change will be beneficial rather than harmful?

A group of social scientists from the United States and one of the Latin American countries recently proposed the following assumptions for guidance in considering certain aspects of these problems:

1. There are important educational, social, economic, and other improvements that should be made in every nation, state, and community. The need for improvement is especially urgent in underdeveloped areas and communities.

2. From a long-range point of view, the best way to assure that needed improvements will be effected in any society is to improve the education of the people. Thus improving the knowledge, insights, understanding, and skills of the people becomes a key to the improvement of a community, state, and nation.

3. Effective planning for social change should be founded on a real desire of people for improvement and a willingness to take action leading to change on the part of the individual members of the group or groups concerned.

4. The objective of all national, state, and community improvement programs should be to promote and facilitate needed and orderly social and economic changes (improvements) by maximizing the improvement and contributions of individuals (as persons and as members of cooperating groups) and thus preserving, protecting, and enhancing respect for the rights and obligations of every citizen.

5. Insofar as practicable, improvements should be carefully and systematically planned, rather than left to chance or caprice. Plans should be developed on the basis of scientific studies and research; goals and objectives should be established by agreement among informed and competent people who should cooperate in their attainment. However, there must be an awareness that social change may occur (1) through a process of evolution, (2) through a revolution, (3) through diffusion, and (4) through planned action.

6. Community, state and national development are interrelated in many ways. Weaknesses in national or state planning and development handicap all communities; weaknesses in communities of any kind retard national and state planning and progress.

7. National plans should include policies for national, state and community development. They should provide for the national government to (1) implement directly only those aspects of the general plan which must be undertaken at that level, and (2) stimulate and encourage state and local planning in those aspects which are appropriate for state and local decisions and which, if undertaken nationally, would retard or discourage local creativity and initiative and tend to increase and to perpetuate needless centralization and control.

8. Careful development and implementation of appropriate plans for the improvement of the rural life and economy are essential for the well-balanced development and continuous progress of any nation. No aspect of the economy or culture can be neglected or permitted to lag seriously without handicapping other aspects. Changes are often interrelated.

9. While wisely and carefully developed national plans are essential for sound national progress, state and community studies and development programs need not and should not be neglected or delayed because of the lack or inadequacy of such plans. In fact, meaningful state and community development programs may stimulate and facilitate the national planning process.

10. The process of planning involves many little-understood aspects and factors and, therefore, should be continuously studied and improved as a means of safeguarding against mistakes or correcting them. Optimum safeguards are provided when competent people who are genuinely interested in bona fide community, state, and national improvements cooperate in the process of developing and appraising plans. The process is most likely to be defective or dangerous when undertaken by uninformed or selfish people who are concerned primarily with their own vested interests.

11. All plans should incorporate procedures for evaluation designed to assure that imperfections will be discovered as promptly as possible, so steps can be taken to assure needed adjustments and to avoid undesirable developments and outcomes.[25]

In what respects should these assumptions be supplemented or modified? What are some of the implications for programs and procedures for preparing teachers, administrators, and technicians who are concerned with aspects of community, state, or national improvement? for educational programs and for the organization and administration of education?

How Much Centralization Is Desirable?

There are many people who believe in a considerable amount of centralization for the purposes of efficiency. Many others vigorously

[25]Developed by the Staff, Instituto de Estudos Rurais, Fundação Escola de Sociologia e Política de São Paulo (Brazil).

resist the idea, especially at the stage of practical application. One difficulty is that the terms "centralization" and "efficiency" mean different things to different people. It is, therefore, difficult even to discuss these concepts without giving some attention to definition and interpretation.

Centralization in the field of education is often used to mean the organization of larger schools or larger school systems. On the other hand, it may mean that an increasing number of things are done—and decisions made—centrally, that is, by the central office of the school system, by the state, or even by the national government.

Such questions as the following are frequently raised: Are there certain things that can be accomplished more effectively and satisfactorily in some central office, by the state, or by the federal government than where they are now attempted? What would be the effect on the educational program of assigning additional functions to a more central organization? Could the following criteria be used for general guidance in resolving such questions: (1) *those things should be done (or decisions made) centrally that do not require or involve local initiative and responsibility and which can be done more efficiently and economically on a centralized basis; (2) those things should be decentralized and carried out at the local level which require decisions relating particularly to local needs and which, if done centrally, would prevent or limit desirable initiative and handicap the development of effective local leadership and responsibility.*

Americans generally believe that maximum provision should be made and encouragement given to local responsibility and to the development of local leadership, which becomes a major source of state and national leadership. However, the people in many other countries do not seem to be especially concerned about this concept.

It is becoming evident to many people in this country that, while primary emphasis should be on the development of a state-local partnership in education, there are probably certain things that can and should be centralized. For example, both the state and the federal government are in a much better position than most local school systems to tap and utilize effectively certain sources of revenue that should be used for support of the schools. On the other hand, teaching must be carried out in the local community, but effective teaching is made possible by resources and materials, some of which must come from without the community and state.

Issues such as the following must be resolved if some of the disadvantages of extreme decentralization or extreme centralization are to be avoided: What aspects of the program should be centralized and to what extent? How can the state, the intermediate unit, and the local school system best cooperate in developing the educational program without creating a situation in which desirable local initiative and responsibility are discouraged?

Who Should Control Education?

One of the major concerns of the American people has been to assure that public schools and educational institutions are not directly subject to control by groups or organizations that might seek to use them for their own purposes. In no other country have the people provided the safeguards sought in most sections of this country. However, the schools are always in some danger. Certain individuals and groups are constantly seeking to influence or even to control education for their own advantage. Control of education offers one promising opportunity to control the thoughts and destinies of the people in the community, state, or nation.

Most people apparently believe that education is so basic and has such tremendous possibilities for good or evil as far as community, state, and national progress is concerned, that special provisions are essential to assure that the schools will not be diverted from their major purposes. But the people are not yet fully agreed on how this can best be accomplished.

By constitutional provision, the public schools are nonsectarian. However, in some Protestant communities, school officials have collaborated in introducing or maintaining practices that have Protestant biases. In certain predominantly Catholic communities the public schools, in effect, have been operated as Catholic institutions. These practices and many others have resulted in sharp, often bitter controversies in many communities. Some of them have been held by the courts to be unconstitutional; yet they have persisted in other communities or states. How can the public schools best be operated as nonsectarian institutions in all communities, or should they be?

Most states have made a determined effort to ensure that schools will be safeguarded from attempts to use them for partisan political purposes. There are still states, however, in which not only the county superintendent but the state superintendent is elected as a Republican or as a Democrat, rather than as a professional educational leader. There are also a number of communities and some states in which board members are elected by political parties and, consequently, may owe some allegiance to those parties. Attempts to use the schools for partisan political purposes have occurred from time to time in many communities, but fortunately such attempts are usually vigorously resisted. What additional safeguards, if any, are needed to assure freedom from partisan political influences?

In almost every community and state, there are some individuals or organizations who are constantly seeking to keep the schools from doing certain things or to see that they do other things that would be contrary to the basic purposes of education. Bitter attacks have sometimes been made on boards of education and school administrators who resisted these efforts. Certain groups would, if they could, prevent children from studying about UNESCO, about evolution, about family relationships, in fact about many other matters that must be studied if children are to learn to understand and think through some of the problems of the modern world. Groups that have "axes to grind," sometimes deliberately set about to control the board of education and consequently the school program, by supporting candidates, openly or secretly, who are committed to their particular point of view. What steps can be taken to ensure that minority or even majority groups do not take over control of the schools for their own particular purposes? How can attempts to get the schools to do something that is contrary to their proper functions best be resisted?

How Can Greater Agreement Be Reached on Purposes and Objectives of Education?

Among the distinctive features of the educational program as developed in many of the democratic nations of the world, Kandel pointed out one that seems especially significant:

> A system of administration conceived as it is in England and the United States is itself educative; it demands intelligence and it elicits intelligence; it relies for the progress and success of education on public opinion and that public opinion must be enlightened; it calls for cooperation and participation of all who are concerned with education but it also creates that concern.[26]

At no time has there been adequate understanding of this unique role of education, nor has there been agreement on purposes and objectives. Complete agreement probably should not be expected. Yet, when there are significant differences of opinion, there are bound to be controversies regarding the schools, criticisms, and difficulties in working out a satisfactory program of education. The public schools need the support of the people. To the extent that this support is not forthcoming from any substantial number, the schools will be handicapped.

There are marked differences of opinion concerning the tasks of the public schools, "the fundamentals," the nonsectarian nature of public schools, adult education, vocational education, preparation of teachers—in fact, about almost every significant aspect of the educational program.

[26]I. L. Kandel, *Types of Administration* (New York: Oxford University Press, Inc., 1938), p. 43.

What procedures can be used to bring about greater agreement than exists at present on purposes and goals and in establishing priorities? In areas where substantial agreement is impossible, what should the schools do?

What Kind of Organization Is Needed to Facilitate the Attainment of Acceptable Purposes?

All citizens should have a direct concern about education. If it is seriously neglected in any state, the nation may be handicapped. The fact that a good program of education is essential for the development and continuation of a sound democratic form of government has been recognized by many from the beginning. If the federal government had been given more responsibility for education when the nation was organized, could some of the mistakes and weaknesses found in various parts of the country have been avoided? Are there any respects in which steps should be taken to develop a national system or program of education?

A few states have left public school education to be developed pretty much by communities, with comparatively little state direction or influence. In fact, schools throughout the country are often thought of as "local" schools. Would it be feasible to consider education as a local rather than a state responsibility? What should be the major responsibilities of the state for the educational program? What kind of local organization for schools is needed to facilitate the attainment of purposes generally agreed upon?

What Should Be the Place of Nonpublic Education in American Life?

The American people have overwhelmingly placed their faith in public tax-supported schools. But many individuals and groups from the beginning have vigorously opposed the development of such schools. On the other hand, the significant contributions of the nonpublic schools, and especially of the nontax-supported institutions of higher learning, have sometimes not been fully recognized.

Not only the number but the proportion of children attending nonpublic schools has increased during the past quarter of a century. By far the greatest proportion of the increase has been in attendance at Roman Catholic parochial schools. This growth apparently has resulted primarily from the policy of Catholic church officials that: "Catholic children must not attend non-Catholic, neutral or mixed schools . . ." except with special permission.[27] There has also been some growth in Jewish and Protestant schools during the past few years.

27From Title XXII, "Concerning Schools," Catholic Canon Law.

A majority of parents representing most denominations apparently prefer that their children attend public schools. Many Catholics also take this point of view. In fact, there is currently a vigorous debate within the Roman Catholic Church in this country about the future of Catholic elementary and secondary schools. Some contend that the present policy should be continued; others that it should be materially revised. Several writers have vigorously supported the latter point of view.[28] The issue of financial support and criticisms of education in parochial schools have helped to bring the problem into focus.

The controversial provision for "shared time" in the Elementary and Secondary Education Act of 1965 may have considerable impact on this situation. Some contend that it may result in an increase in parochial schools, partly because the financial pressure will be decreased to some extent; others that parochial schools may become primarily institutions for religious instruction for pupils who take most of their regular class work in public schools. Still others think the provision may be declared invalid by court action.

Up to the present time, a relatively small minority of all children have attended nonpublic schools. Suppose the time comes when a majority attend nonpublic schools of one type or another. What will be the effect on American life and attitudes? Will the ability to look at problems from a common background and point of view, and to resolve most differences of opinion satisfactorily, be decreased? Would the divisive influences in American life become more serious than they are at present?

The public schools necessarily depend on the support of the people and cannot be expected to do an adequate job unless that support is provided. When an overwhelming majority of the people in any community believe in the public schools and what they are trying to accomplish, the climate is favorable for these schools to continue to improve and to make increasing contributions to the life and welfare of the American people. When they do not have that support, they may be so seriously handicapped that they cannot provide a satisfactory educational program.

There are communities in some states where a majority of the people are supporting nonpublic schools and sending their children to them. In certain cases, these people have elected representatives to the board of education who, for one reason or another, have failed to support the public school program. In some of these communities the children who are attending public schools are being denied the opportunities to which they should be entitled. What is likely to happen to the public

[28]See, for example, Mary Perkins Ryan, *Are Parochial Schools the Answer?* (New York: Holt, Rinehart & Winston, Inc., 1964).

schools and to their contribution to American life in those communities or states in which a majority of the citizens send their children to and support nonpublic schools? Do some of the developments in Holland have any implications for people in America?[29]

Some competition between public and nonpublic schools is unavoidable and may to a certain extent be beneficial. However, Americans have learned that competition in any phase of life may have its unwholesome as well as its wholesome aspects. There has been some unfair criticism of nonpublic schools by public school supporters. Criticism of the public schools by some supporters of nonpublic schools has also, on occasion, been not only unfair but misleading. For example, the charge has frequently been made that the state is attempting to establish a monopoly of public schools even though the Supreme Court has held that cannot be done. Another criticism charges that there is an unfair system of "double taxation" on those who send their children to nonpublic schools, in spite of the fact that this is a voluntary choice.

In what respects has the American public generally been unfair in its attitude toward or criticism of public schools? of nonpublic schools? What would be the "best" solution to the problems in this area?

Selected References

Bennis, Warren C., *The Planning of Change: Readings in the Applied Behavioral Sciences.* New York: Holt, Rinehart & Winston, Inc. 1962.

Brameld, Theodore, and Stanley Elam, eds., *Values in American Education.* Bloomington, Ind.: Phi Delta Kappa, 1964.

Carlson, Richard C., and Keith Goldhammer, *Change Processes in the Public Schools.* Eugene, Ore.: Center for the Advanced Study of Educational Administration, University of Oregon, 1965.

Cramer, John Francis, and George Stevenson Browne, *Contemporary Education.* New York: Harcourt, Brace & World, Inc. 1956.

Graff, Orin B., and Calvin M. Street, "Developing a Value Framework for Educational Administration" in *Administrative Behavior in Education,* ed. Roald F. Campbell and Russell T. Gregg. New York: Harper & Row, Publishers, 1957.

Graff, Orin B., Calvin M. Street, Ralph B. Kimbrough, and Archie R. Dykes, *Philosophic Theory & Practice in Educational Administration.* Belmont, Calif.: Wadsworth Publishing Company, Inc., 1966.

Lippitt, Ronald, Jeanne Watson, and Bruce Wheatley, *The Dynamics of Planned Change.* New York: Harcourt, Brace & World, Inc. 1958.

[29]See Reller and Morphet, *op. cit,* Chap. 4.

Miles, Matthew B., ed., *Innovation in Education.* New York: Bureau of Publications, Teachers College, Columbia University, 1964.

Reller, Theodore L., and Edgar L. Morphet, eds., *Comparative Educational Administration.* Englewood Cliffs, N.J.: Prentice-Hall, Inc., 1962, Chaps. 1, 18–21.

Russell, James E., *Change and Challenge in American Education.* Boston: Houghton Mifflin Company, 1965.

Selznick, Philip A., *Leadership in Administration.* New York: Harper & Row, Publishers, 1957.

2

The Legal Basis for Education

In this chapter, major attention is devoted to the origin, development, and implications of constitutional provisions, laws, board policies, administrative regulations, and court decisions relating to education. There must be a rational authority—that is, a legal basis—for everything that is done in the way of formal education. In this country the legal basis for education, as well as for other aspects of government, has been developed and modified from time to time by the people or their representatives. The constitutional and other legal provisions, as interpreted in many instances by court decisions, determine the kind of educational program that can be provided and the provisions that can be made for organizing, administering, financing, and operating the program. In addition, the perceptions and attitudes of state and local school board members and the competencies and points of view of the educational personnel they employ have an important and often a significant influence on the effectiveness and quality of the program provided. An understanding of the major legal provisions is important for all who are concerned with education and is essential for those who have administrative responsibilities.

BASIS FOR LEGAL PROVISIONS

In all countries the legal provisions (ranging from those incorporated in the constitution, if there is one, through enactments of a legislative body, decrees or other official policy statements, administrative regulations, and court decisions) grow out of the value structure, beliefs, and concerns of the people or their rulers. The legal system may be designed primarily to protect the privileges of the group in control, to assure the perpetuation of certain customs or practices, or to provide the basis for orderly progress. In the United States, the legal provisions (of the federal government and of the states) that relate to education are a direct outgrowth of the value systems and beliefs of the citizens of the nation and of the various states regarding the place and role of education in the lives of people and in the governmental structure. These provisions are an integral part of a comprehensive legal system that constitutes a body of rules for many aspects of human conduct and that are prescribed and enforced by representatives of the organized society.

The Conceptual Design

In general, the legal provisions for education are based on what Hamilton and Mort have termed the "conceptual design."[1] This is the expression of purposes to be achieved through education and is an outgrowth of the beliefs, values, and aspirations of the people. These legal provisions are organized into a more or less consistent and rational system, and provide a place for policies and practices that are considered "good" or desirable, and a basis for rejecting those that are considered "bad" or undesirable. The conceptual design for education is not static; however, many of the basic elements are relatively constant, such as the purpose of developing a system that will provide for the education of all the children of all the people.

The evolving design is affected by changes in society that have implications for education and by new ideas and concepts regarding education. Basically, the design is affected by such factors as the following, which are often interrelated: (1) a developing theory or series of related theories concerning education and its organization and administration, (2) the findings and conclusions based on important research studies in areas ranging from learning through finance, (3) the evaluation of experiences resulting in conclusions as to what works well and what does not, and (4) new and challenging ideas and concepts which seem to hold promise.

Histories of education have directed attention to the differences in purposes and provisions that developed in the New England area, in the Middle Colonies, and in the South. Had some of the original elements of the emerging design for education in any one of these areas been accepted, the nation might have developed primarily parochial or church-

[1]Robert R. Hamilton and Paul R. Mort, *The Law and Public Education,* 2nd ed. (New York: Foundation Press, Inc., 1959), Chap. 2.

controlled schools, fee or tuition schools to which many children of poor families would not have had access, public pauper schools for the poor and private schools for the more wealthy, or some other kind of school system based on purposes quite different from those finally accepted and incorporated in the national design. However, the purposes eventually accepted were those that seemed best suited to meet the needs of the new nation. Had different purposes been accepted, the legal structure for education would necessarily have differed in basic respects from that found at present.

Apparently only a few early leaders, such as Jefferson, had much insight into the place and significance of education in a government of, by, and for the people. The process of thinking through and envisioning the kind of educational program and structure needed by the evolving democratic nation presented many problems and difficulties. While conflicting views and important differences of opinion have continued throughout the history of the nation and will undoubtedly continue into the future, the majority of the people eventually began to agree upon such concepts as the following:

1. All citizens must be reasonably well educated if a democratic form of government is to survive and to function satisfactorily.
2. The citizens themselves are responsible and must make provisions through public schools for the opportunities that are necessary to assure that everyone will be educated, since education cannot satisfactorily be left to parents, to church groups, to private institutions, or even to the discretion of local communities.
3. The people of the entire nation should be concerned about education and should be interested in helping to provide for and stimulate the development of a satisfactory program.
4. The people of each state should directly assume the responsibility for education implied by the Tenth Amendment to the federal Constitution, and should recognize and provide for the implementation of that responsibility by appropriate provisions in the state constitution and laws.

Thus the people in each state and throughout the nation began to agree on some of the chief characteristics of an educational program that they considered essential for a democratic nation. Neither the people of the nation nor those in the areas that later became states started with laws relating to education. They started with beliefs, attitudes, and ideas—with the elements of a conceptual design—that constituted the basis for legal provisions. This design is still evolving with some differences among the states, is still not entirely consistent or rational in certain respects in the minds of many people, and some aspects continue to be controversial.

Many different procedures have been used in arriving at purposes and objectives that should underlie the legal provisions for education. During recent years the people in a number of states have developed more definite plans for reviewing explicit or implied statements of purposes and objectives and for attaining agreement on those that seem appropriate for the state. This has sometimes been done by committees comprised of laymen and educators officially designated to carry on a study of the state program of education. In other cases it has been done by legislative committees. In still others it has naïvely been assumed that the people agree on purposes that are implied by laws on the statute books, and that revisions will be indicated when new laws are enacted whether or not there has been any formal statement.

Continuing or periodic study and review of basic purposes and objectives should be considered essential in every state and community. To the extent that agreement can be reached, there is an acceptable basis for developing legislation and for planning the educational program. New purposes and objectives or new emphases will emerge from time to time, and these, of course, will have implications for developments throughout the state.

There must also be policies or general guides for action that are agreed upon as useful in attempting to attain the purposes and objectives. Policies may either be expedient devices which provide for some immediately acceptable steps, or guides for carefully planned courses of action designed to facilitate the attainment of the objectives. Soundly conceived policies should result in a program of legislation and education that is consistent with statements of purposes and objectives and should promote their attainment.[2]

Cooperatively developed policies involving participation of leaders from throughout the state should help to avoid laws and actions that are inconsistent with the accepted purposes and objectives. Properly developed local policies serve for guidance of the board of education, citizens in the community, and the educational staff in planning and carrying out the local program. They should constitute the basis and serve as guides for any standards or regulations approved by the board.

The Structural Pattern

Since public education is "one instrumentality of society for the carrying out of a function which society has decreed to be a desirable

[2]See James Bryant Conant, *Shaping Educational Policy* (New York: McGraw-Hill Book Company, 1964), Chaps. 2 and 3.

one,"[3] it is not surprising that the basic provisions for the organization and operation of education are determined by the society in which it operates. Thus, the society, in the final analysis determines not only the conceptual design for education but also the structural pattern. Educators, through their concepts, ideas, and research studies, undoubtedly influence both the design and the structure in many ways, but they do not necessarily determine what either is to be. This means that educators must recognize that they are operating to some extent in the public domain and in the political arena and cannot go much beyond what the people will accept. In other words, educators can neither expect to be successful in attempting to preserve the *status quo* when the people are prepared for progress, nor to institute changes the people or their representatives are unwilling to accept. Effective two-way communication is essential. Educators must communicate and interpret research findings and new concepts and their implications, and the people must communicate effectively their own concerns and concepts. Understanding and agreement should constitute the basis for progress.

Ideally, the structural pattern for education should emerge from the conceptual design and be consistent with it. Actually, the structural pattern is determined basically by the legal system that establishes the plan for organization and operation by creating the agencies to be utilized in attaining the desired ends and allocating functions among them within prescribed limits. However, the legal system is often supplemented or extended by practices and procedures in areas not closely defined or restricted by law.

The structural pattern tends, in certain respects, to lag behind the evolving conceptual design for education. In other words, constitutional provisions, laws, and even court decisions are based on elements of the conceptual design as of a particular time. As the design changes, the legal system usually continues to require some practices and concepts that are outmoded. Many examples can be given: the continuation of small obsolete school districts, the county as an intermediate unit with an elected superintendent in areas where districts have been reorganized, the apportionment of funds on bases found by research to be unsound, and so on. Moreover, the structural pattern, for one reason or another, often omits important elements of the conceptual design or includes nonrational aspects that prevent the development of an effective program of education, at least in certain parts of the state. For example, Section 183 of the Kentucky Constitution of 1891 requires the general assembly to "provide for an effective system of common schools throughout the state." However, Section 186, until significantly revised some sixty years later, required that all state school funds be apportioned to districts on the basis of the number of children of school census age, thus making

[3]Hamilton and Mort, *op. cit.*, p. 3.

an effective system of schools impossible in many areas. Several states have so limited the authority of the board and even of the voters in local school districts that they cannot provide the funds needed to assure effective schools, even if the people may want and are expected to do so on the basis of other legal provisions.

Such inconsistencies and limitations should not be surprising. Constitutional conventions and legislatures often include some people who do not subscribe to the generally accepted conceptual design for public education or do not understand the implications of some of the provisions they advocate. The problem is likely to be particularly acute in states in which there are sharp differences of opinion concerning elements of the conceptual design, the design itself is vague or poorly formulated in certain respects, or the people are relatively uninformed or indifferent about changing needs and the characteristics of an effective program of education.

Some steps that might well be taken in any state in an effort to ensure that the structural pattern is as consistent as possible with the evolving conceptual design are the following:

1. Educational and lay leaders should systematically review the conceptual design for education periodically, in an effort to ensure that all appropriate concepts are included, that it is internally consistent, clearly stated, and has the concurrence of everyone involved.

2. Legislators and citizens in all parts of the state should be encouraged to discuss this tentative statement and to propose revisions or clarifications. This procedure should result not only in improving the statement and making it more meaningful but should facilitate understanding, agreement, and support.

3. All major legal provisions should then be reviewed as a means of identifying any handicapping lags or inconsistent aspects, and proposing revisions.

4. The legislature should be encouraged to incorporate into the legal structure elements that seem to be fully substantiated by evidence and experience, so as to make the structure as consistent as possible with the design.

5. The legislature should be expected to refrain from mandating any aspect of structure that is inconsistent with the design or that is based on an emerging concept that has not yet been adequately tried out or tested.

6. As a basis for assuring greater flexibility in introducing locally promising innovations, the legislature should provide for considerable local discretion and should refrain from restricting local boards to those educational policies and practices that are specifically authorized by law.

CONSTITUTIONAL PROVISIONS

The basic legal provisions relating to or having implications for education are found in the federal and state constitutions. Those in the federal Constitution are of significance for education throughout the country, whereas provisions found in each state constitution are applicable only to the educational program within the state.

The Federal Constitution

As far as education is concerned, one of the most significant provisions of the federal Constitution is found in the Tenth Amendment, which—like other sections of the Constitution—does not even mention education. This amendment reserves to the states or to the people all powers not delegated to the federal government by the Constitution. The power of each state to provide and maintain public schools is thus inherent in state sovereignty as established by this amendment. The provision of education for all citizens is one means the state may use to assure its own preservation. Without such a system, which provides for the development of citizens who can act rationally and intelligently on matters of public concern as well as on their own affairs, the future of a state might be jeopardized. The system of education provided by the state, therefore, is to be considered as a service to the citizens for benefit of the state, rather than as a service to the individual primarily for his own benefit, or as a charitable or philanthropic service.[4]

Four other provisions in the federal Constitution and its amendments, commonly recognized as having considerable significance for education, are discussed in Chapter 8. Most of them are concerned with the protection of what is often referred to as the inherent rights of individuals. Sections 8 and 10 of Article I prescribe, respectively, that Congress shall have power to provide, among other things, for the general welfare, and that no state shall pass any law impairing the obligation of contracts. The First Amendment prohibits Congress from making any law "respecting an establishment of religion, or prohibiting the free exercise thereof." One clause of the Fifth Amendment, which is concerned with the protection of individuals against self-incrimination in criminal cases, has been invoked in cases in which investigation committees have sought to inquire into connections teachers and others may have had with so-called "subversive organizations." The Fourteenth Amendment prohibits any state from making or enforcing any law

[4]Lee O. Garber, *Education as a Function of the State* (Minneapolis: Educational Test Bureau, Inc., 1934), p. 21.

abridging "the privileges or immunities of citizens of the United States," or from depriving any person of "life, liberty, or property, without due process of law," or from denying "to any person within its jurisdiction the equal protection of the laws." Each of these provisions has been the basis of a number of controversies involving education, as pointed out later.

Although each state has the responsibility for developing its own public school program, it cannot through its constitutional provisions or laws violate any of the provisions of the federal Constitution or of its amendments. There are thus important controls on what states may do in certain respects, but as long as these limitations are observed, the people of each state are free to develop their own educational program as they see fit.

State Constitutional Provisions

The people of each state have incorporated in their constitution some of their basic beliefs about education as well as about other aspects of government for which they are responsible. However, as new information has become available, insights and points of view have gradually changed. Some of these changing concepts have tended to be reflected in most states either in new constitutions adopted by the people or in amendments to the original constitution.

The constitution, of course, does not incorporate all the beliefs or points of view regarding any aspect of government. Others are expressed through laws, court decisions, policies, and regulations. All of these constitute the rational—and legal—authority for organizing and operating school systems and schools. Constitutional provisions are usually more difficult to modify or repeal than statutes. For that reason, it is generally considered wise to include in the constitution only those fundamental expressions of policy that guide but do not handicap the development of the educational program and are not likely to need revision in a relatively short time.

One of the policies that has found expression in some form in every state constitution (but was modified in a few of the southern states following the 1954 Supreme Court decision on segregation) is that the state legislature must provide for a uniform and effective system of public schools. Thus the people generally have not left the legislature any discretion as to whether public schools shall be established. Usually, however, it has considerable discretion as to steps and procedures that may be used in establishing such schools.

Other policies relating to education that have been expressed in the constitution of nearly every state include the following: the permanent school fund is to be kept sacred and inviolate, and only the income from the fund may be used for public school purposes; public schools are to be provided at public expense, and public tax funds made available for educational purposes are to be used only for the support of public education.

Although one objective of the people in each state seems to have been to incorporate in their constitution those provisions that require and facilitate the development of an adequate program of public education, experience has shown that restrictive or handicapping provisions have from time to time been included. For example, constitutional provisions in some states prescribe such rigid limits on taxes or bond issues for school purposes that the people in many communities cannot make the effort they would be willing to make to support schools. Thus the provisions relating to education that are incorporated in a state constitution have vital significance. They may either stimulate and facilitate the development of an adequate program of public education or make such a program difficult if not impossible of attainment until they are repealed.

The legislature of a state has full power, commonly referred to as plenary power, to enact laws regarding the schools as well as other aspects of government. However, such legislation should not conflict with provisions of the state or federal Constitution. If any such conflict exists and the matter is taken to the courts, the law will be declared unconstitutional. The following statement in a New York court decision is significant: "The people, in framing the constitution, committed to the legislature the whole law making power of the state which they did not expressly or impliedly withhold. Plenary power in the legislature for all purposes of civil government is the rule."[5]

LAWS RELATING TO EDUCATION

Laws as well as constitutional provisions relating to education should be of concern to everyone interested in education or government. Laws express policies of the people for implementing constitutional provisions and intent, and may be as significant in certain respects as constitutional provisions in determining the scope and adequacy of the educational program that can be provided. Unsound or unwise laws may be as serious as limiting constitutional provisions.

Federal Laws

Since education has been established as a function of the respective states, the basic laws relating to the organization, administration, and operation of schools are state rather than federal laws. However, the

[5] *The People* v *Draper*, 15 N.Y. 532.

people of the entire nation have always been interested in education, and as a consequence, from the time of the early land grants there have been federal laws relating to one aspect or another of education (see Chapter 8). While many of these laws are concerned with direct responsibilities of the federal government (for education of the military forces or wards of the federal government, education in certain federal areas and territories, and educational services provided by the federal government through various agencies), others are designed to aid or stimulate education in and through the states. These laws have provided for grants and services to the states for various educational purposes.

The chief problems from the point of view of many people have arisen over the requirements or controls that have been incorporated in some laws relating to financial assistance. Congress undoubtedly has a right to establish requirements that are not inconsistent with provisions of the federal Constitution. The issue is basically one as to the kind and extent of controls that seem to be needed and are prudent. Usually, states have been given the right (theoretically, at least) to decide whether they will accept the funds authorized. However, if a state is willing to accept the funds authorized by any law, it must observe the conditions attached to the acceptance.

State Laws

State laws supplementing the constitutional provisions presumably express the will and policy of the people of the state regarding education and its operation. The number and complexity of laws relating to education have increased rapidly during the last few years in practically every state. Compilations of laws relating to education that required only a few pages to print fifty years ago have in some instances grown into a volume of more than a thousand pages. In some states several hundred bills relating to education are introduced at each session of the legislature and many may be enacted. A large proportion of these usually are concerned with minor amendments or with relatively brief proposals for new sections, but others may require several printed pages and incorporate many details regarding some one aspect of the educational program.

The basic question underlying educational legislation in each state is: What kinds of laws are essential to provide for the development of an adequate and effective program of public education? Appropriate laws are those that facilitate the attainment of this objective; those that do not are undesirable. Undoubtedly, every state has some laws that, properly assessed, would be found undesirable.

The process of evaluating laws is constantly taking place in every state. Sooner or later, unwise or hastily enacted laws are likely to be found unsatisfactory on the basis of studies and experiences in various parts of the state and may be repealed or materially modified. Unfortunately, however, once laws are enacted, the process of evaluation often tends to be slow or ineffective. Many inappropriate laws tend to be continued indefinitely.

Some state legislatures have accepted quite literally the concept that education is a function of the state, and tend to assume that local school systems should have no responsibility or authority unless it is specifically granted by the state. Such states have developed very detailed laws, because such detail has been found necessary in order to enable school systems to operate reasonably satisfactorily. A system of laws prepared on the basis of this premise is referred to as a "mandatory" system or code. California is a good example of a state that has a mandatory system of school laws, since school districts are prohibited from doing anything that is not authorized or clearly implied by legislation. Some years ago, the state attorney general advised that:

> The question is not whether the payment of expense [as proposed by a school board] would contribute to the education of pupils, but whether the authority is vested in the board to make such an expenditure. . . . School districts are *quasi* municipal corporations of the most limited power known to law.[6]

Such a system results in a vast volume of detailed legislation that places a burden not only on the legislature but also on school officials who are attempting to conform to the provisions of law. Perhaps even more significant, it tends to stifle local initiative and may prevent local school systems from experimenting or instituting some promising innovations until the legislature has authorized the action. Especially during this period of rapid change and search for helpful innovations, such a policy can be defended only on the basis of tradition.

Several states have attempted to observe the principle that, while basic responsibilities must be prescribed, some discretion should also be granted to local school systems to assume responsibilities not inconsistent with law that are found necessary for an effective program of education. Provisions of this type, sometimes called a "mandatory-discretionary" system of laws, seem to be favored by an increasing number of states. In a study of the powers and duties of local school boards in selected states with "mandatory" and others with "mandatory-discretionary" types of school codes, Hall found the difference in wording to be small but significant.[7] In the latter group of states, a clause, worded somewhat as

[6]California Attorney General Opinion 47–38, 1947.

[7]Donald Ellis Hall, "Discretionary and Mandatory Provisions of State Education Law" (Ph.D. dissertation, University of California, Berkeley, 1959).

follows, was added to the section giving the powers and duties allocated to local school boards: ". . . and in addition thereto, those which it may find to be necessary for the improvement of the school system in carrying out the purposes and objectives of the school code." After analyzing court decisions in these states, Hall concluded that, in the absence of abuse of discretion, the courts generally ruled in favor of the board in its use of the discretionary authority granted.

Most states have found it necessary, especially during the past half-century, to organize their laws relating to education into a code. When many different laws are enacted at each session of the legislature, some provisions are likely to be inconsistent with provisions in older laws. Under these conditions, it may become difficult or impossible for school officials or even lawyers to determine what the law on a given subject may mean in terms of responsibilities of local school officials. A plan for codification of the laws on any subject means in essence a plan for organizing the laws logically so that they can be more readily located and understood. In many states the school code (or education code) is one of a series of codes comprising laws on different subjects or aspects of government.

Studies show that there is great variation in the progress states have made in organizing and codifying their laws relating to education. Although many state codes met reasonably well almost all standards and criteria used in a 1954 study, some of them met none satisfactorily.[8] School laws, unlike laws on many other subjects, have to be used by both professional educators and laymen serving on boards of education. Few of them have had much legal training. Even well-drafted laws may have relatively little meaning for laymen unless they are well organized, written so they can be readily understood, presented so they can be easily located, and properly indexed. For this reason, many states are giving increasing attention to standards for codification.

Several plans have been proposed for organizing and codifying laws relating to education. One of the simplest of these provides for a code comprising two or three major parts. The first part would include laws that have implications for all aspects of education, with appropriate divisions, chapters, and sections; the second part would include the more specific provisions with divisions, chapters, and sections incorporating laws dealing with personnel, pupils, program, plant, finance, and so on; a third part, or separate code, would include laws relating to institutions of higher learning and other aspects of the educational program.

[8]National Education Association, "The Codification of School Laws," *NEA Research Division, Research Bulletin*, 32, No. 1 (February 1954), 45.

BOARD POLICIES, STANDARDS, AND REGULATIONS

In some cases, laws have included details that have resulted in needless handicaps to the educational program. An extreme illustration is afforded by a law enacted some years ago in one of the states providing that a course on safety education be "taught by lectures." A more common illustration is found in laws providing that a designated number of minutes each day be devoted to a certain subject in every school.

Experience has shown that it is not practicable and usually not desirable to include all minor policies or details in laws enacted by the legislature. In every state, therefore, provision is made for the development and adoption by some state agency (usually the state board of education) of policies, standards, and regulations that have the effect of law. Similarly, local boards are authorized to adopt policies and regulations that are not inconsistent with state laws or regulations and which, if properly developed and adopted, have the effect of law in the local school system.

If the legislature were to attempt to grant unlimited regulatory powers to a state board of education or to a chief state school officer, the courts could be expected to hold that the legislature cannot delegate its responsibilities, that the powers granted are too broad and, therefore, null and void. When the legislature prescribes the general policies and establishes definite limits within which administrative policies or regulations must come, difficulties should be avoided. But, the policies and regulations adopted as authorized by law must be consistent with the provisions of law and must be reasonable.[9]

A good example of legislation that requires the adoption of administrative policies and regulations can be found in the field of teacher certification. In many states the law sets forth the purposes of certification, the general procedures to be used, and perhaps, the major kinds or classes of certificates authorized. The responsibility for prescribing detailed policies, standards, and regulations is usually delegated to the state board of education. The state board should establish application procedures and prescribe requirements to be met before a certificate can be issued. These regulations, however, would have to be reasonable and consistent with the purpose of the law to assure fair treatment for all applicants. The board could not reasonably require that the applicant have blue eyes, a designated racial background, or come from a certain type of family, nor could it alter the requirements for the issuance of certificates without giving reasonable notice.

[9]Newton Edwards, *The Courts and the Public Schools*, rev. ed. (Chicago: University of Chicago Press, 1955), p. 31.

All major policies and directives should, therefore, be incorporated in law, but details that might handicap the program or might need to be changed from time to time should be avoided. Laws should clearly delegate responsibility, when appropriate, for administrative policies and regulations but should carefully define the limits. Boards or agencies to which such responsibilities are delegated should take steps to assure that their actions are authorized by and consistent with provisions of law, are reasonable, and do not constitute an impulsive or arbitrary exercise of delegated power.

The process of developing policies in a local school system often involves some difficulties. Each proposed policy must be considered in relationship to other policies; otherwise, there may be conflicts and crosscurrents with resultant confusion, dissension, or inefficiency. Studies by a competent and representative committee in advance of board consideration should mean that if the board adopts the recommended policy, it is not only likely to be sound but to have a reasonably good prospect of being accepted by the staff and by the community. Adoption of the policy by the board means that the board then has a guide for action in that field, subject to possible revision on the basis of further studies. Once a policy has been adopted, a board should not need to spend time in considering individual problems that arise in that area. Nor should it have to risk the possibility of inconsistent action while attempting to work out a solution for each problem without reference to previous decisions.

As is pointed out in Chapter 13, the board should not enact, nor should the administrator prescribe, detailed rules and regulations governing the implementation of board policies. Unless reasonable flexibility is provided for management, there will be little innovation in a school system. It is not good policy for the legislature, the state board of education, the local board of education, or the administrator to prescribe in detail the activities of principals and teachers. Better educational programs are found in those systems which provide for a considerable amount of decision making at the operating level.

COURT DECISIONS

Any law or any board regulation may be constitutional or unconstitutional. However, in America, laws and board or administrative regulations are presumed to be constitutional, unless or until they are declared unconstitutional. The courts do not on their own initiative or volition rule on the constitutionality of a law. The ruling comes only when appropriate legal steps have been taken in connection with a controversy that results in a challenge regarding the constitutionality of a particular law or some aspect of the law.

The Role of the Courts

Many provisions in both federal and state constitutions are stated in rather broad general terms; they are designed to set forth basic policies, rather than specific guides to action or conduct. Such general provisions leave to Congress and state legislatures greater latitude in making adaptations to changing conditions than would be the case if the constitutional provisions were more specific. Such latitude is generally considered desirable. However, in many areas the broad constitutional provisions make it difficult, if not impossible, for many legislators, congressmen, or even lawyers to determine by reading a proposed law whether it is constitutional. They may have their own opinions, but these opinions have no legal significance. It has often been necessary, and will continue to be necessary on many occasions when controversies arise, for some person or group to resort to the courts to determine whether a particular law is constitutional or unconstitutional.

For example, the power to provide for the general welfare is so broad that many kinds of legislation could be considered desirable by substantial numbers of people. The courts eventually may have to determine whether a given law is consistent with the intent of the constitutional provision. Since more than one interpretation is often possible, especially when the arguments and evidence presented by both parties have almost equal validity, it is evident that the courts have considerable power in determining what is or is not constitutional. Thus, in one sense, the courts in directing the course of law may, from time to time, tend to determine the course of various aspects of social policy, including education.[10]

Many questions in addition to those involving constitutionality are constantly coming before the courts. There are frequent differences of opinion among the citizens of a community or state regarding their legal rights and liabilities or those of others. Many such differences are either resolved through study and discussion of the problems at issue or are considered of such limited importance that no appeal is made to the courts. Many others, however, of both major and minor importance, are taken to court for a decision.

Since education affects practically all people in one way or another at some time during their lives, there are many differences of opinion regarding the rights, privileges, and obligations of people relating to schools. As society becomes more complex, as attempts are made to adapt education to the rapidly changing needs, and as educational

[10]Clark Spurlock, *Education and the Supreme Court* (Urbana: University of Illinois Press, 1955), p. 13.

laws increase in number and scope, more and more questions regarding the purposes and intent of those laws are likely to arise. Thus, the courts in every state are called upon from time to time to interpret one aspect or another of the laws relating to schools. Since in many cases more than one interpretation is possible, the courts may in some situations find themselves in the position of establishing certain educational policies, although that is presumed to be the prerogative of the legislature and boards of education. Conservative courts by making conservative and strict interpretations of new laws may nullify the intent of the legislation and handicap the development of the educational program.[11] On the other hand, courts may, and usually do, attempt to interpret legislation in accordance with its stated or implied purposes and thus help to make it possible for schools to meet emerging needs.

The courts have been established to attempt to resolve the many controversies that are certain to arise in a pluralistic society. They function in accordance with established rules or criteria in an effort to assure equity and justice for all in every aspect of life, including education. Fortunately, courts do not always decide issues merely by precedent or weight of evidence. As the United States Supreme Court stated in ruling on the Social Security Act, "Nor is the concept of general welfare static. Needs that were narrow or parochial a century ago may be interwoven in our day with the wellbeing of the Nation. What is critical or urgent changes with the times."[12]

In this way, controversies are rationalized in the legal and judicial frame of reference. The result has been a slowly changing conceptual pattern to which the courts have made significant contributions. At times, they have helped to free education from some outmoded legislative constraints, and, in a way, have served as an adapting agency between legislation and educational administration.[13]

In addition to the federal system of courts, to which recourse may usually be had only when a federal question or statute is involved, each state has its own judicial system. Practically all educational controversies except those involving federal questions are resolved in state courts.

In most states the courts have been faced with the necessity of attempting to resolve two kinds of controversies relating to education: (1) those involving questions that are clearly legal in nature, and (2) those involving technical and clearly educational problems. In view of the rapidly increasing burden on the courts as civilization and laws become more complex, and of the relative unfamiliarity of courts with educational problems, there are many who believe some other plan

[11]Hamilton and Mort, *op. cit.*, p. 23.
[12]*Helvering* v *Davis*, 301 Cr. S 619, 57 Sup. Ct. 904.
[13]Hamilton and Mort, *op. cit.*, pp. 1 and 11.

should be devised for resolving strictly educational controversies. The precedent has already been established for certain other agencies of government (for example, utility commissions), and progress in the field of education has been made in some states. In New York, the decision of the state commissioner of education on technical educational matters is final and presumably is not subject to review by state courts. In some other states it is final unless reversed by the courts. In many states, however, no such authority or responsibility has been granted to the chief state school officer or to the state board.

Federal Supreme Court Decisions

Since education is not mentioned in the federal Constitution, it is never involved directly in questions that come before the United States Supreme Court. The involvement is always incidental, and comes through other questions, but often is quite significant.

According to Spurlock, 45 cases involving education to a rather significant extent came before the Supreme Court between the time the Constitution was adopted and 1954.[14] Most of these cases were concerned with questions of (1) state or federal power and functions, (2) civil rights under the First and Fifth Amendments, and (3) due process of law and equal protection of law under the Fourteenth Amendment. The cases were also classified under the following headings: (1) contests involving rights of parents and students, (2) contests involving rights of teachers and touching on property rights and personal freedoms, (3) contests involving rights of races in schools in states maintaining segregated schools, (4) contests involving powers of school authorities in fiscal matters or in matters involving rights of citizens, (5) contests involving rights of nonpublic schools.

It is interesting to note that most of these cases occurred after 1925. Before that time, only eighteen cases had concerned education rather directly. Of these, only nine had occurred before the beginning of the present century. Between 1925 and 1954, however, there were 27 cases. Many of these touched on conflicts between individual rights and state requirements, conflicts relating to separation of church and state, and conflicts over civil rights or segregation. Most of the cases relating to education since 1954 have been concerned, in one way or another, with segregation and with the separation of church and state.

The *Brown* Case in 1954 established the controlling legal or judicial principle that *racial discrimination in the public schools is in violation of provisions of the United States Constitution.*[15] In 1964 and 1965, by the refusal of the Supreme Court to review decisions by U.S.

---

[14]The authors are indebted to Spurlock, *op. cit.*, for much of the basic information presented in this section.

[15]*Brown* v *Board of Education of Topeka*, 347 U.S. 483.

Courts of Appeals, four, or perhaps five, other judicial principles seem to have been added:

1. Because a particular public school is completely or predominantly Negro does not necessarily mean that the school authorities are unlawfully maintaining a segregated school system.

2. The U. S. Constitution does not compel racial balance in the public schools; hence a local school board is under no constitutional obligation to correct existing racial imbalance in the schools.

3. A "neighborhood school" plan, constructed originally with no intention to segregate the races, need not later be abandoned because it results in racial imbalance in certain schools, unless it can be shown to be operating so as to discriminate against students because of their race or color.

4. School authorities, rather than the courts, must initiate actions to correct the racial imbalance in the schools.

5. While local school authorities may have no affirmative constitutional duty to correct racial imbalance in the schools, there is no constitutional bar to prevent them from taking reasonable steps to do so should they so desire.[16]

Some of the newer federal laws, especially certain provisions in the Elementary and Secondary Education Act of 1965, are likely to result in controversies that may eventually be decided in the federal courts, perhaps by the Supreme Court. Many people believe the act includes provisions that, in effect, provide aid for denominational schools. The purpose of some sections is to assure reasonably adequate educational opportunities for all students. But if students from denominational schools are sent to the public schools for some classes that involve "nonreligious" subjects, do the funds used to pay for this instruction result directly or indirectly in aid to the denominational (religious) schools in which they are enrolled? How much financial assistance can be provided directly or indirectly for students enrolled in religious schools without breaching the "wall of separation" between church and state? Questions such as these are highly controversial and probably will be resolved through the courts.

In some cases the Supreme Court has indicated that it is reluctant to consider matters that might pertain to state educational policies, in view of the fact that education is clearly recognized as a function of the respective states. Nevertheless, it is apparent that the Court has exercised significant influence in a number of respects on the design and pattern for American education. Without such decisions, the American system of education would undoubtedly have been different in many respects from what it is today. Thus the federal government, through Supreme Court decisions, has controlled more aspects of the develop-

[16]Stephen F. Roach, "The Federal Courts and Racial Imbalance in the Public Schools," *Phi Delta Kappan*, 47, No. 5 (Jan. 1966), 257.

ment of education in the various states than most people realize. This control has been in the direction of stabilization and of unification in certain aspects of the conceptual design for education.[17]

In a case some years ago, one of the justices expressed concern that the Supreme Court might be tending to become a national board of education. However, it seems apparent that the Supreme Court, in its expressed philosophy underlying decisions, has generally tended to reflect the point of view of the American people and has avoided questions involving state policy except where provisions of the federal Constitution are at issue.

State Supreme Court Decisions

United States Supreme Court decisions, by implication at least, affect education throughout the United States. On the other hand, a decision by a state supreme court is of direct significance for education only in that state, although it may have indirect significance in other states if it is used or cited by courts in those states. Courts do not legislate, but their decisions have the effect of law. Consequently, reference is frequently made to *statute law* or law enacted by legislature, and to *case law* or law interpreted in specific instances through court cases.

The courts have no responsibility for determining the *wisdom* of a particular law, but they have a legitimate concern with the *reasonableness* of a law. The guide for determining what is reasonable in a given situation has to be established by the court itself. One court may hold unreasonable a provision of a law that might be held reasonable by a court in another state, or a higher court may, on appeal, reverse a decision by a lower court in the same state. Thus there have been variations in decisions regarding similar laws among the different states, and from time to time state court decisions have been modified or reversed.

Almost every aspect of the educational program has at some time been involved in court decisions in each of the states. The laws among the states differ so widely and there are so many different types of court decisions that generalization would seem to be difficult if not impossible. Yet there are many basic similarities in state laws and, likewise, many basic similarities in court decisions relating to fundamental issues. Although it is necessary to consult the laws and court decisions of a particular state before authoritative statements can be made regarding many aspects of the educational program, there are certain legal principles that have become sufficiently well established to permit generalization. Among the most important are the following:

[17]Spurlock, *op. cit.*, p. 238.

1. The courts are generally agreed that education is a function of the state and that the control and management of the public schools is an essential aspect of state sovereignty.
2. The legislature has full and complete power to legislate concerning the control and management of the public schools of the state, except in respects in which that power is restricted by the state constitution or by the federal Constitution.
3. The legislature may delegate certain powers and responsibilities for education to designated state and local agencies, but it may not delegate all of its powers. It must establish reasonable limits that are required to be observed by state or local agencies as they exercise their delegated responsibilities.
4. Public schools are state not local institutions. In reality the public school program is a partnership program between the state and the local unit created by the state. The state may create and reorganize local school districts and delegate to them definite powers for the organization, administration, and operation of schools. These districts may be especially created for school purposes or may be municipal or county districts. However, the municipality or county has no authority or power over the schools within its boundaries except as such authority or power is definitely granted by the state.
5. On the basis of an old common-law principle, school districts are not liable for the negligence of their officers or agents acting in their official capacity unless there is a state law imposing such liability. Although only a few states have such laws, there has been a tendency during recent years for the courts to recognize increasingly the responsibility and liability of the state and its agencies.[18]

SOME IMPORTANT PROBLEMS AND ISSUES

A few of the many important issues relating to the legal aspects of education are discussed briefly on subsequent pages.

How Much Educational Policy Should Be Incorporated into Law?

Although it may not be possible in any state to get complete agreement on educational policies, majority concurrence on all or most aspects of the conceptual design for education is both feasible and desirable. Without such concurrence, some laws would probably deviate sharply from a rational pattern, and the educational program could be seriously handicapped.

[18]Adapted from Garber, *op. cit.*, pp. 68–70.

One of the first concerns of many who want to change the school program seems to be to incorporate their "idea" into law. Some apparently believe that when a law has been placed on the statute books, the problem has been solved. However, those who understand the situation recognize that laws do not necessarily solve problems. A law requiring counseling in all schools or providing for conservation education does not necessarily mean that all local school boards, administrators, or teachers are in a position to implement rationally the intent of the law or will do so.

Difficulties often arise as a result of the situation in small school districts that cannot afford competent leadership, or in certain other districts in which the leadership or personnel may not have developed a sound program. Inept and incompetent local leadership on the part of the board, the administrator, or the staff has frequently helped to set the stage for laws that handicap other districts.

Laws, of course, are necessary if local school systems are to operate, because their basic authority and responsibilities must be established by the state. For example, because of differences in wealth among school districts, legal provision must be made for financial support to supplement that provided by local effort. Beyond such basic provisions, what other laws are necessary? How can the number of laws be kept to a reasonable minimum, when there are so many demands by different groups for laws to protect their interests?

In an effort to avoid the need for many detailed laws, a number of states, as previously noted, have incorporated in their code a section providing that each local school board is authorized to assume such responsibilities and perform such duties, in addition to those prescribed, as are necessary in the opinion of the board for the development of an effective educational program in the district, and as are not in conflict with provisions of existing law. What are the advantages and disadvantages of such a discretionary provision?

How Should School Legislation Be Developed?

Laws originate in many different ways. Sometimes they grow out of careful studies by some appropriate group concerned with the conceptual design and needs and ways of meeting those needs. In other cases, some individual or group may become concerned because school expenditures have increased rapidly, because some board has inaugurated a controversial type of program, or for some other reason, and may seek legislation designed to prevent the schools from doing those things they consider undesirable. Ignorance, selfishness, and provincialism are likely to lead to bad legislation in any state. While there is probably no way to prevent some unwise or handicapping laws, there are some important safeguards. The most fundamental is widespread understanding of the role and significance of high-quality education by citizens and legislators. However, even this needs to be supplemented by effective political activity by those who believe in and support public education and vigorous leadership by competent leaders who understand the conceptual design and appropriate means of achieving it. This kind of climate should contribute to the development of a "conscience" by the people and in the legislature that will be favorable to sound legislation for education.

Below are some elements of a proposed plan for developing and evaluating legislation relating to education:

1. Proposed legislation should be designed to aid in attaining appropriate purposes and objectives—that is, to implement the conceptual design for education—and should be evaluated on the basis of the extent to which it seems to contribute to that end.

2. The bills or proposed laws should be carefully prepared by competent people who are in agreement with the purposes and objectives and who understand the conceptual design; bills should be systematically checked to assure that they are free from undesirable features including inappropriate controls and limitations and, when the basic features are generally agreed upon, should be presented to the legislature for consideration.

3. There should be a systematic review of the laws enacted at each session of the legislature to determine whether there are conflicts or provisions that are not in harmony with the objectives of the educational program. The findings should be used as a basis for planning needed revisions.

What other criteria should be used in determining whether proposed legislation is desirable or undesirable?

SPONSORING LEGISLATION.   There are always a number of groups interested in legislation pertaining to schools. The educational groups that may sponsor legislation from time to time, include the state department of education, the state education association, the school boards association, and others. Almost any noneducational organization may sponsor certain types of legislation pertaining to schools.

The concerns of some of these groups are likely to differ and their objectives to be conflicting. For example, one group may be primarily interested in providing for more local leeway and initiative, while another may be so concerned with efficiency that it attempts to limit local responsibility. The resulting conflicts and differences of opinion pose difficult problems for the legislature and for the people of the state. The problem becomes especially serious when educational organizations have different proposals and objectives. When educators fail to agree, the legislature finds itself in the position of having to decide what it believes to be the best educational policy.

In several states, reasonably effective plans have been developed for coordinating the interests and efforts of major lay and educational groups. Councils composed of representatives of important educational and lay groups concerned with education have been established to sponsor studies, evaluate findings, and attempt to get agreement on objectives. What steps should be taken to avoid serious conflicts of interest concerning legislation among educational groups? Among lay and educational groups?

PREPARING LEGISLATION.   When bills are to be prepared for consideration by the legislature, there is often a question as to how and by whom they should be written. Most bills relating to education have probably been prepared by lawyers or by persons with some background in law. Since such laws have to be used and understood primarily by board members and school officials, they should be written, insofar as possible, to be understandable by laymen. For that reason, in some states the original drafts of many proposed bills have been prepared by educators who understand law as well as the purposes and objectives upon which agreement has been reached. These drafts have then been checked and necessary revisions made by competent attorneys, legal consultants, or bill-drafting specialists. How can a satisfactory plan be worked out for assuring cooperation between educators and legal experts in drafting legislation relating to schools?

LEGISLATIVE ETHICS.   The point of view and attitude of the public and of the legislators they select is usually a decisive factor in determining the kind of legislation relating to education that is enacted in each state. This attitude is determined by the concepts and philosophy of each individual involved but, no doubt, is greatly influenced by his understanding of the role, contributions, and problems of education in an evolving society. Hamilton and Mort have suggested the need for a legislative "code of ethics" with reference to education.[19] Would such a code be feasible and helpful? How could its acceptance be facilitated? How should the following criteria, adapted in part from their proposal, be modified and supplemented?

1. Legislative committees and the legislature (and the courts when they are called on to resolve conflicts over law) should keep in mind the basic purposes (conceptual design) of education and should attempt to obtain and utilize pertinent valid information as a basis for evaluating, revising, and acting on

[19]*The Law and Public Education*, pp. 619–620.

proposed legislation. Proposals that would not contribute to the attainment of the basic purposes should be rejected.

2. The methods used by the legislature in exercising its powers should always encourage and facilitate meaningful local responsibility and orderly procedures in local school administrative units. Uncertainty and disruptive changes resulting from legislation should be reduced to a minimum.

3. Legislatures should delegate to the state agency for education only those responsibilities and functions that can most appropriately be assumed by that agency, and should clearly delegate to the local school systems the responsibility for organizing and operating the schools and educational program needed in their respective areas. Legislatures should not make changes in details of the educational structure without appraising the implications for the basic structural pattern. They should never impose restrictions on all districts that would interfere with bona fide local responsibility because of problems that may have arisen in a few districts.

What Kinds of Standards and Regulations Should Be Developed?

Because of changing conditions and new insights, every state and every school system is almost constantly in the process of developing or revising policies, standards, or regulations for certain aspects of the educational program. These have often been worked out by the administrator and members of his staff and presented to the board for approval. On the other hand, during recent years there has been a tendency to organize representative committees to study all aspects of the problem and to prepare tentative proposals. These proposals are reviewed by everyone concerned before being submitted for approval. What are the advantages and disadvantages of each of these procedures?

STATE REQUIREMENTS. Each state has established standards and other requirements for certain aspects of the educational program. State and local officials should always consider carefully the kind of standards that should be established, the purposes to be accomplished, the details to be included, and how standards should be developed. Adoption of unattainable standards would be meaningless. Establishment of handicapping regulations would be unfortunate. Acceptance of properly developed minimum standards or requirements, however, may help local school systems to improve their own programs and may facilitate progress in the state. When is a state standard desirable? How can the state avoid prescribing details that may handicap local school systems? What criteria should be used in evaluating proposals for standards or requirements?

LOCAL POLICIES AND REQUIREMENTS.   No local school board can take any action contrary to the requirements established by law and by the state board. Within these limits, however, every local board finds it necessary to establish a number of policies and requirements that are considered important for a well-planned and well-organized program.

General and specific objectives and the policies considered necessary to aid in attaining those objectives should be agreed upon and used for guidance in developing administrative standards and regulations. It is now generally recognized that anyone concerned with an objective, a policy, or even a regulation should have an opportunity to participate in some way (directly or through representatives) in its development.

Many boards have followed the policy of organizing committees to study and propose policies and regulations relating to the various aspects of the educational program. Any such committee might be comprised of lay citizens (assisted by competent members of the staff in assembling information, interpreting findings, or arriving at conclusions), of both lay citizens and educators, or entirely of educators (see discussion in Chapter 6). However, no committee can adopt policies or standards for a school system. That is the prerogative of the board.

Committees usually proceed slowly, because understanding must be developed as they proceed. Some problems do not need committee consideration. When should a committee be organized to study a problem and submit policy recommendations to the board? Is it better to organize such a committee after difficulties have arisen or when there are no serious difficulties? Why?

Selected References

Counts, George S., *Education and American Civilization.* New York: Bureau of Publications, Teachers College, Columbia University, 1952. Chaps. 13, 17, and 18.

Drury, Robert L., ed., *Law and the School Superintendent,* Legal Problems of Education Series, Vol. I. Cincinnati: W. H. Anderson Co., 1958.

Drury, Robert L., and Kenneth C. Ray, *Principles of School Law with Cases.* New York: Appleton-Century-Crofts, 1965.

Edwards, Newton, *The Courts and the Public Schools* (rev. ed.). Chicago: University of Chicago Press, 1955. Chaps. 1, 7, and 21.

Garber, Lee O., *Yearbook of School Law.* Philadelphia: University of Pennsylvania Press, Annual Yearbook Series beginning 1950.

Gauerke, Warren E., *School Law.* New York: Center for Applied Research in Education, 1965.

Hamilton, Robert R., and Paul R. Mort, *The Law and Public Education* (2nd ed.). New York: The Foundation Press, 1959. Chaps. 1, 2, 4, and 17.

Remmlein, Madaline Kinter, *The Law of Local Public School Administration*. New York: McGraw-Hill Book Company, 1953.

Spurlock, Clark, *Education and the Supreme Court*. Urbana: University of Illinois Press, 1955.

3

The Use of Theory and Research
in Educational Administration

Some executives have been inclined to scoff at the use of theory in educational administration. The expression "That is all right in theory but it won't work in practice" has been frequently used by self-styled "practical" school administrators. The myth that theory and practice are incompatible has been attacked by Coladarci and Getzels. "Theorizing is not the exclusive property of the laboratory or the ivory tower. Everyone who makes choices and judgments implies a theory in the sense that there are reasons for his action. When an administrator's experiences have led him to believe that a certain kind of act will result in certain other events or acts, he is using theory."[1] The authors also state that when an administrator learns from experience, he is theorizing, ". . . it may be poor theorizing, but it is theorizing nevertheless."[2]

Much progress has been made in recent years in laying the foundations for a science of educational administration. No systematic science in any discipline has ever been developed by the trial-and-error process; however, until comparatively recently that was the principal method used to develop our knowledge of educational administration. Progress in the physical sciences was very slow as long as knowledge was derived

[1]Reprinted with permission of the publishers from *The Use of Theory in Educational Administration*, by Arthur P. Coladarci and Jacob W. Getzels (Stanford: Stanford University Press, 1955), p. 5.
[2]*Idem.*

primarily from trial-and-error methods, folklore, and superstition. When the scientific method was applied, our knowledge of the physical sciences developed at an astounding rate.

In recent years, we have begun to apply the scientific method to develop knowledge in the social and behavioral sciences. The scientific method involves the conceptualization of theories from which hypotheses may be formulated and tested. The development of theory and research in the disciplines of psychology, sociology, social psychology, anthropology, political science, and economics has provided a number of useful theoretical bases for developing a science of educational administration. Some of these theories will be presented and discussed briefly in this chapter. These theories and some other concepts will be applied to organizations in Chapter 4, leadership in Chapter 5, and to cooperative procedures in Chapter 6.

GENERAL SYSTEMS THEORY

There is a discernable linkage among all the sciences. Systems theory provides an important part of that linkage. According to Hearn:

> General systems theorists believe that it is possible to represent all forms of animate and inanimate matter as systems; that is all forms from atomic particles through atoms, molecules, crystals, viruses, cells, organs, individuals, groups, societies, planets, solar systems, even the galaxies, may be regarded as systems. They are impressed by the number of times the same principles have been independently discovered by scientists working in different fields.[3]

The journal *Behavioral Science* is devoted to general systems theory. The following statement was made in an editorial appearing in the first issue published in January 1956.

> Our present thinking—which may alter with time—is that a general theory will deal with structural and behavioral properties of systems. The diversity of systems is great. The molecule, the cell, the organ, the individual, the group, the society are all examples of systems. Besides differing in the level of organization, systems differ in many other crucial respects. They may be living, nonliving, or mixed; material or conceptual and so forth.[4]

Griffiths defines a system as follows:

> A system is simply defined as a complex of elements in interaction. Systems may be open or closed. An open system is related to and exchanges matter with its environment, while a closed system is not

---

[3]Gordon Hearn, *Theory Building in Social Work* (Toronto: University of Toronto Press, 1958), p. 38.

[4]*Behavioral Science*, 1, No. 1 (1956).

related to nor does it exchange matter with its environment. Further, a closed system is characterized by an increase in entropy, while open systems tend toward the steady state. (Given a continuous input, a constant ratio among the components is maintained.) All systems except the smallest have subsystems and all but the largest have suprasystems, which are their environment.[5]

Each system and subsystem is conceptualized as having a *boundary*. There is more interaction among the units included within the boundary of a system than between units within the boundary and units outside it. It also requires more energy to transmit energy across the boundary from within to without or from without to within than to exchange matter or information among the units included within the boundary of a system.[6]

The environment of a system, subsystem, or suprasystem is everything external to its boundary. There are numerous factors both within a system and its environment that affect the behavior, structure, and function of both the system and its environment.[7]

In Chapters 1 and 2, considerable attention was given to the value structure of our society. There has been much controversy concerning whether scientific research should be "value free." Since values are factors both in a social system and in its environment, the social scientist cannot ignore values. But, he will treat a value in the same manner as he would treat any other factor affecting a system or its environment.

The School as a Social System

The system theory discussed in this book deals only with open, living systems.[8] A school system is an open, living social system which can be conceptualized in a number of ways in terms of system theory. For example, an individual school might be conceptualized as a system; its departments, sections, and divisions as subsystems; and the central staff, the board of education, the state education agencies, and, if present trends continue, even federal education agencies may all in the order listed be conceptualized as suprasystems. The environment of any given system consists not only of its subsystems and suprasystems, but also of all of the other systems in the society with their attendant beliefs, values, and purposes.

Parsons has suggested a useful conceptualization of the formal

[5]Daniel E. Griffiths, ed., *Behavioral Science and Educational Administration.* Sixty-third Yearbook of the National Society for the Study of Education (Chicago: University of Chicago Press, 1964), p. 116.

[6]James G. Miller, "Toward a General Theory for the Behavioral Sciences," *American Psychologist,* 10 (1955), 516–517.

[7]Hearn, *op. cit.,* p. 42.

[8]For an extensive theoretical analysis, see James G. Miller, "Living Systems: Basic Concepts," *Behavioral Science,* 10, No. 4 (1965), 193–237.

school organization.[9] He proposed that the hierarchical aspect of school organization be broken down according to function or responsibility. Using this concept, Parsons classified the hierarchical levels of authority in school systems as the "technical" system, the "managerial" system, and the "community" or "institutional" system. The teaching function is in the technical system, the management system controls the technical system, and the community legitimizes the management system through creating agencies for the control of schools or by direct vote.

Systems theory can also be used to conceptualize informal organizations in social systems. This topic will be treated more completely in Chapter 4.

Research and Systems Theory

Systems theory has proven to be extremely useful for conceptualizing and organizing research dealing with organization and administration. It provides a systematic method for utilizing research from the social and behavioral sciences to understand and control organizational and administrative phenomena. Research on administration and organization conceptualized on meaningful theoretical bases will bring that research into the mainstream of valid research in the social and behavioral sciences and should eventually produce a science of administration.

Miller, after making an exhaustive study of research based on systems theory, listed 165 hypotheses which had been proposed by various researchers including himself.[10] He noted that some of these hypotheses had been confirmed by research but that some were probably entirely wrong or partially wrong and needed to be modified. Miller also observed that, undoubtedly, many other hypotheses relating to living systems could be formulated. His work is highly significant for practicing educational administrators and for researchers in educational organization and administration. Because of their significance, a few of the 165 hypotheses listed by Miller are quoted below and their significance for educational systems indicated.

1. "In general, the more numbers or components a system has, the more echelons it has."[11] The larger the school system, the more pupils and teachers and the longer the chain of command. As we lengthen the chain of command, it can be hypothesized that we retard communication and increase the internal friction of the system. There are many econ-

[9]Talcott Parsons, "Some Ingredients of a General Theory of Formal Organization," Chap. 3 in *Administrative Theory in Education*, ed. Andrew W. Halpin (Chicago: Midwest Administration Center, University of Chicago, 1958), p. 41.

[10]James G. Miller, "Living Systems: Cross-Level Hypotheses," *Behavioral Science*, **10**, No. 4 (1965), 380–411.

[11]*Ibid.*, p. 383.

omies of scale that can be obtained by making school systems larger. If, however, as we make school systems larger, we must increase the echelons of control, how large can we make school systems until the disadvantages of internal friction and difficulty of communication arising from increasing the echelons of control outweigh the advantages of economy of scale gained by increasing the size of school systems? Available research on educational administration has not yet provided the answer to that question.

2. "System components incapable of associating, or lacking experience which has formed such association, must function according to strict programing or highly standardized operating rules."[12] The armed services are sometimes criticized for the regimentation inevitably arising from "highly standardized operating rules." However, when consideration is given to the situation facing officers dealing with recruits and constantly changing personnel, it is probable that the armed services could not function efficiently by any other plan. Is the school system similar to or different from the army? Does the fact that the school system and the army have different purposes affect the validity of the processes of control of each? Those who believe that the purposes of a school system can best be achieved by strict programing and highly standardized rules probably assume a set of purposes for the schools different from those who disagree with them. If research sustains the hypothesis, then the educational administrator who wishes to avoid strict programing or highly standardized operating rules in any system or subsystem he is administering should select as components of that system or subsystem persons who are capable of working with each other and provide them with opportunities to do so in group situations.

3. "The larger a system is and the more components it has, the larger is the ratio of the amount of information transmitted between points within the system to the amount of information transmitted across its boundary."[13] A number of the largest city school systems in the United States have experienced serious crises in recent years. Is it possible that these large school systems have lost some public support because of failure to transmit sufficient information across their boundaries?

It might also be hypothesized that the larger the school system, the greater the difficulty in getting information from the environment across the boundary into the school system.

4. Miller presented several hypotheses, supported by some research, concerning communication channels. Following are two examples: "The further away along channels a subsystem is from a process, the

[12]*Ibid.*, p. 384.
[13]*Ibid.*, p. 385.

more error there is in its information about that process."[14] "The probability of error in or breakdown of an information channel is a direct function of the number of components in it."[15] The application of these hypotheses to educational organization and administration is obvious. The further the teachers are removed from contact with the central administration and the more the echelons placed between the teacher and the central administration, the greater the chance of error in the teachers' perceptions of the actions of the central administration and the greater the number of errors in the factual information reaching the teachers.

SOME THEORETICAL MODELS

In the remainder of this chapter, some theoretical models will be presented and applied to problems of organization and administration.

Toward a General Theory of Action

A bold attempt was made in 1951 by a group of psychologists, sociologists, and anthropologists to develop a general theory of the social sciences.[16] Their frame of reference for a theory of action was based on personality, social system, and culture. Personality was defined ". . . as the organized system of the orientation and motivation of action of one individual actor."[17] A social system was defined as "Any system of interactive relationships of a plurality of individual actors . . ."[18] Although culture can be conceptualized as a body of artifacts, and systems of symbols, it is not organized as a system of action and, therefore, is on a different plane from the personality and social systems. However, cultural patterns tend to become organized into systems.

The personality is viewed as a relatively consistent system of need dispositions which produce role expectations in social systems. Roles rather than personalities are conceptualized as the units of social structure.

Cultural patterns may be internalized both by the individual personality system and by the social system. These patterns are not always congruent, and the integration of personalities in social systems with different cultural patterns frequently presents serious difficulties.

Rewards, roles, and facilities in a social system are scarce and must be allocated. Therefore, the social system, or organization, must deal

14*Ibid.*, p. 388.
15*Ibid.*, p. 389.
16Talcott Parsons and Edward S. Shils, eds., *Toward a General Theory of Action* (Cambridge: Harvard University Press, 1951).
17*Ibid.*, p. 7.
18*Idem.*

with the problems of allocation and integration. Furthermore, "The regulation of all of these allocative processes and the performance of the functions which keep the system or the subsystem going in a sufficiently integrated manner is impossible without a system of definitions of roles and sanctions for conformity or deviation."[19]

The formulation presented by Parsons and his associates seems highly general and abstract. But, the conceptualization of the reciprocal integration of the personality, the social system, and the culture through interaction processes stimulated much creative thinking by other social scientists.

Can the theories of Parsons and his associates be applied to the development of solutions of educational problems? From what theoretical bases will we develop solutions to the problems of integration of the races in the schools? From what theoretical bases will we develop educational programs to accomplish the purposes of the Economic Opportunity Act of 1964 and Titles I and III of the Elementary and Secondary Education Act of 1965? The educational provisions of these acts both deal with the educationally and culturally disadvantaged. It may be inappropriate to refer to pupils as "culturally disadvantaged." It may be more appropriate to use the term "culturally different." For example, a child reared in a slum develops a culture which enables him to cope with his environment in a slum. A child from the middle class has acquired a culture that ill equips him to survive in a slum environment but serves him well in his own environment. The problem of developing educational programs for culturally different children and adults and educationally disadvantaged children and adults is one of the greatest challenges to the educational leadership of the nation. Solutions to this problem by trial-and-error methods will be very slow. The intelligent application of appropriate theory should greatly speed up the development of education programs to alleviate this problem.

The Organization and the Individual

Perceptive administrators have long recognized that the administrator must deal with the organization, the individual, and the environment. The organization and the environment must come to terms with each other—the organization establishing and attaining purposes wanted by the environment, and the environment supporting the organization that satisfies its wants. Similarly, the individual and the organization must come to terms with each other by the individual accepting and facilitating the attainment of the purposes of the organization, and the organization satisfying the wants of the individual.

One of the earliest writers placing these propositions in theoretical

[19]*Ibid.*, p. 25

form was a business executive, Chester Barnard.[20] He conceived of an organization as a system which embraced the activities of two or more persons coordinating their activities to attain a common goal. He considered organization as the binding element common to all cooperative systems. According to Barnard's theoretical formulation, the continuance of a successful organization depends upon two conditions: (1) the accomplishment of the purposes of the organization, which he termed "effectiveness," and (2) the satisfaction of individual motives, which he termed "efficiency." Two types of processes were required for meeting these conditions: (1) those relating to the cooperative system itself and its relationship to its environment, and (2) those related to the creation and allocation of satisfaction among individuals.[21]

Getzels has developed a model for explaining social behavior which has been extremely fertile in producing hypotheses and stimulating research.[22] He started with the assumption that the process of administration deals essentially with social behavior in a hierarchical setting: ". . . we may conceive of administration *structurally* as the hierarchy of subordinate-superordinate relationships within a social system. *Functionally,* this hierarchy of relationships is the locus for allocating and integrating roles and facilities in order to achieve the goals of the social system."[23]

He conceived ". . . the social system as involving two classes of phenomena which are at once conceptually independent and phenomenally interactive."[24] Those two phenomena are the institution with roles and expectations fulfilling the goals of the system, and the individuals with personalities and need dispositions who inhabit the system. The observed interaction he termed social behavior. He asserted that ". . . social behavior may be understood as a function of these major elements: institution, role, and expectation, which together constitute what we shall call the *nomothetic* or normative dimension of activity in a social system, and individual, personality, and need-disposition, which together constitute the *idiographic* or personal dimension of activity in a social system."[25]

Getzels summarized his theoretical formulation in a simple model, which he presented pictorially as follows:[26]

[20]Chester I. Barnard, *The Functions of the Executive* (Cambridge: Harvard University Press, 1938).

[21]*Ibid.,* Chap. 1.

[22]Jacob W. Getzels, "Administration as a Social Process," Chapter 7 of *Administrative Theory in Education,* ed. Andrew W. Halpin (Chicago: University of Chicago, Midwest Administration Center, 1958). NOTE: Getzels credits Egon Guba with assisting him in developing his theoretical formulations.

[23]*Ibid.,* p. 151.

[24]*Idem.*

[25]*Ibid.,* p. 152.

[26]*Ibid.,* p. 156.

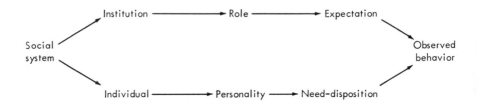

Nomothetic Dimension

Institution ⟶ Role ⟶ Expectation

Social system

Observed behavior

Individual ⟶ Personality ⟶ Need-disposition

Idiographic dimension

This model has already become a classic because of its simplicity and seminal properties. It clearly demonstrates the utility of models in presenting abstract theoretical concepts. A number of empirical research studies have been based on hypotheses originating in Getzels' formulation.[27]

Organizational Equilibrium

Any system has a tendency to achieve a balance among the many forces or factors operating upon the system and within it.[28] Chin distinguishes between different types of equilibriums as follows: "A *stationary equilibrium* exists when there is a fixed point or level of balance to which the system returns after a disturbance. . . . A *dynamic* equilibrium exists when the equilibrium shifts to a new position of balance after disturbance."[29] Current literature on systems theory usually refers to stationary equilibrium as "equilibrium," and to dynamic equilibrium as "steady state." In this chapter, steady state and dynamic equilibrium will be used as synonymous terms. Chin theorized that a system in equilibrium reacts to outside impingements by: "(1) resisting the influence of the disturbance, refusing to acknowledge its existence, or by building a protective wall against the intrusion, and by other defensive maneuvers . . .; (2) By resisting the disturbance through bringing into operation the homeostatic forces that restore or re-create a balance . . .; (3) By accommodating the disturbance through achieving a new equilibrium."[30] Strategies (1) and (2) are designed to attain a stationary equilibrium without making changes; strategy (3) is designed to attain a dynamic equilibrium or steady state by making changes.

---

[27]*Ibid.*, pp. 159–165.

[28]Robert Chin, "The Utility of Systems Models and Developmental Models for Practitioners" in *Planning of Change*, ed. Warren G. Bennis, Kenneth D. Benne, and Robert Chin (New York: Holt, Rinehart & Winston, Inc., 1961), pp. 201–214.

[29]*Ibid.*, p. 205.

[30]*Idem.*

The concepts of stationary equilibrium and dynamic equilibrium or steady state are of great significance to educational administrators because of the consequences of alternate strategies to the social system called the school system, which is at the present time receiving more signals from its environment than ever before.

The concept of "feedback" is closely related to the concept of equilibrium. "Cybernetics" is the study of feedback control. Lonsdale defines feedback as follows: "As applied to organization, feedback is the process through which the organization learns: it is the input from the environment to the system telling it how it is doing as a result of its output to the environment."[31] It is hypothesized that if any social system fails to learn from its environment, it will eventually fail to survive in that environment or the environment will force changes in the system. If research sustains this hypothesis, what will be the eventual fate of a school system that makes continuous use of strategies (1) and (2)?

There are other concepts of equilibrium which are of great importance to administrators. As has been pointed out already, every living system strives to maintain a steady state. It will resist a disturbance if it can, and adjust to it if it must. "Entropy" is the tendency toward homogeneity or state of equilibrium.[32] Every system produces entropy, but at a minimal rate when the system is in a steady state. When a system is under such stress or strain that its components cannot bring it back into a steady state, the system may collapse. Systems under threat will usually use first the most available and least costly processes to relieve the strain to the system by returning the disturbing variable to a steady state. Later, the less quickly available and more costly processes will be utilized if necessary to restore the equilibrium of the system.[33] Thus, any living system, including such social systems as the school system, has a precarious existence. It needs feedback in order to receive the information necessary for the system to serve the environment and to adjust to it, if the system is to survive. But the feedback disturbs the equilibrium and if the steady state cannot be restored, the system will break down. Change is necessary for the survival of the system, but it usually causes stress and strain. These times, which require a rate of change greater than ever before, present an unparalleled challenge to the educational administrator to provide leadership for making desirable innovations and at the same time maintain a dynamic equilibrium in the school system.

[31]Richard C. Lonsdale, "Maintaining the Organization in Dynamic Equilibrium," Chap. 7 in *Behavioral Science in Educational Administration*, ed. Daniel E. Griffiths, Sixty-third Yearbook of the National Society for the Study of Education, Part II (Chicago: University of Chicago Press, 1964), p. 173.

[32]Hearn, *op. cit.*, p. 41.

[33]See James G. Miller, "Living Systems: Cross-Level Hypotheses," *Behavioral Science*, **10**, No. 4 (1965), 394–397.

Compliance Relationship

It is assumed that any formal organization must fulfill its purposes at least to the extent required by its environment or it will cease to exist or be substantially restructured. It is also assumed that the actors in an organization must accept the organizational roles assigned to them and comply with the directives of superordinates, if the organization is to accomplish its purposes. Etzioni has formulated a middle-range theory of organization, utilizing compliance as the primary variable for the classifications in his typology. He defines compliance as "a relation in which an actor behaves in accordance with a directive supported by another actor's power, and the orientation of the subordinated actor to the power applied."[34] Etzioni assumed that the exercise of power involved the manipulation of physical, material, and symbolic means to secure rewards and deprivations, depending upon a person's perception of the legitimacy of the exercise of power by his superordinate and the need disposition of his subordinate. These factors determine the involvement of the individual in the organization, ranging on a continuum from positive to negative. The term "alienative" was used to refer to an intensely negative orientation; "calculative" to a low-intensity involvement, either positive or negative, and "moral" to a high-intensity commitment.[35]

Another basic assumption of Etzioni's theory was that social order in an organization was accounted for by three sources of control: coercion, economic assets, and normative values. He constructed the following typology of compliance relations based on these assumptions.[36]

A Typology of Compliance Relations

Kinds of power	Kinds of involvement		
	Alienative	Calculative	Moral
Coercive	1	2	3
Remunerative	4	5	6
Normative	7	8	9

The terms coercive and remunerative in his typology are self-explanatory. Normative power depends upon the regulation of symbolic rewards and deprivations involving esteem, prestige, social acceptance, ritualistic symbols, and other factors associated with values.

The numbers in Etzioni's typology model are used to identify the

[34]Amitai Etzioni, *A Comparative Analysis of Complex Organizations* (New York: Free Press of Glencoe, Inc., 1961), p. 3.

[35]See Douglas Richard Pierce, *An Analysis of Contemporary Theories of Organization and Administration* (Uupublished doctoral dissertation, University of Florida, 1963), for an interesting analysis of Etzioni's theories as well as a number of other contemporary theories.

[36]Etzioni, *op. cit.*, p. 12.

types of possible involvement resulting from the use of a kind of power. That is, Type 1 is alienative involvement from the use of coercive power, Type 2, calculative, and Type 3, moral. Each number identifies a different type of power-involvement response.

Etzioni further theorized that organizations exhibiting similar compliance structures exhibit similar goals. Goals were classified as follows: (1) order goals to control actors considered deviant, (2) economic goals to provide production and services to outsiders, (3) culture goals to institutionalize attempts to preserve and create culture and to create or reinforce commitments to these ends. A prison would be an example of an organization with an order goal, a factory, an organization with an economic goal, and a school system, an organization with a culture goal.

Following are some other hypotheses Etzioni derived from his formulation: (1) organizations tend to emphasize only one means of power, and when two means of power are used on the same actors in an organization simultaneously, they tend to neutralize each other; (2) organizations exhibit all three kinds of power but emphasize only one kind or segregate the application of different kinds of power; (3) Types 1, 5, and 9 from the preceding model represent the responses most likely to be received from the application of the different means of power.

Etzioni's theories have many applications to educational administration. Should the same means of power be used on all classes of actors in an educational organization to obtain compliance? For example, should there be any differences in the types of power used with teachers, custodians, secretaries, and students? Assuming that the goal of the total school system is cultural, can it be assumed that the goal of each subsystem is cultural? If a new principal uses normative power at the first meeting of his faculty, coercive power at the second meeting, and normative power again at the third meeting, what kind of involvement on the part of the faculty can he anticipate at the third faculty meeting?

Innovation and Change

Numerous theoretical formulations have been developed to account for innovation and change. Only a few examples are discussed here.

Presthus has developed an interesting theory relating to the individual's reaction to the organization in which he finds himself.[37] He assumes that organizations have manifest as well as latent goals. The manifest goals are in terms of the organizational purposes, particularly productivity. The latent goals are in terms of the need dispositions of

[37]Robert Presthus, *The Organizational Society* (New York: Alfred A. Knopf, Inc., 1962).

members for security, recognition, and self-realization. He hypothesized that the attainment of the manifest goals would be promoted by recognition of the legitimacy of the latent goals of the actors in the organization. It is noteworthy that Presthus' formulation bears a close resemblance to the assumption on which Getzels' model was based.

Presthus developed a comprehensive analysis of complex hierarchical organization and hypothesized that there are three types of personal accommodations of actors who remain with the organization: (1) upward-mobiles; (2) indifferents; and (3) ambivalents.

According to this hypothesis, the upward-mobiles become "organization men" and internalize organizational values that become the premises for action. Personal goals are synthesized with organizational goals. The upward-mobiles recognize authority as the most functional value and are sensitive to authority and status differences. They tend to perceive their superiors as nonthreatening models and their subordinates with organizational detachment.

Indifferents adapt to big organizations by withdrawal and redirecting their interest to nonorganizational activities. Since they lack identification with organizational values, they withdraw from organizational activities and decisions.

Ambivalents exhibit dysfunctional behavior in relation to both personal and organizational goals. They depend upon rational values that might be in conflict with the values of the hierarchical organization. The ambivalents are a source of conflict, but they provide the insight, motivation, and the dialectic that inspire change. Therefore, the conflict created by ambivalents is considered as a creative catalyst. Should school administrators deliberately include on a school faculty some ambivalent persons who disturb the "equilibrium" from time to time?

The concepts "local" and "cosmopolitan"[38] have some relationship to the formulations of Etzioni and Presthus. Local actors tend to identify closely with their organization and to have a stronger allegiance to the vertical institutional subculture than do cosmopolitan actors. The latter tend to have a stronger allegiance to the horizontal subculture of the profession to which they belong than to the subculture of the particular organization in which they are actors. It can be hypothesized that the cosmopolitan actor is more likely to initiate change in an organization than is a local one. He is also more likely to be ambivalent than either indifferent or upwardly mobile. It can also be hypothesized that normative power would be more effective than any other means of power in dealing with a cosmopolitan actor.

[38]See Alvin W. Gouldner, "Cosmopolitans and Locals: Toward an Analysis of Latent Social Roles," *Administrative Science Quarterly*, **2** (Dec. 1957), 281–306; **2** (Mar. 1958) 444–480.

Thompson has theorized that the bureaucratic, hierarchical type of organization advocated by Max Weber retards innovation.[39] He hypothesized that "other things being equal, the less bureaucratized (monocratic) the organization, the more conflict and uncertainty and the more innovation.[40] Based on this hypothesis, Thompson proposed that the hierarchical organization be "loosened up" and made less tidy, if innovation and change were desired:

> In the innovative organization, departmentalization must be arranged so as to keep parochialism to a minimum. Some overlapping and duplication, some vagueness about jurisdictions, make a good deal of communication necessary. People have to define and redefine their responsibilities continually, case after case. They have to probe and seek for help. New problems cannot with certainty be rejected as *ultra vires*.[41]

Thompson assumed in his organizational model that some immediate production must be sacrificed in order to assure innovation within the organization.

Carlson has developed a typology of client-organization relationships in service organizations, as opposed to production organizations, from which he has formulated a number of useful hypotheses.[42]

Following is Carlson's typology:[43]

Selectivity in Client–Organization Relationship
in Service Organizations

		Client control over own participation in organization	
		Yes	No
Organizational control over admission	Yes	Type I	Type III
	No	Type II	Type IV

According to this classification, Type I organizations select their clients and the clients select the organization. Type IV represents the opposite set of conditions under which the organization does not select its clients nor the clients the organization. Private universities, hospitals, and legal

[39]Victor A. Thompson, "Bureaucracy and Innovation," *Administrative Science Quarterly,* **10,** No. 1 (1965).

[40]*Ibid.,* p. 4.

[41]*Ibid.,* p. 15.

[42]Richard O. Carlson, "Environmental Constraints and Organizational Consequences: The Public School and Its Clients," Chap. 12 in *Behavioral Science and Educational Administration,* Sixty-third Yearbook of the National Society for the Study of Education (Chicago: University of Chicago Press), 1964.

[43]*Ibid.,* p. 265.

firms are examples of Type I, while public schools, state mental hospitals, and reform schools are examples of Type IV.

Carlson designated Type IV organization as "domesticated" for the following reasons: "By definition, for example, they do not compete with other organizations for clients; in fact, a steady flow of clients is assured. There is no struggle for survival for this type of organization. Like the domesticated animal, these organizations are fed and cared for. Existence is guaranteed."[44]

He classified Type I organization as "wild" because: ". . . they do struggle for survival. Their existence is not guaranteed, and they do cease to exist. Support for them is closely tied to quality of performance, and a steady flow of clients is not assured. Wild organizations are not protected at vulnerable points as are domesticated organizations."[45]

It was hypothesized "that domesticated organizations because of their protected state, are slower to change and adapt than are wild organizations."[46] Following are some of the hypotheses that Carlson formulated from his model concerning how an organization adapts itself to unselected clients: (1) An adaptive response of domesticated organizations to not being able to select its clients is segregation. Example: "dumping" students unsuited to academic programs into vocational areas, special sections, or even special schools. (2) Segregation may lead to goal displacement, which is the replacement of the original goal by some other goal. Example: discipline may be substituted for learning. (3) Preferential treatment may be given the clients that accommodate themselves to the purposes of the organization. Example: research has shown that preferential treatment is frequently given in the public schools to middle- and upper-class children in such matters as discipline, punishment and curriculums.[47]

It was also hypothesized that the inability of the student client to select his organization resulted in the following adaptations: (1) receptive adaptation, (2) drop-out adaptation, (3) situational retirement, (4) rebellious adjustment, and (5) side-payment adaptation.

There is much interest at the present time in innovation and change in education. Griffiths has identified some propositions aiding or inhibiting change which have been derived from the system theory model. They are as follows:

> The major impetus for change in organizations is from the outside.
> The degree and duration of change is directly proportional to the intensity of the stimulus from the suprasystem.
> Change in an organization is more probable if the successor to the

[44]*Ibid.*, p. 266.
[45]*Ibid.*, p. 267.
[46]*Idem.*
[47]*Ibid.*, pp. 269–273.

chief administrator is from outside the organization than if he is from inside the organization.

When change in an organization does occur, it will tend to occur from the top down, not from the bottom up.

"Living systems respond to continuously increasing stress first by a lag in response, then by an over-compensatory response, and finally by catastrophic collapse of the system."[48]

The number of innovations expected is inversely proportional to the tenure of the chief administrator.

The more hierarchical the structure of an organization, the less the possibility of change.

The more functional the dynamic interplay of subsystems, the less the change in an organization.[49]

In this chapter, we have presented only an introduction to some of the theoretical formulations which are useful in studying the phenomena of change. Some additional concepts relating to innovation and change are applied to organizational and leadership problems in the chapters immediately following.

Community Power Structure

Kimbrough and Johns and their research assistants have developed a typology of community power structure and related it to community decision making.[50] It was assumed from existing research that a small minority of elite influential persons in each school district had more influence on the political decisions made in that district than did the unorganized majority. It was hypothesized that this elite formed informal organizations in order to communicate and exercise influence. It was also hypothesized that different communities had different types of power structures. Kimbrough and Johns and their assistants in their investigations formulated the following typology for community power structures:[51] Type I: the *monopolistic-elite* single-group power structure

[48]James G. Miller, "Toward a General Theory for the Behavioral Sciences," *American Psychologist*, 10 (1955), 525.

[49]Daniel E. Griffiths, "The Nature and Meaning of Theory," Chap. 5 in *Behavioral Science and Educational Administration*, Sixty-third Yearbook of the National Society for the Study of Education (Chicago: University of Chicago Press, 1964), pp. 117–118.

[50]Ralph B. Kimbrough and R. L. Johns, Co-directors of Cooperative Research Project 2842, *Relationship Between Socioeconomic Factors, Educational Leadership Patterns, and Elements of Community Power Structure and Local School Fiscal Policy* (Gainesville, Fla.: College of Education, University of Florida, 1967).

[51]This typology was first described by William Robert Marsh, a research assistant for Cooperative Research Project 2842, in his unpublished doctoral dissertation: *Characteristics of the Power Structures of Six Florida School Districts Selected on the Basis of Population, Educational Effort, and Elasticity of Demand for Education* (Gainesville, Fla.: College of Education, University of Florida, 1965).

described by Hunter as existing in Regional City;[52] Type II: *multigroup noncompetitive elite* comprised of two or more overlapping groups of elite members who generally agree on community issues with little regime conflict; Type III: *multigroup competitive elite* comprised of two or more groups of elite members with limited overlapping, who disagree on some community issues and engage in some regime conflict; Type IV: *segmented pluralism,* a segmented or diffused structure with numerous competing groups which have very little overlapping, but with regime conflicts among many groups.

It will be noted that this typology of power structures constitutes a continuum ranging from a single-group monopolistic structure to the political scientists' ideal of pluralism.

The following hypotheses were developed from this formulation: (1) that school districts with Type I and II power structures tended to make less financial effort in relation to ability than districts with Type III and IV structures; (2) that the influential persons in districts with Type I and II power structures tended to be more conservative in their civic and economic beliefs than those in districts with Types III and IV; (3) that educational innovations and change were less likely to occur in districts with structures of Types I and II than in districts with structures of Types III and IV. At this writing, research has not confirmed or rejected these hypotheses, although it has confirmed that these types of power structures (and perhaps others) do exist.

These different types of conditions existing in the environment of the social system called the school system undoubtedly require different strategies on the part of the school administrator if he is to succeed in obtaining political decisions favorable to the public schools. There are no recipes available to the administrator for dealing with each situation. Even if there were, the situation might change with great rapidity. The administrator is more likely to develop a successful strategy if he conceptualizes his problem theoretically and develops his solution in accordance with sound theory. Bailey and his associates,[53] Kimbrough,[54] and others have amply demonstrated that public school administrators are inevitably participants in political decision making when public school issues are decided by the political process.

Theories From Economics

There are many theoretical formulations from economics that have significance for educational organization and administration. Theories of investment, input—output, division of labor, economic growth, the

[52]Floyd Hunter, *Community Power Structure* (Chapel Hill: University of North Carolina Press, 1953).

[53]Stephen K. Bailey, Richard L. Frost, Paul E. Marsh, and Robert C. Wood, *Schoolmen in Politics* (Syracuse: Syracuse University Press, 1962).

[54]Ralph B. Kimbrough, *Political Power and Educational Decision Making* (Skokie, Ill.: Rand McNally & Co., 1964).

allocation of resources, marginal utility, taxation, and credit are only a few examples. Fortunately, in recent years a number of economists have directed their research toward a study of the economics of education. For example, Fabricant in 1959 presented estimates showing that a large portion of the economic growth of the nation between 1889 and 1957 could not be explained by increased inputs of land, labor, and capital.[55] The classical economists had long used an economic model that included land, labor, and capital as the only factors for explaining production. Fabricant hypothesized that investments in education, research, and development and other intangible capital might account for the unexplained difference in economic growth. In 1961, Schultz tested this hypothesis and found that approximately one half of the unexplained increase in national income could be attributed to investment in education.[56] He concluded that a large part of the resources allocated to education could be classified as an investment, because it resulted in the formation of human capital.

The educational literature on school finance is beginning to include numerous concepts based on theories from economics.[57] Space does not permit discussion of these concepts.

Mathematical Models of Theory

Economics is the first of the social and behavioral sciences in which theoretical models were developed and utilized for formulating hypotheses to be tested by scientifically acceptable methods of research. Economists discovered that many concepts in economics could be expressed in mathematical form. This was a great advantage. The preciseness of the language of mathematics made it possible for researchers to express hypotheses exactly in mathematical equations and to test these hypotheses by valid methods. The extensive use of this approach to the study of economics gave rise to a new specialty in economics called econometrics.

Recently, there has been a trend toward the use of mathematical models in research on organization and administration. Simon was one of the first social scientists to make extensive use of mathematical formulations for expressing theoretical concepts in administration and organization. For example, Simon expressed in mathematical form

[55]Solomon Fabricant, *Basic Facts on Productivity Change,* Occasional Paper 63 (New York: National Bureau of Economic Research, 1959).

[56]Theodore W. Schultz, "Education and Economic Growth," Chap. 3 in *Social Forces Influencing American Education,* Sixtieth Yearbook, National Society for the Study of Education (Chicago: University of Chicago Press, 1961).

[57]See Charles S. Benson, *The Economics of Public Education* (Boston: Houghton Mifflin Company, 1961), Chaps. 1, 2, 3, 11; and Roe L. Johns and Edgar L. Morphet, *Financing the Public Schools* (Englewood Cliffs, N.J.: Prentice-Hall, Inc., 1960), Chaps. 3 and 4.

Homans' theoretical system of group relationships in 1954.[58] Subsequently, March and Simon made extensive use of mathematics in presenting a comprehensive theoretical approach to organizations.[59] Miller used a considerable number of mathematical formulas in presenting 165 cross-level hypotheses on living systems.[60] Griffiths has been the pioneer among professors of educational administration in using mathematical formulations of organizational theory.[61] It is probable that mathematical formulations for research in educational organization and administration will be used even more extensively in the future. Furthermore, mathematical formulations adapted to computers are already used widely in decision making by the armed services and some types of business and industry. It is anticipated that a considerable amount of middle-management decision making may be done by computers in the near future. Thus, as so often happens, theoretical mathematical formulations, which were originally applied primarily to pure research problems, are now being applied to day-to-day operations.

SOME IMPORTANT PROBLEMS AND ISSUES

In this chapter we have presented only a sampling of the rich body of significant theory already available. No general field theory of educational organization and administration has yet been formulated. Nor is this likely to occur soon. However, system theory does provide an extremely useful means by which it is possible to tie together much significant research in educational organization and administration. In the following paragraphs, some further applications of theoretical formulations to educational problems and issues are presented.

Can Theory Be Used as a Basis for Obtaining Support for a Bond Issue?

The board of education of a large, rapidly growing urban school district employed a firm of educational consultants to make a school plant survey. It was a competent firm, and it made a thorough and accurate engineering-type, school plant survey. The technical report was submitted to the board, which accepted the major part of the recom-

[58]Herbert A. Simon, "Some Strategic Considerations in the Construction of Social Science Models," in *Mathematical Thinking in the Social Sciences,* ed. Paul F. Lazarsfeld (New York: Free Press of Glencoe, Inc., 1954).

[59]James C. March and Herbert A. Simon, *Organizations* (New York: John Wiley & Sons, Inc., 1958).

[60]James G. Miller, "Living Systems: Cross-Level Hypotheses," *Behavioral Science,* 10, No. 4 (Oct. 1965).

[61]Daniel E. Griffiths, *Administrative Theory* (New York: Appleton-Century-Crofts, 1959).

mendations. Among those recommendations was the proposal that a bond issue of $30 million be submitted to the electorate for approval. The evidence in support of the bond issue seemed overwhelming. At the time the issue was submitted, 10,000 pupils were on double session and thousands of other children were in overcrowded rooms or housed in substandard facilities. The school population was increasing at the rate of 6,000 per year, but current revenue was sufficient to provide new housing for only approximately 2,000 pupils per year. The district had very little outstanding indebtedness, and the legal limit on indebtedness was more than adequate to cover the proposed issue. There had been no school bond issue for fifteen years.

The board voted to call a special election for a referendum on the bond issue. Numerous news releases on the bond issue were given by the superintendent to the press, and to radio and television stations. Great quantities of mimeographed material explaining the bond issue were sent to parents through the pupils. The superintendent and individual board members made frequent speeches to service clubs, parent-teacher associations, womens' clubs, and other organizations. The superintendent and board members also were frequently on radio and television programs.

When the bond election was held, it was soundly defeated. What theoretical formulations could help explain the defeat of this bond issue? What strategies based on these concepts might be used to pass such a bond issue?

How Can Change Be Initiated
in a Junior College Faculty?

The public junior college in a thriving, growing city of 100,000 has been in existence for seven years, but it was started by taking over the facilities and staff of a private junior college. That college had been in existence for 37 years, when it was changed to a tax-supported institution. The private junior college had selective admissions and a good academic reputation, but it was designed to provide only a two-year program equivalent to the first two years of a four-year college. The board of trustees of the private junior college was willing to turn the institution over to the board of education for operation as a public institution because of financial difficulties.

When the institution became a public junior college, the board of education continued the president, his administrative assistants, the deans, and the faculty in their positions. However, additional faculty members were provided because of a large increase in enrollment. The junior college president was administratively responsible to the superintendent of schools and thence to the board.

When the board of education assumed responsibility for the junior college, it inaugurated nonselective admissions and defined the purposes of the junior college as including vocational, technical, and general adult education as well as the two-year college parallel program. It requested the superintendent of schools and the president of the junior college to change the curriculum of the institution to include these purposes, and it provided the necessary funds for staff and facilities.

The superintendent of schools supported the broad-purpose program and the open-door policy, but the president of the junior college and most of his staff opposed both. The new facilities were constructed and some staff members provided for implementing the additions to the program. But the new programs in vocational, technical, and general education for adults did not flourish. The new faculty members added for these new purposes were not accepted by the other faculty members as peers. The president, instead of promoting the new programs, seemed to apologize for their existence. No effort was expended to advertise them and to recruit students for these new programs.

A new situation developed when the president of the junior college resigned and accepted the presidency of a senior college. He took two of his deans with him. When the president resigned, he recommended one person on his staff to succeed him and two other persons on his staff to succeed to the vacant deanships. His recommendation, submitted to the superintendent, was accompanied by a petition signed by 85 per cent of the faculty.

The board of education expected the superintendent of schools to make recommendations to fill vacancies. The board also desired some substantial changes in the program and in the general climate of the junior college.

What theoretical formulations would help the superintendent to plan recommendations for bringing about change in this junior college? What are some strategies that would be consistent with these formulations?

How Can the Recent Increase in Teacher Unrest Be Explained?

During recent years, classroom teachers in the public schools have become increasingly vocal, active, and aggressive. The membership of teachers in labor unions has increased, and many local education associations have adopted some of the tactics of labor unions, such as collective bargaining and withholding of services for certain functions. Sanctions have been imposed on entire states as well as on a number of local school systems. Teachers have been demanding a more aggressive professional leadership at local, state, and national levels. In one school system of 400,000, the classroom teachers by a majority of 90 per cent voted in 1964 to censure their superintendent, their board of education, their legislative delegation, the state superintendent of schools, the state legislature and the governor, and then voted to impose sanctions on their local school system.

What theories can be used to conceptualize this problem? What hypotheses can be derived from these theories to explain this phenomenon?

Selected References

Argyris, Chris, *Interpersonal Competence and Organizational Effectiveness.* Homewood, Ill.: Richard D. Irwin, Inc. 1962.

Barnard, Chester I., *The Functions of the Executive.* Cambridge: Harvard University Press, 1938.

Bennis, Warren G., Kenneth D. Benne, and Robert Chin, *The Planning of Change.* New York: Holt, Rinehart & Winston, Inc., 1961.

Berelson, B., and G. A. Steiner, *Human Behavior: An Inventory of Scientific Findings.* New York: Harcourt, Brace & World, Inc., 1964.

Blau, Peter M., and W. Richard Scott, *Formal Organizations: A Comparative Approach.* San Francisco: Chandler Publishing Co., 1962.

Charters, W. W., Jr., *et al.*, *Perspectives on Educational Administration and the Behavioral Sciences.* Eugene, Ore.: Center for the Advanced Study of Educational Administration, University of Oregon, 1965.

Culbertson, Jack A., and Stephen P. Hencley, *Educational Research: New Perspectives.* Danville, Ill.: Interstate Printers and Publishers, Inc., 1963.

Etzioni, Amitai, *A Comparative Analysis of Complex Organizations.* New York: Free Press of Glencoe, Inc., 1961.

Golembiewski, Robert T., *Behavior and Organization.* Skokie, Ill.: Rand McNally & Co., 1962.

Griffiths, Daniel E., *Administrative Theory.* New York: Appleton-Century-Crofts, 1959.

Griffiths, Daniel E., ed., *Behavioral Science and Educational Administration.* Sixty-third Yearbook of the National Society for the Study of Education. Chicago: University of Chicago Press, 1964.

————, *Taxonomies of Organizational Behavior.* Skokie, Ill.: Rand McNally & Company, 1967.

Halpin, Andrew W., ed., *Administrative Theory in Education.* Chicago: Midwest Administrative Center, University of Chicago, 1958.

Hearn, Gordon, *Theory Building in Social Work.* Toronto: University of Toronto Press, 1956.

March, James C., and Herbert A. Simon, *Organizations.* New York: John Wiley & Sons, Inc., 1958.

Miller, James G., "Living Systems: Basic Concepts," *Behavioral Science*, **10**, No. 3 (July 1965).

————, "Living Systems: Structure and Process," *Behavioral Science*, **10**, No. 4 (Oct. 1965).

————, "Living Systems: Cross-level Hypotheses," *Behavioral Science*, **10**, No. 4 (Oct. 1965).

Parsons, Talcott, *Structure and Process in Modern Society*. New York: Free Press of Glencoe, Inc., 1960.

Parsons, Talcott, and Edward A. Shils, eds., *Toward a General Theory of Action*. New York: Harper & Row, Publishers, 1962.

Presthus, Robert, *The Organizational Society*. New York: Alfred A. Knopf, Inc., 1962.

Thompson, Victor A., *Modern Organization*. New York: Alfred A. Knopf, Inc., 1961.

Tope, Donald E., *et al.*, *The Social Sciences View School Administration*. Englewood Cliffs, N. J.: Prentice-Hall, Inc., 1965.

Weber, Max, *The Theory of Social and Economic Organization*, trans. A. M. Henderson and Talcott Parsons, ed. Talcott Parsons. New York: Free Press of Glencoe, Inc., 1947.

NOTE: The following periodicals emphasize theoretical concepts significant for educational organization and administration: *Behavioral Science, Administrative Science Quarterly, Educational Administration Quarterly, Journal of Applied Behavioral Science.*

4

Concepts and Principles of Organization and Administration

A number of authorities on organization and administration have insisted that most, if not all, of the currently accepted principles of administration are unscientific. For example, Simon wrote in 1950 that the currently accepted principles of administration are "little more than ambiguous and mutually contradictory proverbs."[1] He found many so-called principles of administration to be mutually incompatible when applied to the same situation. For example, it had been stated as a principle that administrative efficiency is improved by keeping the number of persons supervised (span of control) at any given level to a small number. It had also been stated as a principle that administrative efficiency is improved by keeping to a minimum the number of levels through which a matter must pass before it is acted upon. Simon considered these two principles contradictory. He asked, how is it possible to keep the span of control at any given hierarchical level to a small number and at the same time hold the number of hierarchical levels to a minimum? One can agree with Simon that current statements of principles of span of control and number of hierarchical levels leave much to be desired. Nevertheless, every administrator of an organization, especially a large complex organization, must make decisions on how many persons to place under the control of one administrator at each level in the organization, how

[1]Herbert A. Simon, *Administrative Behavior* (New York: The Macmillan Company, 1950), p. 240.

many persons for each type of task to place under the control of one administrator, and how many hierarchical levels to establish in the organization. Perhaps research based on systems theory discussed in Chapter 3 might develop a principle (or perhaps valid criteria), incorporating both the concept of span of control and number of hierarchical levels, which would be useful in making decisions on these matters.

Another example of contradiction is the statement of principles presented by a number of writers relating to "flexibility" and "stability." These two concepts seem to be contradictory. Actually, many concepts of administration and organization are like some mathematical functions that are valid only within certain limits. Unfortunately, the limits of the applicability of many concepts of administration and organization have not yet been determined. When these limits are defined, it should be possible to state more generalizations in the form of principles that can be used as reliable guides for decision making.

Griffiths wrote in 1957, "At the present time, there appear to be no established principles of administration."[2] He generally agreed with the point of view expressed by Simon.

Blau and Scott commented as follows concerning the development of principles:

> The object of all science is to explain things. What do we mean by a scientific explanation? An observed fact is explained by reference to a general principle, that is, by showing that the occurrence of this fact under the given circumstances can be predicted from the principle. To first establish such an explanatory principle as theoretical generalization, many particular events must be observed and classified into general categories that make them comparable. To explain a principle requires a more general proposition from which this and other specific principles can be inferred.[3]

Very few (if any) principles of administration have been developed in strict compliance with the standards proposed by Blau and Scott. Nevertheless, the literature on administration is filled with statements of principles of administration.[4] In this chapter, some of the most commonly accepted "principles" will be presented and discussed. These cannot be considered as scientifically determined but rather as operating rules of thumb which have been developed largely from experience. They constitute a part of the "folklore" of administration, and should be studied

[2]Daniel E. Griffiths, "Toward a Theory of Administrative Behavior," Chap. 10 in *Administrative Behavior in Education,* ed. Roald F. Campbell and Russell T. Gregg (New York: Harper & Row, Publishers, 1957), p. 368.

[3]Peter M. Blau and W. Richard Scott, *Formal Organizations: A Comparative Approach* (San Francisco: Chandler Publishing Co., 1962), p. 10.

[4]Mary Elizabeth Schlayer, *Certain Principles and Criteria for the Internal Organization and Administration of Institutions of Higher Learning* (Unpublished doctoral dissertation, University of Florida, 1951).

because they point to the areas in which principles of administration are needed.

Principles of administration developed in accord with the standards proposed by Blau and Scott are value-free. That is such principles should be equally applicable in authoritarian and democratic societies. However, values are variables and, since democratic administrators and authoritarian administrators have different value structures, administrative processes and organizational structures will vary even though the same principles are applied. The implementation of principles of organization will vary widely in different countries and different communities, depending largely upon the philosophical assumptions of those in a position to make decisions. The administrator holding an authoritarian philosophy will make many assumptions concerning the implications of theories of administration and organization that differ from those made by the person holding a democratic philosophy. Therefore, some of the assumptions underlying contrasting philosophies of administration will be presented.[5]

No attempt is made in this chapter to distinguish between the principles of organization and the principles of administration. In accord with systems theory, the school administrator is conceptualized as an actor in a social system interacting with the environment. Since the administrator is always an actor in an organization, it is extremely difficult to distinguish between principles of organization and principles of administration.

SOME CHARACTERISTICS OF ORGANIZATIONS

In this chapter, we are concerned primarily with the administration of certain types of formal organizations, although certain propositions and theories are probably applicable to all types of organizations. It is difficult to define a formal organization in precise terms. March and Simon observed that "It is easier, and probably more useful to give examples of formal organizations than to define them."[6] Thus, a business firm and a public school system are examples of formal organizations, as contrasted with such face-to-face groups as work groups in a factory or office and groups of interacting influential persons in the community power structure, which are examples of informal organizations.

[5]Some of the concepts presented in the following pages were adapted from Chap. 9 of *Better Teaching in School Administration* (Nashville, Tenn.: Southern States Cooperative Project in Educational Administration, George Peabody College for Teachers, 1955).

[6]James C. March and Herbert A. Simon, *Organizations* (New York: John Wiley & Sons, Inc., 1958).

Classification of Organizations

With reference to formal organizations, Blau and Scott stated, "Since the distinctive characteristics of these organizations is that they have been formally established for the explicit purpose of achieving certain goals, the term 'formal organization' has been used to designate them."[7] These authors have developed a useful typology for classifying organizations. They started with the assumption that the following four basic categories could be distinguished in relation to any formal organization: the members or rank-and-file participants, the owners or managers, the clients and the public-at-large.[8] The following typology was then developed in terms of who benefits from the organization: "(1) 'mutual benefit associations' where the prime beneficiary is the membership; (2) 'business concerns' where the owners are prime beneficiary; (3) 'service organizations' where the client group is the prime beneficiary; and (4) 'commonweal organizations' where the prime beneficiary is the public at large."[9] Examples of mutual benefit associations are unions, teachers associations, and clubs; examples of business concerns are factories, stores, and private utilities; examples of service organizations are public schools, hospitals, and social work agencies, and of commonweal organizations are the armed services, police forces, and fire departments.

Crucial Problems of Different Types of Organizations

Blau and Scott made the following observations concerning the crucial problems of these different types of organizations:

> Thus the crucial problem in mutual benefit associations is that of maintaining internal democratic processes—providing for participation and control by the membership; the central problem for business concerns is that of maximizing operating efficiency in a competitive situation; the problems associated with the conflict between professional service to clients and administrative procedures are characteristic of service organizations; and the crucial problem posed by commonweal organizations is the development of democratic mechanisms whereby they can be externally controlled by the public.[10]

Attention is directed to the fact that these observations concerning the crucial problems of the different types of organizations are applicable only to organizations located in countries with a capitalistic economy and a democratic value system, such as the United States. These are not the crucial problems of the same types of organizations in a country with a socialist economy and an authoritarian value system, such as Russia. In

[7]Blau and Scott, *op. cit.*
[8]*Ibid.*, p. 42.
[9]*Ibid.*, p.43.
[10]*Ibid.*, p. 43.

fact the business concern, as we know it in the United States, does not even exist in Russia.

It seems that all these problems for different types of organizations are crucial in a public school organization, with the possible exception of "maximizing operating efficiency in a competitive situation." However, a crucial problem of public school administration is competition with other governmental services and also with the private sector of the economy for allocation of the national product. Furthermore, public school administrators are under pressures quite as severe as administrators of private firms to make efficient use of resources.

Relationship of Informal Organizations to Formal Organizations

Attention has already been directed in Chapter 3 to a number of other typologies by which organizations may be studied. It is obvious that the study of organization is a very complex matter. Since we are concerned primarily in this chapter with the phenomena of formal organizations, it would seem that our problem should be simplified. However, numerous authorities have pointed out that it is impossible to ignore informal organizations in the study of formal organizations, because informal organizations of actors are factors in the functioning of formal organizations. Therefore, considerable attention will be given to informal groups in Chapter 5.

One of the important distinctions between formal and informal organizations is that formal organizations usually have a longer life than the actors in the organization, while the informal organization usually has a shorter life than the actors in it. In a formal organization such as a school system, the organization will continue after the services of a particular group of teachers are terminated, but the informal organization of a particular group of teachers dies when that group of teachers severs its connection with the school system. The formal organization has long-term purposes which must be continuously met, and the personnel of the organization must be replenished to do this. The informal group usually has a short-term purpose directed toward satisfying the personal needs of the actors in the informal organization. When those needs are met, the group may disappear. These differences between formal and informal organizations affect organizational structure, which is discussed in the following section of this chapter.

Need for Organizations

The purpose of an organization is to provide the means by which the actors in the organization may cooperate.

An organizational structure is necessary when any group has a common task.[11] This is true for gregarious animals as well as human groups.[12] An unorganized group is only a mass of people. It can neither determine its purposes nor accomplish its ultimate objectives. Therefore, in order to survive, the group must organize. The organization, no matter how simple, must provide for at least the following procedures for making decisions and taking action:

1. a procedure for selecting a leader or leaders;
2. a procedure for determining the roles to be played by each member of the group;
3. a procedure for determining the goals of the group;
4. a procedure for achieving the goals of the group.

Advocates of democratic procedures sometimes infer that organization and administration are less necessary in a democracy than in an authoritarian government. Thomas Jefferson's statement, "The least governed is the best governed," is sometimes quoted as authority for that belief. Even Plato, who was not an advocate of democracy, contemplated in *The Republic* the idea of a simple communistic society without government. He rejected the idea, because he believed that man was naturally ambitious, acquisitive, competitive, and jealous. The researches of social psychologists, anthropologists, political scientists, and authorities in business and educational administration do not reveal less necessity for organization and administration in democratic than in authoritarian government. Patterns and procedures of organization and administration will differ, of course, but organization and administration are equally necessary in all forms of human society.

Decision Making

Every organization must make provision for decision making. Decisions must be made concerning what goals, purposes, objectives, policies, and programs will be accepted by the organization as legitimate. Decisions need to be rendered continuously with respect to the implementation of policies and programs. Therefore, every organization, in order to be effective, must have the ability to make decisions. These decisions may be made by the leader, by the group, by authorities external to the group, or by a combination of methods. Regardless of how decisions are made or who makes them, an organization cannot operate unless decisions are rendered.

The processes of decision making are so vital to the understanding

[11]George C. Homans, *The Human Group* (New York: Harcourt, Brace & World, Inc. 1950), Chaps. 4 and 5.
[12]W. C. Allee, "Conflict and Cooperation: Biological Background," in *Approaches to National Unity, Fifth Symposium*, ed. Lyman Bronson, Louis Finkelstein, and Robert MacIver (New York: Harper & Row, Publishers, 1945).

of administration and organization that significant progress has been made in their theoretical analysis. Simon has suggested that the understanding of the application of administrative principles is to be obtained by analyzing the administrative process in terms of decisions.[13] He theorized that the effectiveness of organizational decisions could be maximized by increasing the rationality of organizational decisions. He assumed that there are limits to human rationality and that this creates a need for administrative theory. According to Simon:

> Two persons, given the same possible alternatives, the same values the same knowledge, can rationally reach only the same decision. Hence administrative theory must be concerned with the limits of rationality, and the manner in which organization effects these limits for the person making the decision.[14]

Griffiths has formulated a theory of administration as decision making based on the following assumptions:

1. Administration is a generalized type of behavior to be found in all human organization.

2. Administration is the process of directing and controlling life in a social organization.

3. The specific function of administration is to develop and regulate the decision-making process in the most effective manner possible.

4. The administrator works with groups or with individuals with a group referent, not with individuals as such.[15]

He presented a set of concepts on decision making, perception, communication, power, and authority, and formulated the following major propositions:

1. The structure of an organization is determined by the nature of its decision-making process. . . .

2. If the formal and informal organization approach congruency, then the total organization will approach maximum achievement. . . .

3. If the total organization is not approaching maximum achievement, then, in all probability, the formal and informal organization are divergent. . . .

4. If the administrator confines his behavior to making decisions on the decision-making process rather than making terminal decisions for the organization, his behavior will be more acceptable to his subordinates. . . .

5. If the administrator perceives himself as the controller of the decision-making process, rather than the maker of the organization's decisions, the decision will be more effective. . . .[16]

[13]Simon, *op. cit.*, p. 240.

[14]*Ibid.*, p. 241. Also see Daniel E. Griffiths, *Administrative Theory* (New York: Appleton-Century & Appleton-Century-Crofts, 1959), pp. 57–60 for a discussion of Simon's theories.

[15]Griffiths, *Administrative Theory*, p. 91.

[16]*Ibid.*, pp. 89–91.

Using these concepts, Griffiths presented the view that the central process of administration is decision making, which is composed of the following aspects:

1. Recognize, define, and limit the problem.
2. Analyze and evaluate the problem.
3. Establish criteria or standards by which solution will be evaluated or judged as acceptable and adequate to the need.
4. Collect data.
5. Formulate and select the preferred solution or solutions. Test them in advance.
6. Put into effect the preferred solution.
   a. Program the solution.
   b. Control the activities in the program.
   c. Evaluate the results and the process.[17]

Griffiths' approach to the study of administration is an example of the modern scientific methods being used in the study of administration, as contrasted with the work of Fayol[18] and Gulick.[19] Gulick saw administration as the processes of planning, organizing, staffing, directing, coordinating, reporting, and budgeting. Griffiths presented his assumptions, stated his hypotheses, which can be tested, and stated his conclusions in the framework of a theoretical formulation. Fayol and Gulick did not really present any theoretical formulation. They only described what they had observed about administration in accordance with certain functional classifications of administrative processes. The work of Griffiths and other similar theorists is seminal *for the creation of new knowledge;* the approaches of Fayol and Gulick, terminal.

Miller has proposed a number of significant hypotheses of decision making in social systems.[20] Further research on these and other hypotheses related to the processes of decision making will undoubtedly produce significant advances in understanding principles of administration and organization.

Selecting a Leader

There are many methods by which a group may secure necessary leadership. The leader (here not distinguished from the administrator) may be selected by instinct, as in the case of bees, or by a test of physical

[17]*Ibid.,* p. 113.

[18]Henri Fayol, *Industrial and General Administration,* trans. J. A. Courborough (Geneva: Industrial Management Association, 1930).

[19]Luther Gulick, "Notes on the Theory of Organization" in *Papers on the Science of Administration,* ed. Luther Gulick and L. Urwick (New York: Institute of Public Administration, Columbia University, 1937).

[20]James G. Miller, "Living Systems: Cross-Level Hypotheses," *Behavioral Science,* 10, No. 4 (Oct. 1965), 394–397, 406.

strength, as in the case of the wolf pack. The leader may be selected by force or chicanery, in accordance with the patterns usually followed in dictatorships. The leader may be selected by the group itself or by representatives of the group, as in a democracy or a republic. Regardless of the method of selection, an effective group will always have leadership. The role of the leader will vary widely in different types of groups, depending upon the goals and values of the group, the leader's perception of his role, the group's perception of the leader's role, and other factors.

The group cannot attain its maximum productivity and the maximum satisfaction of individual members unless functions, activities, interests, and assignments are coordinated. That is one of the principal functions of executive leadership.

The executive head of an organization, in order to be of maximum usefulness to the organization, must also be a leader. The functions of leadership are many and varied. The definition of the term "leadership" itself is an involved undertaking. This subject is discussed in detail in the following chapter.

Determination of Roles

The organization must also provide for the determination of the roles of each member of the group. Again, the method of determining these roles will vary widely among different groups, depending upon the nature of the group. In the lowest order of animals, the individual role of a group member may be assigned largely by instinct. In a higher order of animals, such as human beings, the roles of individual members may be determined arbitrarily by the leader, or they may be determined largely by the choice of individual members of the group, or by various combinations of these methods. Regardless of how roles are determined, each member of the group or organization must have an appropriate role for the social system to function with maximum efficiency.

Determination of Goals and Purposes

The organization must provide some method by which a group may determine its common goals. This is very easy in the case of some groups, such as the wolf pack. The common goal of obtaining food was the reason the group was formed. Even in animals of a higher order, such as human beings, common goals are usually the basis of group formation. When human beings are arbitrarily forced together, they cannot become an effective group until common goals have been determined. This phenomenon is sometimes observed in faculties of schools which do not have common purposes. Conflicts sometimes develop within a group over the determination of purposes. If these conflicts are not resolved, the group will either disintegrate or break into two or more factions.

Miller has stated the following two hypotheses concerning the determination of goals and purposes which have been supported by some research:

1. Lack of clarity of purpose or goals in a system's decisions will produce conflict between it and other components of the suprasystem.
2. If a system has multiple purposes and goals, and they are not placed in clear priority and commonly known by all components and subsystems, conflict among them will ensue.[21]

Attainment of Goals

All groups must develop procedures for taking action to attain goals. If these goals are not attained, the group will either disintegrate or be reorganized. The goals must include the goals of individual members as well as those of the organization if it is to maximize its production possibilities (see Getzel's model presented in Chapter 3). It is impossible to attain organizational goals with efficiency if there is a crucial conflict between organizational goals and the goals of the actors in the organization.

A distinction should be made at this point between goal attainment of formal organizations and of informal organizations. An effective organization must be an active one. In fact, activity is essential for organizational survival. Since formal organizations usually have long-range goals which must be continuously met, the need for activity is continuous. But informal organizations usually have short-range goals arising from the needs of the actors in the informal organization. If the goal is attained and no other goal is substituted for it, activity ceases and the organization disappears. The same thing is true even of some types of formal organizations, such as a political organization formed to elect a particular candidate at a given election. After the election, the goal is either attained or abandoned, activity ceases and the organization dissolves. Thus, we have the paradox of the necessity for the organization to attain its goals in order to succeed but the probability of nonsurvival once it attains its goals. This points to the necessity for the public schools to formulate new goals from time to time, consistent with the changing purposes of the schools.

Nature of Organizational Structures

The tendency in formal organizations is to develop pyramidal, hierarchical structures with superordinate-subordinate relationships among the actors in the organization. This phenomenon has been observed in all societies, regardless of stage of civilization, economic system,

[21]Miller, *op. cit.*, pp. 404–405.

or political philosophy. The larger and more complex the organization, the more bureaucratic and hierarchical is the structure of the organization. For example, the organizational structure for a rural elementary school district that provides educational services for only 150 pupils in a six-teacher school is far less hierarchical and bureaucratic than the organizational structure for a municipal district with a population of 500,000 providing numerous elementary and high schools, a junior college, and many special educational services. Further attention will be given to the structure of formal organizations later in this chapter.

Informal organizations are usually small in size and have a very simple structure with few organizational hierarchies. Berelson and Steiner have reported that most informal groups have an upper limit of fifteen to twenty persons.[22] Informal organizations usually have face-to-face relations in small groups.

CONCEPTS OF ORGANIZATION AND ADMINISTRATION

In the following sections of this chapter, a number of concepts of organization and administration are presented. Although each of these "principles" is stated in terms of its relationship to the effectiveness of the organization in surviving in its environment and attaining its goals, it could just as readily be stated in terms of "administrative efficiency." For example, the proposition concerning the single executive could be stated: (1) administrative efficiency is increased by having a single executive head of an organization; or (2) the effectiveness of an organization is enhanced by having a single executive head. These two statements illustrate the relationship of principles of administration to principles of organization. However, the ultimate purpose of an organization is not to establish conditions that increase administrative efficiency but to establish conditions that will enhance the effectiveness of the organization in attaining its goals. Sometimes this important point has been forgotten by an administrative hierarchy snarled in red tape. Administrative efficiency is valid only to the extent that it contributes to the attainment of the goals of the organization, the goals of the actors in the organization, and the extent that it meets the requirements of the environment for the survival of the organization. In the future, more meaningful and useful principles of administration and organization than those presented here will no doubt be developed from current and future research, much of it based on systems theory. Educational administrators administer social systems usually comprising a complex of suprasystems and subsystems. Therefore, useful principles must deal with cross-level factors

[22]Bernard Berelson and Gary A. Steiner, *Human Behavior—An Inventory of Scientific Findings* (New York: Harcourt, Brace & World, Inc., 1964), p. 325.

as well as factors at one system level. The work of Miller may well point the direction for future research on theories of organization and administration.[23]

Single Executive

THE EFFECTIVENESS OF AN ORGANIZATION IS ENHANCED BY HAVING A SINGLE EXECUTIVE HEAD.   The executive must provide central coordination for the activities of an organization. Although an organization may have a number of leaders, one of these leaders must serve as the coordinating head of the group. Unless this is done, no organization can achieve its purposes, because division of central leadership will prevent the coordination of its activities. The necessity for the recognition of this principle becomes more imperative as the size of the organization's membership increases. This principle of administration was among the earliest generally recognized. Despite the fact that numerous experiments in divided central executive leadership have failed, proposals are still being advanced to provide an organization with two executive heads. In educational administration numerous attempts have been made to divide the executive functions for education into educational and business administration. Boards of education have sometimes employed two superintendents, one for educational and one for business administration, each directly responsible to the board and neither responsible to the other. These experiments have almost invariably resulted in friction and in the failure of the organization to attain its objectives effectively. The activities of any effective organization must be coordinated, and this can best be achieved through a single executive head.

Unity of Purpose

THE EFFECTIVENESS OF AN ORGANIZATION IS ENHANCED BY CLEAR DEFINITION OF GOALS AND PURPOSES.   The processes of determining goals and purposes may be formal or informal. The members of a simple organization may have tacitly agreed upon its purposes before the organization was formed. However, a complex organization such as an educational structure has many purposes and goals. In such an organization these must be carefully determined. Unless that is done, the organization is likely to operate with conflicting objectives. Such an organization will almost inevitably end in conflict among members of the group or between the group and the official leadership. Unresolved conflicts will eventually destroy informal organizations and "wild" formal organizations (defined in Chapter 3). The members of a public school organization are members of a "domestic" organization. Such a group, with undetermined or conflicting purposes, may legally continue in existence past its period of

[23]See Miller, *op. cit.*

usefulness. The turnover in such a group is high and the group is ineffective. Therefore, it is vital that any organization determine its purposes and goals if it wishes to continue serving a useful function.

Unity of Command

THE EFFECTIVENESS OF AN ORGANIZATION IS ENHANCED WHEN EVERY PERSON IN THE ORGANIZATION KNOWS TO WHOM AND FOR WHAT HE IS RESPONSIBLE. This principle, as its name implies, was first recognized by the armed services. As pointed out later in this chapter, there is much disagreement concerning the validity of this proposition. Following are some of the assumptions underlying it.

The organization should provide for the definition of the role of each individual. It is demoralizing to the individual and destructive to the productivity of the organization to have individuals uncertain of their duties. Whether the individual is assigned his duties by the status leader or participates himself in their selection, he will not be an effective member of the organization unless he knows what his obligations are. Unless the lines of responsibility and authority are clearly defined, chaos is inevitable. It follows that no individual in the organization should be compelled to take direct orders from more than one person, because conflicts will inevitably arise.

Delegation of Authority and Responsibility

THE EFFECTIVENESS OF AN ORGANIZATION IS ENHANCED WHEN SUPERORDINATES DELEGATE AUTHORITY TO SUBORDINATES.   It would seem that this is a self-evident fact rather than a principle. However, the problem of delegation of authority and responsibility has plagued mankind since the development of organizations. One of the assumptions back of this principle is that when a superordinate delegates responsibility for a task to a subordinate, he should at the same time delegate to the subordinate the necessary authority to accomplish the task.

As is true with many principles of organization and administration, there are limits to the operation of this principle. Miller has hypothesized that segregation (compartmentalization) increases conflict among subsystems.[24] He cited in support of that hypothesis the observation of March and Simon that the delegation of authority to departments in firms increased the disparity of interests and created conflict among them.[25]

Division of Labor

THE EFFECTIVENESS OF AN ORGANIZATION IS ENHANCED BY THE DIVISION OF LABOR AND TASK SPECIALIZATION.   Provision for an appropriate division

[24]Miller, *op. cit.*, p. 403.
[25]March and Simon, *op. cit.*, pp. 41–42.

of labor in order to increase productivity was the basic reason private firms were established. Adam Smith presented an excellent illustration of this principle in his famous book, *The Wealth of Nations,* published in 1776. In his illustration, he demonstrated that if a group of men making pins divided the labor and each specialized on a task, the same number of men could greatly increase their production of pins in a given length of time.

Much of the increase in the productivity of the economy of Western civilization during the past two centuries has been due to the formation of large numbers of complex organizations which have applied the division-of-labor principle. The growth in technology and the industrialization of society have greatly increased the emphasis on division of labor and specialization during the past 25 years. This trend has created some critical problems which will be treated later in this chapter.

Miller has hypothesized that the segregation of functions in a system is increased by structurally increasing the types of its members or components.[26]

Standardization

THE EFFECTIVENESS OF AN ORGANIZATION IS ENHANCED BY THE DEVELOPMENT OF STANDARDIZED PROCEDURES FOR ROUTINE ADMINISTRATIVE OPERATION. Standardized procedures are applicable to such operations as accounting, data gathering, statistical reporting, and record keeping. Standardization of routine operations saves labor on the part of all members of the organization. In many instances such procedures are also essential to collecting the data necessary for evaluation.

Span of Control

THE EFFECTIVENESS OF AN ORGANIZATION IS ENHANCED BY ASSIGNING TO EACH ADMINISTRATOR NO GREATER A NUMBER OF PERSONS THAN HE CAN DIRECTLY SUPERVISE. This is an extremely controversial principle, as will be shown later. However it is a time-honored principle, generally accepted by military and business organizations. Perhaps this principle is applicable to some types of organizations and not applicable to others. Or perhaps the most efficient span of control differs for different types of organizations and for different types of tasks within an organization.

Stability

THE EFFECTIVENESS OF AN ORGANIZATION IS ENHANCED BY CONTINUING POLICIES AND PROGRAMS UNTIL RESULTS CAN BE EVALUATED. An organization which changes its policies or programs capriciously is almost certain

[26]Miller, *op. cit.,* p. 384.

to be an ineffective organization. If policies and programs are carefully defined and given a thorough trial before being abandoned or changed, "sunk costs" are minimized and the probability of establishing a favorable ratio between input and output is increased.

Flexibility

THE EFFECTIVENESS OF AN ORGANIZATION IS ENHANCED WHEN IT MAKES PROVISION FOR INNOVATION AND CHANGE. Innovation and change are facilitated when policies are stated in broad enough terms to permit reasonable flexibility in management. The principle of flexibility also implies that, once a program or policy has been continued long enough for evaluation, provision should be made for change. Therefore, the principle of flexibility might be interpreted as a contradiction of the principle of stability. However, these two principles do not contradict each other as much as they tend to balance one another. What is sought in effective administration is an appropriate balance between stability and flexibility. The need for flexibility of administration and organization increases in these times of rapid change.

Security

THE EFFECTIVENESS OF AN ORGANIZATION IS ENHANCED WHEN THE ORGANIZATION PROVIDES SECURITY FOR ITS MEMBERS. Different members of the group have many different individual needs, but the need for security is universal. This universal craving for security makes it essential that this need be met in any group, regardless of political philosophy. As a matter of fact, security itself is frequently the goal or purpose for which informal groups are formed. The need for security is no less present in formal groups, such as educational organizations, than in informal groups.

Personnel Policies

THE EFFECTIVENESS OF AN ORGANIZATION IS ENHANCED BY PERSONNEL POLICIES, WHICH INCLUDE SELECTING THE COMPETENT, TRAINING THE INEXPERIENCED, ELIMINATING THE INCOMPETENT, AND PROVIDING INCENTIVES FOR ALL MEMBERS OF THE ORGANIZATION. Even informal organizations such as street gangs follow these procedures. Personnel policies in formal groups, such as school faculties, must be carefully defined. Selecting the competent is essential to recruiting potentially effective group members. Training the inexperienced is essential to obtaining maximum productivity from individual members of the group. Eliminating the incompetent is essential to maintaining the integrity and cohesiveness of the group. Providing incentives by meeting the individual needs of group members is essential to maintaining group morale and assuring maximum productivity.

Evaluation

THE EFFECTIVENESS OF AN ORGANIZATION IS ENHANCED WHEN PROVISION IS MADE NOT ONLY FOR EVALUATING THE PRODUCTS OF THE ORGANIZATION BUT ALSO THE ORGANIZATION ITSELF. Activity without evaluation may be fruitless. The ability to evaluate is one of the characteristics which distinguish the human species from lower orders of animals. Evaluation is provided not only by actors within the organization, but also by the environment of the organization if evaluation is effective. Evaluation by the environment is obtained by making provision for the organization to receive feedback, as pointed out in Chapter 3.

Leavitt has presented evidence indicating that two-way communication in an organization providing feedback reduces error.[27] Feedback provides one means of continuous evaluation.

There are numerous technical and scientific methods available for evaluation of the material products of an organization. The instruments available for the evaluation of the nonmaterial products of the educational system are far less precise. This does not relieve the educational system of the necessity for evaluation. It only makes the problem more difficult.

TRADITIONAL AND EMERGING CONCEPTS

OF ORGANIZATION AND ADMINISTRATION

There are two principal competing concepts of organization and administration, which we will call the traditional monocratic, bureaucratic concept and the emerging pluralistic, collegial concept. The use of the terms "traditional monocratic, bureaucratic concept" and "emerging pluralistic, collegial concept" should not be interpreted as suggesting that we have a clear dualism in types of administration and organization.

As Bennis has said, "So we hear of 'Theory X vs. Theory Y,' personality vs. organization, democratic vs. autocratic, task vs. maintenance, human relations vs. scientific management, and on and on. Surely life is more complicated than these dualities suggest, and surely they must imply a continuum—not simply extremes."[28]

Therefore, in this section we will describe not dual concepts of administration and organization but the extreme ends of a continuum. The principles of administration discussed in the previous section are

[27]Harold K. Leavitt, *Managerial Psychology* (Chicago: University of Chicago Press, 1958), p. 123.
[28]Warren G. Bennis, "Theory and Method in Applying Behavioral Science to Planned Organizational Change," *Journal of Applied Behavioral Science*, 1, No. 4 (1965), 356.

equally applicable throughout this continuum. However, as will be shown in this chapter, the structure of the organization and administrative procedures will vary greatly, depending upon the assumptions made and the value systems of those applying these principles.

The Traditional Monocratic, Bureaucratic Concept

The traditional monocratic, bureaucratic concept of organization and administration is defined as a pyramidal, hierarchical organizational structure, in which all power for making decisions flows from superordinates to subordinates. This concept has been described by Weber.[29]

We are indebted to Abbott for the following succinct description of Weber's monocratic, bureaucratic model:

For Weber, the essential and distinctive characteristics of a bureaucracy were somewhat as follows:

1. The regular activities required for the purposes of the organization are distributed in fixed ways as official duties. Since the tasks of an organization are too complex to be performed by a single individual, or by a group of individuals possessing a single set of skills, efficiency will be promoted by dividing those tasks into activities which can be assigned to specific offices or positions. This division of labor makes possible a high degree of specialization which, in turn, promotes improved performance in two ways. First it enables the organization to employ personnel on the basis of technical qualifications; second, it enables employees to improve their skills by limiting their attention to a relatively narrow range of activities.

2. The positions in an organization are arranged on the principle of office hierarchy and of levels of graded authority. This means that there is a firmly ordered system of superordination and subordination in which the lower offices are supervised by the higher ones. Although specialization makes possible the efficient performance of specific tasks, specialization also creates problems of coordination. To achieve the required coordination, it is necessary to grant to each official the requisite authority to control the activities of his subordinates.

3. The management of activities is controlled by general rules which are more or less stable, more or less exhaustive, and which can be learned. These rules are general and abstract, and they constitute standards which assure reasonable uniformity in the performance of tasks. They preclude the issuance of directives based on whim or caprice, but require the application of general principles to particular cases. Together with the hierarchical authority structure, rules provide for the

[29]Max Weber, *The Theory of Social and Economic Organization,* trans. A. M. Henderson and Talcott Parsons, ed. Talcott Parsons (New York: Free Press of Glencoe, Inc., 1947).
NOTE: Max Weber (1864–1920) was a remarkably productive German scholar. He began with the study of law but soon went on to study economics. After writing a number of outstanding works on economics, he turned to the development of a science of sociology. Every serious student of administration should read *The Theory of Social and Economic Organization.*

coordination of organizational activities and for continuity of operations, regardless of changes in personnel.

4. Bureaucracy develops the more perfectly the more completely it succeeds in eliminating from official business love, hatred, and all purely personal, irrational, and emotional elements which escape calculation. The essence of bureaucratic arrangements is rationality. A spirit of formalistic impersonality is necessary to separate organizational rights and duties from the private lives of employees. Only by performing impersonally can officials assure rationality in decision making, and only thus can they assure equitable treatment for all subordinates.

5. Employment in a bureaucracy is based upon technical competence and constitutes a career. Promotions are to be determined by seniority, or achievement, or both; tenure is to be assured; and fixed compensation and retirement provisions are to be made. Since individuals with specialized skills are employed to perform specialized activities, they must be protected from arbitrary dismissal or denial of promotion on purely personal ground.[30]

Weber wrote as follows concerning the superiority of his model for human organization:

> Experience tends universally to show that the purely bureaucratic type of administrative organization—that is, the monocratic variety of bureaucracy—is, from a purely technical point of view, capable of attaining the highest degree of efficiency and is in this sense formally the most rational known means of carrying out imperative control over human beings. It is superior to any other form in precision, in stability, in the stringency of its discipline, and in its reliability. It thus makes possible a particularly high degree of calculability of results for the heads of the organization and for those acting in relation to it. It is finally superior both in intensive efficiency and in the scope of its operation, and is formally capable of application to all kinds of administrative tasks.[31]

Weber was definitely at one end of the continuum. He insisted that, considering the needs of mass administration, the only choice was between bureaucracy and dilettantism in the field of administration. His opinion of "collegiality"—the formal requirement that legitimate acts of a body require the participation of all its members in decision making— was expressed as follows:

> Furthermore, it divides personal responsibility, indeed in the larger bodies this disappears almost entirely, whereas in monocratic organizations it is perfectly clear without question where responsibility lies. Large-scale tasks which require quick and consistent solutions tend in general, for good technical reasons, to fall into the hands of monocratic "dictators" in whom all responsibility is concentrated.[32]

[30]Max G. Abbott and John T. Lovell, eds., *Change Perspectives in Educational Administration* (Auburn, Ala.: School of Education, Auburn University, 1965), pp. 42–43.

[31]Weber, *op. cit.*, p. 337.

[32]Weber, *op. cit.*, p. 399.

Strangely enough, Weber did not consider his idealized bureaucracy as authoritarian. On the contrary, he thought that it foreshadowed mass democracy, because according to his model, technical experts would be placed in the executive, decision-making positions in the hierarchy, instead of staffing these positions through the traditional methods of patriarchalism, patrimonialism, and charisma. Viewed from this standpoint, the development of the modern bureaucracy was a step toward democracy because, theoretically, positions of power in the hierarchy would be opened to experts who could come from the masses.

Thompson has pointed out, however, that at the present time one of the crucial problems in modern organizations is the reconciliation of conflicts between specialists on the staff of an organization who know and executives in the power structure of the line organization who do not know.[33]

Weber's monocratic, bureaucratic model has been severely criticized, in ways discussed later in this chapter. Despite such criticism, the monocratic, bureaucratic concept of administrative organization is the prevailing model of organization found in every advanced country of the world, regardless of its political philosophy or economic organization. It is the basic model for organizing the public school systems of the United States, especially the larger systems.

In the following section, some of the assumptions underlying the monocratic, bureaucratic concept are presented. It will be noted that a number of these assumptions are not value-free.

Some Assumptions Underlying the Traditional Monocratic, Bureaucratic Concept

Administrators differ widely in theory concerning the application of the principles of organization and administration to: first, those activities relating to the formulation of goals, programs, and policies; second, those activities relating to goal attainment through the implementation of programs and policies; and third, those activities relating to maintaining the group. There is no recognized field theory of administration. Furthermore, it is difficult for the student to find anywhere in the literature of educational administration a coherent statement of theory on how the principles of organization and administration should be implemented.

Critics of administrators, sometimes administrators themselves, have tended to categorize administration as good or bad, efficient or inefficient, without attempting to differentiate carefully between different concepts of administrative theory. In this chapter, an attempt is made to distinguish between the traditional monocratic, bureaucratic and the emerging

[33]Victor A. Thompson, *Modern Organization* (New York: Alfred A. Knopf, Inc., 1961), pp. 81–113.

pluralistic, collegial concepts of administration and organization, but even these words unfortunately, have good and bad connotations to many people. Sometimes the arbitrary classification of administrative theory by labels that have good and bad connotations retards a scholarly analysis. It is better to assume that administrators are neither good nor bad but that they differ in their assumptions concerning these concepts. In the following paragraphs, an analysis is made of some of the important assumptions underlying the monocratic, bureaucratic concept.

LEADERSHIP IS CONFINED TO THOSE HOLDING POSITIONS IN THE POWER ECHELON. Those accepting such a premise generally assume that the population is divided into two groups, the leaders and the followers. The leaders should be assigned to power positions in the hierarchy, where it is their responsibility to exercise leadership. If persons other than power holders exercise leadership, conflicts are bound to arise. A capable person should secure a power position if he wants to be a leader. If such a person attempts to exercise leadership when he does not hold a power position, he will become a trouble maker and interfere with the administrative leadership of the person holding the superordinate position. If the superordinate permits leadership to develop, his own position is threatened. If a person does not exercise his authority, he will lose it. The superordinate must carefully protect his prerogatives, or he is likely to lose his leadership position.

GOOD HUMAN RELATIONS ARE NECESSARY IN ORDER THAT FOLLOWERS ACCEPT DECISIONS OF SUPERORDINATES. The decisions of the officials in the power hierarchy must be accepted and implemented, or the enterprise fails. The power holder can use force on his followers and require them to accept his decisions, but force requires rigorous inspection and supervision, which is expensive in time and energy. Therefore, he should establish good relations between his followers and himself so that they will voluntarily follow him without question.

AUTHORITY AND POWER CAN BE DELEGATED, BUT RESPONSIBILITY CANNOT BE SHARED. The top executive may delegate power and authority to subexecutives, and he may hold them responsible for the proper exercise of the power and authority he has delegated to them. Nevertheless, all responsibility is ultimately his if things go wrong.

FINAL RESPONSIBILITY FOR ALL MATTERS IS PLACED IN THE ADMINISTRATOR AT THE TOP OF THE POWER ECHELON. The top executive in the organization is ultimately responsible for everything that happens. He should receive the credit and he should receive the blame. This assumption logically follows the assumption with respect to responsibility. Certainly, if the executive is ultimately responsible for everything, he should have the authority to veto any decision of his subordinates.

The individual finds security in a climate in which the superordinates protect the interests of subordinates in the organization. The person holding the top position in the power echelon should defend his subordinates, right or wrong, so long as they take his orders and are loyal to him. This assumption is similar to the assumptions of feudalism, whereby a person made himself a vassal of a feudal lord for protection. The success of the feudal system was based upon the loyalty of vassals and on the effectiveness with which the feudal lord protected his vassals. Thompson made the following comment concerning this point:

> Bureaucratic hierarchy has inherited the rights and privileges of the early charismatic leader and his retainers, the traditionalistic king and his nobility, and the entrepreneurial owner-manager and his family protégés. Consequently, to be socially defined as "successful" in our culture, one must proceed up some hierarchy.[34]

Unity of purpose is secured through loyalty to the superordinate. Since the superordinate will protect his subordinates, right or wrong, his subordinates owe him their undivided loyalty. This loyalty requires that subordinates defend him and also accept his decisions without question. This, too, is an essential assumption of the feudal system.

The image of the executive is that of a superman. According to Thompson, "The impression is fostered that occupants of hierarchical positions are, of all people in the organization, the ablest, the most industrious, the most indispensable, the most loyal, the most reliable, the most self-controlled, the most ethical, which is to say the most honest, fair, and impartial."[35]

Since money is one of the most important factors in determining prestige and status, the person occupying the top position in the hierarchy, should be paid the highest salary. For example, a requirement for accreditation of high schools by the Southern Association of Schools and Colleges is that no person in the school system may be paid a salary higher than that of the superintendent of schools.

Maximum production is attained in a climate of competition and pressure. People excel in their efforts when they compete with each other. Life is a competitive struggle for survival, and greater rewards should be given to the persons who are successful. This competition should be supplemented by pressure, taking the form of either rewards or punishment. Competition and pressure are good for people.

The line-and-staff plan of organization should be utilized to formulate goals, policies, and programs, as well as to execute policies and programs. Since the best leadership is placed in the line-and-staff

[34]*Ibid.* p. 96. Reprinted from *Modern Organization* by Victor Thompson by permission of Alfred A. Knopf, Inc. Copyright © 1961 by Victor Thompson.
[35]*Ibid.* p. 143.

structure, this leadership is most competent to formulate goals, policies, and programs. That structure has the responsibility for implementing the goals, policies, and programs, and therefore should have the responsibility for formulating them.

AUTHORITY IS THE RIGHT AND PRIVILEGE OF A PERSON HOLDING A HIERARCHICAL POSITION. Authority is inherent in the position itself. The authority should be given to the person who has the greatest ability. Superordinates have the greatest ability, or they would not be in the hierarchy. This assumption can be traced back to the divine right of kings theory.

THE INDIVIDUAL IN THE ORGANIZATION IS EXPENDABLE. The purpose or goal of the organization is more important than the individual. For that reason, the individual should be sacrificed if necessary to accomplish the goals of the organization. The individual exists in order to serve the organization, rather than the organization to serve the individual.

EVALUATION IS THE PREROGATIVE OF SUPERORDINATES. Since the superordinate is finally responsible for everything, logically he should have the exclusive authority to evaluate persons and production. Evaluation is one of the means by which he enforces discipline in the organization.

THE EMERGING PLURALISTIC, COLLEGIAL CONCEPT

Unfortunately, no scholar with the brilliance of a Weber has attempted to describe the model for the pluralistic, collegial concept of administration and organization. Many writers have described in detail the defects of the bureaucratic model, but none has suggested its complete abandonment.[36] The emerging pluralistic, collegial concept of organization can perhaps best be described as a modification of the monocratic, bureaucratic concept, providing for a pluralistic sharing of power to make policy and program decisions on a collegial basis. Under this concept, the organization is structured hierarchically, as in Weber's bureaucracy, to implement programs and policies, and is structured collegially on an egalitarian basis for making policy and program decisions. Perhaps the best example of this model is a college which: (1) emphasizes academic freedom, scholarship, and the dignity of the individual; (2) provides that the faculty, and not the administrative hierarchy, shall

[36]For example, see Victor A. Thompson, *Modern Organization* (New York: Alfred A. Knopf, Inc., 1961); Chris Argyris, "The Individual and Organization: Some Problems of Mutual Adjustment," and Wallazz B. Eaton, "Democratic Organization: Myth or Reality" in *Educational Administration: Selected Readings*, ed. Walter G. Hack *et al.* (Boston: Allyn & Bacon, Inc., 1965).

make major policy and program decisions, and (3) pays distinguished professors salaries as high as or higher than those of persons holding positions in the administrative hierarchy. This is not a hypothetical case. This concept of organization and administration is actually found in most of the leading colleges and universities of the nation.

Thompson noted that the monocratic, bureaucratic organization is not innovative.[37] Following is a summary of his proposals for making a bureaucratic organization more innovative: (1) the organization will be more loosely structured, with less emphasis on a precise definition of duties and responsibilities; (2) jobs will be described in terms of professional responsibilities, as contrasted with duties; (3) communications will be freer; (4) appropriate types of decisions will be decentralized; (5) there will be less stratification in the organization, and salary scales will no longer reflect chiefly "awesome status differences"; (6) greater use will be made of group processes and less emphasis made of authority; (7) work assignments will be made broader; (8) more opportunities will be provided for multiple group membership and interpersonal communication; (9) departmentalization will be so arranged as to keep parochialism to a minimum; (10) the organization will not be as tidy as the monocratic bureaucracy, because some overlapping of functions and vagueness concerning jurisdictions promote interdepartmental communication.[38] While Thompson did not attempt to conceptualize the pluralistic, collegial organizational model, he made the following proposals, which take us a considerable distance on the continuum toward this model.

> If formal structures could be sufficiently loosened, it might be possible for organizations and units to restructure themselves continually in the light of the problem at hand. Thus, for generating ideas, for planning and problem solving, the organization or unit would "unstructure" itself into a freely communicating body of equals. When it came time for implementation, requiring a higher degree of coordination of action (as opposed to stimulation of novel or correct ideas), the organization would then restructure itself into the more usual hierarchical form, tightening up its lines somewhat.[39]

Thus, he has recommended a major modification in Weber's model in order to promote innovation.

Argyris has presented an extremely interesting analysis of the conflict between the healthy human personality and a monocratic bureaucracy established in accord with the principles of formal organization

[37]Victor A. Thompson, "Bureaucracy and Innovation," *Administrative Science Quarterly*, 10, No. 1 (June 1965).

[38]Adapted from Victor A. Thompson, "Bureaucracy and Innovation," *Administrative Science Quarterly*, 10, No. 1 (June 1965).

[39]*Ibid.*, p. 16.

already discussed in this chapter.[40] He did not accept the arguments of some advocates of formal organization that the choice was between the monocratic, bureaucratic organization or no organization at all. Nor did he accept the arguments of some human-relations researchers that formal structures are "bad" and that the needs of the individual actors in the organization should be given priority over organizational goals. He assumed that, to date, no one has defined a more useful set of formal organizational principles than those discussed in this chapter. He then proceeded to demonstrate how each of the formal principles of organization, such as division of labor, unity of chain of command, unity of purpose, and span of control, was in conflict with the psychological needs of a mature, healthy human personality. He cited research showing that the self-actualizing personality through the process of growth passes from a state of being passive as an infant to a state of increasing activity as an adult, tends to develop from a state of dependency upon others as a child to relative independence as an adult, tends to develop from being only able to use a few of his capacities as an infant to the ability to use many capacities as an adult, tends to grow from a subordinate position as an infant toward an equal position as an adult, and tends to grow and mature in many other ways.[41] After comparing the needs of the human personality with the requirements for strict application of the principles of formal organization, Argyris observed:

> If the principles of formal organization are used as ideally defined, then the employees will tend to work in an environment where (1) they are provided minimal control over their work-a-day world, (2) they are expected to be passive, dependent, subordinate, (3) they are expected to have a short-time perspective, (4) they are induced to perfect and value the frequent use of a few superficial abilities, and (5) they are expected to produce under conditions leading to psychological failure.[42]

Argyris concluded that these conditions lead to conflict. He made no proposals for major changes in the bureaucratic organization. But he stated that the basic problem was the reduction in the degree of dependency, subordination, and submission required of the employee, and suggested that "job enlargement and employee centered (or democratic or participative) leadership are elements which, if used correctly, can go a long way toward ameliorating the situation."[43]

[40]Chris Argyris, "The Individual and Organization: Some Problems of Mutual Adjustment," Chap. 14 in *Educational Administration: Selected Readings*, ed. Walter G. Hack *et al.* (Boston: Allyn & Bacon, Inc., 1965).

[41]*Ibid.*, pp. 161–162.

[42]*Ibid.*, p. 176.

[43]*Ibid.*, p. 182.

Some Assumptions Underlying the Emerging
Pluralistic, Collegial Concept

Some of the assumptions underlying the pluralistic, collegial concept of administration differ sharply from those underlying the traditional monocratic, bureaucratic concept. In the following paragraphs an
analysis is made of some of these assumptions.

LEADERSHIP IS NOT CONFINED TO THOSE HOLDING STATUS POSITIONS IN THE
POWER ECHELON. Any person who helps a group to formulate goals,
programs, and policies, any person who assists a group to attain its goals,
or any person who helps maintain the group, is providing leadership.
Therefore, leadership is not a narrow or restricted function, exclusively
reserved to superordinates, but leadership potential is widely dispersed
throughout the organization. The superordinate will be more effective if
he develops, rather than restricts, this leadership potential throughout
the group. Instead of losing his leadership by sharing it, he will increase
his own potential. He can prevent conflicts from multiple leadership by
the appropriate use of the coordination function of executive leadership.

GOOD HUMAN RELATIONS ARE ESSENTIAL TO GROUP PRODUCTION AND TO
MEET THE NEEDS OF INDIVIDUAL MEMBERS OF THE GROUP. Good human
relations improve group morale, and high group morale generally facilitates production. Individual members of the group feel the need for
acceptance by other members. When individual needs as well as group
needs are met, the organization is more productive.

RESPONSIBILITY, AS WELL AS POWER AND AUTHORITY, CAN BE SHARED. If
leadership can be shared, responsibility can be shared. If potential
leaders in the organization are permitted to exercise their leadership
potential, they will voluntarily accept responsibility as well as authority
and power. Since all responsibility is not placed in the executive at the
top of the power echelon, he should not receive all the credit or all the
blame.

THOSE AFFECTED BY A PROGRAM OR POLICY SHOULD SHARE IN DECISION
MAKING WITH RESPECT TO THAT PROGRAM OR POLICY. This assumption
is stated as follows in the Declaration of Independence: ". . . Governments are instituted among men, deriving their just powers from the
consent of the governed. . . ." Lincoln stated basically this same assumption in the following words: ". . . Government of the people, by the
people, for the people. . . ." Perhaps traditional and emerging administrative theories differ more on this assumption than any other. Due to the
development of large, complex educational organizations, not all mem-

bers can participate directly in all types of policy decisions. But all members can participate through their representatives.

THE INDIVIDUAL FINDS SECURITY IN A DYNAMIC CLIMATE IN WHICH HE SHARES RESPONSIBILITY FOR DECISION MAKING. A person is more secure in implementing goals, policies, and programs if he understands them. He will understand them better if he helps to formulate them. A person is more secure if he helps to determine his own fate. A free man is more secure than a vassal.

UNITY OF PURPOSE IS SECURED THROUGH CONSENSUS AND GROUP LOYALTY. When members of a group participate in the formulation of goals, policies, and programs, the group is more likely to accept them than if they are handed down through the hierarchy. As the group works together, interactions occur which make the group more cohesive. If the leader works effectively with the group, he will be accepted by the group as a member. When the group develops goals, policies, and programs, they tend to be the property of the group, and the group will be loyal to what it has developed and to the members who have shared in that process. Unity of purpose is secured through these interactional processes.

MAXIMUM PRODUCTION IS ATTAINED IN A THREAT-FREE CLIMATE. The by-products of competition and pressure may ultimately reduce, rather than increase, production. A threat-free climate does not mean a problem-free situation.

> The solution of problems promotes the growth of the individual and also gives him a feeling of satisfaction. External pressures are sometimes exerted on an individual in order to force him to accept a value or achieve a goal. A pressure is a threat if it is resented by the individual concerned and is destructive of his personality. A threat is particularly destructive to the individual if the pressure is exerted to force him to accept a value or attain a goal which he does not believe is valid. If the individual participates in the determination of acceptable values and goals and they become his own values and goals, he will be under pressure to attain goals that are consistent with his values, but the pressure will be internal rather than external. This internal pressure will then become a felt need of the individual. As he meets his needs, he will solve problems which promote his growth and give him satisfaction.

> The emerging theory of administration provides a climate which avoids the use of external pressures that are destructive of human personality. The traditional theory of administration does not hesitate to use external pressures in order to attain production.[44]

THE LINE AND STAFF ORGANIZATION SHOULD BE USED EXCLUSIVELY FOR THE PURPOSE OF DIVIDING LABOR AND IMPLEMENTING POLICIES AND PROGRAMS

[44]*Better Teaching in School Administration* pp. 92–93.

DEVELOPED BY THE TOTAL GROUP AFFECTED. It will be noted that the emerging collegial concept, as well as the traditional monocratic concept of administration, accepts the necessity of a line-and-staff organization. However, these two concepts differ in the way the line-and-staff organization is used. Under the monocratic concept, it is assumed that the line-and-staff organization determines and also executes policies and programs. The emerging collegial concept of administration calls for group participation in decision making. Therefore, the line-and-staff organization alone will not meet the requirements of emerging theory. Two structures are needed under the emerging theory of administration: one structure for determining goals, policies, and programs, and another structure for executing policies and programs. Under the emerging theory of administration, the structure for implementing policies and programs is usually a line-and-staff organization. The structure for developing policies and programs is usually some type of a committee organization in which all members of the organization have a peer status, regardless of position in the power echelon.

THE SITUATION AND NOT THE POSITION DETERMINES THE RIGHT AND PRIVILEGE TO EXERCISE AUTHORITY. Authority arises out of the situation, rather than out of the position. The point of decision making should be as near the scene of action as practicable. The situation itself demands that authority be exercised by someone. The administrator finds himself in a situation in which he must exercise authority in order to meet the needs of the group. Therefore, he exercises that authority due to the necessities of the situation not due to the prerogatives of his position. The teacher is in a situation which requires that authority over certain matters be exercised. He exercises that authority, not because of privileges he holds by reason of being a teacher, but because the situation demands authority.

THE INDIVIDUAL IN THE ORGANIZATION IS NOT EXPENDABLE. The ultimate purpose of an organization is to meet the needs of individuals in human society. The individuals in the organization are a part of that society. Government was created to serve people, and not people to serve government. Therefore, the worth of the individual should not be ignored by the organization. Furthermore, the organization can better achieve its own purpose by conserving and improving the members of the organization.

EVALUATION IS A GROUP RESPONSIBILITY. If there is broad participation in the formulation of goals, policies, and programs, then there must be broad participation in evaluation. Participation in evaluation by the group is necessary to develop the competencies of the group. Collegial group evaluation is more valid and reliable than evaluation by one individual. Furthermore, broad participation in evaluation provides valuable feedback.

SOME CONTRASTS BETWEEN THE MONOCRATIC, BUREAUCRATIC AND THE PLURALISTIC, COLLEGIAL CONCEPTS

It has already been pointed out that the assumptions made and the values held by those in a position to formulate the structure of an organization and to administer it determine largely the point on the monocratic, bureaucratic—pluralistic, collegial continuum (hereafter shortened to monocratic-pluralistic continuum) on which an organization can be located. Although the principles of formal organization are generally applicable to all types of formal organization, there are vital differences between school systems on one end of the monocratic-pluralistic continuum and those on the other end. Some of those differences are discussed in the following section of this chapter.

Climate

The climate of human relations is different in school systems operating under the monocratic and pluralistic concepts of administration. The absence of fear of the hierarchy, the feeling of equality, and the knowledge that one is master of his own fate beget different personalities in systems at the opposite ends of the monocratic-pluralistic continuum. The monocratic school system tends toward a *closed climate*, as contrasted with the tendency toward an *open climate* in a pluralistic system.[45]

Structure

It has already been pointed out that there are wide differences in organizational structures developed in accordance with the assumptions underlying the monocratic concept and with the pluralistic concept. Structures based on the monocratic concept of administration emphasize centralized authority for planning, controlling, and decision making. Such structures also usually exercise a close inspectional type of supervision. Since the executives in such organizations are responsible for all decision making and planning and, at the same time, for exercising

[45]See Andrew W. Halpin and Don B. Croft, "The Organizational Climate of Schools," *Administrators Note Book*, 2, No. 7 (Mar. 1963). These researchers did not specifically study the variations in climate of school systems at opposite ends of the monocratic-pluralistic continuum; they did define carefully the characteristics of schools with open and closed climates. Although not intended to do so, those descriptions rather accurately distinguish between the climates of school systems at opposite ends of the continuum.

highly centralized control over all operations, the span of control or the number of persons supervised by the executive in the monocratic organization is usually less than the executive span of control in the pluralistic organization. Therefore, the monocratic organization requires more echelons of authority and tends to have longer chains of command supervised by each executive.

There has been some misunderstanding concerning the line-and-staff structure. Some writers have even inferred that the line-and-staff structure is outmoded and should be abandoned. This reasoning seems to be based on the assumption that structure is inherently undemocratic. Actually, the line-and-staff structure is not at fault; the fault lies with the way in which it is used. For instance, in one organization the line-and-staff structure may be so used as to require that all decisions, even routine ones, be cleared with the executive head of the organization before action is taken. This method of operating ignores the possibility of increasing the efficiency of the organization by a judicious delegation of authority. Furthermore, it violates the principle that the decision should be made as near the point of action as practicable. In another organization, line-and-staff structure for the implementation of programs and policies is accompanied by proper delegation of authority and supplemented by machinery for broad participation in decision making with respect to policy and program. Both organizations use a line-and-staff structure, one inappropriately and the other appropriately.

Structures for pluralistic, collegial administration emphasize wide sharing of authority for planning, controlling, and decision making, and such centralized authority as is necessary for coordinating the total organization. The organizational structure may actually be more complex than that for the monocratic, bureaucratic organization. However, this additional complexity is introduced for the purpose of making the arrangements necessary for broad participation in decision making.

It is sometimes said that there is less emphasis on structure in pluralistic than in monocratic organization. It is probably true that the skeleton of monocratic structure is more stark, because of its constraints, than the skeleton of pluralistic structure. On the other hand, the structure for pluralistic organization is designed to give maximum freedom to the individual; therefore, the individual is less conscious of the structure itself.

Communication

The communication patterns differ widely in monocratic and pluralistic organization. The communication pattern for monocratic organization is quite simple. It goes up and down a vertical line organization. A communication from the top must pass through all intermediate echelons of authority before it reaches the bottom, but no intermediate echelon can stop the communication from the top down. A communication from the bottom to the top must also pass through each intermediate echelon, but any intermediate echelon can stop the communication from a lower level from reaching the top. Therefore, the channel of communication is not strictly a two-way channel. Furthermore, great emphasis is given to "going through channels," and any communication from the bottom to the top which does not go through channels is frowned upon. The administrator in the monocratic hierarchy uses his control over communications to increase his status, power, and prestige.

There are many channels of communication in pluralistic organizations. Such organizations have provisions for communicating through a vertical channel, but it is a two-way channel. Communication is also circular and horizontal in pluralistic organization. The organization provides for a committee structure or some other arrangement whereby members at the bottom of the line structure may communicate in a face-to-face relationship with the top executives. Since communication is much freer among all members of the organization in a pluralistic structure, the opportunity for beneficial interactions is much greater.

Administrative Behavior

For want of better terminology, we have already referred to democratic and authoritarian administration. The assumptions underlying traditional monocratic, bureaucratic concepts of administration are largely authoritarian, and the assumptions underlying emerging pluralistic, collegial concepts of administration are largely democratic by popular definition. It should not be inferred, however, that democratic administration is *ipso facto* good and that authoritarian administration is *ipso facto* bad. History provides numerous examples of successful and unsuccessful democratic administration and successful and unsuccessful authoritarian administration. Furthermore, it is not strictly accurate to classify administration as democratic and authoritarian. It would be difficult, if not impossible, to find an administration which is completely authoritarian or completely democratic. It is more accurate to think of democracy and authoritarianism as part of the same continuum. Democratic and undemocratic behavior were defined in a series of studies at the University of Florida of school principals. The definitions are as follows:

Democratic behavior:
  (a) Action involving the group in decision making with respect to policy and program.
  (b) Implementation in line with democratically determined policy.
  (c) Action promoting the group or individual creativity, produc-

tivity, and satisfaction without harm to other groups or individuals.

(d) Behavior or attitude respecting the dignity of individuals or groups.

(e) Action that indicates that the principal seeks to become an accepted member of the group.

(f) Action that indicates that the principal seeks to keep channels of communication open.

Undemocratic behavior:

(a) Action that indicates that decision making is centered in the status leader or his inner circle.

(b) Implementation that ignores democratically determined policy.

(c) Action that frustrates group or individual creativity, productivity, and satisfaction.

(d) Action that indicates that the principal attains objectives by pressures that jeopardize a person's security.

(e) Action that indicates that the principal considers himself above or apart from the group.

(f) Action that indicates that the principal discourages or blocks free communication.[46]

These definitions were developed to describe the behavior of school principals, but they are equally applicable to other types of administrators. According to these definitions, the words "undemocratic" and "authoritarian" are synonymous terms.

Innovation and Change

Attention has already been directed to the fact that a number of investigators have found that monocratic, bureaucratic organizations are not as innovative as pluralistic, collegial organizations. This is not surprising, because monocratic control limits feedback both from the environment and the subsystems of an organization. Furthermore, in monocratic organization the upwardly mobile person must become an organization man; follow the chain of command, observing closely all rules, regulations and norms of the organization; and above all things, avoid becoming a threat to his superordinates by being an innovator. Consequently, innovation and change, when it does come, usually comes from the top of the hierarchy downward.

In pluralistic, collegial organization, there is more feedback from the environment and from subsystems in the organization. Leadership which promotes change is encouraged at all hierarchical levels. Therefore,

[46]Carroll D. Farrar, *Refinement of an Instrument to Determine Certain Characteristics of the Working Patterns of School Principals* (Doctoral dissertation, University of Florida, 1956), pp. 14–15.

in the pluralistic organization, there tends to be more change and inno-vation, and it may come from the bottom of the hierarchy as well as the top.

SOME IMPORTANT PROBLEMS AND ISSUES

A summary of some of the most commonly accepted concepts and principles of organization and administration was presented in the first part of this chapter. It is apparent that many of these concepts and principles are not sure guides to administrative action because of possible wide differences in interpretation and application. Perhaps what is needed is a unifying theory of administration which will make possible a rational interpretation and application of principles. Additional prob-lems associated with the interpretation of these concepts and principles are presented in the following paragraphs.

How Can Principles Be Validated?

It has already been pointed out that principles of organization and administration have been developed largely by the empirical process. How can these principles be scientifically tested? Griffiths has tentatively suggested the following steps for theory development in administrative behavior:

1. A *description* of administrative behavior in one situation.
2. A *definition* of certain basic concepts.
3. A more *general statement* which is descriptive of the average be-havior in a limited number of situations.
4. A statement of one or more *hypotheses*.
5. An *evaluation* and *reconstruction* of the hypotheses in accordance with later observations.
6. The statement of one or more principles.[47]

It would seem that some procedure, such as that suggested by Griffiths, should be used to test principles of organization and admini-stration. The scientific approach would certainly sharpen the statements of those principles, define the operating limits of a principle, and might reveal that some are not even principles. A principle should serve as a guide to action. If these guides are invalid or crudely defined, they are not of much use to school administrators. Therefore, research on theory is probably one of the most needed types of research. Can the so-called principles of administration presented in this chapter be validated by the procedures recommended by Griffiths?

[47]Daniel E. Griffiths, "Toward a Theory of Administrative Behavior," Chap. 10 in *Administrative Behavior in Education*, ed. Roald F. Campbell and Russell T. Gregg (New York: Harper & Row, Publishers, 1957), p. 379.

How Can Assumptions Be Tested?

It has already been pointed out that traditional monocratic concepts are based on somewhat different assumptions than emerging pluralistic concepts of administration. How can these assumptions be tested? Some are philosophical in nature and cannot be tested by objective research. Philosophical assumptions must be tested against the value system of the society in which the organization finds itself. This test of philosophical assumptions would yield somewhat different results in the United States of America than in Russia. For instance, the assumptions underlying traditional monocratic administration are fairly consistent with the assumptions of Plato and Nietzsche. Emerging concepts of administration, however, are fairly consistent with the philosophy of John Dewey and the philosophy expressed in the great political documents of this country, such as the Declaration of Independence and the Constitution with its amendments.

Assumptions dealing with such factors as production, group morale, and human relations can be tested by objective research. As a matter of fact, a considerable body of research dealing with these assumptions is already available.[48] The weight of available evidence indicates that the assumptions underlying pluralistic, collegial concepts of administration relating to production, group morale, and human relations are more valid than the assumptions of monocratic concepts. Some of that research is reviewed in the following chapter. However, this research has been done largely in the United States, a country with a democratic orientation. Whether the same research would yield the same results in a country such as Russia with an authoritarian orientation, is unknown. Much additional research needs to be done on identifying the assumptions underlying different concepts and theories of administration. Furthermore, those assumptions should be subjected to much more rigorous testing and examination than has been the case up to the present time. This will involve the development of more precise theoretical models than have yet been developed, from which appropriate hypotheses may be formulated and tested.

The testing of assumptions is not as simple a matter as it might seem. For instance, before assumptions with respect to production can be tested, production itself must be defined. Production may be defined solely as the output of the organization, or the definition may include what happens to members of the organization along with the output. If

---

[48]See, for example, Bernard Berelson and Gary Steiner, *Human Behavior: An Inventory of Scientific Findings* (New York: Harcourt, Brace & World, Inc., 1964), and Darwin Cartwright and Alvin Zander, *Group Dynamics: Research and Theory* (New York: Harper & Row, Publishers, 1960).

one accepts the first definition, process and product are separable, because members of the organization are expendable. If one accepts the second definition, process and product are inseparable, because members of the organization are not expendable. To state the problem in another way, if one accepts the second definition, production will be measured not only in terms of the quantity and quality of production over a definite period of time, but it will also include the future production potential of the organization. Similar difficulties will no doubt be encountered as other assumptions are tested. Can values be ignored when testing assumptions?

How Can Individuals and Minorities Be Protected from Group Domination?

The group can be quite as authoritarian as the executive in suppressing individuals and minorities. The group itself, if it so chooses, can exercise powerful sanctions against its members to force compliance with group norms, values, and goals. The rights of individuals and minorities are likely to be jeopardized if the administrative group shifts suddenly from the benevolent, paternalistic, directive authoritarian style to a permissive, democratic style. A sudden change from monocratic decision making to pluralistic decision making is likely to create a power vacuum. Group members with authoritarian tendencies are likely to rush into this power vacuum and take over. Thus, a group inexperienced in democratic group operation will hardly become democratic overnight, simply because the administration is changed. There is no assurance that the group will act democratically, unless group members are dedicated to democratic values. Even such dedication does not always protect individuals and minorities from capricious group action. The government of the United States is based on a constitution with amendments that incorporate a bill of rights protecting individuals and minorities from capricious group action. Should educational organizations also develop constitutions incorporating a bill of rights and an internal judicial system for protecting the rights of individuals and minorities?

How Much Collegiality in Decision Making Is Practicable?

When large numbers of people are involved, it is impracticable to submit all matters to the total group for decision. The government of the United States is a republic rather than a pure democracy. Nevertheless, certain matters are submitted to a vote of the total electorate.

In large school systems and even in large schools, it is impractical to submit all matters to the total faculty. The problem then arises as to what matters should be decided by the total faculty, what matters should be decided by committees representing the faculty, and what matters should be decided by the executive head.

There is also the problem of lay participation in decision making. Boards of education are selected to represent the people. But the existence of thousands of citizens' committees and parent-teacher associations throughout the nation is evidence that present legal means of lay participation in decision making with respect to the schools do not meet the demand for wider participation. This problem is so important that it is treated more adequately in another chapter of this book.

What criteria could be used to determine the matters that should be decided by the faculty or its representatives and the matters that should be decided by the hierarchy?

How Wide Should the Span of Control in a Large School System Be?

Recently, one of the authors made studies of two relatively large school systems which differed widely in their interpretations of the span of control principle. Each of these school systems had approximately 36,000 pupils, 1,200 teachers, and 90 separate schools, but the organizational structures were quite different.

System "A" had organized the district into ten areas of approximately nine schools each. A supervising principal served as a line officer between the superintendent and the building principals in each area. The central office provided the usual services, but a building principal had to clear all communications with the central office through the area supervising principal. The superintendent in turn cleared all communications with a building principal through the area supervising principal. The ten area supervising principals met monthly with the superintendent, and the building principals of each area met monthly with their supervising principal. This was a very neat scheme of organization, but the building principals complained that service was very slow from the central office and that the supervising principals of the different areas gave different interpretations of the rules and regulations of the board. They also complained that they had very little to do with policy making.

System "B" had no area supervising principals. The central office had an adequate central staff for providing administrative and supervisory services. Each principal dealt directly with the member of the central staff who had the responsibility for the particular matter concerned. Action was taken in accordance with policies established by the board, but if the matter was not covered by an existing policy, it was presented to the superintendent. The superintendent and his central staff met monthly with a committee of principals and teachers. The principals met monthly as a group. In this system, the building principals were warm in their praise of the central office for the promptness of service. They also felt that they had a part in policy making.

It is apparent that each of these school systems needed an organizational structure. No superintendent can deal directly with 1,200 teachers. The superintendent of System "A" believed that all operations should be coordinated through a line structure in which the number of persons dealing with each person in the organization was held to a minimum. The superintendent of System "B" believed that most members of the central staff should serve as executive as well as staff personnel. He also assumed that each person in the central office could deal with a great number of persons for a specific function. What are the points for and against these two interpretations of the span of control principle?

Are the Monocratic, Bureaucratic and Pluralistic, Collegial Concepts of Administration Equally Suitable for All Types of Organizations?

Earlier in this chapter, reference was made to Blau and Scott's typology of organization based upon who benefits.[49] These authors classified organizations as mutual benefit, business concerns, service organizations, and commonweal organizations.

A public school system is a service organization operated for the benefit of its clients, as contrasted with a mutual benefit association operated for the benefit of its members, a business concern operated for the benefit of its owners, and a commonweal organization operated for the benefit of the general public. Will organizations with such widely different functions as a labor union serving its members, a factory making automobiles to provide profits for the stockholders, a school system serving children, or an army protecting the general public be equally effective in utilizing either the monocratic, bureaucratic concept of organization of the pluralistic, collegial concept?

Teachers are becoming "cosmopolitans" rather than "locals" in their orientation.[50] Therefore, teachers may be oriented to the goals of the profession quite as much as to the goals of an organization. Most college professors are also cosmopolitans. There is considerable evidence that teachers and professors are more productive in pluralistic, collegial organizations than in monocratic organizations. Would the same thing be true of army personnel? Would the type of organization that is most effective for producing automobiles be equally effective for educating students?

[49]Peter M. Blau and W. Richard Scott, *Formal Organization, A Comparative Approach* (San Francisco: Chandler Publishing Co., 1962), p. 43.

[50]Alvin W. Gouldner, "Cosmopolitans and Locals: Toward an Analysis of Latent Social Roles," *Administrative Science Quarterly* 11 (Dec. 1957), 281–306, 11 (Mar. 1958), 444–480.

Selected References

Argyris, Chris, *Interpersonal Competence and Organizational Effectiveness.* Homewood, Ill.: Richard D. Irwin, Inc., 1962.

Berelson, B., and Gary A. Steiner, *Human Behavior: An Inventory of Scientific Findings.* New York: Harcourt, Brace & World, Inc., 1964.

Blau, Peter M., and W. Richard Scott, *Formal Organizations: A Comparative Approach.* San Francisco: Chandler Publishing Co., 1962.

Etzioni, Amitai, *A Comparative Analysis of Complex Organizations.* New York: Free Press of Glencoe, Inc., 1961.

Golembiewski, Robert T., *Behavior and Organization.* Skokie, Ill.: Rand McNally & Co., 1962.

Griffiths, Daniel E., ed., *Behavioral Science and Educational Administration.* Sixty-third Yearbook of the National Society for the Study of Education. Chicago: University of Chicago Press, 1964.

March, James C., and Herbert A. Simon, *Organizations.* New York: John Wiley & Sons, Inc., 1958.

Miller, James G., "Living Systems: Cross-Level Hypotheses," *Behavioral Science,* **10**, No. 4 (Oct. 1965).

Presthus, Robert, *The Organizational Society.* New York: Alfred A. Knopf, Inc., 1962.

Thompson, Victor A., *Modern Organization.* New York: Alfred A. Knopf, Inc., 1961.

Weber, Max., *The Theory of Social and Economic Organization,* trans. A. M. Henderson and Talcott Parsons, ed. Talcott Parsons. New York: Free Press of Glencoe, Inc., 1947.

5

Educational Leadership

Concepts of leadership and administration are rapidly changing. Since 1925, hundreds of research studies on group characteristics, leader behavior, human relations, formal and informal organization have been creating a new and exciting body of knowledge. The implications of these studies are so significant that the demand for new theoretical concepts of administration and organization is widespread. Such interest is not limited to educational administrators. In fact, much of the significant research in these areas has been conducted by business and industry, the armed services, the National Training Laboratories, and university research centers such as the Personnel Research Board at Ohio State University, the Research Center for Group Dynamics at the University of Michigan, the Graduate School of Business Administration at Harvard University, and the Yale Labor and Management Center.

This movement has had a significant impact on educational administration. An organization called the National Conference of Professors of Educational Administration was formed in 1947 primarily to improve preparation programs for school administrators. The Cooperative Program in Educational Administration, sponsored by the American Association of School Administrators and supported in part by grants from the W. K. Kellogg Foundation, was established in 1950 to improve the theory and practice of educational administration.

The National Conference of Professors of Educational Administration in 1954 approved a project involving the preparation of a book to synthesize research findings of significance to educational administration and to preparation programs for educational administrators. A committee of eighteen professors prepared this synthesis, which was published in 1957.[1] The findings of this study indicated clearly that many traditional concepts of leadership or leader behavior are not supported by the latest evidence.

An organization called the University Council for Educational Administration was formed in 1956. The council encourages basic research and the dissemination of important research findings through seminars and publications including the *Educational Administration Quarterly,* the only research-oriented journal in this field published in the United States. It has also fostered the use in educational administration of theoretical concepts developed in the social and behavioral sciences. This has contributed significantly to the beginnings of a science of educational administration, because most of the significant research on leadership, organizations and social systems has been done by social and behavioral scientists.

SOME CONCEPTS OF LEADERSHIP

In Chapter 3, major attention was given to systems theory and the value of theory and research in dealing with problems of organization and administration. In Chapter 4, systems theory was applied to the examination of concepts and principles of organization. In this chapter, attention will be given to the leader and his role in the social system. This is not a simple task for a number of reasons. In the first place, there is no general agreement among researchers and writers on the meaning of the word "leader." For example, some writers, especially historians, do not distinguish clearly between a leader and the holder of a position with status in the organizational hierarchy. These persons, as well as lay persons generally, assume that the holder of an important position in the hierarchy is, by virtue of that, a leader. Most behavioral scientists do not hold that view.[2] Lipham has attempted to solve this problem by suggesting in effect that the term leader be restricted to the role of change agent and the term administrator to the role of maintaining the organization. Some valid reasons exist for accepting this definition, but it is not the concept of leadership utilized in the research designs

[1] Roald F. Campbell and Russell T. Gregg, eds., *Administrative Behavior in Education* (New York: Harper & Row, Publishers, 1957).

[2] James M. Lipham, "Leadership and Administration," Chap. 6 in *Behavioral Science and Educational Administration,* ed. Daniel E. Griffiths, The Sixty-third Yearbook of the National Society for the Study of Education, Part II (Chicago: University of Chicago Press, 1964).

of most behavioral scientists. It is the position of the authors that leadership can be provided by an administrator in his acts of maintaining an organization as well as in his acts as a change agent. Furthermore, leadership can operate to prevent change as well as to facilitate it. Therefore, Lipham's typology is not used in this book.

Cartwright and Zander in 1953 wrote:

> It is not possible at the present stage of research on groups to develop a fully satisfactory designation of those group functions which are peculiarly functions of leadership. A more promising endeavor, at least for the present, is to identify the various group functions, without deciding finally whether or not to label each specifically as a function of leadership, and then to discover by empirical investigation such things as what determines this distribution within the group and what consequences stem from various distributions among members.[3]

Since 1953, considerable research has been based on role differentiation in a social system. Many behavioral scientists now conceptualize leadership in that context.[4] In this chapter *we conceptualize leadership as the influencing of the actions, behaviors, beliefs, and feelings of one actor in a social system by another actor with the willing cooperation of the actor being influenced.* The top leader in any system, subsystem, or suprasystem, is the actor who most often influences in critical matters the actions, behaviors, beliefs, and feelings of the greatest number of other actors in that system with the willing cooperation of the actors being influenced. Under this concept, there are many leaders with different degrees and kinds of influence in a social system, and a leader may or may not hold a position in the hierarchy of the formal organization.

We are confining ourselves in this chapter to leadership in formal organizations and in informal groups. There are other types of leaders which are worthy of study, but they are beyond the scope of this book. Some examples are: (1) opinion leaders such as interpreters of news events, (2) intellectual leaders such as Albert Einstein, and (3) societal leaders such as Marx and Engels.

In examining the leadership phenomena of educational organization and administration, we are concerned primarily with concepts and theories of leadership that are applicable to those who hold decision-making positions in the various hierarchies of educational organizations and in informal organizations that interact with formal educational organizations. These persons include superintendents of schools, school principals, college and university presidents, leaders in teacher organizations, leaders in parent-teacher organizations, and leaders of informal

[3]Darwin Cartwright and Alvin Zander, eds., *Group Dynamics—Research and Theory* (New York: Harper & Row, Publishers, 1960), p. 494.
[4]See Paul F. Secord and Carl W. Backman, *Social Psychology* (New York: McGraw-Hill Book Company, 1964).

organizations. Educational organizations commonly include suprasystems, subsystems, and numerous informal organizations or groups. Educational administrators not only deal with a complex of systems within the educational organization but also with a complex of social systems in the environment of the school system, all of which are exchanging inputs and outputs of information, energy, and matter with each other. Unfortunately, most research on leadership has been confined to leadership in small face-to-face groups. Most of the literature on group dynamics is based on research with small groups. Lipham commented on this situation: "Leadership roles in structure organizations are, indeed, complex. Thus, the methodology and findings of leadership studies concerned with small, unstructured, randomly selected groups are likely to be of only limited value when transplanted indiscriminately to large, complex, hierarchical organizations."[5]

Berelson and Steiner published a comprehensive review of the research relating to human behavior in 1964.[6] They compiled from the research available in the behavioral and social sciences 1045 propositions or hypotheses of moderate generality dealing with groups, organizations, social processes, and other phenomena of human behavior. Most of the propositions they advanced concerning leadership are based on research in small face-to-face groups.[7] Their propositions relating to leadership in organizations did not seem to be based on much research.[8]

Miller has pointed out that a hypothesis or proposition which does not apply to two or more levels of systems does not have much generality.[9] He listed 165 cross-level hypotheses (applicable across different levels of suprasystems and subsystems within a social system) which could reasonably be supported by available research. He did not list a single cross-level hypothesis on leadership.

How many of the conclusions concerning leadership that have been reached from research in small face-to-face groups are applicable to administrators of complex, bureaucratic, hierarchical organizations such as medium and large school systems, colleges and universities? We will not know until more cross-level research is carried out, and this will require sophisticated designs conforming to rigorous standards.[10] With the above limitations in mind, we present certain generalizations and phenomena relating to leadership in the remainder of this chapter.

[5]Lipham, *op. cit.* p. 125.
[6]Bernard Berelson and Gary A. Steiner, *Human Behavior: An Inventory of Scientific Findings* (New York: Harcourt, Brace & World, Inc., 1964).
[7]*Ibid.*, pp. 341–346.
[8]*Ibid.*, pp. 372–377.
[9]James G. Miller, "Living Systems: Cross-Level Hypotheses," *Behavioral Science*, 10, No. 4 (1965).
[10]*Ibid.*, pp. 382–384.

TRENDS IN STUDIES OF LEADERSHIP

Leadership is very highly valued in human society, so it is not surprising that many books have been written and many studies conducted concerning leaders and leadership. Classical literature is filled with references to leaders and leadership. The need to lead and the need to be led is a pervasive characteristic of the human animal. Some approaches to the study of leadership are presented next.

Studies of Traits

Prior to 1945, most of the studies of leadership were devoted primarily to the identification of the traits or qualities of leaders. These studies were based in part on the assumption that human beings could be divided into two groups—the leaders and the followers. Therefore, leaders must possess certain traits or qualities not possessed by followers. Some persons in each generation since the dawn of recorded history have believed that "leaders are born, not made."

In 1948, Stogdill examined 124 studies on the relationship of personality factors to leadership. A summary of his findings follows:

1. The following conclusions are supported by uniformly positive evidence from fifteen or more of the studies surveyed:

   A. The average person who occupies a position of leadership exceeds the average members of his group in the following respects: (1) intelligence, (2) scholarship, (3) dependability in exercising responsibilities, (4) activity and social participation, and (5) socioeconomic status.

   B. The qualities, characteristics, and skills required in a leader are determined to a large extent by the demands of the situation in which he is to function as a leader.

2. The following conclusions are supported by uniformly positive evidence from ten or more of the studies surveyed:

   A. The average person who occupies a position of leadership exceeds the average member of his group to some degree in the following respects: (1) sociability, (2) initiative, (3) persistence, (4) knowing how to get things done, (5) self-confidence, (6) alertness to and insight into situations, (7) cooperativeness, (8) popularity, (9) adaptability, and (10) verbal facility.[11]

Stogdill, however, after further study of the evidence, concluded:

A person does not become a leader by virtue of the possession of some combination of traits, but the pattern of personal characteristics of the leader must bear some relevant relationship to the characteristics,

[11] Ralph M. Stogdill, "Personal Factors Associated With Leadership, A Survey of the Literature," *Journal of Psychology*, **25** (1948), 63.

activities, and goals of the followers. Thus, leadership must be conceived in terms of the interactions of variables which are in constant flux and change.[12]

Therefore, leadership is not a matter of passive status, nor does it devolve upon a person simply because he is the possessor of some combination of traits. Rather, the leader acquires leader status through the interactions of the group in which he participates and demonstrates his capacity for assisting the group to complete its tasks.[13]

In 1954, Myers analyzed more than two hundred studies of leadership that had been made in the previous fifty years.[14] Following is a summary of some of Myers' conclusions concerning the relationship of personality traits to leadership:

1. No physical characteristics are significantly related to leadership.
2. Although leaders tend to be slightly higher in intelligence than the group of which they are members, there is no significant relationship between superior intelligence and leadership.
3. Knowledge applicable to the problems faced by a group contributes significantly to leadership status.
4. The following characteristics correlate significantly with leadership: insight, initiative, cooperation, originality, ambition, persistence, emotional stability, judgment, popularity, and communication skills.[15]

Myers observed the following concerning the characteristics just enumerated:

These characteristics denote qualities of an interactional nature. They are present in leadership situations much more often than are characteristics that denote status or qualities of more individualistic nature. Some characteristics of the latter kind are socioeconomic background and self-confidence.

The research indicates, however, that the personal characteristics of leaders differ according to the situation. Leaders tend to remain leaders only in situations where the activity is similar. No single characteristic is the possession of all leaders.[16]

Thus it is seen that Stogdill and Myers are substantially in agreement concerning the relationship of personality traits to leadership. The study of personality traits alone will not explain leadership. These studies have shown clearly that the assumption, "leaders are born, not made," is largely false. The only inherited trait that has been identified as having some relationship to leadership is intelligence. Even this relationship is quite low.

[12]*Ibid.*, p. 64.
[13]*Ibid.*, p. 66.
[14]Robert B. Myers, "The Development and Implications of a Conception for Leadership Education" (Unpublished doctoral dissertation, University of Florida, 1954).
[15]*Ibid.*, pp. 105–106.
[16]*Ibid.*, p. 107.

Stogdill investigated 33 separate research studies on the relationship of intelligence to leadership.[17] He found that the average of the coefficients of correlation between intelligence and leadership was only .28. A coefficient of correlation this low is only slightly better than a chance guess. Hopper and Bills made a study of the relationship of the intelligence of school administrators to success as administrators.[18] They reported that the school administrators studied were considerably above average in intelligence but that there was very little correlation between intelligence and success within the group of administrators studied.

All the other personality traits identified as being related to leadership are acquired traits and, as such, are subject to modification by training and experience. Actually, most of the personality traits or characteristics that have been found to be associated with leadership should be classified as skills or competencies rather than personality traits. Therefore, it should be possible within limits to attain these skills and competencies through an appropriate program of learning experiences. This emphasizes the importance of preparation programs for school administrators.

It must not be assumed that the many studies of personality traits in relation to leadership have been totally unproductive. Although the traits approach has not provided a comprehensive description of leadership, it has opened the way for further research that gives promise of great significance. Researchers in this area have had great difficulty in defining and measuring leadership and the traits being studied. Different researchers have used different definitions and different instruments. Situational factors have been ignored in most studies. It is not surprising that the conclusions of a number of studies have been contradictory. With sharper definitions, improved instruments, and better control of conditions, researchers in the future will undoubtedly contribute additional knowledge needed in this area.

The "Times Make the Man" Approach

When it became apparent that the traits approach to the study of leadership had limited value, other approaches were sought. The "times make the man" approach captured the imagination of some about 1940. Hitler, Mussolini, and Stalin were certainly leaders. Yet each lacked many of the qualities that rationally should be associated with leadership. Perhaps they were products of their times. Historians in other days have frequently speculated on that point with respect to other figures in history. This approach produced much speculation but little research. Perhaps its principal contribution was to give emphasis to the need for studying the leader in relation to his social environment.

---

[17]Stogdill, *op. cit.*
[18]Robert L. Hopper and Robert E. Bills, "What's a Good Administrator Made Of?" *The School Executive*, 74 (1955), 93–95.

The Interactional or Group Approach

Another approach is known as the interactional or group approach to the study of leadership. It is generally accepted as being the most productive to the understanding of leadership. Although the individual leader is still an important object of study, it is now generally recognized that he cannot be studied in isolation. The leadership behavior of Robinson Crusoe could not be studied until Friday came to his island. The focus of most research on leadership is now on "leader behavior" in a social system, rather than on "leader traits."

The remainder of this chapter presents some generalizations concerning leadership that have been derived principally from studies of leadership in relation to a social system.

Some Definitions and Concepts

Before we proceed further, it is advisable that a few definitions be given of some of the concepts and terms used in this chapter. Leadership has already been defined in terms of the influence of one actor in a social system on another actor in that system with the willing cooperation of the actor being influenced. But the many concepts of leadership cannot be encompassed by a single definition. Following are some additional concepts necessary to the understanding of leadership.

LEADERSHIP ACTS. A person performs leadership acts when he: (1) helps a group to define tasks, goals, and purposes, (2) helps a group to achieve its tasks, goals, and purposes, (3) helps to maintain the group by assisting in providing for group and individual needs.

ATTEMPTED LEADERSHIP, SUCCESSFUL LEADERSHIP, AND EFFECTIVE LEADERSHIP. Hemphill has defined these terms as follows:

1. Attempted leadership acts are acts accompanied by an intention of initiating structure-in-interaction for solving a mutual problem.
2. Successful leadership acts are acts that have initiated structure-in-interaction during the process of mutual problem solution. An attempted leadership act may or may not become a successful leadership act depending upon subsequent observation of its effect upon the structure of interaction.
3. Effective leadership acts are acts that have initiated structure-in-interaction and that have contributed to the solution of a mutual problem. An effective leadership act is always also a successful leadership act, but a leadership act may be successful without being effective for solving mutual problems.[19]

SOME INFORMAL GROUP CHARACTERISTICS. The informal group, sometimes called an informal organization, has the following characteristics:

[19]John K. Hemphill, "Administration as Problem Solving," Chap. 5 in *Administrative Theory in Education*, ed. Andrew W. Halpin (Chicago: Midwest Administration Center, University of Chicago, 1958).

1. Each member of the group is able to interact with every other member of the group.
2. The group develops its own structure and organization.
3. The group selects its own leader or leaders.
4. The group has been voluntarily formed to achieve certain common tasks, goals, and purposes.
5. It does not have an officially prescribed hierarchical structure.

SOME FORMAL ORGANIZATION CHARACTERISTICS. The formal organization, sometimes called the formal group, has the following characteristics as contrasted with the informal group:

1. Each member of the group usually is not able to interact with every other member of the group.
2. The formal organization of the group is usually structured by authority external to the group.
3. The holders of positions of status in the organization are usually determined by authority external to the group.
4. The tasks, goals, and purposes of the group may be determined in part by authority external to the group.
5. It usually has an officially prescribed hierarchical structure.

There are many variations in types of human groups other than those identified above. For example, a state education association is a voluntary group with some of the characteristics of an informal group and some of a formal organization. Attention was directed in Chapter 4 to four types of formal organizations based on who benefits. It would require an extensive treatment to present a comprehensive analysis of all types of human groups. Attention has been directed to the fact that much of the research on leadership has been done in small informal groups and only a limited amount in large formal organizations. However, all educational administrators deal with informal groups as well as with a formal organization. Furthermore, if the assumptions back of general systems theory are valid, it is possible that more of the findings concerning leadership in small groups are applicable to leadership in formal organizations than has been assumed by some behavioral scientists. Therefore, in the next section we will examine some group phenomena that are important to an understanding of leadership.

THE GROUP

School administrators spend much of their time working with groups. The most effective administrators are leaders as well as holders of "headships." Effective administrative leadership involves an understanding of the behavior of people in groups. Many studies of group behavior and structure have been made. Some principal findings of one of the most significant of these studies, that of Homans, are presented in the following paragraphs.[20]

The Human Group

Homans, after studying numerous small groups sometimes called "face-to-face groups," concluded that the underlying human relationships differ from group to group in degree rather than kind. This concept is of great significance because, if it is valid, it is possible to make a systematic analysis of group behavior.

Each group is conceived of as having a boundary, outside of which lies the group environment. Each person may belong to many different groups, and large groups may be subdivided into smaller groups and cliques. Each group has an external environment that differs for every group, and the behavior of each group must be such that it can survive in its environment.

The elements of the behavior of a group are sentiment, activity, and interaction. These elements are all mutually interdependent. Homans analyzed these elements of behavior with respect to the external and internal systems of the group, these two systems together being conceived of as making up the total social system.

The sentiment, activity, and interaction of a group are conditioned by the external environment of the group. That is why Homans calls it the external system. Sentiment in the external system is defined as the motives, drives, and attitudes that individual group members bring to the group from the external environment. Activity in the external system is defined as the activities demanded by the job. The environment conditions the behavior of the group, but the group will in turn change its environment in order to survive. For instance, the behavior of a school faculty is certainly affected by its environment. But the faculty will attempt to change its environment with respect to salary, tenure, community attitudes, and working conditions if it feels this to be necessary for survival. Thus, in the external system of the group, the elements of sentiment, activity, and interaction are mutually dependent and are in constant flux. These elements are being conditioned by the external environment, and the group is changing its environment. Therefore, the entire external system of the group is constantly changing.

Homans then examined these same three elements of behavior in the internal system of the group. He defines the internal system as "group behavior that is an expression of the sentiments toward one another de-

[20]George C. Homans, *The Human Group* (New York: Harcourt, Brace & World, Inc., 1950).

veloped by members of the group in the course of their life together."[21] The life together of the group could be considered the internal environment of the group as contrasted with the external environment. Sentiment, activity, and interaction are also mutually dependent in the internal system. Sentiment in the internal system is defined as the feelings that people develop toward each other and their group as they work together. As a group works together, it develops norms as part of the internal system. A norm is "an idea in the minds of the members of a group, an idea that can be put in the form of a statement specifying what the members or other men should do, ought to do, are expected to do, under given circumstances."[22] Since norms and the various elements of behavior in the internal system are all mutually dependent, the internal system of a group is constantly changing. But this is not all, because the total internal system of the group affects the total external system, and vice versa. Therefore, the total social system of a group is constantly changing.

Homans presented some hypotheses concerning these interactions that are of great significance to the understanding of leadership. Some of these hypotheses are as follows:

1. If the frequency of interaction between two or more persons increases, the degree of their liking for one another will increase, and vice versa.
2. If the interactions between the members of the group are frequent in the external system, sentiments of liking will grow up between them, and these sentiments will lead in turn to further interactions over and above the interactions of the external system.
3. A decrease in the frequency of interaction between the members of a group and outsiders, accompanied by an increase in the strength of their negative sentiments toward outsiders, will increase the frequency of interaction and the strength of positive sentiments among the members of a group, and vice versa.[23]

Let us apply these hypotheses to a school. We might generalize as follows:

1. The more all people—faculty, students, and parents—interact with each other, the more opportunity they have to like each other.
2. Sentiments of liking grow up between teachers and administrators who work on the job together, and these sentiments will lead to other activity beyond the requirements of the job.
3. If the communications between a faculty group and a community group are reduced and this lessening of communications is accompanied by an increase in the negative sentiments of

[21]*Ibid.*, p. 110.
[22]*Ibid.*, p. 123.
[23]*Ibid.*, p. 112–113.

each group toward the other, then the members of each group are drawn closer together, but intergroup hostility is increased.

Let us apply this same reasoning to the relationships between the superintendent or principal and the teacher group. If the administrator is not accepted by the teachers as a member of the teacher group, then he is an outsider and a part of the external environment of the group. As already pointed out, a group has sentiments and norms in its internal system. A group endeavors to survive in its environment. In order to do so, it protects its norms and sentiments. Any attack on these norms and sentiments, especially from an outsider, solidifies the group and develops negative group sentiments toward the source of the attack. If a member of a group violates or offends the norms and sentiments of the group, the group itself disciplines the group member. The group may discipline the administrator by making him an "outsider." The American Federation of Teachers excludes administrators from membership. The National Education Association accepts administrators as members. What are the implications of this difference in the policies of the two organizations?

But group norms and sentiments are not likely to be positively changed by interaction unless the sentiment climate is positive. This seems to be a defect in Homans' hypotheses. He assumes that the liking of group members for each other will always increase as interactions increase. It is conceivable that the negative sentiments of group members for each other might increase with an increase in interactions if the climate of the group is such as to stimulate negative sentiments.

Summarizing: Human society is comprised of innumerable groups, each with a different environment. But all groups have certain common elements of behavior, and those elements are sentiment, activity, and interaction. The elements of behavior differ in degree in each group, but they are always present and mutually dependent. In the external system of the group, each element of behavior conditions the other, the external environment conditions the elements of behavior, and the group conditions its environment. In the internal system, each element of behavior conditions the other, interactions produce group norms, and the internal and external systems of the group are mutually dependent. Within a formal organization such as a large school system, groups tend to increase in number. For instance, the board, the superintendent and his central staff, the principals, and the teachers might each be a tight, separate group. This is especially true if interactions between these groups are minimized. In addition, there will be innumerable informal groups.

Homans' remarkable work has become a landmark in the study of leadership. He was the first to make extensive use of systems theory in the study of groups. There have been numerous studies of groups since Homans' original study,[24] but that study has had more influence on the conceptualization of group phenomena than any other study.

Group Dimensions

Further light has been thrown on group characteristics by the studies of Hemphill.[25] He identified fifteen measures of group characteristics or dimensions and studied leadership in relation to those dimensions. Hemphill's group dimensions are: *size*, the number of persons in the group; *viscidity*, the feeling of togetherness or cohesion of the group; *homogeneity*, the similarity of group members to each other; *flexibility*, the degree to which the group adheres to fixed modes of behavior; *permeability*, the degree to which the group maintains an exclusive membership; *polarization*, the degree to which the group's goals are clear and definite; *stability*, the degree of turnover in group membership; *intimacy*, the degree of mutual acquaintance; *autonomy*, the degree of independence from other groups; *control*, the amount of control the group exercises over its members; *position*, the status of each member within the group; *potency*, the extent to which vital individual needs are satisfied by group membership; *hedonic tone*, the degree of satisfaction group members obtain from group membership; *participation*, the spread of participation among group members; and *dependence*, the degree to which group members depend upon the group leader.[26]

Hemphill found that only two of these group dimensions had a significant positive correlation with leadership behavior. Those dimensions were viscidity and hedonic tone, and the correlations were .52 and .51 respectively.[27] It is interesting to note that Hemphill's dimensions of viscidity and hedonic tone are similar to Homans' element of sentiment. Hemphill's concept of group dimensions is of value in describing, analyzing, and evaluating group behavior.

SOME GENERALIZATIONS ON LEADERSHIP

A number of generalizations and hypotheses concerning leadership have developed from studies in this area. Although these propositions have not all been completely confirmed by research, they are worthy of study.

[24]See A. Paul Hare, Edgar F. Borgatta, and Robert F. Bales, eds., *Small Groups: Studies in Social Interaction* (New York: Alfred A. Knopf, Inc., 1965).

[25]John K. Hemphill, *Situational Factors in Leadership* (Columbus: Ohio State University Press, 1949).

[26]*Ibid.*, pp. 31–33.

[27]*Ibid.*, pp. 51–57.

Generalizations Proposed by Myers

As has already been pointed out, a great number of studies have been made of leadership and the relationship of leadership to the group. Myers, after making an extensive analysis of these studies, proposed the following generalizations which are supported by two or more studies:

1. Leadership is the product of interaction, not status or position.
2. Leadership cannot be structured in advance. The uniqueness of each combination of persons, of varying interactional patterns and of varying goals and means, and of varying forces within and without impinging upon the group will bring forth different leaders.
3. A leader in one situation will not automatically be a leader in another situation.
4. Leadership does not result from a status position, but rather how a person behaves in the organization.
5. Whether a person is a leader in a group depends upon the group's perception of him.
6. The way a leader perceives his role determines his actions.
7. Most groups have more than one person occupying the leadership role.
8. Leadership fosters positive sentiments toward the group activity and persons in the group.
9. Leadership may be democratic or autocratic but never laissez-faire.
10. Leadership protects the critical group norms.
11. Leadership is authority rendered to some who are perceived by others as the proper persons to carry out the particular leadership role of the group.
12. Program development that involves only persons of a single position (such as principals, or supervisors, or teachers) is not as comprehensive or lasting as that which involves people of various positions in the organization.[28]

Although each of these generalizations is supported by some research, it must not be assumed that each generalization is completely valid. Much additional research needs to be done for the further validation of these and other generalizations.

Some Hypotheses Formulated by Berelson and Steiner

Berelson and Steiner made an extensive survey of the scientific findings in the behavioral sciences and formulated a number of propositions and hypotheses. Following are a few of their most important formulations related to leadership in small groups:

[28]Robert B. Myers, "A Synthesis of Research in Leadership" (Unpublished paper presented to A.S.C.D., Mar., 1957), pp. 4–9.

1. The closer an individual conforms to the accepted norms of the group, the better liked he will be; the better liked he is, the closer he conforms; the less he conforms, the more disliked he will be.
2. The higher the rank of the member within the group, the more central he will be in the group's interaction and the more influential he will be.
3. In general, the "style" of the leader is determined more by the expectations of the membership and the requirements of the situation than by the personal traits of the leader himself.
4. The leadership of the group tends to be vested in the member who most closely conforms to the standards of the group on the matter in question, or who has the most information and skill related to the activities of the group.
5. When groups have established norms, it is extremely difficult for a new leader, however capable, to shift the group's activities.
6. The longer the life of the leadership, the less open and free the communication within the group and probably the less efficient the group in the solution of new problems.
7. The leader will be followed more faithfully the more he makes it possible for the members to achieve their private goals, along with the group's goals.
8. Active leadership is characteristic of groups that determine their own activities, passive leadership of groups whose activities are externally imposed.
9. In a small group, authoritarian leadership is less effective than democratic leadership in holding the group together and getting its work done.[29]

Berelson and Steiner also formulated some hypotheses concerning leadership in organizations. However, these authors did not distinguish between leaders as defined early in this chapter and holders of power positions in the hierarchy of an organization. But their formulations do point up some of the difficulties of an executive in the hierarchy when he attempts to provide leadership. They point out that holders of intermediate positions in the hierarchy are under pressure from their superiors for productivity and under pressure from their subordinates for human consideration, and this cross-pressure is the source of actual or potential conflict in their behavior.[30] Following are a few of the hypotheses proposed by Berelson and Steiner relating to leadership (more properly, headship) in formal organizations:

1. The leader's style of leadership tends to be influenced by the style in which he is led.

[29]Bernard Berelson and Gary A. Steiner, *Human Behavior: An Inventory of Scientific Findings* (New York: Harcourt, Brace & World, Inc., 1964), pp. 341–344. NOTE: This important work should be read by every serious student of administration.
[30]*Ibid.*, p. 372.

2. The more the member holds to the organization's professed values, the more likely he is to be promoted within the organization.

3. The requirements for organizational leadership change with the life of the organization: at the start the leader is characterized more by doctrinal loyalty, aggressiveness, and personal quality ("the charismatic leader"); later, when the organization is well established, by administrative skills ("the bureaucratic leader").

4. Within an organization, conflict between leader and subordinates tends to increase the number and the concreteness of the organization's regulations, and vice versa—i.e., regulations go along with conflict.[31]

Although these hypotheses relate to management rather than leadership, they are quite provocative.

Homans' Exchange Theory of Leadership Determination

Homans has developed an interesting theory of exchange for explaining social behavior.[32] It can be used to explain when a person decides to lead and when he decides to follow. The exchange theory is a complex formulation. Homans attempts to explain behavior in terms of costs incurred and rewards exchanged by actors interacting in a social system. He incorporates some of the market exchange concepts from economics and reinforcement concepts from psychology. Exchange theory incorporates four basic concepts: reward, cost, outcome, and comparison level.

Let us apply these concepts to a leadership situation. Let us assume that an actor in a group is contemplating initiating a leadership act in a problem situation. He considers what rewards he may receive if he provides leadership in terms of increased status, need for dominance, desire to see the problem solved, etc. He then considers the cost in terms of loss of status if the group rejects him or his solution fails, increased effort and responsibility on his part, etc. He then attempts to determine the outcome by subtracting the costs from the rewards. If the outcome is positive, it is a profit, and if negative, a loss. His decision to act will also depend on the comparison level. The profit must be sufficiently above a "break-even" point, and his past experiences in comparable situations must have been successful often enough for him to take the chance of leadership. The more frequently he has succeeded in leadership attempts in the past, the more likely is he to attempt another leadership act (reinforcement).

In a similar manner, the actor in a social system who decides to follow also seeks a fair exchange. He weighs the costs against the re-

[31]*Ibid.*, pp. 376–377.
[32]George C. Homans, *Social Behavior: Its Elementary Forms* (New York: Harcourt, Brace & World, Inc. 1961).

wards, considers the qualifications of the person offering to lead, and how successfully he has led in similar situations in the past. He then decides whether there is a fair profit for him if he follows rather than leads.

LEADERSHIP AND EDUCATIONAL ADMINISTRATION

An understanding of leadership, group phenomena, and systems theory is of vital importance to educational administrators. The job of the school administrator is much more complicated than the process of dealing with a primary group. He deals with many groups, both formal and informal, within and without the school system. Many of these groups have conflicting goals and purposes. In addition, he must operate within the limitations of statutory and constitutional law, both state and federal, and within the regulations of the state board of education and his own board of education. He is far from autonomous.

Campbell has described the conflicting expectations faced by administrators.[33] Different groups within the community and within the school system have different perceptions of the role that should be played by the administrator. The board of education also has its perception of the administrator's role. Individuals even within the same group have different perceptions of the role of the administrator. The administrator has his own perception of his role, and somehow he must reconcile all these differences in role perceptions. Therefore, many situational factors condition the behavior of the educational administrator.

The following paragraphs indicate the relationships of some of the concepts of leadership to educational administration presented earlier in this chapter.

A Model for the Study of Administrative Behavior

Halpin has proposed a model or paradigm for the study of administrator behavior in education.[34] He developed this model to facilitate research in administrative behavior and to contribute to the development of a theory of administration. This model has been useful in examining leadership theory as related to educational administration.

Halpin defines administration as a human activity with at least the following four components: (1) the task, (2) the formal organization, (3) the work group (or work groups), and (4) the leader (or leaders).[35]

[33]Campbell and Gregg, *op. cit.*, Chap. 7.

[34]Andrew W. Halpin, "A Paradigm for the Study of Administrative Research in Education," in *Administrative Behavior in Education*, ed. Campbell and Gregg (New York: Harper & Row, Publishers, 1957), Chap. 5.

[35]*Ibid.*, p. 161.

Halpin points out that the Office of Strategic Services, Cartwright and Zander, Barnard, and others have defined the fundamental group goals as group achievement and group maintenance.[36] They also find that the group leader must be committed to these goals. Halpin then reasons that leader behavior associated with group goals must be delineated. He accepts as the two major dimensions of leader behavior "initiating structure in interaction" and "consideration," dimensions that were identified by the Ohio State group.[37] A study was made by Halpin of the relationship between the two leader-behavior dimensions, initiating structure and consideration, and the two group goals, group achievement and group maintenance.[38] He found that effective leaders are those who score high on both dimensions of leader behavior.

Using these concepts, Halpin developed a paradigm for analyzing leader behavior.[39] He presented the paradigm in a series of diagrams. In brief outline form, the paradigm or model follows:

Panel I   Organizational task
Panel II   Administrator's perception of the organization's task
            1. Behavior as decision maker
            2. Behavior as group leader
Panel III   Variables associated with administrator's behavior
            1. Administrator variables
            2. Intraorganization variables
            3. Extraorganization variables
Panel IV   Criteria of administrator effectiveness
            1. Evaluation of administrator as decision maker
                a. Organization maintenance
                b. Organization achievement
            2. Evaluation of administrator as a group leader
                a. Organization maintenance
                b. Organization achievement[40]

This scheme was designed for studying the organization at Time A and Time B, and the change is used as a measure of leader effectiveness. This brief description does not do justice to the implications of the paradigm for the study of leader behavior, but it is sufficient to suggest

[36]*Ibid.*, p. 170.
[37]John K. Hemphill *et al.*, "Relation Between Task Relevant Information and Attempts to Lead," *Psychological Monographs*, 70, No. 7 (1956).
[38]Andrew W. Halpin, "Studies in Aircrew Composition III: The Combat Leader Behavior of B-29 Aircraft Commanders," HFORL MEMO No. TN–54–E (Washington, D. C.: Bolling Air Force Base, Human Factors Operations Research Laboratories, Air Research and Development Command, 1953).
[39]For a complete description see Andrew W. Halpin, "A Paradigm for the Study of Administrative Research in Education," in *Administrative Behavior in Education*, ed. Campbell and Gregg (New York: Harper & Row, Publishers, 1957), Chap. 5.
[40]*Ibid.*, adapted from Fig. 6, p. 190.

the following relationships between the concepts of leadership presented earlier in this chapter and the job of educational administration:

1. The school system's task may be largely defined by authorities external to the group by means of laws and regulations.
2. The administration's perception of the school system's task may be different than the perceptions of other members of the organization. This is a potential source of conflict.
3. Different groups within the system may have goals that are in conflict with the task of the organization. This is a potential source of difficulty.
4. The administrator, in order to be effective, must be a group leader, and this may be difficult if the goals of primary groups are in conflict with the goals of the formal organization. When such a situation occurs, informal organizations develop in order to achieve the goals of primary groups. The task of the administrator-leader is then to bring the formal and informal groups into congruence with respect to goals, if he is to be an effective leader.

Although Halpin developed his model some years ago, it is still useful for the study of administrative behavior when adapted to take into consideration the basic concepts of systems theory.

Coffey and Golden have made the following observations concerning the formal and informal structures:

> Along with the formal structure are the informal functions which have much less structure, are characterized by more spontaneous flow of interpersonal relationships, and are often effective in either aiding the formal structure in reaching goals or working as a very antagonistic core and in a private way against the public goals of the institution. An institution is likely to function more effectively and with greater satisfaction to its employees if the needs which are expressed in the informal social relationships are dealt with in the formal structure.[41]

The Administrative Process

Gregg has made an excellent analysis of the administrative process.[42] He describes the administrative process in terms of the following seven components: (1) decision making, (2) planning, (3) organizing, (4) communicating, (5) influencing, (6) coordinating, and (7) evaluating.

In describing each of his seven components, Gregg dealt with some of the concepts of leadership, group process, and human behavior.

[41]Hubert S. Coffey and William P. Golden, Jr., *In-Service Education for Teachers, Supervisors, and Administrators,* Fifty-sixth Yearbook of the National Society for the Study of Education, Part I (Chicago: University of Chicago Press, 1957), pp. 101–102.
[42]Campbell and Gregg, *op. cit.,* Chap. 8.

As he observed, "Leadership and group processes as well as the whole matter of human relations, are unquestionably important aspects of the administrative process."[43]

There has been less emphasis in recent years on studying administrative processes as separate entities. As Gregg pointed out, these processes are all interrelated.[44] Fortunately, systems theory provides a framework by which the interrelationships of administrative processes may be studied. Gregg complained in 1957 that "Empirical research relating to the administrative process is notably lacking."[45] Unfortunately, the research in this area is still very meager. With greater use of systems theory, especially hypotheses that cut across various levels of social systems, more useful generalizations concerning administrative processes will surely be developed.

Power and Authority

There has been a tendency on the part of some to abhor the terms "power" and "authority" as being inconsistent with democracy. Those who hold that belief seem to assume that if proper leadership is provided, power and authority are not essential to the social system. Let us take a look at power and authority.

For the purposes of this chapter, it is best to conceive of power in terms of behavior. Hunter has presented such a definition. Power, according to Hunter, is "the acts of men going about the business of moving other men to act in relation to themselves or in relation to organic or inorganic things."[46]

Dubin defines authority as "institutionalized power."[47] Simon defined authority in behavioral terms. According to him, "a subordinate may be said to accept authority whenever he permits his behavior to be guided by a decision reached by another, irrespective of his own judgment as to the merits of that decision."[48] Authority is always backed by power. Therefore, it might be said that a person has authority when he is perceived by the group to have the institutionalized right to "move other men to act in relation to themselves or in relation to organic or inorganic things."[49]

Griffiths has presented a thoughtful analysis of power and author-

[43]*Ibid.*, pp. 273–274.
[44]*Ibid.*, p. 274.
[45]*Ibid.*, p. 316.
[46]Floyd Hunter, *Community Power Structure* (Chapel Hill: University of North Carolina Press, 1953).
[47]Robert Dubin *et al.*, *Human Relations in Administration* (Englewood Cliffs, N.J.: Prentice-Hall, Inc. 1951), p. 188.
[48]Herbert A. Simon, *Administrative Behavior* (New York: The Macmillan Company, 1951), p. 22.
[49]Hunter, *op. cit.*

ity as affecting human relations.[50] Following are two of his conclusions concerning power which are of particular significance to the study of leadership:

1. Power is the cement which holds our society together as well as the societies of totalitarian states such as Soviet Russia and Nazi Germany. . . .

2. A democratic society is one in which the power command is held by a large number of people and is subject to the will of all of the people.[51]

We see that power cannot be ignored in a democracy any more than in an authoritarian state. School administrators certainly are not the only wielders of power in the school systems of the United States. Back of the superintendent is the board, and back of the board the people. Teachers and pupils also have power in certain situations.

Wiles has pointed out that power is used differently by persons with different concepts of leadership.[52] He distinguishes between "power over" and "power with" the group. "A 'power over' approach decreases the possibilities of releasing the full power of the group. It limits the potential accomplishment of the group."[53] Wiles states his concept of "power with" the group as follows:

Under the group approach to leadership, a leader is not concerned with getting and maintaining personal authority. His chief purpose is to develop group power that will enable the group to accomplish its goal. He does not conceive of his power as something apart from the power of the group. He is concerned with developing the type of relationships that will give him "power with" the group.[54]

Wiles insists that there is greater control over group members under the "power with" approach, because the group itself will bring pressure to bear on individual group members to achieve group goals.[55] It should not be assumed, however, that Wiles is advocating a system in which the official leader of the group has nothing to do with power. On this point he states: "The official leader administers the controls the group imposes on itself."[56] This is perhaps the ideal for which to strive. However, as has already been pointed out in this chapter, informal group goals are sometimes inconsistent with the goals of the total organization. In that event, the administrator may be compelled to resort

[50]Daniel E. Griffiths, *Human Relations in School Administration* (New York: Appleton-Century & Appleton-Century-Crofts, 1956), Chaps. 5 and 6.
[51]*Ibid.*, p. 105.
[52]Kimball Wiles, *Supervision for Better Schools*, 2nd ed. (Englewood Cliffs, N.J.: Prentice-Hall, Inc., 1955), pp. 161–167.
[53]*Ibid.*, p. 163.
[54]*Ibid.*, p. 164.
[55]*Ibid.*, p. 167.
[56]*Ibid.*, p. 223.

to the "power over" approach, and this will reduce his acceptance as a leader. Therefore, one of the primary objectives of the administrator-leader must be to bring informal group goals and organizational goals into congruence.

Since authority in an organization is backed by institutionalized power, it cannot be exercised effectively unless the person exercising the authority is perceived by the members of the organization as having the right to do so. There are further limitations on authority. Griffiths makes this point:

> Although there is a line of authority in each organization, there are also modifying conditions which change the effectiveness of the power being exerted. We note that the authority of an administrator is affected and modified by the board of education, the teachers, non-teaching staff, parents, students, patrons, the state school law, the customs and traditions of the community, and the authority of the profession.[57]

This concept is also extremely important to each group within the school faculty. No school group is completely autonomous in authority. All school groups, both formal and informal, are subgroups of the total organization. The ultimate "group" that has the final authority to determine school goals is the people. Therefore, no group within a school system has the legal or moral right to consider itself a completely autonomous primary group. Participation in decision making by all groups and individuals concerned is now being widely advocated. As groups participate in decision making, it is vital that the limits of authority of each group be clearly defined. The administrator-leader must also make clear to groups and individuals participating in decision making the decisions that he reserves for executive decision making and the decisions in which they can share. To do otherwise would result in chaos. These implications are important for state school administration as well as for local school administration.

Areas of Critical Behavior

The School-Community Development Study Project, coordinated by the College of Education of the Ohio State University, identified nine areas of critical behavior of educational administrators.[58] Those areas are as follows: (1) setting goals, (2) making policy, (3) determining roles, (4) appraising effectiveness, (5) coordinating administrative functions and structure, (6) working with community leadership to promote improvements in education, (7) using the educational resources of the community, (8) involving people, and (9) communicating.[59]

[57]Griffiths, *op. cit.*, p. 142.
[58]John A. Ramseyer *et al.*, "Factors Affecting Educational Administration," Monograph No. 2 (Columbus: College of Education, Ohio State University, 1955), p. 20.
[59]*Idem.*

These nine areas were identified for the purpose of classifying observations of administrator behavior with respect to interpersonal and environmental factors that have been found to make a difference in administrator behavior. A conceptual scheme for studying administrator behavior was then developed, based upon these nine critical areas. This approach is contrasted with an approach to the study of administration based upon the application of learned technique. It has facilitated the development of research on administrator behavior. It is interesting to note that these nine critical areas of administrator behavior are closely related to several of the administrative processes identified by Gregg.

The emerging concepts of leadership described in this chapter have great significance for administrative action. Some of the problems and issues associated with the application of these concepts are discussed in the following paragraphs.

Can a Person Be a Leader and at the Same Time
Hold an Executive Position in an Organization?

Attention has already been directed to the fact that the executive holding a position in the hierarchy of an organization is under pressure from his superordinates to attain the goals of the organization, and he is under pressure from his subordinates to meet their personal needs (the nomothetic vs. idiographic dimensions of the social system). Thompson commented as follows concerning this dilemma:

> Modern social scientists are coming to the conclusion that headship and leadership are incompatible or that their consolidation in the same hands is very unlikely. Leadership is a quality conferred upon a person by those who are led, and in this sense the leader is always elected. An appointed person on the other hand, must work to advance the interests of his sponsors. He cannot be a leader for his subordinates and still serve his sponsors unless there is complete harmony between the two, an unlikely event.[60]

Is the situation as hopeless as Thompson infers? Would the application of the emerging pluralistic, collegial concepts of organization and administration help to resolve this dilemma?

Is There a Need for Role Differentiation Among Leaders?

Leadership acts include those acts intended to help meet group goals and also acts intended to maintain the group by meeting group

[60]Victor A. Thompson, *Modern Organization* (New York: Alfred A. Knopf, Inc., 1961). Reprinted by permission of Alfred A. Knopf, Inc. Copyright © 1961 by Victor Thompson.

and individual needs. Berelson and Steiner have pointed out that even in small face-to-face informal groups the "intellectual leader" who structures the group and initiates action to attain group goals is usually not the same person as the "social leader" who meets group and individual needs by promoting mutual acceptance, harmony, liking, etc.[61] That is, the top position in an informal group on both "liking" and "ideas" is not frequently held by the same person. If this hypothesis is sustained by research on informal face-to-face groups, can it be assumed that the same findings would be applicable to different leadership roles in formal organizations? Some organizations have placed a "tough" man to say no as a second man to the top executive. Is the purpose of this arrangement to give a better image to the top executive, so that it will be possible for him to play a leadership role when the situation seems to require it? Despite the myth that the top executive in an organization must assume final responsibility, sometimes a subordinate in the executive hierarchy is sacrificed when a serious mistake has been made, in order to preserve the favorable image of the top executive. This policy has been justified because "it was for the good of the organization." What would be the long term effect of this policy on the leadership potential of the top executive?

What Officials Should Be Elected by the Group?

Research indicates that if a group elects its head, the person elected is perceived by the group as being its leader. He is accepted by the group as a group member, and he is in a strategic position to provide leadership for the group. But research has also shown that the person chosen by a group to be its leader is likely to be the person who most nearly is representative of the norms of the group. Rate of production is one of the norms in a factory group. The production norm is the average rate of production that the group believes ought to be maintained. If a group member produces considerably more or considerably less than the group norm, he is not likely to be accepted by the group as its leader.

A school faculty is a formal school group, but the elements of behavior of a face-to-face formal group are similar in some respects to the elements of behavior of a primary or informal group. The executive officer of the faculty is the school principal. The almost universal practice in the United States is for the principal to be appointed by the board of education upon the nomination of the superintendent. Considering the concepts of leadership presented in this chapter, should the present practice be continued, or would it be better for the principal to be elected by the faculty?

[61]Berelson and Steiner, *op. cit.*, pp. 244–245.

In some large high schools and in some institutions of higher learning, department heads are elected by the members of the department concerned. Is this good practice?

In some states the county superintendent of education, who is presumably the executive officer of the board, is elected by the people. What are the advantages and disadvantages of this procedure?

The prevailing practice in the United States for the selection of board members is election by the vote of the people. The board of education is a legislative and policy-forming group. Do the concepts of leadership and group dynamics presented in this chapter justify that practice?

Committee members in school faculties are sometimes appointed by the principal and sometimes elected by the faculty. What criteria should be used to determine whether members of a committee should be elected or appointed?

When the Goals of Two Groups Are in Conflict, How Can They Be Harmonized?

The school community is an aggregation of many groups, some of which have conflicting goals. Sometimes these groups make the school a battleground. Following is an example of such a situation.

In a certain school community, a patriotic group is violently opposed to the United Nations and insists that the school teach a doctrine of extreme nationalism. It demands that all UNESCO materials be removed from the school library and that the school faculty indoctrinate students in national isolation. The League of Women Voters, however, takes exactly the opposite view, believing that one of the school's goals should be to promote international understanding. The majority of the board of education supports the patriotic group, but the teacher group supports the point of view of the League of Women Voters.

What can the administrator-leader do to help the community arrive at mutually acceptable goals? How can Homans' theories of interaction be applied to this situation?

What Is the Relation Between Group Morale and Task Achievement in the Formal Organization?

Let us first consider informal groups that are subgroups of the formal organization. Each informal group, as has been pointed out, has two principal goals: group achievement and group maintenance. Each group defines its own achievement goals. The group maintenance goal is attained when both group and individual needs are substantially met and members get satisfaction from group membership. When a group continues to attain its two primary goals, the morale is high; but if it fails, the morale is low. An informal group with high morale is more productive in terms of its own standards of measuring production than a low-morale group. However, a high-morale group may not be productive as measured by the achievement of the tasks of the organization.

Let us now consider the formal organization of which the informal groups are subparts. The formal organization also has two principal functions: achievement of its goals and organizational maintenance. Let us assume, for example, that we have a formal organization such as a school faculty that has no real achievement goals accepted by its members. Let us assume further that the formal organization has been ineffective in meeting group and individual needs. In fact, the formal organization is not an entity, but rather a collection of individuals subdivided into primary groups and cliques. The informal organization, rather than the formal organization, holds the real power and authority. The morale of the actors in this organization is low.

What can the administrator-leader do to make the formal organization a real group?

How Can the Administrator-Leader Bring About Change and Innovations?

The public school system must constantly change its tasks, goals, and purposes if it is to meet the changing needs of society. This involves changes in the curriculum, the organizational structure, and the services provided. But the administrator always encounters some resistance to change. This is especially true if the changes conflict with critical group norms or threaten the status roles of individuals in the organization. But the administrator, if he is to be a leader, cannot assume a laissez-faire role and avoid change, because change is inevitable. On the other hand, if the administrator in bringing about change ignores certain vital factors of human relations, he will lose the leadership of his group. Under what conditions can institutional changes be made? Coffey and Golden, after an extensive review of applicable research, suggested the following conditions for facilitating organizational change:

> (a) When the leadership is democratic and the group members have freedom to participate in the decision-making process; (b) when there have been norms established which make social change an expected aspect of institutional growth; (c) when change can be brought about without jeopardizing the individual's membership in the group; (d) when the group concerned has a strong sense of belongingness, when it is attractive to its members, and when it is concerned with satisfying member needs; (e) when the group members actually participate in the leadership function, help formulate the goals, plan the steps toward goal realization, and participate in the evaluation of these aspects of leadership; (f) when the level of cohesion permits members of the group

to express themselves freely and to test new roles by trying out new behaviors and attitudes without being threatened by real consequence.[62]

Recently, there has been much interest in planned change. Bennis, Benne, and Chin and their associates have presented a design for planned change.[63] Under this concept there is ". . . the application of systematic and appropriate knowledge to human affairs for the purpose of creating intelligent action and change."[64] The process involves the deliberate collaboration of the change agent and the client system. These authors objected to the conceptualization of a change agent exclusively as a "free" agent brought in as a consultant from outside the client system. They comment on this issue as follows:

> For one thing, client systems contain the potential resources for creating their own planned change programs under certain conditions; they have inside resources, staff persons, applied researchers, and administrators who can and do act as successful change agents. For another thing, we contend that a client system must build into its own structures a vigorous change-agent function, in order for it to adapt to a continually changing environment.[65]

Is the change-agent role a leadership role when the change is made with the "willing cooperation" of the members of the client system? What theoretical concepts discussed in this chapter can be used to predict the by-products of imposing change on a group against its will? Should outside consultants be used as change agents as well as personnel within an organization?

Selected References

Bennis, Warren G., Kenneth D. Benne, and Robert Chin, *The Planning of Change*. New York: Holt, Rinehart & Winston, Inc., 1961.

Berelson, Bernard, and Gary A. Steiner, *Human Behavior: An Inventory of Scientific Findings*. New York: Harcourt, Brace & World, Inc., 1964.

Campbell, Roald F., and Russell T. Gregg, eds., *Administrative Behavior in Education*. New York: Harper & Row, Publishers, 1957.

Carlson, Richard O., Art Gallaher, Jr., Mathew B. Miles, Roland J. Pellegrin, and Everett M. Rogers, *Change Processes in the Public Schools*. Eugene, Ore.: Center for the Advanced Study of Educational Administration, University of Oregon, 1965.

[62]National Society for the Study of Education, *op. cit.*, pp. 101–102.

[63]Warren G. Bennis, Kenneth D. Benne, and Robert Chin, eds., *The Planning of Change* (New York: Holt, Rinehart & Winston, Inc., 1961).

[64]*Ibid.*, p. 3.

[65]*Idem.*

Cartwright, Darwin, and Alvin Zander, *Group Dynamics: Research and Theory.* New York: Harper & Row, Publishers, 1960.

Griffiths, Daniel E., ed., *Behavioral Science and Educational Administration.* The Sixty-third Yearbook of the National Society for the Study of Education. Chicago: University of Chicago Press, 1965.

Hare, A. Paul, Edgar F. Borgatta, and Robert F. Bales, *Small Groups: Studies in Social Interaction.* New York: Alfred A. Knopf, Inc., 1965.

Homans, George C., *The Human Group.* New York: Harcourt, Brace & World, Inc. 1950.

————, *Social Behavior: Its Elementary Forms.* New York: Harcourt, Brace & World, Inc., 1961.

Kimbrough, Ralph B., *Political Power and Educational Decision-Making.* Skokie, Ill.: Rand McNally & Company, 1964.

Lionberger, Herbert F., *Adoption of New Ideas and Practices.* Ames: Iowa State University Press, 1960.

Petrullo, Luigi, and Bernard M. Bass, eds., *Leadership and Interpersonal Behavior.* New York: Holt, Rinehart & Winston, Inc., 1961.

Saunders, Robert L., Ray C. Phillips, and Harold J. Johnson, *A Theory of Educational Leadership.* Columbus, Ohio: Charles E. Merrill Books, Inc., 1966.

Secord, Paul F., and Carl W. Backman, *Social Psychology.* New York: McGraw-Hill Book Company, 1964.

6

Cooperative Procedures

In Chapter 3, major emphasis was given to systems theory in order to introduce a rational, scientific theoretical framework for studying the phenomena of organization and administration. In Chapter 4, systems theory was applied to organization and in Chapter 5 to leaders and administrators of social systems. In this chapter, systems theory as well as other theoretical concepts from the social and behavioral sciences are applied to an analysis of the procedures by which living systems (individuals as well as social systems) relate themselves to each other in order to survive and in order to promote growth beyond survival.[1] We call this relationship "cooperative procedures," and it is similar to Kropotkin's concept of "mutual aid." As will become apparent later in this chapter, this is not entirely a value-free concept as used by the authors. The cooperative concept of human relationships as contrasted with the individual struggle for existence is undoubtedly partly a choice of values arising from a cultural background of political democracy, but we present in this chapter what we believe to be some solid, scientific evidence supporting the validity of this position.

[1]See James G. Miller, "Living Systems: Basic Concepts," *Behavioral Science,* **10,** No. 4 (Oct. 1965).

TRENDS IN COOPERATION RELATING
TO EDUCATIONAL DECISION MAKING

The historical record of public education in America shows the birth, the decline, and the rebirth of cooperative procedures in educational administration. In colonial New England, a public school was a genuine community enterprise. The building itself was frequently constructed by the school patrons. The purposes of the school were defined and understood by the lay people. The policies and budget were usually determined in the town meeting by people in a face-to-face relationship.

As towns grew into cities, and the industrial revolution spread during the nineteenth century, education began to assume new functions. The urban districts grew too large to be managed by town meeting procedures. Representative government was substituted for direct government by the people. Boards found it increasingly unsatisfactory to assume administrative responsibility, and consequently the need for professionally trained administrators began to be recognized. Prevailing theories of administration and organization were adapted to educational administration and organization. These theories were drawn largely from business and industry, which had attained high prestige by the end of the first quarter of the twentieth century.

The public school system had made great strides between 1900 and 1925. Public elementary and secondary education was well on its way to becoming available everywhere in the United States. Professional school administrators were employed to serve most of the larger school districts. A literature on school administration was being written. The words "efficient" and "businesslike" appeared frequently in that literature. The dynamic, bustling, aggressive administrator was confident that he could use the proven methods of business and industry to solve all the important problems of educational administration.

The "gospel of efficiency" dominated the thinking in the first third of the twentieth century.[2] Frederick Taylor, Henri Fayol, Luther Gulick, and Lyndall Urwick were all influential promoters of administrative and organizational efficiency. All of these men with the exception of Gulick were identified primarily with engineering. The efficiency formulations developed by these men did not conceptualize human beings as living systems but rather as inanimate parts of an organization. Consequently,

---

[2]See Bertram M. Gross, "The Scientific Approach to Administration," Chap. 3 of *Behavioral Science and Educational Administration*, The Sixty-Third Yearbook of the National Society for the Study of Education (Chicago: University of Chicago Press, 1964).

these men gave but little emphasis to human relations and the interactions of social systems. They were concerned primarily with getting more from the workers, the managers, and the organizational structures, without giving much consideration to what happened to the human components of organizations.

Then came the Great Depression. Procedures that had seemed so infallible a short while ago began to be questioned. Some of the theories of business and industry were found to be unsupportable. The depression was followed by World War II. That war had a profound effect on the thinking of people everywhere. To the people of the United States, that war was a struggle between the free democracies and the totalitarian states. Following the war, they wanted the freedom for which they had fought.

In the meanwhile, the schools had grown away from the people in most school systems. Boards of education set policies, and superintendents administered the schools. It was a simple scheme of things, but unfortunately it did not provide adequate solutions for many vital educational problems. Following World War II, the need for major expansions in the public school system became imperative. But the people were confused and divided on many educational issues. Even the purposes of the public schools were no longer clear to the people. This is not surprising, because for many years the mass of the people had not had the opportunity to really study, and reach agreement on, the purposes of the schools. There was little consensus in many districts on such vital issues as: what should be taught, how it should be taught, who should be educated, what it should cost, and how the funds should be provided. Administrators and boards of education found it difficult, even impossible in many districts, to develop adequate educational programs when there was but little agreement on these and other vital issues. An educational crisis of major proportions began to develop after World War II.

But long before World War II, pioneering superintendents and boards of education had already begun to experiment with methods to resolve these issues. The methods which had most frequent success usually included cooperative efforts involving many people. Space does not permit the detailing of the history of cooperative efforts in education. They have probably always been present to some extent, but the relative emphasis on cooperative effort versus directive control has certainly shifted from time to time. For instance, the Parent-Teacher Association was organized in 1897. But most administrators for many years did not permit Parent-Teacher Associations to share significantly in decision making.

It is interesting to note the influence of John Dewey and his students on "cooperative procedures," a term he used practically synonymously with "democratic procedures." Dewey wrote his *Democracy and Education* in 1916, placing great emphasis on cooperative efforts as being essential to the growth and development of children. However, even though Dewey and his colleagues have had a profound influence on the thinking of many people, numerous surveys have shown that both administrative and instructional practices have changed at a slow rate.

Although both teachers and administrators have been slow to accept genuinely cooperative procedures, the use of these procedures has been widely extended in recent years. In fact, it seems safe to predict an accelerated rate of acceptance of cooperative procedures by both classroom teachers and administrators in the future.

The National Citizens' Commission for the Public Schools was established in 1949, primarily to promote the welfare of the public schools. The commission was particularly active in developing lay interest in public education. As a means of doing this, it stimulated the creation of citizens' advisory committees on education throughout the United States. The National Citizens' Commission was in direct communication with some 2500 state and local citizen committees by 1955, and it is estimated that approximately 7500 additional committees were also operating at that time.

The National Citizens' Commission for the Public Schools was superseded by the National Citizens' Council for Better Schools in 1955. The council promoted the improvement of both public and private schools. It operated for a few years and then dissolved itself in 1959, in accordance with the original plan, when it appeared that lay-professional cooperation for better schools had become firmly established throughout the nation. The number of *ad hoc* lay-professional committees that operate at the present time is unknown. The practice has become so universal that it is now considered standard operating procedure.

The Year-Book Committee of the National Society for the Study of Education made a national survey of citizen cooperation for better schools in 1954.[3] The committee found a great increase in educational activities involving the cooperation of citizens. These activities were of many types, and they were being carried on at all levels of school government. The study also presented analyses of the reasons for the success or the failure of cooperative activities involving citizens.

It is not the purpose of this chapter to present recipes for successful cooperative procedures in educational administration. Each situation is different and, although some generalizations are justifiable, recipes may not be too helpful. Cooperative procedures in administration may

[3]National Society for the Study of Education, *Citizens Cooperation for Better Public Schools* (Chicago: University of Chicago Press, 1954).

involve lay citizens, teachers, or pupils, or all three groups. They may involve cooperative relationships with other governmental agencies. They may also involve cooperation among local, state, and national educational groups. The primary purpose of this chapter is to present some of the concepts and theories upon which cooperative procedures are based. Almost everyone in the United States professes to believe in democratic procedures. But democracy means so many different things to so many people that the authors have deliberately used the words "cooperative procedures" rather than "democratic procedures." Even the term "cooperative" may be subject to different interpretations. The authoritarian administrator may describe a person in his school system as cooperative if he accepts his orders without question. Any other person is considered noncooperative. The term "cooperative procedures" as used by the authors has quite a different meaning.

SOME BASIC THEORIES

Fortunately, there is a rich body of research produced by anthropologists, sociologists, psychologists, physiologists, social psychologists, biologists, and others from which we can secure much evidence concerning the validity of cooperative procedures. It is not possible in a book of this length to present even an adequate review of the pertinent research. However, a few of the more important findings are presented in the following paragraphs.

Early Theories of Economics

The economist Adam Smith gave great emphasis to self-interest. His monumental work *The Wealth of Nations* was published in 1776. He believed that the natural unfettered effort of every individual to improve his own condition "is so powerful a principle that it is alone and without any assistance, not only capable of carrying on the society to wealth and prosperity but of surmounting a hundred impertinent obstructions with which the folly of human laws too often incumber its operations." The postulates of Adam Smith dominated economic theory during the nineteenth century and have had great influence even during the twentieth century. His emphasis on extreme individualism also had a significant influence on theories of human relations during this same period of time.

Ricardo, a close friend of Malthus, accepted Malthus' population theory (though not most of his economic theories) and published in 1817 a brilliant exposition of economic theory in his *Principles of Political Economy*. Of interest here is Ricardo's "iron law" of wages. According to Ricardo, a worker should be paid only a subsistence wage, defined as a wage sufficient for the worker to survive and reproduce a sufficient number of workers to meet the needs of the economy. If a worker were paid wages above the subsistence level, the reproduction rate would increase to the point where a surplus of workers would be produced, which would drive wages back down to the subsistence level. At that level, poverty, misery, disease and reduced reproductive activity would hold the number of workers down to the number needed. Ricardo saw little need for cooperation of workers with the managers and owners because in his view their interests were conflicting.

The "Survival of the Fittest" Theories

The "survival of the fittest" theory of life reached a high point of acceptance during the latter part of the nineteenth century. It was even held by many to be the law of life. In fact, this theory has a powerful influence on the social thinking and actions of many people on the contemporary scene.

Malthus laid the foundation for the "survival of the fittest" theory in his famous *Essay on Population*, written in 1798. In that essay he stated the theory that poverty and distress were unavoidable, since population increases in geometric ratio whereas the food supply increases in arithmetic ratio. He accepted war, famine, and disease as necessary to human survival, because the population must be kept in balance with the food supply.

Darwin, stimulated by the work of Malthus, wrote his *Origin of the Species* in 1859. He started with the assumption that more of each species are born than can possibly survive. The surplus starts a struggle for existence, and if any individual in the species varies in any way profitable to itself, it has a better chance of survival. Thus, the surviving individual has been "naturally selected."

The scientist Huxley supported and advanced still further the theories of Darwin in his *Struggle for Existence*, written in 1888. But the theories of Darwin and Huxley needed philosophical justification. This was done in masterly fashion by Nietzsche in his *The Will to Power*, written in 1889. He looked upon life as a battle in which strength rather than goodness, pride rather than humility, unyielding intelligence rather than altruism, and power rather than justice are needed. He concluded that theories of equality and democracy had been disproven by the laws of selection and survival; therefore, democratic procedures were decadent.

The Smith-Darwin-Huxley-Nietzsche theories found a fertile ground indeed in the last half of the nineteenth century. The industrial revolution was in full swing. Industrial and business empires were being established. The demands for cheap labor were great. The business and industrial barons needed ethical justification for exploitation of the weak and the ruthless conflicts they had with one another. They found it in these theories.

The "survival of the fittest" theories gave rise in the latter part of the nineteenth century to a school of thought known as Social Darwinism.[4] Herbert Spencer, a brilliant English thinker, was the intellectual leader of this movement. His *First Principles,* published in 1864, *The Study of Sociology,* published in 1872–73, as well as his other publications, were widely read in the United States.

The Social Darwinists applied Darwin's theories of biological evolution directly to social institutions and the life of man in society. The "struggle for existence" and "survival of the fittest" concepts suggested that natural law demanded that these factors be permitted to operate in human sociey or that society would degenerate. Competition would eliminate the unfit, and this would assure continuing improvement.

Social Darwinism was embraced wholeheartedly by the economic and political conservatives of the nineteenth century. It sanctified by natural law the ruthless activities of the "robber barons" and their imitators. It preserved the *status quo,* because it suggested that social change should come about very slowly by evolution, as contrasted with revolution. It is interesting to note that the conservatives, including many industrialists not only of the nineteenth but also of the twentieth century, oppose social change bitterly and yet are the leaders in promoting revolutionary technological changes in business and industry. This glaring inconsistency has never seemed to bother conservatives in the economic power structure.

Another strange thing about Social Darwinism is that Karl Marx, the arch-enemy of the conservative industrialists, also embraced Darwin. He saw in Darwin's "struggle for existence" scientific justification for his "class struggle" theories.[5]

Students of political science have long known that there is not a great ideological difference between the extreme right and the extreme left. Each denies the dignity of the individual, each uses ruthless power to make decisions, each is based on the authoritarian concept of human relations, and each uses the same tactics to gain its ends. This should not be too surprising because the extreme right and the extreme left are both basing their ideologies on the same value assumptions with respect to what man's life in society should be.

[4]See Richard Hofstadter, *Social Darwinism in American Thought* (New York: George Braziller, Inc., 1959).

[5]*Ibid.,* p. 115. Hofstadter quoted the following from a letter written by Marx to Engels in 1860: "Darwin's book is very important and serves me as a basis in natural science for the class struggle in history."

Opposition to Social Darwinism developed, as discussed later in this chapter. Most intellectuals had rejected Social Darwinism by the close of the nineteenth century. Although the open advocacy of this doctrine by the business community had declined by the turn of the century, the basic belief in that doctrine persisted unabated. In fact, the full flowering of this type of thinking was not reached until the first quarter of the twentieth century.

The term "rugged individualist" was coined, and was considered to be a compliment. Teachers were expected to prepare children for this struggle by emphasizing competition and survival of the fittest in the classroom. The Great Depression, the rise of Hitler, and World War II were some of the fruits of actions based on the theories of Smith, Darwin, Huxley, and Nietzsche.

The "Class Struggle" Theory

Marx and Engels, who were contemporaries of Darwin and Huxley, advanced some political theories that were as ruthless as Social Darwinism. Marx and Engels published the *Communist Manifesto* in 1847, and Marx published the first volume of *Das Kapital* in 1867. These writers took a materialistic view of history and developed a theory of human relationships on that basis. According to Marx and Engels, the arrangement of social classes and political institutions is for the purpose of production. As the conditions of production change, the arrangement of social classes and political institutions must change. But this cannot be done by voluntary cooperation, because political and social institutions lag behind and can be changed only by revolution.

The only real value of goods is the labor it takes to produce them (an idea advanced by Adam Smith nearly a hundred years earlier). The capitalistic class exploits the workers by the extraction of "surplus value" from them. This is done by adding profits, interests, and rents to the price of goods and services. The capitalist system produces unfavorable conditions for production. The only solution is for the working class to revolt, seize the state, and create a new state in its own image. The first step is to establish a "dictatorship of the proletariat" as a temporary state for the purpose of liquidating all opposition. When the dictatorship has abolished all classes and all exploitation of man by man, all classes are merged into one. Then the state gradually withers away. It is replaced by a kind of social administration of a classless society in which all conflicts have been eliminated. This is the Marxist utopia. It is a forced type of cooperation in which, initially at least, no confidence whatsoever is placed in voluntary cooperation.

It is interesting to note that the Communists make a perverted use of the group process in accomplishing their goals. This is done through

168 Principles, Concepts, and Issues*

establishing large numbers of Communist cells throughout the society being penetrated, a step preliminary to revolution. These cells are face-to-face groups, but all goals are determined by authority external to the group. The group is not established for the purpose of providing opportunity for broad participation, but rather to give external authority an instrument for the control of the masses. Each group must think and feel as every other group. There is no place for any degree of group autonomy, for each must follow the party line. The penalty for deviation is liquidation. Thus the theories of Marx and Engels are as antagonistic to theories of democratic cooperative action as the "survival of the fittest" theory.

Mutual-Aid Theories

It should not be thought that the "survival of the fittest" theory went completely unchallenged. Many voices were raised against the sweeping conclusions being drawn from this theory. Many religious leaders opposed the doctrine, because of its association with the theory of evolution which they considered atheistic. The fact of evolution could not be refuted, so the opposition of the ministry was not very effective.

Some intellectuals soon began to reveal the fallacies of Social Darwinism. The early pragmatists were among this group. In 1867, William T. Harris started the *Journal of Speculative Philosophy,* in which he and others attacked many of Spencer's propositions. The pragmatists accepted evolution but rejected Social Darwinism. William James, the famous philosopher and psychologist of Harvard University, first accepted Spencer, but by the middle 1870s he was exposing the fallacies of Spencer's theories.[6]

The influence of John Dewey and his *Democracy in Education,* published in 1916, has already been mentioned. Dewey was greatly influenced by Harris and James.

Kropotkin, an anthropologist, wrote a series of essays between 1890 and 1896 in which he attacked some of the theories of Darwin and Huxley.[7] He rejected the Darwinian concept that the struggle for existence pitted every animal against every other animal of the same species. He contended that competition within the same species was of only limited value and that mutual aid was the best guarantee for existence and evolution. Kropotkin's conclusions were based on studies of conditions for survival of animals, savages, barbarians, a medieval city, and of the times in which he lived. He found that the unsociable species were doomed to decay. But the species that reduced to its lowest limits

[6]*Ibid.,* p. 128.
[7]Peter Kropotkin, *Mutual Aid, A Factor of Evolution* (London: William Heinemann, Limited, 1902).

the individual struggle for existence and developed mutual aid to the greatest extent were the most numerous, the most prosperous, and the most likely to develop further. His studies of human beings, regardless of the stage of civilization, led to the same conclusions.

Montagu, another anthropologist, has also boldly challenged the Darwin-Huxley thesis that the nature of man's life is a conflict for the survival of the fittest. He assembled an array of evidence from the investigations of many scientists and concluded that the true nature of man's life is cooperation. He stated his position as follows:

> Evolution itself is a process which favors cooperating groups rather than dis-operating groups and "fitness" is a function of the group as a whole rather than of separate individuals. The fitness of the individual is largely derived from his membership in a group. The more cooperative the group, the greater is the fitness for survival which extends to all its members.[8]

He studied the researches of Allee on lower order animals,[9] and concluded that animals confer distinct survival values on each other. For Montagu, the dominant principle of social life is cooperation and not the struggle for existence. The findings of Montagu are particularly significant because they are based on the researches of biologists, anthropologists, physiologists, psychologists, and many other scientists. He accepts the theory of evolution but insists that, for the human animal, the fitness to survive is based more on the ability to cooperate than on "tooth and claw." It is interesting to note that both Darwin and Huxley recognized in their later years the importance of cooperation in the evolutionary process, but many of their followers would have none of it. Nietzsche died holding firmly to his thesis.

LaBarre, an anthropologist, has presented a synthesis of the sciences of man, an integration of human biology, cultural anthropology, psychiatry, and their related fields.[10] According to LaBarre, man is a polytypical anthropoid and not a polymorphous arthropod. The polytypical anthropoid is a species in which all individuals have essentially the same characteristics. A polymorphous arthropod is an insect species that has been structured into many physical castes by evolution. Each of these castes is a proper slave to the codified instincts of the hive. Since man is a polytypical anthropoid, he cannot grow maximally under a rigid caste or class system. Biologically, all men are brothers; therefore, man can grow best in a society of peers or equals.

He also concluded that racial traits have nothing to do with the

[8]Ashley Montagu, *On Being Human,* 2nd ed. (New York: Hawthorn Books, 1966), p. 45.

[9]Ward C. Allee, *Animal Aggregations* (Chicago: University of Chicago Press, 1931).

[10]Weston LaBarre, *The Human Animal* (Chicago: University of Chicago Press, 1954), p. 225.

survival of the individual or the races. Therefore, the ultimate survival of societies depends on "what the people in them believe," and not on physical differences. Social organisms are the means of survival of mankind. The findings of LaBarre support the thesis that the evolution and growth of mankind is primarily dependent on cooperative procedures which assume that all members of human society are essentially equal.

Hofstadter has demonstrated that racism and imperialism are essentially based on the theories of Social Darwinism.[11] Hitler's "master race," the assumptions back of the "white man's burden," and racial segregation are all based on the assumption that some segments of the human race are more fit to survive than others.

Teilhard de Chardin, a distinguished paleontologist and a Jesuit Father, accepted the theory of evolution but rejected Social Darwinism. After a lifetime of research in his chosen field, he concluded as follows: "No evolutionary future awaits man except in association with other men. The dreamers of yesterday glimpsed that. And in a sense we see the same thing."[12]

Kelley has advanced the interesting thesis that man has no common world. Each individual is born with his own hereditary equipment which is different from that of any other human being. He builds on this hereditary foundation through his own perceptions of experiences.

"Since perception is the usable reality, and since no two organisms can make the same use of clues or bring the same experimental background to bear, no two of us can see alike; we have no common world."[13]

Kelley and Rasey further developed this thesis later.[14] They seemed to consider it a handicap to cooperation but pointed out that people could communicate with each other by working together toward common goals and thereby achieve a large degree of "commonty." They also noted that there seemed to be a therapeutic value for the individuals involved in working together.

If a man's perceptions constitute his only reality, in isolation he is possessed of but a small world because of his limitations. But if one can share and compare his perceptions with others, he can extend the limits of his reality. By this process, each individual member of a cooperating group may grow. Furthermore, each individual has learned by bitter experience that his own perceptions cannot always be sure guides to wise action. This may give rise to personal insecurity. When one verifies his

[11]Hofstadter, *op. cit*, Chap. 9.

[12]Pierre Teilhard de Chardin, *The Phenomenon of Man*, trans. Bernard Wall (New York: Harper & Row, Publishers, 1959), p. 246.

[13]Earl C. Kelley, *Education for What Is Real* (New York: Harper & Row, Publishers, 1947), p. 34.

[14]Earl C. Kelley and Marie Rasey, *Education and the Nature of Man* (New York: Harper & Row, Publishers, 1952), pp. 38–41.

perceptions with others, he gains a feeling of security that probably accounts to some extent for the therapeutic value of cooperative group action. In fact, participation by the individual in a cooperating group may constitute the continuing action research by which he validates his perceptions. The distinction is made between a perception and a fact, because each individual may bring to the group a different perception of group. Growth of the human being is promoted by belonging, not isolation.

Giles has developed an extremely interesting field theory of the basic motives of human behavior.[15] This theory is intended to describe "not only the dynamics of interpersonal and group relations, but those forces which operate in individual development, all within one system of thought." It is a field theory, in contrast with an atomistic theory. According to his growth-belonging theory, "growth" is the inclusive purpose of human behavior and "belonging" the chief condition for growth. He defines growth in general as "continuous development toward increasing adequacy for: (1) survival; (2) progress toward human purposes beyond mere survival, such as the continuous exploration and enlargement of human capacities through their free exercise in increasing fields of opportunity."[16] Belonging is one of the basic needs of the human being. It is a basic need of the single cell, the individual, and any social group. Growth of the human being is promoted by belonging, not isolation.

Giles, in his studies of growth, noted a number of factors related to growth that have significant relationships to cooperative procedures. Freedom of choice is a fundamental prerequisite to human growth. The human being in isolation or in a rigid authoritarian society has little freedom of choice. Status is necessary for growth. The individual needs not only to belong but to have a role in which he has opportunity to grow. It is possible that when an individual struggles for power, he is merely trying to achieve a status in which he has the opportunity to grow. Giles noted that all living things exhibit irritability, that irritability leads to action, and that action leads to growth. Therefore, cooperative procedures in order to promote growth must be active, not passive, and designed to satisfy some of the personal motivations of participants.

Giles, like Dewey, believes that many human goals such as eating, drinking, and procreating are not ends in themselves, but means to growth. Selfishness and altruism may both be aspects of growth. "For selfishness may turn out to be only a narrower, more limited realization of growth possibilities, while altruism, 'social mindedness,' is the same basic desire for growth possibility on a larger scale, with realization of

[15]Harry H. Giles, *Education and Human Motivation* (New York: Philosophical Library, 1957).
[16]*Ibid.*, p. 76.

larger opportunities in a larger theater through cooperative effort."[17]

Giles also points out that "the physiologists, the psychologists, and the anthropologists seem to agree that only a small part of the potential of the organism and the society has ever been developed." Thus, both Giles and Montagu seem to agree that belonging to an accepting or cooperating group is essential to the growth or evolution of the human being.

Nurses in hospital wards have long noted that babies whose mothers had abandoned them would grow faster both mentally and physically if they were cuddled occasionally. Research has verified those observations. It is quite possible that the human infant is born with the basic need for affection and belonging.

The implications of the growth-belonging theory for cooperative procedures are evident. If growth is the major purpose of human behavior, and belonging is essential to growth, then cooperative procedures which provide the opportunity to belong are valid.

This concept is particularly applicable to the public schools. In America, the schools belong to the people. Therefore, public education cannot possibly be the exclusive preserve of professional educators. Cooperation between educators and laymen is essential to the development of a satisfactory program. Cooperation is impossible unless laymen have a feeling of belonging.

Summarizing, the evidence available from many fields of science indicates that the conditions for survival of mankind are minimized by living in isolation and maximized by cooperative living. Conditions for survival are probably somewhere between maximal and minimal in an authoritarian society, and may approach closest to the ideal in a democratic society.

The adoption of cooperative procedures for resolving human problems is not as general as the evidence would justify. This is particularly true concerning the relationship of one social system to another or of one society to another. As Heilbroner has pointed out, man has faced the problem of survival since he came down from the trees, "not as an individual but as a member of a social group."[18] But the task is not easy, because "he is torn between a need for gregariousness and a susceptibility to greediness."[19]

Some Hypotheses Related to Cooperative Procedures

In this chapter we have introduced the concept of intergroup cooperative procedures and shown that it has a sound theoretical basis.

[17]*Ibid.,* p. 26.
[18]Robert L. Heilbroner, *The Worldly Philosophers* (New York: Simon and Schuster, Inc., 1953), p. 9.
[19]*Idem.*

Miller has formulated some hypotheses, supported by research, which are applicable to this concept. Following is a summary of the applicable hypotheses.[20] Under systems theory, each social system has a boundary, and the actors within that boundary interact with each other more frequently than with the actors external to the boundary of the system. It is easier for actors within a social system to pass information to each other than it is to pass information across the boundary of the system to actors in the environment who also may be within another social system. Furthermore, it takes less energy to exchange information within a social system than to pass information from without a social system across the boundary to within a social system. Therefore if Actor A is in one social system and Actor B in another, the boundaries of two social systems must be crossed in order for A and B to exchange information. The problem is further complicated when numbers of social systems are involved. The strategy of formulating a new cooperating group, such as a joint professional and lay committee to study school problems, is based on the hypothesis that the actors from a number of different social systems when placed in the same face-to-face group, will interact with each other, form a new *ad hoc* social system and exchange information with each other without the necessity of crossing so many systems boundaries.

Behavioral scientists have formulated a number of hypotheses based on evidence produced by research which are related to cooperative procedures. Following are some hypotheses proposed by Berelson and Steiner, which they derived from their inventory of scientific findings in the behavioral sciences:

1. That a small group after discussion finds a more satisfactory solution to a problem than individuals working alone when the problem is technical rather than attitudinal, when a range of possible solutions is available, when the task requires each member to make a judgment, when rewards and punishments are given to the group as a whole, when the information and skills needed are additive, when the task can be subdivided, and when the task includes "traps" that might be missed by individuals.[21]

2. Active participation in the communicating itself is more effective for persuasion and retaining information than is the passive reception of information.[22]

3. The more people associate with one another under conditions of

[20]James G. Miller, "*Living Systems: Cross-Level Hypotheses,*" *Behavioral Science,* 10, No. 4 (1965), 382.

[21]Adapted from Bernard Berelson and Gary A. Steiner, *Human Behavior: An Inventory of Scientific Findings* (New York: Harcourt, Brace & World, Inc., 1964), p. 355.

[22]*Ibid.,* p. 548, adapted.

equality, the more they come to share values and norms and the more they come to like one another.[23]

4. The more interaction or overlap there is between related groups, the more similar they become in their norms and values; the less communication or interaction between them, the more tendency there is for conflict to arise between them. And vice versa: the more conflict, the less interaction.[24]

TYPES OF COOPERATIVE PROCEDURES
IN EDUCATIONAL ADMINISTRATION

As has been previously pointed out, the practice of using cooperative procedures involving citizens has greatly increased since World War II. But the trend toward the wider use of cooperative procedures includes many other areas of cooperation. Chief state school officers, state boards of education, and state departments of education in many states are now involving state education associations, the state congress of parents and teachers, citizen groups, and representatives of local school systems before making important decisions on policies and programs. Cooperative school surveys of both state and local school systems are now commonplace. Local school superintendents and boards of education in progressive school systems are involving teachers, principals, citizens, and representatives of other governmental agencies before making vital policy decisions. Modern school principals are now involving teachers, other school employees, citizens, and even pupils before making many policy decisions. There is evidence available that indicates that teachers are making much wider use of pupil-teacher planning as a part of the learning process than was the practice in the 1930s.

Space does not permit a description of the procedures used in implementing all of these different types of cooperative procedures. Attention is directed, however, to the fact that most of these procedures involve group activities. These groups frequently take the form of committees. In Chapter 4, it was pointed out that modern administrators consciously plan for cooperative procedures by incorporating a structure for committees within the organizational plan. A committee in order to be effective must become a group, rather than an aggregation of individuals in a struggle for survival. Therefore, the administrator in order to use committees effectively must be aware of the characteristics of effective groups. Some of these characteristics were described in Chapter 5.

[23]*Ibid.*, p. 327.
[24]*Ibid.*, p. 331.

State Cooperative Procedures

Johns and Thurston, after studying the activities of a large number of cooperative state projects, concluded that the most satisfactory state projects had the following characteristics:

1. Opportunities were given for broad participation of organizations, groups, agencies, and individuals in the development of educational policies and programs.

2. The state organization worked with local groups organized to provide opportunities for citizen cooperation. State groups have frequently stimulated the organization of local groups and have rendered valuable services in coordinating their activities.

3. Work procedures emphasized the making of studies. Decision making based upon discussion only has not proved as effective as decision making after considering the facts.

4. Educators were used in a consulting capacity by decision-making and study committees.

5. The project developed an action program for educational improvement. Nonaction state groups which have been organized primarily for orientation have had some value, but a group which does not have the opportunity to participate in decision making, at least in an advisory capacity, does not really have the opportunity to cooperate.

6. The members of the council or committees were selected in such a manner as to be representative, but they were free to cooperate with each other.

7. The group defined its policies of working together, developed its plan of work, and organized to carry out its activities.

8. Cooperative activities were genuine and sincere on the part of all persons involved.[25]

These characteristics of successful state cooperative projects seem equally applicable to local projects.

Working With Citizens' Committees

Morphet, after analyzing the factors affecting the success or failure of numerous citizens' committees, suggested some general guides for cooperative procedures. Although these guides were designed primarily for application to citizens' committees working on education problems, they are also broadly applicable to all types of committees and co-

[25]R. L. Johns and Lee M. Thurston, "State School Programs Are Being Improved Through Co-operation," Chapter 8, *Citizens Co-operation for Better Schools*, Fifty-third Yearbook of the National Society for the Study of Education, Part I, (Chicago: University of Chicago Press, 1954), pp. 212–213.

operative procedures. His proposals are summarized in the following
paragraphs.

> *Both educators and lay citizens have responsibilities to meet and con-*
> *tributions to make in the development of the educational programme.*
> Both have a vital stake in the schools and have important responsibilities
> to meet if the schools are to function satisfactorily. However, there
> are certain things pertaining to the operation of schools which educators
> are better prepared to do than other citizens. On the other hand, deci-
> sions involving policies for education should be made by citizens general-
> ly, rather than by educators alone. Lay citizens need the counsel of
> educators in order to arrive at the best answers as to what should be
> done, and educators frequently need the counsel and support of lay citi-
> zens concerning how certain things should be worked out under exist-
> ing circumstances.
>
> *The development of a sound educational programme requires the best*
> *cooperative efforts of both educators and lay citizens.* Policies can be
> sound or unsound educationally, as well as desirable or undesirable
> from a community point of view. Well-trained and competent educa-
> tional personnel are needed to help in planning a sound programme of
> education, yet it cannot be done satisfactorily by educators alone. The
> cooperation and support of parents and other citizens is essential.
>
> *Educators and other citizens should share the responsibility for stimulat-*
> *ing, encouraging, and facilitating cooperation in connection with the*
> *educational programme.* People need to learn to work together con-
> structively for the common good. If they learn how to cooperate effec-
> tively in improving the programme of the schools which affects the home,
> the community, and the nation, they should be in better position to
> participate constructively in improving other aspects of community life.
>
> *All cooperative effort to improve the educational programme should*
> *utilize the basic principles of satisfactory human relations.* Among the
> most important of these are the following:
>
> (a)   There should be respect for the individual, yet continuing
>   recognition of the fact that the common good must always be
>   considered.
>
> (b)   The talents and abilities of all persons who can make a contri-
>   bution to the development of the programme should be utilized.
>
> (c)   The thinking and conclusions of two or more interested persons
>   with a good understanding of the problems and issues are
>   likely, in the long run, to be more reliable than the conclusions
>   of one individual.
>
> *The major purpose of every individual and group should be to help*
> *improve education.* The basic objective of any individual or group can be
> positive or negative, constructive or destructive. Individuals can work
> for their own self-interest or for the public interest. Persons who parti-
> cipate in any cooperative effort relating to the schools should be genuine-
> ly interested in seeking ways to help the schools.
>
> *The kinds of cooperative activities which should be developed are*
> *those considered to be most appropriate and meaningful in each situation.*
> There is no one kind of cooperative activity which is most appropriate

for all conditions and communities. There are many kinds of cooperative activities, each of which is best suited to meet a particular need. Committees or study groups are likely to be desirable when policies are being formulated but may be a handicap when there is need for prompt and efficient administration.

Cooperation should always be genuine and bona fide. Mutual trust and confidence are essential for the success of any project. Confidence and understanding are basic to successful cooperation.

Insofar as practicable, all cooperative projects should be cooperative from the beginning. There is usually little basis for cooperation when any person or group is asked merely to approve conclusions previously reached by one person.

The procedures used in a cooperative programme should be designed to assure that conclusions will be reached on the basis of pertinent evidence and desirable objectives. Rumors, vague or unfounded reports, or the omission of pertinent evidence are almost certain to result in unsound conclusions and thus destroy the value of cooperative effort.

Insofar as practicable, decisions should be reached on the basis of consensus and agreement. In cooperative procedure it is important that agreement be reached on all points, if at all possible. The fact that a majority favours a certain point of view does not necessarily mean that is the only point of view to be considered. Reasonable people should be able to reach agreement if all evidence is considered and sound procedures are followed.

Leaders who understand and believe in cooperative procedures are essential. If the head of a school or the chairman of a committee is interested in getting things done quickly, regardless of the wishes or feelings of individual members, a satisfactory cooperative procedure is likely to be slow in developing or may not develop at all. Cooperation works out most satisfactorily when it has the support of leaders who understand and believe in cooperative processes.

Persons involved in cooperative projects should be broadly representative of all points of view in the school or community. If minority groups, students, or others who should be concerned with the educational programme are ignored, there are likely to be difficulties. If a group is organized merely to "put across" a certain point of view, regardless of the wishes of others, serious opposition to the entire procedure is likely to develop.

Cooperative activities should be so planned as to be beneficial to the individuals and groups involved as well as to the schools. The process of cooperation is important because, if desirable procedures are used, all participants should become more understanding and helpful as a result of their experience.

School officials should give the most careful consideration to all proposals and recommendations growing out of a cooperative programme, and should approve those which seem to be for the best interests of the schools. If the participants in any cooperative project relating to the schools are assured that their proposals will receive careful and fair consideration, their efforts will be much greater than if they have serious doubts about this matter.

All persons and groups interested in any form of cooperation should constantly seek to improve the procedures and outcomes. Every effort at cooperation can be improved on the basis of study and experience. Those engaged in any cooperative effort should therefore make a continuous appraisal of their own procedures in an effort to improve the process and outcomes.

The procedures used in cooperative activities should be consistent with these fundamental principles but should be designed to meet the needs of the particular situation. It should be apparent that there is not likely to be any pattern or blueprint that will fit all types of conditions and every aspect of group cooperation. It should be equally evident, however, that basic principles and criteria such as those proposed above should be carefully followed in planning and carrying out any cooperative procedure.[26]

Although Morphet developed his proposals primarily from experiences with and meticulous observations of citizens' committees at work, students of group dynamics will readily note that Morphet's conclusions are consistent with the findings of social psychologists. For instance, (1) opportunities are provided for group work; (2) group members work with peer status; (3) opportunities are provided for group interactions; (4) common goals are determined; (5) the total resources of each member of the group are utilized; (6) leadership is shared and opportunities are provided for leadership to emerge; (7) the group is an active group; (8) plans are developed for goal achievement; (9) individual needs as well as group needs are recognized; (10) opportunities for belonging and sharing are provided, and (11) opportunities for communication are maximized.

The Administration and Committees

The necessity for cooperative action has been emphasized in Chapters 4, 5, and 6. The latter part of this chapter has given particular emphasis to citizens' committees. The role of citizens' committees and even faculty committees is sometimes misunderstood. The use of committees is an excellent procedure for developing policies and programs and for securing agreement on goals and purposes. However, a committee is a poor instrument for the administration of programs and policies. The administrator cannot and should not expect a committee to make executive decisions for him. He should make the executive decisions in line with democratically determined policies. All members of the staff including administrators, teachers, custodians, clerks and others

[26]E. L. Morphet, *Cooperative Procedures in Education* (Monograph distributed by the Associated Students' Bookstore, University of California, Berkeley) (Hong Kong: Hong Kong University Press, 1957), pp. 5–9. These guides were adapted from the proposals presented in E. L. Morphet, *Citizen Cooperation for Better Schools,* Fifty-third Yearbook of the National Society for the Study of Education, Part I (Chicago, 1954).

must make executive decisions. Therefore, each member of the staff from time to time must be the administrator for some particular activity. Consequently, it is essential that careful distinction be made between those decisions that should be made by group action and those decisions that should be made by the administrators of programs and policies.

Attention is also directed to the fact that the board of education is the legally constituted policy-making body for a school district. Therefore, citizen committees and faculty must serve in an advisory capacity to the board of education. The board of education cannot abdicate its responsibility for policy making to committees. Neither should it make policies without providing opportunity for wide participation in decision making by all persons concerned.

SOME IMPORTANT PROBLEMS AND ISSUES

Cooperative procedures may seem to be a way for delaying decisions that should be made by school administrators and boards of education or for dodging responsibility. In fact, cooperative procedures could be used for those purposes, but these procedures are especially important when there are differences in value systems that need to be resolved before a decision can be satisfactorily implemented. Certain problems and issues related to cooperative processes are presented in the following paragraphs.

What Consideration Should Be Given to Persons Who Have a Low Need for Participation?

Bennis stated the following values were held by some theorists on planning for change in organizations:

> The values espoused indicate a way of behaving and feeling; for example, they emphasize openness rather than secrecy, collaboration rather than dependence or rebellion, cooperation rather than competition, consensus rather than individual rules, rewards based on self-control rather than externally induced rewards, team leadership rather than a one-to-one relationship with the boss, authentic relationships rather than those based on political maneuvering.[27]

Bennis then raised the question whether these values are natural, desirable, or functional, and what then happens to status or power drives. "What about those individuals who have a low need for participation and/or a high need for structure and dependence?"[28] He suggested that the needs of these people could best be met through

[27]Warren G. Bennis, "Theory and Method in Applying Behavioral Science to Planned Organizational Change," *Applied Behavioral Science,* 1, No. 4 (1965), 356.
[28]*Idem.*

bureaucratic systems and wondered whether these people should be changed or forced to yield and comply.

Assuming that Bennis has presented a real problem, how could a superintendent, a college president, or a school principal deal with it?

What Is the Function of Social Controls?

A great number of scientific studies have shown that growth or evolution is more the result of the cooperative process than the product of a ruthless struggle for survival. These studies have not overthrown the theory of evolution, but they have shown that evolution is affected by many factors other than the struggle for survival. The fitness of the human individual or human society to survive is determined more by the ability to cooperate than by the sharpness of tooth and claw. These are not pious platitudes. They are the findings of objective scientists. It is interesting that these findings are consistent with the assumptions of democracy.

Despite the evidence supporting cooperative behavior, much human behavior even in the United States is based on the assumptions of Darwin, Huxley, and Nietzsche. The pessimist would say that most of it is based on those assumptions. Many social controls have been developed for regulating human relationships. Those controls have taken the form of laws, administrative regulations, codes of ethics, and many other forms. Many people have felt that laws and regulations restrict the individual and deny him the freedom to develop. But if controls enhance the opportunity of the individual to cooperate with his fellow human beings in order that the individual and society may have maximum freedom to grow, then they are good. However, if the controls established by society perpetuate the privileges of the few or establish a society based on the assumptions of Darwin, Huxley, and Nietzsche, then they restrict the growth and development of humanity and are bad. Perhaps this is as good a test as any to apply to any social control. Is the Fourteenth Amendment a control or a freedom, or both? What are some undesirable social controls affecting education?

Does the Need for Quick Action Invalidate Cooperative Procedures?

The administrator sometimes meets situations in which it seems that quick action is needed. For instance, the newly employed administrator may find that faculty members are quarrelling with each other, pupil discipline is bad, school attendance is poor, the curriculum is inadequate, and the public has little confidence in the schools. The board is back of him and expects him to "clean up the mess." Does this situation call for cooperative procedures or for authoritarian action?

What changes could the administrator expect to make by issuing unilateral orders and taking direct action, and what changes could he
expect to make by cooperative procedures?

When Can Conflict Be Constructive?

Cooperative procedures involving group operation will very frequently result in conflict both within a group and among different
groups. This is especially true if the membership of a group was deliberately selected to represent different points of view. However, conflict
itself, if properly understood and dealt with, may present an opportunity
for growth. Therefore, conflict can be either constructive or destructive.
This point of view was originally presented by Mary Parker Follett in
1925.[29] Miss Follett was one of the pioneer thinkers in the field of human
relations. In her great paper on "Constructive Conflict," she advanced the
point of view that the three main ways of dealing with conflict are
domination, compromise, and integration.[30] Domination, the victory of
one side over the other, is the easiest and quickest but the least successful method for dealing with conflict. Compromise, the most commonly
used method, involves each side moderating its demands in order to have
peace, neither side obtaining all its objectives. If the ideas of both sides
are integrated into a solution that encompasses the desires of both sides,
the highest level of dealing with conflict is reached. Miss Follett's
illustration of her point is worthy of repetition here. It seems that a
dairymen's cooperative league was on the point of breaking up over the
question of precedence of unloading. The creamery was located on the
side of a hill. The men who came uphill thought that they should have
precedence, but the men who came downhill thought their claims to
precedence were stronger. If the method of domination had been followed, one side or the other would have been given precedence. If the
matter had been compromised, the uphillers and downhillers would each
have been given precedence on alternate days. But a consultant suggested that the platform be so arranged that unloading could be done on
both sides, so that the uphillers could unload on one side and the downhillers on the other. This solution was adopted. Each side got what it
wanted, and the conflict was completely resolved. She pointed out that
thinking is too often confined between the walls of two possibilities. The
integrator is inventive and examines all possible alternatives, not just the
ones being advocated by the parties in conflict.

Unfortunately, more differences are settled by compromise than
by integration. Undoubtedly, conflicts have been resolved many times

[29]Henry C. Metcalf and L. Urwick, eds., *Dynamic Administration, The Collected
Papers of Mary Parker Follett* (New York: Harper & Row, Publishers, 1940).
[30]*Ibid.*, pp. 30–49.

by compromise when the possibilities of developing integrated solutions had not been fully explored. Incidentally, Nehru once suggested that compromise that represents a step toward attaining a desirable objective may be good; compromise that results in abandoning an objective or substituting an inferior principle may be bad. The most effective groups, however, will not resort to compromise to resolve conflicts without first attempting to find an integrated solution.

Conflict is destructive when it continues or increases social disorganization or is damaging to individual personalities. Conflict is constructive when it can serve as the impetus for growth in human relations and the finding of better solutions for meeting the needs of the group.

What should be the role of the administrator in resolving conflicts? What procedures can be used to help groups grow in their ability to resolve conflicts constructively? Under what conditions are destructive conflicts likely to be encountered in educational organizations?

How Can Pseudocooperation Be Avoided?

There are three main types of cooperation: authoritarian, controlled, and voluntary.[31] Authoritarian cooperation is essentially the master-slave concept of human relations. The leader or leaders do all the thinking and give all the instructions. The followers or workers cooperate by carrying out all instructions to the letter.

Controlled or pseudodemocratic cooperation is the same in principle as authoritarian cooperation. The leader decides on what he wants done, but he uses subtle and clever means to assure that the "right" decision is made by the group. This type of cooperation is insidious, because the group is frequently led to believe that it is operating on a democratic basis. The leader manipulates the group into agreeing with his previously determined conclusion. This gives him more power than the leader using authoritarian cooperation, because he obtains group support by his artifices. The leader using this type of cooperation may use any or all of the following devices: he appears to promote free discussion, but slants the information made available to the group; he plants persons in the group with his own point of view with instructions to steer the thinking of the group; or he commends certain suggestions and passes lightly over others. He must be very clever, because the group would be resentful if it realized it was being "guided." It is surprising, however, how often the techniques of securing controlled cooperation are used in the United States by authoritarians who insist that they are using democratic processes. It is interesting that these methods are almost identical

[31]Morphet, *op. cit.*, pp. 38–41.

with the methods used by communist cells in gaining converts.

Voluntary cooperation is secured when people are not only free to think for themselves but are encouraged to do so. It is the opposite of the master-slave relationship, because all citizens are peers. People are not manipulated, but each person is given a real opportunity to contribute to the thinking of the group.

How can the schools train citizens to detect the leadership that would govern them by controlled cooperation? What relationship does the concept "brainwashing" have to controlled cooperation?

Some Other Problems and Issues

1. Generally speaking, citizen committees have been made up largely of "leaders." Is this really in keeping with the broad representation idea, or does it hold to the idea that there is a certain elite in the community who knows what is best for the community and all the people in it? What should be the criteria for committee membership? Should it be representative in terms of geographic areas, employment groups, racial groups, religious groups, and the like; or should the membership be determined in terms of competence, willingness to work, interest, perspective, and similar factors?

2. Cooperative procedures take a great deal of time and energy. Good solutions can frequently be developed in a much shorter time by the use of expert professional personnel. In such circumstances, are cooperative procedures really worthwhile?

3. Administrators sometimes find communities where the community values and goals with respect to education are relatively low or limited. Should the administrator accept community values and goals as they are, or should he attempt to bring about change? What procedures can be used to change community values and goals?

4. Parent-Teacher Associations have long promoted cooperative relationships between the school and the home. But frequently school administrators have used Parent-Teacher Associations primarily for money-making activities or as a device by which the administrator can "sell" his program to the community. What can be done to give Parent-Teacher Associations more opportunities to participate in significant cooperative activities?

5. Citizens' committees sometimes consider technical problems, the proper answers to which can best be determined by professional educators. For instance, parents are very much interested in methods of teaching reading. Should a citizens' committee determine the methods of teaching reading used in their schools? Should all educational decisions be made by the

group process? What types of decisions are best determined by group processes and what types by the professional expert?

6. Many school principals are making wide use of cooperative procedures. Decisions on programs and policies are made by the entire faculty after appropriate study. Should the principal reserve the right to veto decisions of the faculty, if he believes the judgment of the faculty to be wrong?

7. Sometimes a school administrator has been reluctant to involve citizens in cooperative activities, for fear that citizens would believe him to be incompetent to find the answers to school problems. Does an administrator gain or lose prestige if he becomes a peer member of a group that is working on an educational problem?

What Are the Implications of the Concepts
   Presented in Chapters 3–6
   for Preparation Programs for School Administrators?

It is apparent from the concepts presented in Chapters 3, 4, 5, and 6 and elsewhere in this book that the study of educational organization and administration in depth requires a knowledge of many of the theoretical concepts of the social and behaviorial sciences. The evidence is clear that this applies both to practicing school administrators and professors of educational administration. Modern educational administration requires not only a knowledge of its theoretical bases but also a knowledge of management techniques, the findings of operations research, and many other facets of administrative "know-how." This raises the question of specialization in preparation programs for school administrators. Should we train generalists or specialists in administration? If it is assumed that it is necessary to have some specialization in order to have depth, what common core of learning experiences should be included in all advanced graduate programs for school administration? Should each institution of higher learning offering a doctoral program in educational administration provide a general program and limit the number of specializations in that program in accordance with its strength and resources?

It is beyond the scope of this book to present an analysis of trends in preparation programs for school administrators. The American Association of School Administrators already requires that all new voting members must have completed at least a two-year graduate program in educational administration at an institution approved by the National Council for Accreditation of Teacher Education. Many boards of education already require the doctorate for the superintendency. Present trends indicate that two years of graduate work or the doctorate will soon be required of principals, supervisors, and assistant superintendents in the leading school systems of the nation.

Professors of educational administration being recruited by the leading institutions of higher learning today must be able to do research and to publish as well as to teach. The "publish or perish" issue is found in all colleges of the larger universities but it is particularly urgent in graduate schools and colleges.

The University Council for Educational Administration is taking the leadership in stimulating improvement in preparation programs for school administrators.[32] The Council is encouraging the development of new curriculum designs, the production of new types of instructional materials and basic research for the production of new knowledge. The cross-disciplinary approach to the preservice preparation of school administrators is being used by a number of universities. The acceleration of the rate of educational change is creating an increased demand for continuing in-service training programs for school administrators and professors of educational administration. The participation in exchange and postdoctoral programs is rapidly increasing. One of the principal problems of the departments of educational administration in modern universities is to attain a "dynamic equilibrium" or "steady state" in this period of rapid interchange of matter, information, and energy of the department with its environment. The practicing administrators of school social systems find themselves dealing with inputs and outputs of matter, information, and energy of those social systems with their environments in a complex and rapidly changing world. The scientific study of the politics and economics of education and the application of systems theory and other theories formulated by the behaviorial sciences to educational administration and organization are relatively recent innovations. These conditions require far more sophisticated programs for the preparation

[32]Following are a few of the publications relating to the preparation of school administrators that have been produced by or sponsored by the University Council for Educational Administration: Lawrence W. Downey and Frederick Enns, eds., *The Social Sciences and Educational Administration* (Edmonton, Canada: Division of Educational Administration, University of Alberta and the University Council for Educational Administration, 1963); Jack A. Culbertson and Stephen P. Hencley, eds., *Preparing Administrators: New Perspectives* (Columbus, Ohio: University Council for Educational Administration, 1963); Jack A. Culbertson and Stephen P. Hencley, *Educational Research: New Perspectives* (Danville, Ill.: Interstate Publishers and Printers, Inc., 1963); Keith Goldhammer, *The Social Sciences and the Preparation of Educational Administrators* (Columbus, Ohio: The University Council for Educational Administration, 1963); Donald J. Teu and Herbert C. Rudman, eds., *Preparation Programs for School Administration, Common and Specialized Learnings* (East Lansing: College of Education, Michigan State University, 1963); Donald J. Willower and Jack A. Culbertson, eds., *The Professorship in Educational Administration* (State College: University Council for Educational Administration and College of Education, Pennsylvania State University, 1964).

of educational administrators and professors of educational administration than have been generally available.

Selected References

Argyris, C., *Interpersonal Competence and Organizational Effectiveness.* Homewood, Ill.: Richard W. Irwin, Inc., 1962.

Berelson, Bernard, and Gary A. Steiner, *Human Behavior: An Inventory of Scientific Findings.* New York: Harcourt, Brace & World, Inc., 1964.

Cartwright, Darwin, and Alvin E. Zander, *Group Dynamics: Research and Theory.* New York: Harper & Row, Publishers, 1960.

Heilbroner, Robert L., *The Worldly Philosophers.* New York: Simon and Schuster, Inc., 1953.

Hofstadter, Richard, *Social Darwinism in American Thought.* New York: George Braziller, Inc., 1959.

Kropotkin, Peter, *Mutual Aid, A Factor of Evolution.* London: William Heinemann, Limited, 1902.

LaBarre, Weston, *The Human Animal.* Chicago: University of Chicago Press, 1954.

Metcalf, Henry C., and L. Urwick, eds., *Dynamic Administration, The Collected Papers of Mary Parker Follett.* New York: Harper & Row, Publishers, 1940.

Miles, M., ed., *Innovation in Education.* New York: Teachers College, Columbia University, 1964.

Montagu, Ashley, *On Being Human,* 2nd ed. New York: Hawthorn Books, 1966.

National Society for the Study of Education, *Citizen Cooperation for Better Schools,* The Fifty-third Yearbook, Part I. Chicago: University of Chicago Press, 1954.

Schein, E. H., and W. G. Bennis, *Personal and Organizational Change via Group Methods.* New York: John Wiley & Sons, Inc., 1965.

7

The External Environment
and the Schools

Throughout history, the relation of the school to its community has been a matter of major significance. To what extent may a faculty teach what it is committed to teach without regard to the wishes of the people? How much support can a school or school system expect if it is pursuing values not accepted with enthusiasm by the community? The historic gown-versus-town conflicts regarding the university have some parallels in every active school community today. The problems have grown more difficult to understand as the nature of the community has grown more vague and the problems of education have become infinitely more difficult.

The rising expectations regarding education which have been noted in many countries of the world add to the problem. The expectations may be so high that they cannot be fulfilled, or at least not as rapidly as desired. Frustration, alienation, and antagonism may then result. Education has become the nation's and the world's most important business; therefore, everyone tends to be involved in it and desires in some manner to contribute to it. Many have rather simple solutions to propose to complex problems. The problem in our society is accentuated by the tendency to equate schooling with education to too great a degree.

Some educators who have sought the participation of the "people" in education (school affairs) and who might indeed be elated over developments, have recently at times tended to draw back. The implications of many current developments are difficult to assess, and the road ahead is somewhat unclear. Confronted by an almost incomprehensible power to chart his own destiny—to build or destroy—man may tend to withdraw or to seek quick and "certain" solutions. In such an uneasy world, schools may expect to feel the impact of uncertainty and changes in the society. They must also re-examine their relation to and their impact upon the society. Of this vast arena of the school or school system and its environment, a few issues will be examined as one way of getting a better understanding of the problem which confronts the educator and the citizen interested in education today.

SOME BACKGROUND CONSIDERATIONS

Education in our society has been characterized by the following:

A VERY GREAT BELIEF IN THE EFFICACY OF SCHOOLING. The people of the United States have long viewed the school as the most important agency of social and economic mobility for the individual. They have assumed that if schools were provided and made accessible, children and youth would avail themselves of the opportunity. To a rather remarkable extent, this has indeed occurred. The mobility which has characterized our society has been highly related to educational provisions. The children of immigrant groups have thus in the second or third generation achieved a status to which they could scarcely have aspired in the countries from which they came. This mobility in our society was, of course, the product of other factors also. However, the point to be noted here is that this concept came to be so widely accepted that there was too little recognition of the extent to which it was not operative, of the individuals and groups which were not involved, of the considerable numbers who did not "see" the opportunity and were not "motivated" to achieve. The society and even many teachers may thus have placed the burden of failure to achieve on the student.

A TENDENCY TO REGARD SCHOOLING AND EDUCATION AS ONE. In the commitment of our society to equal educational opportunity, attention has been given largely to the provision of rather formally established opportunity in schools. This concept of equality of educational opportunity has been sharply challenged by the civil rights movement in recent years and by the attack on poverty. Teachers in many instances accepted the achievement of Negro children and other "lower class" children as being in accord with their potential to a much greater degree than was justified. They found it difficult to think of the kinds of experiences which children had in their homes and communities in the

preschool years and while in school, as an important aspect of education. They assumed that the formal school opportunity could overcome
that which preceded and accompanied it. Actually, of course, in many
cases it overcame much, and their faith in education (schooling) was an
important element in the strength of the school. However, this faith
was also a factor which may have prevented educators from seeing
the problem of the education of the culturally different in more valid
terms. In recent years the society has called for a redefinition of education—one which sees the growth of an individual in light of many factors
and forces, only one of which is the school. Thus there is the growing
concern about poverty, housing, the community, and the attitudes of
parents as matters of large importance for the education of the child.

A TENDENCY TO SEE THE SCHOOL AS AN ISOLATED SOCIAL AGENCY RATHER
THAN AN INTEGRATED ONE. The people of the United States have seen
the school as an institution which is most unique in their society. Here,
long before most other societies, they have attached great importance to
the school and have wished to ensure conditions for it which would be
strongly supportive. Thus, out of philosophical considerations and as a
result of the widespread corruption that characterized city government
in the last half of the nineteenth century, they moved toward *ad hoc*
boards of education. These boards of education enjoyed a very considerable measure of independence from city government and from the
political machines that controlled city government. This development
was facilitated by the acceptance of the view that education was a
function of the state and thus not the proper concern of the city government.

Very probably, the schools advanced much more rapidly in the
United States because of the fact that they were thus isolated from other
activities of city government. They enjoyed greater support and lived
with higher expectations than other governmental agencies. This removal
of schools from the usual political controls gave them a political position
and support of importance. They were removed from politics thus only
in the sense of being removed from manipulation by the political bosses.
However, the view developed that they were nonpolitical. This and other
factors caused them to develop somewhat in isolation from other local
governmental agencies and services which were more responsive to
political party controls. Teachers and administrators supported the view
that they should be independent and that thus they would contribute
most to the development of citizens of independence and the advancement of the society.

While, as has been suggested, there were large gains made as a
result of this independence, it must also be noted that this was done at
certain costs. Among the gains were: the more rapid advancement of

education than would probably have occurred otherwise, the development of merit plans for appointment of teachers and administrators prior to such developments in other governmental services, the strengthening of the responsibilities of the administrator, the establishment of a plan through which the people could center attention upon the schools and seek their improvement.

On the other hand the independence led to a lack of responsiveness on the part of boards of education to the changing needs of the society, a concern on the part of teachers and administrators with academic learning rather than with the total situation in which the child lived and which had a large impact on his education, an inability of educators and others engaged in public services such as housing, public health, libraries, and social welfare to work together with understanding, a belief that educational services were removed from politics (not recognizing the politics of the nonpolitical), a view which in the long run may have hindered rather than advanced the quality of educational services.

This "isolation" may have indeed been justified in the late nineteenth and early twentieth centuries. In rural areas and small towns it was readily understandable because of the limited nature of local government services. However, it must be noted that the growing complexity of the society, with its enormous concentrations of population and expanding programs of governmental services calls for a thorough reexamination of this question. So also does the theory of government which requires a less naïve, less simple, and quite possibly a less satisfying concept of how decision making is and probably will be carried on in our democracy.

CHANGED LOCAL CONDITIONS

While the concepts briefly discussed here have persisted, the world in which schools and school systems have existed has been in process of extremely rapid change. Among the more important of the changes are the following:

From a Rural to an Urban to a Metropolitan Nation

Until relatively recently, the United States has been a predominantly rural nation. From the 24 urban places of 2500 population or more in 1790, there was a steady population growth in rural and urban areas for more than a century. While the urban growth at times exceeded the rural, it did not make spectacular gains until the early decades of the present century. By 1960 the urban population was approximately 70 per cent and it was continuing to grow far more rapidly than other areas.

Much more striking than the change from rural to urban has been the transformation of the nation from urban to metropolitan. Victor Jones has noted that "The people of the United States became metropolitan before realizing their change from rural to urban."[1] In 1900 approximately one third of the population lived in "metropolitan areas" (according to the Bureau of the Census, a city of at least 50,000, including its county and adjacent counties that are "metropolitan in character" and "economically and socially integrated" with the county containing the city). By 1960, approximately 63 per cent were metropolitan dwellers and the expansion was expected to continue. This percent is slightly smaller than the urban percentage because, by definition, the urban figure includes many small towns and cities which are not part of a metropolitan area.

Related to this metropolitan growth was the matter of rapid population growth of the nation. In 1960 the official count of our population was over 179 million. Four years later, the federal government estimated that another 11 million had been added. Further, approximately 90 per cent of this population increase was in metropolitan areas. This population growth and concentration was such that during the sixties the question of population control became a major issue not only in the newly developing countries but in the United States. The question was not one of how many people could be fed but rather what quality of life was likely to be maintained with the population explosion. Some people began inquiring as to what quality of life now existed in parts of the core cities of the great metropolitan areas.

"A Mosaic of Social Worlds"

The simplicity of the structure of the former town with its "other side of the tracks" is in marked contrast to the metropolitan area. It is described as "heterogeneous, constantly changing, fragmented"; "arranged spatially in an often confused and seemingly incompatible pattern"; "numerous neighborhoods and suburban groupings of varying social, ethnic and economic characteristics scattered throughout the metropolitan complex." "The luxury apartment casts its shadow on the tenement houses of workers. The Negro ghetto is ringed by a wall of white neighborhoods. The industrial suburb lies adjacent to the village enclave of the wealthy."[2]

[1]John C. Bollens and Henry J. Schmandt, *The Metropolis: Its People, Politics and Economic Life* (New York: Harper & Row, Publishers, 1965), p. 12.
[2]*Ibid.*, p. 83.

Thus, the metropolitan area is a balkanized one. Homogeneity characterizes many neighborhoods. Some neighborhoods are affluent, others are populated heavily by refugees of a rapidly changing society. Many live where they do partly because of financial resources, others because of a type of enforced segregation. These neighborhoods have vastly different educational needs and expectations of a school system, and differ in their participation. These different neighborhoods may be described in various ways such as: social rank, urbanization, and segregation.[3]

In terms of social rank, the range is from the neighborhood composed largely of broken homes, minorities, considerable unemployment, unskilled workers, to those made up largely of professionals, business executives, and college graduates. Urbanization refers to the family and home situations which prevail. They range from the suburban area marked by single family units, no or few working mothers, and young families with small children, to the rooming house and apartment areas with many single men and women, and married couples with few children and both working. The factor of segregation relates to the ethnic composition. This segregation may be an imposed one, as is frequently the case of the Negro, or it may result from other forces such as the tendency for a religious group to settle around a school. The tendency for segregation to increase in metropolitan areas is one of the major challenges to our society. Only recently has serious consideration been given to its fuller implications. Even today, the middle class continues to escape from the core city and to settle in a suburb, perhaps unconsciously hoping to avoid the problems of the metropolitan area. Thus, in spite of the expressed desire of the society to have less segregation, it may have more. This poses large problems for education and its governmental structure, and raises the question of whether men are citizens of a metropolitan area or only of a neighborhood.

Further analysis of the neighborhoods can well be done regarding such matters as mobility of the people, the age structure of the population, the percentage of youth in the population, fertility of the population, recreational needs and opportunities, occupational patterns, occupational mobility. Regarding all of these matters, attention must also be given to changes which are occurring, for the metropolitan areas are especially characterized by rapidity of change.

Large Resources and Larger Needs

The metropolitan areas contain enormous economic wealth, scientific and technical skills, human resources. They are home to a large per cent of the great corporations that produce the economic wealth of the

[3]Eshref Shevsky and Wendell Bell, *Social Area Analysis* (Stanford: Stanford University Press, 1954).

nation. The income of their people is above that of the nation. Here also are found the large financial institutions and the commercial establishments. The accumulation of resources is so great that the metropolitan area achieves ends that were not even sought in a simpler society. It is the golden age of the industrialization and specialization which marks the twentieth century. It acts not only for itself but sets the patterns and trends which substantially dominate the nation.

In its economic life, it too is marked by change. The core city or the downtown area threatens to die and needs major attention. Industries scatter widely over the area. Workers commute long distances and under increasing stress as the transportation system (too often the automobile) breaks down or takes over an increasing land area with far from satisfying results. The distribution of economic resources is often unrelated to the needs of the people or the resources may be more effectively tapped by the state and federal governments. The wealthy center of the metropolitan area can scarcely "afford" to purchase the land for schools and recreation that is absolutely essential to maintain a defensible quality of life.

Local Governments in Great Number and Variety

During the last fifty years, the legal boundaries of cities have not been extended as the city or metropolitan area has grown. In fact there has been very strong resistance to permitting the growth of the city through annexation. As a result, very strong municipal governments have frequently grown up around the city. They have been committed to preventing the expansion of the city. Further, many small municipal governments have either continued or have been established in the metropolitan areas. They have frequently been viewed as a means of avoiding the high taxes of the city and of keeping "undesirable" developments such as factories and low-cost housing out. The boundaries of these local government units are too frequently the result of "cherry-stemming" or similar procedures through which more powerful authorities secure wealthy or otherwise desirable areas. They are not logical, planned, or necessarily in accord with existing community-of-interest patterns.

In addition to the general local governments which are found in the metropolitan area there is an increasing number of *ad hoc* authorities. Some of these exist to meet areawide problems, such as water, sewage, transportation, smog. Others serve to meet special needs or desires of the people in a given area, such as mosquito control or recreation. School districts also continue to be found in large numbers.

The variety and complexity of the local government structure is shown by the Bureau of Census report which indicates that in 1962 the

212 Standard Metropolitan Statistical Areas of the country contained 18,442 local governments.[4] This number included 6004 school districts, 5411 special districts, 4142 municipal governments, and 2575 towns and townships. Interestingly in these metropolitan areas 44 per cent of the school districts have fewer than 300 childen in school, and 900 do not maintain schools but transport children to other districts. Chicago, one of the larger metropolitan areas, contains over 1000 local governments.

These figures suggest that those interested in school district consolidation have possibly been giving more attention to rural areas than to metropolitan areas. In fact, little has been done to establish minimum standards to be achieved through consolidation in metropolitan areas. It is reasonable to assume, however, that the minimum numbers of pupils, for example, to be accepted as the base for a local district should be considerably larger than is the case in rural areas. The somewhat shocking picture of school districts in metropolitan areas should not be accepted as an indication that the situation in regard to school districts is worse than in the case of municipal governments and other special districts. In fact, because of the interest of the states in education, there has been substantial improvement in the school district situation and there is reason to believe that it will greatly improve in the next few years. This is probably less true of municipal governments and other special districts.

For the school administrator, the situation with reference to municipal governments and special districts other than for schools is of utmost importance. For it is with this multitude of districts that the school administrator must work if schools are to be integrated into and developed in light of the life of the metropolitan area of which they are a part. There can be little doubt that in these highly interdependent metropolitan areas there is large need for the coordination of governmental services and great difficulty in achieving it. Further, this proliferation almost certainly has a debilitating effect upon all the local governments involved and tends to reduce the accountability to the public, which has been traditionally regarded as one of the values of local government. Financial disparities and a wide range in standards of service also result. And only in a rather reluctant and stumbling manner do citizens tend to accept the fact that they are indeed citizens of a metropolitan area as well as, probably, of a municipal government and several special districts. If it is true that participation in local government itself is an important educational experience, it would appear that not much progress has been made in making this experience realizable and satisfying.

[4]U.S. Bureau of the Census, *Census of Governments: 1962*, Vol. I, Governmental Organization (Washington, D.C.: 1963), p. 11.

CHANGES IN FEDERAL AND STATE ACTIVITY

The growth in the metropolitan areas in economic power, in population, and in unresolved issues has stimulated the federal government to action in many matters that have hitherto been regarded as matters of state and local responsibility. Establishing the Department of Housing and Urban Affairs in 1965 in the United States Government was one evidence of the growth of this interest in an area with important implications for education. Other extremely significant developments which may be regarded as important aspects of the revolution in education in the sixties are discussed briefly in the next sections.

The Curriculum Development Programs

The last half of the decade of the fifties and the first half of the sixties was a period in which important changes in the curriculum were effected in fields such as mathematics, physics, and chemistry. Almost as important as the changes themselves were the procedures through which they were brought about. They were effected through federal government grants to private or semiprivate individuals and groups, which brought university personnel and public school personnel together. They involved the preparation of materials by authorities in the academic fields, the development of a plan for the dissemination of the concepts, the development of competence on the part of teachers to use materials, the provision of carefully worked out instructional materials to be employed by the teachers.

In a sense, these curriculum programs became a model illustrating how curriculum change can be effected in a decentralized educational system. These programs reached into a very large percentage of the school districts of the nation and altered matters without creating great concern on the part of local board of education members, teachers, or administrators. This was accomplished even though the effects of the programs had not been determined in any highly valid manner. These programs have large significance regarding the procedures to be employed in curriculum development activities of the local school districts. They had an important bearing on the Vocational Education Act of 1963, suggesting how advances might be attained in that field, and on the Elementary and Secondary Education Act of 1965.

The Elementary and Secondary Education Act of 1965

This act may well prove to be one of the more important federal education acts of our country. It broke new ground in its effort to sidestep the parochial school aid controversy. Developments resulting from this action may influence nearly all local school districts. Of more immediate significance here, however, are its provisions for the establishment of regional educational laboratories. These laboratories which are intended to bring the resources of the universities and colleges into close relation to the needs (curriculum development, research, and change) of local and state school systems and private schools may usher in a new period in American education.

In this period, it may well be expected that applied research will be pursued with a competence and a vigor that has not marked educational efforts in the nation heretofore. No local school system could wish to remain apart from this movement; however, no local system can expect to be a part of it without being affected in highly significant ways. These laboratories will hopefully not be controlled by the universities, by the state departments of education, or by local school systems. They will be responsible to all of these and more, but yet provide an essential independence for one engaged in research and development. They will also be related in an important manner to various smaller program and instructional development centers developed in various sections of the states.

Equally important were the act's provisions making substantial federal funds available to improve the educational provisions for children from low-income groups in public and private schools. The provision of funds for this one group was bound to have large implications for the total school program. It raised in sharp manner the question of what differences should be made in the expenditure of funds and in educational provisions for "poor" children. The making of additional provisions would almost certainly result in the demand for extended provisions by other groups. Thus there was promise that an important policy question was likely to be carefully considered with supplementary federal, state, and local action developed.

The Economic Opportunity Act

Not quite as directly or completely seen as an education act but with education (broadly viewed) as its major goal was the Economic Opportunity or Poverty Act of 1964. It was conceived of as a broad attack upon the problems of the relatively uneducated and poor. It proposed to enable them to help themselves. It provided massive programs, such as Headstart, to improve the cultural opportunities of poor children in preschool years and during the years in school. It encouraged the development of councils with substantial representation of the poor to determine the program to be undertaken. It thus challenged the established local government councils and boards, raising the question of the adequacy with which they spoke for the poor or of the extent to which they were seen as being representative of the poor by the poor. Further, this act provided a direct attack on the problem of employment for youth through job corps centers and related activities. This, too, was a highly important issue which was an educational one in major respects. This act also was important in terms of local school administration in that it brought other local government departments such as those concerned with health, welfare, employment and libraries much more actively into matters closely related to education. The poor were not going to make their way ahead through the use of the formal school programs only.

Finally, in considering the changing federal and state programs, the Higher Education Act of 1965 with its provisions for teacher education programs and urban extension education must be noted. All of these federal acts had important implications for the states, pushing them into the consideration of many policy questions and developing a framework, as in the case of the educational laboratories, which did not recognize district and state boundaries in the organizational plan. In the meantime, both the states and the federal government were showing increased interest and activity in securing more adequate indications of the accomplishments of the schools.

OTHER ORGANIZATIONS AND AGENCIES

As should have been anticipated, the great expectations regarding education also had an important stimulating effect on agencies other than public schools. While many others could be identified such as Parent-Teacher Associations, political parties, research and testing services, taxpayers' associations, associations of school boards, labor unions, business and professional groups, attention will be given here to only three groups.

The Foundations

The number of foundations and the wealth in the hands of the foundations increased greatly in recent decades. Probably it is also true that the foundations increased their interest in education. The largest of the foundations, the Ford Foundation, centered and promises to continue to focus attention on educational developments. A considerable part of the federal action previously described was based at least in part upon programs sponsored in part by foundations. The foundations, being free from the need to support mass programs, were able to exert an influence far beyond that which the dollars they provided would suggest. For theirs was the "venture" money so frequently not forthcoming from the public authorities. While an actual assessment of the influence exerted by the foundations is difficult, it is noteworthy that in recent years it has been sufficient to be the subject of considerable controversy. Some educators have felt that the foundations have not been interested in advancing money to make possible the appraisal of an idea, but rather only to advance an idea to which a commitment existed. The American Association of School Administrators conducted a study of the influence of the foundations because of the concern found among some of its members.[5]

Educational Organizations

In recent decades, educational agencies and individuals involved in the educational process have become increasingly organized. Through their organizations, they have gained greatly increased influence in regard to educational matters.

The colleges and universities, for example, have played an increasing role in public education in the last decade. They have had important influence in such areas as curriculum, achievement testing, and accreditation. Through their own admission policies and their concern for the gifted student, they have also influenced secondary schools. The development of research programs in the field of education and the growing interest of psychologists, sociologists, and political scientists in education and the school as an institution suggest that the influence of higher educational institutions and their staff on public education will be felt more significantly in the future.

The growth of organizations of the professional staff of the schools has also been marked in recent years. Related to this growth has been a notable increase in their activity and influence. In this area, reference may well be made to organizations of administrators, curriculum and supervisory staff, guidance personnel, and teachers. The large number of different organizations has reduced the influence which these groups might have had; however, they increasingly accept the view that it is only through organization that they can be effective and correspondingly reject the idea that they should not be a militant group working toward goals which they formulate. Especially noticeable is the growth of militancy among teachers' associations and teachers' unions. They have gained a substantial increase of influence in recent years not only in salary matters but in a wide range of curricular and instructional matters. While teachers and teachers groups have had large influence in many schools and school systems, they are now gaining a new image in this regard and in the public expectations that they have a more explicit and direct role in decision making.

[5]American Association of School Administrators, *Private Philanthropy and Public Purposes* (Washington, D.C.: The Association), 1963.

Private and Parochial Schools

Recent decades have been marked by continued action on the part of certain private school groups, notably the Roman Catholic, to which attention is given here, for greater public recognition and for support in one form or another. They have been ably represented by their spokesmen in state legislatures, in the federal Congress, and in the core cities of the metropolitan areas where enrollments in their schools have become quite substantial. During recent years, they have won certain gains in terms of federal legislation for their students. They have also tended to accept the limitations on aid such as have been stipulated or implied by the Supreme Court decisions and to seek new solutions. One of these solutions is the release of their children to attend the public schools for such subjects as mathematics and science and their retention of them for social sciences, language, and other subjects held to be more directly relevant to their central purposes. The legality of these arrangements has not yet been fully established. Their impact and desirability also remains unclear both in terms of the parochial school and the public school.

More than formerly, the religious schools and their supporters also are troubled. Both financially and philosophically, they are far less sure that it would be desirable to have all children of their faith in a separate school system. The results are not conclusive in terms of values achieved. They have not met the problems of the culturally different or of the gifted more effectively than the public schools. Further, every step such as the release of children for instruction in mathematics and science to the public schools, raises important questions regarding instruction. Many had claimed that all aspects (subjects and textbooks) of instruction should be permeated by the special values of the faith. And each step toward public support must be made at some cost to the values of being private and separate. Fair-employment practice acts do not suggest that religious tests may be employed in selection of teachers, principals, or other staff if there is any public support. The minority status and feeling of being discriminated against which was long a force for the religious school is losing its meaning as change in status occurs. The church also is seeking a new relation to the world outside, and some of its members are unsure that the separate school contributes in this direction. Then, too, its problems are so great with the expansion of educational services, the technological advances in education, the decline in the availability of members of orders to meet teaching needs that it is re-examining its position regarding many educational problems and the relation of education to other religious issues.

It would thus appear that we may be in a new period of "openness" regarding the relations of public schools and various private bodies engaged in education. Quite possibly some of the barriers to communication and development will be reduced when it is more generally recognized that many problems are common to public and private bodies interested in education. Possibly also we are beginning to re-examine the question of pluralism in our society, the form of it we wish to attain, and its relation to the education question.

POWER IN THE LOCAL SCHOOL DISTRICT AREA

The school administrator is thus in a position of leadership in a district which is but a segment of an area, metropolitan or otherwise. It is not truly a separate unit except legally, and frequently its nature is to be explained by tradition rather than logic. He has responsibilities for a single service, which however is expanding and is increasingly linked to a great number of other services that are administered by other bodies. What is done in his unit and service is highly related to what is done in other units providing a similar service and to what is done by local authorities providing related services.

The Power Structures

As pointed out in Chapter 3, the power structure of this unit is not clearly established. Depending upon the nature of the population, the traditions and wealth of the unit, and its relation to the metropolitan or other area, it may appear to be of the Hunter power-elite type. More likely however, it is somewhat of the process-pluralist type, where power and influence on most occasions are dispersed and where decision making involves a measure of bargaining, compromise, conflict, and agreement. If an elite once ruled educational decision making, it is perhaps less likely to do so now because of the growing interest in education on the part of various groups.

The manner in which the power structure in one school district may relate to that in other school districts of the area is unclear. The question of the nature of the metropolitan area power structure and its relation to educational developments in various school districts remains relatively unexplored. This is a matter of importance both because of the fact that a metropolitan or other area is a reality and because many educational services and developments must be conceived in larger terms. The usual school district is greatly handicapped or with extremely limited resources for the development of educational TV, programed learning, research and development, technical education, adult education, and junior college education needed for the area. It may also be extremely limited in its capacity to engage in professional negotiation or bargaining, since it is dealing with agents of groups representing the resources of the whole area.

Impact of Federal and State Activities

In this situation, it is also important to note that the state and federal agencies will be playing an increasingly important role. They have already played a more important one than is generally recognized. For example, the very system of state grants-in-aid to many suburban school districts has made it possible for them to remain independent of the core city or industrial areas of which they are a part. Without such grants, probably the integration of outside areas into a single government unit would have proceeded much more rapidly. But the federal programs in education and related matters, previously referred to, will be of far greater significance in determining the decisions made.

This development of federal-state programs will also further the influence of the professionals, as will the necessary increasing cooperation among the districts of an area. This is not to deny the fact that members of boards of education and other legislative bodies will have a large role in decision making; however, they will be dependent upon the comprehensive information and data development which must occur in the increasingly complex metropolitan and other areas. And it is the bureaucracies of the local, state, and federal governments that will be responsible for the development of these data, for their interpretation and communication regarding them.

Power thus tends to be diffuse, not only in terms of elite or pluralist views regarding the local unit but also in terms of networks of power extending through an area larger than the unit and in terms of federal and state action. And finally, it tends to be diffuse in terms of the inevitable and necessary bureaucracies.

BUILDING AN INTEGRATED SCHOOL COMMUNITY

The educational administrator and the local board of education are thus confronted with the problem of building an integrated school system and community. The people of a school district or of a school system cannot achieve the desired educational program without some cohesion and a measure of *community.* The people must be held together at least in the educational world by some mutual ties that provide a feeling of identity and belonging. Since we may well begin with school communities that are quite heterogeneous and lacking in *community* or integration, this may be among the most important tasks facing the schools.

As a first step in this process, study of factors related to integration may well be essential. Jacob and Teune have suggested that some elements to consider as a possible base for developing an integrated political community are: proximity, homogeneity, transactions, mutual knowledge, functional interest, communal character, political structure, sovereignty, governmental effectiveness, and integrative experience.[6]

Studies of this type may provide the understanding in light of which steps can be taken to develop ties among the people regarding educational issues and goals. Only with some development of this type is the local system likely to be effective, in relation to the larger immediate area of which it is a part, in dealing with the growing organizations of the area, and in working with the stronger state and federal agencies. Unless some *community* is achieved, the district is likely to be pushed along by external forces. Without clean-cut though not rigid goals, it cannot be a strong unit which melds various pressures and considerations into a constructive organization.

The educator should be aware of facts such as the following regarding the community.

Society is characterized by large power organizations.   In a community, for example, at least the following power groups of special interest to education will usually be found: the school power structure; governmental structures other than schools (some of which are directly related to political organizations); organizations of businessmen, professional groups, and labor; mass media of communication; and power leaders who may function informally or through recognized organizations.

The term "power" is not used here in the sense that it is something undesirable. Rather, "power" is a word that will be used to describe the "acts of men going about the business of moving other men to act in relation to themselves or in relation to organic or inorganic things."[7] The power of the individual is extremely limited unless structured through an organization or association. Such structuring may be provided for by statute. It may be highly formal or quite informal.

The school system itself may be viewed as a power structure. It coordinates the efforts of the board of education, administration, teaching, and other staff members in the provision and advancement of education. It generally is supported by such groups as the Parent-Teacher Association, which may be regarded as a part of the power structure that exists to further education.

[6]Philip E. Jacob and Henry Teune, "The Integrative Process—Guidelines for Analysis of the Basis of Political Community," *The Integration of Political Communities*, ed. Philip E. Jacob and James V. Toscano (Philadelphia: J. B. Lippincott Co., 1964).
[7]Floyd Hunter, *Community Power Structure. A Study of Decision Makers* (Chapel Hill: University of North Carolina Press, 1953), p. 2.

Some other power structures in the community may oppose the school system. But it should be noted that the opportunity that groups have to organize themselves in order to be effective is a fundamental right that a free society must guarantee. In fact, the existence of such groups may be regarded as one measure of the level of maturity of the democratic community.

MANY OF THE POWER ORGANIZATIONS HAVE BEEN CONSCIOUSLY CREATED AND HAVE A DEFINITE PURPOSE. The written statement of purposes, if one exists, may or may not be complete. Possibly it will not reveal some of the purposes. Informal organizations may have greater power than many that are formally organized.

MANY ORGANIZATIONS ARE NATIONALLY ORIENTED. Their members think and act more like members of similar organizations in other communities than like other citizens of their own community. This situation is related to the stratification found in the community. It raises the question whether the geographic community is a social community.

INDIVIDUALS ARE FREQUENTLY ASSOCIATED WITH ORGANIZATIONS THAT HAVE CONTRADICTORY PURPOSES. The professional organization to which they belong may oppose the interest individuals have in the education of children and which they demonstrate through work in an association of parents. This lack of consistency suggests the need for involvement of people in an organization if their support is to be secured.

THE COMMUNITY EXISTING OR TO BE DEVELOPED HAS IMPORTANT VALUES, IDEALS, AND CONCEPTS THAT CAN BE SIGNIFICANT LEVERS OF ACTION. The concept of equality of educational opportunity and the understanding that it does not mean identity of opportunity, for example, is extremely powerful. Too little attention is given to such fundamental concepts in many communities, although they also have important implications for education in the state and nation as well as in the community.

THE COMMUNITY WILL NOT ACT IN ACCORD WITH ITS OWN IDEALS, VALUES, AND CONCEPTS, UNLESS IT KNOWS THE FACTS AND IS CHALLENGED. It is easy to profess interest in equality of educational opportunity and to behave in ways that deny it. The challenge of facts may be helpful in causing the people of a community to act in accord with their professed values.

THE SCHOOL DISTRICT IS BUT A PART OF A LARGER COMMUNITY. The district cannot and should not expect to move alone. It must be aware of the larger community (both in terms of its own geographical area and with reference to the metropolitan or similar area) and accept a constructive role in it.

STUDIES OF THE COMMUNITY

Methods of Study

Many methods may be employed to study the complexities of the community and its institutions including the schools. Important methods to be employed are the following:

THE HISTORICAL METHOD.   This method, which is too little employed, may reveal how the community has grown, what the nature of population change has been, how the community has been organized, what educational values and issues have been prominent in it, the reasons for the existing school organization, and the relation of community education to other governmental services.

ANALYSIS OF LAWS AND RECORDS.   Statutes, minutes of boards of education and of other organizations, press treatment of education, census reports, population data, economic reports, success of high school graduates in college and in employment, and records of dropouts are samples of the large quantities of data pertaining to the community that await analysis. The amount of data available suggests the need for careful definition of purpose and study over a period of time, if a comprehensive picture of the community is to be secured.

SURVEYS OF STATUS AND PRACTICE.   What are the existing conditions? Does social stratification mark the community and the school? What have been the objectives, the programs, and the practices of the schools? What is the nature of home life? What is the place of youth, and how are their problems being met? What are the power organizations in the community, who are their members, and how do they operate? Who are the power leaders? Who controls the mass media of communication, and what is the audience and impact of each? How does the school system function as a power organization? What are the community practices and norms? These are a few of the many aspects of status and practice that might be studied as the base for the advancement of the educational system. An approach to these problems will involve the use of many techniques such as observation, interviews, analysis of records, questionnaires, and maintenance of logs and diaries.

STUDIES OF VALUES.   These could be regarded as one phase of surveys of status in the sense that one aspect of status would be the values held. They are listed separately, however, because of their significance and because they are not generally thought of as an aspect of current status. The values held are largely ascertained through interviews, but records of elections and previous community actions may also be highly informative.

CASE STUDIES. Case studies are suggested as a method of studying a community because they make it possible to visualize the interaction of various forces and to view the community or any of its organizations or groups as societies in action. They reveal organizations as dynamic structures. This concept of community life must be accepted if one is to be prepared to work with the forces that shape education.

STUDIES OF THE AREA. The school district must be informed regarding the larger geographical area of which it is a part. Therefore, in cooperation with other districts, it must provide for studies of the larger community and of other school districts. Only in this manner can essential cooperative effort be achieved and programs developed which are beyond the resources of any one district.

STUDIES OF STATE AND FEDERAL PROGRAMS AND THEIR INFLUENCE. Too often districts make little or no attempt to determine the influence of federal programs. In fact many districts are small and understaffed to such a degree that they are not prepared to plan effective utilization of the opportunities opened through federal programs. The districts of an area might well plan to attack this problem through a cooperative effort with a staff jointly employed.

Procedure in Community Study

Equally as important as the methodological approaches used in the study of the community are the procedures by which the study is conducted. Although certain of the suggested methods would need to be carried on individually by highly trained specialists, this would not be true in the great majority of instances. Competent specialists or consultants would, of course, need to participate in planning, formulating hypotheses, constructing the instruments used, preparing research workers, analyzing data, and formulating findings. But many people residing within the community could participate in the work. Local personnel need to do much of the work, not only for reasons of greater economy and a consequent expansion of the program, but because the knowledge gained would more likely result in action.

It would, therefore, be desirable to plan considerable action research. This would involve using available resources under competent leadership. It means systematically collecting and using many data that presently go unused. It would involve many teachers, parents, older students, and other citizens of the community interested in any organization that impinges on education.

In organizing such a program no one form is to be preferred in all situations. Provision should generally be made to involve the following:

1. Both laymen and teachers;
2. Lay leaders of status and laymen representative of a wide variety of groups;
3. Consultants;
4. Resource people and assistants to carry out the routine operations, implement as work proceeds, and relate data to community values;
5. Research and development staff to design and appraise the work undertaken.

Consultants and research and development staff may be supplied by a metropolitan or other intermediate or areawide unit.

Implications of Community Study

Frequently, questions are raised regarding the use of data pertaining to the community. For example, does the administrator become subservient to the power structure when elements of it are known to him? Or is he then in the position to become a manipulator? Or in a better position to provide constructive leadership?

The administrator, board of education, and others are in a position to act with intelligence and with reference to accepted values only when the power structure is known to them. Certainly the administrator and the board of education need to avoid becoming the tools of any single power group that may or may not have knowledge of and belief in the potential of education. At times, permitting such a group to make decisions may appear to be the easy road, but it would scarcely be consistent with the purposes of public education in a democracy.

If being a manipulator is interpreted to mean concealing facts, seeking personal power, controlling or making decisions for others, this concept or role must be rejected. However, if by being a manipulator reference is made to providing leadership and helping the community determine what its status is, how status differs from values held, and how the community can achieve what it seeks for its children and youth, the role should be welcomed. The role of manipulator might well be sought if it means helping a community reconsider and clarify its purposes. In reality, this is leadership, not manipulation.

In serving in a leadership role the school administrator needs also to recognize his power in relation to the decision-making process and the effect of the values he holds upon the processes and action to be taken. Too frequently, he may see his views (values) as objective and the only defensible ones. He may indeed re-examine his values and modify or hold fast to them, but it is important that he understand them in explicit terms. This understanding will provide him a much more adequate base for analyzing the situations which present themselves, for seeing himself in interpersonal relationships, for suggesting processes, for relating to role expectancies. Then he may see and understand the possible importance of deviant values—their potential for new integration or for disintegration. He must provide for them, though unfortunately, contrary to the American dream, there is no assurance that they inevitably will produce a desired integrated school community.

ACTION BASED ON COMMUNITY STUDY

A knowledge of the community is an essential background of action in the school-community relations area. Without this knowledge, any program developed must be based upon various assumptions regarding the community—assumptions that may or may not be sound.

A knowledge of the community includes a knowledge of the school, for the school is one of the institutions of the community. It can be understood only by considering various other conditions existing in the community. Without a thorough knowledge of the school and its relations to the community, the development of a program cannot be carried on in an effective manner.

The study of the community, including the school, should supply answers to such questions as: What have been the media of communication between school and community? What are the areas of ignorance between the school and community? What "publics" exist in the community? What resources are available for use in the program? How competent are school personnel to participate in the program? What mass media of communication service the community, and what contribution can they be expected to make? What power structures and what organizations exist in the community? What are the major limitations of the public education power structure in the community? What are the values of the community? What are the major strengths and weaknesses of the schools?

When data of the types suggested are available, it becomes possible to give careful, considered thought to the development of a program for achieving an integrated school community. In developing the program, it should be recognized that a most difficult task is being undertaken. Fundamentally, the problem is one of communication and of education. It is a matter of assisting the community in gaining knowledge of the schools, of the schools' potential, and of the procedures through which the potential may be realized. Given the diversity of backgrounds, interests, and activities of citizens however, and the variety of media that may be employed, the problem of communication is an exceedingly complex one. A good medium of communication with a few people may have no value with many others. It must be remembered that in communication what is heard may be very different from what is spoken.

And, of course, behavioristic communication may be much more effective than verbalistic.

The inevitability of communications in the school-community relations area must be recognized. A visit to a school, a meeting with children going to school, a child's report regarding events in school, the role of teachers in community organizations, a school building—an infinite number of situations exist through which some type of communication occurs. The problem is whether a sufficient number of media of high validity can be utilized to improve the understanding of school and community and enable them to progress together. If this can be achieved, a substantial benefit will result for the school and community and for education itself, since much of it goes on in the home and in the community outside the school. Thus, although the best school program is central in any school-community relations program, it also must be remembered that education is most likely to achieve significant goals through a high level of school-community understanding. The parent or community organization for youth with little understanding of the school is not prepared to contribute in a highly effective manner to the education of youth. But the parent and the youth group are inevitably "educating" youth.

Suggestions Regarding School-Community Action

In developing a program to promote school-community cooperation the following guidelines should be kept in mind.

MULTI-DIRECTIONAL COMMUNICATION IS ESSENTIAL AND MUST BE BOTH THE BASIS OF THE PROGRAM AND ONE OF ITS PURPOSES. Two-way communication is mentioned frequently. It is necessary but not likely to be effective unless accompanied by communication within the school staff and within various other agencies.

A POLICY STATEMENT REGARDING SCHOOL-COMMUNITY INTERACTION SHOULD BE ADOPTED BY THE BOARD OF EDUCATION, MAKING CLEAR THE PURPOSES OF THE PROGRAM AND THE ROLE OF SCHOOL PERSONNEL. Failure to establish adequate policies in this area sharply reduces the opportunity for effective leadership by school administrators.

THE PROGRAM MUST BE PLANNED. The difficulty of the task as well as the variety of possible ends and media demand careful planning. Without such planning, achievement will probably be extremely limited. A committee of laymen familiar with the organizational life of the community and with the media of communication within it can be of great assistance in this planning. Studies to determine the extent of information about and attitudes toward various aspects of the educational program are an essential base for planning.

AN EFFECTIVE PROGRAM CAN ONLY BE DESIGNED WITH SOME CLEARLY DEFINED GOALS IN MIND. Are there particular problems to be met, groups to be communicated with, or areas of ignorance on the part of the school or community? A planned program can be integrated with the more routine work in the field of school-community relations that is established with reference to legal requirements, events in the school calendar, and seasonal opportunities regarding aspects of the total educational program. While the vision must be large, steps toward it should permit observable progress.

REPORTING IS AN ESSENTIAL ELEMENT OF THE TOTAL PROGRAM AND NEEDS TO BE DEVELOPED IN AN EFFECTIVE MANNER WITH REFERENCE TO THE VARIETY OF GROUPS TO BE REACHED. It may involve report cards or conferences with parents; press relations; the preparation of brief, attractive, and well-illustrated annual or special reports; and reports on achievements and needs of the schools. Above all it must offer satisfaction through achievement by participants.

INVOLVEMENT OF MANY CITIZENS IS DESIRABLE. It facilitates a higher level of understanding and more action than is likely to result from reporting. It avoids the tendency of school people to have the "answer" to the problem and then to attempt to win acceptance for it. Rather, it places the problem in the hands of many more people for consideration and the formulation of tentative solutions. It reveals large, unused personnel resources. It should lead to more sound solutions and to earlier implementation. It is likely to be developed effectively only if the board has adopted policies encouraging it.

A WIDE VARIETY OF MEDIA SHOULD BE EMPLOYED. The error of utilizing only one medium, such as the press or the Parent-Teacher Association, should be avoided. This is not to underestimate the significance of such media, but rather to suggest that consideration should be given to the many that are available. Different media may involve or reach different groups, or may have a different impact.

THE SIGNIFICANCE OF THE INDIVIDUAL SCHOOL IN SCHOOL-COMMUNITY RELATIONS SHOULD BE RECOGNIZED. The most impressive contact that parents will have with the school system will be at the school that their children are attending. They will inevitably think of the system in terms of their personal experiences with teachers and principal at the school they know. If many are going to be involved in working through problems and policies, it is likely to be done at the individual school level. The communities or neighborhoods served by schools vary widely in many systems, and consequently the programs at the school level need to be characterized by variation.

THE CENTRAL OFFICE SHOULD TAKE RESPONSIBILITY FOR A FEW SYSTEMWIDE SCHOOL-COMMUNITY RELATIONS ACTIVITIES AND SHOULD CONCENTRATE ITS ENERGIES ON THE DEVELOPMENT OF A STAFF FOR MORE EFFECTIVE PARTICIPATION IN THE WORK.   Principals need help in developing programs for their schools. Teachers need assistance in developing competency for utilizing parent-teacher conferences effectively. Many staff members need to develop more competency in working as a member of a lay-professional committee or in serving on a panel. Staff members are frequently lacking in group process skills, which are most important if problems are to be worked through cooperatively. Many groups in the community remain relatively uninvolved.

RESPONSIBILITY FOR COORDINATION AND LEADERSHIP IN SCHOOL-COMMUNITY RELATIONS SHOULD BE FIXED UPON SOME ONE PERSON.   Formerly, this person probably would have been drawn from the press. With the broader concept of the work, however, he needs to have much more than press experience—though this would still be desirable in terms of mass media of communication. Today, however, he needs to be skillful in techniques of community analysis and in communication, able to help others develop competency in working with laymen in a wide variety of ways, and competent in the field of education. He must be an expert in public participation and action.

EVALUATION OF THE PROGRAM AND OF ITS VARIOUS ASPECTS IS OF VITAL IMPORTANCE.   Many activities are carried on without any systematic attempt at collecting available data and at evaluating the work done. Many Parent-Teacher Associations carry on programs for years without critically constructive evaluations being made. A citizens committee is formed, operates for several months or a year, submits a report, and dissolves without anyone's studying its procedures and its strengths and limitations. When another committee is formed, there is too little knowledge available as a result of past experience. What are the results of the program of reporting through the press, or through special reports? What coverage of vital issues is offered? Various people have judgments regarding the effectiveness of various techniques and procedures, but all too rarely are they based upon a planned evaluation. Just how is desirable educational change effected?

THE COMMUNITY AND ITS SCHOOLS

In concluding this section, attention is called to the fact that the community (the state, the local school system, or the area served by the individual school) substantially determines the quantity and quality of educational provisions. Its understandings, values, ability to organize its efforts and to act are central elements in the decisions that it inevitably makes.

In making these decisions the community must have concern for children and youth and also for various staff members connected with the schools. It must be aware of the organizational structure of the community and of the schools. It must be familiar with legal structure pertaining to schools and function in accord with it, effecting changes when needed. It must constantly seek facts so that it may make sound decisions. It must periodically re-examine its philosophical commitments and use them as standards for evaluating its practices.

In all of these activities the community should be able to regard the school administrative staff as its agent, providing leadership in its relentless search for a more adequate educational program. The community must have an understanding of the conditions under which leadership can function effectively, and it must scrupulously protect those conditions. The leader must no less scrupulously respect the competency of the community to make decisions.

Under these circumstances, the community and its educational leaders cooperate in planning, in formulating policy, in implementing programs, and in evaluating. School-community relations are not then essentially matters of reporting or interpreting. Rather, they are carrying forward a public enterprise with laymen and educators playing the respective roles that are most rewarding in terms of the education of men. Action now builds mutual understanding in depth.

SOME IMPORTANT ISSUES

In the following pages, consideration is given to a few of the major issues pertaining to the community and its schools.

May Public Opinion Be Too Large a Determiner of Educational Practice?

There is danger that uninformed public opinion or perhaps a small but highly vocal group will have too large an influence on educational practice. Occasionally, a meeting is reported where a vote is taken on a rather technical subject about which the voters are uninformed. The individual or group with the greatest pressure potential does not necessarily have the sound answer.

The school administrator should not abdicate his leadership responsibility, a responsibility that includes presenting the facts and the results of studies that have been carried on regarding the problem, presenting proposals for a more thorough study, and presenting suggestions for essential research. The administrator must assist groups in recognizing that there are important ways to get information regarding a matter other than asking opinions about it. Public interest in an issue needs to be seen as an opportunity for its fuller study—an opportunity for many to learn more about the issue.

This is not to suggest that public opinion should be ignored on many issues. It is an important factor in many situations and must be considered. However, this interest may be of more value in suggesting communication, clarifying goals and practices, or re-examining values than in pointing the way in regard to practice. If public opinion differs widely from the views or understandings of school personnel, an excellent opportunity would appear to exist for some planned research and a cooperative study of the problem.

The development of sound educational practices demands that there be recognition of the limitations of the expert. Often he may be so deeply immersed in the subject that he misses some of the broader implications. It also requires that the contribution of the expert be recognized and capitalized upon. Closer attention to many educational problems will increase the awareness of laymen regarding the complexity of the issues. It will reduce the demand for simple solutions—especially those involving a return to some practice that may have worked reasonably well in a far simpler and quite different society. It may also result in the development of a more soundly based public opinion, that could be a most important element in controlling the influence of groups not seeking constructive ends.

What are the strengths and limitations of the expert? How can a community best use the expert? What types of issues require research rather than a survey of public opinion in order to arrive at sound solutions?

Does the Closeness of the School to the Community Subject the School to the Narrowness of the Community?

Will not the school merely reflect the prejudices of the community if it works closely with it? Will not community lack of concern for human values limit the school in the attention it can give to them? Will the administrator become a part of the business group with which he associates, largely a reflector of its concepts?

In response to these queries, a number of observations may be made. The community may of course contain a wide variety of groups and individuals, some of whom may have better vision regarding educational objectives than the administrator and the teaching staff. Then, too, it is assumed that the administrator has the competence to work with groups without being enveloped by them. His own commitments with reference to society and education are an important source of strength.

Although leadership is recognized as having a relationship to various situational forces, the assumption must not be made that the administrator is without influence, adrift in a nondescript public opinion sea. Rather, knowledge of the complexity of the leadership role enables the administrator to be more effective.

The community also has values that if brought to public attention may be important levers through which it can raise its vision and activities. The administrator has responsibilities in this sphere.

Finally, in the case of the community that does not seek or attain even desirable minimum levels of educational provision, whether in terms of what is taught or how it is taught, there is recourse to the state and to constitutional rights. In general, the state should be seen as a stimulating agency, an agency of cross-fertilization challenging communities with the pollen gathered over the nation. Regrettably, however, there will also be times when the state must make attempts at enforcing minimum standards. This role of the state should remain a minor one, one that is exercised less and less frequently as communities seriously contemplate educational problems. Therefore, there would seem to be much reason for seeking the close integration of the community and the school, recognizing, however, that neither local community nor the local school system will always take a sound position. The interaction of the two, with contributions to thought and practice from school and community leaders and at times from the outside, offers much promise.

Can the schools rise above the community? How can the administrator avoid becoming the instrument of the more reactionary forces in the community?

Is a School Public Relations Program Consistent
with the Educational Purposes of our Society?

Some educators have doubted the desirability of devoting large energies to various aspects of the school-community relations program. They have been suspicious of publicity. This concern is quite understandable in a society in which much publicity has not sought the enhancement of the citizen but rather has sought to make him an unthinking captive of some group. This publicity has sought to influence through offering the half-truth or through hiding essential facts and thus distorting. The fear that man may become merely the dupe of those with the resources to control the mass media should not be discarded without thought.

On the other hand, it must be recoginzed that unless the facts and the case for public education are put forth vigorously through the most effective instruments employed in our society, the gap between the people's desires and practice in education will widen. And even their values and desires may shift farther away from interest in children and young people and concern for the dignity and worth of the individual. In the fierce struggle for the minds and commitments of men the administrator cannot default and remain an educator.

The educator may consider this program as one of adult education regarding the schools. In an age when the school may be playing a less significant educational role than at times in the past—because of the great impact of the mass media of communication—it is especially fitting that fuller consideration be given to educational goals in our society and the relationship of various agencies to them.

Furthermore, if the ability to govern is related to experience in governing, then the public schools may constitute one of the most important opportunities to develop the skills of self-government. In a period of growing central control, decision-making opportunities close to the people take on added significance. Carrying on a public relations program should facilitate rather than militate against the cooperative solution of educational problems.

For these various reasons it appears clear that public relations per se are not inconsistent with the purposes of education in a democracy but are an important factor in achieving those purposes.

Is there a danger that the school system will reveal only the facts that reflect favorably upon it? How can this be avoided?

The fear that government officials may engage in propagandizing and not present the facts in the light of which the people can make decisions, should not be dismissed lightly. However, the growing complexity of the educational enterprise and of the society of which it is a part demands increased expenditure of time and money for the promotion of understanding. Without such understanding the possibility of intelligent citizen action or of sound action on the part of educators is greatly reduced. A sound approach to the problem will recognize these facts and give attention to the manner in which the work can be most desirably carried forward. There are standards regarding the programs of public relations that need to be established. The development of closer working relationships between citizens and educators will in itself constitute an important barrier to the development of undesirable practices.

Are present statutory provisions regarding the expenditure of funds for public relations purposes sound?

*How Much Concentration upon School-Community Relations
in the Local School or School System is Desirable?*

Our society is marked by large organizations. The federal government plays a larger and larger role in our lives. The nation is economically one unit. Is it not rather self-deceptive to be so greatly concerned about the local situation?

Conceivably such concern could be self-defeating. Intense interest and concern about the local school might result in a lack of interest in the utilization of the federal tax power for educational purposes, even though the economic organization of the society would indicate the desirability of this.

Similarly, the local system might be quite incapable of fending off the attacks of a national organization with large resources that is devoted to the weakening of public education. Such a national organization might choose to strike at a few local organizations at any one time and shift its energies to best achieve its ends.

Although there is no completely satisfactory safeguard against these dangers, it must be observed that the local school is probably the most readily available base for interesting and activating the citizen. The citizen is interested in education both within the school and outside. His children are involved and his devotion to their development is as great as that of the educator. From this base his concern for more adequate education in other areas can be developed. The bringing together of strong local forces of different communities could result in the striking advancement of education in the state or nation.

It is not suggested that strength at the local level is sufficient. Increasing attention must be focused upon organization of those interested in education at the state and national levels. Local forces need the assistance of national organizations. Concentration upon the local situation should be desirable if accompanied by the development of an understanding of the nature of our society and of the ability to function effectively in it.

How can the tendency of many laymen and educators to be concerned with education only in their own area be overcome?

*Can the PTA Be a Part of the Educational Power Structure
and Yet Enjoy Independence of Thought and Action?*

In many communities the parent-teacher organization is one of the more important parts of the power structure devoted to the advancement of education. Some people hold that in too many instances the parents' group may become merely a mouthpiece of professional educators. Some "educators" may desire to have parents' groups play this role.

It is surely proper and desirable that the parents associated with the school should be part of the organization of the total forces devoted to education. It must be recognized, however, that the total structure related to education will be better and stronger if various parts of it enjoy a very real measure of independence and initiative. The parent group that does not think for itself is not one of great strength. Neither is it, in the long run, one that contributes significantly to education.

Educators and other citizens need to develop stronger belief in the desirability of honest differences in judgment, in the expression of different points of view. The submissive power structure is not one that will grapple effectively with large issues. Groups motivated by common purposes can gain much through the utilization of all the capacity found in them—and by developing their potential capacity through attacking important issues.

Does the PTA enjoy adequate independence of action in most communities? How can a strong, nonsubservient PTA be developed? Would the same proposals apply to other citizen groups?

What Are the Limits of Involvement as a Practice
Designed to Improve School-Community Relations?

There are limits to involvement in terms of available time, in terms of the contribution of those involved, and in terms of the abilities of the various parties to work together in a satisfactory manner.

Development of plans for and working with large numbers of laymen is time consuming for the educator. He cannot work with too many groups at once without neglecting other responsibilities. This may be remedied in part as more members of the professional staff develop competency in working with lay groups. Laymen also have many demands upon their time and unless adequate resources are available to facilitate the collection of essential data, committees either fail to do the job or do it without adequate knowledge. The limits of time for involvement therefore need to be considered carefully.

Limitations may also exist in terms of the competency of various people to contribute to the specific issue under consideration. Laymen may be profitably involved in a consideration of the uses to which the school buildings will be put in evenings and for which provision should be made in the plans, but there would be little point in having them consider details of structural safety. Various factors have to be considered when determining whether or not there will be involvement and what the nature of the involvement will be.

Limitations to involvement are also found in the competency of people to work together. If they have had little experience in group processes and are emotionally attached to certain proposed solutions, little good is likely to result from their consideration of the problem.

Finally, it should be noted that participation must be carried on in such a manner as not to hamper the operation of the organization. Many decisions need to be made in the operation of a school or school system. Involvement is essential in broad policy and procedural determination but scarcely in the details of administration resulting from the application of the policy.

Unless there is a realization of the limits of involvement, it is conceivable that it will result in increasing the insecurity of the teacher and administrator and in reducing the effectiveness of the educational program. On the other hand, its possible contribution to the teacher, to the administrator, and to the education of children and young people is large. With careful consideration the dangers should be largely avoided while the benefits are secured. Fruitful utilization of involvement requires time and analyzed experience.

Why must much of the involvement secured occur at the school level? How can staff and citizens be prepared for participation in the school-community relations activity? Are teachers prepared to work on studies in cooperation with citizens? What are the practical limits of involvement?

Selected References

American Association of School Administrators, *Public Relations for America's Schools,* Twenty-eighth Yearbook. Washington, D.C.: The Association, 1950.

Bailey, Stephen K., Richard F. Frost, Paul R. Marsh, and Robert C. Wood, *Schoolmen and Politics.* Syracuse: Syracuse University Press, 1962.

Bollens, John C., and Henry J. Schmandt, *The Metropolis: Its People, Politics and Economic Life.* New York: Harper & Row, Publishers, 1965.

Campbell, Roald F., Lavern L. Cunningham, and Roderick F. McPhee, *The Organization and Control of American Schools.* Columbus, Ohio: Charles E. Merrill Books, Inc., 1965.

Campbell, Roald F., and John A. Ramseyer, *School-Community Relationships.* Boston: Allyn & Bacon, Inc., 1955.

Dahl, Robert, *Who Governs?* New Haven: Yale University Press, 1961.

Hunter, Floyd, *Community Power Structure. A Study of Decision Makers.* Chapel Hill: University of North Carolina Press, 1953.

Kaufman, Herbert, *Politics and Policies in State and Local Governments.* Englewood Cliffs, N.J.: Prentice-Hall, Inc., 1963.

Kimbrough, Ralph B., *Political Power and Educational Decision Making.* Skokie, Ill.: Rand McNally & Co., 1964.

Kindred, Leslie W., *School Public Relations.* Englewood Cliffs, N.J.: Prentice-Hall, Inc., 1957.

Kindred, Leslie W., and George N. Fehr, Jr., *Communications Research and School-Community Relations.* Philadelphia: Temple University Press, 1965.

part two

*The Organization
for Education*

8

The Federal Government
and Education

The involvement of the federal government in education has increased dramatically since the early 1950s. In 1952–53, the federal support for all education totaled $1,417,000,000, more than half of which was expended on the education of veterans. In 1966–67, federal support for all education and related activities totaled approximately $8,400,000,000. In this chapter, we will present a brief history of federal relations to education, describe some of the major issues and analyze some of the recent major changes in federal educational policy.

The relationship of the federal government to public education is one of the most controversial and yet one of the most important issues before the American people. This issue has been debated since the adoption of the Constitution in 1789, but during the past 25 years, interest in this issue has been greatly intensified. In 1951, Quattlebaum listed 42 governmental commissions, advisory groups, and voluntary organizations as having made studies and issued recommendations concerning federal educational policies during the preceding twenty years.[1] Since that time, the number of such studies has greatly increased.

The relationship of the federal government to public education has become the battleground for testing many important principles of law,

[1]Charles A. Quattlebaum, *Federal Educational Activities and Educational Issues Before Congress* (Washington, D.C.: U.S. Government Printing Office, 1951), pp. 69–128.

theories of government, and philosophical values. Issues concerning states' rights, the general welfare, the police power, federalism, freedom of speech and press, freedom of religion, separation of church and state, impairing the obligation of contracts, equal protection of the laws, the due process of the law, the power of Congress to tax and spend, and other vital matters have become involved in this problem. Decisions on public education made by the federal government serve as precedents defining the relationship of the federal government to the states and to the people on many other important issues. Fundamental changes in the economy of the nation and in international relationships are bringing about many changes in the respective roles of the federal government and the states. Changes and proposals for changes naturally become political issues in a democracy. Therefore, it is not surprising that interest in the relationship of the federal government to public education is increasing.

A comprehensive treatment of this problem would require a formidable volume. Therefore, this chapter presents only some of the more important facts and issues that will serve as a basis for the further study of the relationship of the federal government to public education.

FEDERAL CONSTITUTIONAL AUTHORITY[2]

The powers of the government of the United States are delegated rather than inherent. The Tenth Amendment provides: "The powers not delegated to the United States by the Constitution, nor prohibited by it to the States, are reserved to the States respectively or to the people." The federal government, therefore, has no powers other than those specifically conferred on it by the Constitution or such as can reasonably be implied from those specifically granted.[3] On the other hand, the governmental powers of the states are plenary except for the powers that have been delegated to the federal government or withheld from the states by some specific provision of the Constitution.

The Constitution of the United States makes no reference to education. Therefore, under the Tenth Amendment the states have been allocated the basic responsibility for public education. Any authority of the federal government to finance, to control, or to regulate education must be found in the implied powers delegated to the central government in one or more clauses of the Constitution. But the Constitution is a very broad statement of principles, and numerous judicial interpreta-

[2]The authors are indebted to Newton Edwards, *The Courts and the Public Schools* (Chicago: University of Chicago Press, 1955), for many of the concepts set forth in this section.

[3]Edwards, *op. cit.*, p. 1.

tions of these principles have greatly extended the application of the implied powers of the federal government since the adoption of the Constitution.

The General Welfare Clause

Clause 1 of Section 8 of Article I of the Constitution provides that "The Congress shall have the power to lay and collect taxes, duties, imposts and excises, to pay the debts and provide for the common defense and general welfare of the United States. . . ." This clause of the Constitution, although it deals with many other important matters, is commonly known as the "general welfare clause." It has been one of the most controversial provisions of the Constitution since the very beginning. It was the center of the famous controversy between Alexander Hamilton and James Madison. It was argued by Madison that this clause conferred no additional powers on the Congress to tax and spend, and therefore it was meant only to be a reference to powers that were specifically granted to Congress by the Constitution. Hamilton held, however, that this clause conferred upon Congress the power to tax and spend for purposes in addition to those specifically enumerated by the Constitution and in fact conferred on Congress the power to tax and spend for any purpose that it deemed to be for the general welfare.

This controversy has continued for more than 175 years, but the battleground has shifted from constitutional authority to wisdom of policy. The Supreme Court, in ruling upon the Agricultural Adjustment Act, declared that "the power of Congress to authorize expenditures of public money for public purposes is not limited by the direct grants of legislative power found in the Constitution."[4] The Supreme Court, in an opinion relating to the Social Security Act, held that the discretion of determining whether some purpose of federal expenditure was for the general welfare laid with the Congress and not the Court, provided it was not clearly a display of arbitrary power. As pointed out in Chapter 2, the Court further declared that the concept of general welfare is not static because what is critical or urgent changes with the times.[5]

The authority of the Congress to tax and spend for public education has not been challenged in the Supreme Court. It seems clear that the constitutional authority of the Congress to spend money for public education has been clearly established by the principles of law enumerated by the Supreme Court in other cases before it. Therefore, the controversy now centers on whether it is good public policy for the federal government to take positive action with respect to public education and not on the constitutional authority of Congress to act.

[4]*United States* v. *Butler*, 297 U.S. 1, 56 Sup. Ct. 312.
[5]*Helvering* v. *Davis*, 301 Dr. S.619, 57 Sup. Ct. 904.

Limitations on the States

Opposition to federal control of education is widespread in the United States. The term "federal control" is interpreted in various ways by different people. Actually, the federal government from the beginning of the nation has exercised substantial control over the educational activities of the states, as explained later. These controls have been found so wise and they are so well accepted that the people have seldom thought of them as controls. Actually, if a movement were started to eliminate them, there would be as much opposition as there is to more federal control of education. Such is the force of custom and propaganda.

The educational policies and activities of the states are profoundly affected by limitations on the powers of the states contained in the Constitution. Some of these limitations are discussed in the following paragraphs.

SEPARATION OF CHURCH AND STATE.   The power of the federal government to control the relationship of the public schools to religion was clearly established by the First and Fourteenth Amendments. The First Amendment provides: "Congress shall make no law respecting an establishment of religion, or prohibiting the free exercise thereof. . . ." The Fourteenth Amendment provides in part: ". . . No state shall make or enforce any law which shall abridge the privileges or immunities of citizens of the United States. . . ." The Supreme Court has held that this amendment makes the First Amendment applicable to the states in defining the relationship between church and state. In the case of *Illinois ex rel. McCollum v. Board of Education*[6] and in *Everson v. Board of Education*[7] the Court declared the First Amendment was intended to erect a "wall of separation between church and state." The Court has made it clear in these two opinions and in other opinions that tax-supported property cannot be used for religious instruction and that neither a state nor the federal government can set up a church or levy a tax, large or small, to support any religious activities or institutions.

A case involving Bible reading in the public schools was brought before the United States Supreme Court in October, 1962. The Court ruled in 1963 that Bible reading in the public schools was a violation of the First Amendment.[8] This ruling at first caused some violent criticism, but it soon subsided.

EQUAL PROTECTION OF THE LAWS.   Neither a state nor an agency of the state such as a board of education can deny a citizen of the United

[6]333 U.S. 203.
[7]330 U.S. 1.
[8]*School District of Arlington Township v. Schempp*, 374 U.S. 203.

States equal protection of the law. The Supreme Court on May 17, 1954, in dealing with five cases before it, ruled that segregation in the public schools was unconstitutional because it denied equal protection of the laws. The Court stated:

> We conclude that in the field of public education the doctrine of "separate but equal" has no place. Separate educational facilities are inherently unequal. Therefore, we hold that the plaintiffs and others similarly situated for whom the actions are brought are, by reason of the segregation complained of, deprived of the equal protection of the laws guaranteed by the Fourteenth Amendment.[9]

This ruling reversed the position of the Court on *Plessy* v. *Ferguson* in 1896, when it ruled in a transportation case that separate but equal facilities were constitutional.[10] The educational policies of seventeen states and the District of Columbia were vitally affected by this decision. The *de facto* segregation by race in the large cities of many other states has also been affected by this decision. It will be noted that this decision controls not only the educational policies of the states with respect to segregation by race but also the policies of boards of education wherever situated. The states' rights theory, insofar as it applies to segregation of the races, was also overthrown by this decision.

The Civil Rights Act of 1964 greatly increased the power of the federal government to eliminate discrimination in public education. Title VI of this act states: "No person in the United States shall on the ground of race, color, or national origin, be excluded from participation in, be denied the benefits of, or be subject to discrimination, under any program or activity receiving Federal financial assistance." This act gives any federal agency disbursing federal funds the power to withhold such funds if the recipient agency or institution violates this act. The United States Office of Education has used this act in recent years to force racial integration by withholding federal funds from both public and private schools and colleges that fail to comply with the provisions of the act. Since federal grants are now quite substantial, this is a powerful control designed to force racial integration. The enforcement of the Civil Rights Act has greatly speeded up this movement.

CONTRACTUAL OBLIGATIONS.   The Supreme Court in a large number of cases has ruled that neither a state nor a board of education could take action "impairing the obligations of contracts" as provided in Section 10 of Article I of the Constitution. This provision of the Constitution has frequently been applied to settling controversies between states and colleges or universities over contractual provisions of charters and to controversies between teachers and governing authorities over tenure

[9]*Brown* v. *Board of Education,* 347 U.S. 483, 74 Sup. Ct. 686.
[10]163 U.S. 537, 16 Sup. Ct. 1138.

and retirement rights. The Supreme Court has held that "a legislative enactment may contain provisions which, when accepted as a basis of action by individuals, become contracts between them and the state or its subdivision. . . ."[11] Thus, the federal Constitution itself provides substantial control over the actions of the states and boards of education, insofar as those actions involve the impairment of obligations under contract.

THE DUE PROCESS OF LAW AND THE POLICE POWER. The Fourteenth Amendment provides in part ". . . Nor shall any state deprive any person of life, liberty, or property, without due process of law. . . ." But the police power is inherent in every state, and this power frequently must be balanced against the due-process-of-law clause that protects an individual. Edwards states: "The police power is that power of the state to limit individual rights in the interest of the social group."[12] The limits of the states in exercising the police power are continually being redefined by the courts. Prior to 1860 the Supreme Court placed almost no restrictions on the states in the exercise of this police power except those restrictions specifically set forth in the Constitution. Since the adoption of the Fourteenth Amendment with its due-process-of-law clause, the Supreme Court has had much greater authority to restrict the police power of the states, but it did not begin to exercise that power until after the case of *Muller* v. *Oregon*[13] in 1908. In that case the Court took cognizance of physiological and social facts bearing on the employment of women. This case set the precedent for considering psychological and social facts in the five segregation cases ruled on in 1954. It is now apparent that the Supreme Court, when making a decision involving a determination of a proper balance between the due process of law and the police power, will make the decision not so much in terms of abstract legal concepts as in terms of psychological, economic, and social facts.

Space does not permit adequate illustrations of these limitations on the educational powers of the states and their subdivisions. Attention has already been directed to the case of *Brown* v. *Board of Education* in which it was ruled that segregation itself was unequal.[14] Psychological and social facts and not abstract legal concepts were the bases for the decision.

On the other hand, the Supreme Court has upheld the constitutionality of the Smith Act.[15] This act makes it a crime punishable by fine and imprisonment to advocate the overthrow of the government by

[11]*State ex rel. Anderson* v. *Brand,* 313 U.S. 95.
[12]Edwards, *op. cit.,* p. 12.
[13]208 U.S. 412.
[14]347 U.S. 483.
[15]*Dennis et al.* v. *United States,* 341 U.S. 494.

force. This act clearly comes within the police power of the federal government. It is definitely a federal control over one aspect of what may be taught in a public or even a private school. Therefore, those who insist that the federal government should have no control whatsoever over the curriculum of the public schools seem to be unaware of the inherent police power of the federal government relating to matters of national concern.

SOME HISTORICAL RELATIONSHIPS

Despite wide differences of opinion concerning the role that should be played by the federal government in public education, it has shown an interest in and has participated in the support of public education since before the adoption of the Constitution in 1789. The educational activities of the federal government include (1) financing and administering its own educational programs and (2) aiding the states and territories and institutions and agencies therein in financing and otherwise promoting education.[16] A brief review of some of those activities is presented in the following paragraphs.

Land Grants for the Public Schools

The Ordinance of 1785 provided that "There shall be reserved the lot number 16 of every township for the maintenance of public schools in each township." This provision was repeated in the Ordinance of 1787 providing for the government of the Northwest Territory. The interest of the federal government in public education was clearly demonstrated in these words contained in the Ordinance of 1787: "Religion, morality, and knowledge being necessary to good government and the happiness of mankind, schools and the means of education shall be forever encouraged."

Ohio was the first state admitted to the Union under the Ordinance of 1787. The Ohio policy of setting aside the sixteenth section of each township for the public schools was followed for states admitted to the Union up to 1848. Congress set aside two sections in every township for public education when the Oregon Territory was established in 1848. This policy was followed until 1896, when Utah was granted four sections in every township. Similar grants were given to Arizona and New Mexico when they were admitted to the Union in 1912.

The federal government made many other types of early grants for the benefit of the public schools. Some of those were as follows: (1) grants of funds in lieu of land grants in Indian territory; (2) additional

16Quattlebaum, *op. cit.*, pp. 69–128.

land grants under the Internal Improvement Act of 1841; (3) grants of saline lands; (4) grants of 5 per cent of the funds received by the federal government from sale of public lands in the states; (5) payment to the states of 25 per cent of the income from national forests and 37.5 per cent of the income received from the extraction of non-metallic minerals for the benefit of roads and public schools; and (6) the allocation of surplus federal revenues to the states in 1836.

Swift has estimated that the early grants of land given by Congress to the thirty public land states aggregated an area ten times as large as Maryland and that grants given to the states in whole or in part for the public schools totaled more than 76 million acres.[17]

Most of the states did not handle these grants very wisely. The land in many states was sold at very low prices. In other states much land was settled by private parties without the state's protesting, and title to the land was lost to the state. In still other states, funds derived from the sale of school lands were lost owing to fiscal mismanagement or misappropriation. However, the income derived from these early land grants is still an important source of revenue in a few states.

Opponents of federal aid for public education almost invariably argue that it is impossible to have federal aid for education without federal control. Nevertheless, the federal government has never exercised any control over these land grants. Perhaps if the federal government had exercised enough control over the land grants to protect them from wastage and misappropriation, these grants would have been of greater benefit to the public schools. Such protection could have been given these funds without the federal government's interfering with the prerogatives of the states to determine the school curriculum, organize and administer schools, and exercise all other legitimate powers with respect to education.

The activities of the federal government in administering the territories and making land grants had other important effects on the public schools. The federal government itself organized school systems in each territory, and when the territory became a state, the federally established school system was taken over by the state. The funds arising from land grants served as precedents for state aid for the public schools.

The Land Grant Colleges

The Morrill Act passed by Congress in 1862 granted 30,000 acres to each state for each representative and senator then in Congress or when a state was admitted to the Union. Provision was made for com-

[17]Fletcher Harper Swift, *Federal and State Policies in Public School Finance in the United States* (Boston: Ginn and Company, 1931), p. 59.

pulsory military training in the colleges established. The proceeds from the sale of the land grants were required to be used for "the endowment, maintenance and support of at least one college where the leading object shall be, without excluding other scientific and classical studies and including military tactics, to teach such branches of learning as are related to agriculture and mechanic arts." This act also had as one of its purposes "to promote the liberal and practical education of the industrial classes in the several pursuits and professions of life."

This act is of great significance, because it has demonstrated (1) that the federal government, when it deemed it necessary to do so for the common defense or the general welfare, could and would take positive action with respect to education, and (2) that the federal government could and would take positive action with respect to vital areas of education that were neglected by the states. Prior to 1862, most institutions of higher learning catered primarily to the sons and daughters of the wealthy. Cultural and classical education was emphasized. Education in agriculture and engineering was not considered a proper activity for an institution of higher learning. This was a carry-over from European traditions concerning higher education. The Morrill Act might therefore be considered a layman's revolt from the prevailing educational leadership of that day.

Other acts of Congress have supplemented the activities of the land grant colleges. The Hatch Act of 1887, the Adams Act of 1906, the Purnell Act of 1925, the Bankhead-Jones Act of 1935, the Research and Marketing Act of 1946, and subsequent amendments have increased the funds available for agricultural experiment stations. These experiment stations made it possible to develop a scientific knowledge of agriculture which was the basis for the remarkable productivity of American agriculture.

The Smith-Lever Act

The Smith-Lever Act in 1914 provided for extension services by county agricultural agents, home demonstrators, 4-H leaders, and specialists in agriculture and homemaking, and for the professional training of teachers in these subjects. The Coffee-Ketchum Act of 1928, the Bankhead-Jones Act of 1935, the Bankhead-Flannagan Act of 1945, and subsequent amendments have broadened the scope and increased the funds provided by the Smith-Lever Act. The Smith-Lever Act for the first time required the states to match educational funds provided by the federal government.

The extension workers provided by the Smith-Lever Act have made a significant contribution to the education of farmers and housewives.

The agricultural agents have been particularly effective in bringing the findings of the experimental farms to the farmers. The extension workers have also made significant contributions to the lives of rural youth. Field demonstrations and the "group process" were first used extensively by these workers. The extension workers were among the first educators to experiment with the techniques of group dynamics and the dynamics of change. They have clearly demonstrated the value of the role of "change agents."

The extension service provided under the Smith-Lever Act is not an integral part of the system of public education. The act is administered on the federal level by the Department of Agriculture. The extension workers are employed by the governing bodies of counties. The state director of extension services is almost always associated with a land grant institution of higher learning, but this is about the only connection between the extension program and the program of public education.

The Smith-Hughes Act

The Smith-Hughes Act of 1917 was the first federal act providing funds for vocational education below college level. This act provided a continuing appropriation for vocational education in agriculture, trades and industry, and homemaking, and for teacher training in those fields. It is administered on the federal level by the U.S. Office of Education. The original act required that the states and local school units match the federal appropriation on a dollar-for-dollar basis. Federal assistance for vocational education was further extended by the following acts: the George-Reed Act of 1929, the George-Ellzey Act of 1935, the George-Deen Act of 1937, the George-Barden Act of 1946, and the Vocational Education Act of 1963.

Public interest in vocational education increased rapidly with the beginning of the twentieth century. By 1909, some 500 agricultural high schools had been established. By 1911, 44 of the 47 states offered instruction in home economics in some high schools. A number of trade schools had been established in city school systems. Nevertheless, comprehensive vocational education opportunities were not available to most high school pupils. Lay organizations such as the American Federation of Labor, the Grange, the National Association of Manufacturers, and the Chamber of Commerce of the United States all urged the expansion of vocational education in high schools. The National Education Association made certain studies of vocational education but did not play a very active role in promoting the development of vocational education. The educational leadership administering the high schools in the early part of the twentieth century was concerned much more with college preparatory education than education to meet the needs of all pupils of secondary school age. Therefore, the federal acts providing financial support for vocational education represented, in actuality, a lay revolt from the prevailing educational leadership.

The Smith-Hughes Act provided some federal control of vocational education, but in practice much of the control was delegated to the states. The Smith-Hughes Act and subsequent acts provided a great stimulus for vocational education. All states now spend far more for vocational education than the minimum matching requirement.

Relief Measures Affecting Education

The nation was deep in its greatest financial depression by 1933. Franklin D. Roosevelt was inaugurated President in March, 1933, and almost immediately he started his New Deal to break the depression. The New Deal included a large number of new and experimental measures that had as their principal purpose the improvement of the economic condition of the people. Many of these measures affected education, but they were designed primarily as relief measures. Some of the programs are discussed briefly in the following paragraphs.

THE CIVILIAN CONSERVATION CORPS.   The Civilian Conservation Corps, or CCC, was created by an act of Congress in March, 1933. The purpose of this act was primarily to relieve unemployment through the performance of useful public work and to provide for the restoration of depleted natural resources of the country. The CCC had developed an extensive educational program by 1937. More than 3 million men, most of whom were young, enrolled in the CCC between 1934 and 1941, and more than 2.7 million of this number participated in some type of organized educational activity. Shortly after World War II began, war and defense activities largely eliminated unemployment, and the CCC was abolished in 1943.

THE NATIONAL YOUTH ADMINISTRATION.   The National Youth Administration was established by the executive order of the President in 1935. The NYA program provided many benefits to needy college and secondary school students. It carried on a great variety of useful work projects. In the beginning, the young people it aided usually lived at home. Later, an increasing number were housed in NYA residences and dormitories. The NYA even began constructing some special schools in some states. In the later 1930s the educational leadership began to fear that the NYA was beginning to develop a competing federal system of schools. In the defense period prior to 1941, the NYA was charged with competing with defense agencies for manpower. Opposition to the NYA caused it to be placed under the Federal Security Agency in 1939, transferred to the War Manpower Commission in 1944, and liquidated in 1944.

OTHER RELIEF AGENCIES.   Many other federal relief agencies carried on programs between 1933 and 1940 that gave significant aid to the public schools and institutions of higher learning. Some of the more important were: the Civil Works Administration, the Federal Emergency Relief Administration, the Works Progress Administration, and the Public Works Administration. The CWA was primarily for the purpose of providing work for the unemployed. Many school houses were repaired and renovated under this program. The FERA distributed many millions of dollars of funds for relief of the unemployed. Thousands of teachers, especially in rural areas, benefited from those funds. The FERA also provided funds for adult education, vocational rehabilitation, and nursery schools. However, the primary purpose of the FERA was to provide work for unemployed persons.

The Works Progress Administration superseded the FERA in 1939. It carried on all the FERA projects, and in addition it provided substantial funds for the construction and repair of school buildings.

The Public Works Administration, established in 1933, made grants for school buildings. Initially, these grants amounted to 30 per cent of the cost of construction, but they later rose to 45 per cent. The PWA also made loans for part or all of the remaining cost.

All these agencies were liquidated in the early 1940s. It is impossible to make an accurate appraisal of all the educational benefits provided by these relief agencies.

Apparently the only permanent federal aid for the public schools that originated from all the relief measures was federal aid for the school lunch program. The CWA, FERA, and later the WPA provided some aid for the school lunch program in the form of labor. The Federal Surplus Commodities Corporation was established by Congress in 1935. It purchased and distributed surplus commodities to nonprofit school lunchrooms. This was a relief act for agriculture, and it was administered by the Department of Agriculture. Surplus commodities were distributed to both public and private elementary and secondary schools. Some cash was also provided primarily for the purchase of surplus foods to be used in school lunchrooms. School lunch aid for private schools was justified on the grounds that it was an aid to the child and not the school. These policies finally culminated in the National School Lunch Act of 1946, which has apparently made federal school lunch aid a permanent policy. This act was supplemented in 1954 by an act providing special aid for the school milk program. Undoubtedly, these acts greatly stimulated the development of the school lunch program.

Federal Educational Activities for Defense and War
  Prior to 1958

It would require a formidable volume to describe all federal educational activities for defense and war. The federal government has operated elementary schools, high schools, institutions of college grade, and various other types of educational programs. Some are on service posts, some are in territories, and some are abroad. In fact, all of these activities are still being carried on by the federal government. Furthermore, the federal government has carried on many types of war and defense educational activities through state and local agencies and institutions. Space will permit only a few examples.

THE ARMED FORCES.   The Military Academy was established at West Point in 1802, the Naval Academy at Annapolis in 1845, and the Air Force Academy at Colorado Springs in 1954. The Army Medical School was established in 1893, the Army War College in 1902, superseded by the National War College in 1946, and the Air University in 1947.

The educational system for enlisted men began with an act of Congress in 1866 which provides that "Whenever troops are serving at any post, garrison, or permanent camp, there shall be established a school where all men may be provided with instruction in the common English branches of education, and especially in the history of the United States." Thousands of men have been taught to read and write and also have been given much additional postschool education under this program. The act of 1866 probably set the precedent for the development of the Armed Forces Institute in 1945. This institute now provides very extensive programs of educational opportunities for all career and active duty personnel. It is a voluntary off-duty program.

In summary, the educational activities of Army, the Navy, the Air Force, the Marines, and the Coast Guard now make it possible for all personnel to obtain a wide range of educational opportunities that will not only benefit the armed services but will be of great benefit to the service personnel in civilian life.

THE TRAINING OF WAR PRODUCTION WORKERS.   In the period immediately prior to World War II, the federal government initiated a crash program for the training of workers in war industries. This program was administered through the U.S. Office of Education which worked through the state educational agencies in administering the program. Approximately 7.8 million workers were trained through this program. The Office of Education was also authorized to cooperate with degree-granting institutions in organizing short courses for the training of engineers, chemists, physicists, and production supervisors. More than 2 million workers were trained under this program. Other significant programs administered by the Office of Education were the program for training rural war production workers, which benefited 4.2 million students, and the student war loans program.

WARTIME USES OF INSTITUTIONS OF HIGHER LEARNING.   When the United States entered World War II, the federal government made wide use of the facilities of institutions of higher learning. By 1943, the Army specialized training program had been established on more than 300 campuses.[18] The Navy V-12 program provided college opportunities of a similar nature for naval personnel. These two programs enabled many thousands of youth to obtain advanced educational training.

FEDERAL IMPACT AREAS.   The Lanham Act of 1941 provided federal financial assistance to local governments for the construction, maintenance, and operation of community facilities in areas where war-incurred federal activities created financial burdens that the local governments could not bear. Federal authorities worked through the U.S. Office of Education in administering this act insofar as it applied to public education. This act was superseded in 1950 by Public Laws 815 and 874, which continued approximately the same federal benefits to areas adversely affected by federal activities.

It is interesting to note that the educational activities of the federal government during the war years affecting the public schools and colleges were carried on largely through the U. S. Office of Education, which in turn worked through state educational agencies as contrasted with the uncoordinated federal relief activities of the 1930s. This newer policy proved to be far more satisfactory from an educational standpoint.

AID FOR VETERANS.   Certain postwar but war-related educational activities of the federal government are deserving of mention. The Congress in 1918 provided for the vocational education of disabled veterans of World War I, and the Vocational Rehabilitation Act of 1943 made similar provisions for disabled veterans of World War II. In 1920, the federal government provided funds for the rehabilitation, including training, of disabled civilians. This law required the states to match federal funds. This act was superseded in 1943 by Public Law 113, which provides for federal assistance to the states that develop approved plans for the vocational rehabilitation of injured persons.

The most important postwar educational activity of the federal government was the veterans' training program. Public Law 178 of 1918 provided for the vocational training of World War I veterans at federal expense. Approximately 180,000 veterans received training under this act. Public Law 16 of 1943 provided for the vocational rehabilitation of

[18]Quattlebaum, *op. cit.*, p. 30.

disabled veterans of World War II. More than 500,000 veterans have received training under this act.

The most important of the veterans' education acts was Public Law 346 of 1944, popularly known as the G.I. Bill. This act provided training for all veterans of World War II, the length of training depending upon the length of service. The educational provisions of this act were very liberal, covering almost every kind of training desired by the veteran from ballroom dancing to advanced graduate research. Approximately 8 million veterans had received some training under this act by 1954. Several millions of veterans were enabled to attend college by this act, and college enrollments more than doubled following World War II. Public Law 550 of 1952 provided educational training for the veterans of the Korean War. More than a million veterans of the Korean War have received the benefits of this act. In 1966, the Congress extended the benefits of the G.I. Bill to veterans of the Cold War. It is possible that these benefits will be continued indefinitely for all service personnel. The recent veterans' education acts have been administered by the Veterans' Administration.

The various veterans' education and vocational rehabilitation acts have made educational opportunities available to millions of persons who otherwise would not have had those opportunities. Some studies have shown that the increased income taxes paid by veterans and vocationally rehabilitated persons resulting from increased earning power more than reimburse the federal government for the funds expended on their education.

THE NATIONAL SCIENCE FOUNDATION. The National Science Foundation was established by Public Law 507 in 1950. Its purpose is "to promote the progress of science; to advance the national health, prosperity and welfare; to secure the national defense; and for other purposes." The foundation initiates and supports programs to strengthen research in mathematics, the physical and biological sciences and the engineering sciences through contracts, loans, grants, fellowships, institutes and other means. Of particular interest to the public schools are the new curricula in science and mathematics that have been developed under the sponsorship of the Foundation. These curricula have been widely disseminated by means of institutes for high-school teachers which have been financed by the Foundation. The success of the Foundation in changing high-school curricula has demonstrated that an adequately financed federal agency can have a powerful influence on curriculum change.

THE COOPERATIVE RESEARCH PROGRAM. Public Law 83-531 established the Cooperative Research Program in 1954. This act is administered by the U.S. Office of Education. It authorized the U.S. Commissioner of

Education to enter into jointly financed contracts with universities, colleges and state education agencies for conducting research, surveys, and demonstrations in the field of education. Educational research has received a major impetus from this act. Far more educational research is now being financed under the provision of this act than from all other public sources combined. This act is potentially extremely significant. It may have more permanent effect on the improvement of the educational program than any other federal act.

Federal Educational Activities Since 1958

The year 1958 marked the beginning of a new era in the relationship of the federal government to education. The scientific success of the Russians in launching the first earth satellite in 1957 jarred the people of the United States out of their complacence. We were carrying on the Cold War with Russia, fully confident of our superiority in science and technology. With the launching of Sputnik I came the realization that our potential antagonist might be gaining on us rapidly. This fear triggered the passage of the National Defense Education Act in 1958 which was the beginning of a large number of federal acts relating to education that have been enacted since 1958. Kurth listed what he considered to be the 47 most significant federal acts relating to education or major amendments to such acts.[19] Seventeen of those laws were enacted prior to 1958, and thirty between the years 1958 and 1965 inclusive.

The basic federal policies toward education have not changed since 1958. All federal funds provided for education since that date have been earmarked for special purposes. Therefore the federal government has continued its long-time policy of providing special-purpose grants rather than grants for general purposes. However, as has been pointed out, the amounts of these grants have been enormously increased since 1958. The federal government no longer takes a laissez-faire attitude toward education. Education is now being deliberately used by the federal government to implement its policies of providing for the common defense, promoting the general welfare, eliminating poverty, promoting economic growth and social change and in other ways to attain "The Great Society."

Although the recent federal grants are all categorical or special-purpose aids, there has been very little coordination in the planning of these acts to prevent duplication of attempts to accomplish a given purpose. Kurth identified 36 major purposes of the 47 acts he studied.[20]

[19]Edwin L. Kurth, *A Chronology Summarizing Important Federal Acts Aiding Education* (Gainesville, Fla.: Florida Educational Research and Development Council, College of Education, University of Florida, 1966).
[20]*Ibid.*

However, numerous separate acts have been passed which deal with the same purpose. For example, of the 47 acts Kurth studied, 15 different acts deal with adult education, 19 with educational facilities and equipment, 17 with research, and 10 with guidance.

A few of the more important federal laws relating to education which have been enacted since 1958 are treated briefly in the following paragraphs.

THE NATIONAL DEFENSE EDUCATION ACT OF 1958—PUBLIC LAW 85-864. Congress defined a new role of education as follows in this act:

> . . . that the security of the nation requires the fullest development of the mental resources and technical skills of its young men and women. The present emergency demands that additional and more adequate educational opportunities be made available. The defense of this Nation depends upon the mastery of modern techniques developed from complex scientific principles. It depends as well upon the discovery and development of new principles, new techniques, and new knowledge.

The ten titles of this act authorized grants and loans assisting both public and private education from the elementary school through graduate school. The original act provided financial aid primarily for science, mathematics, modern foreign languages, technical and vocational education and counseling and guidance. This act was amended and broadened in 1964 by authorizing financial assistance for instruction in history, geography, civics, English, and reading. The grants, loans, fellowships and other forms of financial aids provided under this act have had a significant impact on education in this nation. This act is administered by the U.S. Office of Education.

MANPOWER DEVELOPMENT AND TRAINING ACT OF 1962—PUBLIC LAW 84-415. The basic objective of this act is to reduce the hard core of unemployment by retraining workers whose skills had become obsolete. The costs of training and training allowances for the unemployed were financed under this act. Although the primary purposes of this act were to provide occupational training for unemployed adult workers and to encourage manpower planning based on research, it also provided for "the testing, counseling, and selection of youths, 16 years of age or older, for occupational training and further schooling." This act is administered jointly by the U.S. Department of Labor and the Office of Education in the U.S. Department of Health, Education and Welfare.

HIGHER EDUCATION FACILITIES ACT OF 1963—PUBLIC LAW 88-204.   This act authorized $230 million a year for three years beginning in 1964 for the construction of facilities for higher education. Of this amount 22 per cent was earmarked for construction of public community colleges and public technical institutes. Public or other nonprofit higher institutions are eligible for financial assistance under this act. It is administered by the U.S. Office of Education.

THE VOCATIONAL EDUCATION ACT OF 1963—PUBLIC LAW 88–210. This act more than quadrupled the federal appropriations for vocational and technical education. It has much broader purposes than the original Smith-Hughes Act for vocational education. The major purpose of the 1963 act is to provide occupational training for persons of all ages and achievement levels in any occupational field that does not require a baccalaureate degree, to provide for related services which will help to ensure quality programs, to assist in the construction of area vocational facilities and to promote and to provide financial assistance for work study programs and residential schools. This act is administered by the U.S. Office of Education. As pointed out in Chapter 9, the organization for vocational education contemplated by this act creates some undesirable duplication with public community junior college programs.

THE ECONOMIC OPPORTUNITY ACT OF 1964—PUBLIC LAW 88–452. The major purpose of this act is "to mobilize the human and financial resources of the Nation to fight poverty in the United States." Section 2 of the act declares, "that it is the policy of the United States to eliminate the paradox of poverty in the midst of plenty in this Nation by opening to everyone opportunities for education, training, work, and a life of decency and dignity, and the purpose of the act is to strengthen, supplement, and coordinate efforts in furtherance of that policy." This act, probably more than any other act of Congress, clearly recognizes the social value of education as well as its economic value. Education is recognized not only for its value to the individual but also for its contribution to production and to the distribution of the fruits of production.

The Office of Economic Opportunity in the Executive Office of the President was established by this act. This office is headed by a director who coordinates all the programs supported by this act. The director operates some programs directly and other programs through the following federal agencies: the Office of Education, the Department of Agriculture, and the Small Business Administration.

THE ELEMENTARY AND SECONDARY EDUCATION ACT OF 1965—PUBLIC LAW 89–10. This was the most important federal act affecting the elementary and secondary schools passed by Congress up to 1965. It provided approximately $1,300,000,000 annually to support the programs included in the act. It doubled the federal aid available for elementary and secondary schools, increasing the per cent of total revenue receipts provided by the federal government for public elementary and secondary schools from 4 to 8.

There are five major titles of this act. The financial aid under the first three titles is allocated to the elementary and secondary schools and under titles four and five to institutions of higher learning and state departments of education. Of the appropriations, 90 per cent is earmarked for elementary and secondary schools.

Title I provides financial assistance for educational programs especially designed to benefit the children from families with an income below $2,000 per year or who are receiving welfare aid for dependent children; Title II provides funds for libraries, textbooks and audio-visual materials; Title III provides funds for supplementary education centers for students in both public and private schools; Title IV provides funds for regional educational research and training laboratories; and Title V provides funds for strengthening state departments of education. This act is administered by the U.S. Office of Education.

Analysis of Recent Developments

Jackson and Steinhilber reported in 1960 that "Over 50 major administrative units in 22 federal departments and agencies reported expenditures in programs which provided funds for educational activities of the States and of educational institutions, or which provided educational services or funds for financing the education of individuals."[21] Even more federal agencies were involved in administering federal funds for education by 1966. Despite this scattering of federal responsibility for the administration of educational funds, considerably more than half of all the federal funds, exclusive of contract research, allocated to elementary and secondary schools and higher institutions in the United States in 1966 were administered through the U.S. Office of Education or the National Science Foundation. Furthermore, most of the recent federal appropriations to education are allocated through the U.S. Office of Education. Therefore, the problem of the control of federal educational funds by noneducational agencies is not as serious as it might seem.

The critical problem is the earmarking of all federal appropriations for special purposes. Although the public elementary and secondary schools were receiving more than $2 billion in federal funds by fiscal 1966, many boards of education could not provide educationally balanced budgets because of this earmarking policy. This problem will not be solved until a substantial amount of general-purpose funds is made available annually by the federal government or until the number of federal special-purpose grants is increased sufficiently to cover all major

[21]Penrose B. Jackson and Dolores A. Steinhilber, *Federal Funds for Education: Fields, Levels, Recipients 1959 and 1960*, U.S. Department of Health, Education and Welfare, Office of Education (Washington, D.C.: U.S. Government Printing Office, 1962), p. 5.

educational needs. In this latter event, the difficulty of administering so many funds might result eventually in their consolidation into a general-purpose fund. However at this writing there are no signs that the federal government intends to substitute general-purpose grants for special-purpose grants in the near future. Instead of the federal government's adopting policies to avoid or reduce federal control of education, recent federal acts all extend federal control of education. This is apparently due to the fact that education is now seen as a major instrument for accomplishing national purposes. Therefore, the Congress enacts legislation which controls educational objectives to the extent deemed necessary to attain national purposes.

Following is a summary of the estimated expenditures in fiscal 1967 of federal funds for education, training and related programs by category (in millions of dollars):[22]

1.	Preschool, elementary and secondary	2,436
2.	Higher education	2,382
3.	Vocational education, work-training and other adult or continuing education	1,333
4.	Educational research, curriculum development, etc.	125
5.	Training of federal government military personnel	1,496
6.	Training of federal government civilian personnel	86
7.	International educational activities	255
8.	Other	272
	Total	8,385

But the above table presents only a part of the expenditures of the federal government for education, research, and development. The National Science Foundation estimated the federal expenditures of the Department of Defense, the National Aeronautical and Space Administration, the Atomic Energy Commission, and other agencies for research, development, and research and development plants in fiscal 1966 to have been 15.5 billion dollars.[23] It is estimated that the expenditures for these purposes were even greater in fiscal 1967. There was an overlap of only approximately 1.2 billion dollars in the expenditures estimated by the Bureau of the Budget for education, training, and related programs and the expenditures estimated by the National Science Foundation for

[22]Bureau of the Budget, *Federal Education Training, and Related Programs,* Special Analysis G (Washington, D.C.: The Bureau, 1966), p. 89.
[23]National Science Foundation, *Federal Funds for Research, Development and Other Scientific Activities,* Vol. XIV (Washington, D.C.: U.S. Government Printing Office, 1965), p. 4.

research and development. Therefore, the total expenditure of the federal government in 1966–67 for education, training, research, development and related programs totaled approximately 22.7 billion dollars. There is a very close functional relationship between education and research because each complements the other.

It is apparent that education is no longer the exclusive responsibility of the states. Research is no longer the exclusive responsibility of the private sector of the economy. Education, research, and development are now major activities of the federal government.

THE UNITED STATES OFFICE OF EDUCATION

The present U.S. Office of Education had its origin in an act of Congress in 1867 that established a federal Department of Education headed by a commissioner. The original purposes of the act were to create a federal service for: (1) "collecting and diffusing such educational information as shall aid the people of the United States in the establishment and maintenance of efficient school systems, and (2) otherwise promoting the cause of education throughout the country."[24] The name, functions, and administrative control of the federal agency designed to serve education have been changed from time to time by acts of Congress or executive orders. For many years the Office of Education was in the Department of the Interior. It was made a part of the Federal Security Agency in 1939. In 1953 the Office of Education became a part of the newly created Department of Health, Education and Welfare, where it has remained since that time. The Office is headed by the Commissioner of Education, who is a political appointee of the President. However, for a long number of years, regardless of the political party in power, the appointee has always been an educator. The professional staff of the Office of Education consists of educators, most of whom are selected under the provisions of the federal Civil Service System.

The principle functions of the Office are as follows: (1) to collect and publish educational information, (2) to engage in educational research, (3) to provide educational leadership and consulting services, (4) to cooperate with various state and local public and private educational agencies and institutions to promote the cause of education, and (5) to administer the federal funds for education provided for the states and territories when the authority to do so is provided in the appropriation acts.

Due to the recent increase in the numerous categorical federal

[24]Quattlebaum, *op. cit.*, p. 8.

appropriations administered by the U.S. Office of Education, the administration of funds is rapidly becoming the most important function of the office. All of these categorical appropriations contain substantial federal controls and the office administers the controls contained in those acts allocating funds to the Office. Actually at this writing, the acts administered by the Office are controlling to a considerable extent its organizational structure because separate sections of the Office have been set up to administer a number of acts. Therefore, the organization of the Office is being structured into a bureaucracy for administering federal acts rather than for providing leadership and services. If Congress would consolidate its numerous categorical appropriations into general aid, most of the federal controls over educational appropriations could be abolished, and the Office could then emphasize its functions of leadership and service rather than control.

SOME IMPORTANT PROBLEMS AND ISSUES

The problems and issues of federal relationships to education are far from being resolved. As we previously pointed out, general issues of taxation, states' rights, centralization, and other important matters are interwoven with educational issues. Therefore, it is not likely that the issues of federal relationships to education will be speedily settled. A few of the more important problems and issues concerning federal relationships are presented in the following paragraphs.

What Should Be the Role of the Office of Education?

A number of noneducational federal agencies have administered educational programs directly affecting the elementary and secondary educational policies and programs of the states. Sometimes these agencies have bypassed the state education agency and dealt directly with local boards of education. This has frequently caused conflicts between federal and state policies.

It is confusing and frustrating to the states to be compelled to deal with so many different federal departments and agencies on educational matters. Educational authorities generally recommend (1) that when the federal government deals with a state on educational matters it should operate through the central state education agency and not deal directly with local boards of education, and (2) that all federal grants for public education be administered by the U.S. Office of Education. What federal funds now administered by other federal departments and agencies should be transferred to the U.S. Office of Education?

The establishment of a federal Department of Education with a Secretary in the President's cabinet has been advocated for many years by some educational authorities. This issue has come to the front in recent years because of the rapidly increasing federal involvement in education. There is probably more support for this position among the educational leadership of the nation than ever before. It is argued that adequate consideration of educational problems will not be given until education is given cabinet status. It is further argued that the efficiency of administration of federal funds for education would be greatly enhanced by establishing a Department of Education with full responsibility for administering federal funds for education and for coordinating and providing the educational services which can best be provided at the federal level.

The opponents of this policy generally fear that the establishment of a federal Department of Education would lay the base for further increases in federal funds for education and also extend federal control over education. What other arguments for and against the establishment of a federal Department of Education can be advanced?

How Much Federal Control of Public Education Is Desirable?

The issue of federal control of education is a very broad one. Federal control of education has usually, in the public mind, been associated with federal financing of education. However, as pointed out early in this chapter, the federal government under the authority of constitutional limitations on the powers of the states exercises important control over the educational systems of the states. Those controls have no relation to finance.

Furthermore, there seems to be no necessary relationship of federal financing to federal control. In its history, the federal government has made grants for public education with little or no controls. On the other hand, it has made a number of grants with a great amount of federal control. When the Congress desires federal control over a particular appropriation, it writes the desired controls in the act. If it desires to exercise no federal control over a particular appropriation, it writes no controls in the act. There is no evidence of "creeping" federal controls over education. If it can be assumed that Congress represents the people, it can also be assumed that the people from time to time have desired some types of federal controls over education and that at other times they have not. Federal controls over education will be extended or reduced at the will of the people so long as our form of government endures.

What types of federal control are desirable and what types undesirable? What criteria can be used to determine whether a particular educational control should be exercised by the federal government, by the states, or by local school administrative units? Should all federal controls over education be eliminated? Has our time-honored doctrine of state responsibility for education under the Tenth Amendment become obsolete?

Selected References

Allen, Hollis P., *The Federal Government and Education.* New York: McGraw-Hill Book Company, 1950.

American Association of School Administrators, *The Federal Government and Public Schools.* Washington, D.C.: The Association, 1965.

Campbell, Roald F., Luvern L. Cunningham, Roderick F. McPhee, *The Organization and Control of American Schools.* Columbus, Ohio: Charles E. Merrill Books, Inc., 1965, Chap. 2.

Hutchins, Clayton D., Albert R. Munse, and Edna D. Booker, *Federal Funds for Education and Welfare.* Washington, D.C.: U. S. Government Printing Office, 1961.

Johns, Roe L., and Edgar L. Morphet, *Financing the Public Schools.* Englewood Cliffs, N.J.: Prentice-Hall, Inc., 1960, Chap. 13.

Miller, Van, *The Public Administration of American School Systems.* New York: The Macmillan Company, 1965, Chap. 4.

Munger, Frank J., and Richard F. Fenno, *National Policies and Federal Aid to Education.* Syracuse: Syracuse University Press, 1962.

Quattlebaum, Charles A., *Federal Educational Activities and Educational Issues Before Congress.* Washington, D.C.: U.S. Government Printing Office, 1951.

9

State Educational Organization
and Administration

The strategic and significant position of each state in the education of the children and youth of the nation has not been fully understood or appreciated by many American citizens. The people of each state who face their educational responsibilities courageously and make adequate provision for a sound program of education are contributing not only to the development of the citizens of their own state but also to the progress of the nation. To the extent that they are shortsighted or unwise in their provisions for education, they not only handicap the development of children in communities throughout their state but limit national progress.

In all states except Hawaii much of the responsibility for the organization and operation of schools has been delegated to local school systems. For this and other reasons, most people have become accustomed to appraising the strengths and weaknesses of local schools without considering the relationship of the state provisions to the program that can be carried on in those schools. Actually, adequate and farsighted provisions by the state make it possible for good schools to operate in every part of the state, and for an effective program of higher education to be developed for all. The adoption of unsound policies or failure to make adequate provisions in any state inevitably means that the schools, at least in certain parts of the state, will be handicapped.

DEVELOPMENT OF STATE SYSTEMS OF EDUCATION

State systems of education in America have evolved slowly and with considerable unevenness. Everyone concerned with education should be familiar with the major issues, controversies and trends, a few of which are summarized in this section.[1]

The beginnings may be traced to the Massachusetts Acts of 1642 and 1647. The ordinances of 1785 and 1787 represented a major step toward establishing a policy regarding the role of education in the new nation. The adoption of these ordinances and the provisions of the federal Constitution indicated that the American people had begun to recognize that (1) education is a concern of the people of each state and therefore should be a state function, (2) the federal government has an interest in education and feels an obligation to aid education in states and territories, and (3) public funds or resources may not be used to support religious organizations or schools.[2]

By the time the nation was organized, all the original thirteen states had made some legal provisions for education. These varied from authorization of pauper schools in Pennsylvania and low-priced schools in North Carolina to a strong mandate directing the legislature to encourage schools and colleges in Massachusetts. These provisions tended to reflect the early attitudes toward education in the different colonies.[3] Soon, however, both Congress and the people began to expect each new state to make some definite provision for education. Early in the nineteenth century, this idea became accepted as policy. States that adopted new constitutions or made revisions in their original constitutions tended to include stronger and more clear-cut provisions relating to state responsibility for education. Unfortunately, the legislatures of many states failed to make adequate provisions to implement such directives.

The first state board of education was established in New York in 1784 but was given responsibility only for the colleges and academies authorized during colonial days. Not until 1904 was it made responsible for the public schools. It was only after Massachusetts established a state board of education in 1837 that the movement made any significant headway. By 1870, most states had established boards of education but, among the older states, Georgia, Pennsylvania, and Maine did not do so until after the beginning of the present century.[4]

[1]See Ellwood P. Cubberley, *State School Administration* (Boston: Houghton Mifflin Company, 1927), and more recent publications dealing with the subject.

[2]Adapted from Lee M. Thurston and William H. Roe, *State School Administration* (New York: Harper & Row, Publishers, 1957), p. 56.

[3]Cubberley, *op. cit.*, Chaps. 1 and 5.

[4]Ward W. Keesecker, *State Boards of Education and Chief State School Officers,*

Before 1830 only three states—New York, Maryland and Michigan—had provided for the position now known generally as state superintendent or chief state school officer. During the ensuing twenty years, however, another 21 states authorized a position of this type, and by the beginning of the present century all states had provided for a state superintendent. In many, however, the first chief state school officers were designated on an ex officio basis; that is, some state official serving in another capacity was at first given the additional responsibility of serving as superintendent. The movement to provide a chief state school officer in every state was given considerable impetus in the second quarter of the nineteenth century by three developments: (1) the significant contributions of Horace Mann, the first state superintendent of Massachusetts, who was appointed in 1837; (2) the need for some state official to keep track of the school lands and account for the funds derived therefrom in each of the states; and (3) the growing awareness of the need for someone representing the state to collect information, make reports, and answer inquiries regarding common schools that were being organized in most communities.[5]

Recognition of the responsibility of the people of the state for education developed slowly in most states but much more slowly in some than in others. There was no pattern to follow and no design that had been agreed upon. The people in each state had to develop their own plans and policies, but of course in some cases they were greatly influenced by what had happened in leading states such as Massachusetts. It seems evident that state systems of education in this country are still in process of evolution.

STATE PLAN FOR EDUCATION

In some states the constitutional provisions, the laws, and the leadership provided by the people all contribute to the development and operation of a reasonably adequate and efficient program of education that is consistent with the ideals and objectives generally accepted in this country. In others, there are so many handicaps inherent in certain legal provisions that the ideal seems impossible of attainment under present conditions.

The State Constitution

The basic provisions for education are found in the constitution of a state, as pointed out in Chapter 2. Although the phraseology varies considerably, the constitution in most states includes a mandate or direc-

U.S. Office of Education Bulletin No. 12 (Washington, D.C.: U.S. Government Printing Office, 1950), p. 8.
[5]*Ibid.*, p. 25.

tive requiring the legislature to provide an effective system of public instruction, free of tuition charges and equally open to all. Other sections in the constitution incorporate additional policies considered essential in the state.

The people of each state thus determine the basic policies relating to the plan of organization for education within the state. These policies may be sound and forward looking, vague and indefinite, or narrowly restrictive in certain respects. The criterion that should be used in evaluating constitutional provisions relating to education may be stated as follows: *The state constitution should set forth the basic policies for the organization, administration, and support of an adequate program of public education; it should empower and direct the legislature to establish the general plan for carrying out these basic policies; and it should be free from detailed or restrictive provisions that may handicap or prevent the development of a sound program of education.*[6]

The Legal Provisions

The people in each state depend on the legislature to enact laws that provide for the implementation of the basic policies and provisions incorporated in the constitution. The legislature may act wisely or unwisely and may thus facilitate or handicap the development of the educational program.

A serious problem in some states arises from a tendency of the legislature to incorporate restrictive details into the law and to pre-empt a number of functions that should be assigned to the state board of education. The criterion that should be used in evaluating legislative policy may be stated as follows: *The legislature should make a serious effort to implement the constitutional directives by enacting into law the basic framework of the educational system and the important principles and policies to be observed in operating that system; the authority for prescribing minimum standards and the technical requirements consistent with those policies should be delegated to the state board of education.*[7]

The plan of organization for education—that is, the framework within which education operates in any state—is of great importance. Although some good schools and educational institutions can be found in a state with a poor plan of organization, it is likely that even these will be handicapped. Any plan of organization that creates overlapping functions, facilitates the introduction of partisan politics into any phase

[6]Adapted from Edgar L. Morphet, ed., *Building a Better Southern Region Through Education* (Tallahassee, Fla.: Southern States Work-Conference on Educational Problems, 1945), p. 173.

[7]*Ibid.*, p. 174.

of the educational program, discourages meaningful local initiative and responsibility, rewards inefficient organization and operation, or makes desirable organization and coordination difficult, obviously needs to be improved.

The legislature of each state presumably is elected to represent the people. If many of the people are not seriously concerned about the kind and quality of education provided, if powerful pressure groups are more interested in low taxes than in good schools and institutions of higher learning, if people in the wealthy communities are not concerned about education in the less wealthy areas, or if other similar attitudes and conditions exist, the state plan and provisions for education are likely to be defective, at least in certain respects. Moreover, if the educators themselves are sharply divided regarding the purposes of education or means for achieving them, the people and the legislature may tend to become confused and fail to provide for an effective program. Only when a majority of the people are agreed on objectives and the best means for attaining them, is significant and continuing progress in improving the plan and provisions for education to be expected.

The state education agency usually comprises the state board of education, the chief state school officer, and the state department of education. The manner in which this agency is organized, the functions assigned to it, the way it operates, and the educational responsibilities assigned to other agencies all have a rather direct bearing on the potentialities of the educational program.

THE STATE BOARD OF EDUCATION

Since education is concerned with the development of the mind and capabilities of each citizen and is the foundation for many of the beliefs, aspirations, and actions of the people, American citizens have always insisted that the control should be kept in their hands. To that end they have established state and local boards of education that are responsible to them for determining policies, subject to the provisions of the constitution and the laws of the state.

Number and Composition

According to a study by Beach and Will, there were 231 state boards concerned with public schools, institutions of higher learning or other aspects of education in the 48 states in 1954.[8] While some additions

[8]Most of the information for this section is based on Fred F. Beach and Robert F. Will, *The State and Education,* Office of Education, Miscellaneous No. 23 (Washington D.C.: U.S. Government Printing Office, 1955), and on Robert F. Will, *State Education, Structure and Organization,* Office of Education, Miscellaneous No. 46 (Washington, D.C.: U.S. Government Printing Office, 1964).

and reorganizations have been made, the total has not changed materially since that time.

The number of states having state boards of education for the public schools increased from 31 in 1900 to 48 in 1964. (North Dakota has a state board that is primarily responsible for vocational education but has some responsibilities for district organization, certification, special education, and other aspects of the program.) It seems to be only a matter of time until all states will have such a board, because the people generally believe that a policy board at the state level is desirable for at least the public school program. The two states that do not have a state board of education responsible for most or all aspects of the public school program are Illinois and Wisconsin.

There has been a marked tendency toward the elimination of ex officio state boards of education. In 1890, 20 of the 29 state boards of education were of the ex officio type. By 1940 the number had decreased to 8 out of 39, and by 1964 to 2 out of 48. The two states having ex officio boards are Florida and Mississippi. Arizona has predominantly an ex officio board, but three members from designated educational groups are appointed to the board by the governor.

Not only the ex officio board but also ex officio board members have been disappearing. Whereas in 1920, 35 boards had ex officio members, only 17 included such members in 1964. In 8 states the governor was included, in 16 the chief state school officer, and in 6 still other state officials held ex officio membership. In 10 states the board included only one or two ex officio members.

Partly because of the provisions of the Smith-Hughes Act, most states provided for a state board for vocational education shortly after 1920. In a number of states that had already established a state board of education, the two boards were, in effect, merged because the membership was identical. Thus, the state board of education also served as the state board for vocational education. In 1945, thirteen states had boards for vocational education that included at least some members who were not on the state board of education. By 1964, only four states had a separate or independent board for vocational education: Colorado, Illinois, Massachusetts, and Wisconsin. It will be noted that two of these (Illinois and Wisconsin) had no state board of education. The state board of education or vocational education also serves as the state board for vocational rehabilitation in all states except Colorado, Massachusetts, New Jersey, Pennsylvania, and South Carolina, but in some of these states there is an overlapping of membership.

State residential schools for the blind and deaf are under the state board of education in almost half the states, under some noneducational state agency in a few, and have their own governing board or boards in the remainder of the states that have such schools. In four states (Florida, Idaho, Montana, and New York) the state colleges and universities come under the state board of education. In a few others the state colleges but not the state university are under the state board. Various other combinations are found in the remaining states.

Selection of Members

When the number of ex officio boards began to decrease some years ago, appointment by the governor became the favored method of selecting members for the state board of education. During the past fifteen years a few states have changed to popular election of state board members or to selection in some other manner than appointment by the governor. In 1964 the governor appointed at least a majority of the members of the board in 32 of the 48 states having state boards of education. In 20 he appointed all members; in the other 12 there are some ex officio members. In New York the state board is elected by the legislature; in Wyoming it is appointed by the elected chief state school officer with the approval of the governor; in Iowa and Washington (except for one ex officio member) it is elected by local school board members or their delegates; in South Carolina one member is selected from each judicial circuit in the state (with rotation required among counties in the circuit) by the legislative delegation from that circuit; and in nine states—Colorado, Louisiana, Michigan, Nebraska, Nevada (two members appointed by the elected members), Ohio, Texas, New Mexico, and Utah—the members are elected by vote of the people. In Colorado, Louisiana, Michigan, New Mexico, and Texas, they are elected on a party ballot.

In most states, except in the case of ex officio members, the board members are elected or appointed from congressional judicial, or other residence areas. In many states the board members may not be employed by schools or educational institutions; in others, such as Arizona and Indiana, at least a certain percentage must be educators. In a few, representation from certain occupations is required.

Size and Term

The 48 state boards for public schools ranged in 1964 from 3 ex officio members in Mississippi to 21 popularly elected members in Texas and 23 in Ohio. The range in size in most states was from seven to thirteen members. Only eight states had fewer than seven members and only four more than thirteen.

The length of term for appointment or election of state board members ranged from four years or less in fourteen states, to thirteen years in New York. There has been a distinct tendency to increase the length of term in many states, partly because of the desire to provide for a term of sufficient length to prevent a governor from appointing a majority of the members—except in case of resignation or death—during his first term of office, and partly because a term of only three or four years is considered by many to be too short. The tendency has been to increase the length of term to seven or nine years and to provide for overlapping terms so as to assure some continuity in service of experienced persons.

Responsibilities

In some states the differences between the functions of the chief state school officer and those of the state board of education have not been made clear. In most cases an attempt has been made to designate the state board as the body responsible for policies and regulations, and the state superintendent as executive officer of the board. Where the state superintendent is appointed by the state board such a differentiation seems to work out satisfactorily. In most states where the state superintendent is responsible to the people because he is elected by popular vote, there have been, and probably will continue to be, conflicts and uncertainties from time to time.

It is generally recognized that the state board of education should have the legal responsibility for the general supervision, control, and management of all aspects of at least the public school program of the state. However the board would not only be ill advised but would be inviting difficulties for itself and the educational program if it did not expect the chief state school officer and his staff to prepare reports and make recommendations for its consideration in arriving at decisions regarding policies and standards. The major functions of a state board of education may be listed as follows:

1. to appoint and fix the compensation of a competent chief state school officer who should serve as its secretary and executive officer;
2. to determine areas of service, establish qualifications, and appoint the necessary personnel for the state department of education;
3. to adopt a budget for the operation of the state education agency;
4. to authorize needed studies and, with the assistance of appropriate committees and consultants, to develop and submit to the governor and legislature proposals for improving the organization, administration, financing, and other aspects of education in the state;
5. to adopt policies and minimum standards for the administration and supervision of the state educational enterprise;
6. to approve jointly with other appropriate state agencies, policies, regulations, and standards in those areas that involve responsibilities of these boards and agencies that relate to education;
7. to represent the state in determining policies on all matters per-

taining to education that involve relationships with the federal government; and

8. when authorized to do so, to adopt policies for the operation of institutions of higher learning and other educational institutions operated by the state or to approve major policies recommended by the board or boards of control for such institutions.

THE CHIEF STATE SCHOOL OFFICER

Potentially the most important educational position in any state is that of a chief state school officer. However, in some states this position has been one of relatively minor significance as contrasted with those occupied by superintendents of some of the larger school districts or presidents of state institutions of higher learning.

Although a few states, particularly in the New England area, adopted from the beginning the concept that the chief state school officer should be selected by and responsible to a state board of education, many states for one reason or another assumed that he should be elected by popular vote, appointed by the governor, or selected in some other manner. Several states, beginning with Iowa in 1846, included a constitutional provision requiring the chief state school officer to be elected. Although Iowa eliminated this requirement several years ago, many other states have not been able to effect such a change.

In 1896 there were only three states in which the chief school officer was appointed by the state board of education. In 31 states he was elected by popular vote, in most cases on a partisan political ballot along with the other officials. In nine states the governor appointed the state superintendent and in three he was appointed by the general assembly. A few still had no regular chief state school officer. Since that time many significant changes have occurred.

In 1964, there were 24 states in which the chief state school officer was appointed by the state board of education, 5 in which he was appointed by the governor, and the number in which he was elected by popular vote had decreased to 21. The states in which he is appointed by the governor are: Alaska, New Jersey, Pennsylvania, Tennessee, and Virginia. It is interesting that in sixteen states the chief school officer serves ex officio as a member, and in some states as chairman, of the state board of education. This seems to place him in an anomalous position, since as a superintendent he would recommend policies and standards to the board, as a board member he would vote on them, and again as a superintendent he would implement those that are approved.

These trends are shown in the following table.[9]

[9] Adapted from Beach and Will, *op. cit.*, Table 17, p. 30; and Will, *op. cit.*, p. 26.

Years	No Chief State School Officer	Appointed by General Assembly	Appointed by Governor	Popular Election	Appointed by State Board of Education
1896	2	3	9	31	3
1909	1	1	9	33	4
1930	–	–	7	33	8
1950	–	–	6	29	13
1964	–	–	5	21	24

Two of the factors that have retarded the development of the position of chief state school officer in several states have been the low compensation provided and failure to recognize that special qualifications are needed. Generally, as states have changed from popular election to appointment by the state board, salaries have been improved and higher qualifications have been recognized as necessary. Most people in some states now recognize that the person selected for the position as chief state school officer should be the most competent educator who can be found and that the compensation must be adequate to attract such a person.

The duties and responsibilities of the chief state school officer vary considerably from state to state. In a number of states that provide for popular election the responsibilities are limited and the position carries comparatively little prestige. In the more progressive states they usually include the following:

1. to serve as secretary and executive officer of the state board of education;
2. to serve as executive officer of any board or council that may be established to facilitate coordination of all aspects of the educational program;
3. to select competent personnel for and serve as the administrative head and professional leader of the state department of education to the end that it will contribute maximally to the improvement of education;
4. to arrange for studies and organize committees and task forces as deemed necessary to identify problems and to recommend plans and provisions for effecting improvements in education;
5. to recommend to the state board of education needed policies, standards, and regulations relating to public education in the state;
6. to recommend improvements in educational legislation and in provisions for financing the educational program;
7. to explain and interpret the school laws of the state and the regulations of the state board of education;
8. to decide impartially controversies and disputes involving the administration of the public school system;

9. to submit frequent reports to the public and periodic reports to the state board, to the governor, and to the legislature giving information about the accomplishments, conditions, and needs of the schools.

THE STATE DEPARTMENT OF EDUCATION

The term "state department of education," as used here, includes the chief state school officer and his staff, authorized by and functioning in accordance with provisions of law and policies adopted by the state board of education. The duties and responsibilities of all state departments of education have increased greatly during the past quarter of a century. For many years these duties were carried out by the state superintendent with the assistance of a secretary or two. In 1900, there were only 177 professional and other staff members in all state departments of education. This number increased to 3,718 in 1940,[10] to approximately 15,000 by 1955, and has more than doubled since that time.

Increases in the number of staff members have been associated with the major stages in the development of state departments of education. At first, these departments were chiefly concerned with accounting and reporting functions. A second stage of development placed considerable emphasis on inspection. A more recent stage has placed emphasis on leadership in planning and effecting improvements. As a result of these changes, increasing emphasis has been placed on the importance of competent professional personnel who work with educators in the field, organize conferences, plan studies, lead in facilitating improvements in the state educational program as well as in local programs, and work effectively with the governor, the legislature, and representatives of other state and federal agencies.

In a study of state departments of education, Beach identified three major types of functions, which he classified as leadership, regulatory, and operational responsibilities.[11] In some states considerable emphasis has been given to regulatory functions and limited attention to leadership. In other states the reverse has been true.

The leadership functions include planning, research, advising and consulting, coordinating, and public relations. The regulatory functions are designed to help protect the welfare of children and youth of the state, guarantee prudential procedures in the use of educational funds, assure efficiency in the management of the educational enterprise, and

[10]Fred F. Beach and Andrew H. Gibbs, *Personnel of State Departments of Education*, Office of Education, Miscellaneous No. 16 (Washington, D.C.: U.S. Government Printing Office, 1952), p. 6.

[11]Fred F. Beach, *The Functions of State Departments of Education*, Office of Education, Miscellaneous No. 12 (Washington, D.C.: U.S. Government Printing Office, 1950), pp. 3–17.

provide a framework and a basic minimum for the instructional program in order to assure an educated citizenry.

There are a number of states in which state departments of education and state boards of education have some operational functions assigned by the legislature. These include responsibilities for certain schools that are to provide instruction on the elementary, high school, or college level; area vocational schools; classes in citizenship, adult education, and trades; cultural and educational institutions or programs of service directed to the public at large; and programs of service to individuals including especially vocational rehabilitation, teacher placement, and teacher retirement services. Questions have been raised during recent years by many authorities regarding the desirability of assigning such operational functions to state departments of education.

The need for greater emphasis on leadership functions in many state departments of education is evident to all who study state educational problems. If this need is to be met satisfactorily, it seems apparent that (1) the chief state school officer who administers the department should be selected because of his ability to provide professional leadership in improving the state program of education, (2) the professional members of the department staff should be carefully selected on a basis which will assure that they are not only leaders in their respective fields of education but can work effectively with others in studying and solving educational problems, (3) the department should be so organized and administered that effective functioning is facilitated, and (4) the people and the legislature should insist on and support the kind of services that can be provided through competent leadership in the state department of education.

STATE RESPONSIBILITIES AND RELATIONS

Various authorities have directed attention to such basic concepts as the following: education is in the public domain; it is "political" in a broad sense, because it is operated by an agency of the formal political government; its nature and functioning are affected by the social climate in which it operates; as a formal, specialized structure and organization, education is a subsystem of the broader process of socialization in the nation.[12]

Thus, in order to understand why a state system of education, or its state agency for education, is organized and operated in certain

[12]See, for example, J. K. Galbraith, *The Affluent Society* (Boston: Houghton Mifflin Company, 1958), p. 355; and Howard Dean, "The Political Setting of American Education," in *The Social Sciences View School Administration* (Englewood Cliffs, N.J.: Prentice-Hall, Inc., 1965), pp. 213–217.

ways, it is necessary to know the beliefs and values of the people and
the forces that have been operating in the state as well as those in the
national setting. It is not surprising, therefore, to find some marked
differences, as well as a number of similarities, among the states. In this
section, attention is directed to some of the major problems, functions,
and kinds of relations that are encountered to a greater or lesser extent
in all states.

Relation of Education to Other State and Federal Agencies

STATE AGENCIES.   In a number of states, responsibilities for certain
functions or services involving or related to the public schools have been
assigned to agencies other than the state board or department of education. These include not only the responsibilities for vocational education or junior colleges, which in some cases are assigned to separate
boards, but also, in some states, responsibilities for certain aspects of
finance, school plant construction, safety education, health education,
or other aspects of the educational program. Some of these assignments
have been made capriciously and unwisely. In such cases, local school
officials have often become involved in red tape and delay, because they
were required to attempt to work with a variety of state agencies whose
services were not satisfactorily coordinated.

There are undoubtedly certain services for schools that should be
rendered by agencies other than the state department of education. For
example, there is no need for the department to employ a sanitary en-
gineer if this service is available through the state board of health, or to
check on all aspects of fire safety for school buildings if the state fire
marshal has personnel who render this service. On the other hand,
another state agency that might have responsibility for school buildings,
for safety education, for school finance, or for other aspects of public
education, would have to add educational personnel to its staff, or it
might seriously handicap the educational program.

The following criteria are generally recognized as desirable for
guidance in planning state services and developing coordination:

1. Services primarily educational in nature should be provided by
    the state department of education, and those chiefly noneduca-
    tional should be provided by other state agencies.
2. The state education agency or some other appropriate educa-
    tional agency established by the state should be charged with
    the responsibility of coordinating the entire state program of
    education. It should work in close cooperation with other
    agencies of state government in planning services in areas of
    joint concern.

3. When two state agencies are concerned with policy matters involving the schools, any minimum standards or regulations that are found to be necessary should be jointly approved and adopted by both agencies. For example, in matters involving school health the standards should be jointly approved by the state board of education and the state board of health.

4. The state department of education should serve as a coordinating agency and clearing house for matters involving contacts with or applications from local school systems to other state or federal agencies. For example, in the school plant field, the state department of education should be able to save local school systems much confusion and delay if it has the responsibility for obtaining approval of plans by the state fire marshal, the state health department, and any other state agency that is responsible for approving any aspect of the plant program.[13]

FEDERAL AGENCIES.   Many agencies of the federal government have been concerned with one or another aspect of education for some years (see Chapter 8). Problems of federal-state-local relations have been encountered from time to time. As a result of recent legislation and decisions regarding new programs, other kinds of problems have developed. Some of these will be difficult to resolve satisfactorily. Many people are seriously concerned that an increasing number of important decisions regarding education may be made at the federal level during coming years. Some realignment is probably inevitable, but this does not mean that the concept of state responsibility for education is outdated. What it does mean is that *all states must face up to their responsibilities and prepare promptly to meet them realistically.* Patterns and practices that have been complacently followed in the past in many states will not be adequate to meet future needs. The people in every state will need to re-evaluate their system as a basis for developing better ways of meeting their responsibilities for education in the future. Such improvements will not only provide needed safeguards against inappropriate federal encroachments but will establish a basis for constructive cooperation that should assure more adequate programs of education for all.

State Board Policies and Standards

Since the legislature should not attempt to prescribe by law all details of policies and standards that may be needed for education, an important question that arises is: How much responsibility or discretion should be delegated to the state board of education? A generally recog-

[13]Adapted from National Council of Chief State School Officers, *The State Department of Education* (Washington, D.C.: 1952), pp. 25–26; and Beach, *op. cit.,* pp. 7–8.

nized principle of law provides that *limits or boundaries should be established for any discretionary authority that is granted.* Thus the legislature should prescribe the basic policy and authorize the development of more specific policies, standards, or regulations by an appropriate administrative agency, such as the state board of education.

Some minimum standards have been found necessary in every state as a means of helping to assure adequate educational opportunities. However, states have learned by experience that the establishment of minimum standards alone will not solve the problem. Those standards cannot substitute for good local planning or leadership, nor can they result in a satisfactory program of education unless the state plan ensures that sufficient funds will be available to finance the program.

There are several criteria relating to standards and regulations that have generally been accepted by authorities. Among the most important are the following:

1. Although the major responsibility of the state should be to provide adequate leadership and service, it should, when necessary, establish those minimum standards and only those that are universally applicable, are designed primarily to assure minimum educational opportunities for all children and youth, and that in no way limit the freedom of the local school system to go beyond the established standards.
2. In making decisions regarding the desirability of minimum standards or other controls, preference should be given to retaining control locally, particularly for those elements concerning which there is no certainty that central authority will provide the best long-term results.
3. The advantages of close popular control over local educational programs should be protected and promoted by avoiding inhibiting controls over boards of education, local school programs, or school funds by noneducational authorities.[14]

State Leadership and Coordination

Among the most important functions of state leadership are planning and coordination. Planning, to be effective, must be based on carefully developed studies, research, and bona fide cooperation in determining purposes and objectives and agreeing upon steps to be used in attaining them. Improvements in the state program of education cannot safely be left to chance developments. Failure to formulate sound

[14]Adapted from National Education Association, Committee on Tax Education and School Finance, *Guides to the Development of State School Finance Programs* (Washington, D.C.: The Association, 1949), pp. 5–10.

plans and proposals for improving the program may result in unfortunate changes sponsored by groups with vested interests, perpetuation of inefficiencies that handicap the entire program, or even failure to obtain the support of the people and the legislature in providing funds to meet growing school needs. Soundly developed and well-formulated plans should, on the other hand, result in constantly improving programs that are strongly supported by the people because they believe in the value of what is being accomplished.

Few people realize the amount and extent of coordination needed in any state if education is to be developed satisfactorily. In states where there is one state board for public schools, another board for vocational education, and separate boards for each of the institutions of higher learning, the problem of coordinating all aspects of education presents serious difficulties. However, there has also been some concern about the possibility of establishing a board that would have so many functions and responsibilities for different aspects of education that it would not be able to operate effectively.

There must also be coordination and cooperation within the state department. No member of the staff can operate satisfactorily without relating his work to what others are doing. No bureau or division can function in isolation. Most educational problems are interrelated. Finance is not merely a matter of money; it also involves the provision of necessary services and facilities. Curriculum improvement requires consideration not only of subject matter but also of students and their needs and the relationship of each phase of learning to other phases.

In every state there are a number of agencies and organizations that are interested in, concerned with, or have responsibilities for certain aspects of education. If each operates in isolation and without reference to what others are doing, the result can only be confusion, inefficiency, and dissatisfaction. Many hold that the state education agency should be in a position to provide needed coordination in order to assure, insofar as possible, that there is agreement on common purposes and that no agency or organization in education promotes its own special interests and objectives without reference to other phases of the program.

The need for coordination in research and planning should be obvious. Without coordination, there is likely to be much duplication of effort and failure to give proper attention to matters of considerable importance. Competition and rivalry may be disastrous when there is no effective coordination.

Many services provided by the federal government are not coordinated and result in some confusion in local school systems unless these groups agree upon a plan and leadership to provide needed coordination. In most situations the state education agency is necessarily involved in developing plans for such coordination.

The Provisions for Education

State education agencies have many important responsibilities to meet and decisions to make with reference to the provisions for education. Some of the most important are considered briefly below.

THE EDUCATIONAL PROGRAM.   Adequate attention must be given to the scope of the program (whether nursery schools, kindergartens, junior colleges, adult education and so on are to be included or required); the length of the school year; requirements for attendance, promotion and graduation; the curriculum, courses of study, textbooks and other instructional materials including libraries; standards and accreditation for schools; measurement of achievement and progress, and other similar matters.

PREPARATION AND CERTIFICATION OF PROFESSIONAL STAFF.   Most states prescribe requirements for the preparation of teachers and other staff members. Some approve programs or institutions whose graduates may be recommended for certification. All states have established requirements for certification but certain large cities in a few states are authorized to assume this responsibility for their own personnel.

VOCATIONAL EDUCATION.   Each state develops, and revises from time to time, plans including standards for vocational education, personnel and programs. Some states administer area vocational schools and all provide programs of vocational rehabilitation. In a number of states professional personnel in other aspects of education have been little concerned with the vocational program and vocational people have given little attention to other aspects of the educational program. The need for better cooperation and coordination seems to require further consideration.

JUNIOR COLLEGES.   With two or three notable exceptions, few states have done much about planning for junior colleges until the last few years. In some states, junior colleges have been developed as a part of the university system, and they give little attention to vocational technical or other terminal programs. In a few, a separate board has been established; in others, junior colleges come under the supervision of the state board of education and are a part of the public school system. Much further attention will need to be given to this aspect of education in the future.

HOUSING AND TRANSPORTATION.   Housing and transportation traditionally have been considered primarily matters of local concern. In terms of operation and maintenance, they still are in most states. However, many developments have led to an increasing recognition of the need for states not only to establish minimum standards for sites, buildings, and buses, but to assist in planning and financing housing and transportation programs as a means of helping to ensure more effective education. Few states, however, have developed a realistic state-local-partnership procedure for dealing with developments in this area.

FINANCE AND BUSINESS ADMINISTRATION. All states have made considerable progress toward assuring uniformity in the minimum essentials of record keeping, accounting and reporting as a means of obtaining pertinent and reasonably comparable information and of safeguarding and encouraging efficiency in the use of school funds. Most states have recognized that some districts cannot provide satisfactory schools on the basis of local funds alone, but few have developed plans of financial support that make possible equality of opportunity or adequate programs. Some seem to be more concerned with using financial support as a means of controlling the program or restricting local initiative than of facilitating the attainment of objectives with which most people seem to agree. While much attention of state department staff members has been given to both major and minor problems in this area, the efforts of economy-minded pressure groups or inept or misguided efforts of other kinds have left some of the major issues unresolved in a number of states.

PREPARING FOR THE FUTURE

The state agencies for education, as organized and operated in many states, are not prepared to contribute significantly to the improvements that must be made in education during the next few years. Unfortunately some groups—even some educators—have not been making any obvious effort to cooperate in effecting needed changes in these agencies. If present trends continue, in some states there may soon be only a weak agency concerned primarily with assuring compliance with the requirements of law and regulations and promoting efficiency in conducting the required program. Under such conditions, federal agencies or officials might conceivably consider it their responsibility (as some have already advocated privately) to find better ways of working with local school systems in order to "help them avoid the dangers of state control." As a means of assuring that all states are prepared to meet their constitutional responsibility for education, everyone should be concerned with plans and proposals for developing a dynamic and effective state agency for education in every state.

Fortunately, there have been some encouraging and challenging developments in certain areas during the past few years. Some of the implications of the studies in New York, for example, are being seriously explored and a number of changes are being made not only in the climate for innovation but in the organization and in operating procedures. Many states are beginning to recognize that they can make more progress in resolving certain problems by cooperation than would be possible by working in isolation. For example, five states in the Southwest have learned much, through a cooperative project, about procedures for improving programs in small isolated schools; eight states in the Rocky Mountain area are attempting to envision changes in society that will have implications for education and to plan reorganizations designed to meet the needs; twenty states across the country are cooperating in a plan to improve state education department personnel; several others are attempting to find more effective ways of locating and making available important educational information for the use of personnel in each state. These and other proposals being considered suggest that many state education agencies may be preparing for some of the most significant changes that have been made since they were first established.

Purposes, Plans, and Policies

One of the problems in most states arises from the fact that many people who give lip service to the commonly accepted purposes of public education apparently have reservations about some of them. Moreover there are sharp differences of opinion as to how they can best be achieved. Such differences complicate the problem of developing a soundly conceived state agency for education and assuring that it is properly organized and assigned an appropriate role. They may make it impossible for the agency to provide the leadership required to redefine or reinterpret purposes, conduct needed studies, establish goals and develop policies and procedures for attaining them. A primary problem in many states, therefore, is to get agreement on the need for an effective state agency for education, get it established on a sound basis and define its functions realistically in terms of emerging needs.

There have been comparatively few studies of state boards of education, chief state school officers, state departments of education, or of state operations in the field of education.[15] In view of the potentially significant role of the state in shaping educational policy, in influencing in many ways the development of education and in effecting the course of federal-state-local relations in education in this country, it is apparent that more fundamental and searching studies are needed.

Some recent studies have focused attention on state organization

[15]For example, *Research Studies in Education, 1953–63* (Bloomington, Ind.: Phi Delta Kappa, Inc., 1965), pp. 55–57, which lists doctoral dissertations, reports, and field studies for the eleven years, included fewer than a dozen studies, most of which are restricted to some aspect in a single state.

for educational change. Proposals have been made for major reorganization and new roles for the state education agencies to involve them more directly and aggressively in research development and dissemination of new instructional practices. Brickell's study resulted in some important observations concerning the dynamics of instructional change in the elementary and secondary schools of New York.[16] He proposed that (1) there should be established in the state education agency a semiautonomous research service to deal separately with program design and evaluation; and (2) regional or area school development units should be created to disseminate new practices through demonstrations, inservice education, and other ways. The California study focused on the needs that can be met effectively by a state education agency.[17] The conclusions included the following: (1) there is need for a formal process to provide plans for educational development within the state; (2) the state board of education appears to be the logical agency to lead in such developmental planning; (3) the state department of education should make extensive use of *ad hoc* project teams for research development and evaluation activities and should provide a bureau of educational reference to serve the local and intermediate units.

Four political scientists undertook studies of the dynamics of educational policy making at the state level in the northeastern states.[18] They were concerned with the role of educators in initiating and formulating public school policy in eight northeastern states, especially in New York. This study brought out clearly the importance of leadership from the ranks of professional schoolmen and state department personnel, as well as of other key personnel, in helping to effect changes in state educational policy. Three other political scientists studied the processes of arriving at decisions affecting public schools in three midwestern states.[19] They noted that much of the state politics in those states has been concerned with public schools, and that ". . . the ways in which the state is involved in education vary and so do the political processes." Missouri was classified as a state with "low-pressure politics," Illinois as a state with a structural plan for obtaining consensus, and Michigan as a state characterized by lack of consensus.

The state education agency, like any other similar agency, tends to continue doing what it was established to do, holding itself relatively

[16]H. M. Brickell, *Organizing New York State for Educational Change* (Albany: New York State Department of Education, Dec. 1961).

[17]Arthur D. Little Co., Inc., *The Emerging Requirements for Effective Leadership for California Education* (Sacramento: California State Department of Education, Nov. 1964).

[18]Stephen K. Bailey, Richard T. Frost, Robert C. Wood, and Paul E. Marsh, *Schoolmen and Politics: A Study of State Aid to Education in the Northeast* (Syracuse, N.Y.: Syracuse University Press, 1962).

[19]Nicholas A. Masters, Robert A. Salisbury, and Thomas H. Eliot, *State Politics and the Public Schools* (New York: Alfred A. Knopf, Inc., 1964), Chaps. 2–4.

stable and resisting attempts at restructuring. Brickell noted that in New York the climate for educational change had been improved by recent state department interest in instructional innovation, but that this spirit represented by the top echelon officials apparently had not permeated the department.[20] Thus, sufficient consensus seems to have developed, or the kind of leadership has begun to emerge in some states, that a climate somewhat favorable to innovation is beginning to be evident. But this climate needs to be even more favorable, and to be developed in all states if the education agency is to become effective in adapting to changed conditions and needs and is to provide the leadership required to encourage rational acceptance of desirable innovations. To become effective, the state agency will need to have the necessary assistance and support to (1) redefine its role and functions and reorganize accordingly, (2) develop a plan for determining the implications for education of major changes, (3) identify promising innovations and seek to create conditions favorable for their adoption, and (4) develop plans for designing needed innovations, evaluating them and disseminating the most promising primarily through demonstration. If this is to be done satisfactorily a favorable and relatively threat-free climate must be created by developing a staff that is interested and has the competency to utilize change as a basis for effecting improvements, and by reducing or eliminating the emphasis on compliance with customary requirements that might discourage innovation.

Research

Few state departments of education have had the personnel or resources to undertake significant research in the past. Assembling and analyzing pertinent data, which has been done reasonably well in a number of states, is important to determine trends, to make projections and, in some cases, to identify certain kinds of problems. However, carefully planned research is basic for appraisal of many developments and for the discovery of problems for further study. The development of long-range goals and plans for achieving them will be facilitated by utilizing appropriate data and the findings from related research studies as bases for the carefully considered value judgments that must be made.

There is serious doubt as to whether state departments of education should undertake basic research, since this can be done better and more appropriately by universities under the Cooperative Research Program of the U.S. Office of Education, or with funds from other sources, or by independent research agencies. State departments, however, should be interested in encouraging such research and seeking to identify practical implications.

The state department of education should have a research, or a

[20]Adapted from Brickell, *op. cit.*, p. 19, 37–38.

research and reference agency, but Brickell and some other authorities believe this agency should have a semiautonomous status. It should not become involved in the process of obtaining or analyzing routine information. Rather, it should be concerned with the development of a state-wide research plan and program, with facilitating coordination and cooperation, and with undertaking certain projects on its own initiative. Most of these projects might well be concerned in one way or another with innovations designed to effect improvements in the educational program or organization. The permanent staff should probably be small, but funds should be available for extensive use of consultants and for assisting other agencies to plan and conduct special studies as needed.

The research functions of the state department of education should probably include the following: (1) helping to create a favorable climate not only for research but for utilizing the findings of research, (2) devising ways of identifying major problems and issues concerning which research is especially needed, (3) stimulating ideas for research and the development of research projects, (4) helping to coordinate the research efforts in the state and to focus attention from time to time on certain problems that need special study, (5) assisting, or locating qualified consultants who can assist with research design, (6) developing, organizing, and keeping up-to-date, perhaps in cooperation with other states and agencies, a "library" of research findings in areas that would be of interest and value in the state, (7) developing a plan for assuring that the research findings in appropriate areas are summarized, synthesized, and interpreted in such a way that they will be of maximum benefit to educational leaders in the state who should utilize them.

Organizing and Staffing

There is little likelihood that a department of education staff that provides effective leadership in improving education will be found in a state in which the members of the state board of education owe their primary allegiance to political parties or powerful pressure groups, the state superintendent is primarily a "politician" or a manipulator, the people are complacent about inequities and inadequacies, or other similar conditions prevail. In such states, leading lay citizens and educators will need to join forces to convince legislators that a drastic but soundly conceived reorganization is essential. Even the state education agencies that have functioned well in the past will probably need to re-evaluate and revise their policies and operating procedures within the next few years as a basis for continuing to provide effective guidance and leadership.

When a sound plan has been developed to ensure, insofar as possible, the selection of competent members of the board of education who are dedicated to the improvement of education and the appointment of a chief state school officer who is the most competent educational leader available, criteria such as the following should be observed in defining the functions and operating procedures of the state department: (1) the members selected for the staff should not only be highly qualified in their respective areas, but should recognize that all aspects of education are interrelated; (2) the organization should, in itself, facilitate communication and cooperation within the department and within the field, and discourage unnecessary formality and red tape; (3) ways should be found to utilize the human resources of the state to study and solve the varied problems of education (this means teamwork and cooperation should replace rivalry and petty struggles for power, and that the department staff members will generally serve as leaders and facilitators rather than as problem solvers or builders of bureaucratic power structures requiring ever enlarging staffs); (4) sufficient funds will be made available not only to provide adequate salaries for staff members but also to obtain the services of consultants from universities, local school systems and other agencies as needed, and to provide for the operation of appropriate committees or task forces; (5) the fact that social scientists who are interested in education can make important contributions should be recognized and provision made for utilizing their services; (6) compacts or agreements probably should be made with one or more state education agencies in nearby or appropriate states to provide for cooperative studies and other projects from which each state should benefit.

SOME IMPORTANT PROBLEMS AND ISSUES

A few of the problems and issues in the area of state educational organization and administration are discussed briefly on the following pages. What others are important? Why?

What Should Be the State Organization for Education?

Although some differences in organization among the states should be expected, the question as to which of the existing differences are necessary and defensible should have careful consideration. One important difference involves the question as to whether there should be one state board for all aspects of education, or several boards.

Some of the arguments that have been advanced in favor of separate boards for different aspects of education are as follows: (1) each major aspect is sufficiently important that it should be controlled or directed by a board that is chiefly concerned with and responsible for its development; (2) the educational program is so complex that no one board could be expected to keep up with and do justice to all developments; (3) the problems of coordination involving vocational and general education, or higher and public school education, are not as serious as some people maintain and can be resolved by voluntary cooperation which is more wholesome than forced coordination.

In some states that have a board for each institution of higher learning, a board for the public schools and, in effect, separate boards for vocational education and for vocational rehabilitation (even though the membership may be the same or have some overlapping), there seems to have been far more competition than cooperation. Rivalry for difficult-to-obtain state funds can have unfortunate consequences for one or more state institutions or for certain aspects of the public school program. All aspects of education are interrelated in many ways, and serious imbalance is likely to retard the development of the state.

Many people have proposed that an advisory board or council should be established to facilitate coordination in education within the state and in dealing with agencies of the federal government. Some think this should become a policy board on financial affairs, planning and other similar matters of concern to all aspects of education. California, which has one state board responsible for the public school program, another for the state colleges, and a third (board of regents) for the several campuses of the university, established a few years ago a Coordinating Council for Higher Education, that has made a number of important contributions in that area.

There seems to be some trend toward establishing a board for higher education or, at least, for state colleges, to replace separate boards still found in a number of states. Is this desirable? How and why are traditions or special interest groups likely to retard the development of an improved plan? What seems to be the best plan of state organization for education?

How Should the State Board of Education Be Selected?

A state board of education may be comprised of competent persons who devote their best efforts to the development of a program designed to meet the educational needs of the people of the state. On the other hand, it may include members who are primarily interested in keeping down expenses, are more concerned with partisan political affairs than with public education, who hold certain beliefs and want to use their position on the board primarily to promote these ideas, or who in other respects are not "good" board members.

Apparently, the American people generally believe in a lay state board of education. Only a few states provide specifically for professional educators to serve on the state board. Among the professions, the idea of a lay board seems to be restricted largely to education. Is a lay board in the field of education desirable? If so, why? Should any of the members be required to be educators?

The method of selecting the members of the state board of education has caused much concern in a number of states. A major controversy has arisen in several states during recent years as to whether the state board of education should be elected by the people, appointed by the governor, or selected in some other manner. The chief points presented in favor of appointment by the governor include the following: (1) the governor should be in a position to select and appoint the best qualified people in the state; (2) by providing for appointment by the governor, a step is taken that will assure his continued interest in education; (3) by providing for overlapping terms of eight or nine years, there is assurance that no governor will control the board by appointing a majority of the members during his first term.

Election by popular vote is cumbersome, expensive, and tends to lengthen a ballot that is already long. There is no assurance that the best-qualified people in the state will risk the hazards or be willing to meet the expense involved in a statewide election for a position that normally provides no salary. Under such conditions there is always the possibility that certain powerful vested-interest groups, not primarily interested in education, will finance the campaign for people they select with the expectation that these people would at least be favorable to their points of view. On the other hand, some people who favor popular election say that a governor might appoint people to the board who would tend to favor his point of view, or might otherwise be able to control many of the decisions of an appointive board. Some years ago the Council of Chief State School Officers proposed that:

> In each state there should be a non-partisan, lay state board of education composed of seven to twelve able citizens broadly representative of the general public and unselfishly interested in public education, elected by the people in a manner prescribed by law. The members of this board should serve for long overlapping terms without pay.[21]

Unfortunately differences of opinion regarding the best method of selecting the members of the state board of education in some states have tended to involve other issues, especially the matter of how to select the chief state school officer. Additional states would probably have changed from the elective to the appointive superintendent if the problem of how to select members of the state board could have been

---

[21]National Council of Chief State School Officers, *Our System of Education* (Washington, D.C.: The Council, 1950), p. 20.

satisfactorily resolved. A basic question is: What plan will be most likely to ensure that all persons selected to serve on the state board of education will be highly competent and qualified to serve the best interests of education and of the state?

An increasing number of people have apparently reached the conclusion that both appointment by the governor and election by the people present some hazards unless safeguards are provided. In most states where the governor appoints members of the state board, concurrence by the legislature or by one house of the legislature is required. Most authorities now favor a nine- to eleven-member board whose members serve for eight- or nine-year overlapping terms. Several have proposed that regardless of the method of selection, there should be a small nominating committee established by law (somewhat as is done in North Dakota) to identify persons who should be considered for board membership. This committee might be comprised of one or two representatives from such groups as the state bar association, the school board members association, the state chamber of commerce, the AFL-CIO, the education associations, or others. If the appointments are to be made by the governor, three nominations might be made for each vacancy and he would be required to appoint one of the three. If the election is to be by popular vote, only one name would be proposed (with the consent of the nominee) for each vacancy. This name would go on the ballot, but another name or names could be added by petition. What are the advantages and disadvantages of each of the plans discussed above?

The board is usually expected to be representative of the state and residence areas are sometimes prescribed, but when members are elected, the election must usually be by statewide vote. What would be the disadvantages, if any, of election by vote of the people of the district or area in which a candidate resides? What should be the best plan and procedure for selecting members of the state board of education? Why?

How Should the Chief State School Officer Be Chosen?

Election by popular vote, which early became established as the procedure for selecting the chief state school officer in a majority of the states, has not been very satisfactory from the point of view of most educators. In fact, the Council of Chief State School Officers approved the following policy some years ago:

> It is desirable that the board elect a chief state school officer on a nonpartisan basis and determine his compensation and his term of office. He should serve as executive officer of the board and head of the state department of education.[22]

[22]*Idem.*

Appointment by the governor has usually not been considered satisfactory by educational leaders, partly because the chief state school officer then becomes directly responsible to the governor, rather than to the state board for educational policy. However, some political scientists favor appointment by the governor, in theory at least, because the governor should be held responsible for all aspects of state government. In such a situation the state board, if there is one, presumably would be largely an advisory body.

What arguments are usually used by those who favor election of the chief state school officer by popular vote? What arguments are advanced by those who favor appointment by the state board of education? Which of these arguments is most defensible?

Some political scientists have been interested in the assumption that generally persons elected by popular vote will tend to observe the norms accepted by a majority of the people, and therefore are not likely to encourage innovations or help to effect significant changes in the traditional system regardless of the need. Some evidence has been given that seems to support this assumption. What does the evidence indicate about the appropriateness of this assumption in the field of education at the local or state level?

To what extent should the chief state school officer be interested in stimulating the introduction of promising changes? What are the implications for education of the selection of a chief state school officer who is politically ambitious or who knows little about the problems and potential of education? What procedures should be used and safeguards observed in selecting the chief state school officer?

What Procedures Should Be Used in Improving State Programs of Education?

Whether the people of a state are successful in identifying and solving their educational problems is determined by many factors. Certain forces and factors contribute to or delay progress. One important factor in every state is likely to be the position and role of the state education agency.

In several states, the state education agency has seemed to be mainly interested in checking on requirements or preserving the *status quo*. In such states, those groups or organizations in position to take leadership in attempting to deal with emerging educational problems often proceed to do so. In some of these states the more active groups, including on occasion the state education association or representatives from the larger school systems, seem to be well satisfied with the situation and would probably oppose directly or indirectly more active leadership by the state agency of education.

In many states the education agency is actively interested in encouraging studies needed to evaluate various aspects of the educational program and provide a basis for planning improvements. Representative committees or task forces are organized to study various problems as they arise, obtain the facts, and propose solutions. Although the state education association has its own program, its members and representatives cooperate by working on state committees and helping to plan needed improvements. Much of the leadership and responsibility for coordination is assumed by the state department of education. Who should lead in planning and conducting studies of various aspects of the state program? What should be the role of other groups? If the state department of education provides leadership for improving education, how can state domination or control be avoided?

Sooner or later, in almost every state the need for a careful study of all major aspects of the state provisions for education is recognized as desirable. A comprehensive study of the entire program may direct attention to imbalances and problems that might be overlooked in studying only certain aspects. Three kinds of procedures have been used in planning and conducting such studies. The one most commonly used, until recently, was to employ a team of outside experts to conduct a survey and prepare a report. A second procedure has involved a study by people from within the state. A third procedure, used in many states during recent years, has been to utilize a combination of competent outside consultants and leaders from within the state. This procedure has the advantage of involving both consultants, who should bring new perspectives, and people who will continue to live and work in the state and thus should be interested in implementing recommendations on which there is agreement.

A related question concerns the respective roles that should be played by educators and lay citizens in conducting such studies.[23] A rather typical procedure during the past few years has been to select a state study or policy committee that is often comprised largely of laymen. An educator from within the state is usually employed to serve as executive secretary and coordinator. Special study committees, commonly comprised of both educators and lay citizens, may then be organized for each of the major areas of the study, such as personnel, housing, organization, instruction, and finance. These committees work under the direction of the general policy committee in planning and conducting their studies and report periodically to the central committee their findings and recommendations for consideration. These are coordinated with the assistance of all groups involved and presented to the public.

[23]Edgar L. Morphet, Chmn., *Citizen Cooperation for Better Public Schools*, Fifty-third Yearbook, National Society for the Study of Education, Part I (Chicago: University of Chicago Press, 1955), Chaps. 8 and 10.

Under what conditions should a comprehensive study be undertaken? What should be the respective roles of lay citizens and educators in planning and conducting studies of any kind? How should such studies be financed? How should the sponsoring group be created and how should it function?

Sometimes state policies, standards and regulations have been developed entirely by the department of education staff or chief state school officer and submitted to the state board of education for adoption. In a number of states, the state board of education has adopted a policy that all standards and regulations are to be developed by representative committees selected to study the problems and submit proposals. The state department staff, appropriate research organizations, and institutions of higher learning cooperate in planning and conducting any special studies or assembling any information that may be needed. After study, discussion, and consultation with people who have special competencies in the field, the committee submits its report that constitutes the basis not only for policies and standards to be adopted by the state board of education but often provides suggestions for improvements that may be effected without the necessity of regulations. During the process, committee members usually grow considerably in their insight and understanding of the problems and needs.

What procedure should be followed in a state in developing or revising policies and standards? What should be the role of state department staff members in connection with this procedure?

What Should Be the Responsibility of the State for Nonpublic Education?

In the past, almost any person or organization interested in establishing a nonpublic school or educational institution could proceed to do so in most states without having to be concerned about many state requirements. However, there have been some serious abuses of this relative freedom from requirements, and several states have found it desirable to enact laws and prescribe regulations that are designed to safeguard the interests and welfare of those enrolled in such schools. While the right of the states to establish reasonable standards and requirements for nonpublic schools is generally recognized, nearly one half of the states have taken no action to establish standards relating to instruction; some have done little in other important areas. However, the people in every state have expressed their interest in adequate educational opportunities for all children. How can these opportunities best be assured for children who attend nonpublic schools? What, if any, state requirements should be established for all nonpublic schools and educational institutions? What problems are likely to arise from attempts to assure that nonpublic schools meet desirable requirements?

Selected References

Butts, R. Freeman, and Lawrence A. Cremin, *A History of Education in American Culture*. New York: Holt, Rinehart & Winston, Inc. 1953, pp. 241–259, 429–433, 571–584.

Chase, Francis S., and Edgar L. Morphet, *The Forty-eight State School Systems*. Chicago: Council of State Governments, 1949.

Conant, James Bryant, *Shaping Educational Policy*. New York: McGraw-Hill Book Company, 1964.

Cubberley, Ellwood P., *State School Administration*. Boston: Houghton Mifflin Company, 1927.

Knight, Edgar W., *Readings in Educational Administration*. New York: Holt, Rinehart & Winston, Inc., 1953, Chap. 2.

National Council of Chief State School Officers, *Our System of Education*. Washington, D.C.: The Council, 1950.

Pierce, Truman M., *Federal, State and Local Governments in Education*. New York: Center for Applied Research in Education, Inc., 1964.

Thurston, Lee M., and William H. Roe, *State School Administration*. New York: Harper & Row, Publishers, 1957.

Wills, Robert F., *State Education: Structure and Organization*, Office of Education, Miscellaneous No. 46. Washington, D.C.: U.S. Government Printing Office, 1964.

10

Local School Districts
and Intermediate Units

There are three sets of terms relating to the organization for schools that have often been misunderstood or misinterpreted by both laymen and educators. These are (1) the school district or local school administrative unit (sometimes referred to as "the local school system"), (2) the local school center or attendance area, and (3) the intermediate district or unit for school administration.

A *local school district,* or local school administrative unit is a quasi-corporation,[1] authorized or established by the state for the local organization and administration of schools. It is comprised of an area within which a single board or officer has the responsibility for, and commonly has considerable autonomy in, the organization and administration of all public schools. It usually has certain powers, including the power to specify tax levies for school purposes, that have been delegated by the state. It may include from one to a hundred or more schools and attendance areas.[2]

[1]As defined by Edwards, "A quasi-corporation . . . is purely a political or civil division of the state; it is created as an instrumentality of the state in order to facilitate the administration of government. . . . A municipal corporation proper is a city or town incorporated primarily for purposes of local government." Newton Edwards, *The Courts and the Public Schools* (Chicago: University of Chicago Press, 1955), p. 63.

[2]Adapted from Howard A. Dawson *et al., Your School District.* National Commission on School District Reorganization (Washington, D.C.: Department of Rural Education, National Education Association, 1948), p. 47.

A *local school attendance area* is that part of a school district whose population is served in part at least by a single school. The school may comprise the kindergarten and primary grades, the elementary, the junior high or intermediate school, the senior or four-year high school, the community or junior college, or some other combination of grades. The *school or educational center* is the place where a school, which may be comprised of one or several buildings, is located.[3] In small districts the boundaries of the district and of the attendance area are usually coterminous, and from this situation much of the confusion has arisen.

An *intermediate unit* or district is a unit for school administration or service that has been organized to provide educational services in an area comprised of two or more local school districts. It usually is expected to function intermediately between the state department of education and local school districts in its area and to provide services for both.[4]

LOCAL SCHOOL DISTRICTS

The early settlers and leaders in this country could have made an assumption similar to the one made by those who went to Australia, that is: each state should be responsible for organizing and operating the schools and programs of education. However, the settlers in America made quite a different assumption: each state should be responsible for the education of its citizens, but school districts should be organized as needed, and the responsibility for organizing, administering and operating schools and programs of education in accordance with state standards and requirements should be delegated to them. Each assumption had many implications for the development of education. Each also has directed attention to certain problems. For example, in America many of the school districts eventually proved to be too small to provide an effective program of education, the people in some districts did not take their responsibilities seriously, and in many areas the local resources were so inadequate that only limited education could be provided.

Origin and Development of School Districts

Every state except Hawaii has designated or created local subdivisions, commonly called school districts, for the purposes of administering and operating the public school program. In some instances

[3]Adapted from Henry F. Alves and Edgar L. Morphet, *Principles and Procedures in the Organization of Satisfactory Local School Units*, U.S. Office of Education Bulletin No. 11 (Washington, D.C.: U.S. Government Printing Office, 1938), p. 4.

[4]Adapted from Shirley Cooper and Charles O. Fitzwater, *County School Administration* (New York: Harper & Row, Publishers, 1954), p. 103.

(for example, cities, townships, or counties) these subdivisions already had been created for other governmental purposes. In others, new districts, frequently with the same boundaries, were established specifically for school purposes. In most instances, the local school districts were made autonomous in that they were not subject to control by local governmental agencies. However, in some instances a local government agency was either granted some authority over the local school district or was even organized to encompass education within its framework of responsibility (as in some cities with special charters).

Local school districts vary in many ways. There are only 17 districts in Nevada, 24 in Maryland, 30 in Alaska, 40 in Utah, 41 in Rhode Island and 55 in West Virginia. However, in 1965-66 there were in excess of 2000 in Nebraska and South Dakota and more than 1000 in California, Illinois, Iowa, Kansas, Michigan, Minnesota, Oklahoma, and Texas. Enrollments vary from fewer than fifteen pupils in many districts operating one-room schools to hundreds of thousands in large city systems. Some districts provide only for elementary, secondary, or community college education; others provide for education of all groups through the junior college. Many of the large districts are directly responsible to the state, while the smaller districts in a number of states have more limited responsibilities and are subject to some control or supervision by an intermediate unit. There are more than 100 districts in Iowa, Kansas, Missouri, New York, and Nebraska, and about 900 in South Dakota that do not even operate a school but have the power to levy taxes to pay the tuition of pupils who attend other districts and to meet other expenses. In fact, there are so many variations among local school districts that about their only common characteristic is that they serve as an agency of the state for the administration and operation of one specialized state function: public school education.

The organization of local school districts for the administration of education within each state developed out of the political philosophy and the geographic circumstances of the growing nation. Although early Massachusetts legislation placed local educational responsibility and control in the town (township), the people were not long satisfied. As the colonists spread out and new communities developed, the residents wanted their own institutions such as churches and schools. As a result, towns were divided into school districts. This was natural in a time when population was scattered and sparse, when communication and transportation between communities were difficult, and when isolation was the condition of life. As the frontier moved westward, this tendency continued. The idea of "home rule" in education is historical.[5] The result

[5]American Association of School Administrators, *The American School Superintendency*, Thirtieth Yearbook (Washington, D.C.: The Association, 1952), p. 103.

has been that in most states the legislatures authorized small settlements and rural areas to be organized as local school districts. Many districts still have the same limited boundaries established under frontier conditions.

For a long period the small district, with its schools in physical proximity to the students and in control of residents of the small community, was looked upon as the epitome of educational organization. Every community came to look upon itself as independently competent to choose its teachers, determine the conditions and program of learning, and govern and finance the school. It was this extremity of provincialism and isolationism that caused Horace Mann to refer to the Massachusetts law establishing small independent local school districts as "the most unfortunate law on the subject of education ever enacted by the State of Massachusetts."

Factors Affecting District Organization

Since frontier days, the people in each state have been attempting more or less seriously to adapt their schools and school district organization to new and changing circumstances. However, as pointed out in Chapters 1 and 3, a local school system is, in a sense, a "domesticated organization." Historically, this type of organization has been slow to change. Some factors that continue to require serious consideration are discussed briefly in the following paragraphs.

IMPROVEMENTS IN TRANSPORTATION AND COMMUNICATION.   The time and distance limitations on the communications and movements of man have been greatly extended. Each person has contact with persons, places, and organizations that are much farther removed from his place of residence, and they in turn have impact on him. School districts in many areas have had to be expanded or reorganized to meet the needs of rapidly growing communities and other developments in modern society.

THE EXPANDING EDUCATIONAL PROGRAM.   The citizens have made continually increasing demands on the public schools. Schools that offered only the rudiments of instruction to a restricted number of youth have been generally replaced by institutions that offer a broad scope of learning experiences to nearly every segment of society. Efforts to provide adequate educational opportunities, to avoid duplication of offerings, to facilitate articulation between different grade levels, and to meet many other needs have stimulated the development of larger districts.

CHANGING ECONOMIC CIRCUMSTANCES.   As long as schools remained small and the basis of economic wealth was largely the land from which man produced his sustenance, the matter of financing education was, perhaps logically, considered to be a local problem. However, the economy has changed greatly. Other types of wealth have come into existence or increased in importance with the result that economic resources are much more unevenly distributed than during pioneer days.

CHANGING PATTERNS OF EDUCATIONAL LEADERSHIP. In face of the increasing complexities encountered in organizing and administering a program of education, the lay school boards in smaller districts, with increasing frequency, have either operated with evident inefficiency or have had to turn to county or state educational leaders for advice and direction. Well-prepared and competent administrative leaders and supporting staff have been available generally only to the larger districts. Increasingly, the fact has been recognized that only districts of sufficient size and ability to attract, support, and retain competent education leadership are actually able to exercise local control of their school systems.

Thus, many school districts (and schools) that were organized to meet a pioneer situation have become inadequate in terms of needs arising from changes in transportation and communication, an expanding educational program, the changing economic situation, the necessity for competent educational leadership, and other factors.

Some Significant Trends

As early as 1837, Horace Mann advocated the abolition of the newly created common school districts and re-establishment of the township system in Massachusetts. Since that time, numerous states have engaged in programs for reorganizing school districts through a variety of procedures including permissive legislation, compulsory reorganization, semicompulsory plans, and legislation embodying financial incentives. Many states have relied chiefly on educational leadership, generally on the state and county level, to accomplish their objective. Several have created state commissions with expert personnel to provide guidance for reorganization.

NUMBER OF DISTRICTS. As a result of such efforts there has been a steady decrease in the total number of school districts during the last 30 to 35 years. In 1932, the first year reasonably complete information was assembled, there were 127,244 local school districts in the United States; in 1941–42 there were 115,384; in 1951–52 there were 70,993; in 1955–56 there were approximately 57,000; and in 1965–66 there were 26,800 of which 2,420 did not operate any schools. In 1966, more than 50 per cent of all school districts in the nation were in the states in the Great Lakes and Plains areas. Practically all states had fewer local school districts in 1966 than in 1932. However, nearly 60 per cent of all districts in the nation still have fewer than 1,200 pupils, and approximately 15 per cent do not operate any schools. On the other hand, more than 40 per cent of all pupils in the nation are enrolled in districts having more than 12,000 pupils, and fewer than 14 per cent are in districts enrolling under 1,200. The evidence available indicates that about 5,000 properly organized districts could more adequately meet the needs of education in modern American society and provide opportunity for more meaningful local responsibility for the operation of schools than would ever be possible under the present district structure.

KINDS OF DISTRICTS.   There are many kinds or types of school districts. For example, in Florida, Nevada, and West Virginia, all counties are organized as school districts. In most southern states and Utah, all county areas are organized as school districts, but the major cities usually constitute school districts separate from the county units in which they may be geographically located.

Arizona, California, Illinois, Wisconsin, and certain other states have distinctly different prevailing patterns. A wide variety of districts is found within each state. Only the unified districts have a single board of education responsible for all education, kindergarten through high school, and in some cases including the junior or community college. In other areas of each of these states, and in many rural areas in some other states, there are separate districts for elementary and secondary school students with separate governing boards and administrative officers for each level. However, the separately organized elementary and high-school districts are gradually being replaced by unified districts.

The basic types of school districts can be classified, for the most part, into six main categories: (1) the common school district, most frequently found in the rural areas of several states, is generally relatively small both in area and in enrollment, frequently has a single school, and usually provides education only on the elementary level; (2) county-unit districts with boundaries coterminous—or nearly so—with county lines; (3) city school districts that are usually coterminous—or nearly so—with city boundaries; (4) county districts in which the cities constitute separate districts; (5) special "independent" districts organized by legislative act in some states to provide education on an elementary or high-school level or both; (6) town or township districts found in several of the New England states as well as in some areas in Indiana.[6] To this list should be added high-school districts, usually covering two or more elementary school districts, found in several states, and separately organized junior college districts that have been created in some states dur-

[6]Adapted from National Society for the Study of Education, *American Education in the Post-War Period*, Forty-fourth Yearbook, Part II (Chicago: University of Chicago Press, 1945), pp. 135–136.

ing recent years. Most county-unit, city and town or township districts, and many of the county districts in which the cities constitute separate school districts, are unified; that is, they offer programs extending through the twelfth grade and in some cases include junior colleges.

ORGANIZATION AND RELATIONS. In most instances the local school district is a relatively autonomous unit operating by authorization of the state and not responsible to other governmental units except in specified instances. Each district has a governing board that is usually elected by the people. Except in the small districts (and in some of the county districts where the superintendent is elected), a superintendent is appointed by the governing board as its chief administrative officer and policy consultant. Under his professional leadership the local district has opportunity, subject to minimum requirements established by the state and in certain respects by the federal government, to develop its own program of education. This near-autonomy of the local school district is uniquely American, and the preservation of "local control" is a rallying issue in many public debates about a variety of school problems.

Nevertheless, as already pointed out, school districts are instruments of the state for the accomplishment of the state's educational function. The state legislature, subject to the state and federal constitutional limitations and court decisions, has complete authority over such districts and may instruct, advise, direct, create, or abolish them in accordance with its judgment regarding the welfare of education in the state. A statement by the State Supreme Court of Washington illustrates the commonly held legal point of view regarding the relationship of school districts to the state:

> Local subdivisions of the state can be created by the sovereign power of the state without solicitation, consent, or concurrent action by the people who inhabit them. This being so, it follows that legislative authority over school districts is unlimited except as that limitation is found in the state constitution.[7]

Characteristics of Effective School Districts and Schools

The chief function of a school district is to make it possible for the citizens of the area to provide for the organization, operation, and administration of an adequate, economical, and effective educational program for those who should be educated in and through the public schools. Any district that fails to carry out this function satisfactorily is an ineffective district. The ineffectiveness may be due to the attitude of

[7] 18 Washington (2nd) 37, or 137 Pacific (2nd) 1010, 1943.

the people, to the limited size of the area, to inadequate human or economic resources, to failure to recognize or meet emerging needs, or to any combination of these factors.

Since some of the major characteristics of a satisfactory program of education, and of provisions for its organization, administration, and support, are discussed elsewhere in this book, major attention will be centered here on other criteria, including size, that must be observed if a district is to be in a position to operate effectively. However, size should not be the only determining factor, because size does not assure effectiveness; it only makes it possible when other conditions are favorable.

When an area is too small in terms of population, it cannot provide an adequate program at an economical cost. When it is too large in terms of distance or population, the citizens who are responsible for the educational program may have difficulty in communicating, agreeing on objectives, and cooperating in developing plans for the program. The possibility that people may be able to learn to cooperate effectively, therefore, becomes an important consideration in determining whether a particular area proposed for a reorganized school district might become an effective district. Largely for this reason some authorities have advocated that districts be organized to encompass communities whose residents have been accustomed to cooperating in certain matters of common interest. However, many rural communities and towns are too small to make effective school districts. Furthermore, "homogeneous" districts, particularly in suburban areas, would tend to result in economic or even racial segregation. It seems evident that in school districts, as well as in other aspects of government, people with widely divergent backgrounds will need to find effective ways of cooperating in the solution of problems of mutual interest.

Authorities are agreed that every district should be in a position to provide an educational program that extends through at least the high-school grades. Separate districts for elementary and for high schools, even though they may be fairly large, are not considered desirable. Education should be a continuous process, unhampered by unnecessary complications for voters, for children, or for the educational staff.

Research shows that reasonable economy of scale cannot be attained in districts with a school population of fewer than 10,000 pupils. Districts that are smaller in size are faced with rapidly increasing unit costs for an adequate educational program as the number of pupils decreases. In districts with fewer than 1,200 pupils, the unit costs become so great that such opportunities can seldom be provided. Therefore, the minimum acceptable size of school districts should be 10,000 pupils in all except the most sparsely settled areas where the minimum should be established at not less than 5,000. These minimum sizes should not be confused with optimum sizes, which in many areas should probably be at least 50,000 pupils.

Proper organization of districts lays the foundation for the solution of the small-school problem in all except isolated and sparsely populated areas where small schools may have to be continued regardless of cost. However, the continued existence of small districts usually means that the small school in each district is likely to be perpetuated even when it should be consolidated.

Whenever practicable, an elementary school should have sufficient pupils to warrant at least two teachers per grade or age group, and a junior or senior high school should have at least 100 pupils in each age group. Elementary and high schools having at least twice this minimum are usually in a position to provide a more adequate program at a more reasonable cost.[8]

Reorganization of School Districts

On the basis of experiences in the various states and studies made thus far, the following criteria have been proposed for guidance in developing state plans and laws relating to district reorganization:

1. Legislation relating to district reorganization should be kept as simple as possible and should make it easy for districts to effect desirable reorganization.

2. All state laws and regulations should be reviewed periodically to determine their effect on district reorganization. Those that encourage the continuance of inadequate districts or retard needed reorganization should be revised or repealed.

3. All reorganization proposals should be based on careful studies and planning. Many reorganizations based on the desires of local groups have been found to be unsatisfactory because facts pertinent to the situation were overlooked or ignored.

4. The people of the state should define and agree upon and the legislature should prescribe basic criteria or minimum standards to be used for guidance in planning reorganization of districts.

5. In all states with a large number of small districts the law should provide for a state reorganization commission. This commission must be properly financed and staffed if it is to function effectively. County or area committees on reorganization should also be established.

6. The responsibilities of the state and local reorganization commissions and of all groups and persons officially involved in the reorganization program should be clearly defined.

[8]R. L. Johns and Edgar L. Morphet, eds., *Problems and Issues in Public School Finance* (New York: Bureau of Publications, Teachers College, Columbia University, 1952), pp. 77–84.

7. Provision should be made for the participation of a maximum number of people working cooperatively for effective district reorganization. Only when the people involved in a plan of reorganization understand all the pertinent facts are they in a position to make wise decisions.

8. A favorable vote by a majority of the electors in an area proposed for a reorganized district (or both in a major center of population and in the remainder of the area) should suffice to make the proposal effective.

9. If the people in any separate elementary or secondary district or in any inadequate district choose to continue their separate district beyond a designated date, the taxpayers of each such district should bear the extra expense involved in providing adequate school services and facilities for the children of the district.

10. Needed funds for an adequate educational program including buildings and transportation should be assured for any properly reorganized district.

11. A three- or four-year deadline within which reorganization is to be completed on a voluntary basis should be prescribed by the legislature, which should also provide that, for any reorganizations not completed by that time, the state education agency (or district reorganization commission) is to develop a plan for approval by the legislature.[9]

Problems and Prospects

While considerable progress has been made in reorganizing school districts in many states, the pace has been too slow to meet the needs. Few legislatures have adopted a harmonious set of laws that have removed all obstacles and afforded effective incentives. A piecemeal approach, involving only minor changes in existing laws or failure to provide effective machinery, has commonly been used. The reluctance of legislatures to deal realistically with this problem can be understood in light of the pressures frequently exerted by local and sometimes statewide groups to maintain a traditional system that seems to many to have worked reasonably well. However, the evidence that much more reorganization is needed in most states in the immediate future should be convincing to everyone concerned. Some of the problems and prospects are considered briefly below.

NONOPERATING DISTRICTS. Nearly one half of the states still have from a few to nearly one thousand districts that exist legally but do not operate any school. Several states also have some areas not included in any

[9]Adapted from Edgar L. Morphet and others, "State Laws Can Aid District Reorganization," *Phi Delta Kappan*, **32** (Mar. 1951), 319–320.

district. The reason these situations are permitted to exist is that legislatures have been lax in dealing with them, perhaps because they have failed to recognize the inequities and the unfair tax advantages that are usually provided.

SMALL DISTRICTS.   More than three fourths of all existing districts are too small to be effective. Most of these are elementary school districts, but a rather substantial number of high school and unified districts (some of which are county districts in southern states in which separate city districts have been organized) are included. Yet every study that has been made shows that these districts are costly to operate and most provide inadequate programs. Hanson, for example, reported higher costs ranging from $19 to $96 per pupil in districts of 1500 than in districts of "optimum" size in nine states from the east to the west coast.[10] The average difference was $27 per student.

Morphet and Ross directed attention to what seems to be one of the most serious shortcomings of the smallest school districts in California (unified school districts with fewer than 1500 pupils, elementary school districts with fewer than 900 and high school districts with fewer than 300).[11] They pointed out, on the basis of an analysis of the laws relating to the districts and county school services: "It is clear . . . that small school districts are not expected to assume full responsibility for the nature and quality of the educational program." They also made a study of the operations of small school districts and concluded that ". . . local responsibility and control in small school districts is not as complete or as vigorous as has often been assumed. . . . These findings do *not* support any conclusion that the elimination of small districts would reduce local responsibility for education. On the contrary, the findings suggest that the elimination of small districts may increase the potential for effective local responsibility and control of education."

SEPARATE DISTRICTS FOR ELEMENTARY AND HIGH-SCHOOL PURPOSES.   This pattern began to develop in some states as high schools were established, partly because existing elementary school districts were too small to include the attendance area for the high school. A high-school district that included two or more elementary districts was then established with a separate board, tax levies, and so on. In spite of the complexities and confusion, the lack of coordination and other problems, the pattern, once established, was continued, expanded, and vigorously defended by

[10]Nels W. Hanson, "Economy of Scale in Education: An Analysis of the Relationship Between District Size and Unit Costs in the Public Schools" (Unpublished Ph.D. dissertation, Stanford University, 1963).

[11]Edgar L. Morphet and John G. Ross, *Local Responsibility for Education in Small School Districts,* Legislative Problems No. 1 (Berkeley, Calif.: Bureau of Public Administration, University of California, 1961), pp. 23 and 33.

educators in a number of states. This plan of organization has persisted even in some cities and many suburban areas. The deficiencies have been pointed out by numerous authorities. Such districts are all-too slowly being replaced by a more defensible plan of organization. However, this statement does not necessarily apply to the organization of separate junior college districts, especially in sparsely populated rural areas.

LARGE DISTRICTS.   The evidence available indicates that costs per pupil tend to be lowest in districts having more than 10,000 pupils and fewer than 40,000 to 50,000. Beyond 50,000 costs tend to rise again and may increase as much as $10 or more per pupil in much larger districts; however, this may result from increased services or quality. When factors other than costs are considered (e.g., adaptability and adoption of innovations) the evidence seems to indicate that special problems are encountered in very large districts for a number of reasons. In very large as well as very small districts, conditions relating to school quality tend to become less favorable. In both kinds of districts, special arrangements seem to be necessary to achieve the best possible quality of education.[12]

On the basis of such evidence, and for other reasons, some authorities have advocated that the large city districts should be divided into smaller districts. However, if that were done, some of the districts would be much more wealthy than others and serious inequalities would result. This may mean that the large city base should be retained for over-all planning and financial purposes, and that districts should be organized within the city for administrative and operating purposes. Further studies and adjustments are undoubtedly needed to provide a sound basis for resolving the problems inherent in such situations.

SUBURBAN AREAS.   Many suburban areas present particularly troublesome problems. If districts are organized about "communities" some are likely to be quite wealthy, others (especially tract housing bedroom communities) will have limited tax bases and other kinds of problems. The optimum plan for school district organization in such areas will probably have to ignore subdivision boundaries; yet, this will present special problems of coordination and cooperation. The development of a defensible plan for district organization in such areas will require high-quality statesmanship on the part of educators as well as lay citizens.

RURAL AREAS.   The problems of district organization in rural areas are quite different from those in urban and suburban communities. In most rural communities the people have been accustomed to the idea that they are responsible for operating their own schools. When districts are

[12]*Relations Between Community Size and School Quality,* Institute of Administrative Research (New York: Teachers College, Columbia University, **2**, No. 1 (Oct. 1961), 1–3.

reorganized, they are concerned that local responsibility will be lost, even though they may never have assumed much real responsibility. Ways need to be found to continue this sense of responsibility in a different context. Although many reorganized districts will necessarily be fairly large in area, most will not be large in population.

JUNIOR COLLEGE DISTRICTS.   Special districts for junior college purposes have been organized in a number of states during the past few years; in others, most junior colleges are operated by the larger local school districts as a part of the public school system. In some states no definite plans for junior colleges have been implemented thus far; in a few, these institutions are operated by the university. The need for each state to develop a plan in the near future to provide for the orderly development of junior or community colleges should be apparent. For some time to come, districts that provide junior colleges, especially in rural areas, will have to be considerably larger than existing elementary and high-school districts. In many of the larger districts the educational program has been or is being extended to include the community college program as a part of the district function. This seems to be a logical development and will probably be extended to more areas as district reorganization progresses.

FURTHER REORGANIZATION.   Many of the reorganizations that have occurred in rural areas, and some in suburban areas have been inadequate from a long-range point of view. Further reorganization involving new combinations of reorganized districts will be needed in many states. However, the fact that reorganization or further reorganization is not a panacea should be clearly recognized. But reorganization does make it possible to solve problems that could not otherwise be solved.

FISCALLY INDEPENDENT SCHOOL DISTRICTS.   While more than 90 per cent of the school districts in the United States are fiscally independent from a legal point of view, none is autonomous in any fundamental sense. The people in most states obviously believe that school districts should be free to determine their fiscal needs and, within limits, to certify and obtain the local funds needed for their operation. In four states—Hawaii, Maryland, North Carolina and Virginia—and in some districts in a number of other states, the fiscal needs are determined by an agency other than the school board. As a matter of fact, in all states some limits of one kind or another have been placed on what school boards may do in terms of finance, either on the basis of constitutional or legislative provisions, or by the requirement for approval by vote of the citizens under certain conditions. Moreover, no district is politically independent or autonomous. School district officials must, if they are realistic, work with other officials and agencies of government in developing plans and proposals. To fail to do so would mean sooner or later isolating themselves from some of the support they need, and maybe even failing to win the approval of the voters in an election involving needed school funds.

LOCAL RESPONSIBILITY.   While the people in school districts insist they believe in local responsibility, in far too many instances they have failed to exercise much responsibility. Often only a minority has participated in elections for board members, and too many boards have failed to meet some of their responsibilities for developing an effective program of education in the district. During recent years, control of education has gradually moved toward the state, and in some respects, toward the federal government. Some assumption of state control in certain respects is probably inevitable and may be desirable from a long-range point of view, but the process is in danger of being carried too far in some states. Only when districts are properly organized and vigorously supported by citizens who demonstrate that local responsibility can be met can a wholesome local-state-federal partnership be assured.

THE INTERMEDIATE UNIT

The intermediate unit of school administration in America began to develop during pioneer days, primarily in the Midwest, when most school districts were small and communication was slow and difficult. The need for some agency to perform certain services both for the small, relatively isolated districts and for the state soon became apparent.

Since counties had been established by most states as local units of government, following somewhat the pattern in England, it was logical that they would be designated as the intermediate units for schools in many states. However, the township was actually the first intermediate unit established in some of the midwestern states, notably Michigan and Indiana. The earliest demand seemed to be for an agency to oversee small districts, to enforce certain state regulations, to gather information for the state, to direct the distribution of state funds within the area, and to provide certain services for the districts.

The primary concern and responsibility of these intermediate units was for rural schools, although at first they were also legally responsible for some general oversight of city schools. As cities began to increase in population in many states, they tended to develop separate organizations for government and for schools, to bypass or ignore the intermediate units, and to insist on an independent status. Legislatures were frequently persuaded to pass special laws granting city school systems either partial or complete independence from the intermediate units. Thus the intermediate unit in most states became predominantly an organization for limited control of and service to rural schools and for service to the state.[13]

In some instances, intermediate organization was resisted as an unwanted arm of the state. In others, the intermediate organization was considered at times as a protector of the local district against unwanted state-level control. But in all instances, the intermediate unit, when established, was created by state action and was a political subdivision of the state organized in part to assist in carrying out the state's educational function.[14]

Intermediate Unit Organization

Twenty-seven states have some type of intermediate unit organization for schools. Generally, in the states where all local school districts are county units, except for some independent city districts, these are basic local school administrative units that deal directly with the state, so there are no intermediate units. There are two basic types of intermediate units.

COUNTY INTERMEDIATE UNITS. In 26 states, the intermediate units are coterminous, or nearly so, with county boundaries. Generally, the intermediate administrative functions have been assigned to a county superintendent of schools who, in eighteen states, is an elective official. In eleven of these states he administers the intermediate unit program without a board of education. In eight the board of education is elected and appoints the county superintendent. In New Jersey he is appointed by the state commissioner of education. In other instances the county board may be appointed by the district board members or in some other manner. The county boards may act either in a governing or in an advisory capacity to the county superintendent, depending upon the laws of their respective states.

THE NEW YORK PLAN. A different type of intermediate unit has been established in New York State. It is not coterminous with, nor related to, the county. Provision was first made for this type of unit a few years after the Revolution. Beginning with a town commission which had limited responsibilities relating to the districts in its area, it has undergone a number of changes. In 1948 a new intermediate unit law was enacted providing for boards of cooperative services to consist of representatives of boards of local school districts in the area. These representatives, comprising the board, appoint a superintendent of schools who

[13]William P. McLure, *The Intermediate Administrative School District in the United States* (Urbana: University of Illinois Press, 1956), p. 3.

[14]Shirley Cooper and Charles O. Fitzwater, *County School Administration* (New York: Harper & Row, Publishers, 1954), Chaps. 4 and 5.

has general supervision over the services provided in the component districts. On the basis of recent studies this plan may undergo further revision.

OTHER PROVISIONS. The New England states have established supervisory unions composed of contiguous local school districts or town school units. These have some characteristics of intermediate units but also differ from such units in several respects. Under permissive legislation these unions were often somewhat transitory in character and concerned with the many problems of an impermanent organization, but more recently the laws in several of these states have become mandatory upon districts under certain conditions. Generally, each of these supervisory unions has a board of education frequently selected by the composite town boards. The board either elects a superintendent or nominates one to the state department, which makes the appointment.

The township form of intermediate unit has been the least common; in fact, it has disappeared as an intermediate unit in all states that had it. However, the transition from the township to the county intermediate unit was not easily accomplished and involved many bitter struggles.

The Changing Character of the Intermediate Unit

When local school districts in a state have been reorganized and are large enough to justify the employment of competent administrative leadership and few enough in number to allow for direct state-district cooperation, the intermediate units have usually either been discontinued or the need for their continuation has been increasingly questioned. The continued existence of inadequate school districts, the apparent impossibility of eliminating all of them in the near future, and the development of new problems have seemed to make at least the temporary continuation of some kind of intermediate unit essential in many states. However, the changing socioeconomic situation and the emergence of new concepts and points of view have tended to result in new perspectives concerning the organization and functions of such units.

CHANGING CONCEPTS. In the first place, many people now recognize that, in many areas, the county is no longer defensible as the basis for establishing or continuing intermediate units. In most areas it is as outmoded as the township became several generations ago. Yet it will tend to persist in many states, partly because of tradition but, perhaps equally important, because there are powerful vested interests that will resist any change. These interests may even seek to prevent or delay the development of realistic alternate plans.

In the second place, the provision for elective county superintendents in many states tends to handicap the county as an effective intermediate unit. The elected superintendent all too often is not particularly well qualified professionally to develop the kind of intermediate unit program needed under modern conditions. The concept that election by popular vote is a satisfactory method of selecting the highly competent professional leader needed to provide services for reasonably well-organized school districts, is indefensible. Yet this practice has persisted for many years and will tend to persist for some years to come, partly because in some states this procedure is prescribed by the constitution.

In several states, including California and New York, and perhaps Ohio and Wisconsin, there is a tendency to encourage intermediate units to assume the responsibility for providing the professional services needed to help make possible equality of educational opportunity for children in all districts of the state. The implementation of this concept requires a sound plan, adequate financial support, and highly competent professional personnel who can work effectively with all types of districts. In all instances the emphasis is or should be on service and not on control. The general policies and plan need to be developed cooperatively by the districts and the intermediate unit, leaving to each district the functions and responsibilities that can best be carried out by the district. This point has been well presented by the superintendent of California's largest intermediate unit:

> We try to lean over backwards to work under the philosophy that the center of gravity of education is within the local district. It is not in the county office. We do not try to run the districts—we try to serve the districts.[15]

Even in California, where the county intermediate unit has been reasonably well financed from a combination of state and local funds and has been given strong state support in providing a variety of services, there is a growing recognition that a number of improvements are seriously needed. In the first place, in areas where all districts have been reorganized, or where only a few hundred children are enrolled in all schools, the county is a costly and unrealistic unit. In the second place, some of the superintendents elected by popular vote (a constitutional requirement in all but a few counties) have not been able to provide the kind of leadership required for a satisfactory intermediate unit program. Finally, the cities and suburban areas need an entirely different kind of program and services than can be provided by counties whose bound-

[15] C. C. Trillingham, "The County Superintendent and the County Service Fund," *Second Report of the Assembly Interim Committee on Public Education* (Sacramento: Assembly of the State of California, 1949), p. 113.

aries were established long before modern metropolitan areas began to develop. The awareness of problems such as these has been stimulated by many developments including some findings and recommendations in the report of a recent study.[16]

On the basis of a study of public education in the San Francisco Metropolitan Bay Area, Reller proposed that the number of school districts be reduced from 264 to 30 or 40, each of which would be prepared to meet certain basic needs more effectively.[17] He concluded that, even after reorganization, these districts would not be in a position to provide effectively for all aspects of the educational program. He, therefore, recommended the creation of a regional or metropolitan district for education that in certain respects would serve as an intermediate unit for the area. This proposed metropolitan district would have its own board and administrative staff and would be responsible for financial matters, for providing educational assistance for the component districts, for special educational services for certain types of students such as the severely handicapped, for special junior college programs, and for the development of programs for older youth and adults.

IMPORTANT CONSIDERATIONS.   Some leaders in a number of states believe there will be no place in a few years for an intermediate unit that, to a certain extent, is local in nature and thus has a distinctly dual function. A number believe that services such as those for certain kinds of handicapped students that cannot well be provided by a single district except in the large cities, will be provided by agreements involving two or more districts that will cooperate in financing and providing for the administration of the program. Others doubt whether this would work satisfactorily except in cooperation with an intermediate unit. Some authorities believe the time has come for most state departments of education to establish regional offices staffed with personnel selected to serve the needs of the area as well as those of the state (thus the staff in a predominantly rural and small town area might be different in several respects from one serving largely metropolitan areas). Others doubt whether such a plan would meet the needs and are fearful it would tend to result in increased state control.

Recent developments and proposals suggest that intermediate units of the future in most states (if they are continued) will probably be comprised of other than county-coterminous areas. The need for intermediate units embracing areas larger than a single county in many areas

[16]Arthur D. Little Co., *The Emerging Requirements for Effective Leadership for California Education* (Sacramento, Calif.: State Department of Education, Nov. 1964), pp. 27–31, 49.

[17]Theodore L. Reller, *Problems of Public Education in the San Francisco Bay Area,* (Berkeley, Calif.: Institute of Government Studies, University of California, 1963).

or cutting across county lines in others is apparent even in many places where districts have been reorganized.

Generally speaking, it seems evident that the place and functions of the intermediate unit still have to be determined in many states. In some, this unit has been abolished and may not be restored. In others, where little attention has been given to the problem, it has continued with functions that are largely traditional. In a few, a genuine effort is being made to develop a unit that is prepared to render the high level of services required for a modern educational program. Whether the intermediate unit will continue largely because of the political support it can muster, be abolished in areas where some such unit is needed, or be reorganized to meet the needs of an evolving educational program will largely be determined by the willingness of the people in each state to face the problem and work out a defensible solution.

SOME IMPORTANT PROBLEMS AND ISSUES

Several important issues have been suggested by the discussion in this chapter. If there were no small school districts, unnecessary small schools, or ineffective or outmoded intermediate units in any state, the quality of education might be considerably improved over that found in many areas at present. What steps should be taken to improve the unsatisfactory aspects of the present situation? Why have they not already been taken? A few of the major issues relating to these questions are further considered on the following pages.

What, If Any, Responsibilities Now Delegated to Districts Should Be Assumed by the States?

Since districts have only the powers and responsibilities delegated to them by the state in which they are located, the legislature would have the right to withdraw some or many of these powers. For example, the legislature could prescribe all salaries for school personnel; determine what subjects are to be taught in the various grades; prescribe uniform standards for testing, grading, and promotion of pupils; reorganize all school districts, and take other similar steps. Many people favor more state control, on the assumption that it would result in greater efficiency and improved quality of education throughout the state. The evidence shows that most states have added many new standards and requirements to be met by school districts and have assumed greater control over education during the past few years. Some of these developments have been helpful; others have brought complications and probably have been harmful. Many local school boards (perhaps partly because of lack of interest on the part of citizens in the area or of leadership by the administrative staff) have been lax about meeting some of the responsibilities delegated to them. Some have shown little interest in developing high-quality programs of education for their area.

A number of authorities believe that the solution to many of the present problems can best be effected by organization of districts of adequate size and the delegation of even greater responsibilities to them. They contend that withdrawing more responsibilities from properly organized districts would only weaken them further and discourage local leadership. This in turn would encourage the state to assume even more responsibilities and, in turn, further weaken local districts.

There is almost certain to be at least some further realignment of state and local responsibilities during coming years. It is important that the implications of such shifts in power be carefully thought through in each state so wise decisions may be made. What criteria should be used in determining responsibilities that should be reserved for the states and those that should be assigned to the districts? What kinds of responsibility shifts to the states would be advantageous from a long-range point of view? What kind would be disadvantageous?

What Should Be Done About School Districts That Are Too Small To Operate Efficiently?

There are four ways of attempting to deal with the small-district problem: (1) eliminate all such districts through reorganization; (2) provide additional funds so they can do a better job, (3) place all sparsely populated areas in one large state-operated district, as Alaska has done, (4) attempt to provide more adequate services through properly organized intermediate units. Small districts tend to persist in many states for reasons such as the following: (1) people in many communities believe they can keep in closer touch with their school when the district is small; (2) boards frequently do not like to give up their "power"; (3) small districts in some states receive sufficient subsidies to operate with a lower tax rate than would be required if they reorganized; (4) people are afraid they would lose their local school if the district were reorganized; (5) administrators of the small districts do not like to lose their status and title as superintendent.

To what extent can services by an intermediate unit ensure that all needs will be met satisfactorily without encouraging the continuation of unnecessary small districts? What steps should states take to solve the small-district problem?

How Can School District Reorganization Best Be Effected?

The people of each state are responsible for determining the basic policies to be followed in providing for the organization of school districts and schools. It seems evident that the plan of organization is not likely to be materially altered unless most citizens believe a change is desirable. Likewise, voluntary reorganization in any area is likely to occur only when a majority of the citizens are convinced that the proposed plan of organization will be beneficial. Therefore, popular understanding of the major educational needs and how they can be met most satisfactorily is of considerable importance.

Many contend that if the principles of American democracy are to be observed, reorganization must be permitted to proceed voluntarily. However, experience shows that in many situations the people in districts with considerable wealth hesitate or refuse to join with districts having limited wealth. Moreover, residents of one or more districts have often prevented reorganization in situations where state laws require a favorable vote in each district. Some contend that a time should be set by which all districts must reorganize voluntarily, and after that reorganization should be effected by the legislature on the basis of a plan prepared by the state education agency.

What is the best policy for bringing about needed reorganization of districts? How can unwise reorganizations be avoided?

What Can Be Done to Encourage Local Interest and Initiative in Large Districts?

Research has reasonably well established the minimum size for an effective school district, but there has been inadequate attention to the maximum size or to some of the problems of the largest districts. There seem to be two major problems in all large districts (several hundred thousand students) that are particularly difficult to solve: (1) What can be done to prevent the staff from becoming enmeshed in a web of impersonal relationships, red tape requirements, and prescribed procedures that tend to discourage initiative and responsibility and to place a premium on conformity? (2) What can be done to help citizens keep in close touch with their schools, to demonstrate to them that the educational program is designed to meet the needs of the area in which they live, and to eliminate the feeling that they and their children are insignificant factors in a vast educational machine?

Various proposals have been made for solving these problems, but little has been done. Some have suggested that the largest districts and especially the large cities should be divided into smaller districts. However, such a step would often create other problems. Others have proposed that the city or metropolitan district should be retained as a basic planning, taxing, budgeting, and bonding unit, but several special districts should be organized in the area for operation and administration of schools. Thus, the original district would continue to have a policy board and an administrator or coordinator with a staff that would include competent consultants. Each subdistrict would also have a board elected by the residents of the area, a superintendent and a staff for its schools. As an additional means of providing more opportunity for citizens to help make decisions about their schools, especially those involving financial support, the subdistricts might have some leeway in taxing. The large district would thus become a kind of intermediate unit that would provide basic support and coordination, and the subdistricts would become basic units for the operation of the educational program in their respective areas.[18]

What should be done to solve the unique problems confronting some of the largest and most populous school districts?

How Much Local Autonomy Should Be Preserved When Districts Are Reorganized?

Many small districts have more board members than teachers. In such districts almost every citizen knows every board member personally. When these districts are reorganized, the board usually has from five to seven members elected from the entire area in which from two to a dozen or more small districts may have previously existed. Thus, the number of school board members representing the area is usually considerably reduced.

This problem is important in many rural sections, and may be serious in places where small isolated schools have to be continued. People who live in the outlying areas may not know a single member of the new board. They tend to feel that they no longer have much of a voice in school affairs. Not much has been done to help to solve this problem in many reorganized districts. The new board takes over, selects an administrator and a staff for the district, and the school program moves on from there.

One step commonly taken is to provide for board-member residence districts (but with election by districtwide vote) to assure that not more than two or three of the board members will be elected from a major population center in the district. Another provides safeguards to assure that small schools will not be arbitrarily consolidated. But such steps do not satisfy many people from rural areas.

Several districts have experimented with the idea of an informal advisory board or committee for each school. Members of each such committee may be elected informally, usually for three-year overlapping terms, at an annual meeting of the patrons of the school. Of course, such advisory boards or committees cannot be given legal responsibilities that conflict with those of the central board. However, it seems logical that the advisory board should be encouraged to work with the principal

[18]See, for example, McLure, *op. cit.*, p. 153.

and his staff in studying problems and needs, in developing policies for the school, and in presenting to the central staff and board proposals that have implications for improvements in the program of the school.

The concept of such advisory boards seems to have considerable merit, in light of the discussion in Chapter 6. It has not gained very wide acceptance because it is relatively new to most people, some central boards are afraid they might run into conflict or competition that would weaken their authority, and many principals are concerned as to how it would work. Some have frankly stated they are afraid they would not have a "free hand" to run their schools if they had an advisory board.

Is the concept of advisory boards or committees for individual schools worthy of careful consideration? Would this be appropriate for city districts? If so, how should such committees be selected and what should be their responsibilities? What problems must be faced in developing and implementing such a plan?

Should All Local School Districts Be Eliminated?

During the past few years several writers and speakers have contended that all local school districts should be abolished and that the states should operate the schools. They grant that districts may have been useful under pioneer conditions but believe they have outlived their usefulness and are inappropriate under modern conditions. These people are disturbed by the inequities existing at present and by the complexities and problems found in what they consider to be a cumbersome and outdated system.

Only a few countries have organized special districts for the purpose of operating schools. In many nations all schools are operated and controlled by the central government. In Australia they are operated by the states. Hawaii is the only American state thus far that operates all schools and has not established districts for that purpose such as are found in other states.

Most people in this country would probably be opposed to the establishment of state systems. While they recognize some of the weaknesses in district operation, they contend that the advantages greatly outweigh the disadvantages. They believe that the state-local partnership plan that is still evolving is best adapted to meet emerging needs. They point out that the farther decision making is removed from local schools, the greater the danger of developing a cumbersome and slow-moving bureaucracy that ignores local needs and discourages innovations. What would be the advantages and disadvantages of a state-operated system of schools in any or all states? Does social systems theory support or justify the establishment of local school districts?

Under What Conditions Are Intermediate Units Needed?

In the early days, the intermediate unit for schools met a definite need in most parts of the country. Many things have happened since that time. However, the intermediate unit in some states has changed very little. Much of the work it conducts is often routine in nature and does not demand particular competence or ability.

In a number of states the intermediate unit has developed on a professional basis. It is attempting to meet the needs of modern, rapidly growing schools and reorganized districts in metropolitan as well as in rural areas. The superintendent is selected because of his professional competence to head a staff qualified to provide services needed by more adequately organized school districts.

The people in most states have not yet faced this issue realistically. Some of the larger districts have tended to ignore established intermediate units, perhaps because they believe they can provide all the services needed by the schools. Some of the smaller districts have sought more "independence," whether or not they are prepared for it. In some cases, county superintendents have organized to defend the county as the intermediate unit, or the elective system, or both. It should be apparent that the problem of the intermediate unit, the manner in which it should be organized, and the services it should render needs careful study.

How should intermediate units be organized and what services should they provide for what kinds of districts? Should area centers be established by the state department of education to replace intermediate units? What would be the advantages and disadvantages?

Selected References

American Association of School Administrators, *School District Organization*. Commission on School District Reorganization. Washington, D.C.: The Association, 1958.

Chase, Francis S., and Edgar L. Morphet, *The Forty-eight State School Systems*. Chicago: Council of State Governments, 1949.

Chisholm, Leslie L., *School District Reorganization*. Chicago: Midwest Administration Center, University of Chicago, 1957.

Cooper, Shirley, and Charles O. Fitzwater, *County School Administration*. New York: Harper & Row, Publishers, 1954.

Dawson, Howard A., et al., *Your School District*. National Commission on School District Reorganization. Washington, D.C.: Department of Rural Education, National Education Association, 1948.

Fitzwater, C. O., *School District Reorganization Policies and Procedures,* U.S. Office of Education, Special Series No. 5. Washington, D.C.: U.S. Government Printing Office, 1957.

Gregg, Russell T., "The Intermediate Unit of School Administration," *Administrators Notebook,* Vol. **8**, No. 2 (Oct. 1959).

McLure, William P., *The Intermediate Administrative School District in the United States.* Urbana: University of Illinois Press, 1956.

Morphet, Edgar L., *et al., The Unified School District in California.* Sacramento: California State Department of Education, Sept. 1956.

11

The Local School System

In previous chapters the fact has been emphasized that the educational system in the United States is legally a state system. Decisions of the courts establishing this fact have been cited. Considerable attention has also been given to the structure of education at the state level and to the manner in which the state discharges its responsibilities.

THE SIGNIFICANCE OF THE LOCAL SYSTEM

The sharp decline in the number of school districts in the last decades, as shown in previous chapters, might be interpreted to indicate that the local school system is of decreasing importance. The growing national and state interest and action in education could be used to support this thesis. Further, the tendency of states to pass legislation which sharply limits the scope of the decisions to be made at the local level would also seem to support this view. In fact, the significance of the local system may seem to be declining.

It is the view of the authors, however, that this should not be the inference to be drawn from these and other factors that may be cited. Rather, it is our view that the decrease in the number of school districts creates the potential for much more vigorous initiative and responsibility on the part of the local system. Most of the systems which have been eliminated were too small to have the resources essential for the development of excellent education. The states and the federal government have generally been restrictive because of a lack of confidence in the local authority, rather than because of a desire to establish a state system operationally or a federal system. The growing belief in or recognition of dependence upon education in our society, as in other societies, indicates that the role of the local system needs to expand sharply in the years immediately ahead.[1]

The traditions and myths of our society regarding local control as well as present societal needs constitute an impressive base upon which to develop local school systems of great vitality and unique characteristics.

If this is to be accomplished, it will be necessary not only to avoid restrictive state regulation but also to recognize that a school system is a social system, closely related to external and internal traditions, needs, and forces. Provision will need to be made to facilitate change within it as a result of experimentation and research. Its own differences from other systems and the variety within it will be valued. Then it may become the instrument of its staff and its people to achieve to the fullest basic values drawn from the past struggles and experiences in the development of men. Whether the society achieves these values with the aid of education will depend upon the vision and action which is found within local systems. There would be little reason to expect them to be achieved in a monolithic system, which would dominate a state or the nation, and which was not built upon the resources, energies, inspirations, initiatives of the people (staff and citizens) in local units or systems. This view, of course, does not deprecate the essential role of the state and federal government in guaranteeing minimum standards, ensuring the rights of all people, in providing leadership, in facilitating experimentation and local initiative, and in providing financial resources. The case for a stronger, more vital partnership appears to be unassailable.

THE STATE-LOCAL PARTNERSHIP

Even though the educational system has been a state operation in accord with statute and judicial interpretation, it has also been a system characterized by partnership. In the early years of the nineteenth century

[1] In this regard see Jesse Burkhead, *Public School Finance Economics and Politics* (Syracuse: Syracuse University Press, 1964), p. 284. "The consideration of who would lose power in such a new working arrangement—the local school board, state department of education, the professional, academic, or layman adviser—is a meaningless one because a new institutional framework for the educational process would increase the responsibility of all and would make the tasks more difficult, but surely more interesting, provocative, and meaningful. As institutions grow in size and complexity, the challenge of all concerned increases. To be sure, individuals who are unwilling to accept change or different ways of doing things are bypassed and become disgruntled. But the persons and groups accepting change and challenge usually find the new situation brings greater responsibility."

the state did not exercise its interest in education vigorously. Some local areas established schools and developed them, but other communities provided little in the way of educational opportunity. Whether a community had good schools or not was probably more the result of local forces and factors than because of any special activity on the part of the state. This is not to deny that general or special state laws existed with reference to education or that there were some state leaders such as Mann and Barnard who supplied much encouragement. But education actually developed as a local activity. State educational personnel was exceedingly limited and quite unable to serve the great number of local districts in a direct manner.

When the state did become more interested in the development of an educational service that would meet the needs of children and youth, it generally chose to do so through local school districts. Thus the partnership was strengthened. The state offered certain financial aid and stimulated local districts by making available trained state personnel who could work with them in meeting their problems. The direct provision and management of the schools was a responsibility of local authorities. Thus it could be said that the school system was actually a local one. It was a system marked by variety, by wide differences in opportunity, and by excellent provisions in some cases and extremely inadequate ones in others. In later years the state became much more active and sought to guarantee all children and youth at least a minimum level of opportunity. Even this, however, was done through local districts. The system was scarcely a decentralized one, for it had never been centralized. It was rather a partnership with the state rendering much assistance and giving attention to the development of more competent and responsible local partners.

A system was achieved in which it was hoped that desirable experimentation would result from the independence of local districts in developing schools to meet needs. Many of the advances that have marked education have come from the exercise of initiative by local districts. After the worth of these practices was demonstrated in some communities, they gradually spread to other communities. In some instances the spread of the practices was aided by the state department personnel—in other cases by the enactment of legislation supporting them financially. Our state system of education is also a local system and a partnership.

The nearness of the schools to the people has always been a distinguishing feature of the school system. In few other countries has there been such a close relationship between the schools and the people. This has had both advantages and disadvantages. It has been a major factor in the strong interest that the people have had in their schools. The development of the schools has been closely related to this interest. It has stimulated the making of adaptations in educational practice. It has resulted in a school system of remarkable vitality and excellence with relatively little exercise of rigid controls by state and federal governmental agencies.

On the other hand, it did result in the continuance of many small school districts that did not provide reasonably adequate educational opportunity even though their costs were high. Furthermore, the "interest" of certain pressure groups in education has at times known no bounds, and interference with the schools has harmed them. Materials have been introduced or eliminated from the curriculum as a result of pressure by some group—not always one interested in or competent to judge "what education is of most worth." Teachers also have been subjected to pressure or even discharged without adequate reason or even the opportunity to be heard. The responsibility of the trained educator has at times been seriously hampered by the unsound action of citizens.

Despite the difficulties that have been encountered, few desire to increase the distance between the school and the people. The desire is to move in the other direction, especially in larger communities where the distance separating them may be greater than is generally recognized. In this development, however, there is a growing awareness that some guidelines need to be established. Such guidelines should facilitate close relationship and high public interest without undesirable interference.

THE BOARD OF EDUCATION

While, generally, there has been this close relationship of the citizenry to the schools, there has been a legal structure for the establishment and development of the local school system. The legal responsibility has rested upon the education committee of the town in New England and in other sections of the country upon the board of school trustees, school directors, or board of education.

Election of Board Members

The members of boards of education are generally elected by popular vote. In the majority of instances they are not sponsored by political parties and are not elected as members of a political party. In some of the larger cities, board of education members are appointed by the mayor. In a few cases they are appointed by another agency such as judges of common pleas courts. The appointment procedures have been employed in some cases to effect a closer relationship between the education service and local government services. In other cases appointment reflects some lack of belief in the ability of citizens to elect competent school board members. Opinion in general, however, strongly supports popular election, though it is recognized that board members of a wide range of competence are found under any plan of selection.

Formerly, many board of education members were elected as representatives of wards or areas within the district. This tended to result in board members representing the ward from which they were elected. Consequently, there has been a long-term trend toward election at large. Despite this trend some boards continue with election of members for subdistricts or areas within the school district. This arrangement may be necessary where smaller parts of the district feel they will be completely overshadowed by a more populous section. In some instances members are required to be residents of specified areas though elected by vote of all of the people of the district. Election from subdistricts should be viewed as a somewhat temporary expedient to be replaced when the confidence of the people in the district as a unit has been established.

Board members are generally elected for overlapping terms of three to six years. In order to ensure reasonable continuity, the longer term (with no more than one or two members elected in any one year, or two elected every second year) appears to be preferable.

Size of Boards

The size of boards has varied greatly. Many small rural districts have had only three members. In some of the cities the boards grew as the city added territory, until late in the nineteenth century some boards had several hundred members. During the current century, with the elimination of many of the smaller districts and with an awareness of the problems resulting from extremely large boards, the trend has been toward boards of five to seven or possibly nine members.

Board Duties

The board of education is responsible for the establishment and operation of the local public school system. This usually includes responsibility for kindergartens and grades one through twelve. In some states, depending upon the size of the district, the board also makes provisions for adult education, various special education offerings, and junior college education. Statutes fix this responsibility upon local boards of education either by mandating broad and implied powers or by specifying in more detail the duties and powers of the local board of education. In either case it should be clear that the local board derives its power legally from the state. It thus is an agent of the state and also of the people of the district whom it serves. It serves the people of the district in accord with the mandate of the powers vested in it by the state.

Among the many powers of the board of education the following are of outstanding importance:

1. The selection of a chief administrator, the superintendent of schools;

2. The establishment of policies and procedures in accord with which the schools are administered;

3. The adoption of the budget and the enactment of provisions for the financing of the schools;

4. The acquisition and development of necessary property and the provision of supplies;

5. The appointment of necessary personnel to staff the varied services;

6. The appraisal of the work of the schools and adoption of plans for improvement and expansion.

Board Organization and Functioning

When boards of education were large, dependence upon administrative staff limited, and board members represented subdistricts, the practice of administering schools through the standing committee system was widespread. Then, also, it was not uncommon for individual board members to get deeply involved in the details of administration. They individually interviewed applicants for teaching positions and selected instructional materials.

Today, it is agreed that board members need to recognize that they as individuals do not have powers regarding the schools. Statute fixes responsibility upon the board of education, rather than upon individual members. Furthermore, the standing committee is not favored, though boards may from time to time appoint temporary committees to consider a special problem and report back to the board. The desirability of having the board recognize the establishment of policies and procedures, rather than involve itself in administrative details as a major responsibility, is increasingly clear. This, of course, assumes that the board has competent leadership and staff to secure and provide it with the data that are essential as the basis for the determination of policies and procedures. It also assumes that the board has an administrative staff that can administer the schools in accord with the policies and can report results, including the inadequacies of established policies and procedures.

Thus, the board of education comes to be a unified body devoted to the provision and advancement of the educational service with the cooperation of the teaching, administrative, and other groups of personnel. Its cooperative relationship with the administrative staff is especially important because of the close understanding that must exist between them if the organization is to function properly.

If the board of education is to discharge these difficult responsibilities in an effective manner, it needs to give attention to and make provision for procedures to be followed at board meetings and to records regarding board actions. Otherwise, it will spend its time in the discussion of details rather than policies, and it will frequently engage in lengthy discussions of matters about which it does not have essential data.

The successful board of education meeting is dependent upon a number of factors such as preparing the agenda and related materials effectively, planning the meeting, giving adequate hearings to individuals and groups, and reviewing the meeting.

The agenda should be prepared several days before the meeting and should be submitted to the members of the board along with various reports containing the essential data that must be studied by the board members if they are to be prepared to make decisions. At the opening of the meeting, brief consideration should be given to the plans for the meeting, with tentative allocation of time made to different matters on the agenda. The rules of the board should establish procedures for getting items on the agenda. The rules should provide that under certain circumstances brief presentations may be accepted from individuals or groups regarding matters not on the agenda. The time for such presentations, however, should be limited, and discussion and action generally should be delayed until essential related data may be gathered and presented to the board. At the conclusion of meetings, at least occasionally, the procedures followed should be reviewed. If considerable time was wasted through lack of planning, this should be recognized and plans made to avoid similar situations at later meetings. Meetings can be made fruitful and effective if adequate attention is given to the manner in which they are conducted. Attention can be given to important instructional issues frequently overlooked because of lack of time, if plans are made to do so. Many boards in recent years have given more attention to developing plans for a consideration of these matters. Otherwise, the details of buildings, finance, and business administration will consume the total energies of the board.

The successful functioning of the board is largely a result of the assistance it has in planning its meetings. No other person can render as large a measure of assistance as the superintendent of schools. Partly in recognition of his central relation to sound board functioning many boards appoint the superintendent their secretary.

THE SUPERINTENDENT OF SCHOOLS

The great importance of the position of the superintendent of schools has already been implied in the consideration of the work of the board of education. The position is at least the equal in significance of any other position in the community. If schools are to contribute to the development of the values of the people and not just reflect the community, it will in no small part be because of the leadership furnished by the superintendent.

Selection of Superintendent

No single act of the board of education is more important than its selection of a superintendent. If one is chosen who provides the needed leadership and who is an excellent administrator, the work of the board can be far more effective. An inadequate administrator will make it virtually impossible for the board to render excellent service. The board therefore should devote great care to the selection of the superintendent.

It may do this by first clarifying the role that it desires of a superintendent and then indicating the personal characteristics and educational background and experience that it believes relate significantly to this role. It may also want to assess the local school and community situation as a basis for defining the role. Many boards desire the assistance of professional educators in doing this job. The retiring superintendent, members of the state department of education, or professors in neighboring colleges or universities may be able to render valuable assistance to the board in the work of defining the position and the type of man needed and in doing at least preliminary screening of applicants.

After the position has been defined, recommendations for the position should be sought from colleges and universities. The position is too important to be filled merely by receiving applications of those who by chance hear of it and apply. In the last analysis the board itself will have to choose the man—but it can do a far better job if it has followed procedures such as suggested here and does not find its energies consumed in interviewing large numbers of men who hold administrative certificates but vary widely in competence.

The quality of man secured will, of course, be dependent in part upon the situation. Important considerations in the local situation will be the board and its procedures and attitudes, the quality of the professional staff, the community attitudes toward education, and the nature of the contract and the salary. The initial contract should be long enough to give the superintendent the opportunity to study the situation, to develop plans, and to have a chance to test them through application. This suggests that a four-year contract is a minimal one. After the first contract it would be desirable for the superintendent to hold a continuing contract during satisfactory service.

Responsibilities of the Superintendent

Another important factor related to the quality of superintendent who can be secured is the concept of the position held by the board. Few excellent men will go into a situation in which they are denied opportunity to perform the duties that they regard as those properly vested in the superintendent. In this respect, it should be noted that the duties of the superintendent are largely determined by action of the board—except in a few large cities where a charter or statute partially defines the duties. There are relatively few powers conferred on the superintendent by statute. Although some strengthening of the powers of the superintendent through statute is probably desirable, most laymen and educators favor keeping major responsibility for defining the responsibilities of the superintendent in the hands of the board of education.

Among the important duties of the superintendent are:

1. To serve as chief executive officer of the board of education and thus to be responsible for all phases of the work;
2. To provide leadership in the planning and evaluation of all phases of the instructional program;
3. To select and recommend all personnel for appointment and to guide the in-service growth of said personnel;
4. To prepare the budget for submission to the board and to administer it after its adoption by the board;
5. To determine building needs and to administer building programs—construction, operation, and maintenance;
6. To serve as leader of the board, the staff, and the community in the improvement of the educational system.

If the superintendent is to render superior service, it is important that his duties be clearly defined, but this should not be done by the statement of a multitude of details that tend to limit his activity and produce a rigid administration lacking vision and initiative.

Staff Organization

The growth in responsibility and the larger size of local school systems as a result of the elimination of many of the small districts, the growth in population, the changing concept of what constitutes an adequate education, the increasing aspirations of the people regarding education, and the growing relations with the state and federal governments —all have led to substantial increases in administrative staff. These increases have at times resulted in sharp criticism of administrators and in the charge that too large a percentage of the budget is devoted to administration. Most of this criticism is probably unjustified. However, it should be recognized that the organization of staff, the determination of special competencies needed, the definition of responsibilities, and the appraisal of administrative functioning are highly essential in what is more generally becoming a large-scale organization.[2]

[2]William B. Castetter, *Administering the School Personnel Program* (New York: The Macmillan Company, 1962), pp. 101 ff.

Consideration of the responsibilities of the superintendent listed here suggests the importance of an administrative staff of adequate numbers and high quality. The administrative staff consists not only of the assistant superintendents, directors, and administrative assistants found in the central office but also the principals and assistants located in the respective schools. In a small system the superintendent will need to discharge many of his responsibilities with very little administrative assistance. In a large system his work may be largely the identification of needed development and leadership in securing it, the coordination of the work of others and the direction of the growth of other administrators in the discharge of their responsibilities.

A few decades ago, there was some question as to whether the school system should be organized on a unit or dual or even multiple basis. This was fundamentally a question of whether the superintendent of schools should be the chief executive of the system or whether there should be no one chief executive. It is almost universally agreed today that the organization should be a unitary one and that, since the super-intendent of schools is most basically concerned with instruction (the educational program), he should be the chief executive.

The superintendent of schools has an important decision to make regarding the manner in which the staff is organized. A few decades ago the line-and-staff organization was generally accepted as the most desir-able type. With changing concepts of the meaning of educational lead-ership, this concept of organization has undergone further examination.[3] Can the school principal be effective, both as a line and a staff officer? Or is the term "officer" acceptable? Does the line-and-staff organization facilitate the cooperative effort that the school administrator seeks in the school system today? Is there some other type of organization that is more in accord with present day concepts of leadership and that has larger potential? (See discussion in Chapter 4.)

To what extent should the new administrative staff be located at the central office? At the school level? At selected secondary schools which serve as centers for a number of schools? Or in large systems should there be area superintendents with an office and staff located in the area served? If so, which services shall be decentralized and which centralized?

Fundamental also is the question of the staffing pattern of the local school district. Rapid change in education demands new personnel or reassignment of those with other responsibilities. An old organization is called upon to meet new challenges, to plan, to provide new services, to coordinate services. The organization is frequently subjected to criticism

[3]Alfred A. Skogsberg, *Administrative Operational Patterns* (New York: Bureau of Publications, Teachers College, Columbia University, 1950).

by legislative committees and by teachers' organizations. Teachers' organizations criticize the type and amount of supportive help provided for them.[4] The growing specialization of staff and range of services provided in a school system as well as the increasing rate of change emphasize the need for developing staffing patterns and defensible staffing ratios. Without such guidelines, essential staff provisions to facilitate constructive change are not likely to be made.

Probably the most difficult of the chief administrator's responsibilities is that of selecting and stimulating the development of the members of the administrative team. If his assistants in the central office are highly competent in their respective fields and if they can work effectively as a team and with other people, the superintendent's burdens are greatly reduced. If the principals of the schools are competent and provide leadership in the study of children, the development of the educational program, the stimulation of child growth, and in the area of home-school coordination, then a superior school system results. In a large system the superintendent cannot hope to work directly with large numbers of the teaching staff, but he can influence them greatly through the administrative staff he develops.

THE ADMINISTRATIVE GUIDE

As a way of summarizing this conception of the role of the board of education and the superintendent of schools, attention will be turned briefly to the significance of developing an administrative guide. It should contain policy statements that guide the board, the superintendent, and other staff in the administration of schools in the system, and it should outline procedures regarding some of the more important activities. It can be of great value for the orientation of new board members and new staff. It serves to give to each party involved a better understanding of his responsibilities and thus lessens misunderstandings. It aids the public in understanding how the schools are operated. It facilitates getting the work of the schools done and helps center attention upon the various phases of work that need to be planned and carried through. In the development of a guide all those who are affected by it should be involved. The past practices of the board and system should be analyzed as one basis for it. In the preparation of the guide it is very important that attention be given not only to the specific duties to be discharged by each party but also to the fact that many of the activities can be effectively discharged only through the cooperative action of a number of parties.

The guide should, for example, give to the principal an under-

[4]Arthur D. Little, Inc., *Guidelines for Staffing School Districts to Facilitate Constructive Change* (San Francisco, 1965), p. 20.

standing of the major responsibilities that are his—and also of the extent to which he should serve as a leader of others in decision-making rather than just as a decision-maker. The development of too detailed a code that would result in rigid organization and operation should be avoided. A rigid organization which fails to recognize that the informal organization may be as important as the formal one is not likely to result in an effective educational system.

SOME IMPORTANT PROBLEMS AND ISSUES

In the following pages, consideration will be given to some of the more important issues pertaining to the local administration of schools.

How Can a Community Secure the Most Competent Board of Education?

Election to boards of education has come to be on a nonpartisan basis in most of the states. It has been held that the education service should be carried on independently of the usual political organizations through which the people make choices regarding many questions of public policy.

Everyone would probably agree that a spoils system would not be desirable in education. However, the attempt at avoiding political relationships may have resulted, in some cases, in the concept that education is and should be noncontroversial—that there are no major public policies regarding education that can best be resolved through extended discussion. This may have resulted in the practice of re-electing board of education members without opposition and thus without the vital debate of policies that should take place. It is not the view here that controversy per se is desirable and that elections of school board members should always be contested. Instead, education is considered a service of great public significance. In the long run, educational advances are likely to be related to the extent to which there is public discussion and decision making on important issues. One of the ways to facilitate this discussion is through contests for board of education positions.

There is of course the danger that the contest may not pertain to public policy matters but rather to details of practice or to personalities. This can probably be avoided through careful planning and by developing through public understanding a situation in which a change in board members does not inevitably or even generally mean a change in the chief administrator. The tendency to change the administrator frequently may be related to our spoils tradition, and especially to the immaturity of our communities in the procedures they employ in electing board members and the expectations that they have of them.

If the community is going to secure outstanding board members, it is not likely to secure them through inaction. Rather, interested citizens and groups, preferably in a cooperative manner, need to take various steps. They need to define the qualifications that board members should have, to attempt to identify men and women who have good potentials, to encourage such individuals to run for office and to offer them assistance, to stimulate citizen interest in voting, to take steps to avoid the view that contested elections are undesirable, and to avoid the thought that the new board member is or should be the instrument of the group that supported him. One of the qualifications for the board member should surely be the ability to study objectively the facts and participate in decision making in the interest of those served through education. Prior fixed pledges to some group regarding what will be done about specific services and personnel must therefore be scrupulously avoided. How can a competent man make a commitment without a knowledge of the situation, which knowledge can only be gained in full measure after election?

Such study and encouragement of men to serve as members of boards of education should be applied to incumbents as well as to other citizens. Other things being equal, the incumbents should generally be preferred.

Through the development of attitudes and practices such as are briefly outlined here it is believed that more outstanding boards of education could be secured in many communities, desirable public discussion of policies related to education could be greatly increased, some of the tendency of the new board member and of the community to expect a quick radical turnover of practices and staff could be eliminated, and the problems confronting the public schools could be met in a more intelligent and effective manner.

Unless the public accepts responsibility for securing excellent board members, minorities may control. How can citizen action regarding board member selection be increased and improved?

Should Boards of Education Be Organized
with a Number of Standing Committees,
or Should the Board as a Whole Be a Standing Committee?

When boards of education were large and when they still engaged in direct administration, standing committees were generally used. In some cases, there were many standing committees organized to care for various services or to look after the schools in different sections of the community. It was one way to get the business completed when the administrative staff was extremely limited. Through standing committees it was also believed that the talents of the respective members could be utilized most effectively. The banker chaired the finance committee; the retired contractor, the maintenance committee; the ex-athlete, the committee on athletics. The standing committee did give some members of the board an opportunity to learn a considerable amount regarding some phase of the work.

On the other hand, standing committees led too frequently to the exercise of large influence and even participation in the details of administration by individual board members. In extreme cases they became administrators. Then, too, as a result of the amount of board business and the number of standing committees, the board as a whole came too often to have little time for or interest in major policy matters. Its energies were spent in receiving and generally approving with little discussion the reports of numerous committees. Thus the board came to be less informed than it would have been had it devoted its energies to considering the major issues that confronted it. Another of the problems resulting from the standing committee system was that in effect it resulted in decisions in reality being made in committee—the meetings of which were not open to the public.

The organization of the board as a committee of the whole probably resulted from the desire to have all members involved in decision making and to avoid having board meetings marked by the public presentation of conflicting views. The board could make its decisions in committee and at the board meeting quickly and harmoniously transact its business.

With the growing acceptance of the idea that individual board members should not engage directly in the administrative process and that public business should be conducted in open meetings, the case for standing committees has declined. Approaching the matter positively, it can be said that boards have come increasingly to see the desirability of acting upon major policy matters in public session after adequate data have been collected and analyzed to constitute a base for intelligent action. Of course, it is recognized that in some matters such as certain personnel problems it is in the public interest as well as the interest of individuals to act in closed session. Such matters, however, constitute a very small part of the total activity of the board.

Under what circumstances, if any, are board of education committees desirable?

How Can the Board of Education Appraise the Results of the Educational Service?

Probably the most difficult of the responsibilities of the board of education is that of appraisal. It has selected its staff, provided resources to carry the program through, devoted long hours to a consideration of many policies and procedures, and now it must evaluate. For without evaluation it lacks the basis for decision making regarding future planning and development. Several steps are suggested. They assume that board members are competent.

Each board member should, with the help of the state association of school boards and that of the local staff, develop considerable knowledge about education. He will not be an educational expert—and must avoid assuming that he has become one. But he must become familiar with schools, educational practices, problems, and issues. Unless he does so, he cannot exercise that judgment that appraisal requires on his part. Some of this knowledge he can get through planned visits to schools. For such visits he must have some background and assistance in order that he may understand the significance of what he observes.

Considerable knowledge can be gained through board of education meetings that are planned with this purpose. Materials need to be developed regarding the services or issues under consideration and distributed prior to the meeting. Various staff members may make presentations. Board of education meetings that greatly increase the board members' knowledge of the educational service are not likely to occur unless the need for them is recognized, plans are made for them, and specified times are set for them.

The development of more adequate research provisions and the conducting of continuous evaluation programs are other essential steps. Regrettably, prior to the federal programs developed in the sixties, few resources were provided for research in most school systems. Also, too little is done in planning for a continuing evaluation program which over a period of years would collect large amounts of data about the variety of programs and services that are provided in the schools. The board that will insist upon the development of such plans has taken a long step in the direction of developing a base in the light of which appraisals can be made.

Finally, the board may periodically seek a more comprehensive appraisal. It, too, like the continuous appraisal referred to above, may be carried forward under the direction of the administrative staff. It also may involve the assistance of consultants. It generally should be cooperative— involving teachers and citizens—in many of its aspects. Further suggestions regarding the manner in which such a study can be carried forward are contained in Chapters 5 and 20 dealing with cooperative procedures and with appraisal.

Board of education members and the staff associated with them should recognize that appraisals are inevitably going to be made. Attention therefore needs to be centered upon the problem of insuring that appraisals have a real measure of validity and avoiding the too readily available alternatives of making appraisals on the basis of few or no facts, on the spur of the moment, or in consideration of personalities.

*Can and Should the Work of the Board of Education
and That of the Administrator Be Sharply Separated?*

In an effort to assist individual board members to avoid getting involved in the details of administration it is frequently pointed out that the individual board member, except when the board is in session, has no legal powers not possessed by all other citizens. Further, it is held that the board should see its role as that of policy maker, and the administration should administer in accord with established policy. This view may be sound enough. However, it is unrealistically simple. Consider, for example, the question of the selection of personnel.

A desirable policy would doubtless be that the most competent personnel should be secured—that personnel which can render the greatest service to children. The board however would probably wish to go well beyond such a general policy statement in discharging its responsibility in this area. It would probably wish to adopt procedures that were judged most likely to implement the policy effectively. In the consideration of the policy and especially in the consideration of procedures related to it, the board needs the assistance of the administrative staff. Studies would be required outlining various possible procedures and indicating their probable results. The administrative staff would seek the assistance of members of the instructional staff in formulating such proposals. Periodically, also, the board would wish the assistance of the executive arm in evaluating the procedures in the light of results produced and in effecting modifications. Thus, although the board would adopt the policies and the procedures through which they are to be implemented, it generally could not hope to do the job without very important assistance from its administrative staff. In a sense, therefore, policy making is engaged in by board, administrator, teachers, and other interested parties. Only policies developed through cooperative effort are likely to be sound and have genuine promise of implementation.

Approaching the issue from the other side it can be observed that policy making is a part of administration. Furthermore, such actions as adopting the budget, fixing the tax rate, and authorizing borrowing for capital outlay purposes are important phases of administration. Regarding all these matters, the administrative staff has a highly significant role to play, though the final decision is legally that of the board. In these matters, both the board and administrators are significantly involved in reaching a decision. Other groups such as the teachers and community groups may also play important roles. With the increase in community interest in education and the growing strength of the organized educational profession, it is likely that the problem of determining "who makes the decision" may be more difficult in the future. The growing complexity of the situation, however, demands that attention be given to fixing the responsibility for initiation, for example, and clarifying the expectations of the various groups involved. What thus appeared to be a rather simple problem—the separation of the powers of the administrator and of the board—is a very complex one, one that will be satisfactorily resolved only through extended cooperative effort based upon mutual confidence and respect among the parties involved.

All of this is not to suggest that the board or its members should again become involved in the details of selecting teachers. The procedures adopted should outline clearly the steps to be followed by a competent professional staff in making the selection. The board would confirm the appointments, maintain an interest in the results, and receive reports regarding them. This it would need to do in order to meet its legal responsibility regarding the employment of personnel and in order to be enabled to discharge its appraisal function.

How can the essential cooperative relationship and the recognition of the respective responsibilities of the superintendent and board be attained?

Is the Superintendency a Defensible Position, or Are the Expectancies of the Position too Great?

The superintendency which has long had a reputation for insecurity, short tenure, and being an anxious profession, is in one of its most troubled periods. This is a result of many factors, including the growing expectations for education, the increased role of teachers in administrative and policy decisions, and the view that educational leadership must mean community leadership. Thus *de facto* segregation, an important community problem, has become a major challenge to the school system and to the superintendent.

With the growing awareness of the great variation in the expectancies regarding the superintendency, the question has been raised whether the position is not an impossible one. Should the administrative organization be changed to reduce the varying "demands" on the superintendent? Has there been a tendency to regard the superintendent as the one who can resolve inevitable conflicts—and then to condemn him when they are not resolved?

The board of education looks to the superintendent as its chief executive and perhaps even more importantly as its adviser, guide, and leader. The teachers expect the superintendent to reflect their point of view in his work with the board. Various groups of citizens have widely varying views regarding education and they expect the superintendent to represent their respective views. He also must keep children and youth in mind and decide what would be in their interest. This decision will, of course, be related to his philosophy of life and of education. He has a loyalty to these innermost convictions as well as to the groups just mentioned.

It also should be noted that in an organization the point of view of the chief executive is extremely important. Many individuals are influenced by it, because in a sense the viewpoint of the chief executive sets the tone of the organization or system. His views or attitudes even though not verbalized are known or assumed to be known and rapidly communicated.

Certainly it is true that the superintendency is one of the most difficult positions conceivable because of the impact of expectancies. And even boards of education, for example, may have widely varying views regarding the superintendency and may over a period of time change their expectancies. In communities in which the local superintendent is largely an administrator and not a leader, the position is a much simpler one to fill. However, it is probable that neither our society nor administrators themselves would choose a system that might be easier for the individual but would lower the vision of the system, for out of the conflict of expectancies may come much desirable educational change.

Thus, the continuance of the present system in its essentials appears likely. Recognizing this, we see that certain things might be done. The varied expectancies might well be more clearly determined. The administrator can make greater effort to understand the perspectives of those with different expectancies. With better understanding of the perspectives of others, communication is more likely to occur. With greater involvement of others in the process of decision making, more common understanding can be developed between and among the various parties, including the superintendent. Administrative guides should emphasize the extent to which cooperation marks administration (if it truly does), rather than rigid, fixed definitions of individual responsibility. Recognition that many decisions that must be made are neither right nor wrong but merely best judgments, and a further willingness to examine carefully all proposed solutions, can also make the superintendency more desirable. Knowledge of processes through which sound answers may be found will frequently be better than answers.

Further, as a result of recent federal legislation regarding education, it is to be expected that in the not distant future highly significant research and experimentation may be carried on regarding many more issues in education. The superintendent should take the initiative in formulating problems for experimentation, in utilizing research facilities which may become available, and in seeking answers through carefully planned study. This emphasis may avoid or blunt both unsound attacks and plans and too much dependence upon past experience.

Acceptance by the superintendent of the fact that others may be equally desirous of serving youth and the society may be helpful. The superintendent must recognize that to be helpful to others—to be a leader of others—he must be perceived by others as one who is helpful, one who is a leader.[5] This perception on the part of others has to be earned through demonstrated ability to understand and to work with others and through demonstrated commitments to the purposes of public education.

Finally, the superintendent must recognize that in the very large difficulties of the position are to be found large opportunities. His position is a highly influential one and he may play a negative role, as Callahan has indicated.[6] He can, however, recognize that it is not too unlike other leadership positions in a vital democracy. Kerr has written of the university presidency in terms not at all unlike the experiences of many superintendents. As Kerr has stated, the position of the leader-initiator is rarely a happy one. But there are goals beyond happiness. "Some abuse" is to be expected. "He wins few clear cut victories; . . . He must find satisfaction in being equally distasteful to each of his constituencies; he must reconcile himself to the harsh reality that successes are shrouded in silence while failures are spotlighted in notoriety." But in return for this he has the satisfaction of knowing that he is "in the control tower helping the real pilots make their landings without crashes even in the fog."[7]

Would it be desirable to state more fully the duties of the superintendent in statutes?

Should the Superintendent of Schools Have Greater Security?

The school superintendency has developed into one of the most important positions in our society. Few, if any, men in other professions discharge a role that has a larger impact upon the development of individuals and of our society. The values that he holds as well as his knowledge impinge upon many people. Quite possibly we have developed an administrative situation that fixes too large a responsibility upon one man. Generally, it has been held that the superintendent should be given large powers by the board of education and then held responsible for the effectiveness of the educational system—and not re-employed if he does not "produce." This was a simple, rather clear-cut arrangement and contributed much.

[5]Harriet O. Ronken and Paul R. Lawrence, *Administering Changes; A Case Study of Human Relations in a Factory* (Cambridge: Graduate School of Business Administration, Harvard University, 1952), p. 305.

[6]Raymond E. Callahan, *Education and the Cult of Efficiency* (Chicago: University of Chicago Press, 1962).

[7]Clark Kerr, *The Uses of the University* (Cambridge: Harvard University Press, 1963), p. 40.

However, it is quite possible that the situation needs to be carefully examined and possibly revised. Increasingly, it is being recognized that effective administration is related not only to the administrator but also to many other factors in the situation. Concerning some of these situational factors the administrator may be able to do little or nothing. The very insecurity that he has known has tended to reduce his ability to cope with some of the situations in an effective manner. Improved administration would thus appear to be probable if the situation surrounding the administrator were improved. Insecurity is unlikely to enable the administrator to function well in the interest of the board, the teachers, the children, or the community.

Greater security is not a matter of protecting incompetency. Because of the nature of the administrator's role it is not at all certain that "tenure" in the sense it is applied to teachers is desirable. Rather, it may be found in a growing understanding on the part of boards of education, of teachers' groups, and of community groups that they must act in relation to some of the situations found and not attribute all difficulties to the administrator alone. They need to come to recognize that in this way they may best advance both their own interests and that of education.

On the other hand, administrators should move to overcome some of the situational difficulties themselves and not turn back the movement toward client-centered administration, even if they could. This is but recognition of the fact that general principles regarding personnel which have come to be widely accepted in government, business, and education also have application in the case of school administrators. When administrators are perceived (and accepted) by themselves and others as having certain strengths and limitations, they will be enabled to render more outstanding service.

Should the superintendent of schools have a tenure status similar to that of teachers?

What Shall the Local System Be in a Metropolitan Area?

One of the most difficult problems confronting our society is that of the metropolitan area. It is in these areas that population growth has been and will probably continue to be greatest. Wide variation in wealth, occupation, racial, and social status mark different sections of a metropolitan area. In a sense the metropolitan area is many communities— some highly stratified and others very heterogeneous. But it is also a dynamic social, economic, and political unit. Until four or five decades ago, as the city grew, so did its legal boundaries through annexation. This process then ceased in large part, and the number of units of local governments within the metropolitan area increased sharply. Today the metropolitan area generally contains within it many populous school districts and a considerable number of suburban or fringe area districts.

Actually, the people of the metropolitan area are in a very real sense citizens of the whole area as well as of the small town, city, or township, and of the separate school district. They will not long be able to ignore the government and education of the districts adjoining them. Many educational services now inadequately provided could be well provided by a metropolitan educational district. Special education provisions, research provisions, programs for development of leaders, and technical and junior college education are a few of the types of service that such a metropolitan unit might desirably provide.

But what shall be the organization? Should the metropolitan district levy taxes and receive all state grants for distribution among the various districts as the Metropolitan Education Board of Toronto does?[8] What shall be the powers, duties, and staff of the metropolitan district and those of the subdistricts? Can an organization be effected through which the subdistricts will remain vital, independent, and characterized by initiative in the development of education provisions? What should be the relationships of the board of education, superintendent, and administrative staff of the subdistricts? How should the subdistricts be determined? And how can a desirable metropolitan-local unit system of education be effected?

If, as many agree, the very large city has witnessed an increase of the distance between the people and the school system, then can this be avoided through the development of a federal system in the metropolitan area? Can a situation be achieved in which both the metropolitan area and the local areas within it will be "systems" of education? Can this development enhance the values that have so long been the strengths of the better local systems of education in the United States?

When the extent to which our population will be housed in metropolitan areas in the decades ahead is realized, it quickly becomes clear that the question of the adequacy of our educational organization will be determined in substantial part by developments in metropolitan areas.

Can a "System" Be Achieved if Individual Schools
  or Area Subdivisions Have Considerable Leeway
  and Opportunity for Initiative?

As local school systems have developed in the United States, considerable attention has been given to the development of the system as a whole. Citizens' groups have frequently been quite vocal in demanding that similar programs be offered in all schools as a way of attempting to

[8]Frank Smallwood, *Metro Toronto: A Decade Later* (Toronto: Bureau of Municipal Research, 1963); John C. Bollens and Henry J. Schmandt, *The Metropolis: Its People, Politics and Economic Life* (New York: Harper & Row, Publishers, 1965).

secure what they have regarded as equality of opportunity. Boards of education and administrators also have not been adverse to developing the central office staff in order that needed data regarding the schools may be readily available and that planning may be done in any part of the system in which it is needed. This development of the system has probably been both desirable and inevitable.

Emphasis upon the development of the system can have the unfortunate effect of reducing the significance of the school or of a small number of schools that may serve a part of the district. All schools may tend to look toward the central office for leadership, rather than utilize the opportunity which is theirs either individually or in cooperation with other schools of their neighborhood. Similarly, the specialized staff may be housed largely at the central office rather than at the schools where the instruction is carried on. Such developments can lead to the view that the central office is apart from the schools and is the place where decisions are made. Complaints by school personnel regarding the "downtown" office then are not uncommon.

The view offered here is that the best system can only be achieved by fixing large responsibility upon individual schools or groups of schools serving an area and challenging them to develop the program that best meets the educational needs of the children involved. This does not mean that systemwide objectives should not be established or that central purchasing should not be carried on. With the wider use of television, there will also probably be an increasing demand for uniformity of class schedules. This again emphasizes the desirability of the adoption of the philosophy which holds that the strong system is the system composed of outstanding schools, each having some distinctive achievements. If some uniformity of schedules results from television, then what are the opportunities to balance this that will give to the staff of each school the knowledge that they are part of a dynamic unit?

Teachers generally will support that system in which they have strong commitments to the school of which they are a part. They will have strong commitments to the school if they have been able to develop pride in the manner in which the school meets its educational problems. Thus, the unity that should characterize the strong system is developed by affording opportunity for diversity, which appears to be essential if education is to develop in consideration of the needs of children and youth.

How Can Initiative Be Fostered within the Local School System?

As has been indicated in the chapter on local school districts and intermediate units, larger local school systems are being achieved as the result of district organization and because increases in population tend to be centered in metropolitan areas. In fact, many exceedingly small systems remain. On the other hand, some of our local systems are extremely large—larger, in fact, in student population than many states.

With larger units, communication becomes more difficult. Decision making may occur at increasing distances from the scene of action. The system may remove itself farther from the many communities it encompasses. With the drives toward conformity that mark our society and the desire to be sure of what happens in each school, there might be more of a tendency toward decision making at the center. "Efficiency" in the narrow sense argues for a well-structured, rigid system.

However, one of the main strengths of the public school system has been its nearness to the people. We have sought adaptation through a noncentralized system—anticipating the bubbling up of experimentation and variation in light of needs. The continuance of local taxes for public education has been advocated in part because of the belief that this will facilitate a "local" system of schools.

Perhaps it has been too easily assumed that adaptation, experimentation, and development in the light of needs of children and youth will occur somewhat inevitably. If the local system is to be characterized by initiative it will be the result of opportunities being provided for initiative within the system—probably largely at the individual school level.

Attention should be turned to the restraints that may exist within school systems and to steps that should be taken to stimulate the exercise of initiative. Study may reveal that individual schools are not moving forward because of factors such as the distance between the school and its community, the policies and practices of the board of education or central office staff that reward conformity, the attitudes of principals (the peer group) or teachers in other schools within the system, rigid rules and regulations, the difficulty of developing sound educational programs, and the qualities that are valued when principals are selected.

As systems grow larger, there appears the need to develop a plan by which each school may achieve a life, a uniqueness, and a vitality of its own. In this manner, staff and community can be energized, and the feeling of inability to effect changes in policy and practice that too often marks teachers in extremely large systems can be overcome. Basic to this type of development is a philosophy of administration that seeks high standards through the development of all people involved, rather than through the imposition of uniform practices. This does not mean that there should be no broad common goals and guidelines to practice that are applicable throughout the system. It does mean, however, that the efficiency of practices must be determined in light of the development of people (principals, teachers, pupils, parents) that occurs under these goals and guidelines, rather than in terms of arbitrary standards. It emphasizes the central role of the principal as a leader of school and community and suggests that the main efforts of the central office should be in the direction of rendering assistance in the growth of that leadership.

In regard to what matters are schools encouraged to and aided in taking initiative in most local systems? Is this desirable?

How Should Educational Services Be Coordinated
with Related Services Such as Library,
Public Health, Youth Agencies, Private Schools,
Housing, and City Planning?

The growing concentration of population in metropolitan areas and the growing complexity of society point to the need for closer coordination of the efforts of the educational services and other public and semi-public services concerned with individual and community development.[9] This appears necessary and inevitable if education and the other services are to be administered effectively. Closer coordination among the services should lead to better understanding of children by the various agencies. It also should result in the strengthening of each agency, because greater understanding would result between and among the lay and professional personnel who are associated with the various agencies including the schools.

Decades of development have tended to separate education from other public and private services in the United States. Public education has been uniquely valued as the road to equality of opportunity and the progress of the society. Thus, it has had its own separate government in our society to a far greater degree than in most societies. Recent federal educational legislation, stimulated by the problems of the great cities and recognition of inadequate achievement of goals, has called for a re-examination of the relation of public education to other agencies involved with the development of children and youth. It calls also for a rethinking of the relation of education and schooling.

Fiscal independence for schools has created some misunderstanding on the part of some people concerned with other community services. Without reopening the question of fiscal dependence or independence at this time, there is little question but that much more coordination of effort could be effected. The school system having a responsibility for the development of youth and legally having a relationship with more of them than any other agency should accept responsibility for initiating and facilitating such coordination.

In a middle-sized city or other large district, some effort at co-

[9]Theodore L. Reller, ed., *The Public School and Other Community Services*, Annals of the American Academy of Political and Social Science, 302 (Nov., 1955).

ordination must be made through the central office of the school system and that of other agencies. Here the criteria for such coordination should be developed in cooperation with the other agencies concerned. New patterns of coordination need to be developed and tested during the present decade.

The heart of the effort at coordination, however, must be at the secondary-school attendance area or neighborhood level. The education of a child or youth is greatly influenced by the home, the community, and the school. It is essential that these parties know one another and know something of the efforts of each other. The necessity of home-school cooperation has been emphasized. There has not been a similar emphasis upon school-community cooperation, even though the school is spoken of frequently as the community school, and improved community living looms as one of the major objectives. The effort at coordination should be related to the neighborhood that may contain three or four elementary schools, a couple of junior high schools, and a senior high school. It may also contain private schools, a public library, youth clubs, state employment offices, and a public health center. The area may be larger or smaller than this, depending upon the area organization of related agencies and upon existing feelings of community or neighborhood. It needs to be large enough to involve some resources in terms of personnel from various agencies, yet small enough to make it possible to know youth and resources well.

The nature of the organization for coordination found in various sections of a large school district will vary widely because of their different needs. Although coordination of existing resources is essential, it should be noted that the identification of needs and the securing of more adequate provisions will be the major challenge to both lay and professional personnel.

Does fiscal independence make it difficult for the schools to achieve the cooperation of other agencies working toward community improvement?

Selected References

American Association of School Administrators, *School Board-Superintendent Relationships,* Thirty-fourth Yearbook. Washington, D.C.: The Association, 1956.

———, *The American School Superintendency,* Thirtieth Yearbook. Washington, D.C.: The Association, 1952.

Anderson, Vivienne, and Daniel R. Davies, *Patterns of Educational Leadership.* Englewood Cliffs, N.J.: Prentice-Hall, Inc., 1956.

Arthur D. Little, Inc., *Guidelines for Staffing School Districts in California*. San Francisco, 1965.

Callahan, Raymond E., *Education and the Cult of Efficiency*. Chicago: University of Chicago Press, 1962.

Campbell, Roald F., John E. Corbally, Jr., and John A. Ramseyer, *Introduction to Educational Administration*. Boston: Allyn & Bacon, Inc., 1958.

Davies, Daniel R., and E. L. Prestwood, *Practical School Board Procedures*. New York: Chartwell House, Inc., 1951.

Dubin, Robert, *Human Relations in Administration*. Englewood Cliffs, N.J.: Prentice-Hall, Inc., 1951.

Educational Policies Commission of the National Education Association and the American Association of School Administrators, *The Unique Role of the Superintendent of Schools*. Washington, D.C.: The Commission, 1965.

Fensch, Edwin A., and Robert Wilson, *The Superintendency Team: Organization and Administration of the School System's Central Staff*. Columbus, Ohio: Charles E. Merrill Books, Inc., 1964.

Griffiths, Daniel E., *The School Superintendent*. Englewood Cliffs, N.J.: Prentice-Hall, Inc., 1966.

Hagman, Harlan L., and Alfred Schwarz, *Administration in Profile for School Executives*. New York: Harper & Row, Publishers, 1955.

Kerr, Clark, *The Uses of the University*. Cambridge: Harvard University Press, 1963.

Miles, Matthew B., *Innovation in Education*. New York: Bureau of Publications, Teachers College, Columbia University, 1964.

Moore, Hollis A., Jr., *Studies in School Administration*. Washington, D.C.: The American Association of School Administrators, 1957.

Reller, Theodore L., *Problems of Public Education in the San Francisco Bay Area*. Berkeley: Institute of Governmental Studies, University of California, 1963.

Spalding, Willard B., *The Superintendency of Schools: An Anxious Profession*. Cambridge: Harvard University Press, 1954.

12

Organization of Schools for Instructional Purposes

The present organization of schools for instructional purposes is the result of long years of experience during which competing purposes and plans have emerged and been tried to a limited degree. Too frequently, inadequately prepared teachers, inadequate instructional materials, poor physical facilities, limited financial resources, growing numbers of children, less than desirable administrative leadership, and invalid evaluation techniques and procedures have resulted in necessary decision making based upon notably inadequate data. When data are not available which establish the worth of one arrangement or plan over another, it is understandable that cost, convenience, or expediency may become the major influences in decision making.

While past decades have seen many plans offered and some movement back and forth from one idea to another, it is nevertheless true that the concept of a single class to a room in a definitely graded school with limited departmentalization has been widely adopted. Also the 6-3-3 plan of organization has come to be widely accepted. Further, schools at the elementary and even high school level have come to be regarded as neighborhood schools. High schools were generally regarded as necessarily comprehensive, though the extent to which they were truly comprehensive in meeting the needs of all youth was inadequately determined. When thus, by about 1960, it appeared that the organizational plans had been substantially set, strong new forces challenged them more sharply than had been done for a long period.

The challenge came from a number of directions and may have large effects. Among the major forces involved in the challenge were: the demand for higher standards of intellectual achievement which involved programs for the gifted as well as programs designed to alter the motivations of the culturally different and thus raise their achievement levels; the redefinition of the concept of equality of opportunity, which ruled out the idea of expending equal dollars per child and insisted that those who had least opportunity in their homes and communities must have more in the school; the technical advance which made many new procedures and organizations potentially valuable (television, programed learning, language laboratories, magnetic tapes, kinescopes) and focused attention once more upon independent study and student acceptance of responsibility for learning; higher teacher competence; recognition of range and variety in teacher competencies, awareness that not all teachers are equally prepared to direct the growing diversity of learning which is necessary and that they should be assisted by subprofessionals; increased knowledge regarding the range of abilities of children to learn and the age at which certain types of knowledges and skills can be learned; increased belief in the effect of environmental forces as a factor in determining the learning potential of children and a related or consequent emphasis upon the preschool years; the attack on *de facto* segregation and the demand that the segregated school be recognized as inherently inferior; the seeking of a heterogeneous rather than a homogeneous student body in terms of social, economic, and racial factors.

From these forces have come demands for such programs and plans as the nongraded school, the Stoddard dual-progress plan, team teaching, prekindergarten instruction, special programs for the culturally different, special programs for the gifted, the 6 or 7-4-4 plan (1 or 2 years preschool, kindergarten, grades 1-4, grades 5-8, 9-12), and education parks.

Many other proposals have been made. For example, a columnist a few years ago proposed through the press that in view of the increasing numbers of children and the growing costs of education, the schools of the future should be designed for efficiency. He stated that the schools should become large institutions, so that their various facilities and personnel could be utilized with little waste of effort. He urged consideration of a plan whereby a city of 100,000 population might have only one school for its 15,000 or even 20,000 students. A school of this size could afford to employ many specialists whose energies would not be wasted in traveling from school to school. Here the plant could be utilized by one or another group—the occasional vacant classroom in elementary schools would not exist. One kitchen and possibly one cafeteria could serve all students and staff. A central file of records would contain detailed information regarding the total years of education of each child. Fewer principals, in fact, very few principals would be needed. Testing could be done by a few highly trained people with the aid of modern machines. Extended student records could be efficiently developed and maintained; modern instructional equipment could be employed by highly skilled personnel.

PURPOSES OF ORGANIZATION

Such a proposal is not presented with the idea that it should be adopted. It is included primarily to indicate that a different plan of organization could conceivably be employed and to raise the question as to why it may not be especially appealing. Is it only that it is new and we are unaccustomed to the thought? What are the purposes of an organizational plan?

The only significant test of the worthwhileness of any organizational plan is its effect upon the educational program, or the opportunity that it affords children to learn. All other tests such as the desires of teachers or parents or taxpayers are relevant only in the sense that they do or may impinge upon the learning of children. This test may appear to be so obviously the valid test that one might wonder whether it is necessary to mention it. Actually, however, it needs considerable emphasis, because institutions tend to formalize, to go their own way without the essential re-examination in light of purposes. Pressure groups exist that may have little or no concern for the education of children. They may seek answers that satisfy their purposes with regrettably little regard for the well-being of the society or of its members. Furthermore an organizational plan may result in a satisfactory operation but not be a stimulant to initiative, experimentation and continued development.

The application of the test is not easy. What is the nature of the learning that is desired on the part of children and young people? How can the school raise the motivational levels of the culturally different children? What are the individual and social needs of children for which provision must be made? Are academic skills, artistic skills, vocational skills, or social skills to be emphasized and to what extent? Are knowledge, appreciation, citizenship, or all of these to be highly valued? Is conformity sought primarily, or is initiative a major goal? Is education the prerogative of the school, or is it desired that the home and neighborhood shall play a large role? What are the basic values toward which the schools should be stimulating growth? Only when these and many related questions are answered in some manner can the test be applied.

Any examination of the problem of organization requires not only an awareness of the relation of purposes to organization but also knowledge regarding how learning takes place. The goals could be clear but relatively meaningless if the nature of the child, the learning process, and the forces influencing learning were not understood.

The difficulties with or inadequacies of the proposal included in the introduction to this chapter may become clear when purposes and knowledge of learning processes are considered. It may not appear to be a plan through which home and school would be encouraged to know one another and to cooperate in the process of education. It may not offer much promise in terms of giving to students or teachers the feeling that they are a responsible part of an institution. It may suggest that the emotional needs of the child be largely ignored.

But are these "inadequacies" of the proposal inherent in it or are they the result of our limited understanding of it? Conceivably under competent leadership the home and school relationship could become very close with important programs to assist parents in their educational role. With competent specialists, adequate numbers of staff, and appropriate facilities students could play an important role in the life of the school. Similarly, emotional needs of children might be far better provided for than in the usually much smaller school. In fact, if such a school were not organized on the basis of a limited concept of the meaning of efficiency (saving expenditures, rather than an investment in human development) it would probably not be a single school but almost inevitably an education park. The size of the school may then be of much less importance than the organization of the school, its living space, staff, and instructional facilities.

SCOPE OF THE EDUCATIONAL PROGRAM

The expansion of the program of public education is another matter that is related to the problem of organization. When the school system was largely an elementary system with an occasional academic high school to provide for the relatively small percent who continued their education, much of the complexity of the problem was absent. The addition of the child care center, the nursery school, preschool programs, the kindergarten, the junior high school, the junior college, various special schools, and the development of an extended adult education program offer new opportunities and challenges for organization.

The scope of the educational program has not only extended further down and up. It has also expanded greatly at the various levels. How different the modern elementary school program is from that of a few decades ago. In addition to the traditional skill subjects, one looks for programs in areas such as science, art, crafts, music, health, and foreign languages. In all areas the well-worn textbook has been replaced by a program that emphasizes concept, principle, meaning, appreciation, understanding, and ability to work as an individual and as a member of a group, as well as skill and knowledge. The sameness of program for all has been replaced by a program that recognizes individual differences and provides for those with special needs as well as for those of outstanding capabilities.

Cafeterias, independent study areas, a wide variety of shops, music, speech, and art facilities, family living centers, and foreign language centers suggest the change in the offerings of the high school. The modern school with its great range of subjects and activities is strikingly different from the school composed of standard classrooms. The provision of the facilities raises the question as to the age for which they should be provided and the organization through which they can best be made available. Are special rooms and facilities needed in the seventh or eighth grades, or is the ninth grade the one in which they become necessary? Or are special facilities mostly related to individual differences? Does provision for the "gifted" mean enrichment or special groups or both? If special groups, are they for the intellectually gifted only or for a number of other categories of giftedness?

Can the wide range of technical programs and the guidance services needed by the fourteen- to eighteen-year-old be provided most effectively in a three-year senior high school and two-year junior college or in a four-year junior college? In what schools providing for what ages can various phases of the general education program be provided in the most desirable manner? Is there no one grade that should be sharply differentiated from the one that precedes it or follows it?

Should adult education programs be developed as an integral part of the community or junior college? Does the high school have any further adult education role after the establishment of the community college? Should adult centers separate from the secondary schools be established? Are special technical training centers necessary for youth and adults? What should be their relation to secondary schools? junior colleges?

ORGANIZATIONAL PLANS

The number of types of organizations that exist in school systems is very great. Various combinations of grades or age groups are established by communities either temporarily or for relatively long periods. The types of special schools also vary considerably. It is not important that the organizational arrangements be similar.

The organization should be determined by the purposes and needs of the area served by the school district. A couple of decades ago, one community with two elementary school plants, concerned about the growth of all of its children and the development of understanding between the children of long-time residents and those of the new "dust bowl" and ethnic group residents, anxious to avoid an "across the tracks" group, established one K-3 school for the kindergarten through the third grade and another for grades 4–6. It did this although it thereby reduced the possibility that each school might become a "neighborhood" school. Two K-6 schools would have been the more usual and more easily justified arrangement. They would have resulted in shorter distances to school and less expense for transportation. The community, however, has been well satisfied with the educational achievements under this plan and does not wish to change. This plan was a forerunner of many that have been adopted in recent years to overcome *de facto* segregation. Other communities have organizational plans that are not widely used or discussed. In many instances the unusual plan may be the result of a building situation, rather than a consideration of educational needs of children. Recognizing that not all organizations can be described, attention will be given to only a few including the more common ones.

Eight-Four Plan

The 8–4 plan is the traditional way of organizing education in the United States. A variant of this was the 7–4 plan in sections of the country where eleven years of public school education were provided. Until approximately 1910, this plan was found very generally. Since that time it has lost ground at varying rates depending upon the growth of the intermediate school or the junior high school concept. The 8–4 plan came under attack principally because it was believed that it provided students too limited a program in grades 7–8. The seventh- and eighth-grade students were thought to be at a period of development when a more varied program and one less repetitious of the elementary subjects should be provided. In the first decades of the present century it was also held that more students would continue in school for a longer period if the break in organization came at some point that did not coincide with the age of fourteen, that was commonly regarded as the end of attendance by large numbers of youth and parents.

In more recent years the 8–4 plan has continued strongest in rural areas, where a more conservative approach to education has been found, and in states with separate administrative units for elementary education. There has also been some support for it on the basis of the belief that under this plan the thirteen- and fourteen-year-old student does not mature socially at a rapid rate. Proponents argue that the seventh grader is too young to be in a junior high school and too greatly influenced in an undesirable manner by the "mature" ninth-grade students. Despite these arguments that have been rather frequently advanced in recent years, few if any school systems are returning to the 8–4 organization.

It should be noted that in the case of the 8–4 plan as well as in other plans of organization, the kindergarten has been widely provided. The growth of the kindergarten since 1940 has been rapid. However, it has not generally been incorporated into another unit of organization, but rather has remained as a separate unit in our thinking even though it has been housed in nearly all cases in the elementary school buildings. The rapid expansion of preschool opportunities in the 1960s also suggests the need for a re-examination of the organization plan. What shall be the relation of preschool programs to the kindergarten and to grades 1 and 2?

Six-Three-Three Plan

This plan of organization is now the most widespread in the nation. It is found particularly in the urban areas and in states that have accepted the desirability of the junior high school. In some states the junior high school has been encouraged not only through the efforts of educational leaders but also through favorable state aid provisions.

Among the advantages claimed for this plan are enriched provisions for seventh- and eighth-grade students, a junior secondary school of adequate length to develop a good guidance program, opportunities for ninth-grade students to develop leadership capacity, and large opportunity to develop a program related to the needs of young people of this age as a result of being freed from the traditional patterns of both the elementary and senior high schools.

Although the percentage of children in school systems organized in accord with this plan has continued to increase, there have been many criticisms leveled at some of the organizational units of this plan in recent years. These criticisms have pertained to the secondary schools rather than to the elementary. It has been argued that many junior high schools have been "overdepartmentalized," are nothing but little high schools, and that the academic achievement in them has been unsatisfactory. Studies have not supported the charges regarding lower academic achievement, but among the critics there are those who believe that the ninth grade should be in the senior high school to raise the achievement level. As mentioned above, it has also been argued that the seventh- and ninth-grade children are too wide apart in development to be members of the same school.

Recently this plan as well as the 8–4 has also come under attack in the large cities as one which does not facilitate desegregation to the desired extent. Including fewer grades in a unit, especially at the elementary level, makes it possible to bring together children from a wider area who may be more heterogeneous socially or racially.

Six-Two-Four Plan

This plan is found in communities or sections of the country where the 6–3–3 plan is unacceptable because of certain conditions or viewpoints such as the following:

1. Separate elementary and secondary school districts with responsibilities respectively for grades 1–8 and 9–12 are in existence.
2. Four-year senior high schools are believed to offer better college preparatory programs than three-year senior secondary schools.
3. The two-year intermediate school offers the opportunity to develop a better, less departmentalized educational program than the three-year junior high school.
4. Economy can be effected because the two-year school does not need all the special facilities that appear necessary in the three-year junior high school.
5. The three-year school provides too wide a range of ages with resultant undesirable development of students in the seventh grade.

Four-Four-Four-Four Plan
    or Four-Four-Three-Three-Two Plan

These plans are not offered as ones which are widely employed at the present time. They are presented, however, to suggest that developments are occurring which may make the emergence of new plans highly desirable. Both of these plans make provision for sixteen years of public education. They incorporate one preschool year, the kindergarten, and two years of junior college into the organizational structure. In many instances these provisions are being made, but in part they remain appendages rather than officially established elements of a structure.

When the preschool and kindergarten are attached to the structure, they would appear to fit well with the first two years of the elementary school. Thus, a four-year institution which would be relatively small and close to the home would result. The second four-year block, including traditional grades 3 to 6 could then be somewhat farther removed from the home and could facilitate desegregation through serving a larger geographical area. The goals of these years may also suggest the desirability of having them in one unit.

It is to be noted that at the top of the structure the junior college is being added at a very rapid rate. A decade ago, only a few states clearly regarded it as essential, but now there are many. The junior college, however, is not universal in many states, and in some states it serves only limited functions. The next decade, however, will almost certainly see it expand rapidly both in terms of provision for it being made and in terms of having it become multipurpose. It will need to serve increasingly not only as a part of higher education but as a vehicle for a new level of vocational-technical education and as an adult education center. These developments offer an important opportunity for a thorough re-examination of the strengths of various organizational plans.

The extension downward and upward of educational provisions suggests that the old designations such as 6–3–3 and 8–4 will be discarded during the 1960s and 1970s and that new, more comprehensive and accurate terminology will become accepted. Possibly, greater structural variation will be found both within and among districts.

ORGANIZATIONAL GUIDELINES

The complexity of the problem of organization makes the formulation of a number of guidelines desirable. They should be of value either in evaluating an existing organization or in developing an organizational plan. In considering these guidelines, we should keep in mind that no one organization will meet the needs of all communities, that organizational plans have varying potentials, and that regardless of the organizational plan the potential may go largely unrealized. Some of the guidelines that follow pertain to the plan for determining the types of schools to be established; others pertain to the schools within the plan. In general, they refer to the basic units such as elementary and secondary schools, rather than to schools for children with special needs.

1. *The value of any organizational plan must be determined fundamentally in terms of the opportunity that it provides for the development of the desired educational program.* The establishment of any units in an organizational plan may have the effect of suggesting that the school in question is much more different from the other units of the school system than it actually is. Educational needs of children and youth are not basically different. It is a matter of emphasis rather than difference in kind. The needs of the sixth-grade student are far more similar to those of the seventh grader than to those of the child in the first grade, even though he is in the elementary school rather than in the junior high school.

2. *The organizational units need to be understood as instruments through which more adequate provisions can be made for caring for individual differences.* The establishment of formal units of organization

may cause some people to have too little regard for the differences among the students within the school. Principals, teachers, and parents may assume that since the children are all within a two- or three-year age bracket their needs may be substantially met through a common program. The idea that the narrow age-range produces homogeneity in many significant areas for education must be sharply rejected. Team teaching and nongrading are both intended to facilitate more adequate provision for individual differences than has been provided in the grade-level system.

3. *The plan of organization involving the various schools must provide for the continuous educational development of children and youth.* Although the plan should be designed to facilitate continuity, it cannot be assumed that this will result. The establishment of any plan of organization requires a positive program to facilitate the necessary relations and understandings between the schools. The most important approach to this problem is the development of a total program of education that has substantial elements of continuity in purposes, content, and methods, and yet provides for the needs of children and youth as they mature. As has been suggested, it is inevitably true that some members of any school are more similar in needs to members of other schools than to the majority of those in the unit of which they are a part.

The nature of growth of children and youth and the extent to which children are characterized by individual patterns of growth emphasize the need of continuity in the educational program. Sharp changes in methods and content are difficult to justify. Despite these facts, any unit or school takes on certain special characteristics. The fact that a school is a society with a measure of independence makes this both inevitable and desirable. The problem of the student who passes from one school to another that makes rather different assumptions about his needs is a large one. How to help each unit play its distinctive role effectively and yet coordinate its efforts with those of related units remains a major continuing problem. Whether or not a given organizational plan is desirable is highly related to the extent to which it effectively integrates the units.

4. *The organizational plan must be continuously or periodically re-examined in a constructive manner with a view to assisting schools to meet educational purposes in a more effective manner or to provide a basis for modifying the plan.* Schools have a tendency to formalize, to develop *a* program, to become too rigid. Thus the excellent school or unit today may become complacent and lose its justification for existing. The community and school system aware of this tendency will avoid it through the development of a program designed to help the unit or school contribute as it should to the total plan. Failing in this, the community will seek the creation of schools or units that will contribute

more effectively to the educational growth of children and young people. Changes in society and changes in educational aims may warrant modifications in the organizational plan.

5.   *The school should be large enough to make available necessary specialized competencies and services at reasonable cost; it should be small enough or be so organized as to be comprehensible to the student and to facilitate the recognition of and the provisions for individual differences.* It should be of such size that the student is encouraged to participate in its functioning. It should be small enough to facilitate the development of competencies that may result from genuine involvement in the life of a society. The desirable size of schools has not been determined through any rigidly scientific procedures. However, it would appear that there is rather widespread agreement concerning approximate desirable ranges of population of schools of various types. Elementary schools with kindergarten through grade six might range from approximately 200 to 700. A student population of 300 to 900 would be regarded favorably for a junior high school. Senior high schools with a population of 400 to 1500 would appear to be desirable. It should be noted that these are approximations and that, while costs would be higher, smaller schools could also be good schools. Similarly, larger schools could be good ones, though special arrangements to overcome some of the undesirable effects of size should be made.

6.   *In large schools many of the advantages of the smaller unit can be attained through the organization of "schools within the school."* The question of at what point a school is too large was an important one when a monolithic organization was assumed. With new organizational patterns providing for decentralization which enables each student and faculty member to identify with "his own school," the traditional views on size need no longer apply. House plans, schools within schools, team teaching when comprehensively developed, and other subschool plans offer large opportunties for improvement. It must be recognized, however, that while there has been much discussion of such plans in recent years and while some school districts have implemented them, much remains to be done. There are important problems in housing, program planning, staff assignment and development, grouping or forming subschools, financing, and related matters that must be worked through if such plans are to become more common. The opportunity to advance such plans appears to be good. However, the problem is so difficult and complex that the attainment of such plans in many communities will require the exercise of all of the change agent power of the school administrator.

7.   *The school should be characterized by both homogeneity and heterogeneity.* Actually, this may be a matter about which relatively little can be done easily in many communities because of the segregated

housing that exists in them. People of a given socioeconomic level or racial or ethnic group tend to reside in one section of the community. In an effort to avoid transporting children and to enable the schools to work closely with the homes and community, a system has frequently provided that a rather homogeneous social group attended a given elementary, junior high, or even senior high school. This had some advantages, for each school should have or develop some community of feeling. Without this it is likely to be an extremely turbulent society. On the other hand, such a school can easily be too complacent and may provide little of the education that may result from associating with children from different groups and working through some of the problems of the society. Perhaps the school that is quite heterogeneous in the backgrounds of its students but that becomes a society in which individuals from the various groups really belong is the school to be desired. The creation of such schools, however, it has been generally argued, does not warrant the shifting of students from one section of the community to another without reference to their residence. In recent years, however, the society has drafted the schools to be the principal change agent to effect racial integration. Further, the potential educational value of the integrated school has become more widely accepted and various plans to facilitate integration, including transportation of pupils, have been urged and adopted.

Careful examination may reveal far greater heterogeneity in the backgrounds of the student body of many schools than is commonly recognized. The question of heterogeneity or homogeneity is one that needs much more careful study and consideration than it has had. This involves not only the nature of those in the school but especially the question of what is done in the school. Have too many communities and professional staffs assumed that being together in a school inevitably results in understanding and mutual respect? Has much of the educational potential of the heterogeneous student body gone unrealized?

These guidelines indicate the complexity of the organizational problem. It is a problem that warrants greatly increased study. The potential of some organizational plans is greater than that of others. Much of the potential of any plan may go unrealized unless there is continuous restudy and development of the plan and of the schools that it provides. Thus, much of the potential value of the comprehensive high school or of the integrated school goes unrealized.

SELECTED ISSUES

A few major issues in the field of organization for instruction are examined in the following pages.

Shall Preschool-Kindergarten-Primary Units
Be Developed as Separate Units?

The kindergarten-primary unit that provides for children in kindergarten through the second or third grade has been regarded by some as a highly desirable unit. It is small, generally with fewer than 200 students, and consequently a school in which the young child may easily find security. It can be designed to be quite like a home and generally does not need to be far removed from the place of residence of the child. It should facilitate home-school cooperation in the early school years. Further, it is a rather natural unit in that it includes the younger children who do not need large play areas but who do need a similar educational environment. In this type of school it may also be easier to have less emphasis upon the division of children into traditional grades than in the K-6 school.

Opponents of this type of school point out that it introduces another division and thus tends to break the continuity of the elementary education experience. Even though this gap may be largely closed by special effort, they believe the gap should not be created. They also point to the administrative problems of a school that is too small to have a full-time principal, a cafeteria, or a health unit, and in which there are no older children to serve on a traffic patrol or in other helpful ways.

Analysis of the experience with the unit suggests that its potentiality in terms of improved home-school relations has not been realized in large measure. It would appear that a case has not been made for this unit as one that should be generally utilized. This is not to deny the fact that there are many situations in which it may readily be justified. It may help reduce the size of an elementary school that is too large or overcrowded. It may assist in overcoming the need of transporting children. It may be desirable in a situation where an adequate site for a large elementary school is not available but where some additional facility is necessary. It may be a desirable way of meeting a bulge in population in an area that can later be served adequately by an existing K-6 school. It may be the first unit of a K-6 school that is developed later, provided the site is adequate.

The preschool-kindergarten-primary unit can provide an educational opportunity at least equal to that of the regular elementary school. Decision to use it or not would appear to depend upon the conditions found. Plans for its use should include consideration of the somewhat special administrative problems that it may bring with it.

When preschool-kindergarten-primary units are established, what steps should be taken to make sure that the unique potential educational values of this type of school will be sought? To what extent and in what manner can the claimed educational advantages of the kindergarten-primary unit be realized in a K-6 school?

Shall the Junior High School Be Two, Three, or Four Years in Length?

Although the six-year elementary school based upon a kindergarten has come to be widely accepted as the unit of organization for the years prior to the approximate age of twelve, there has been no similar agreement regarding the early secondary school years. The three-year junior high school has continued to grow in acceptance, but there has also been some re-emphasis of the two-year junior high school. The four-year junior high school has been found largely in communities that have had a junior college and have followed the K-6-4-4 plan of organization. It is now found less frequently than it was a decade ago.

The three-year junior high school appears to be preferable to the two-year in that it offers a longer period of time for the teachers and staff to get to know the student and for the student to make the school his institution. Three years affords more ample time to provide a program that at the one end must reflect the continuity of the elementary school and at the other end be related to the practices of the senior high school. It must have these relationships and yet not neglect the provision of the most desirable opportunity for young adolescents. In three years the transition from little to considerable departmentalization can be effected more satisfactorily than in two. In three years the change in methods and materials in instruction can also be better carried through. Guidance is difficult in a two-year school because the student is a member for too short a period. Half of the student body changes every year in a two-year school. This is too great a turnover for effective education. In a three-year school the ninth-grade students can offer leadership to others and experience considerable leadership opportunity. Eighth-grade students do not provide similar leadership in a two-year school.

Proponents of the two-year school hold that the differences between the seventh and the ninth grades are too great. They believe that the seventh-grade students are too much influenced by the ninth-grade students and as a consequence "grow up too quickly." The question of rapid or early social development that they associate with the junior high school is very much in their minds. It is also the belief of many of those favoring the 7-8 grade school that in it, as well as in the ninth grade of a four-year senior high school, traditional academic achievement is emphasized to a greater extent and that academic achievement is greater than in the three-year junior high school. Although it is not generally mentioned, it is possible that education in the 7-8 grade schools is less expensive than in 7-9 grade schools. The 7-8 grade buildings generally contain fewer special rooms. In fact, some of them offer extremely meager educational opportunities because of a lack of reasonably adequate facilities for a program including arts, crafts, and music activities, guidance work, physical education, shops, and library. The desire for economy, even though it results in an inadequate program, may be a factor that results in 7–8 rather than 7–9 grade schools in some communities.

In considering the problem of the preferred length of the junior high school, attention must be given to many factors. Other things being equal, probably the three-year school is to be preferred. However, a decision should be made only after consideration of many related factors. A three-year junior high school that is marked by excessive departmentalization may be less desirable than a two-year school without this arrangement. A two-year school that is very effectively articulated with both the elementary school and the senior high school may do a better job than a three-year school lacking such articulation. Probably no division of the school system is in greater need of careful study and development than the junior high school. Much of its promise has not been realized. However, in one form or another it will remain and it will continue to be a challenge to those who can grasp its potentialities.

Do the ninth-grade students "belong" in a junior or senior high school? What do studies regarding the physiological and social maturation of children suggest in this regard? How much departmentalization should there be in two- and three-year junior high schools respectively?

Shall the High School Be Comprehensive or Special Purpose?

This question may be regarded as one that has been answered in our society. Yet despite the long trend toward the comprehensive school there remains a real measure of doubt in the minds of many people. The recent attacks on the high school and the claims that it offers too little encouragement to the development of genuine intellectual interests on the part of even the well-endowed student are not unrelated to this issue. The interest in more adequate provisions for the "gifted" also pertains to it.

Those who favor a special-purpose school believe that its more limited and clear-cut aims are more readily realizable than the aims of the comprehensive school. They believe that higher achievement, especially with reference to the aims most closely related to the special purpose, will result.

Proponents of the comprehensive school emphasize somewhat different aims, though holding that the aims of those favoring the specialized school are also more likely to be desirably achieved in the comprehensive school. They believe that the comprehensive school can better help all youth develop the common goals while also achieving in the light of their individual needs and abilities. They also believe that the comprehensive schools will contribute to the further democratization of our society, to the acceptance of people for their individual worth, to equalitarianism, and to the avoidance or reduction of class tension. They see much greater opportunity to study youth and to attempt to develop a program related to their social and individual needs than is likely to be found in special-purpose schools. It is easier to develop certain common objectives within one school than in a number of schools. It is easier to transfer from one curriculum to another within a school than to transfer to another school. Further, they dislike the separation of children and youth at an early age; they wish to provide more common experiences and to delay career decision-making—which if made early is likely to be more related to economic and social position.

What differences are there in the aims of the proponents of the comprehensive and of the specialized secondary school? Can the desires of those seeking specialized secondary schools be more fully satisfied in the comprehensive school than they have been? Can this be done without doing violence to the comprehensive school?

Shall the Junior College
Be a Two- or Four-Year Institution?

The probable great increase in the number of junior colleges in the next couple of decades makes consideration of the length of the junior college program of considerable importance. The commonly accepted length is two years—grades 13 and 14. There has been some development of the junior college, however, as a four-year institution—grades 11 to 14 inclusive. For a number of years the four-year institution was favorably regarded in California and was adopted by a number of school districts such as Pasadena, Stockton, and Compton. These districts have now adopted the two-year institution. The decision to discontinue the four-year institution, however, was not based upon a careful consideration of educational desirability and consequently should not be regarded as providing a satisfactory answer to other communities. The experience that these cities have had, however, needs to be examined in order that there may be an awareness of the difficulties that were encountered with this plan of organization.

The two-year institution fits into the usual situation more readily than the four. It does not call for the reorganization of the high school. It can take its place as a part of higher education more readily than the four-year institution. If the idea of the junior college is not accepted as a part of free public education to the extent that the high school is, it avoids mixing groups for which different provisions are made. The recruitment of a faculty may be easier because it is a "college." On the other hand two years is a short span for an educational institution to carry through a guidance and instructional program for youth. This short span is further emphasized when the turnover of thirteenth- and fourteenth-grade students is realized. The two-year institution is more definitely a part of secondary education than of higher education and thus it results in three institutions for the eight-year period of secondary education. This would appear to provide more gaps than are desirable. In smaller communities the two-year institution is likely to be extremely small and therefore offer either a very limited program or a very expensive one on a per student basis. In larger communities the two-year institution may have as broad a program at as reasonable a cost as the four-year institution.

The establishment of a four-year junior college preceded by a four-year junior high school reduces the number of gaps, increases the opportunity of developing a guidance and educational program marked by continuity, and makes possible a greatly enriched program at a given cost.

Despite what would appear to be obvious educational advantages of the four-year institutions, they have had many difficulties. They have interfered with the established secondary school athletic practices and made it difficult to schedule games with neighboring traditionally organized schools. This has aroused the highly vocal, athletically minded citizens and press. They have not been able to develop an integrated four-year program. Rather, they have had two two-year programs. This is the result of such factors as tradition, state laws and regulations, and the desire of some youth to transfer to four-year colleges at the beginning of the thirteenth grade. Thus the educational potential of the four-year institutions has not been realized. The control of youth in these institutions has been difficult. Regarding such matters as smoking, the provisions of law in some states are different for the eleventh and twelfth grades from the provisions for the thirteenth and fourteenth grades. Thus, a variety of forces have led communities to discontinue the four-year institutions. This, however, should not be regarded as an adequate answer to the issue of the two- or four-year institution. Only a careful study of the local situation and consideration of the many factors involved can give an indication of which is educationally preferable in a given community. Note should be made of the fact, however, that it is generally much easier to fit into a prevailing pattern, whether or not it is defensible, than to build the new.

Can a more satisfactory technical vocational program be developed in a two- or four-year junior college? Is the general education program of the eleventh and twelfth grades similar to that in the thirteenth and fourteenth? How should locations for junior college centers be determined?

Should the Junior College Be a Part of the Public
School System or of the State University System?

The junior college will experience great expansion in many parts of the country during the next decade. Demands or needs that it will meet will be of various types. It will be expected to render large assistance in meeting the need of providing the first two years of college opportunity for an increasing percentage of young people. Without this development of the junior college, it appears doubtful that even the percentage of young people who are currently enjoying college opportunity will be able to do so. Actually, both individual and social demand will in all probability require that provision be made for a larger percentage. In view of the expansion of this phase of the junior college work, there are those who believe that the junior college should be increasingly associated with and preferably become a part of the university.

On the other hand, it must be recognized that the other functions of the junior college will also expand—and at a rate equal to or exceeding the demand for the provision of the first years of college opportunity. The terminal function involving both general education and technical programs promises large growth. Increasing leisure and the growth of social problems emphasize the need for education for citizenship and individual development. The technological age emphasizes the need for expanded provisions for technical education and re-education for many people. The junior college thus will meet adult needs to an increasing extent and will become more truly a community college.

Considering its functions, the junior college could thus properly be a part of either the public school system or of the university system. Regardless of which of these institutions it is joined to, it will need to maintain exceedingly close relations with the other. The most desirable arrangement may conceivably be different in one state from another, depending upon such factors as the district structure for public education, the concept of role held by the university and the public schools, and the other available higher education facilities.

As a generalization, however, it is believed that it may be preferable for the junior college to be a part of the public school system. Under this arrangement it will probably be more responsive to the needs of the community and serve the terminal, guidance, and adult functions more effectively. It will also be viewed as a part of the community more fully if it is supported in part by revenues raised locally and administered under the general direction of a locally elected board of education. There would also appear no reason why it should not offer as satisfactory a first two years of college education as if it were a part of the university system. Despite the fact that they are a part of the public school system, the junior colleges of California have met this function extremely well— better in general than the terminal functions that prove to be more diffi- cult to develop and more costly to finance. The development of the junior college as a part of the public school system frequently brings problems regarding district structure with it. A district large enough to provide for excellent development of the junior college may be regarded by some as too large for elementary school purposes unless desirable decentraliza- tion can be effected. This is especially true in rural areas and small communities. In metropolitan areas where an adequate district structure exists, there would appear to be less reason why a K-14 plan of organi- zation should not be employed.

Are junior colleges that are developed as a part of the university system less likely to provide adequately for the terminal functions? Can branches of the university become community colleges? How can this be effected? Is considerable turnover of students in a community college to be expected? Why?

Should the High School and Junior College
Be Organized on a Departmental Basis?

Secondary schools have traditionally been organized by subject departments. This has served to give the teachers the opportunity to work with and to secure the assistance of other teachers with similar purposes. It has emphasized the achievement of the dominant goals of the respective subjects. Especially in large schools it has provided a type of decentralized administration. Through the departmental organi- zation it has been possible to exercise supervision, determine instruc- tional materials needed, plan evaluation programs, induct the new teacher, engage in course-of-study evaluation and improvement, and effect neces- sary communication.

In recent years the departmental organization has been subjected to considerable criticism. It is said that it has contributed to the main- tenance of instruction which is not sufficiently related to the stated purposes of the school. In some schools it has separated the staff into tight compartments, the members of which have little understanding of what other departments are doing. At times it has resulted in the neglect of needs of students who do not fit into the purposes of the respective departments. For these reasons, consideration has been given to different types of organization that may be more directly related to the purposes of the institution and that may be more able to provide for the needs of youth. Such organizational plans provide opportunities for members of various subject fields to work with teachers from other areas. Especially in large schools it appears to be necessary to develop an organization through which special services such as guidance may be more effectively integrated with instruction. This may involve some type of "school within the school" plan.

What organizational plan would retain the valuable results of the traditional departmental system and overcome its undesirable features? If "schools within the school" were developed, would it be desirable to have also a subject departmental organization involving all members of the high school or junior college staff? Is there a danger that the school may become overorganized?

Selected References

Association for Supervision and Curriculum Development, *A Look at Continuity in the School Program.* Washington, D.C.: National Education Association, 1958.

Brown, B. Frank, *The Nongraded High School.* Englewood Cliffs, N.J.: Prentice-Hall, Inc., 1963.

Education for All American Youth, A Further Look, rev. ed. Washington, D.C.: Educational Policies Commission, 1952.

Medsker, L. L., *The Junior College: Progress and Prospect.* New York: McGraw-Hill Book Company, 1960.

National Education Association, *Planning and Organizing for Teaching.* Washington, D.C.: The Association, 1963.

National Education Association, *Schools for the Sixties.* New York: McGraw-Hill Book Company, 1963.

National Society for the Study of Education, *The Changing American School,* Sixty-fifth Yearbook, Part II. Chicago: University of Chicago Press, 1966.

National Society for the Study of Education, *The Public Junior College,* 55th Yearbook, Part I. Chicago: University of Chicago Press, 1956.

Otto, Henry J., *Elementary-School Organization and Administration.* New York: Appleton-Century & Appleton-Century-Crofts, 1954.

Shaplin, Judson T., and Henry F. Olds, Jr., *Team Teaching.* New York: Harper & Row, Publishers, 1964.

Trump, J. Lloyd, and Dorsey Baynham, *Focus on Change: Guide to Better Schools.* Skokie, Ill.: Rand McNally & Co., 1961.

Weinberg, Meyer, ed., *Learning Together, A Book on Integrated Education.* Chicago: Integrated Education Association, 1964.

13

The Administration
of the School Center

We have conceptualized the school system as a complex social system comprised of numerous subsystems, some of which are formal organizations and some informal. The school center or the individual school is the operating unit of the school system: it is the critical point of the organizational structure at which the organization produces educational services. The basic function of the superstructure of board of education, superintendent and his central staff is to provide the facilities, staff, and services that facilitate the production of educational services at the school center. The operating school center that houses pupils is the most visible part of the school system. It is at this point primarily that the total school social system interacts with its environment by exchanging "matter, energy, and information."

So far in this book we have applied theories and concepts of organization and administration primarily to the suprasystems of the school center. That is, major emphasis has been given to the federal level, the state level, and the administrative unit; however, there is no area of educational administration deserving of more study than the administration of the school center. If we can judge by prevailing practice, there does not seem to be wide agreement on either policy or theory in this area. There are many reasons why this is true. Our schools started on an extremely decentralized basis, as was pointed out in previous chapters.

Even in city systems during the first half of the nineteenth century, the school center was usually a ward school governed by ward trustees. It was not until shortly before the middle of the nineteenth century that the practice of giving citywide boards responsibility for the schools of a city was initiated. At about this same time, these boards began the practice of employing a professional superintendent to administer the schools.

Rural schools emerged in much the same way. These schools originally were typically one-teacher schools governed by local trustees. In several states this type of organization still exists. However, in most states rural schools were largely reorganized during the first half of the twentieth century. In some states, particularly the southern states, this reorganization took the form of the county-unit system of administration. In other states some type of consolidated or unified school district was formed, as explained in Chapter 10.

These trends can properly be described as trends in the direction of centralization of the administration, supervision, and financing of the public schools. The advantages of centralization have been so clearly demonstrated that we can confidently expect this trend to continue. By the middle of the twentieth century, the large majority of the public school pupils attended school in multiple-school districts. More than one school center in each district was made necessary by the formation of large centralized school districts. Boards of education also soon found that the services of a trained executive were necessary for the efficient administration of the centralized district.

The position of school principal evolved in much the same way. One-teacher schools required no principal. As small multiple-teacher schools were formed, one teacher was named head teacher. As these multiple-teacher schools grew larger, the practice of employing nonteaching principals emerged. When school districts were small, the duties of principal and superintendent were discharged by the same person. As multiple-school districts were formed, it became necessary to employ principals for multiple-teacher schools and superintendents for multiple-school districts. Thus two major types of school executives have evolved in the American school system—the executive of the individual school and the executive of the administrative district. It should not be assumed that all schools in the United States are organized according to this pattern. Actually, almost every stage of the evolution of the organization of American education is still found in existence somewhere in the nation. The primary purposes of this chapter are to describe the decision-making role of the school center and the relationships of the school principal to the central administration, to his staff, to his pupils, and to his community.

THE DECISION-MAKING ROLE OF THE SCHOOL CENTER

The decision-making role of the school center is determined largely by the board and the superintendent. This determination is based on the theories of administration and organization accepted and assumptions made by the board and the superintendent. These theories may not be formally stated; nevertheless, the policies of the board and the actions of the superintendent always reveal their concepts of theory, either stated or unstated.[1] Some emerging theories of modern administration are described in Chapter 4. That these theories are not universally accepted is clearly revealed by wide divergence in the roles assigned to school centers in different school systems.

In some school systems, the area of decision making assigned to individual schools is very narrow. The rules and regulations of the board with respect to individual school administration are written in great detail. The course of study for each grade level and the curriculum generally are prescribed in great detail. Even the method of giving grades to students is sometimes made uniform. For example, as late as 1955 the printed regulations of a medium-size school system included the requirement that the final grades of all students in each subject be determined as follows: one third by class recitation, one third by monthly examinations, and one third by a final examination. That system had a K-6-3-3 organization. How this regulation could be applied to kindergarten children was not explained by the board. The principal in such systems usually has but little to do with the appointment of either instructional or noninstructional personnel, and he must secure the approval of the superintendent on all but the most trivial matters. He and his faculty have but little opportunity for leadership. In fact, he is merely an unimportant official in a monocratic bureaucracy carrying out the superintendent's orders.

In contrast with the school systems that exercise rigid control over the educational activities of individual schools, there are other school systems that give school centers a considerable degree of freedom in decision making. Following are some of the characteristics of the school systems that give important responsibilities to school centers:

1. Board actions with respect to the educational program are expressed in terms of broad policies and objectives rather than in terms of detailed specific regulations.
2. The principal and his staff are expected to take the primary responsibility for the development of the educational program at the school center.

[1]Arthur R. Coladarci and Jacob W. Getzels, *The Use of Theory in Educational Administration* (Stanford, Calif.: Stanford University Press, 1955), pp. 4–8.

3. The principal, in accordance with policies approved by the board, recommends to the superintendent for appointment all personnel, both instructional and noninstructional, employed at the school he administers. This does not mean that the principal should have complete autonomy in the matter of appointments. All persons recommended for appointment by the principal should meet the qualifications set forth in board policies. Further, especially in large systems, the principal cannot possibly do all the necessary recruiting. These systems normally establish a personnel department. This department usually conducts initial interviews, obtains records of college training and experience, writes for recommendations and performs such other services required to provide a roster of qualified personnel available for appointment. This central office, however, should not be given the power to assign personnel to a school until the principal approves the appointment.

4. Representatives from the principals, teachers, the central staff, and others advise with the superintendent concerning any regulations of systemwide application before he presents such regulations to the board for adoption.

5. The budget is based on an educational plan, but that plan is not developed exclusively by the superintendent and his central staff. The over-all educational plan is based on an analysis of the educational needs at each individual school center. Therefore, the principal and his staff at each school are given important responsibilities for participating in developing the educational plan upon which the budget is based. The principal and his staff are expected to work closely with the citizens of their school community in developing the educational plan.

Elsewhere in this book, attention is directed to the fact that one of the most important problems of educational administration is the determination of the appropriate level of government at which a particular decision should be made. Education is a state responsibility; therefore, the legislature has extremely broad powers with respect to public education. Sometimes legislatures exercise those powers unwisely by enacting too many specific laws regulating the curriculum. Laws or regulations of the state board of education that are too detailed and specific with respect to the curriculum sometimes handicap local school systems and individual schools. As pointed out, boards of education sometimes handicap individual schools by rigid rules and regulations.

These problems have arisen in part from a lack of understanding of the functions of centralization. The benefits of centralization have been widespread. The development of state systems of financial support, the enlargement of the size of local administrative units, and the reorganization of small, inefficient individual schools into efficient school centers have resulted in spectacular improvement in educational opportunity. The limitations of centralization have not always been recognized. In Chapter 6 we pointed out that in many school systems the lay public has lost close contact with the public schools. This loss of contact results in lack of understanding that breeds lack of support, and lack of support will inevitably limit the development of educational programs.

But the development of education depends on more than adequate financing, administrative efficiency, and the elegance of organizational structure. Development implies change, but change does not always mean evolution or growth. The anthropologist LaBarre tells about a primitive anthropoid who, in the process of evolution, discovered how to swing by his tail.[2] The monkey had a clever idea, but there was no future in it. Another primitive anthropoid in the process of evolution discovered how to walk on two feet and use his other two limbs for making tools and machinery to extend his capabilities. Man's idea did not seem as clever as swinging by the tail, but it had a future.

Dozens of theories of learning and methods of teaching and curriculum organization are being advocated vigorously by their proponents. Which of these innovations are only clever ideas, like the monkey's swinging by his tail, and which innovations have a future? This question can be determined only by experimentation at school centers. It is true that we have a few university laboratory schools in which some innovations are tried out. However, university laboratory schools usually do not have a randomly selected school membership, and the environment, organizational structure and control mechanisms are usually atypical. Therefore, the usefulness of educational innovations can be determined only by extensive field testing at many school centers. Experimentation at school centers throughout the United States provides the opportunity to make the peculiar adaptations in an innovation necessary for the maximization of its usefulness in a particular situation.

Most inventions originate outside of a given school system.[3] There are only a few truly inventive persons. Changes in a school system are usually adoptions of innovations or adaptations of innovations. But the diffusion and adaptation of innovations are vital steps in the change process.[4] If the school program at the operating level of the school center changes in accordance with the needs of the times, then not only must the central administration give the school center the freedom to change, but it must also stimulate and encourage desirable change.

[2]Weston LaBarre, *The Human Animal* (Chicago: University of Chicago Press, 1954), p. 81.

[3]Matthew B. Miles, ed., *Innovation in Education* (New York: Bureau of Publication, Teachers College, Columbia University, 1964), p. 640.

[4]See Herbert F. Lionberger, *Adoption of New Ideas and Practices* (Ames: Iowa State University Press, 1960).

This does not mean that the public school system should revert to the one-teacher school of the past century. The benefits of centralization in many areas of educational organization and administration are tangible and real. The problem is to retain the benefits of centralization without destroying the initiative of the school center. The emerging theories of administration, organization, leadership, and cooperative action described in Chapters 3, 4, and 5 and 6 suggest procedures for resolving this problem. There is considerable reason to believe that the logical extension of these theories to the school center would result in greater freedom and the possibility of more productive initiative at local school centers than is now prevailing in many large centralized school systems.

THE PRINCIPAL

The role of the principal is determined largely by the role assigned to the school center and his perception of that role. However, his role is also determined to some extent by the perceptions of his role held by the local community and the staff of his school. The trend in progressive school systems is to assign primary responsibility for the educational program in a school center to the principal and his staff. The principal and the staff are expected to develop and administer the educational program at the school center within the broad framework of policy established by the people through the legislature and their board of education. This is a major responsibility, and it requires leadership of the highest order.

What specific competencies are needed by principals? Wherein do those competencies differ from the competencies needed by superintendents or supervisors of instruction? What implications do the answers to these two questions have for preservice training programs for principals? Some of the studies made under the auspices of the Cooperative Project in Educational Administration have dealt with this subject. Moore, after reviewing the CPEA studies, stated:

> First, there is no general agreement on the differentiation between the role of the principal as contrasted with the superintendent. The conclusions reached on this point have importance for training programs, certification, and other decisions for the profession. Some universities have altered their professional courses in such way as to recognize wide differences between these two major divisions of administrative jobs. Other colleges appear to be eliminating distinctions that now exist between preparation for the two jobs.[5]

[5]Hollis A. Moore, Jr., *Studies in School Administration, A Report on the CPEA* (Washington, D. C.: American Association of School Administrators, 1957), p. 30.

Woodard made an extensive study of competencies needed by superintendents, principals, and supervisors.[6] He reviewed the professional literature and identified 203 competencies as essential for superintendents, principals, or supervisors. Of these 203 competencies, 188 were listed as essential for the superintendent, 171 as essential for the principal, and 163 as essential for the supervisor. But he found that 70 per cent of these competencies were common to all three types of positions. Furthermore, he found that 84 per cent of the competencies listed as essential for the principal were also listed as essential for the supervisor. The major differences in competencies needed according to the professional literature are as follows:

1. Superintendents need a greater knowledge of finance, buildings and public administration, and how to work with the board than do the principals or supervisors.
2. Supervisors need to know more about curriculum and supervising teachers than do superintendents.

Woodard also had selected juries of superintendents, principals, supervisors, and professors of administration to identify the competencies needed for each position. The findings derived from the jury studies were practically identical with the findings derived from the study of the professional literature.

Those engaged in the Southern States Cooperative Project in Educational Administration made a detailed study of the competencies needed in educational administration.[7] This study identified the critical tasks of educational administration and the theory and know-how necessary to perform those tasks. The researchers made no effort to distinguish between the competencies needed by principals and superintendents.

If we assume that the principal should be the responsible educational executive of the school center and if we accept the modern theories of organization, administration, leadership, and cooperative action presented in Chapters 3, 4, 5, and 6, then the preservice training program for principals will include many of the same concepts included in the preparation programs for superintendents. In larger school systems, principals often become superintendents. In progressive multiple-school systems, the principals are given important executive and leadership responsibilities, and they should be competent to discharge those responsibilities. It is true that there are some important differences

---

[6]Prince B. Woodard, "A Study of Competencies Needed by School Administrators and Supervisors in Virginia with Implications for Pre-Service Education" (Doctor's dissertation, CPEA Project, University of Virginia, 1953).

[7]Southern States Cooperative Project in Educational Administration, Better Teaching in School Administration, a CPEA Project (Nashville, Tenn.: George Peabody College for Teachers, 1955).

between the job of the superintendent and the job of the principal, but the differences in the nature of the critical tasks performed are not great.

RELATIONSHIP OF THE PRINCIPAL
TO THE CENTRAL STAFF

Reference has already been made to the fact that an executive in the line organization is in a position of potential role conflict because he is under pressure from his superordinates to attain the goals of the organization and he is under pressure from his subordinates to assist them in attaining their individual goals. The principal holds a position in the line organization which is very vulnerable to this type of role conflict because he is closest to the teachers. In fact, he frequently is perceived by the teachers as a leader in the informal organization as well as the holder of status in the hierarchy. This enhances the leadership potential of the principal. But when the teachers expect the principal to express their norms, sentiments, and needs, even when they are not congruent with organizational purposes, he is placed in an embarrassing situation.

There is no known way of completely eliminating this potential source of role conflict. However, the undesirable effects of this type of role conflict can be minimized by utilizing cooperative procedures involving classroom teachers and principals in decision making at the school system level. This type of procedure will tend to develop policies and programs that are not in conflict with the need dispositions of the members of the organizations.

Another potential source of conflict is lack of clear definition of the role of the principal in relation to the central staff. The relationship of the principal to the central staff of the school system should be clearly defined and understood by all parties concerned. The nature of that relationship varies in different school systems, as has been pointed out above. In school systems that provide a considerable degree of freedom for school centers and that expect the principal to be a real rather than a nominal leader, the relationships are somewhat as follows:

1. Lines of communication between the principal and the superintendent are direct rather than circuitous. District superintendents or supervising principals who serve as line officers between the superintendent and the building principal sometimes retard action rather than facilitate it. In large school systems, the superintendent will have deputy or assistant superintendents who may serve as line officers for certain matters. The operating arrangements should be so designed that these officers facilitate rather than retard the development and operation of the educational program.

2. There is direct functional communication between the principal and the business office, the maintenance department, the central film library, and similar central services where the matters concerned are within the limits of established policy or within the budget for that school. On matters outside of the budget or established policy, the principal communicates with the superintendent or his designated representative, and he does not act without securing proper approval.
3. The principal is recognized by the central staff as the executive head of the school he administers.
4. No one from the central staff has direct control over the employees at a school. The principal has that responsibility.
5. The principal and not the supervisory staff of the central office is administratively responsible for the educational program of the school he administers. The supervisory staff of the central office are staff officers and not line officers. Therefore, they act in an advisory rather than administrative capacity.
6. The principal is responsible for executing board policies at his school center. If he does not believe that a particular policy is sound, he has the right and the responsibility to seek a change in policy. However, until the policy is changed, he either executes it or resigns from his position.
7. The board of education does not adopt a policy or educational program until it has been carefully studied. Such studies should involve principals, teachers, lay citizens, and others when appropriate.
8. The relationship between the principal and the central staff is friendly and cooperative. The principal is not an isolate, but rather a member of a team that has the characteristics of an effective group.

This may seem a somewhat formal statement of relationships. It represents an application of the tenets of organization and administration described in Chapter 4 for determining the relationships between the principal and the central office. The cooperative procedures described in Chapter 6 cannot be effectively implemented unless the respective roles of the principal and the central office are clearly defined.

ORGANIZING THE STAFF

Very small schools present few problems of staff organization. As schools become larger, organizational structure becomes necessary. There is a national trend toward increasing the number of schools that could be classified as medium or large-size schools. Elementary schools of

600 to 800 pupils, junior high or intermediate schools of 1000 to 1500 pupils, and senior high schools of 1200 to 2000 pupils are becoming common in urban and suburban areas. Much larger schools are found in many school systems. Large schools, especially junior and senior high schools, require some type of staff organization for effective work.

Size is not the only factor creating organizational problems. As was pointed out in Chapter 12, almost every type of grade organization conceivable is found in the public schools of the nation. A 1000-pupil senior high school presents quite different organizational problems than does a 1000-pupil school including grades 1–12.

The local school staff can be roughly classified as follows: (1) the instructional staff, (2) the clerical and secretarial staff, (3) the custodial staff, (4) the lunchroom staff. The instructional staff of a large school may include many different types of personnel. Following are some of the types of instructional personnel that may be employed in large elementary or high schools: (1) regular classroom teachers with many specializations, (2) teachers of exceptional children, (3) adult education teachers, (4) intinerant teachers, (5) assistant principals, (6) curriculum consultants, (7) deans, (8) counselors, (9) librarians, (10) psychologists, (11) teacher aides, (12) physiotherapists. School nurses are also employed in a number of school systems.

The size of the school, the variety of programs, the school level, and the organization of the program all influence the organizational structure. For example, there are a number of variations in the way the work may be divided for administering an elementary school. In a small elementary school, one teacher may teach children in two or three grade levels, while in a large school there may be a number of sections at each grade level. An elementary school may be organized on a "self-contained" classroom basis, a departmental basis, a team teaching basis, an ungraded basis or some other basis. A number of innovations in elementary school organization are being experimented with at the present time and new concepts will no doubt be developed. The old type of elementary school, where each teacher taught in his own little cubicle with the school being administered by a head teacher who also taught full time, is a thing of the past. Such a school was hardly an organization. It was basically little more than an aggregation of one-teacher schools under one roof. The modern elementary school is an organization rendering a variety of educational services, and it is staffed with highly competent teachers assisted by specialists rendering specialized services. Therefore, sound organizational structure is essential to a properly functioning elementary school.

Large high schools are commonly organized on a departmental basis, each subject matter area making up a department. This plan has the advantage of providing for vertical articulation of subject matter, but it does not facilitate interdisciplinary coordination. This type of organization has sometimes developed into a monocratic bureaucracy.

It has been proposed that high schools be "purpose organized" and that the basic purposes of education be the predominant basis of organization.[8] Under this plan, coordinators for basic purposes are placed in the line organization between the principal and the teachers. As one group of authors describes the plan:

> In such schools there are supervisors or coordinators of citizenship objectives, of activities objectives, of aesthetic objectives, of health objectives, and of life work objectives. Each supervisor is charged with the responsibility of helping every teacher in the school attain the educational outcomes desired in each subject with relation to his particular objective.[9]

This proposal has not proved to be very popular.

It is not the purpose of this chapter to review all different patterns for organizing elementary and high schools or to evaluate those patterns. Modern high schools as well as modern elementary schools require types of organizational structures different from those utilized in the limited-purpose schools operated in the first quarter of this century.

There is no specific plan of organization that is useful for all types of high schools. The same is true of elementary schools. The principal and the staff at each school should have the freedom to develop the particular plan of organization that best meets the needs of that school. The plan of organization should be the servant and not the master of a school. It should be accepted as desirable and necessary by every member of the organization. Therefore, the principal should not construct the plan of organization by himself. He should involve the staff actively in developing and evaluating the plan of organization. In developing this plan, it is suggested that the principal and his staff give careful consideration to the basic tenets of organization and administration. If the principal and his staff accept the emerging theories of administration, provision will be made in the organizational plan for broad participation in the development of policies and programs developed by the group. These two broad generalizations apply to all types of schools. Generally speaking, staff organization will be more elaborate in high schools than in elementary schools. But the organizational plan for broad participation in the development of programs and policies is just as important for elementary schools as for high schools. In fact, this part of the organizational structure is important even for small schools.

---

[8]David B. Austin, Will French, and J. Dan Hull, *American High School Administration: Policy and Practice*, rev. ed. (New York: Holt, Rinehart & Winston, Inc., 1962).
[9]*Ibid.* pp. 161–162.

WORKING WITH THE STAFF

The organizational plan lays the basis for the procedures by which the principal works with his staff, both instructional and noninstructional. Therefore, all members of the staff should participate in the development of the plan of organization. They should understand it and accept it. No better method of achieving acceptance and understanding has been devised than the method of participation.

The differences between a school that is a monocratic bureaucracy and a school that is a collegial pluralism can readily be observed in faculty meetings. Following are some of the characteristics of faculty meetings in this latter type of school:

1. Faculty members and not the principal usually preside at meetings. The principal is the chief executive officer of the faculty, but that responsibility does not require that he preside at all meetings.

2. The agenda is prepared by a committee of the faculty. The principal has the same right as other members of the faculty to place matters on the agenda.

3. The major amount of time at faculty meetings is spent on program development and policy formation, and only a minor portion of time is spent on announcements and routine matters.

4. *Ad hoc* study committees frequently make reports to the faculty on matters being considered.

5. The principal participates in faculty discussion on a peer basis with other members of the faculty.

6. The faculty strives to reach consensus before taking action.

7. The faculty considers the recommendations on appropriate matters from the Parent-Teacher Association, citizens' committees, and student groups before taking action.

8. When the faculty is making decisions on matters involving noninstructional employees, those employees are involved in the decision-making process.

9. The principal does not veto actions of his faculty unless the actions are in conflict with state law or with the regulations of the board. The principal should avoid having to make this type of veto by making clear to the faculty the limits of their decision-making authority. There is nothing more frustrating to a faculty than to be invited to make a decision on a matter and then be advised later that the faculty did not have the authority to make the decision.

The Principal as Instructional Leader

It is much more than a truism to state that the most important task of the principal is to provide leadership for the development and implementation of the instructional program at his school. He is the executive in the line organization at the scene of action. No amount of elaborate services at the system level can overcome a weakness in leadership at the school center. The principal is at the school center, and he has far greater opportunity to interact with the components of that subsystem of the total school system than an outside agent. Despite this obvious fact, it has been argued that modern teachers are professional "cosmopolitans" and therefore do not need supervision. In fact, it has been argued that since it is impossible for a principal to be an expert in all the subject areas in his school, it is an insult to a teacher to assume that he could provide her with instructional leadership.

Gross and Herriott directed a carefully designed research project which explored the effect of the educational leadership of elementary school principals.[10] These researchers found a positive relationship between the amount of professional leadership provided by elementary principals and staff morale, the professional performance of teachers and the pupils' learning.[11] They also found that the stronger the professional leadership provided by the principal's immediate superior, the greater the professional leadership of the principal. Although this study was confined to elementary principals, it seems reasonable to hypothesize that the findings are also applicable to high-school principals.

While it is true that a principal cannot be a technical consultant in each subject matter area taught in his school, he can be a change agent by bringing innovations to the attention of his staff and by encouraging the members of his staff to experiment with innovations. That is, the principal can not only be a change agent himself, but he can encourage his teachers to be change agents also. Change should not be sought for its own sake but for the purpose of maximizing the productivity of the school. There is no evidence available that shows that either the school system or the teachers are benefited by the principal's assuming the "disappearing leader" role.[12]

As has been pointed out, the principal is in a strategic position to serve as a change agent in introducing adoptions of innovations in his school. He is also in a strategic position to prevent change. This is a

[10]Neal Gross and Robert E. Herriott, *Staff Leadership in Public Schools: A Sociological Inquiry* (New York: John Wiley & Sons, Inc., 1965).

[11]*Ibid*, p. 150.

[12]See John E. Corbally, Jr., T. J. Jenson, and W. Fredrick Staub, *Educational Administration: The Secondary School*, 2nd. ed. (Boston: Allyn & Bacon, Inc., 1965), pp. 42–43.

serious problem in many school systems. Some principals become staunch defenders of the *status quo,* and sometimes the schools they administer are in "stationary equilibrium" rather than in "dynamic equilibrium" or steady state as described in Chapter 3. The schools they administer are more like "closed, dead systems" than "open, living systems." This creates a serious problem, especially in school systems in which the principal is on tenure. These conservative principals frequently have strong support from the conservative elements in the communities in which the schools they administer are located. In such schools, the change agents must come from outside the school center. Some school systems have at least partially solved this problem by providing highly competent instructional supervisors at the system level, by engaging outside consultants and by developing extensive in-service training programs. Probably the best strategy to use in dealing with this problem is to prevent it from developing by exercising extreme care in the appointment of principals, by providing a continuing program of in-service training for principals and by giving both principals and teachers sabbatical leave for advanced study.

The point of view has been advanced in this chapter, that the principal and his faculty should have wide decision-making authority. However, this does not mean that the principal and his faculty should have the authority to operate a school center as though it were an "independent city state." The courts require that even a board of education must be "reasonable" in the exercise of the powers given to it. Therefore, if a principal does not provide adequate leadership for initiating desirable change in the school he administers, that leadership should be provided by outside change agents, or the leadership of the school should be changed.

WORKING WITH PUPILS

If the principal and his staff accept the collegial, pluralistic theories of administration and organization, that commitment must also include pupils. The teacher is an administrator of instruction in the classroom. The teacher who insists on democracy for himself and is an autocrat with his pupils is in a strangely inconsistent position. If we accept "education for living in a democracy" as one of the valid purposes of our educational program, then life in the school should provide experiences in democratic living. Those experiences should be provided in the classroom, on the playground, in the principal's office—in fact, in all phases of school life.

School experiences for living in a democracy start in the classroom. Pupil-teacher planning has long been practiced in progressive schools.

The ability of pupils to participate effectively in decision making is frequently underestimated by both teachers and parents. It is frequently assumed that pupils cannot participate wisely in decision making until they are fairly mature. But skillful teachers make extensive use of pupil-teacher planning even in the kindergarten. These experiences develop the leadership competencies of pupils and maximize the conditions for effective learning. They also minimize discipline problems. As pupils grow in their ability to solve problems and make decisions, they develop competency to participate in many phases of classroom management.

There are many school programs and policies that affect pupils so directly that they should share in the development of those programs and policies. Some examples are: extracurricular activities, school discipline, class and club activities, and similar activities. Many schools have had long and successful experiences with student participation in school government, student councils, student advisory committees, and similar means for pupil participation in decision making. Students not only participate in planning, but frequently administer or participate in the administration of many activities. Administrators who fail to provide these opportunities for pupils fall far short of providing "education for what is real."[13]

WAYS OF WORKING WITH THE COMMUNITY

As was pointed out in Chapter 3, feedback is the process by which a living system such as a school learns "How well am I doing?" It is very important for any system to receive feedback from its environment. If it does not do so, it will not have the knowledge needed to adjust to its environment or to change the environment so it will suit the system. Failure to follow either one or both of these alternatives will result in the decline in the efficiency of a system or even its failure to survive.

However, each system has a tendency to keep itself in a steady state by manipulating the variables both within its system and in its environment that cause strain. Miller, after reviewing a number of researches, formulated the following hypothesis: "A system gives priority processing to information which will relieve a strain (i.e., which it 'needs'), neglecting neutral information, and positively rejects information which will increase strain."[14] In other words, the school social system, like a person, will hear and see what it wants to hear and see and

[13]Earl C. Kelley, *Education For What Is Real* (New York: Harper & Row, Publishers, 1947).

[14]James G. Miller, "Living Systems: Cross-Level Hypothesis," *Behavioral Science,* **10**, No. 4 (1965), 390.

screen out what it does not like to hear and see. The same thing is true of social systems in the environment of the school system. Researches on radio and television listening during political campaigns have shown that most people tune in on the programs that support the point of view they already hold and will tune out programs advancing opposing views. This characteristic of human beings and social systems makes it difficult for the school to receive full and accurate feedback information from its environment and it also makes it difficult for persons and social systems in the school environment to receive full and truthful information concerning the school. Some suggestions are presented in this section for dealing with this problem.

Working Patterns of School Principals

The way the principal works with the community not only vitally affects the educational program of his school, but it also has a major influence on the entire school system. Henderson studied school-community relationships in 48 school centers all within one large school system.[15] He found that the quality of school-community relations improved as principals increased their use of procedures that involved other people in decision making. Community differences in educational level and income were held constant in this study. Henderson found that community attitudes toward the superintendent, the board, and the central staff were affected by the working patterns of principals as well as by community attitudes toward the local school.

Thomsen synthesized the data from seven doctors' dissertations on the same schools.[16] He developed a composite measure of attitudes and interpersonal reactions of parents, teachers, and pupils. He used this as a measure of leadership effectiveness. He found that the pattern of behavior of the principal accounted for 37 to 48 per cent of the variance in the measure of leadership effectiveness.

Numerous other studies have shown that the way a principal works has a vital influence on the climate for the total educational program. His working pattern must be consistent in his relationships with teachers, pupils, and parents if he is to attain maximum effectiveness as a leader. No group can be ignored.

The principal who achieves the best community relations uses cooperative procedures whenever and wherever practicable, in accordance

[15]Lee G. Henderson, "A Study of Certain School-Community Relationships with Special Reference to Working Patterns of School Principals" (Doctor's dissertation, CPEA Project, University of Florida, 1954).
[16]Donald R. Thomsen, "An Analysis of Certain Objective Measures for the Prediction of the Community's Reaction to a Principal's Behavior" (Doctor's dissertation, CPEA Project, University of Florida, 1956).

with the procedures described in Chapter 6. Many community groups are ready and willing to cooperate with the principal if given a chance. The Parent-Teacher Association is one of the oldest and has one of the most distinguished records of service of any organization. It has rendered magnificent service for more than a half-century. Numerous civic groups, labor organizations, professional groups, governmental agencies, and many private citizens who do not even have children in school are able and willing to participate cooperatively in the development of an adequate educational program. In recent years, citizens' advisory committees have made many contributions to improvement of the educational program. These committees tend to cut across all organized groups and are particularly helpful in providing for communitywide participation.

It is impossible in a book of this length to describe all the possibilities for involving the community in the educational program. School visiting days for parents, individual parent-teacher conferences, educational trips to community industries and agencies, the use of members of the community as resource persons, and many similar activities are commonplace in modern schools. Resourceful principals and teachers are discovering new and fruitful activities every year.

The principal who works well with the community does not neglect publicity. He and his staff make good use of the mass media of communication such as newspapers, the radio, and television. Newsletters and school publications are widely distributed. Not only the principal but members of the staff speak to community groups when requested. The public is interested in school news, both favorable and unfavorable, because it wants to know the whole story. Therefore, school publicity should be honest. The community that really understands its schools will usually cooperate with the principal and the faculty in remedying unfavorable conditions.

In a study of community attitudes in a school system of 56 individual schools, the researcher found one school in which community attitudes were extremely positive and another school in which community attitudes were particularly negative. The researcher, in an interview with the principal of the first school, asked him what he did to improve community relations. His reply in part was, "We do everything we can think of. We try to make this a community school. We give the parents a chance to help where they can and we don't neglect publicity." The interviewer asked the same question of the principal of the other school. His reply was, "I know that our community relations are not what they should be, and I brought the subject up to the Parent-Teacher Association. But they haven't done a thing about it."[17]

[17]Unpublished interview data files of College of Education, University of Florida. CPEA Project.

SOME IMPORTANT PROBLEMS AND ISSUES

The school center serves an attendance area, the boundaries of which are defined by the board. Sometimes that area is a neighborhood, sometimes a community, and sometimes it may embrace a sizable territory in sparsely settled areas. The school attendance area is the smallest subdivision of the administrative district. Its boundaries can be changed from year to year by the board. In some school districts the boundaries of school attendance areas are very loosely defined. Schools located near the borders of a district may have an attendance area in two or more districts. Accessibility to the school and the capacity of a building have usually determined the school attendance area. Thus, the school attendance area is not rigidly defined by law in a multiple-school district; nevertheless, the individual school is the principal focus of interest of parents who have children in school.

One of the authors directed a survey of a school system with sixteen different schools. At the request of the board, the survey staff gave its report in a large auditorium at a meeting to which the general public was invited. The meeting was well advertised through a daily newspaper and by radio. Only approximately 250 people attended the meeting, half of whom were teachers. Following the meeting, the president of the Parent-Teacher Association of one of the larger elementary schools asked the staff if it could go through its data and make a report to the P.T.A. for that particular school. The staff agreed to do so, and that meeting was attended by more than 600 very interested persons.

One of the problems of a large school district is to obtain lay support for the total school system. This intense interest in the school center is both an asset and a liability. It is an asset because it is real and intimate to parents. It is a liability because overzealous efforts for a particular school may create unwholesome rivalry among individual schools. One of the problems of educational administration is to keep this vital interest in the school center and at the same time to relate this interest to the common good of all the schools in the district. Some other problems and issues are discussed in the following paragraphs.

How Should the Attendance Area of a School Center Be Determined?

Although the capacity of the plant and the accessibility of pupils to the school have traditionally been the most common determinants of what pupils attend a particular school, these have not been the only determinants. Prior to the U.S. Supreme Court decision in 1954 outlawing racial segregation in the public schools, some seventeen states had laws authorizing or requiring racial segregation. Furthermore, *de facto* segregation was practiced prior to 1954 and still is practiced in most states where there are large numbers of Negroes living in urban districts. Most of the *de facto* segregation is the by-product of the housing pattern of Negroes. There is a tendency for low-income groups to seek housing in low-rent sections of a city. Negroes usually have about one half the per capita income of whites. Therefore, most Negroes are compelled to seek low-cost housing which tends to be concentrated in certain limited sections of a city. This situation is aggravated by the fact that some boards of education have deliberately gerrymandered attendance lines in order to segregate pupils by race. Furthermore, real estate interests have frequently followed a policy of racial segregation in the development, sale, and rental of housing.

There has been a demand recently in a number of cities for the board of education to transport Negro pupils to predominantly white schools and white pupils to predominantly Negro schools in order to achieve some kind of a racial balance in the public schools. This policy has caused bitter controversy. What are the pros and cons of this policy?

Many school systems in the seventeen states that had legal segregation prior to 1954 have established what is called a "freedom of choice" policy. Under this policy a pupil has a priority right to attend the school of his grade level nearest his home but he has the privilege of attending any other school in the district not filled to capacity. There have been some transfers of Negro pupils to predominantly white schools under this policy but almost no transfers of white pupils to predominantly Negro schools.

Some boards of education have established rigid attendance lines for each school and require all pupils living in the attendance area of a school center to attend that school. This policy has frequently resulted in all the whites' moving out of the attendance area of a predominantly Negro school. Under this policy, segregation of the races has been increased rather than decreased.

There are some who insist that segregation by social class is as harmful educationally as is segregation by race. Housing patterns in the urban and suburban sections of the United States follow rather closely the income levels of the owners. This results in schools filled almost entirely with pupils from middle- and upper middle-class homes and in other schools filled with pupils who come largely from the lower socioeconomic classes. The differences in the achievement levels of schools with such great student body differences are striking. Furthermore, when pupils attend a school which is filled with disadvantaged pupils, they do not have the opportunity to associate with pupils who have middle-class norms. It is claimed by some that this policy of segregating pupils in the public schools by income and social class tends to strengthen rather than weaken the barriers between caste and class in American society. Can boards of education deal with this problem, or is it a problem that must be solved by zoning boards and housing authorities? Is the basic problem of determining attendance areas, segregation by race or segregation by income class? Can one problem be dealt with without also dealing with the other problem?

What Policies Should Be Systemwide in Application,
and What Policies Should Be Determined at the School Center?

Many controversies have arisen over this issue. Following are a few examples.

In one school system there was considerable controversy over the method used to report the progress of pupils to parents. The board required all schools of the same grade level to use the same type of report card. This card provided for a five-point grading system, and marks were given only on formal school subjects. The Parent-Teacher Association of some schools wished to retain this method. Other schools wanted to revise the report card and include marks for citizenship and certain personality characteristics. Still other schools desired to do away with the formal report card and substitute letters written to parents that would describe the pupils' progress. Should the method of reporting pupils' progress be uniform throughout the system, or should individual schools determine this matter?

An intensive curriculum study was carried on for two years in a school system. Districtwide curriculum committees were appointed and a number of curriculum consultants were employed. Less than 5 per cent of the teaching staff of the system served on these committees, but each school was represented. The committees made recommendations for major changes in the curriculum. The board accepted the recommendations. One of the recommendations was that a core curriculum be established for English and social studies in the junior and senior high schools and that separate courses in English and social studies be abolished. The principals and the faculties of two of the five high schools requested that this policy not be applied to their schools. The principal reason given was the lack of staff trained in the core curriculum approach. Should all high schools in a system be required to have the same curriculum organization?

A school system made a survey of its school lunch program. It was found that school lunches varied greatly in quality and quantity. Also the lunch programs of some schools were in financial straits whereas others had surpluses. Each school did its own purchasing, school lunch planning, and financing. Schools were paying retail prices for most foods purchased. The board decided to centralize the financing, purchasing, and menu planning for all schools. The plan worked very well except for the requirement that all menus be uniform. The pupils in different areas of the district preferred different kinds of food, and considerable resistance was encountered.

These are but a few illustrations of policies or programs that could be made systemwide or that could be left to individual school determination. What criteria might be used to determine whether a policy should be made systemwide or be left to the school center?

How Can the Central Business Administration Serve the School Center?

Many business administration services can be provided more efficiently by the central office than by each school. When services are centralized, there is always the danger of inflexibility in providing for the needs of each school center. This is particularly true of central purchasing of instructional supplies, library books, textbooks, and equipment. Business officials know that usually the larger the quantity of a particular item purchased, the lower the unit cost. Furthermore, the problems of storage, distribution, and cataloging are reduced when the different types and sizes of the same item are reduced. Before items can be purchased on competitive bids, specifications of some type must be drawn. If the specifications are drawn exclusively by employees of the central office, there is little assurance that the instructional supplies and school equipment purchased will be of maximum value to the educational program. What should be the role of the instructional staff in preparing specifications for instructional supplies and school equipment?

How Should a Parent-Teacher Association Be Organized?

Some studies have shown that membership of the Parent-Teacher Association in many communities is drawn largely from the higher-level socioeconomic groups. The membership of most citizens' advisory committees is also generally selected from the higher-level socioeconomic groups. Is there leadership potential in the lower-level socioeconomic groups? Will the inclusion of leaders from the lower-level socioeconomic groups in Parent-Teacher Associations and citizens' advisory committees help or hinder the development of the educational program?

A new elementary school with 24 teachers was opened in a suburban area. The principal believed that he should have a Parent-Teacher Association. He was new to the community, but he made discreet inquiries concerning who were the most influential people in the school community. For a preliminary conference he called six people to his office whom he had identified as leading citizens. No teacher was present. At this meeting the citizens invited suggested the names of four other persons who should be included in the planning. At the next meeting the principal and the ten citizens made plans for organizing a Parent-

Teacher Association. A slate of officers was picked for nomination. All the persons selected for nomination came from this group of ten. The principal sent mimeographed notices to all parents inviting them to come to the school on a specified date for the purpose of organizing a Parent-Teacher Association. The meeting was well attended. The principal presided and discussed the need for a Parent-Teacher Association. He then asked for nominations for officers. The only nominations made were by persons who had been invited to the principal's office. The slate was elected with no opposition and the meeting proceeded smoothly.

The Parent-Teacher Association of this school seemed to function efficiently for two years. Then, however, the association broke up due to a struggle for power among the ten persons who originally founded the association. The issue which brought on the crisis was the selection of a slate of officers for the third year. How could the concepts of collegial, pluralistic organization and administration discussed in Chapter 4 be applied in organizing a Parent-Teacher Association?

Selected References

Anderson, Lester W., and Lauren A. Van Dyke, *Secondary School Administration*. Boston: Houghton Mifflin Company, 1963.

Austin, David B., Will French, and J. Dan Hull, *American High School Administration: Policy and Practice*, rev. ed. New York: Holt, Rinehart & Winston, Inc., 1962.

Berelson, Bernard, and Gary A. Steiner, *Human Behavior: An Inventory of Scientific Findings*. New York: Harcourt, Brace & World, Inc., 1964.

Burr, James B., William Coffield, Theodore J. Jenson, and Ross L. Neagley, *Elementary School Administration*. Boston: Allyn & Bacon, Inc., 1963.

Corbally, John E., Jr., T. J. Jenson, and W. Fredrick Staub, *Educational Administration: The Secondary School*. Boston: Allyn & Bacon, Inc., 1965.

Graff, Orin B., Calvin M. Street, Ralph B. Kimbrough, and Archie R. Dykes, *Philosophic Theory and Practice in Educational Administration*. Belmont, California: Wadsworth Publishing Company, 1966.

Gross, Neal, and Robert E. Herriott, *Staff Leadership in Public Schools: A Sociological Inquiry*. New York: John Wiley & Sons, Inc., 1965.

McCleary, Lloyd E., and Stephen B. Hencley, *Secondary School Administration: Theoretical Bases of Professional Practice*. New York: Dodd, Mead & Co., 1965.

Wiles, Kimball, *The Changing Curriculum of the American High School*. Englewood Cliffs, N.J.: Prentice-Hall, Inc., 1963.

Williams, Stanley W., *Educational Administration in Secondary Schools: Task and Challenge*. New York: Holt, Rinehart & Winston, Inc., 1964.

part three

*Administering
the Program*

14

The Educational Program:
Basic Considerations

During the past few years, there have been so many changes in the educational program that many teachers have had difficulty in keeping informed about developments in their respective areas. Even greater changes are in prospect; indeed, they are essential if the schools are to meet future needs. The school board, the superintendent, and the facilitating staff, without neglecting the difficult problems of housing, staffing, finance, and other important aspects of administration, must find time to devote even more attention to the educational program than, in many cases, they have given to it in the past. Everyone needs to understand that the progress of the schools in achieving their basic purposes is determined by the adequacy and quality of the educational program they provide.

A satisfactory educational program cannot be developed by groups of specialists working in and concerned with only their own fields of specialization. Each group and its members, however, should contribute to the development and implementation of a comprehensive plan and program that is designed to meet the needs of the students. This can best be done when all members of the staff know that the community, the board, and the superintendent believe a high-quality program is essential and will support such a program in every way possible.

The board, with the assistance of the staff, needs to develop and adopt policies that will encourage innovation and progress and discourage complacency. The administrator not only needs to keep informed about major developments and their implications and to provide leadership in effecting improvements but also to develop a competent staff that is interested in keeping up to date and in cooperating to assure progress. Every aspect of the climate in a school system needs to be as favorable as possible if the schools are to develop and provide the kind of educational program needed under modern conditions.

THE CHANGING EDUCATIONAL PROGRAM

Most citizens know something about the newer developments in education, but many do not understand some of them or their implications. Three major factors seem to be involved in the confusion and uncertainty that exists in some areas: (1) many people do not realize that new knowledge and changes in civilization inevitably require adjustments in education; (2) some school systems have made changes without proper study or understanding; and (3) educational leaders in some communities have made comparatively little effort to help lay people understand the need or basis for adjusting the educational program or the significance of some of the newer practices. Back of recent improvements are factors such as the following:

1. *New information provides additional insights into the teaching-learning process.* For example, repetitive drill is no longer considered desirable merely as a mental discipline. The emphasis is on learning experiences that will enable children to understand relationships between means, ends, and consequences. Knowledge is valued as a means to an end, rather than an end in itself.

2. *Increasing emphasis is being placed on research and the application of scientific methods and findings.* When people know how to find and use pertinent evidence in a scientific way in the solution of problems, they are much better prepared to make progress than when they rely merely on tradition or subjective judgment. The change from reliance on tradition to the use of scientific findings has had tremendous implications for procedures in the educational program.

3. *Studies have shown that how people learn may be as important or, in some cases, even more important than what they learn.* With the acceptance of this concept, emphasis has been changed in many classrooms from the formal recitation to group or individual activities organized around problems or topics for study. Teachers and pupils cooperate in finding out how to study, learn about, and solve these problems.

4. *The most meaningful improvements in the educational program*

are being effected on the basis of cooperative study and agreement. The idea that the curriculum in a school system can be revised only by an expert or that teaching can be improved largely on the basis of administrative directives has been discredited. Widespread participation of teachers in studying problems and needs has helped to bring about significant improvements in teaching. Participation by laymen in studying and determining desirable educational goals and policies is tending to result in better support for needed improvements in the educational program.[1]

Factors Affecting the Program

The educational program in any school system at any time is the result of the interplay of many different factors. It represents the contributions of the excellent, the mediocre, and the poor teachers. It cannot, except perhaps in unusual classrooms, rise much above the ability and vision of the administrator and his staff, the policies and regulations of the board, or the understanding and support of leading citizens.

The educational program in any school, or important aspects of it, may be appropriate for some students and inappropriate for others. It may free the minds of some to create and contribute to the improvement of the society in which they live; to others it may provide major frustrations or give only the knowledge and skills that will help them to become more clever in exploiting their fellow human beings.[2] To a great extent, the educational program reflects the culture of the society and of the community in which it is found. It also tends to alter that culture to some extent, either directly or indirectly. Some schools lag behind the needs of a changing society, do little to improve the people they serve, and may even do an unsatisfactory job of transmitting the cultural heritage. Others not only transmit quite successfully the best of the accumulated heritage but make a substantial contribution to civilization by helping those they serve become better able to solve their own problems and to contribute to the solution of the problems facing their respective communities and the nation.

Among the important factors and conditions that affect the educational program are the following:

1. *Important discoveries and significant advances that have implications for education are constantly being made in all fields.* The rate

---

[1]Adapted from Prudence Bostwick, J. Cecil Parker, and Gladys L. Potter, "One Hundred Years of Curriculum Improvement, 1857–1957," Association for Supervision and Curriculum Development (Washington, D.C.: National Education Association, 1957), pp. 1–8.

[2]Florence B. Stratemeyer *et al.*, *Developing a Curriculum for Modern Living,* rev. ed. (New York: Bureau of Publications, Teachers College, Columbia University, 1957), p. 1.

of progress is rapidly increasing. We analyze the structure of the atom, launch satellites, and create electronic machines that can do things considered impossible a few years ago. We not only know what causes a large proportion of the diseases of mankind but have at our command the means of preventing or curing many of them. Studies have provided considerable insight into many aspects of human relations and behavior. Discoveries, insights, and understandings such as these have many implications for the educational program.

2. *Studies have resulted in much new information regarding growth and development of children.* We know, for example, that individuals differ more significantly than had been assumed some years ago, and we have considerable insight into the nature and meaning of some of these differences. We also know that children learn many things regardless of the efforts of a teacher, but that learning proceeds more significantly and meaningfully under the guidance of a competent teacher; and that the learning process is essentially one of problem solving, rather than of acquiring fragments of knowledge students may not be able to integrate or retain.

3. *As a result of such developments, the conceptions of the people regarding goals and purposes of education have been changed in a number of respects.* As new purposes have emerged or new emphasis has been given to a particular purpose or goal, the educational program has had to be changed so it will contribute more effectively to the attainment of the revised purposes and goals.

4. *Changes in the organization, administration, and financing of education have resulted in or contributed to improvements in the educational program.* The elimination of small districts in many parts of the country has made it possible to develop school systems in which more adequate and effective educational programs can be provided. The establishment of a foundation program for financing schools has provided the basis for more adequate educational opportunities in a larger proportion of the districts in each state. The recognition of the need for competent and well-prepared administrators as leaders and for properly qualified teachers in all schools has made it possible to provide more effective educational programs than could have been done with a less competent staff.[3]

PLANNING IMPROVEMENTS

All aspects of the educational program must be carefully planned and continuously evaluated and revised. If improvements are to be made as needed, the planning procedures should be systematically and skill-

[3]Adapted from Vernon E. Anderson, *Principles and Procedures of Curriculum Improvement* (New York: The Ronald Press Company, 1956), pp. 104–105.

fully developed. Among the important considerations are the following:

1. *A broad perspective should be maintained at all times.* Any phase or area that is being studied should be considered in light of its relationship to the total program. Failure to maintain a broad perspective and to take steps to ensure coordination is likely to result in a program that has some serious weaknesses and consequently lacks balance. Maintaining a reasonable balance among all goals is essential.

2. *Proposals for improvement should be based on systematic studies of problems, needs, and possibilities.* No school system should make changes merely on the basis of what other schools are doing or of impulsive ideas. Any changes should be based on careful study and evaluation of the situation and needs, of the alternatives available, and determination of what seems to be the best policy. A well-organized school system has a plan for providing for, encouraging, and assisting with such studies, and for utilizing the findings and conclusions as they become available.

3. *Needed studies should be planned and conducted cooperatively.* The group responsible for making a study of any or all aspects of the educational program should be comprised of persons who are interested in the problem, and have the necessary competencies and time to conduct the study and to arrive at sound conclusions. The study group should include competent people with a wide range of interests as well as specialists in the area under study.

4. *Competent resource people should be located and utilized in carrying out the study.* The kind of resource people required will be determined by the nature of the problem. If the committee is concerned with the science curriculum, scientists who have a contribution to make can probably be found in the area. If it is concerned with teaching procedures, there may be psychologists who can contribute to the understanding of children and the learning process.

5. *The findings and conclusions should be carefully considered by the superintendent and the board with due attention to implications for the total program.* If the study has been properly developed and the relationships to the other aspects of the program have been kept in mind throughout, the conclusions and recommendations should contribute substantially to the process of developing a sound program. The board should then be in excellent position to consider and adopt any policies that are needed to assist in implementing the proposals.[4]

Some of the important and closely related steps in planning improvements in the educational program are: (1) identifying and obtaining agreement on desirable educational objectives, (2) planning sequen-

[4]Adapted from Van Miller, *The Public Administration of American School Systems* (New York: The Macmillan Company, 1965), Chap. 8.

ces of appropriate learning experiences to assure continuity, (3) locating and organizing subject matter and instructional resources to make the learning experiences meaningful and effective, and (4) planning effective instructional procedures.

Agreeing on Objectives

An objective is something people want to attain. It gives direction and purpose to action. An objective, then, is a goal leading to the accomplishment of a purpose that is determined by the beliefs and values people accept. These purposes lead them to accept objectives or goals that, if attained, will safeguard their values.

Differences of opinion about the educational program grow out of the beliefs and points of view or "frames of reference" people use in looking at education and other aspects of life. Some of these beliefs and points of view may be based on understanding, others on ignorance or prejudice. These opinions become a part of the value system and philosophy accepted by each person and to which he tends to have a strong emotional attachment. They may be roughly classified under such philosophical positions as realism, idealism, or pragmatism,[5] or perhaps others that are related in one way or another to these major positions. All are concerned with the ultimate nature and purpose of man's relation to the universe and, of course, with the nature and purpose of education. All are concerned also with (1) what is real or true (the metaphysics), (2) a theory of knowledge or how we know (epistemology), (3) a theory of values, or what is worth while (axiology), and (4) a theory of reasoning or a method of reaching conclusions (logic).[6]

The differences of opinion regarding the educational program (based fundamentally on differences in philosophies accepted) lead inevitably to controversies or criticisms of the schools and the way they are organized and operated. These criticisms and controversies tend to become most widespread following major changes in society or in the educational program.

One major difficulty arises from the fact that although people have many common values and beliefs, there are also marked differences and even inconsistencies in these values. The Lynds provided some excellent illustrations of the inconsistencies in a typical American community.[7] These inconsistencies lead to confusion and sometimes to conflict for the individual or group. They also may prevent the attainment

[5]For a discussion of some implications of each of these positions for the educational program, see J. Cecil Parker, T. Bentley Edwards, and William H. Stegeman, *Curriculum in America* (New York: Thomas Y. Crowell Company, 1962), Chap. 2.
[6]*Ibid.*, p. 38.
[7]Robert S. Lynd and Helen Lynd, *Middletown in Transition* (New York: Harcourt, Brace & World, Inc., 1937), Chap. 12.

of one objective, because to accomplish that objective would mean that another would have to be abandoned or modified. Many people are not willing to make that concession. Every school system and every school within the system has the problem of attempting to reconcile differences in values and beliefs relating to the educational program, to resolve inconsistencies, and to obtain agreement on appropriate objectives.

The first step in designing or revising an educational program or an instructional system is the specification of its purposes and objectives.[8] These purposes and objectives should be agreed upon by the staff and representatives from the community, after careful study and consideration, before there is any action by the board. A similar procedure should be observed in developing policies designed to ensure that satisfactory progress will be made in achieving the objectives. Insofar as practicable, such policies should provide that the professional staff in each school has the responsibility for developing more specific objectives designed to meet the needs of that school and the students it serves.

The objectives accepted by a local school system and by each school should grow out of a number of cooperative studies, including: a study of the community in relationship to the state, the nation, and the world; a thorough analysis of the community and its problems and needs to determine the implications for the educational program; and a study of the students in the community and of learners in general, to obtain information that may be used in developing appropriate objectives relating to learning needs and processes.

Some purposes, objectives, and policies have already been established nationally by court decisions and laws, as noted in Chapter 8. Others have been established by each of the states. The development of some major policies and objectives concerning the educational program by agreement among the people of the nation, and of each state, is appropriate. However, these generally are and should be, sufficiently broad that they do not prevent or discourage the people in local school systems from developing objectives, policies, and programs that are designed to meet their own needs.

Planning Learning Experiences

All members of a society must share certain common learnings if that society is to be cohesive. In addition, all members will need some more or less specialized learnings to meet the needs of the society. The common learnings are sometimes referred to as "general education,"

[8]Robert Glaser, "Implications of Training Research for Education," in *Theories of Learning and Instruction*, Sixty-third Yearbook of the National Society for the Study of Education, Part I (Chicago: University of Chicago Press, 1964), p. 154.

which has been described by a prominent industrialist and former university professor as consisting of "the highest common factors—the parts of education we all need to achieve a full, useful and rewarding life."[9] He listed the main objectives of general education as: "first, to help the student develop those qualities and abilities that will serve him and the community well, no matter what his calling in life; and second, to foster in him those interests and abilities that will induce and enable him to continue to grow—to learn by himself and in whatever joint activity he may be engaged." He also observed: "There are abilities and skills, generally useful in all fields of endeavor and largely transferable from one to another. These are also the same abilities and skills most durable and useful throughout life." The basic transferable skills and abilities were listed as: (1) the ability to perceive problems and solve them; (2) the ability to understand people, to communicate with them, to deal with them well, as individuals and in groups; (3) the ability to organize, to structure data into an ordered pattern, to marshal scarce resources for given ends; (4) the ability to devote full effort to the task at hand; and (5) the development of a good memory.

Parker, Edwards, and Stegeman listed the educationally important processes as those having to do with (a) communicating, (b) thinking, (c) associating with others, and (d) creating.[10] For all aspects of the educational program, they emphasized the necessity for teaching problem-solving skills, building necessary attitudes, stressing decision making, and helping students to learn values and develop a willingness to work for a deferred value. They noted that: "What keeps people apart are not differences of opinion, but the absence of any common basis for discussion."

For many years, learning opportunities and experiences outside the classroom were largely ignored by the schools. Studies have shown, however, that learning takes place in a variety of situations. School programs are being adjusted accordingly. Certain learning experiences, by the nature of the situation, must be centered in the classroom. This does not mean, however, that they should be restricted to the classroom. The concern should be to determine what experiences would be most meaningful and appropriate and to plan procedures that will make it possible to utilize a wide range of such experiences.

Many learning experiences can be most meaningful when planned in an individual classroom by the teacher and pupils. However, in every school system and school it is possible and desirable for committees of teachers, parents, and children to explore learning opportunities for the

[9]Theodore O. Yntema, *The Enrichment of Man*, Benjamin F. Fairless Memorial Lectures (Pittsburgh: Carnegie Institute of Technology, 1964), pp. 54–56.
[10]*Op. cit.*, pp. 74–91.

various classes and age groups and to prepare suggestions that, of course, will need to be revised from time to time so they may be kept up to date.

Locating, Organizing, and Utilizing Resources

A well-prepared textbook that organizes and classifies knowledge is still considered essential by most teachers. However, there are a great many other resources that, with the aid of a skilled teacher, may become as meaningful or even more meaningful than a textbook. Since the modern emphasis in many aspects of the educational program is on teaching children how to think, the development of some appropriate plan for locating, organizing, and utilizing knowledge is essential for effective thinking. An individual or a group, in or out of school, that is attempting to discuss problems and issues without obtaining, studying, and using effectively all pertinent information, is making little or no contribution.

There may be some disadvantage as well as advantage to knowledge that is fully organized and classified for students. In fact, there are many occasions when students need the experience of seeking out pertinent information and organizing it themselves in order to bring it to bear on the problem under consideration. On such occasions the typical textbook might be a liability rather than an asset. Regardless of its source, the subject matter should not determine, but should contribute to, the learning experiences. During recent years, considerable emphasis has been placed on what has been called "discovery learning."[11] The discovery method, like most other methods, has limitations as well as advantages. It is consistent with the concept of autonomy of character and motivation and should be used when it provides the kinds of experiences that would be most helpful to students in the learning process.

Once objectives have been agreed upon, the means of attaining those objectives determined, and learning experiences appropriate for learners in various age groups and aspects of the educational program tentatively selected, the problem of choosing and organizing appropriate resources for learning for each group must be considered and resolved. Some of the basic aspects of this process can be carried out by specialists and committees representing the school system. This procedure, however, should result only in general guides and suggestions and should not stereotype or limit the procedures that must be followed by each teacher and his students, if the learning experiences are to be most meaningful.

The kind and quality of resources potentially available for learning have been greatly expanded within the last few years. As a result, it is important in most school systems (1) to help teachers and other staff

[11]John D. McNeil, *Curriculum Administration: Principles and Techniques of Curriculum Development* (New York: The Macmillan Company, 1965), Chap. 1.

members become well acquainted with, and to understand the advantages and limitations of resources of each type; (2) to identify and arrange to make available those that should make maximum contributions to the teaching-learning processes for students, consistent with their ability, achievement, maturity, and other pertinent factors; and (3) to assist teachers and students to learn how to make optimum use of the resources provided. Since some excellent discussions, guides and, in many cases, evaluations of each of the many kinds of resources have been published,[12] only brief comments on some of the developments will be given here.

Most teachers have been making effective use for some time, not only of encyclopedias, monographs, magazine articles, and other pertinent printed materials found in the greatly improved school libraries, but also of film strips, motion pictures, recordings, radio and television programs, and community resources of various types. More recent developments such as instruction on closed circuit or other educational television stations, programed learning including, in some cases, a variety of "teaching machines," language laboratories, team teaching and flexible scheduling, have brought many new challenges and problems.

Some of these developments, especially television instruction and programed learning, have been promoted by a few enthusiasts almost as panaceas. A few people have even indicated that they might largely replace teachers in some areas. The experiences and results of studies made thus far indicate strongly that the role of the teacher will continue to be crucial in the learning process. They point definitely to the necessity for better-qualified teachers and staff and for more effective planning, if optimum benefits are to be obtained from recent innovations in this area. Unwise decisions, poor planning, or resistance to change could adversely affect the quality of the educational program in some districts. The school systems that select and utilize wisely the "tools" and other resources for teaching and learning now available, as well as others that will almost certainly become available in the future, should be in excellent position to improve the quality of their programs.

Improving Instructional Procedures

From one point of view, the curriculum of a school or school system is not separable from teaching or, in some respects, from the program of teacher improvement. Every consideration of the curriculum or of the in-service program has to include teaching and teaching procedures. A revised statement of objectives, an enriched range of experiences, or a new organization of subject matter means little for a large propor-

[12]For a more detailed discussion and list of references, see, for example, J. Galen Saylor and William M. Alexander, *Curriculum Planning for Modern Schools* (New York: Holt, Rinehart & Winston, Inc., 1966), Chap. 14.

tion of the learners unless the teacher understands the implications, believes that improvements are possible and desirable, and utilizes appropriate procedures in working with the learners.

In a typical school system the teachers will have been trained at different times, in different institutions, are at different stages in keeping up with developments of recent years, and frequently hold widely varying beliefs and values. In most school systems some teachers continue to believe that many of the older practices are best and perhaps accept only with reservations some of the newer ways of doing things. Other teachers, genuinely interested in utilizing findings of recent studies, attempt to devise and make use of the best possible approaches to the problem of teaching and learning.

Although improvement of teaching is basic to improvement of the educational program, it is a slow process. Fundamentally, it is a process of helping people to become acquainted with and understand the significance of important studies and developments relating to the educational program, to analyze their own points of view and procedures in light of these findings, and to want to make meaningful changes in the program.

EFFECTING CHANGES IN THE PROGRAM

Any program of planning improvements in education involves an understanding of changes in human relations within an organization and how they occur.[13] People who are complacent and satisfied are usually unwilling to change even when what they are doing is ineffective. On the other hand, a person who becomes dissatisfied with the results he is attaining or who begins to believe he has not kept pace with progress is likely to be willing to examine his procedures and to attempt to determine what changes should be made.

As explained in Chapter 4, institutions such as school systems find it necessary to develop some kind of formal structure designed to facilitate the process of carrying out their work. Thus, a school system has a board, a superintendent, a central staff, principals of individual schools, teachers, and pupils—all concerned in one way or another with learning. In connection with each position, there are distinctive responsibilities and privileges. On the basis of this situation, a status system soon develops. The persons in each kind of position are expected to play certain

[13]The authors are indebted to Hubert S. Coffey and William P. Golden, Jr., "Psychology of Changes Within an Institution," *In-Service Education for Teachers, Supervisors, and Administrators,* Fifty-sixth Yearbook, National Society for the Study of Education, Part I (Chicago: University of Chicago Press, 1957), Chap. 4; and to Vernon E. Anderson, *op. cit.,* Chap. 2, for many of the concepts discussed under this topic.

formal roles that grow out of the structural organization. In addition, there are a number of informal rules that develop and have many implications for the functioning of the organization. The informal roles may tend either to facilitate or to thwart the efforts of the organization to attain the officially recognized goals. Any change in an institution or its organization tends to threaten the roles to which certain persons have been accustomed and in which they find security. The greater the number of persons or roles threatened by the change, the greater the feeling of instability and insecurity is likely to become.

Changes in the educational program are most likely to be made successfully when the principles and concepts of leadership and of cooperative procedures, presented in Chapter 5 and 6, respectively, are carefully observed by everyone concerned. The situation is particularly favorable for improvements to be made when (1) the conditions within the school or school system permit and encourage reappraisal of objectives and the means that may be used to attain those objectives, (2) members of the staff are encouraged to participate in studies and prepare recommendations they can help to implement, (3) the entire group has come to recognize the necessity for improvements in the educational program, (4) the climate and morale are such that members of the group can express themselves freely and can participate and provide leadership in determining goals and procedures and in trying out new ideas and ways of doing things.

Any defensible change or innovation should be encouraged and supported by the school system. Policies should be adopted that will give direction to the program and security and encouragement to members of the staff who are interested in attempting to carry out those policies. When there is substantial agreement, changes can more readily be made than when there are sharp disagreements. When there are marked differences of opinion, proposed changes might best be tried out by small groups instead of being required for all. Another possibility would be to obtain the assistance of a competent consultant, who might also play the role of change agent.

Effecting improvements in the educational program may be thought of as *planned social change*. Good human relations tend to facilitate improvements, because the threat to the security of individual members of the staff is far less than when relationships are unsatisfactory. Changes based on arbitrary action of the board or by administrative decree are far more threatening to members of the staff than changes that come about as a result of participation and consensus. The greatest progress, therefore, should be expected in those school systems in which (1) effective administrative leadership is provided; (2) there is good understanding between teachers, members of the staff, and the board; (3) teachers feel that both the community and the board want and expect a better program of education, and (4) satisfactory cooperative procedures have been developed for planning and implementing improvements.

In such a situation, the teachers and staff members who are contributing to the studies and decisions are likely to be the ones who feel secure when improvements are being made and insecure when there is no progress. The teachers and others who are attempting to hold on to their traditional ways of doing things regardless of the evidence are the ones who are likely to feel most insecure until they can begin to make adjustments.

THE ROLE OF LEADERSHIP IN IMPROVING THE PROGRAM

In some communities, most of the leaders tend to be "tradition oriented" while in others they are "progress oriented." Such contrasting points of view may both reflect and affect the attitude of the residents about many aspects of life, including schools and the educational program. Partly on the basis of their orientation, the people tend to elect a "conservative" or a "progressive" board, and the board tends to select an administrator whose philosophy is not sharply inconsistent with theirs. However, in every community there are many differences of opinion about education. Moreover, the reactions and proposals from the professional staff must be considered; state requirements must be met, and major developments in other school systems and in society can hardly be ignored. Whether needed improvements in the educational program (other than those required by laws or court decisions) can be made in a school system will be largely determined by the kind and quality of leadership that influences the decisions affecting education. Gross emphasized the significance of (1) the quality of the school board, (2) the perception, strategies, and courage of the superintendent, and (3) the interest of the community which, if it is concerned, "will not tolerate nefarious pressures on the schools."[14]

In any school system the professional leaders, including not only the superintendent and members of his facilitating staff but teachers and others who head up special studies and projects, may either encourage those who want to continue the traditional aspects of the program regardless of their value, or support and provide stimulation for those who are seeking to make improvements. Leadership, then, can be considered as the natural accompaniment of goal-seeking behavior of human beings in any organization.[15]

[14]Neal Gross, "Who Controls the Schools," in *Education and Public Policy*, ed. Seymour E. Harris and Alan Levensohn (Berkeley, Calif.: McCutchan Publishing Corporation, 1965), p. 9.

[15]Gordon N. Mackenzie and Stephen M. Corey, *Instructional Leadership* (New York: Bureau of Publications, Teachers College, Columbia University, 1954), p. 4.

The superintendent is the chief executive of the school system; the principal is the chief executive of the school. These executives may or may not be "leaders," as defined in Chapter 5, but each of them is in a powerful position to influence educational decision making. In each case, the executive identifies himself, because of his own point of view and inclinations, either with those who are seeking to maintain *status quo* or with those seeking to effect improvements. In the former case, most of the innovations will be effected by individuals or small groups and the prospects for systemwide improvement, or of improvement in a particular school, will not be encouraging. In the latter case, the principal or superintendent, provided he proceeds wisely and helps to set the stage, can greatly facilitate the process of change.

Studies have shown that interpersonal staff relations are important factors in encouraging or discouraging innovations. The principal of a school plays an important role, directly or indirectly, in influencing this process. If the teachers know he favors promising changes or innovations, they not only will be encouraged to utilize some of them but also to exchange ideas and observations with other teachers.[16] These findings are important also for the school system. If the staff and teachers know that the "climate," as established by the board and superintendent, is favorable, tendencies to innovate will be encouraged.

THE CURRICULUM

The term "curriculum" is no longer considered by most people to mean only the subjects taught in a school. A suitable modern interpretation is: "The curriculum encompasses all learning activities provided by the schools."[17] Although an appropriate definition is always helpful in providing perspective, the point of view accepted by educators in a school system as a basis for planning and implementing the curriculum is far more important for teaching and learning than any definition. What happens or does not happen to children should be one of the most important considerations in any school. All children make progress in one way or another because learning is inevitable. Through the curriculum of their school they may learn to dislike books and learning experiences, or they may be challenged by the opportunities to increase their knowledge and understanding of the world in which they live.

The kind and quality of learning experiences become important because, through appropriate experiences, children grow and develop

---

[16]Mark Chesler, Richard Schmuck, and Ronald Lippitt, "The Principal's Role in Facilitating Innovation," *Theory and Practice*, 2, No. 5 (Dec. 1963), 269–277.

[17]Saylor and Alexander, *op. cit.*, p. 5.

insights, understanding, and skills, as they must if they are to become effective and productive citizens. To facilitate this process, the total environment should be favorable. It must enable each student to acquire his experiences under conditions that are most conducive to the kind of learning he needs.

Since people in every community develop widely differing beliefs and sets of values, it becomes apparent that lay citizens cannot be left out of the basic processes of curriculum development. Most lay citizens may not be in a position to decide upon the scope, sequence, kind, and quality of experiences needed by children. However, they can and should help to determine the values and objectives that should be accepted as a basis for planning the curriculum. The experience of helping to validate and reach agreement on educational objectives can be most challenging and meaningful for lay citizens and educators in any community. The major steps in curriculum development are (1) determining how to select and selecting subject matter, (2) determining the grade location or sequence of learning materials, and (3) deciding upon the allotment and distribution of instructional time.[18] The important criteria that should be observed in carrying out each of these steps are presented in most of the recent books dealing with curriculum development.

Curriculum Organization

The traditional curriculum organization is based on subjects. In this type of organization the learning experiences are grouped according to the generally accepted subject areas such as English, mathematics, history, and geography. It has the advantage of providing a logical organization that appeals to many. However, it tends to compartmentalize learning experiences, when in reality they cannot be fully compartmentalized on this basis. Some allege that it tends to ignore the real interests of the learners and that it may not provide effectively for the development of good habits of thinking about problems.

Another plan, sometimes called the project curriculum, provides for the organization of some experiences in terms of activities or projects. This plan places considerable emphasis on identification of problems, the organization of experiences about problems, and problem solving. To supplement the project curriculum, provision usually is made for other needs to be cared for through certain subjects. This type of curriculum has encountered considerable criticism. However, the concept seems to have considerable merit, but competent teachers and well-qualified lead-

[18]B. Othanel Smith, William O. Stanley, and Harlan J. Shores, *Fundamentals of Curriculum Development*, rev. ed. (Yonkers, N. Y.: World Book Company, 1957), p. 106.

ership may be even more important than in the case of the subject curriculum.

The core curriculum represents another attempt to cut across rigid subject lines. To some, the core curriculum represents a variation of the subject curriculum with correlation between or integration of certain subject areas. By others, it is considered a variation of the project curriculum. Fundamentally, the core curriculum comprises the major learning activities that are considered essential for the education of all students. The core curriculum generally has been organized on some basis other than traditional subject lines.[19] Among other features, it utilizes a relatively large block of time to make possible diversified activities. It also encourages cooperative planning.

The problem of curriculum improvement is one that constantly faces all schools. Experience has shown that improvements can be made only with the understanding, cooperation, and leadership of competent personnel who recognize the need and are willing to make the effort. Certain aspects of curriculum planning can best be conducted through the cooperation of committees representing the entire school system. However, many aspects must be developed in individual schools through the cooperation of teachers, students, parents, and the principal, with assistance from the central staff as needed. Improving the curriculum is one way of improving teaching and, consequently, of providing better learning experiences for all children.

Recent Developments and Concerns

During the past few years, more people than ever before have become concerned about the quality of the program provided in the schools. Partly as a result of this concern, many improvements have been made. But there are still differences of opinion as to what constitutes the kind and level of quality desired. Improvements in the curriculum and in teaching constitute important steps. But to what extent should the curriculum be subject-centered? How much emphasis should be placed on acquiring information and on tests that indicate the extent to which certain kinds of information have been acquired? For what kinds of students is more drill and additional homework needed? There is a possibility that in the pressure to achieve loosely defined "quality" the commendable goal of excellence has been or may be all but ignored in some school systems.

A number of authorities insist that more attention should be given to the formulation of an integrating theory of curriculum, instruction,

[19]See Harold Alberty, *Reorganizing the High-School Curriculum* (New York: The Macmillan Company, 1947), pp. 154–155.

and learning that can be used as a guide for procedure,[20] and as a basis for planning and conducting more meaningful research in these areas. Thus, they believe, better guidance can be provided for the present somewhat fumbling efforts to improve teaching and learning.

Some people have become convinced that the solution to many of the present problems will come only from the development of a national curriculum, at least for certain aspects of the educational program. They point to the fact that the limited information now available shows wide variations in educational opportunity and achievement among school systems in the same state, as well as among the states. A few have advocated a national testing program as a means of obtaining more accurate information to provide a better basis for national planning and perhaps for curriculum requirements. Others point to improvements that have already been made by a large proportion of the school systems, and to the fact that many have voluntarily accepted and implemented the recommendations of major nationwide committees. Many people are concerned that more harm than benefits might come from a national testing program or curriculum.

There has certainly been much ferment. Many improvements have been made in most aspects of the curriculum and in teaching during the past few years. Even more may be expected in the future. The mathematics program in a large proportion of the districts has been materially revised (and teachers have had to be retrained) as a result of the work done by such groups as the Commission on Mathematics of the College Entrance Examination Board, and the School Mathematics Study Group. As a result of the work of various groups, the science curriculum, especially in physics and chemistry, has been materially revised. Studies are in progress in a number of other areas that will probably result in substantial changes. The details of these significant developments that have materially affected schools and learning opportunities throughout the country have been reported in numerous publications.[21]

IN-SERVICE EDUCATION

In every community in which there is an interest in better schools, the need for improving staff members, teachers, and teaching has been recognized. Many procedures and devices have been used to that end.

[20]Jerome S. Bruner, *Toward a Theory of Instruction* (Cambridge: Harvard University Press, 1966).

[21]An excellent discussion of these developments, along with references to important publications in the various areas will be found in Saylor and Alexander, *op. cit.,* Chap. 9.

The improvement of the professional staff and of teaching is a continuous process; only limited results should be expected from an intensive short-time effort, especially when teachers themselves do not actively participate in the planning.

As one promising means of improving instructional procedures and the entire educational program, considerable attention has been devoted to the reorganization and improvement of college and university programs of preparation. Increasingly, both university and public school authorities have been studying the program in institutions of higher learning on the assumption that improvements in their curriculum can and should result in better preparation for professional personnel. However, regardless of the excellence of the work in institutions of higher learning, every school system needs a good in-service program for the improvement of its personnel. No one approach will suffice because the problems and needs of teachers, principals, and others differ, and appropriate procedures must be devised to help in the solution of their problems.

The improvement of teaching requires provisions designed to help teachers recognize their problems, determine their own strengths and weaknesses, revise some of their goals and objectives, and develop and utilize procedures that will be effective in attaining the revised objectives. Most approaches that are planned to meet bona fide needs are likely to be helpful. Those that become a formality or degenerate into routine may be meaningless or even harmful. Basic to any satisfactory program are competent staff, good planning, and constructive human relations.

Parker has presented a number of guidelines for in-service education from which the following are adapted:

1. There is a general expectation in the community and in the school system that the educational program and the contributions of the staff will be constantly improved;

2. The climate is conducive to building mutual respect, confidence, support, and creativeness;

3. All members of the group are encouraged to propose and discuss new ideas and to try out those that seem promising;

4. The fact that individual members of the group differ is recognized and each is encouraged to make his own contribution in his own way;

5. People are encouraged as individuals and as members of groups to propose goals and plans and to work on problems that are meaningful to them;

6. Procedures for moving from decisions into programs of action are kept as simple as possible;

7. Appropriate resources are identified, made available, and utilized as needed;

8. Provisions for appraisal are developed as an integral aspect of the program and the results are utilized in effecting improvements.[22]

SOME IMPORTANT PROBLEMS AND ISSUES

Since education has such great significance for the lives of people and for the welfare of the nation, it is not surprising that, in a pluralistic culture, many controversies arise about the program. When people come to accept different values and points of view, whether these are based on understanding or ignorance, they are likely to challenge any aspect of the program that conflicts with their values. Most of the issues considered on the following pages are related to this problem. What additional issues should have attention?

To What Extent Should the Schools Help To Improve the Culture in Which They Exist?

There are two extreme points of view regarding the role the public schools should play in American life. One holds that the schools should do little more than transmit the social heritage. Another insists that the schools should help to make needed improvements in the social order. Which, if either, point of view is appropriate?

If the schools do little more than transmit the accumulated culture, by implication the emphasis should be placed on acquiring and organizing accumulated knowledge and related information. Major changes in the present curriculum or the need for exploring and experimenting with other types of organization might not be particularly urgent. If they undertake to help to prepare students to face current and emerging problems, almost continuous change will be needed in the program.

The American people have always been concerned that their public school system be free from control by groups that would use the schools for their own purposes. They want children to be educated to believe in and support the American form of government, but many do not want them to support or to advocate any specific proposals regarding change.

The fact remains that the American culture is changing. If the schools merely transmit the social heritage, will they be helping future citizens to prepare to evaluate prospective changes, determine what is best from a long-range point of view, and assist in preventing undesirable changes from occurring? Should schools help students to understand

[22]Adapted from J. Cecil Parker, "Guide Lines for In-Service Education," "*In-Service Education for Teachers, Supervisors, and Administrators,*" Chap. 4.

the weaknesses as well as the strengths in capitalism, in the labor movement, or in the purposes and objectives of organizations and institutions? Can the schools help to bring about improvements in the culture without coming under the domination or control of groups interested in a particular type of reform?

What Should be Done About Pressure Groups Concerned with the Educational Program?

Throughout the country, there are hundreds of special-interest groups, some of which have been organized for the specific purpose of protecting and perpetuating certain aspects of the educational program or of bringing in new emphases and points of view. Such groups recognize that what happens or does not happen in the schools may have tremendous significance for the future of America and, consequently, are interested in attempting to influence the educational program. These developments are inherent in the American form of democracy. There is, however, concern that well-organized and highly persuasive groups may be able to get certain things accomplished merely on the basis of pressure. Pressure and propaganda do not constitute sound bases for evaluating and revising the educational program.

One important safeguard against undesirable changes in the educational program is an intelligent and informed public. Many local school systems have organized joint committees of professionals and laymen to represent the citizens of the community in studying various aspects of the program, attempting to get agreement on objectives, and submitting proposals for improvements to the board. But minority groups have sometimes attempted to obtain control of such committees and even to infiltrate the P.T.A., and occasionally have been successful. What safeguards can and should be established to prevent undesirable changes in the curriculum that result from the efforts of pressure groups? What should be done when the legislature or a board of education proposes or approves unwise policies relating to some aspects of the educational program?

From one point of view, the colleges and universities constitute a "pressure group" concerned with the program provided at least in the secondary schools. The admission requirements established for college entrance are designed for prospective college students but tend in many cases to have considerable impact on the entire program. To what extent should public school people be involved in developing these requirements?

How Should Controversial Issues Be Handled?

Many of the learning experiences of pupils in schools are relatively noncontroversial. Few people would challenge the theorems and postulates of geometry or many of the principles and findings in the field of science. Most of the standard literature is considered relatively non-controversial, but some contend, for example, that *The Merchant of Venice* is not suitable for study in the high-school grades because of its treatment of certain characters. In the areas of social science and current events, there are many learning materials that may be considered controversial by a substantial proportion of the people.

Difficulties have arisen in a number of school systems because the board of education has not adopted a policy relating to treatment of controversial materials. Thus, by implication, the question of what issues might be considered controversial and how such issues are to be dealt with in the classroom is left to the judgment of individual teachers. Some teachers may do an excellent job, while others may make mistakes that cause dissension. A few boards have adopted policies so rigid and limiting that discussion of certain issues is practically precluded. Such a policy would probably be less satisfactory than no policy at all.

Any sound policy should recognize the need and value of discussing current issues. It should probably provide that, in considering controversial issues, each teacher should attempt to ensure that students have access to all related information and that in the discussion all pertinent facts and points of view are considered. Teachers should accept the objective of helping the learners follow sound procedures in thinking through any problem and attempting to arrive at defensible conclusions or alternatives. What issues, if any, should not be discussed in certain states or communities? What safeguards should teachers use in planning learning experiences on issues considered controversial? What policies should be adopted by the board?

During the past few years, controversies have arisen in a number of communities regarding both library and textbooks. Some people have charged that school libraries have included books or other material that should not be placed in the hands of students. In some communities certain citizens have checked the school library and submitted a list of books which they demanded be removed from the shelves. In many communities, individuals or groups have insisted that certain textbooks contain passages that are objectionable and have demanded that those books no longer be used. Who should select library books for the schools? Should lay citizens participate in the selection? What about textbooks?

How Can the Effectiveness and the Adequacy of the Educational Program Best Be Determined?

Differences of opinion are to be expected regarding what the schools are accomplishing. People tend to judge the schools on the basis of their own value systems. For example, those who believe in learning as good mental discipline are likely to be disturbed by the programs that place emphasis on meaningful learning experiences and minimize drill except when it is important in connection with some significant activity. Most judgments regarding the educational program are subjective. The range varies from highly favorable opinions on the part of a number of people to almost complete condemnation by others.

There are a number of approaches that may be used in studying this problem, such as: (1) attempting to get agreement as to whether present objectives and directions are satisfactory, or how they should be revised; (2) organizing a committee to study the scope and adequacy of learning experiences and the procedures used in providing them; (3) using various types of tests to obtain pertinent information about pupils and their progress in the different grades or classes; (4) making studies of pupils who fail to complete the secondary program for one reason or another; (5) making studies of graduates whose reactions may be helpful in determining the strengths and weaknesses in the program.

What criteria should be used in judging the effectiveness of the program in a school system? How much weight should be given to criticisms by lay people? What are some important steps that should be taken in every system to provide for a continuous and effective evaluation of the program?

New York State has used "Regents' examinations" for many years as a basis for ascertaining the achievement of students at certain grade levels. There is considerable interest in several states in using uniform standardized tests to determine the status and progress of students in certain grades. California has recently instituted such a program. The published results show that some of the large cities "rank" considerably lower than certain suburban districts. Many people have become confused and disturbed. Some school systems have been sharply and unfairly criticized. Some teachers think they may now have to start "teaching for the tests." As previously noted, some people strongly believe there should be a national system of tests for all students. What are or would be the advantages and disadvantages of a state or a national system of tests for determining the adequacy and effectiveness of the educational program in each district?

How Can Current and Prospective Innovations Best Be Evaluated?

During the past few years, a number of experiments have been concerned with different means of facilitating learning experiences for children. Some of these developments have resulted from concern over the shortage of qualified teachers. Most have grown out of a genuine interest in improving the effectiveness of education. For example, several school systems have experimented with assistant or cadet teachers. Some hold that it may be possible for most experienced teachers to assume the responsibility for larger classes than customary at present, if competent assistants are available to relieve the teacher of much of the routine, particularly in the lower elementary grades. Is there sufficient evidence in support of this point of view to justify a change in all schools?

Some of the recent experiments with television tend to indicate that under certain conditions large numbers of students can be taught successfully by master teachers. As far as lectures and demonstrations are concerned, the number of people who might benefit from a good television program in education is almost unlimited. There are advantages to a good lecture or demonstration provided by experts that cannot be achieved by less competent teachers even in small classes. When does learning proceed best on the basis of lectures and demonstrations? When is guided student activity and discussion in small groups essential? How can demonstrations by master teachers most advantageously be supplemented by other types of related and meaningful learning experiences?

Team teaching has been introduced in many school systems. In some it has worked well; in others it has not. Why should it succeed in some areas and fail in others? Programed instruction or learning is widely used, but in some cases has been abused, perhaps because administrators or teachers have not understood its limitations. What are they? Other recent developments include ungraded schools, flexible scheduling to provide blocks of time for certain activities at intervals during the week and to give students more leeway in planning their own programs. There are filmstrips and recordings to accompany some of the new books, laboratories in which the teaching of foreign languages and certain subjects has been revolutionized, and many other challenging developments. What steps should be taken to encourage effective selection and use of such materials and developments? How can abuses be prevented?

Other proposals for improving learning opportunities or, in some cases, for relieving a shortage of teachers include: (1) extend the school year either by increasing the number of days schools are in session or by providing a program of special educational activities and learning opportunities during the summer months; (2) provide for a four-quarter, twelve-month program, by dividing the students into four groups and arranging a schedule so that three fourths would be in school and one fourth would be on vacation each quarter. The first proposal should increase learning opportunities and achievement, which many consider essential. The second, some claim, would greatly reduce the building space required, decrease the number of teachers needed, and increase salaries of those willing to teach on a twelve-month basis. However, the practical problems of obtaining community support for different vacation periods for children and of making such a plan operate economically in

any except the larger schools seem to have prevented serious consideration in many communities. What are the advantages and disadvantages
of each of these proposals?

Some of the newer curriculum materials have been developed
largely by specialists outside the field of education; others have been
cooperatively developed. Some of them seem to be based on the assumption that everyone who takes the course should become a specialist in
the area; few such courses have been prepared for people who should
become well-informed "consumers" interested in understanding developments in the field. There has been some tendency to increase the emphasis on subject areas and to reduce the attention on learning experiences that cut across subject lines. What are the implications of tendencies
such as these?

What prospective developments during coming years are likely to
be most significant for teaching and learning? Which of these, if any,
may have a bearing on class size and on the number and qualifications
of teachers needed? What steps should be taken in a school system in an
effort to resolve these problems satisfactorily?

Selected References

Bruner, Jerome S., *The Process of Education.* Cambridge: Harvard University Press, 1961.

Harris, Ben M., *Supervisory Behavior in Education.* Englewood Cliffs,
N.J.: Prentice-Hall, Inc., 1963.

Hilgard, Ernest R., ed., *Theories of Learning and Instruction,* Sixty-third
Yearbook of the National Society for the Study of Education, Part I.
Chicago: University of Chicago Press, 1964.

In-Service Education for Teachers, Supervisors, and Administrators,
Fifty-sixth Yearbook of the National Society for the Study of Education, Part I. Chicago: University of Chicago Press, 1957.

Mackenzie, Gordon N., and Stephen M. Corey, *Instructional Leadership.*
New York: Bureau of Publications, Teachers College, Columbia
University, 1954, Chaps. 1–4.

McNally, Harold J., A. Harry Passow *et al., Improving the Quality of
Public School Programs.* New York: Bureau of Publications, Teachers College, Columbia University, 1960.

Parker, J. Cecil, T. Bentley Edwards, and William H. Stegeman, *Curriculum in America.* New York: Thomas Y. Crowell Company, 1962.

Saylor, J. Galen, and William M. Alexander, *Curriculum Planning for
Modern Schools.* New York: Holt, Rinehart & Winston, Inc., 1966.

Social Forces Affecting American Education, Sixtieth Yearbook of the National Society for the Study of Education, Part II. Chicago: University of Chicago Press, 1961.

The Superintendent as Instructional Leader, Thirty-fifth Yearbook. Washington, D.C.: The American Association of School Administrators, 1957.

15

The Educational Program:
Special Aspects

In addition to the basic problem of developing and conducting a good program of education for all, every school system and school has the special problem of making adjustments and adaptations to meet individual needs. Students not only should be prepared to meet their obligations and make their maximum contributions to the society in which they live, but they also should be given opportunity and encouragement to develop fully their potential as individuals. From a fundamental point of view, the purposes of socialization cannot be met satisfactorily unless the purposes of individualization are also attained. As pointed out by the Educational Policies Commission, "Social progress and individual freedom interact; each is essential to the other."[1]

GENERAL AND SPECIAL EDUCATION

Although the need for certain essentials (sometimes referred to as common learnings or general education) is common to all students, the program should not be identical for everyone, because there are wide differences in abilities and needs. The schools generally are organized to work with students in groups. Such an orientation is appropriate and,

[1] *The Purposes of Education in American Democracy* (Washington, D.C.: National Education Association, Educational Policies Commission, 1938), p. 23.

within limits, has many advantages and values. However, these limits must be clearly recognized and other provisions made as needed to assure for each child a wholesome and stimulating climate for growth. In other words, individuality must also be encouraged and nurtured. The implications of the following comments should receive careful consideration and lead to appropriate action in all school systems:

> The foundation of our nation is its supreme commitment to the individual human being. . . . Now this foundation is threatened . . . because increasing massiveness and complexity have led in many subtle ways toward a great cultural shift. Individuality tends to be submerged in gigantic organizations, in chain-belt production, in monolithic economic enterprise, and in the complex cultural interdependencies of our society. Caught in this cultural drift, the schools too are veering toward impersonal solutions to vital educational problems. Mass grouping, standard curriculums, texts, and examinations, and standardized institutions are squeezing individuals into a common mold. . . . With an eye to masses rather than to individuals, the schools are departing from their unique historic character by manipulating pupils and teachers into organizational patterns and by leaning on administrative and mechanical devices that tend to destroy the very quality which has made them great.[2]

The committee responsible for this timely report directed attention to the marked difference between taking care of individual differences and nurturing individuality. The former is usually concerned with caring for differences in rates of progress, achievement, competence, interest, and motivation; the latter with personality and character, of integration and integrity, ego strength, and moral fiber.[3]

While much learning takes place in group situations, that are supplemented in most schools by individual approaches to learning, all teachers must recognize that *only individuals learn.* The goals accepted and the procedures utilized by administrators, teachers, and students create a climate in all schools, colleges, and universities that may favor mass production or individual growth and development.

From the point of view of organization and administration there are two kinds of special education: (1) the special education that, in reality, is a part or aspect of general education but is designed to meet the needs of individual students; and (2) the specialized education that is provided for students with certain abilities and aptitudes and which differs in many respects from that provided for students with different aptitudes and abilities. Both should contribute to the full development of each student and to the flowering of his individuality.

The special aspects of general education are provided in regular classes, often with appropriate provisions for groupings of students with

[2]*A Climate for Individuality* (Washington, D.C.: American Association of School Administrators, Association for Supervision and Curriculum Development, National Association of Secondary School Principals, and NEA Department of Rural Education, 1965), p. 9.

[3]*Ibid.,* p. 10.

different abilities, and in special classes for those who are handicapped or have special abilities and need experiences that can be provided only through such classes. Specialized education includes vocational and professional education, and also the provisions for persons interested in developing special talents, abilities, and competencies regardless of their relationship to vocational objectives.

Those who are responsible for planning the educational program in individual schools or school systems should keep in mind the basic distinctions between common or general education and specialized education. Different methods of organization, different teaching materials, and perhaps different standards may be applicable to the two areas.[4]

In high schools and colleges, the educational program usually includes course offerings that may be classified as follows: (1) the constants, that is, those courses that must be taken and the requirements that must be met by every student (general education); (2) the variables, that is, the courses that must be taken and the requirements that must be met by certain groups of students, such as those who are interested in advanced music or certain business skills (specialized education); (3) the "free" electives, that is, the courses that may be chosen by any student in accordance with his interests and needs, providing he meets the requirements for constants and variables for his particular area (another form of specialized education).

One of the common criticisms, especially of high schools, comes from people who believe there should be few, if any, variables or electives in the program. Most of them apparently assume that all students should take college preparatory courses, that only through these can they be satisfactorily educated. In fact, during the past few years there has been so much pressure to extend the list of "respectable" required subjects in schools that many students have little or no opportunity to continue their special interests in other areas. Although this point of view cannot be defended satisfactorily, there is a valid basis for criticism if students are permitted to choose courses without guidance. A carefully developed program that includes adequate diagnosis and counseling for every student should be recognized as essential.

SPECIAL NEEDS OF STUDENTS

Three assumptions, each based on recognition of the fact that there are marked individual differences among students, may be made with reference to the educational program: (1) major attention should be

[4]Van Miller, *The Public Administration of American School Systems* (New York: The Macmillan Company, 1965), Chap. 9; and Will French, J. Dan Hull, and B. L. Dodds, *American High School Administration: Policy and Practice*, rev. ed. (New York: Holt, Rinehart & Winston, Inc., 1957), pp. 190–191.

given to the development of likenesses among people, rather than to the encouragement of differences; (2) major attention should be given to the differences with little attention to the development of common interests and points of view; (3) there should be a reasonable balance between the development of common interests and points of view and the improvement of each person as an individual.

Most educational authorities in this country support the third assumption. If this is accepted as a basis for discussing the special needs of students, and if the fact is recognized that each student has certain needs that will differ at some time and in certain respects from the needs of others, the foundation for planning and developing the program of general and specialized education has been established. However, before such a program can be planned in any school system, it is necessary to develop procedures for identifying the needs of the individual students.

Determining Needs

The plan for identifying individual needs should include at least the following elements:

1. From the beginning of his school career, each student should be systematically observed and studied as an individual by teachers and counselors. On the basis of this study, each teacher or counselor should note on the record of the student any needs that seem to be important. Any such notation should be subject to modification or supplementation as the result of further study or developments. Notations should be based on studies of the home situation, class work, test results, relations with other children, and other pertinent factors. Any tendency to "classify" a student on the basis of early impressions should be vigorously resisted.

2. An appropriate testing program should be planned to aid in discovering the status, problems, and needs of each student. This program should include a variety of measures designed to discover special aptitudes, abilities, and needs, and to diagnose difficulties when necessary. The findings that seem to be significant should be noted on the record along with any special comments as to indicated needs.

3. Each teacher should, from time to time, have conferences with other teachers who have or have had responsibility for teaching or working with any student who needs special attention and, when necessary, with specialists including counselors, nurses, social workers, psychologists, and perhaps psychiatrists. Appropriate notes regarding needs should be made on the basis of these conferences.

4. From time to time, the teacher should discuss with each student and his parents appropriate matters relating to his work and

progress. These conferences should be carefully planned to aid in assessing, and in helping the student and his parents to assess his progress and to determine problems and needs that should be met. Appropriate notations should, of course, be made on the basis of such conferences.[5]

Planning the Program To Meet Student Needs

Many policy decisions must be made as a basis for planning the educational program. These decisions will have important implications for teachers, students, and the teaching-learning process. If the students in each grade or subject are not assigned to sections or classes on the basis of ability, achievement, or related criteria, each teacher will have to attempt to assist students that vary widely in learning progress and motivation. If they are assigned on some such basis, what criteria are to be used? No single criterion, such as intelligence quotients or achievement test scores, seems to be defensible. Even if two or three of the most defensible criteria are used, there will still be considerable variation in the progress of students and in other respects. Moreover, the groups should be kept flexible.[6] There must also be decisions as to whether team teaching, independent study, programed instruction, educational television, or other promising procedures are to be utilized for certain or all groups or subjects, what kinds of teachers are to be assigned to what groups, and so on. While wise decisions should resolve many potential problems and prevent others from developing, there will always be many students who will need special attention and consideration. At least until more is learned about children and how to cope with adverse home and community influences, every school will have some students with such serious problems that they will require every possible kind of assistance if they are to make progress.

The matter of effecting needed adjustments in the elementary grades may seem to be simple and easily accomplished. In reality it is not. The process of determining, planning, and carrying out needed adjustments requires not only a thorough understanding of the problems and needs of each child but unusually good judgment on the part of the teacher and others involved. As a basis for planning adjustments, difficulties must be diagnosed, future problems anticipated, and needed remedial or preventive measures decided upon and implemented.

Similar analyses and studies need to be continued through the

[5]See Lawrence H. Stewart and Charles F. Warnath, *The Counselor and Society* (Boston: Houghton Mifflin Company, 1965), Chaps. 7 and 8.
[6]See *Planning and Organizing for Teaching: Project on the Instructional Program for the Public Schools* (Washington, D.C.: National Education Association, 1963), Chap. 3; J. Galen Saylor and William M. Alexander, *Curriculum Planning for Modern Schools* (New York: Holt, Rinehart & Winston, Inc., 1966), Chap. 11.

secondary schools and junior colleges, but there the problems become even more difficult and complicated. In the first place, several teachers may be involved in the process as far as each student is concerned. In the second place, study habits and patterns of thinking and reacting on the part of the students may have become so fixed that changes become difficult. Moreover, the need for determining special interests and planning a program designed to meet those needs becomes especially important, and should involve not only the student and teacher but also his parents and a skilled counselor.

Periodically, during his entire educational career, questions such as the following should be considered for each student: What are his needs and how have they changed since the last time they were carefully considered? In what respects are they being met? What needs are not cared for satisfactorily? What adjustments should be made to care for those needs?

THE COUNSELING PROGRAM

There has always been some informal counseling or guidance of one kind or another for students by teachers, parents, and friends, but the concept of a carefully planned and comprehensive counseling program is comparatively new. Although tests and testing procedures have been greatly improved, they cannot be relied on as the sole, or in many cases, even as the primary, basis for counseling students. The respective roles of the professional counselors, the teachers, and the students vary from school to school and constitute the basis for much discussion and, sometimes, controversy.

Educators generally agree, however, on the basis of evidence now available, on the following:

1. Good counseling is needed and should be available to all students beginning in the elementary grades and extending through the colleges and universities.
2. Some students will need comparatively little counseling, others almost continuous counseling, while the majority will need periodic counseling.
3. Much counseling in the elementary grades and perhaps the early intermediate or high-school grades can and should be carried out by the classroom teacher in cooperation with parents and with the advice and assistance of professional counselors.
4. Professionally prepared counselors should be available not only for all high school, junior college, and college students but also for elementary and intermediate or junior high-school students.

These counselors should assume a major responsibility for leadership in planning and directing the counseling program.

5. Both individual and group counseling should be utilized.
6. Counseling should not be the exclusive domain of professionally trained counselors, but rather should be based on a cooperative program involving counselors, teachers, parents, and students.
7. The purpose of counseling should be to aid in diagnosing and advising, not to tell students what they should do.
8. The many aspects of counseling should constantly be kept in mind, and the program should provide for appropriate recognition and utilization of all aspects. Any student may need counseling at one time regarding relations with people; at another regarding habits of study; and at still others regarding health, educational program, occupational choice, and so on.
9. A major objective of counseling at all times should be to help students become increasingly able to think through their own problems and work out their own solutions.

In planning and developing a counseling program, the school staff will need to study and resolve various issues such as the following: (1) What should be the role of teachers in elementary, junior high, and senior high-school grades? What should be their relationship to students, parents, and professionally trained counselors? (2) What should be the role of expert counselors of various kinds, and what should be their relationship to teachers, parents, and students? (3) How many counselors are needed in relation to the number of students in the various kinds and types of schools, and what should be their preparation? (4) What kind of program for testing and obtaining other information is needed to provide an adequate basis for counseling as well as for resolving other school problems, and how can this program best be developed and utilized? (5) What services should be provided through the central office, and how should these be related to services provided in the individual schools? (6) What in-service programs should be planned to meet the needs of teachers, counselors, principals, and others, and how should each group be involved in these programs?

Many school systems have not yet clearly defined the counselor's function in the school setting. In some situations, he has had to attempt to combine the role of counselor and disciplinarian to the detriment of counseling. In a few others, he has been encouraged to attempt to assume practically the complete counseling function, which he cannot do satisfactorily because teachers have a vital role to play. However, as better programs of training have been developed and state and local policies have been clarified, the situation has generally been improved.[7] Coun-

[7] See Stewart and Warnath, *op. cit.*, Chap. 15; C. G. Wrenn, *The Counselor in a Changing World* (Washington: American Personnel and Guidance Association, 1962).

selors (along with other professional personnel in the schools) have to face and resolve many ethical problems involved in working with people and to develop appropriate standards to use in the solution of those problems.

From time to time, every school system should study and evaluate its counseling program and needs. A special committee could profitably be created for this purpose. Such a committee might well include counselors, elementary and secondary teachers, principals, representatives from the central office, and perhaps representative parents. The committee should recommend counseling policies to be adopted by the board, and procedures to be used by the school system, the individual schools, teachers, counselors, and staff. Everyone should recognize that an adequate counseling program will cost much more than a limited one. Unless the board and the public recognize the needs, such funds as are required may not be forthcoming.

SPECIAL PROVISIONS IN THE GENERAL PROGRAM[8]

Students with similar problems and needs can often be grouped together for instructional purposes. Adequate provisions should be made for these groups and special adaptations devised for the needs of the individual students within each group. Some of the groups with special needs are discussed on the pages that follow.

The Physically Handicapped

The physically handicapped range from those who are so severely handicapped that they cannot attend any school to those who have such minor handicaps that no special adjustments are needed. A major concern in each school system should be to identify each child who is physically handicapped, determine the nature of his handicap, then decide upon the special provisions, if any, that must be made to ensure that he has adequate educational opportunities. Another step will be to determine, on the basis of handicaps, the various kinds and classes of students who will need special instruction. For example, those who have serious sight, hearing, or other physical defects may have to be taught in special classes or schools by teachers who have been prepared to instruct such children. A number of other children can be identified who should receive most of their instruction in regular classes but will temporarily or periodically need special instructional help. Among those would be children with minor speech defects.

[8]Also consult, for example, Lloyd M. Dunn, *Exceptional Children in the Schools* (New York: Holt, Rinehart & Winston, Inc., 1963).

Many school systems have such small numbers of children with certain types of defects (for example, spastics) that they cannot provide at reasonable cost the special facilities and instruction needed. In many areas the most feasible solution is for two or more districts to cooperate in providing facilities and resources for a center that can best be administered by one of them.

There is general agreement that one objective of the program should be to place most students in regular classes as soon as they can benefit from instruction in those classes. Students should be assigned to special classes only as long as necessary to enable them to advance satisfactorily and to prepare for resuming work in regular classes.

Health Handicaps

Fortunately, most students are subject only to temporary illnesses that may necessitate their absence from school for a few days occasionally but do not seriously handicap their educational progress. Some of them will need special assistance from teachers to cover what they have missed. However, in nearly every school system there will be a few students who have serious health handicaps. Some of these will be hospitalized for a while; others may be homebound over an extended period. Teachers who work with such students need to cooperate fully with the teachers responsible for the classes to which these students regularly belong. When the program is properly developed, most students with health handicaps should be in a position to progress nearly as rapidly as those in the regular classes.

The first consideration, of course, for students who are handicapped because of health or physical condition should be to see that they obtain proper treatment or corrective devices so they can resume their regular work as soon as possible.

The Emotionally Disturbed

All children have emotional problems of some kind from time to time. Fortunately, most of these are only temporary and can be resolved by the child himself, or by the child and his parents and teacher, and do not result in serious handicaps. However, some children encounter such serious emotional problems that, unless these can be resolved satisfactorily, they cannot make normal progress with their schoolwork or a normal adjustment to society. These are the ones who need special attention, and unless arrangements are made to assure that such attention is provided as needed, they will be seriously handicapped.

In some cases, students with serious emotional problems can easily be identified by teachers; in others, the problems are more elusive and can be analyzed only by experts. Properly trained teachers can help some of these students, but expert assistance will be needed for many. Such assistance should either be provided by the district or by several districts cooperatively.

The problem of the emotionally disturbed is one of the most serious facing society at the present time. School systems generally have made far less satisfactory provisions for meeting and resolving these problems than for many other aspects of the program. However, the importance of special services for emotionally disturbed students is now generally recognized by authorities and the better school systems throughout the nation are making more adequate provisions to cope with the problem.

The Gifted

The assumption in most school systems for many years has been that teachers in regular classrooms would make special adjustments and provisions for gifted students and that, as a result of these provisions, each student would be challenged not only to develop proper study habits but to maintain standards in keeping with his capacity. In many cases, however, this assumption was unrealistic. The basic consideration is not whether these students do better work than others but whether they achieve and progress in accordance with their capacity.

Among the steps taken in school systems that have made substantial progress in meeting the needs of the gifted are the following:[9]

1. Each student who is especially gifted in one respect or another is identified on the basis of studies and test results, and an effort is made to determine and make adequate provision for meeting his needs.
2. On the basis of conferences involving teachers, the counselor when necessary, the parent, and the student, he is encouraged to undertake special studies and projects in the elementary school and to select an appropriate program in high school, including courses designed to help meet his educational and career needs.
3. A serious effort is made to maintain standards that are appropriate for each student in each class or section.
4. Teachers are encouraged to help the gifted students in each of their classes to carry on special study or projects through which they can make special contributions both to their own progress and to that of the class.
5. In some schools, especially gifted students are assigned or encouraged to enroll in classes or sections that include only other students with similar abilities. In these groups an effort

[9]For a discussion of provisions made in secondary schools, see J. Ned Bryan, *Building a Program for Superior and Talented High School Students* (Chicago: North Central Association, 1963).

is made to provide special challenges and experiences and to encourage high standards of achievement.

6. In other schools, especially gifted students may remain for some of their classes with others pursuing the same general program but join other gifted students in sections or courses in which they work on projects of particular interest and value to them.

7. Teachers with special ability to work with gifted children are assigned to special classes and projects in order to help such students.

8. Teachers who are selected to work with gifted groups are given help through an in-service program to prepare them better for effective work with such students.

Slow Learners

Some students may be slow learners in certain areas and not in others. Others, however, do not have the ability or motivation needed to make satisfactory progress in any of their classes unless they have special help. Some teachers can diagnose difficulties readily and are able to give students the kind of help they need. Others seem not to be disturbed about learning difficulties until the problems become serious.

Many school systems have organized special classes for slow learners and have assigned to those classes teachers who have had special preparation for working with such students. Most students have made much more progress in such classes than they could have made had they continued in regular classes. However, special classes for slow learners (often including problem children) have not always worked out satisfactorily, probably because the problems have not been carefully analyzed or the program has been poorly planned.

The following steps should be beneficial in any school system:

1. The slow learners in each class or grade are identified and classified into at least the following groups on the basis of appropriate criteria developed by the system: (a) Those who have emotional or other problems that need special attention, (b) those who need special attention in their regular classes and should not be assigned to special classes, and (c) those who can make satisfactory progress only when they are assigned to special classes.

2. All teachers are given special help in diagnosing and dealing, in their regular classes, with problems of slow learners.

3. Teachers, especially selected on the basis of preparation and ability to deal with problems of slow learners, are encouraged to accept assignment in special classes in accordance with their competence.

4. The problems of each child are studied and reviewed continuously to determine whether he is making satisfactory progress under the arrangement that has been made for him or whether he should be reassigned to some other group.
5. All teachers are encouraged to accept as the objective for slow learners the development of each to his maximum potential and to strive to attain that objective.

The Culturally Disadvantaged

There have been some culturally disadvantaged or culturally different children in most school systems since they were founded. Many of them became school failures, problem students, and later dropped out of school. Some eventually become social parasites of one kind or another. A few overcame their handicaps and made important contributions to society. Until recent years, the basic problems inherent in this situation were largely ignored, because they were not understood either by educators or laymen. During the past few years, they have been brought into focus and partly identified as a result of studies by social scientists and a growing awareness by many others of some of the factors involved.

School systems and communities across the nation have begun to face the fact that a culturally disadvantaged student has little opportunity to benefit from education until some of the handicaps with which he is confronted, through no fault of his own, can be alleviated or eliminated. These concerns and activities have been stimulated by numerous developments, including some of the new federal programs recognizing that some of the problems of society and communities cannot be solved by schools alone. The dilemma arises from the fact that education cannot solve directly many of the basic social and economic problems that result in cultural handicaps for the children, yet many of these problems cannot be solved unless children have a better and more meaningful program of education.

Some of the promising steps include: (1) realistic urban renewal and slum elimination projects, (2) the organization of effective community groups and agencies that are attempting to resolve some of the problems, (3) retraining and rehabilitation programs for youth and adults with provisions for better economic opportunities, (4) programs such as "Head Start" to introduce children to education at an early age and provide health and other needed services, (5) provisions for small classes, competent teachers, teaching and community assistants and appropriate facilities, equipment and supplies for culturally disadvantaged children, and (6) programs for in-service training of teachers to help them to understand the value systems and problems of the students and to learn to communicate effectively.

Only a small beginning has been made thus far in this long-neglected area. But on the basis of this start, promising new concepts and experiments are being evolved and substantial progress should be made during the next few years.[10]

SPECIALIZED ASPECTS OF THE PROGRAM

One of the most important problems in every school is to identify and determine the needs of all students (both college-bound and non-college) and to develop a program that is designed to meet their needs. Added to this is the communitywide problem of developing and providing a program of education to meet the needs of dropouts and of adults with a wide range of interests and needs.

The College Preparatory Program

By the time most students are ready to enter high school, it should be possible to determine tentatively whether they have the ability to benefit personally and to make a contribution to society by continuing their education in a junior or community college, college, or university. However, there will always be some students for whom this determination cannot be made until later. Others will have the potential but may not have the motivation or be in financial position to attend college, at least for a few years.

Any well-organized school system should have policies that provide for (1) identifying, insofar as practicable, all students who should be encouraged to prepare for college; (2) counseling and encouraging those students to plan a program and select courses that will qualify them for college entrance, and if they have a particular college in mind, to qualify them for entrance to that college; (3) working especially with students who may have college potential but whose records are not satisfactory; (4) counseling students with college potential who have no current interest in or prospect of attending college and helping them to develop a program that will best meet their individual needs and still not exclude them from college if their objectives change; (5) encouraging and helping students to identify their major interests in college and to plan a program that will enable them to pursue those interests, yet not neglect their general educational needs.

Vocational-Technical Education Programs

Discussions have continued for years as to how practical—or how academic—public school, particularly secondary school and junior college,

---

[10]See Benjamin S. Bloom, Allison Davis, and Robert D. Hess, *Compensatory Education for Cultural Deprivation* (New York: Holt, Rinehart & Winston, Inc., 1965); also "Compensatory Education," *Phi Delta Kappan*, 47, No. 2 (Oct. 1965), 64–95.

education should be. It is apparent that for many years to come, a rather substantial proportion of the graduates from many high schools will not go on to college. Probably some 20 to 30 per cent of the elementary school students in many parts of the country will not even complete the high school program. Many believe that most of these students, as well as some of those who will attend college, should have some practical or vocational education as one means of meeting their needs.

Before World War I, several states had made some provision for vocational education. It was becoming apparent that the nation was handicapped by a serious shortage of skilled craftsmen, farmers, and homemakers. As a result of this situation and of the growing demand for more vocational education, Congress passed the Smith-Hughes Act in 1917 to stimulate the teaching of certain vocational subjects. Funds were provided to assist the states in this development. Since that time, various other measures described in Chapter 8 have supplemented the original provisions and appropriations, or provided for new or extended programs.

The purpose of vocational education under federal acts has been:

> . . . to provide training, to develop skills, abilities, understandings, attitudes, working habits, and appreciations, and to impart knowledge and information needed by workers to enter and make progress in employment on a useful and productive basis.[11]

From the beginning there have been conflicting points of view regarding the best plan for organizing vocational education in the public schools. One group envisioned a single system of education with vocational education as an integral part of that system. The other strongly favored a dual system, or at least dual control with a separate board and plan of organization for vocational education. The creation by the Smith-Hughes Act of a separate Federal Board for Vocational Education seemed to imply acceptance of the concept of dual control. However, the decision as to the actual plan of organization was left to the states. It is interesting to note that the American public seems to have favored the policy of unitary control. In fact, Wisconsin is the only state that has developed a dual system, but a number of other states have some elements of such a system.[12]

There are still a number of people, especially in vocational education, who believe strongly in the dual system. The Vocational Education Act of 1963 (P.L. 88–210, Sec. 8) gives some support to the concept. Following the passage of that act, several states began to establish a

---

[11]*Administration of Vocational Education,* Vocational Education Bulletin No. 1, General Series No. 1, Federal Security Agency, Office of Education (Washington, D.C.: U.S. Government Printing Office, 1949), p. 1.

[12]Clayton S. Hawkins, Charles A. Prosser, and John C. Wright, *Development of Vocational Education* (Chicago: American Technical Society, 1951), Chap. 11.

system of area vocational-technical schools, at least partly on the post-secondary level, designed to concentrate on specialized occupational training to "meet the nation's manpower needs." This and other developments have important implications for students and for the evolving junior or community college system. These institutions are already under pressure in some states and communities to become academic institutions offering two years of college work. Thus, some states face the prospect of attempting to maintain two kinds of separately administered post-secondary institutions (sometimes in the same community), and students face the prospect of having to make choices some of them may not be well prepared to make.[13] In such situations, the concept of a bona fide system of community colleges may be impossible to implement and, because of the costs involved, neither type of institution may be able to achieve its potential.

According to Harris, "The entire concept of separating vocational education from the mainstream of public education in the United States is contrary to the basic tenets of a free society."[14] From his point of view, the proposals for vocational high schools that are separate from academic high schools, as well as for area vocational-technical schools, are "based on assumptions about individual differences which are psychologically unsound, on assumptions about 'the world of work' which are outmoded and on European concepts of education which encourage social and occupational stratification."

Venn has noted that there is "a new relationship between man, his education and his work, in which education is placed squarely between man and his work."[15] Several writers believe that while vocational education in high schools will be terminal for some, it will not be terminal at all for increasing numbers of youth, but will constitute for them a form of preparation for advanced post-high school occupational education. Most authorities agree that vocational education in the future must differ in many respects from that provided in the past if it is to meet the needs. There is considerable concern that, in view of this situation and of the emphasis currently given at all levels to college preparatory programs, vocational-technical education may tend to lose prestige in many communities and even be in a less favorable position than previously to prepare youth and adults to meet vital emerging needs.

The typical American secondary school is a comprehensive school that offers two or more types of curricula, including the vocational and college preparatory programs. Many courses in the academic or college

[13]See Leland Medsker, *The Junior College: Progress and Prospect* (New York: McGraw-Hill Book Company, 1960).

[14]Norman C. Harris, "Redoubled Efforts and Dimly Seen Goals," *Phi Delta Kappan*, **46**, No. 8 (Apr. 1965), 364.

[15]Grant Venn, *Man, Education and Work* (Washington, D.C.: American Council on Education, 1964), p. 1.

preparatory curriculum may contribute to some extent to vocational competence, but their central purpose is not to prepare people for a particular occupation or field of work. Most vocational programs have the latter as their central objective but necessarily are concerned with the development of attitudes, abilities, skills, and understandings that are essential for vocational success and civic competence.

The following considerations are important in planning and developing a program of vocational education in the secondary schools:

1. Vocational education should, as far as practicable, be developed as an integral part or aspect of a comprehensive program of education.

2. A good program of general education is as essential for vocational students as for college preparatory students.

3. Since the work in general education as well as in vocational education should be designed to meet the needs of students in the program, vocational teachers should cooperate in planning the work in general education and teachers of the general education courses should cooperate in planning the basic aspects of the work in vocational education.

4. The testing and counseling program in the schools should be designed to determine capabilities and aptitudes of all students and to encourage those, and only those, to enter the vocational program whose need is in that area.

5. The program should be broadly conceived and planned to include all elements and factors that contribute to vocational and civic adequacy.

6. Special steps should be taken to assure that vocational education is flexible and dynamic and that the content and procedures are modified as necessary to meet changing needs.

In the interest of the proper development of the human resources of the nation, it is essential that all school personnel use a positive approach in considering the problems and potential of vocational education. It should never be permitted to become a haven for the academically maladjusted or problem students, or a substitute for general education. It constitutes an important specialized aspect of the comprehensive program of education and should make a definite contribution to the development of good and economically productive citizens.

Other Specialized Interests

There are many kinds of specialized education other than that provided through college preparatory and vocational programs. In many high schools, these have tended to be neglected. However, most of the larger high schools provide special work in the fine and practical arts and free electives in the academic fields and other interest areas, some of which are prevocational or avocational in nature. In addition to, or in place of, special courses of this type, provision is made in many schools for meeting some of these interests and needs through extra- or co-curricular activities or special interest clubs. The required courses, even for college bound students, should not be permitted to crowd out these specialized aspects of the program. A good secondary school program should be considered one in which provision is made, as far as possible, for offerings and opportunities that meet the needs and provide for the interests of all students.

Continuation Education

In many states, students are permitted to drop out of the regular school program when they have reached a designated age, commonly sixteen years. Sometimes they must also have "completed" the work in a designated number of grades. In some school systems, students who are not doing well in school or have presented some problems are encouraged to drop out as soon as they have met the legal requirements. Such systems are abdicating one of their basic responsibilities to society.

Laws requiring students who drop out of the regular program to continue their education on a part-time basis until they reach eighteen years of age have been on the statute books of several states for some years. Often they have been almost meaningless, as few local school systems have made a serious effort to provide an appropriate program. Often the housing and teaching have been inadequate and the courses poorly adapted to the needs of these students.

This situation is changing rapidly in a few states. People finally are beginning to recognize that dropouts constitute a problem for society and a challenge for the schools that have failed, for one reason or another, to challenge them in the regular program. It seems clear that every school system should plan and take two important steps in a serious attempt to deal more realistically with this situation: (1) re-evaluate its program and procedures in an effort to develop more effective ways of providing meaningful learning experiences for the potential dropouts, and (2) develop an adequate and effective program designed to meet the needs of those who do drop out of the full time program. Thus, the schools may find ways of providing one more opportunity for these students to prepare to contribute to society, and to learn that still further education may be helpful as they move into adulthood.

Adult Education

Adult education becomes increasingly important as the rate of change increases in society and civilization grows in complexity. If adults are to keep informed regarding many significant developments or to satisfy special interests and needs, a substantial proportion may find it desirable to enroll for special courses or programs provided through the schools. The fact that almost all students now complete the elementary grades and a large proportion graduate from high school does not lessen the problem, particularly in view of the new demands and rapid changes in the civilization in which they live. Many adults are employed during the day and, if they are to take courses of any kind, must do so at night. Some of them are interested in credit courses but many are not.

Adult education in most communities has grown rapidly during the last two decades. In 1951, the enrollment in adult education activities in public schools was estimated to exceed four million. More than 25 million were estimated to be engaged in all aspects of planned adult education.[16] A decade later, a comprehensive study showed that one person out of every five in the country was active in one kind or another of learning activity. Most of these were engaged in practical (non-academic) studies on their own initiative—many of them outside the regular classroom setting. Fewer than 2 per cent were pursuing courses conducted by television. A larger proportion of high school and college graduates than of the nongraduates, and of younger than of older adults, were engaged in various kinds of learning programs. Approximately seven out of every ten adults expressed an interest in some kind of learning activity relating to special interests or needs, but many indicated that they were too busy or had inadequate resources to pursue these interests. The evidence points clearly to a great increase in adult education in the near future, since a large proportion of the people are beginning to recognize the importance of some learning beyond the formal educational program.[17]

The objectives of adult education are similar to those of public school education. Kempfer listed them as self-realization, human relationships, economic (including vocational) efficiency, and responsible citizenship.[18] Most other authors agree in general but use somewhat different terms or bases for classification. All agree that the subject matter, interests, and methods are exceedingly diverse, that the number of public and private institutions, organizations, and groups engaged in some kind of adult education is almost bewildering, and that it is still in a sense a marginal activity for many groups and individuals. Among the educational institutions conducting programs of adult educa-

[16]Paul L. Essert, *Creative Leadership of Adult Education* (Englewood Cliffs, N.J.: Prentice-Hall, Inc., 1951), p. 37.

[17]W. C. Johnstone and Raymon J. Rivera, *Volunteers for Learning: A Study of the Educational Pursuits of American Adults* (Chicago: Aldine Publishing Company, 1965), pp. 1–22.

[18]Homer Kempfer, *Adult Education* (New York: McGraw-Hill Book Company, 1955), pp. 42–44.

tion are high schools, junior colleges, vocational or technical schools, colleges and universities.[19]

Although the public schools, junior colleges, colleges and universities cannot expect to meet all educational needs for adults, they have definite responsibilities that should be recognized and met. The public schools cannot afford to neglect the elementary or secondary school program; neither can they ignore the needs for continuation and adult education. In planning a program of adult education in any community, the place to start is with the needs and interests of the citizens. A community study will provide valuable information regarding informal or organized programs of adult education already in operation, areas in which citizens are interested, and some indication of the proportion or number of citizens interested in such areas.

A major concern should be to select teachers who can provide leadership for stimulating and challenging courses in adult education. Some teachers from the public schools will also be interested in teaching adults and have aptitudes that should make them successful teachers in that field. Other adult teachers may have to be recruited from among competent citizens in the community who are interested in and have had special preparation or experience in some area in which they can serve effectively. Such persons may have aptitudes for teaching but little or no special training, so programs of in-service training may need to be organized.

The development of the curriculum may in some cases present special problems. Many of the adults, although not interested in credit, will be keenly concerned with the question as to whether the courses offered meet their needs and interests. Some teachers may be able to develop their own curriculum and course plans, but others will need considerable help.

This means that any school system that has an extensive program in adult education will need staff members who can organize and administer the program and develop a plan for providing special assistance where it is needed. The person in charge of the adult education program should, of course, have special preparation and competence in that area. If buildings are properly planned, as many modern buildings have been, there should be no special problem of housing. Classrooms, laboratories, and other rooms usually can be scheduled and made available in accordance with the needs of the group without interfering with the regular school program.

The problem of financing adult education has not been resolved in many states and communities. Some states include adult education in their foundation program, thus assuring that reasonably adequate funds

[19]Jack London and Robert Wenkert, "American Adult Education: An Approach to a Definition of the Field," *Adult Leadership*, Dec. 1964.

are provided even for the poorer districts. Others provide limited special appropriations, but many still do not provide any funds. Some communities include adult education in their budgets and make provision for part or all of the costs through public funds. Others charge fees and attempt to make the program largely self-supporting. In most states and communities the objective seems to be to develop a plan that will assure that at least a reasonable proportion of the expense will be provided through public funds.

SOME IMPORTANT PROBLEMS AND ISSUES

Five important problems and issues relating to special aspects of the educational program are discussed briefly on the following pages. What others are important and how should they be resolved?

*What Should Be the Relative Emphasis
on "Common Learnings" and on Specialization?*

As civilization increases in complexity, many educational problems demand further consideration. Among these are two of particular concern in connection with this chapter: (1) How can people acquire all of the basic understandings, insights, attitudes, and appreciations that are so essential if they are to participate intelligently and constructively in the improvement of the society in which they live? (2) How can each person acquire the special knowledge, skill, and understanding that will be necessary if he is to make his maximum contribution as an individual to the maintenance of a satisfactory standard of living for himself and his family, and to the economic development of society? These are in reality two aspects of the basic problem: how can every person be adequately educated?

Anyone who devotes too much attention to preparing to earn a living may be handicapped as a citizen. A person who neglects the practical problem of preparing for an occupation or profession may find himself handicapped economically. Upon the schools, colleges, and universities of the nation falls much of the responsibility for leadership in attempting to resolve this dilemma. The solutions developed thus far are not satisfactory to many people, including a substantial proportion of educators.

It is generally agreed that major attention in the elementary schools should be centered on common learnings and that considerable emphasis on common learnings should continue through the high schools and colleges. However, if a person has the talent to become an exceptional musician, artist, or linguist, he must begin to develop that talent before he has finished the elementary grades. Consequently, even the elementary schools should not devote their entire attention to common learnings.

Some degree of specialization for many is generally accepted as desirable in connection with the high-school program. But how much specialization should there be? Obviously specialization at this stage can easily be overdone. Colleges and universities continue to wrestle with the same problem in a different form. Potential doctors, educators, and anthropologists need to continue their study of society, its problems and potential, but they also must begin to specialize.

The entire program of specialization should be based on careful study and planning on the part of the student, his parents, and his advisers. It should be built on and integrated with a sound program of general or "liberal" education. Failure to discover special abilities and interests at an early age may result in postponing specialization beyond the time when it should begin. Early discovery without adequate and continuous counseling could conceivably result in too much emphasis on specialization and not enough on general education, and thus handicap both the individual and society.

To what extent should an effort be made in the elementary schools to discover and develop special talents and abilities of students? How can proper balance between general and special education be developed and maintained in the high school?

Can Mediocrity Be Avoided
in the Educational Program of the Public Schools?

In America, the public schools must be prepared to attempt to educate all children except the few who must be cared for in special institutions. There are significant differences in intelligence, study habits, background, emotional stability, aptitudes, and in other important respects. Although not all of the extremes are likely to be found in any one classroom, every study has shown that there are pronounced differences, even when students are grouped on the basis of ability or other factors.

Many have charged that American public schools tend to provide a reasonably good program of education for all students but one that, in reality, is mediocre. They contend that the interest of many teachers is in having their classes achieve or slightly exceed the norm. The fact that the slower learners will probably be somewhat below and the more rapid learners above the average in achievement does not mean that the situation is good. In reality, the group may be setting the pace for the fast learners instead of the fast learners helping to challenge the class.

Many believe this problem can be solved through better homogeneous grouping of students and insist that such an arrangement would not only facilitate the process of learning for many but would simplify the problem of teaching. Others advocate that the problem be solved in some other way. Theoretically, schools should be able to adapt the educational program to the needs of the students, even when there is a considerable range in ability, as well as in other respects, in each of the classes. Presumably, teachers should be in a position to give special attention to slower learners in accordance with their needs and at the same time to find opportunity to challenge the more capable students and stimulate them to go far beyond the average level for the class.

What policies can be developed in a school or in a school system that will help to ensure that all students develop more nearly in accordance with their capacity than has been the case on many occasions in the past? How can students best be challenged to make maximum progress in their educational program?

How Much Attention Should Be Given to Slow Learners?

The slow learners present a special problem in every school. Unless they have considerable help and attention, many of them will miss some of the important concepts or fail to develop some of the basic skills. The slow learner is not only a problem for himself and his teacher but to a certain extent for the group or class. He may require time and attention that should be devoted to other members of the group. As a result, the more able students, as well as the less able, may be handicapped.

Many citizens have had little patience with the idea of incurring much extra expense for slow learners, although many of them may come from culturally disadvantaged homes. They hold that funds for the public schools are limited and that a larger proportion of the budget spent on slow learners means a smaller proportion for the others. The fact remains, however, that these students will be citizens along with the more able, and unless they are given special help in school, many of them may either become delinquents or develop into welfare cases requiring continuing support from the state. An adequate amount of money to help with their education should yield substantial returns to society at a later date.

To what extent and under what conditions can the problems of slow learners who are culturally handicapped be solved by the schools? What policies should a superintendent recommend for guidance in dealing with the problems of slow learners? What can a principal and his teachers do to solve the problems in a school where there are many children with limited ability or some who are culturally different?

Can "Class Education" Be Avoided in Developing Special Programs for the Gifted?

Many people believe that much talent has been and is continuing to be wasted in this country because gifted students have been relatively neglected in the schools. Some of the gifted have developed poor study habits, presumably because they have not been sufficiently challenged.

In other cases their special talents have not been discovered until so late that the schools have not been able to give them much help.

During the past few years, in particular, a number of schools have been making a special effort to give greater attention than ever before to education of particularly capable students. Many colleges and universities have provided courses in the education of the gifted. A number of local school systems have organized in-service training programs for teachers for the purpose of providing an opportunity to study and think through the problems of educating the gifted. Many school systems have organized special classes for the gifted or made other special arrangements with the idea that these students can then be challenged to do superior work and can also be provided with an enriched program.

There seem to be two sharply contrasting points of view among American citizens: (1) if the especially gifted students are segregated and given special opportunities throughout their school career, there is considerable danger that, in effect, we may develop a system of class education or a group of intellectual "snobs;" (2) the only satisfactory way to provide an adequate program of education for the gifted is to place them in special classes and to provide opportunity for special instruction.

During the past few years, many have come to believe that neither of these extremes provides the most desirable learning situation for many students in elementary schools. There has been some tendency in many school systems to place more emphasis on provisions for meeting individual needs in all classes and, at the same time, to arrange for students with special talents and interests to pursue (with appropriate guidance) independent study or to meet in separate groups or classes at designated periods each week for study and discussion designed to meet their particular needs. Some hold that the problem is basically social and that a major change in the school program without proper concern for pertinent social factors would only result in further difficulties.

When should special sections for the gifted be organized or independent study planned? Will ungraded schools help to solve the problem? What policies should a superintendent recommend for dealing with this important issue?

Can Tendencies Toward Compartmentalization Be Avoided in Developing Educational Programs?

The comprehensive high school is as indigenous and typical of America as the public school system. Within many comprehensive high schools, however, certain cleavages and tendencies toward separateness or compartmentalization have developed. As a result, some rather difficult problems have arisen. One of these relates to the differences between the college preparatory and the terminal programs. In many communities the college preparatory program has come to be thought of as the program for the "elite," while the noncollege-oriented program has only limited prestige. This point of view may be held by teachers as well as by students and their families. A student whose family expects him to be in a college group may have very serious adjustments to make if the evidence indicates that he should take terminal courses.

In some schools the principal, or even the superintendent, pays little attention to what is going on in the vocational program as long as no problems are encountered. Similarly, the vocational people seem little interested in other aspects of the program. These attitudes may have come partly from the fact that federal funds have been provided to assist with the financing of the vocational program, but no such funds may be available for some of the other aspects. Moreover, the policies for the vocational program are included in a state plan that is usually developed by specialists in vocational education. This state plan has sometimes been used as an excuse or defense for doing things in certain ways, and thus the impression may have been created that there is little or no leeway to adapt the program to local needs.

However, the tendency toward separateness, or compartmentalization, exists in many other aspects of the program. Teachers in one subject area often know little or nothing about what is going on in other related subject areas and do not seem to be concerned, in spite of the fact that learning is not bounded by subject matter areas. One of the serious administrative problems in many school systems is to determine how best to assure coordination and cooperation and to avoid or eliminate tendencies toward compartmentalization or separateness in various aspects of the educational program.

Why do tendencies toward "compartmentalization" exist in many schools? How can board or administrative policies help to avoid or to solve serious problems in this area? What should be the role of teachers and counselors?

Selected References

Barbee, Walter B., *The Exceptional Child.* New York: Center for Applied Research in Education, Inc., 1963.

Bloom, Benjamin Samuel, *Stability and Change in Human Characteristics.* New York: John Wiley & Sons, Inc., 1964.

De Haan, Robert F., *Accelerated Learning Programs.* New York: Center for Applied Research in Education, Inc., 1963.

Education for a Changing World of Work. Report of the Panel of Consultants on Vocational Education. Washington, D.C.: U.S. Government Printing Office, 1964.

Getzels, Jacob W., and Philip W. Jackson, *Creativity and Intelligence.* New York: John Wiley & Sons, Inc., 1962.

Hawkes, Glenn R., and Joe L. Frost, *The Disadvantaged Child: Issues and Innovations.* Boston: Houghton Mifflin Company, 1966.

How to Educate the Gifted Child. New York: Metropolitan School Study Council, 1956.

Lindeman, Eduard C., *The Meaning of Adult Education.* Montreal: Harvest House, 1961.

Miller, Harry L., *Teaching and Learning in Adult Education: How to Attain the Objectives of Adult and Continuing Education.* New York: The Macmillan Company, 1964.

Stewart, Lawrence H., and Charles F. Warnath, *The Counselor and Society.* Boston: Houghton Mifflin Company, 1965.

"The Swing to Vocational-Technical Education," *Phi Delta Kappan,* **46**, No. 8 (Apr. 1965), 353–413.

Wren, C. G., *The Counselor in a Changing World.* Washington, D.C.: American Personnel and Guidance Association, 1962.

16

Personnel Administration

One of the most important, if not *the* most important, single area of administration is that of personnel. Support for this point of view can be developed from various bases. The statement, "as is the teacher, so the school," emphasizes the supreme importance of this area. When it is noted that there are more than one and one-half million certificated employees in the public schools today and that this number will increase sharply in the years ahead, the significance of this service area may be recognized. To these employees must be added the proportionately increasing numbers who, although not certificated, contribute significantly to the work of the schools. Included here are technical assistants in instruction, bus drivers, secretarial staff, business office employees, custodial staff, and cafeteria workers.

The chief school administrator must think not only of the large number of teachers and those who directly facilitate the educational program, but also of principals, consultants, supervisors, and others who are in status leadership positions. The selection of these people and the creation of the climate in which they work constitutes one of the major opportunities for service that confronts the school administrator.

A further indication of the significance of the personnel area is revealed by an examination of the budget. Salaries of teachers constitute 65 to 75 per cent of the current expense budget of most school systems. To this, 10 to 20 per cent may be added for salaries of other personnel.

The central importance of personnel administration may also be recognized by noting that personnel make the system. A school system is people. Formal structure, rules and regulations, courses of study, and other aids may be developed, but they take on significance only as people make use of them. The formal structure or the administrative guide may give a very different picture from the true one. The way life is lived in the school is of paramount importance. The achievement of a desirable way of living is the challenge to those interested in personnel administration. The difficulty of the task can be realized when the widely different role concepts and desires of personnel are understood. The achievement of the schools' purposes is dependent upon the extent to which all personnel develop and re-examine certain common goals and find genuine satisfaction in participating in working toward them. Any act that causes individuals or groups not to be a part, not to be "in," reduces the likelihood of high attainment of goals.

The participation of various staff members and organizations in decision making increases the potential achievement. It also makes it more likely that conflicts will occur. The administrator needs to be aware of this and to recognize that, while conflict under certain conditions may be destructive, there are other situations in which it may have large value. The growing emphasis upon professionalism and the larger opportunity for recognition within the profession could indeed reduce concern for the individual school or school system. There are those who believe that this has occurred to a substantial degree in higher education. It could also place one staff group more sharply in opposition to another. The administrator must thus be able to recognize the possible significance of organizational stress in a system which may become too monolithic and in which too little is done to facilitate the consideration of various aspects or sides of a problem before action is taken.

THE MEANING OF PERSONNEL ADMINISTRATION

When personnel administration first emerged as a field of study, it dealt largely with the selection, placement, and retention of people in the interest of the organization. In the sense that it did not necessarily give much recognition to the individuals involved, it was "administration" of personnel. Perhaps it is for this reason that a more adequate term was not developed to describe this area of service. Note should be made of the fact, however, that the essence of personnel administration is not the administration of people. Rather, it is the study of various interrelated forces and factors that play upon people. People themselves may, of course, be one of these factors.

In later years, personnel administration was characterized by the "efficiency" movement. It was then hoped that the time would come when it would be possible to determine the capacities of each person so as to be able to put him in a place where he would be needed. This movement was inadequate in that it failed to recognize that people were fundamentally involved and could not be classified without regard to various aspects of their nature and needs. The "scientific" movement was highly unscientific in that it failed to study abilities in light of the total personalities and of the situation in which they were involved.

In more recent years, personnel administration has become considerably more mature. It has been recognized as a staff rather than a line function in its most important aspects. It is seen as a service available to all personnel. Theoretically, it is no more the instrument of the administration than it is of the individual teacher or group of teachers.

Personnel administration is, therefore, not a means for manipulating employees and getting the largest returns out of them. It is, rather, a series of procedures through which the enterprise may establish common goals and may work most effectively toward their attainment. Recruitment, orientation, transfer, and morale thus become responsibilities, not of the administrator alone, but of all members of the staff including the administrator. Studies of teacher effectiveness as well as administrator effectiveness may be carried forward. Problems between groups or among people may be studied and plans for overcoming difficulties developed. If, as Jersild suggests, there is considerable hostility among staff members,[1] the personnel administrator should establish the facts, ascertain the causes and recommend programs of action.

This level of personnel administration is not readily achieved. It depends upon various individuals and groups accepting one another and necessitates overcoming barriers related to status. It requires knowledge of organizations and how they function, and a maturity and objectivity on the part of various people beyond what is generally found. It requires a director of personnel who is thoroughly prepared in social psychology and in personnel administration. The director must be in a position that enables him to be committed to the purposes of the enterprise, rather than to any one individual or group. He must be in a position to identify and lead in the study of any problem pertaining to the interrelationship and tensions found among members of the administrative, teaching, and nonteaching staffs.

With reference to personnel, it should be clear that in addition to the staff functioning, there will also be line responsibilities. These need, under present organization and laws, to be exercised by line officers. They may need to be approved by the board of education. However, as the

---

[1] Arthur T. Jersild, *When Teachers Face Themselves* (New York: Bureau of Publications, Teachers College, Columbia University, 1955), pp. 115–116.

staff aspect of personnel work is strengthened, the line will be greatly influenced by it. The line will become greatly dependent upon the functioning of staff and will have the fuller cooperation of all employees because of the common goals and understandings that result from effective staff personnel work.

The achievement of this level of staff personnel administration is a challenge to all engaged in the educational enterprise. It is fitting that an organization that exists to facilitate the optimum development of children and youth should do no less for those employed by it.

In considering personnel administration it is important to recognize the changing role of the profession in regard to various educational issues. This changing role is nowhere more important than in regard to personnel matters. The teaching profession through its organizations has gained important power in the last decade and is engaged in determining its desirable role. Thus, the selection of a bargaining agent, the conduct of negotiations or bargaining, the application of sanctions, and related matters have risen sharply in importance. These developments have challenged boards of education and school administrators. They have required the development of new concepts of the respective roles and related procedures in working through personnel issues. They have called for such substantial change in the responsibility of the superintendent that in some instances he has believed that the usefulness of the administrative office was being largely destroyed. Actually, the complexity of the situation suggests that this office will be at least as important in the future as it has been, though its functions and functioning will indeed be substantially modified.

Consideration will now be given briefly to some of the large number of personnel administration areas with which the local school administrator must be concerned. These are not matters that concern him alone. Most of them are also matters of great importance to an alert profession. For example, the in-service education of personnel, which is considered in Chapter 14 of this book, and related matters such as salary schedules, teaching certificates, selection and promotion of personnel are extremely important problems confronting the profession. In approaching many of these areas the administrator will be closely associated with the teaching staff both through its formal organization and in an informal manner.

TEACHER EDUCATION AND CERTIFICATION

The desirability of developing programs that will help young people decide whether or not they wish to make teaching their career has been recognized in recent years. This is not a matter of enticing them into teaching. But it requires recognition by the profession of attitudes that may keep young people out of the profession. Positively, it necessitates the development of a plan through which students can obtain an understanding of the satisfactions and problems of service as a teacher. It should involve the opportunity to work closely with teachers in some of their endeavors. It should aim at bringing those people into the profession who have considerable promise and are likely to be successful in the field. Each school system should make a contribution in this direction.

Participation in Teacher Education Programs

Too few school systems and school people have participated actively in the process of helping the profession develop more adequate teacher education programs and of evaluating such programs. The current rather large number of experimental teacher education programs is highly encouraging, since many of them represent more active cooperation in planning and evaluating than has been found generally. Local school systems must do considerably more than provide the opportunity for supervised teaching if highly effective teacher education programs are to be developed. The organized teaching profession also has a larger responsibility in this area than it has been exercising.

Development of Teacher Credential Programs

The issuance of certificates or credentials for teachers has been generally accepted as a responsibility of the state. This does not relieve local school systems of the need for exercising considerable concern about certificates, since the effects of various credential programs are determined largely at the school system level. The wide divergence of practice from state to state indicates that a generally satisfactory program has not been found. For instance, the number of credentials that are issued varies widely, with some states issuing very few and others extremely large numbers. California, in 1957, for example, was issuing 57 teaching and administrative credentials. It has since sharply reduced this number of basic credentials. Should the credentials be issued on the basis of detailed course prescriptions, or should teacher education institutions be encouraged to develop programs with considerable uniqueness though pointed toward certain common goals? The latter would appear desirable. In doing this, cooperation of local school systems and school staffs with the teacher education institutions would appear to be imperative. Another problem pertains to the question of provisional credentials. When and under what circumstances should they be issued? To what extent should special teacher education programs and credentials be developed for teachers of the culturally different? How can abuses, such as the appointment of teachers at lower salaries who are not fully certificated, be avoided?

SELECTION, APPOINTMENT, AND ASSIGNMENT OF TEACHERS

In recent years, there has been an increasing awareness of possible variations in staffing patterns. The growing complexity of the school, the increasing difficulty of school-home cooperation, the recognition of range in competencies of teachers, the increase in the number of specialists needed in a school system, and the growing need for planning and administrative services have centered attention upon the staffing pattern. Questions such as the following have received greater attention: What is the desirable composition of a teaching team? How many subprofessionals should be employed and for what purposes? How many members should be on the administrative-supervisory staff, and where should they be located? What personnel are essential for an effective guidance service? The conduct of studies and development of proposals regarding the staffing pattern has become one of the most important challenges to the director or other person responsible for staff studies. Until such work is completed and decisions made, prudent selection cannot be undertaken.

The selection, appointment, and assignment of teachers are among the most important responsibilities of the administrative staff and of the board of education. The policies regarding selection and selection procedures adopted by the board of education will determine in significant manner the quality of the education offered. At times, the problem has been one of selecting from among many applicants and of resisting pressure from local residents who have desired appointment. Generally, the problem in recent years is one of having policies that make it possible to locate people of ability and of appointing them some months before the school term opens.

The selection procedure must be based upon a definition of the position or positions to be filled and the competencies that are essential in it. The procedure must make clear the role of various members of the administrative and teaching staffs in selection. The present shortage of qualified teachers has unfortunately greatly hampered the development of sound selection procedures. Rather than selecting teachers, the administrator frequently has to recruit and accept them without too much regard for the desirability of the applicant for the situation at hand.

Despite these difficulties there is a desirable trend toward involving more members of the staff in the selection and assignment processes. Appointment should be to the staff of the district, rather than to a school, thus permitting assignment as proves desirable in accord with the policies of the board of education. The principals of the schools should have an established part in the assignment of teachers if they are to be held responsible for the work in their respective schools.

In considering the matter of teacher recruitment and appointment, thought must be given not only to the local system but also to other districts. In the situation in which one district is considerably wealthier than another, how is "raiding" to be avoided? Fortunately, there are other factors than salary that relate to the satisfactions of the teacher in his work. Despite this, each district must have concern for others. Unless this concern exists and action related to it is taken, the decentralized education system and local initiative and responsibility could reduce the goal of equality of educational opportunity to the status of a myth.

The Orientation Program
for Teachers New to the System

The mobility of teachers and the number of new teachers appointed to school systems in recent years has emphasized the need for a program of orientation. Such a program is necessary for both beginning teachers and experienced teachers who are new to the system. This program may take many forms and involve a wide range of activities. It may involve mailing materials about the community and its school system immediately upon appointment, holding sessions for a day or more prior to the opening of school, appointing a "buddy" or a team of teachers in the school to assist the new teacher, and holding conferences by the principal or central office staff on a variety of subjects ranging from the teacher's assignment to a well-developed program of supervision of the beginning teacher. Some phases of this program can be effectively developed and discharged by the organized profession.

PERSONNEL RECORDS AND PROMOTION PRACTICES

An important aspect of any personnel system is the personnel record. It should contain information regarding the education, experience, and state credentials of each staff member. The record of any one person should be jointly developed by the personnel director and the individual concerned. It should be open to the teacher at any time and should contain such material as the teacher may wish to contribute regarding further study, special instructional projects undertaken, and special responsibilities assumed. The notes regarding administrator-teacher conferences should also be included in these records.

The record system should be regarded as a cumulative one that needs to be kept current if it is to have real value either to the teacher or to the system. The development of the individual record system and its administration is exceedingly important, because individual records contain materials that are basic to any analysis or evaluation of many aspects of the personnel program. This record is also important in considering future study or other activities in which the teacher may be interested. The personal nature of such records should be recognized and great care exercised in their use. Unless there is mutual responsibility and concern regarding them, they may defeat rather than facilitate the attainment of their purposes.

The Promotion Program

The promotion area involves a number of issues such as: Shall promotions be made from within the system whenever possible? How can the best candidates for promotion be identified? How can the view (and possibly the fact) be avoided that administrators may at times recommend those for promotion who are "yes men," who see loyalty mostly in terms of personal subservience, or who above all are unlikely "to rock the boat" where rocking is needed?

Most school systems have accepted the desirability of promoting from within the system when equally competent people are available. Large systems with large personnel resources tend to promote from within more generally than do smaller systems. Even large systems at times reach outside, seeking people with different backgrounds and experiences. It must be recognized that systems do become ingrown, but it also must be recognized that failure to promote from within may be unjust and impair morale. The principle of seeking the most promising person for the situation must be observed in promotion practice.

Fortunately, a school system has many opportunities through which individuals may be given an experience related to or in administration. The utilization of these opportunities as a way of identifying and providing for the development of administrative abilities is essential. Some larger school systems have had programs for the development of personnel for promotion for many years. With the rapid growth of student population in recent years, many smaller systems are also developing programs for supplying potential administrators experience and education beyond that required for the state supervisory and administrative credentials. Such programs are frequently developed cooperatively with a university.

The problem of developing confidence on the part of the staff in the procedures through which selection for promotions is made is a complex one. It needs to be long-range. It demands more carefully defined policies and selection programs than are found in some districts. It probably involves more participation by staff in the development of policies pertaining to the identification and selection of those of promise. In this matter again, it is easy to visualize the large contribution that could be made by the personnel administrator.

Contracts and Tenure

One of the most controversial areas of personnel administration has been that of contracts and tenure. Slowly our society has moved from the position in which teachers had contracts for only a single year without any assurance of fair consideration for reappointment, to that in which they may have indefinite tenure during satisfactory service. In the past, dismissals have occurred for personal, political, and other indefensible reasons. They have occurred without adequate opportunity for the teacher to modify unsound practices or to present his side of the case. On the other hand, so-called permanent or life-tenure legislation has enabled some individuals to take advantage of the situation. It has also caused many administrators to pause a long time before taking what may have been desirable action.

With the maturation of personnel administration and of professional organizations of teachers, the years ahead should witness less dependence upon rigid tenure laws that were the inevitable and necessary result of the practices of some school districts. In their place should come more dependence upon the study of personnel problems and consequent adjustments in policies and practices. This can only be done in an effective manner if the public, the administration, and the teachers' organizations agree on and follow certain basic policies. In accord with these policies, transfers to phases of the service other than teaching should be provided for where this is indicated as desirable. In some instances dismissals might occur. However, there would need to be assurance of just and fair treatment of any individual recommended for dismissal. The problems of dismissal are among the most difficult confronting the teachers' organizations and the administration, since they affect people in a crucial manner and have great emotional overtones. Because of the difficulty, it is frequently easier to avoid than to meet such problems. With the growth of stronger professional bodies and the reduction in reprisals or even fear of reprisals, these problems should be attacked more directly.

The Transfer Program

The possibility of transfer in a large school system offers many opportunities to improve the service and satisfactions of the individual teacher and to improve the educational service. The teacher who does not "fit" in one school may do well in another. The system opening a new school may do well to staff it with teachers from a number of schools as well as with teachers new to the system.

However, if the transfer program is to contribute as it might, it needs to be carefully developed and administered. Otherwise, transfer may on the one hand be abused by teachers with seniority, or on the other be regarded as a method of punishment by the administrator. The development of a program involves the definition of what is desirable in terms of the faculty of an individual school. For example, should range in education, experience, special competency, and age be sought in each school faculty? Or should some few faculties be developed as outstanding ones, in comparison with others in the system? What role should the principal and teaching staff play in the development of the faculty of the individual school? How is the transfer program to be related to the induction of teachers into the system? How are the desires of the individual teacher to be related to the needs of the system?

In this area, there are a number of problems that must be cooperatively attacked by the teaching profession and the administration if the potential of the staff is to be more fully realized. Experience suggests that the difficult problem of transfer will not be met satisfactorily by either the administration or the organized profession on its own. It may be resolved by these forces cooperatively. The leadership of a personnel director who is staff- rather than line-oriented is greatly needed in this effort to develop policies and programs.

EVALUATION AND IN-SERVICE EDUCATION PROGRAMS

One of the most difficult aspects of personnel administration is that of evaluation. If attention is centered upon improvement of instruction as a major purpose and evaluation is not tied to salary questions, it is more likely to be handled effectively. Some general guidelines regarding evaluation are: (1) it should be cooperative, involving the teacher and the administrator; (2) it should provide for self-evaluation; (3) it should be carefully planned in light of a definition of the desired role of the teachers; (4) it should involve the collection of pertinent data pertaining to the services rendered by the teacher and should not give undue weight to rating of the work of the teacher in the classroom; (5) it should be seen as a constructive effort, extending over a considerable period of time, to assist the teacher in improving his work, and (6) it should draw upon wide resources of personnel and not be seen as a principal-teacher relationship only.

Effective evaluation requires a maturity that is not easily attained. It assumes that administrators as well as teachers will be evaluated and that evaluation is a constructive professional service and not a matter of personal favoritism or attack. It assumes that people are accepted as people and thus able to communicate regarding a problem that is common to them. A sound program is one in which fellow teachers participate and assist the profession to accept a responsibility that it must accept and thus reduce the tensions that may result from the activity of those in status positions. In regard to this problem, it must be noted that people are not likely to be helped by those whom they do not perceive as a source of assistance. An organization that is helping many is much more likely to be perceived as a source of help than an individual who is in a status position that requires leadership. The status leader must be involved in the process, but he cannot do the job.

In the school system, evaluation is necessary, not only for direct improvement of instruction, though this should be the major purpose, but for other reasons as well. Other purposes of evaluation involve questions of indefinite tenure, of promotion, of reassignment, and of separation. Regarding these as well as the major purpose, it is necessary that clear statements of policy be developed with the assistance of teachers and that procedures be developed in accord with the policies. As the educational profession achieves more of the attributes of a profession, a larger role should be played in all these matters by the members of the teaching staff.

The In-Service Program

This program is closely related to the evaluation of personnel for improvement purposes. The more that is learned about how teachers learn the less it appears likely that a fixed in-service education program can be formulated. It must be very clearly developed in light of the experience, education, competencies, and needs of the staff. It must be substantially developed and carried through by the staff. It will take many forms and cannot be limited to functions frequently regarded as supervisory. In one school or school system it may mean the study of an individual child for some months, the study of a subject matter field or of methods, participation in a workshop, participation in the formulation of the characteristics of the outstanding teacher, cooperation with the business office to insure the provision of materials at the time needed, development of the ability to hold parent conferences, analysis of the role played by various teachers in the school, or engagement in an action research project to determine the worth of certain materials of instruction or of a plan of grouping within the class.

In recent years, the ability of the central administrative and supervisory staff and the principal to provide leadership for teachers in their work has been challenged. This has become an extremely important question with the increase in the power and responsibility of organizations of teachers. Gross and Herriott report that their study of the leadership role of the elementary school principal supports "the staff influence conception of the principalship and strategies to increase the principal's professional leadership."[2] This should not be regarded as a statement in

[2]Neal Gross, and Robert E. Herriott, *Staff Leadership in Public Schools: A Sociological Inquiry* (New York: John Wiley & Sons, Inc., 1965), p. 151.

opposition to the growing responsibility of the profession. However, it emphasizes the need for study, accommodation and cooperation in the in-service area.

Both the administrators and the teachers must recognize that developing and carrying through this program is of greatest significance among the various elements of the personnel administration services. They both must accept it as an opportunity. They must cooperatively seek resources that will be of assistance in the program, and then attempt to create the situation in which these resources can be used with maximum desirable results.

SALARY SCHEDULES AND SALARIES

No other phase of the personnel service area attracts more attention than salary schedules and salary. Because of inflation, it has been necessary to review the salary situation almost annually and to make adjustments in it. Regrettably, a large part of this work has not been a matter of improving the economic status of the profession but rather of running hard to maintain past status.

The salary issue is largely related to the development of a salary schedule and to the formulation of the rules in accord with which it will be administered. The last decade has witnessed the general acceptance of the single salary schedule. It provides the teacher in any part of the school system the same salary for a given education and experience. The adoption of the single salary has meant that elementary teachers have made substantial salary gains in recent years, while in some instances secondary-school teachers have been provided for less adequately in relation to their past position.

In developing or revising a salary schedule, particular attention must be given to the minimum and maximum salaries, the number and size of the increments, the number of classes (generally based upon degrees held or units earned), and the salary differences provided for the various classes. Salary schedules or minimums may be specified by the state, but even in such cases the local district should desire to exceed them.

The determination of the ability to finance a schedule that is presented for adoption is exceedingly difficult. Teachers can be advanced on the schedule for a period of years and estimates of costs can be made. The cost when certain percentages of teachers are in certain classes on the schedule and have certain years of experience can also be determined. However, estimating the probable income of the district through local taxes and from state sources cannot be done with satisfying accuracy. Intertwined in this problem is also the question of whether there will be continued inflation and if so, at what rate. Despite the difficulties, estimates of the future financial impact of a salary program should be developed as one way of testing the proposed schedule.

Among the problems encountered by the administration are those concerned with the placement of teachers on the schedule, the years of experience in other districts that will be recognized, the number of credits that may be earned during the teaching year for salary placement purposes, and the method to be used and the factors to be employed for advancement on the schedule.

One of the more interesting developments pertaining to teachers' salary schedules in recent years has been the movement toward index schedules. "An index salary schedule is one that has one salary for a specified amount of education and experience set as the base and all other salaries on the schedule set at predetermined ratios to the base."[3] This type of schedule focuses attention on structure and relationships, rather than on dollar amounts, and facilitates revision. Generally, the teachers' salary schedule for the minimum acceptable educational level is accepted as the base. All other teacher salaries, without regard to the factors recognized (such as additional years of education, experience, professional status, special responsibilities, or recognition of merit), are then expressed as a ratio of the base. Similarly, all other professional staff, including administrative, can be placed on the schedule with a ratio which provides recognition for time, merit, complexity of assignment, and responsibility. With such a schedule, annual action by the board of education on salary matters can be greatly simplified. Periodically or continuously, study of the ratios should be carried on, especially in light of the changes which are occurring both in the composition of the staff and in the required education and responsibilities of those in specified positions.

Another of the more difficult problems is the question of extra pay for extra work, that frequently arises in connection with extra- or co-curricular activities. Theoretically, most people agree that the most desirable arrangement for these activities is to regard them as a part of the regular teaching load and to relieve of certain other duties those teachers who assume responsibility for them. Thus, all teachers would have an equivalent load. In practice, however, it is frequently difficult to develop satisfactory work schedules for these teachers. Furthermore, since most payments made for extracurricular activities are token payments not very closely related to the hours or responsibility involved, it is frequently considerably less expensive to provide extra payments for them.

If this is the decision, the question arises as to the amount of the

[3]*NEA Research Bulletin,* 43, No. 2 (May 1965), 60.

extra payment and the services for which payment is to be made. Perhaps for some services compensation is provided through reducing the load of other duties, while for others extra compensation is provided. In view of the variety of factors that enter into the teacher's load and also because of the desirability of developing a more adequate salary schedule for all teachers, it is generally desirable to hold extra payments to a token or minimum level. If they mount, they may have adverse effects upon the morale of teachers and will lead to the demand for more and more types of service to be recognized for extra pay.

The procedures employed in working through various salary schedule issues are of great significance. In some systems the superintendent of schools takes major responsibility for making the essential studies. In others one or more organizations of teachers may carry through studies and present salary schedule proposals. In a few communities, committees representing the board of education, teachers, administration, and at times, citizens of special competencies work through the salary problem. Unfortunately, the salary problem has produced considerable tension and misunderstanding among the various interested parties in some school systems. It would appear that an effort should be made in more school systems to define the respective roles of the various parties so that the problem can be met more effectively and more satisfactorily.

NONCERTIFICATED PERSONNEL

In concluding this consideration of various aspects of personnel administration attention is turned to noncertificated personnel. Problems and opportunities in this area parallel in considerable measure those that exist in the case of certificated personnel. The same principles and philosophy of personnel administration apply in the case of these employees as in that of the certificated staff. A part of the responsibility of the personnel administrator is the development of an understanding of this fact on the part of the certificated staff.

The local school system must define the competencies needed by various personnel and then recruit, select, and assign. It must provide opportunities for transfer, machinery for consideration of grievances, and in-service development programs. A salary schedule recognizing education, responsibility, and compensation for equivalent work in other public and private enterprises should be developed for various groups of noncertificated personnel. These workers as well as teachers need to be provided for in case of ill health and when in retirement.

These groups of employees have expanded greatly as the educational services have developed. There is considerable range in the levels of responsibility that different members of this staff have. However, all of them play a significant role as assistants to those with teaching responsibilities. Furthermore, many of them have a direct relationship to children and young people. It is extremely important, therefore, that appropriate action be taken in establishing policies and practices pertaining to noncertificated personnel.

<h2 style="text-align:center">PROBLEMS AND ISSUES</h2>

In the following pages, consideration will be given to a few of the many problems in personnel administration.

How Can Personnel Administration Be Developed Effectively as a Staff Function in an Educational System?

There is probably no aspect of the educational system where the question of line and staff organization is faced more directly than in the area of personnel. It is clear that the administrative line officers will wish and should have decision-making responsibilities within a framework ensuring fair and just treatment for all personnel. It is equally clear that line officers experience considerable difficulty in serving as staff officers. There would seem therefore to be need for a personnel division that is definitely a staff division. This decision, however, does not end the difficulties.

Among the problems[4] are the following: Will the line officers grant to the staff officers the essential autonomy, so that they may be recognized as, and actually be, personnel advisors to various groups of employees as well as to management? Can staff officers escape the cloud that results from the fact that their future promotion will be dependent upon line officers who may be more jealous of the prerogatives of the formal organization than of the concerns of groups of employees? Can staff officers resist the temptation to get more and more deeply involved in actual administration, rather than to conduct research and furnish advice?

The problems related to a line and staff organization for personnel may be so difficult that they may suggest recourse to another type of organization. However, in this area perhaps more than in any other, the tendency to ignore formal organization cannot be readily defended. We may value informal organization especially and proceed as a highly cooperative group in the attack on a curriculum problem. Although

[4]For an excellent discussion of these problems see Dalton's study as reported in Robert Dubin, *Human Relations in Administration* (Englewood Cliffs, N.J.: Prentice-Hall, Inc., 1951), pp. 128–138.

cooperative effort is also essential in matters of personnel and is to be highly valued, it is not sufficient. It will not give to all members of the group that assurance of impartiality that is an imperative of an excellent personnel system.

Possibly, in education there exists an excellent opportunity for study of some of the issues that are found in this field. In a service devoted to the development of people, there should be a basis for a program that is somewhat better than that found in industry. It is clear that much remains to be done in the study, organization, and development of personnel programs in educational systems.

What are the major difficulties the superintendent or the principal experiences when serving both as a line and as a staff officer? What should be the duties of the director of personnel of the school system? Can you propose a structure of relationships in which there will be a balancing of "the need for rationality in organizational performance and a humane concern for personnel"?[5]

Are Schools Organized in a Manner that Provides
that Too Many People Are Responsible to One Person?

In the rapidly growing school or school system there is some evidence that the single administrator frequently attempts to retain too much direct responsibility for too many people. The principal of the large high school cannot work closely with all of the members of the faculty. This is true also in large elementary schools. However, in relatively few instances have "schools within the school" been developed. This direct retention of responsibility by the administrator who cannot work closely with any large percentage of the staff increases the isolation of the individual teacher. This isolation reduces the feeling of the teacher that he can do anything about the situation in the schools, and impairs the effectiveness of the staff.

The old departmentalization plan is quite probably undesirable. However, some plan, whereby teachers will be a part of a team that they can comprehend and do something about, would appear to be quite necessary. Such teams may also offer one of the best opportunities for the integration of such special services as guidance with the instructional program.

The organization of schools and school systems in such a manner that staff members have the opportunity to participate more effectively with consequent satisfactions is imperative. Too many staff members do not accept responsibility for the enterprise. It is not theirs. One approach that may assist in this situation is an organization through which respon-

[5]R. Oliver Gibson, and Herold C. Hunt, *The School Personnel Administrator* (Boston: Houghton Mifflin Company, 1965), p. 153.

sibility will be more widely disseminated. Perhaps more of the staff who are on the immediate operational level need to have certain administrative and coordinative responsibilities. This could also provide for more gradations of responsibility and could thus be significantly related to the demand for merit pay programs for teachers.

What number of administrative personnel should be responsible directly to the superintendent of schools? What organizational plan will facilitate the development of feelings of responsibility for the school program among the staff of the large school or school system?

What Is the Future Nature and Role
of the Teaching Profession?

The teaching profession has been challenged on many fronts during recent years. The challenges remain unmet in substantial part, though new directions of development may be appearing. Among the more important of these issues are: Will there be a teaching profession or a family of professions as a result of developments such as programed learning, teaching machines, educational TV? What will be the respective responsibilities of the professional teacher and of teaching assistants, aides, and subprofessionals? Will staff composition and organization within schools vary widely with greater emphasis upon departmentalization and with important advances through team teaching? Will the profession concentrate more upon academic achievement or will it seek the development of the child on a broader front (not neglecting the academic) as a result of the civil rights movement and a new awareness of problems of the culturally different and of the emotionally disabled?

It appears clear that the direction of learning in the future will be increasingly complex and that it will not be carried on by the individual somewhat isolated teacher in the closed-door classroom to as great an extent as heretofore. It will require the services of a staff possessed of a considerable range of knowledge, skills, abilities. Conceivably, the professional teacher as the central figure in the process will have the assistance of a number of highly trained technicians and experts. He also will very probably have the assistance of a number of nonprofessionals who can render important service to the teaching process or in relation to various matters which impinge on learning, such as the interpretation of the school and community to each other.[6]

Quite conceivably, we shall also see the development of different career lines in teaching. One of these may be the transitional—intended for or pursued by those who may be in the profession for a relatively short period of years; another for the professional teacher who would

[6]Frank Riessman, "The Revolution in Social Work: The New Nonprofessional," *Transaction*, **2**, No. 1 (Nov.-Dec. 1964), 12–17.

assume ever increasing responsibilities, who would engage in extended study beyond that of entering teachers, and who would receive a substantially higher salary.

What "Authority" Shall Be Vested in the Organized Teaching Profession and How Shall It Be Exercised?

Traditionally and in accord with law the board of education has authority for the conduct of the school system. Gradually the development of large scale organizations has resulted in an increase of the authority which is in reality exercised by the necessary bureaucracy. Especially during recent years, the members of the teaching profession as organized groups have been taking increased interest in matters pertaining to personnel, academic freedom, and instruction and have been gaining increased responsibility.

Thus, while legally the board of education remains the responsible body, there has been a growth of responsibility on the part of other groups. Some recognition of this growth is found in the new state laws providing for collective negotiation. The teaching profession, which has for some years exercised important responsibilities at the state legislative level, is now increasing its role at the local level.

This increase of activity by the profession has raised a number of issues. Among them are: the procedures through which the profession determines upon those who will represent it (Shall one organization be "bargaining agent" or shall various teacher organizations be represented on a negotiating committee?), the relations of the negotiating committee to the board of education and the superintendent of schools (What matters, if any, shall be presented to the board of education directly, rather than only after discussion with the superintendent?), the question of sanctions imposed by the profession (the question of whether justified, when justified, and how administered).

Shall Teachers Be Rated?

There is little question regarding the desirability of an evaluation of teacher performance. The issue becomes largely one of who will do the evaluating, how it will be done, and why it will be done.

First, it is important to note that rating based upon an observation or two of a teacher in the classroom is being increasingly recognized as of little value. This does not mean that classroom observation should not be utilized. However, it must be seen as a part of a larger plan for evaluation. An evaluation is very different from a rating in that it is based upon the use of various techniques that produce considerable data pertaining to the individual. The collection of data pertaining to the various activities of the teacher is an essential of evaluation. Without a sound broad base, the evaluation cannot be valid. Among the many data collected may be records of achievement, of study and writings, of work on committees, of work with students and parents, and of ratings and self-ratings and follow-up conferences regarding them.

The aspect of rating that is least subject to criticism is self-rating by means of a scale developed or selected by the staff. It is likely to be helpful to the extent it is effectively used as one aspect of a carefully developed personnel program that has built mutual respect and confidence among teachers, supervisors, and administrators.

As suggested above, the most important purpose of evaluation is improvement of service. This is the major emphasis that evaluation should receive. This requires some definition of what desirable or outstanding teaching service is as a basis for the evaluation. It is extremely important that teachers participate in the framing of the characteristics of the good or superior teacher. They also must participate in the development of the plan of evaluation.

The success of a program of teacher evaluation can only be judged in light of the purposes. Widely varied or confused purposes may sharply reduce the value of any program. The assumption is unsound that evaluation for improvement of instruction can be combined with evaluation for purposes of paying teachers in accord with their "worth." In fact, evaluation programs that have contributed considerably to the improvement of instruction may be largely destroyed by the "threat" of payment in accord with the "contribution made." The development of the plan of evaluation of teachers should be seen as a cooperative activity involving teachers and other staff. Its purposes must be clearly defined and carefully followed if its potential is to be reasonably well realized.

What plan for the evaluation of the work of teachers and administrators would you recommend? Consider the implications for evaluation of the immediately preceding issue regarding the changing nature of teaching and role of the professional teacher.

Can a Transfer Policy Be Developed That Is Equitable Both to Teachers and to Children and Youth?

In some states, because of the large number of school districts, much of what might be regarded as transfer has been a matter of teachers shifting from one school district to another. This movement has been the result of desire for better working conditions as well as for increased salary. Resulting largely from inequalities of wealth among districts, this movement has tended to produce large inequalities in educational opportunity. Frequently, poor districts or geographically remote ones have had to accept a high percentage of beginning teachers or teachers unacceptable to the wealthier and generally more desirable communities in which to live.

As districts have grown larger, the transfer problem within systems has increased. Large districts in many instances are characterized by contrasts in socioeconomic conditions of different sections. Schools reflect these conditions and are regarded as desirable or undesirable by many teachers. Poorer sections socially or economically may also be racially mixed communities with resultant problems.

Some school districts have attempted to meet the wishes of teachers for transfer by providing that transfer will generally be granted to teachers on the basis of the years of service that they have rendered. This has resulted in the development of faculties of schools in the "better" areas that are composed of older teachers, while schools in the less desirable areas have an extremely high percentage of beginning teachers. Thus, the schools that have many difficult problems are staffed largely with inexperienced teachers. Such practices can hardly be regarded as representing an adequate concern for the needs of all students.

On the other hand, in a few districts, transfer is regarded by some teachers as a form of punishment. In these districts, transfer may occur with little opportunity for consideration of the wishes of the teacher.

The question of the extent to which transfers should be initiated by teachers or administrators and the attitudes regarding the initiation of transfers are matters of concern in a considerable number of school districts. Often equally unclear are the procedures followed in the decision making regarding proposals for transfer.

The profession itself has not faced the transfer problem directly in many school systems, and thus has not helped remove some of the confusion and uncertainty regarding practices. Certainly, the interests of teachers and students should not be regarded as being inevitably —or perhaps in any sense—in conflict. The bringing of the "right" teachers and "right" students together should be accomplished in a manner that will raise teacher morale.

The solution of this issue is intimately tied up with the development of considerably more staff personnel research work than is found in most school systems. It may involve improvement of conditions found in some schools through the provision of more staff or facilities. It may also involve the integration of the individual school with many of the resources of the neighborhood. The view cannot be accepted that teaching in the poorer communities is inevitably less satisfying professionally than is teaching in "better" ones.

When a new school is opened, which teachers should be transferred to it? How can the schools in the poorer economic and social sections of the city be staffed with well-balanced faculties? What is a well-balanced faculty?

Should a School System Have Grievance Machinery?

Traditionally, school systems have not had a planned program for receiving and disposing of the complaints of teachers. It has been assumed that this is not necessary, since the teacher could go to the principal and the matter would be satisfactorily resolved. Certainly there are school systems where this was and is true, where there may appear no need for grievance machinery.

On the other hand, it must be recognized that many teachers are extremely hesitant to present matters to the principal that are disturbing them. Some are sure they would not receive an objective consideration of the matter and a few would fear reprisals. As educational organizations have grown larger and traditional ways of resolving issues have been challenged, there has been an apparent need for the provision of a program that will do more to ensure the frank presentation of problems.

There would, therefore, appear to be a need for many systems to give consideration to such a program. Careful study should be given to the program, or it may be only a form and not substantive. Other difficulties such as the tendency to attempt to handle too many different problems should also be avoided. Properly conceived and developed, however, it can offer considerable advantage in many school systems to both teachers and administrators. Similar arrangements may also be desirable in the case of personnel other than teachers.

In setting up such programs the objectives of the program should be clearly defined. In the Houston, Texas study the following broad objectives were suggested:

> . . . (a) to assure an opportunity for the teacher to have direct communication with the person who is responsible for the alleged grievance, (b) to reduce the potential area of grievances between teachers and administrators, (c) to instill in teachers the understanding that channels for redressing grievances are open without fear of reprisal, and (d) to develop teacher morale and responsibility.[7]

The program should make clear what constitutes a grievance; the channels for the presentation of a grievance and, if necessary, appeals from a decision; the method of presentation and assistance therefor; and the time limits for action in order to avoid delay that in itself may become a source of dissatisfaction and tension.

What is a grievance? Should administrators as well as teachers have recourse to the grievance machinery?

[7]National Education Association, National Commission for the Defense of Democracy Through Education, *A Study of Factors Related to Educational Unrest in a Large School System* (Washington, D.C.: The Association, December, 1954), p. 38.

Should Teachers and Administrators Belong
    to the Same Professional Organization?

Teachers and administrators are members of the teaching profession. In one sense they are also members of separate professions. The roles and responsibilities of teachers and administrators are quite similar in that they are the professional staff charged with responsibility for the educational service. The roles and situational factors related to the work of teachers and administrators are significantly different. These contradictions raise the question as to whether teachers and administrators should be members of a single professional group.

The answer to the question may not be a clear yes or no. A recognition of their joint responsibilities suggests that they should be members of the same group. A recognition of their respective roles also suggests that on some matters they may properly have different needs.

Quite possibly the answer to the problem will be found in a more frank recognition of their respective roles, their common goals, and their possible and probable areas of disagreement. With a clearer perception of the responsibility of each, a common organization could provide considerable leeway for the independent action of each as well as for the joint pursuit of common goals. Considerable progress has been made along these lines in some professional organizations. It is believed, however, that there has not been sufficient recognition of the roles and obligations of each party. As a result, tensions and misunderstandings have been too common. Unless this problem can be resolved in an open realistic manner, separate organizations that can then develop cooperative effort may be the solution.

What, if any, are the implications for professional organizations of collective bargaining laws for teachers? Should or could the superintendent be a member of an organization engaged in collective bargaining with the board of education at the same time he is the spokesman for the board?

Are Salary Schedules Adequate That Are Built
    upon Years of Teaching Experience and
    Degrees or Units of Credit Earned?

Salary schedules for teachers have increasingly provided recognition for these two factors only. There is general agreement that they are both important factors that should be recognized. There is, of course, some concern that other factors are not provided for. This is the major element in the recurrent question regarding the establishment of merit pay programs. This is the background of the growing demand for professional salary schedules which will recognize teachers who are career-committed and increasingly competent and responsible.

The credits or degrees earned should have a definite relationship to the quality of service rendered. However, the extent of this relationship may be related to the system of administration of the salary program. Does it ensure the provision of opportunities for further study that are significantly related to the service rendered by the teachers? Is further study carried on under such conditions that it improves the work of the teacher rather than impedes it? A well-developed personnel program will recognize the possible pitfalls in a salary schedule that emphasizes hours of credit earned and will, in cooperation with the profession, avoid them. Unless the program is carefully developed and administered, abuses by a few could seriously impair respect for the salary schedule.

Although there is no established program for recognizing factors beyond years of experience and credits earned, attention should be given to the possibility of developing a different organization and providing some recognition for different amounts or levels of responsibility accepted. Such an approach could meet the challenge of those seeking some further recognition for teachers who accept large responsibilities and render outstanding service while considerably improving the educational results. In the development of such programs, widespread teacher participation would be essential. Care should be taken to avoid placing some teachers in these positions for an indefinite period, and on the other hand to avoid the equally undesirable plan of merely rotating the assignment of the special responsibility.

What plan should a local school system adopt to maximize the educational returns of courses pursued by teachers for salary schedule credit purposes? Should the schedule provide allowances for dependents?

What Should Be the Relation of the Minimum and Maximum Salaries for Teachers, and What Should Be the Size of the Increments?

The problem of relationship of the minimum and maximum salary has been re-examined during recent years. Changes in attitudes toward this relationship are related to the salary philosophy of the community, to practices in other professions, to the financial ability of school districts, to the supply of and demand for teachers, and to the levels of education required or recognized for teachers.

Should the rough ratio of two-to-one for the maximum and minimum salaries be accepted as a desirable goal? During recent years, supply and demand have probably put more pressure on beginning salaries than on maximums, because it has been necessary to compete with other fields in order to get teachers into the classrooms. While higher maximums affect attraction and retention, the loss of teachers may not be as visible, and consequently, supply and demand may not press as hard at this point. Higher maximums also have great impact upon the financial problem of the district—especially if a large percentage of the teachers should approach the maximums. On the other hand, the shortage of teachers has emphasized the need of adequate schedules, since beginning salaries alone will not attract. The development of a group of men and women who have accepted teaching as a profession and not as a temporary employment also emphasizes the need for keeping the maximum well ahead of the minimum. The considerable number of men on many elementary school faculties compared to the situation in the twenties or thirties is a specific illustration of this need. From these facts it would appear that an approximate ratio of two-to-one will be maintained.

Not only is the retention of such a ratio probable, but the span of years required to move from the minimum to the maximum does not promise to increase. A few years ago, a longer period of years was advocated. This shorter span of years is related to the need for the teacher to reach a reasonable income without long years of teaching. This was imperative with low minimums and with more teachers having dependents in the early years of their teaching. Whether there is or may develop a psychological problem from the fact that the teacher may reach his maximum salary when still in the early thirties is not known. Recent years have been characterized by inflation. The resultant need for redeveloping salary schedules annually has made it difficult to determine the possible effects of various salary schedule provisions.

The shorter period of years for increments has been related to an increase in the size of increments. Larger increments were essential, since the increments reduced in purchasing power by inflation were no longer adequate.

What is a desirable annual increment? How many increments should the schedule provide?

Should a Merit Salary Program Be Adopted?

Demands for a merit salary program for teachers have been voiced for more than half a century. The anticipated advantages of such a program are widely recognized. The inadequacies and disadvantages of such programs quickly become evident when presented or applied. Probably the issue is no nearer solution than it was a few decades ago. Although there may be more agreement on what constitutes the excellent discharge of a teacher's duties, there is also much more awareness of the complexity of the problem of evaluating the teachers. There is also more understanding of the school as a social system and more regard for the people in it.

If progress is to be made in this area, the meaning of merit salary programs must be clarified. Present salary schedules make an indirect effort at recognizing merit. If by merit pay programs, reference is to a super maximum, the problem is very different from that which would be encountered if an attempt were to be made to evaluate each teacher each year and to relate salary received directly to the results of such rating. Even in business and industry where the "results" of work are more tangible, there are far fewer programs of the latter type than is assumed in the discussions of merit pay programs for teachers.

If merit pay programs of any type are developed, it is clear that they should be formulated with the assistance of those who will be affected by them. Unless the program is accepted as sound by the various parties who will be involved in it or with it, it is not likely to succeed. Programs thus must be the result of extended work by teachers, directors of personnel, administrators, and lay citizens of communities that are concerned with the problem.

Any community developing such a program will need to clarify the purposes of the educational program; define "excellence" on the part of the teacher; agree on the role of the teacher in the classroom, community, profession; establish a plan for evaluating teacher performances; establish machinery for administration of the program; provide for the collection of data to determine the various effects of the program; determine whether the merit payments will be token or substantial; and plan the periodic review and modification of the program.

Any program of this type should be regarded as a part of a comprehensive personnel program. Standing alone, it can probably contribute little that is constructive and may in fact be highly destructive of morale and effectiveness of teachers. Such programs should not be avoided because of their complexity and difficulty. However, it is well for a community to be informed regarding the nature of the task in order that it may plan effectively. A community that begins a program uninformed of the many problems involved will not be likely to achieve constructive results.

What is meant by a merit salary program? How can the merit of a teacher be determined? Should recognition for merit be in token financial terms or related to actual difference in performance? Is it more feasible to recognize levels of responsibility than merit?

Should the Salary Schedule of Teachers and That of Administrators Be Related?

Salary schedules for teachers have been widely accepted as one of the essentials of an adequate personnel program. As school systems have become larger, the need of schedules for administrators also has been generally recognized.

Traditionally, the schedules of administrators and those of teachers have not been directly related. In an increasing number of school districts they are being directly related through an established ratio or other procedure.

Prior to the economic depression of the thirties, administrators' salaries were much higher in relation to teachers' salaries than they have been since. The reduction in the distance between the earnings of the workers and management personnel that was general in the society was reflected in the educational scene. Perhaps it was reflected in the educational scene to an extreme degree. In any case, around 1950 there were instances in which the range had narrowed to such an extent that principals were receiving a lower salary per month than they would have received had they been teaching in the school of which they were principal. Thus they received no recognition for administrative responsibility. During very recent years, there has been some fuller recognition of the responsibility and role of the administrator, and the distance from the basic teachers' salary schedule has increased slightly. The relationship between the teachers' salary schedule and that of administrators will undoubtedly vary over a period of years, depending upon economic trends in the society, the education of teachers and various groups of administrators, and the public concept of their responsibility. Therefore, any ratio that is established will have to be periodically re-examined. In this re-examination, data regarding the respective responsibilities need to be assembled. An element of judgment will also be involved.

The establishment of a ratio is favored by some, since it reduces the work involved in developing the budget for the year. Instead of two salary studies and considerations, only one is necessary. Action on the teachers' salary schedule results in changes in the administrators' schedule. Furthermore, when the ratio is established through studies in which various personnel are involved, the feeling that exists at times among teachers that administrators are overpaid may be eliminated. It thus facilitates the cooperative effort of teachers and administrators in educational work.

A few board of education members oppose the ratio, believing that it encourages administrators to favor higher salaries for teachers since they also are benefited. Actually, there is little if any evidence to support this view. Some administrators question the ratio, believing that it tends to hold salaries of administrators lower than they would be otherwise. They believe that salaries of administrators are not high enough in respect to those of comparable positions in society or in relation to those of teachers to cause men of great promise to undertake the additional education and to accept the additional responsibilities and demands upon time.

It would appear to be desirable to develop the administrators' schedule in relation to that for teachers. This, however, does not mean that a ratio once established should remain. If this view is accepted, then basic studies should be carried through periodically to determine the ratio, after consideration of the salaries for comparable positions in society and the significance and responsibilities of the administrators' positions.

What should be the ratio of the salary of the superintendent or principal to that of the teacher? Should this ratio express difference in responsibility or in months of service each year, or both? Should all professional employees be on a twelve-month schedule with a specified vacation period?

Selected References

American Association of School Administrators, *Staff Relations in School Administration*, Thirty-third Yearbook. Washington, D.C.: The Association, 1955.

Castetter, William B., *Administering the School Personnel Program*. New York: The Macmillan Company, 1962.

Culbertson, Jack A., Paul B. Jacobson, and Theodore L. Reller, *Administrative Relationships: A Casebook*. Englewood Cliffs, N.J.: Prentice-Hall, Inc., 1960.

Dubin, Robert, *Human Relations in Administration*. Englewood Cliffs, N.J.: Prentice-Hall, Inc., 1956.

Elsbree, Willard S., and E. Edmund Reutter, *Staff Personnel in the Public Schools*. Englewood Cliffs, N.J.: Prentice-Hall, Inc., 1954.

Fawcett, Claude W., *School Personnel Administration*. New York: The Macmillan Company, 1964.

Gibson, R. Oliver, and Herold C. Hunt, *The School Personnel Administrator*. Boston: Houghton Mifflin Company, 1965.

Griffiths, Daniel E., *Human Relations in School Administration*. New York: Appleton-Century-Crofts, 1956.

Homans, George, *Social Behavior*. New York: Harcourt, Brace & World, Inc., 1961.

Jersild, Arthur T., *When Teachers Face Themselves*. New York: Teachers College, Columbia University, 1955.

Lieberman, Myron, and Michael Moskow, *Collective Negotiations for Teachers: An Approach to School Administration*. Skokie, Ill.: Rand McNally & Co., 1966.

Pearl, Arthur, and Frank Reissman, *New Careers for the Poor*. New York: Free Press of Glencoe, Inc., 1965.

Steffensen, James P., *Teachers Negotiate With Their School Boards*, Bulletin No. 40, U.S. Department of Health, Education and Welfare, Office of Education. Washington, D.C.: U.S. Government Printing Office, 1964.

17

The School Plant

The school plant is one of the major concerns and opportunities of the school administrator. It is of great importance because of the impact of the plant on the educational processes and program. While it is generally agreed that the plant should reflect the educational program and needs, it is often true that the educational program bears many evidences of the influence of the plant. This may be the result of a number of factors, such as the tangibility of the school plant and the number of years that it serves.

SCHOOL PLANT—A NEW OPPORTUNITY

In recent years, a considerable number of factors related directly to the school plant have been greatly modified. As a result of this change an unusual or essentially new opportunity has opened up in the field of housing. Not only have there been changes in each of these areas or factors but the changes occurring concurrently in the others have pyramided the opportunity which is open to educators and architects, and thus to the community. Among these factors the following are noted:

A NEW "OPENNESS" REGARDING EDUCATIONAL PURPOSES AND PROCESSES. Value questions are being raised in the educational world to a much greater degree than was true only a few years ago. Is it "democratic" or desirable or defensible to spend considerably more on each gifted child than on each average child? to develop giftedness in regard to what? mathematics? science? music? If so, how much more is to be expended per student?

Is it desirable to spend considerably larger sums on the culturally different? Can it be assumed that somewhat equivalent services would not be of great importance for many of the culturally advantaged? Are they really so advantaged? If so, how should these funds be expended in a way to facilitate maximum returns? Is it primarily a matter of smaller classes? special or new programs of reading instruction? cultural enrichment in preschool and during school years? To what extent does such enrichment involve improving the competencies and tastes of the parents so that they may not be alienated from their children? Can essential language development best be accomplished in the school or through the enlistment and development of affiliated agencies?

Even with an emphasis on preschool and out-of-school experiences, important modifications must also be effected in the school program. Is the great emphasis on mathematics and science to remain? Will a similar emphasis develop in language, social sciences, art, music? Are the old separations between that which is elementary and that which is secondary education disappearing?

CHANGES IN THE ORGANIZATION OF SCHOOLS IN THE SYSTEM. For a considerable number of years it appeared that preschool programs would not develop rapidly, that the neighborhood school was an idea which would become increasingly universal, that the 6–3–3 plan of organization would be employed in an increasing number of districts. Further, important forces were emphasizing the use of tests for purposes of grouping either in the school or the classroom. While there was some discussion of separate schools for the gifted or for vocational purposes, only a few districts made such provisions.

As noted in Chapter 12, all of these questions of organization of schools have been and continue to be re-examined. Is not a 4–4–4–4 or 4–4–3–3–2 organization better than the 6–3–3 or the 1–6–3–3–2? Does it not facilitate desegregation? Did we really hold to or utilize the neighborhood school concept to as great a degree as has been assumed? May we not turn to school parks, established in attractive surroundings, containing a number of schools and providing for more effective use of specialized facilities and the growing number of special-technical personnel? Must we not develop essentially different approaches in the vocational-technical field if the needs of youth and society are to be met in this area? Will job corps centers be institutionalized? Should they be part of the educational system? If there is to be a new relation to the nonpublic schools, with some of their students coming to the public schools for certain parts of the program, what are the implications for structure?

And with the employment problems before us, are we going to at last grasp adult education in terms of its liberal education values? Perhaps we are in the closing days of the period when it was assumed that school experience could be ended at sixteen or eighteen. Or possibly we have passed that period but have not yet fully recognized social developments in educational programs.

CHANGES IN ORGANIZATION WITHIN THE SCHOOL.   Change and the opportunity for change within the school also offer a major challenge to the school plant planner. Team teaching in its many possible definitions and forms has large meaning for the school plant. Related to it are developments in terms of staff such as: the use of teaching assistants, the development of a handful of professions engaged in teaching as distinct from the teacher, the place of guidance staff, social workers and other specialists, the nature and degree of departmentalization in schools at all levels. There are also the major developments related to the expansion of library facilities and programs, the provision of laboratories (language, for example, but why not other areas?), centers for the arts. The provision of proper facilities for independent study is a challenge. The implications for organization of a more adequate staff to provide for the culturally different also are substantial. Surely it is not merely a matter of providing more rooms to care for more smaller classes. Perhaps classroom walls will disappear, and designs other than that of a number of approximately equal-sized boxes can now spread rapidly.

A NEW TECHNOLOGY.   Ready to facilitate the development of schools with a new organization is technology. Improved construction materials make it possible to escape some of the old limits of size and shape. Advances in lighting, heating, and air control also offer new opportunities. In more direct relation to the learning process, developments regarding programing, audio-visual media, computerized instruction offer the teacher vast new opportunities for securing assistance. So large are the opportunities here that the day may be near when the percentage of the total cost of a new plant which is devoted to instructional facilities or equipment will increase very sharply—not unlike the change in this regard which has occurred in the new industrial plant. Correspondingly, the percentage of the cost devoted to the basic structure could decline sharply.

A NEW BELIEF IN THE IMPORTANCE OF INVESTING IN EDUCATION.   The significance of the preceding factors is greatly enhanced by the apparent fact that the society sees in education an area in which it must invest much more heavily. The breakthrough in federal education programs in 1963–65 attests to this.

It would appear therefore that the schoolmen confronted with the need for new plants are facing the most difficult problem of their careers —difficult because the pace of change is extremely rapid; difficult because many of the old forms are weakened, if not broken, while the new have not been institutionalized; difficult because the opportunity is so great; difficult because the results may be more affected by their knowledge and vision, or lack thereof, than in any recent period.

BUILDINGS AND INSTRUCTION

In many instances the organization of schools has been greatly influenced by the available school buildings. The junior high school was given an important push in many communities by the fact that it was an appealing way to relieve overcrowding in both the elementary schools and the senior high school. Similarly the kindergarten-primary unit has been favored in some communities in recent years because of its ability to relieve elementary schools in areas where remaining sites were few, not primarily because of belief in its educational potential. Action based upon building expediency, rather than upon thorough consideration of educational purposes, may be one explanation of the failure of many junior high schools to develop in accord with the professed educational goals of such schools.

More important than organization are matters of instruction. Many teachers have found themselves extremely limited by the facilities with which they work. To develop a social science or mathematics laboratory (rather than a general classroom) in many existing classrooms is extremely difficult. It is much easier to settle down to teaching as one was taught. Many who have a vision of instruction more in accord with sound educational principles may lose it rather quickly when confronted with the problems offered by the school building. The building that should be a stimulating agency thus becomes another force for traditionalism. And after a few years, the teacher would not have it otherwise.

Too seldom has the administrator glimpsed his unique opportunity to contribute to the improvement of instruction through leadership in the planning of a new school plant. To discuss principles of learning is to deal in abstractions. To discuss the school plant—the design of a learning laboratory or classroom—is to deal with the concrete. By means of the tangible, the more abstract can be envisioned. Many people including teachers can get a better and quicker conception of methodology through consideration of the classroom than through a more direct approach. Where adequate learning space is provided, the administrator also has a responsibility and an opportunity to assist a staff in its effective utilization. It cannot be assumed that the teacher who has had years of experience as a student and teacher in a classroom providing 20 square feet of space per student is prepared to use 30 or 35 square feet effectively, or to use but part of a relatively large open space. Here is an excellent opportunity for the stimulation of staff growth—including growth of the administrator.

Not only does the new plant or the prospect of one challenge teachers, it also can challenge parents and help them develop a sounder understanding of educational objectives and of the types of activity and behavior related to the objectives. It may be a better instrument for arousing interest in matters of educational philosophy and method than a direct approach to these matters.

SCHOOLHOUSING NEEDS

The opportunity that administrators have and will have in the next decade to contribute both directly and indirectly to improved education through schoolhousing is emphasized by a consideration of the amount of housing that is necessary. As a result of the delays in eliminating obsolete housing because of depression, war, rising costs, inadequate district structure, inept state and local leadership, and unsatisfactory finance provisions, a large opportunity has been created. To this must be added the fact that buildings become obsolescent continuously. Furthermore, housing needs are increased greatly by the changing concepts of education and the growing variety of educational programs. Special note should be made of the need at the preschool level which heretofore has been largely neglected. Finally, attention also must be given to the greatest single factor, namely, the growth in population.

These factors suggest that the school administrator in the older, more established community, as well as the administrator in the newer, rapidly developing district, will have many opportunities for leadership in education through housing development in the next decade.

Obsolescence, overcrowded classrooms, and double sessions in many systems need to be eliminated through new construction. Further, it is estimated that from 1965 to 1975 the enrollment in public and private elementary and secondary schools in the nation will increase by 15 to 20 million. It would therefore appear probable that in this decade structures will be built to house more than one third as many children as are enrolled in schools today. Since the enrollment increase will be greater at the secondary level, the number of new spaces that will need to be created at that level in relation to enrollment will be higher than at the elementary level. Provision would appear necessary in this decade for more than 25 million children. Of this number nearly 90 per cent or 22 million spaces will need to be provided in public schools.

If this were to be translated into dollars, it would be necessary to assume a unit cost per student. Accepting a figure of $2000.00 per student, the provision of new housing for 22 million children and youth would result in an expenditure of 44 billion dollars. Thus, an average of 4.4 billion dollars per year for this decade is indicated if the housing needs are to be met reasonably well. This figure may actually be considerably higher, especially in the later years of the decade, if construction costs continue to increase as they have in recent years.

From these figures it appears probable that new housing will continue to absorb approximately 20 per cent of the total educational costs in the years immediately ahead. This is a considerably higher percentage than was involved a few decades ago when the percentage was 12 to 15. Increasing instructional equipment costs may push this percentage even higher. This percentage increase emphasizes the growing problem of financing capital outlay and the need for more adequate state plans for equalizing such costs. This increase in percentage is the result of a number of other factors such as: the expansion of population, the greater increase in construction costs than in current expense costs of schools, the demand for schools that provide more adequate footage for regular programs as well as for the greater variety of educational services that have come to be desired.

ADMINISTRATIVE STAFF TIME INVOLVED

Schoolhousing programs thus promise to make large demands upon the board of education and the school administrator. It is upon the superintendent of schools that much of the responsibility for developing and carrying through these programs falls. In the small community he may be called upon only once in a decade to take leadership in this field, and he may be somewhat handicapped by lack of knowledge that is gained through constant application to the problems of schoolhouse construction. It is also highly probable that schoolhousing programs are added to a busy schedule that is already fully concerned with operation of the schools. Too seldom are adequate assistants, in quality or quantity, available to help meet the needs.

In the larger districts and especially in the suburban and fringe sections of metropolitan areas, schoolhouse construction becomes a continuous process. The study of population growth, the raising of new funds, the selection of sites, the formulation of educational programs, the employment of architects, the reviewing of plans, and other related problems are always present. Too frequently, they consume an extremely large part of the time of the superintendent and of the board of education. In many instances too little time is provided for the development of the educational program as a base for the needed housing. Attention is diverted from the ongoing educational program in many communities as the schoolhousing program is carried forward.

The schoolhousing program has a certain tangibility that makes it attractive. It also is extremely demanding of time. A large number and variety of decisions must be made with reference to it. Children are waiting to enter the new schools, and pressure for quick action is great. Many of the steps such as site selection, review, and rereview of plans by various parties are time-consuming. Yet by its nature, schoolhousing is seen as a somewhat temporary activity, rather than a continuous one —an activity related to a given bond issue. For these many reasons the school administrator must recognize the large opportunity and responsibility he has in the housing field and must seek to establish a plan by which children can be adequately housed for the present and for future years while the current operation of the schools is not neglected. He must insist upon more adequate administrative assistance than is usually provided. There is small "economy" in saving the salary of an administrative assistant, perhaps $15,000, and producing an educationally inadequate or obsolete structure costing three or four million dollars.

DETERMINING NEED AND ABILITY

Attention will now be turned briefly to some of the most important steps that are involved in school plant planning and development.

Estimating Pupil Population

Each school district should have an established plan through which it can continuously or frequently estimate student population for a period of five to ten years. The nature of the plan will vary from community to community. Procedures that are very good for an almost saturated community may have little significance or value for a rapidly expanding suburban community. The estimates need to be recognized as such—subject to "error" because of unpredicted changes in social and economic conditions, and subject to probable increase in "error" as the period of years is increased and the size of the area is decreased. Factors to be considered include: births to residents of district by year; past experience of school system as shown by average ratio of students in each grade to preceding one; new construction completed by year and children of various ages per house; mobility of population; preschool census data; enrollments and plans of nonpublic schools; dropout situation in secondary schools; extent to which land area of district is saturated; proposed highway, industrial, and commercial construction projects; zoning; permits secured and planned construction of homes; age of adult population; and size of families. From these factors and with an awareness of the limitations of estimates, pupil population can be estimated. Frequently, it is desirable to develop a minimum estimate based on certain factors and assumptions, and a higher estimate based on certain additional factors. In making an estimate it is important to emphasize the need for periodic —at least annual—re-examination of the estimates.

Not only must the population be estimated for the whole area, but the geographic distribution of pupils of various estimated age groups must be determined in order that best use of the present plant can be established and plans developed for the new plant.

Evaluating Existing Plants

Any school district should periodically evaluate existing plants. This is essential for reasons of safety and the elimination of hazards, for the determination of maintenance needs, and for the determination of optimum utilization. The growing district has additional reasons for evaluating existing plants. Before constructing new plants it must determine the capacity and the best use that can be made of the existing plants. This will also frequently involve questions of rehabilitation.

Evaluation of existing plants may well involve the employment of engineers who can determine structural safety. Hazards may also be located with the assistance of the fire marshal or evaluators provided through the firms handling insurance for the district. The alert administrator and teachers may also identify safety hazards.

The evaluation of the plant in terms of educational needs is more difficult. It involves considerable understanding of the nature of a desirable environment for learning. It requires knowledge of space, lighting, heating, and ventilating needs. It requires a genuine understanding of the educational program that is to be carried on. Further, as the word evaluation implies, it requires the making of judgments.

Various scorecards and guides for evaluating school plants[1] are available for the use of those undertaking this work. Some of them have been designed for the use of laymen as well as for educators. Participation by laymen in evaluation of school plants is highly desirable. If it is undertaken, however, it is important that laymen and teachers also have the opportunity to develop essential knowledge as a base for making judgments. Such training may be provided by reading, discussions, and pilot evaluations.

[1]Such as Jack L. Landes and Merle R. Sumption, *Citizens Workbook for Evaluating School Buildings* (Dubuque, Iowa: W. C. Brown Co., 1951); or New England School Development Council, *Guide for Evaluating School Buildings* (Cambridge: The Council, 1949).

The determination of the capacity of the plant is also difficult, especially in the case of a large secondary school. It involves important judgments regarding such matters as class size and percentage of the student body that should be accommodated in the various special facilities, such as the library and cafeteria. It also is highly related to the type of educational program that is to be offered, and to the extent to which an effort will be made to develop a program in light of the needs of the students. Formulas should, therefore, be employed in making studies of capacity, but it should be recognized that they supply only the base for judgments, not the answers.

Determining Needs

This essentially is a process of bringing the estimated population and the best utilization of existing plant together and determining what additional facilities are needed. This may involve the study of possible use of plants under different organizations such as the 6–3–3, 6–2–4, or 4–4–4–4 arrangement.

Determining Financial Ability

It is appropriate here only to recognize this problem that is treated in greater detail in Chapter 19. It involves determination of the existing indebtedness and retirement schedule of the debt, the ability and bonding limits of the district, and state or federal grants or loans available.

SELECTING AND EMPLOYING AN ARCHITECT

The selection of the architect for the housing program is one of the most important responsibilities of the board of education and superintendent of schools. Upon it will depend the creativity displayed in meeting the educational needs, as well as the general desirability of the plant secured for the funds expended. The architect becomes essentially a partner of the superintendent and board of education in carrying the program through. Employment of the local architect because he is local, or the well-known architect because he is well known, must be rejected.

A plan for selecting the architect should be set up. It should supply evidence regarding such things as: the ability and willingness of the architect to work with the superintendent, principals, and teachers in clarifying and solving educational needs; the adequacy of the staff of the architect for various essential architectural and engineering studies and plans; past experience of the architect as revealed by the adequacy of plans developed, bids secured, and buildings completed. After data are secured regarding these matters, the superintendent and board may choose to interview the three or four architects who appear to offer the best promise, to visit buildings that they have designed, and to discuss their work with school administrators and boards of education in communities that they have served. Then they should be prepared to select an architect in whom they can develop confidence and work with during the months of close cooperative effort ahead. The contract with the architect also needs to be considered carefully in order that there will not be misunderstanding regarding his work and responsibilities.

SELECTING SITES

The selection of sites is one of the important responsibilities of the superintendent of schools. He may wish the assistance of state department of education personnel or of other consultants in this work. It is important that desirable sites be selected early enough to secure them at reasonable cost. This may be some years prior to the time when the site is needed. To delay, however, frequently results in accepting less adequate sites and paying far larger sums for them. Early action may at times result in the purchase of a site that may later prove unnecessary because of changes in zoning or failure of an area to develop as anticipated. Generally, however, such "errors" do not result in financial loss.

Sites should be selected with reference to the location of population to be served. Consideration must also be given to topography, nature of soil, shape, accessibility, convenience to but distance from main highways, utility connections, development potential for beauty and usefulness, and expense involved in purchase and development. Sites should be checked on a scorecard to ensure consideration of all factors of importance. The size of the site will depend upon the type and size of school contemplated. It will also be related to standards for sites that may have been established by the state department of education or recommended by other bodies such as the National Council on Schoolhouse Construction.[2]

Before making the final selection of sites for recommendation to the board of education, the superintendent will want to review the proposals with the city or county planning commission. He also may need to have surveys completed and appraisals made, in order that essential facts are available regarding sites that otherwise appear to be almost equally satisfactory. In selecting sites the superintendent should consult an architect for suggestions regarding the site development and the possible placement of buildings.

[2]*Guide for Planning School Plants*, (East Lansing, Mich.: National Council on Schoolhouse Construction, 1964).

EDUCATIONAL SPECIFICATIONS AND ARCHITECTURAL PLANS

Guiding the staff in the preparation of educational specifications is the most important and probably the most difficult of the superintendent's duties in the schoolhousing field. The educational philosophy, aims, and methods must be stated. The nature of the varied activities to be provided for in the building must be clear to the architect if he is to design effectively for them. What will class size be? What methods of teaching and learning are envisioned? Are self-contained classrooms desired? If so, to what extent? If it is a secondary school, are there to be "schools within the school"? How will the guidance services be related to the instructional program? To what extent will departmentalization be employed? Are provisions to be made for independent study? How broad and varied a curriculum is planned? What new technological provisions are to be made? What learning laboratories and library services are planned? Is the cafeteria viewed as a feeding station or a service with important educational opportunities in addition to health? Will the plant be used for adult education purposes?

These are suggestive of the many questions that have important implications for the building. Unless the school system has been engaged in considerable curriculum work in recent years, it may find the development of the educational specifications difficult and time-consuming. Although some of the specifications need to be formulated by the staff prior to consultation with the architect, there is considerable merit in having the architect share in much of this work.

REVIEWING SKETCHES AND PLANS

A considerable period of time is required for the critical evaluation of proposed solutions to the housing problem. Staff members who participated in the development of the educational specifications should assist in this work. They will need to study the proposed detail of arrangements with great care and through careful inspection make sure that the plans will meet the need as adequately as possible. The administrative staff will need to devote many hours to the careful analysis of plans pertaining to such matters as relationships of various areas, student circulation, and details of various facilities.

Although architects are responsible for the planning, they can make mistakes. They are most likely to avoid doing so if challenged by many intelligent questions. The question might be asked whether this is not intruding on the architect's area of service. Actually, the superintendent and architect must cooperate in finding solutions to many problems.

Although the superintendent does not have the technical and design competence of the architect, he may be more able than the architect to anticipate problems that could result from proposed arrangements. Furthermore, he must be as interested as the architect in making sure, for example, that the rooms will have comfortable balanced lighting without glare or contrast that sharply limits the manner in which the rooms can be used. The superintendent does not need to know the answers, but he surely should be prepared to ask the questions.

In most states, plans need finally to be submitted to and approved by state agencies. They may be checked by a state agency for educational desirability and for safety. Presentation of the plans for approval is made by the architect, though again both the superintendent and architect may be involved.

CONTRACTING FOR AND CONSTRUCTING THE PLANT

Major responsibility for approval of contract forms will rest upon the architect and legal counsel of the board of education. However, the superintendent will need to be familiar with the various provisions of the contracts in order to make sure that the interests of the school district are protected and the needs met. He will also have the responsibility for recommending to the board of education the plans through which the projects are to be financed. As executive officer he will then have the responsibility for carrying through the finance plans with the assistance of specialists as needed. If bonds are to be issued, materials for the prospectus will need to be prepared. A bond attorney should be employed in connection with the issuance of bonds. Concerning contracts and bonding, there are numerous state laws with which the superintendent will need to be familiar if he is to serve as advisor to the board.

SUPERVISING THE CONSTRUCTION

During the period of construction, the superintendent will have many duties of a general supervisory nature. The architect will, of course, have responsibility for direct supervision in accord with the provisions of his contract with the board of education. In addition, it is very important that a building inspector be employed by the board who can exercise a more minute supervision under the general direction of the architect. Even with supervision provided, and in spite of the excellence of the plans and specifications, some questions may arise. There will be change orders resulting from the unavailability of materials or the desirability of modifications that become apparent during the course of construction. There will be questions of delays in construction and compliance with the specified construction period. Upon the completion of the construction of the building and a final inspection of all of its aspects by the architect, engineers, contractors, and the superintendent of schools, a recommendation for its acceptance is made to the board of education.

EQUIPPING AND UTILIZING THE PLANT

The superintendent of schools still has many weighty responsibilities beyond the acceptance of the building. Some equipment has been built into the building in accord with the plans. Much equipment and furnishings, however, are still to be determined and installed through separate contracts. Here again, many members of the staff should be involved. Assistance may also be secured from the educational consultant, the state department of education, or from specialists in the various matters under consideration. Many of the questions pertaining to furnishings and equipment should have been partially solved when the plans were developed, since the building had to be designed with reference to the equipment. Decisions had to be reached at that time regarding what was to be built in. However, many final decisions must now be made.

Attention must also be given to the preparation of the custodial and teaching staff for the utilization of the building. Custodians must be instructed about the operation of various technical facilities. They also need instructions for the care of the chalkboards, floors, walls, and equipment. If teachers have been involved in the development of the educational specifications and the selection of the equipment, they have a good background for using the new plant and its equipment effectively. However, many of them will not have been involved, and unless leadership is offered, they may continue to function as they have been accustomed to, rather than in accord with their new opportunity. The larger classroom does not just mean greater distances between the rows of desks, as one business manager supposed. Rather, it suggests a different kind of living and learning. What is it to be?

The superintendent thus completes his responsibility with reference to the new plant. He is fortunate indeed if he has been able to provide effective leadership regarding many aspects of the educational program while deeply engrossed in the housing program. He has had to devote much thought and action to housing for a period of two or three years. He probably hoped the period would be shorter, but the prospect of greatly reducing the time does not appear good. During all this time he has had to work with many people, become familiar with statutes, and observe and evaluate many proposals. He has had to test all ideas in terms of principles relating to safety, educational desirability, flexibility, expansibility, and initial and operational economy.

The following issues among the many in the school plant field have been selected for more extended consideration.

What Is Adequate Space for Learning?

This issue should be examined from two points of view. There is first the quantitative—expressed generally in square feet per student for the total school or for various areas. Second, there is the question of the quality of the space for learning. What is the climate or tone desired in the cafeteria? the library? the elementary school classroom? Can the community afford adequate space—quantitatively and qualitatively?

Recommended standards in terms of square feet have increased substantially in the last couple of decades. The inadequacy of the old elementary school room of 660 square feet has been widely recognized. Few familiar with the purposes and life of the elementary school desire less than 1,000 square feet. The problem of achieving more adequate space at the secondary level is more difficult. There are greater differences in the needs of youth, and the necessity of attempting to meet some of them through specialization is present. Furthermore, as the desire to keep senior secondary schools below an enrollment of 1500 or 1800 grows, the utilization of special types of spaces may decrease. Whether it does or does not will of course be related to the concept of education that is developed and followed.

How much space would be needed to provide cafeteria or lunch service in such a way as to offer something more than "caloric injection"?[3] What social habits are developed over the lunch table? Does the cafeteria afford relaxation?

Is the social science room a "regular" classroom or a vital laboratory? What space does it need if youth are to attack and work through social problems confronting them or the community? Do we generally recognize the tragic inadequacy of many traditional classrooms? They not only do not invite the development of good learning—they even rebuff the teacher and students who seek it.

Regarding sites, considerable change has also been occurring. Standards have risen and the inadequacies of former provisions are being increasingly recognized.

The whole question of quantity of space in grounds and buildings is one that confronts our society in sharp terms. It applies to recreation

[3]Lawrence B. Perkins, *Work Place for Learning* (New York: Reinhold Publishing Corp., 1957), p. 56.

as well as to education, to adults as well as children. As we develop our ever larger and increasing number of metropolitan areas, are we committed to less and less opportunity for men to have some touch with nature? to have the opportunity to create? to find relaxation in part away from the "madding crowd"? How adequate is our land use planning? Quite conceivably with the increase of leisure and more conscious consideration of the nature of life in our metropolitan areas that just grow, we shall see the need of much more space for learning and living through such institutions as the school. Dare we hope that we may even seek beauty in the school and community environment that we develop? Or are schools not related to community development after all?

Less tangible and equally difficult is the question of the quality of the space provided. Does the school beckon? Can a building attract? Can a building influence taste? Do the hours spent in a classroom intimately related to the out-of-doors have an effect? What are conditions that stimulate creativity? Does the principal's office have to be an "ogre's den"?[4] Does the classroom invite pursuit of knowledge and truth, or is it a "strait jacket"?

Beyond question we are moving in many schools in the direction of developing more adequate space for learning in the qualitative sense. Too many school buildings, however, continue to be built merely to house children, with little thought or attention given to the quality of the housing in terms of its educational influence. Citizens, educators, and architects must recognize and grapple with this problem more effectively.

It may be objected that all of this calls for the use of genuine creative ability; that it costs money. But can a nation with an almost incomprehensible achievement in terms of materials produced do less than devote some of them to the education of its children? Does the ever larger automobile or the second automobile indicate that less actual space and space of less quality is to be provided for children? Here is an issue that raises questions about the values of our society. Can any state take pride in an "austerity" schoolhousing program—a program that rigidly limits the space available because there are so many children and "the funds are not available" to make more adequate provisions?

Have educators developed a clear concept of the quantity and quality of space needed for learning? Are they prepared to lead others in this quest?

Should a School be Planned To Serve
a Heterogeneous or Homogeneous Community?
What About an Education Park?

For many years it was assumed by many that a school should be built to serve a neighborhood that was homogeneous socially and economically. With the housing patterns that developed in metropolitan

[4]*Ibid.*, p. 21.

areas, this frequently resulted in a high degree of racial homogeneity and *de facto* segregation. As a part of the civil rights movement and in an attempt to reduce segregation, the question of schools' serving homogeneous communities has been re-examined. It is now widely agreed that schools generally should be planned to bring together children from diverse backgrounds. Instead of being placed in the center of homogeneous communities, they are desirably placed on the borders of neighborhoods, drawing students who vary considerably from one another in racial, cultural, and economic background.

The provision of a school to serve a heterogeneous group is a recognition of the educational influence of the school itself as an institution. To grow up associated only with children of one race, one religion, or one economic class is limiting. When it is further the result of imposed separation on a group, it may have an additional serious impact. Separate but equal is therefore no longer accepted as equal. While the desirability of these developments should be recognized, it would be a mistake to assume that the educational needs of many of the culturally different (which is not race) are to be regarded as being met through greater heterogeneity in the school population. Rather, it is the hope to establish understandings and a social climate upon which educational opportunity may be built. It would further be an incorrect assumption to believe that the understandings and the climate will result rather automatically. What is provided is but a base for building a better educational program.

The re-examination of the relation of a school to its neighborhood has again suggested in some communities the development of a single large site, an education park, which would have a number of schools—and a school or schools of several levels. Such education parks could also be centers for a wide variety of activities of local government, such as library, recreation, public health, and social welfare. In larger cities a number of such education centers could be developed. It is assumed that each center would have at least one high school, two to four middle or lower secondary schools, perhaps eight to ten elementary schools and centers for preschool children. (The term "education park" may also be used to mean a site with several schools all of a given level, such as preschools, lower elementary schools, elementary schools, or high schools.)

Among the advantages suggested are: the elimination or reduction of segregation in schools, the more effective utilization of specialized technical staff and facilities, increase in ability to use plant and grounds for different purposes during the day and over the years, attractiveness of setting compared to older schools in poorer areas, improved instructional aids because less duplication among schools is needed, ability to provide facilities and services which could not be considered in widely separate schools, opportunity to reduce the gap between elementary and secondary schools and to "articulate" curriculum and guidance services between school levels, opportunity to assign children to greater variety of programs in light of needs, improved possibility of service as an adult center and making less sharp the "end of schooling."

Opponents of the plan suggest that it would increase still further the distance between the home and the school, sharply increase costs for special services such as transportation and thus reduce funds available for the educational program, reduce educational effectiveness because of the vastness of it—especially in the case of younger children, produce an even more conformist mechanical operation, and reduce further the warmth and human quality. They also fear that, while many of its potential disadvantages could be overcome if adequate numbers of staff members and a sufficient number of separate subunits were provided, the drive for efficiency would probably prevent these provisions from being made.

Though there are some disadvantages, there is little doubt that the possibility of effectively using such units is far greater now than at any earlier period. It is, therefore, suggested that the student formulate a plan embodying this idea, describing the plan and appraising it, through contrasting it with the more traditional or established plan of dispersed schools for a given community.

How Can Adequate Educational Planning as a Basis for Schoolhousing Be Assured?

It is quite probable that the most serious inadequacy of schoolhouse planning is to be found in limited educational planning. This results from factors such as the difficulty of the problem, the intangibility of the process, the lack of adequate time on the part of competent people, and the lack of appreciation of the cruciality of the need. If we are to utilize the creative powers of architects and not build facilities that tend toward obsolescence, some of the following conditions must be more fully realized.

1. The meaning of educational planning must be clarified. It must be clearly understood to be the formulation of the educational philosophy, the nature of the activities to be housed, and the manner in which the activities are to be carried on. It is, in essence, a basic curriculum problem that cannot be grappled with effectively without thoughtful consideration of the needs of children, youth, and adults; without clarification of objectives, without consideration of the organization of learning experience, and without consideration of the organization of the school to meet the accepted needs. It must be agreed that educational planning is *not* a list of rooms with square footages.

2. The educator must recognize leadership in educational planning as his most significant responsibility in the school plant area.

He will then insist upon the time and personnel that are essential.

3. Adequate time must be devoted to the formulation of the educational plan. Unless very considerable curriculum work has been done recently in the school system, there are many months of work involved.

4. Provision must be made whereby administrators who are responsible for leadership in this area have sufficient time to do the job.

5. The services of those who can offer leadership in working through the problems in the instructional field must be sought and used. They may be drawn from the school system, the state department of education, universities, and the community. To an extent commitments must be made regarding the kind of educational program and school living envisaged for tomorrow and the years that follow. A concept of function—defined or merely inherited and not thought through—will guide the architect.

6. Even after the best possible educational plan has been developed, thoughts should be given to flexibility and adaptability of the structure. It will probably serve for forty or fifty years. Will it be a constraining or releasing force? Fortunately, with the development of newer materials such as prefabricated building components, we may be near the time when much more flexibility can be built into the building. The large block type structure in which all interior walls are readily and economically movable is illustrative of what may be achieved. The Hillsdale, California, high school is an excellent early example of possibilities along these lines.[5] More recently "open-space schools" or schools without interior partitions have appeared in a variety of shapes and forms. They are among the most significant developments in school architecture in the last decade. They offer important educational advantages.[6]

It would be a mistake to believe that educational planning can be done by the architect or the consultant, though they may play roles in it. The possibility of planning well in a few weeks should be rejected. It calls for extended cooperative effort. Effort is needed to tap the resources of literature and the experiences of other schools and men. Educational planning cannot be done by teachers alone. They may not have had the opportunity to work through the problems and may reflect largely a limited background. But it cannot be done without the involvement of teachers.

[5]John Lyon Reid, "A High School that Wants to Stay Young," *American School and University*, 26 (1954–55), 229–236.
[6]*Schools Without Walls* (New York: Educational Facilities Laboratories, 1965).

*Should a School Plant Be Designed To Serve
Community and Adult Education Needs as Well as
the Needs of Children and Youth?*

Society has witnessed a large growth in the demand for facilities for community groups and adult education. This demand will probably continue to increase sharply in the years ahead. Much of the demand has been met through the use of facilities designed primarily for elementary and secondary school purposes. The cost of schoolhousing as well as the fact that many facilities are not used during certain hours and days suggests the desirability of multiuse in this sense.

On the other hand many facilities if designed for multiuse may be relatively undesirable for any of the planned uses. Then, too, there is the problem of equipment that may not be appropriate for both children and adults. Also, the use of instructional equipment and supplies by more than one teacher frequently leads to dissatisfaction.

It would seem clear that there has been insufficient study of the possibility of the use of facilities by children, youth, and adults. Certain facilities such as auditoriums, multiuse rooms, shops, and gymnasiums have been most widely used. Study of the adult needs of the community should be carried on at the same time the needs for children and youth are being ascertained. In addition, it is extremely important that adequate storage space be provided so that materials and equipment can be removed when the facility is used by the second party. In spite of the efforts that are made to plan facilities to serve more than one need—and an increase in these efforts is very much demanded—there will remain the need to provide an increase in facilities that will serve one need primarily. Many communities have not faced the question of the facilities that will be required as youth and adult programs expand.

When should separate facilities be developed for youth programs and for adult education programs?

*How Can School Plant Planning and City-County
Planning Be Coordinated?*

Coordination and perhaps integration of planning efforts would appear to be increasingly necessary. In a more populous society and one in which an increasing percentage of the people reside in metropolitan areas, land use comes to be of great significance. Without coordination in planning, the probability of achieving an attractive community in which to live and to work appears slight indeed. Furthermore, in addition to the community itself as an educational force, it must be recognized that the library and recreation services, for example, are an aspect of education. We are probably too little aware of the educational impact of the community in which we live. The development of a taste for the beautiful is not unrelated to the opportunity to experience it. We recognize this in our schools. Is it not equally important in our communities?

In addition to the above factors, it must be recognized that there are other arguments strongly favoring coordination. The data collected by a competent city or county planning authority are of great value to the school planner. Data pertaining to highway development, population, land use, zoning, and housing proposals are essential for sound school planning. There is no need to have more than one agency collect these data if through cooperative planning the needs of various public agencies can be met. Furthermore, the schools can render a great service to the planning agency through participation in planning, through assisting in collecting and analyzing data (a project with great educational values), and through a program of education designed to help young citizens develop a knowledge and appreciation of the significance of community planning.

The educator, however, is at times somewhat hesitant to seek the coordination that appears desirable. He has a rather strong attachment to independence—which is related to the struggle for fiscal independence. He draws back when he meets the city planner who may appear to want to "take over" the school planning function rather than to assist in it. And, all too frequently, he finds that the city and county planning office has too little data or staff to be of any considerable assistance, or that it has district boundary lines that confine its interest to only a segment of the school district.

Despite the inadequacies on either or both sides and the frictions that develop at times, there would appear to be no question but that the school and planning agencies should greatly increase their cooperative efforts. This can be to the benefit of both of them, and more especially to the benefit of the community that they both serve. They share responsibility for improving the quality of community living and are likely to discharge this responsibility most effectively only if they develop a high-level cooperative effort.

What arrangements are likely to result in the essential coordination? Who should take the initiative in effecting coordination?

Should School Buildings Be Planned and Constructed for Short-Term or for Long-Term Use?

It can be argued that because of the changing nature of the educational program and methods it is unwise to build school buildings that will be used for a period longer than fifteen or twenty years. They are likely to be educationally obsolete within that period. Furthermore, in many neighborhoods the need for elementary facilities may decrease sharply within such a span of years. In these neighborhoods, almost all adults are of childbearing age today, and there are children of school age in every house. Within a decade or two, this area may be one in which there are relatively few elementary school age children. If permanent structures are built for forty or fifty years of service, it is probable that in order to utilize the facilities it will be necessary to transport children to some of them. How much better it would be if the "old" facilities could be discarded and new ones erected where needed. And is not all this made possible by the present age of light building materials that are attractive and of high quality? Furthermore, would this not be the most economical procedure?

On the other hand, it would appear that the probable decline of children in a neighborhood has been overstated. The mobility of people and the continuing high birth rate suggest that the decline will not be drastic. In most communities if it occurs, it will afford a needed opportunity to abandon some of the quite old buildings that continue to be used. If the buildings are well planned, some of them may be adapted for other purposes—such as recreational. Or a former elementary school may become the nucleus of a junior high school. The problem of the changing program and methods should be able to be met substantially through modifications within the structure of the well-planned building. Regrettably, also the costs of a higher-quality "temporary" are nearer the costs of a more permanent structure than is generally anticipated. Furthermore, the maintenance costs of the temporary are likely to be high.

In the light of these facts this issue remains one for analysis by the individual community. Certainly, greater adaptability and flexibility should be sought and provided. A case can be made in some instances for the building of a permanent structure containing only the basic units plus that number of classrooms that will probably continue to be needed. High-quality, permanent, portable classroom units, planned as part of and integrated into the whole, may constitute good insurance against vacant classrooms in the future.

Are permanent portables a good answer to the continuing demand for portables?

What Shall Be the Role of State Departments of Education in the Field of Schoolhousing?

State departments of education have in some instances had a rather different relationship to schoolhousing than they have had in regard to other aspects of education. Schoolhousing has continued to be regarded almost exclusively as a local matter in some states. In other states an increasing amount of state control, even of details, is apparent. These developments have been related to the programs of state financing of capital outlay that have developed. Without going into the financing question, which is treated elsewhere in this book, it is extremely important to look at the problem of the role of the state department of education and the matter of state controls. It would appear that the state department of education should discharge the following responsibilities:

1. The state department of education should be the administrative agency with which or through which the local school districts and their agents make all school plant arrangements. If it does not provide all the needed state services, it can coordinate the services of all state agencies involved.

2. It should be responsible for seeing that minimum standards of safety and health are established and observed in all school plants.

3. It should exercise a general supervision over school plant provisions to ensure minimum desirable space for learning.

4. The state department of education should be responsible for the planning, coordination, and implementation of research in the schoolhousing field. Quite possibly, much of the research should be done in local systems and in organized programs in the university. Through the development of adequate research programs, the state department should encourage that expansion of knowledge which may improve programs of schoolhousing. The operations of the school Development Group in the Ministry of Education in England[7] is a challenging illustration of a desirable research operation.

5. It should accept as its role the stimulation and guidance of local systems as they develop schoolhousing programs. Emphasis upon this aspect of responsibility may eventually result in the virtual elimination of concern regarding the minimum school plant provisions referred to before.

In carrying out these responsibilities the state department of education, as well as the legislature, needs to avoid exercising detailed controls that stifle local initiative. A state department of education that loses its way in legalisms and minute detail denies itself the chance to provide leadership. Not only must it avoid resisting new ideas—but it must avoid even the development of the suspicion that it does so. Unless it is acutely aware of this trap, it can easily be caught, and architects and educators may prepare plans that will be readily approved, rather than

[7]Theodore L. Reller, "Improved Schoolhousing and Lower Costs; Work of the Development Group," *American School Board Journal*, **130**, No. 3 (Mar. 1955), 49–50.

plans designed to facilitate the best situations. The recent and necessary growth of state financing of capital outlay needs to be carefully watched, or inadvertently the control of details may follow. It need not; but it may, if local districts, the over-all plan, and the prevailing philosophy of administration are inadequate. State control of detail has occurred to too great an extent in some states, although "no one" involved in the service consciously sought this end.

How can state departments of education exercise leadership in an effective manner?

Can the Future School Population Be Estimated
  With Reasonable Accuracy?

The development of schoolhousing plans takes a great deal of time. Therefore, it is very important to have sound estimates of future student population some years ahead. Recent years have witnessed a greater need for such estimates and greater difficulty in developing them. Much of the assumed ability to predict, which characterized population studies of a decade or two ago, has disappeared. The economic and social changes with corresponding shifts made many predictions appear too wide of the mark. Consequently, some of the efforts to predict with exactitude have given way to the need for developing estimates.

Despite the difficulties of estimating the population, the school administrator must assume leadership in devising a plan through which estimates are established and revised continuously or at frequent intervals. The nature of the plan will depend upon the community. The problem of estimating pupil population in the old established community where few opportunities for new construction exist is very different from that of the rapidly growing suburb or fringe area. But in each case a plan that is established as a policy is essential.

When estimating population it is important to recognize that it is easier to estimate for a school system than for a school, and the more years ahead the estimate is made the less valid it is likely to be. In some communities the grade-progression method is the best method to use as the principal estimating technique. In others the grade-progression method will have little value unless supplemented by other techniques. In all cases, attention must be given to general population trends, economic and social developments, housing trends, private school developments, holding power of secondary schools, preschool census figures, and percentage of adult population of childbearing age. In all instances the cooperation of public planning and building approval agencies and of public and private utilities should be sought. These organizations have many data of great value to the schools for use in estimating population. They also frequently have prepared plans of their own that are based upon studies of population that they have conducted.

It would thus appear that all school districts must develop estimates of student population for a period of years ahead. They need to establish a plan for developing such estimates and for keeping them up to date. In this program they can determine the worth of various techniques for their local situation. Such estimates need to be developed with great care. Various factors having a bearing upon the situation need to be considered. Abundant judgment is inevitably involved. Considering the complexity of the factors involved and the change of elements, there should not be overconcern about estimates that need to be adjusted as a result of the continuing periodic studies. Frequently, it is desirable to develop more than one estimate—a minimum as well as a maximum—in part to avoid the tendency to seek exactitude, rather than the essential knowledge for sound planning.

What Quality and Quantity of Artificial or Natural Light Is Desirable?

Questions of materials and of heating, lighting, and ventilation are questions that are more directly the responsibility of architects and engineers than of educators. However, since the whole facility exists to serve educational ends, the final evaluation must be in terms of the effect upon education. The school administrator must, therefore, have an interest in and knowledge regarding these problems. He must at least be prepared to ask intelligent questions regarding the extent to which proposed facilities will meet educational needs.

One of the most complex of these problems has been that of lighting. Fortunately, the time has now passed when the mere quantity of light was the issue. It is now recognized that the quantity can be too great as well as too little. Much more important than quantity, though immediately related to it, is quality. Is the light comfortable? Is it balanced? Is glare avoided? Are contrasts not so great as to cause discomfort? Do the various materials, colors, chalkboards, and outside lights blend and produce a situation that is conducive to the kind of work that is to be carried on? Is the situation one in which there needs to be a minimum of adjustment and change in seating during the day in order to find comfort?

Perhaps no other developments in schoolhousing in the last couple of decades have been so striking as those related to lighting. They have led to the use of increasing varieties and amounts of color; to lighter-colored chalkboards, desks, and floors; to square or different shaped classrooms that displaced the standard rectangle finished in dark drab colors with walls of schoolhouse brown; to bilateral, trilateral, and clerestory lighting, as contrasted with the old established unilateral lighting; to greater width in classrooms; and to greater effort to open classrooms to the world outside. A learning situation has been sought that is comfortable, conducive to work, and conducive to the developing appreciation of color, form, and light in life. In a sense, while much science has been involved in these developments, there has been much art also.

The end of developments in this area has not yet been reached. The present luminous ceiling is probably only a step toward a more truly luminous room. The question of the respective place of artificial and natural lighting is probably not to be answered categorically. There will be many situations in which the general dependence upon artificial lighting will be defensible and easily established—in which a window strip will exist for psychological reasons alone. There will be many rooms in which no provision for natural lighting will be made. For certain services this will be highly advantageous. There will be other rooms in which on many days natural lighting—without undesirable glare—will be quite sufficient. And in many rooms on some days the lighting will be a combination of artificial and natural. Whether it is natural or artificial, however, attention must be concentrated on the quality of the lighting. The fact that quality is the result of many elements found in the situation must be more widely recognized. The achievement of high-quality lighting is fortunately not unrelated to the achievement of an environment that is characterized by taste and charm. How much easier it would be if we could be satisfied that lighting would be adequate when 30 or 50 candlepower is provided in all parts of the room. But given the nature of individual differences and of the learning situation, no such easy solutions can be accepted.

How can the school administrator develop competence for his role in the lighting field?

Other Issues

1. Should a local architect who has not established himself in the field of schoolhousing be given preference?
2. What size elementary, junior, and senior high schools should be planned?
3. Do teachers use effectively the more adequate learning space that is being provided?
4. What is the point beyond which there is no return in the multi-use of facilities?
5. What are essentials in the planning and effective utilization of "schools without walls"?
6. Shall school buildings be used twelve months in the year to enrich and increase the offerings to a given group of children, or shall capital outlay expenditures be reduced by housing more children in a given plant by having some on vacation during each quarter?

7. Are the commonly accepted standards for sites and square footage per student in classrooms, libraries, laboratories, cafeterias, and other rooms defensible?
8. Should school districts employ outside consultants to do the job of schoolhouse planning, or should they do the job themselves with the possible assistance of consultants?
9. What are adequate site sizes for various types of schools in metropolitan areas?

Selected References

Caudill, William, *Toward Better School Design*. New York: F. W. Dodge Corp., 1954.

The Cost of a Schoolhouse. New York: Educational Facilities Laboratories, 1960.

Englehardt, N. L., N. L. Englehardt, Jr., and Stanton Leggett, *Planning Elementary School Buildings*. New York: F. W. Dodge Corp., 1953.

———, *Planning Secondary School Buildings*. New York: Reinhold Publishing Corp., 1949.

———, *School Planning and Building Handbook*. New York: F. W. Dodge Corp., 1957.

Guide for Planning School Plants. East Lansing, Mich.: National Council on Schoolhouse Construction, 1964.

Herrick, John H., *et al.*, *From School Program to School Plant*. New York: Holt, Rinehart & Winston, Inc., 1956.

Leu, Donald J., *Planning Educational Facilities*. New York: Center for Applied Research in Education, Inc., 1965.

Perkins, Lawrence B., and Walter D. Cocking, *Schools*. New York: Reinhold Publishing Corp., 1949.

Schools Without Walls. New York: Educational Facilities Laboratories, 1965.

18

Business Administration
Services

The primary purpose of business administration is to help assure that maximum educational returns will be received per dollar invested in education. The purpose definitely is not to hold educational expenditures to a minimum, though too often that concept has prevailed. Economical and efficient administration does not mean parsimonious administration. Business administration should be the servant of the educational program, and not the master. Business and industry have long known that the investment of additional funds in an enterprise will frequently return more profits per dollar invested than could be obtained from a smaller investment. There is much evidence available showing that this same principle applies to the educational enterprise. On the other hand, the wasteful or unnecessary expenditure of funds does not bring the desired returns in either business or education.

MAJOR ASPECTS OF BUSINESS ADMINISTRATION

Many concepts of sound business management are equally applicable to education. However, the purpose of a business enterprise is to earn profits and the purpose of an educational enterprise to earn educational dividends. Profits in business are returned to the investor annually, monthly, weekly—even daily. Educational dividends may not be returned to the investor until years after the original investment. Business can, therefore, evaluate its policies much more quickly than can education. However, there are many operations in business that are similar to the operations in education. Some of these operations are as follows: the receipt and disbursement of funds; the construction, operation, and maintenance of buildings; the operation of motor vehicles; the operation of lunch programs; and the operation and maintenance of many similar types of equipment. Where operations are similar, the concepts of sound management are likely to be similar. School business administration should not be thought of as something entirely different from management in business operations. On the other hand, the purposes differ; therefore, procedures differ at many significant points.

Since educational business administration is concerned with procuring the maximum amount of educational dividends per dollar expended, it should not be thought of as consisting entirely of the handling of money and the keeping of records. Sound business administration of a school system is impossible without careful over-all planning of the total educational program, a sound organization, and efficient administration of policies and programs. Some administrators have mistaken neat, accurate records for business administration. Such records are commendable, but they cannot substitute for policy and program.

In Chapter 10, it is pointed out that there are many thousands of school districts so small that it is impossible to provide good educational programs at a reasonable cost in those districts. Therefore, the only sound business administration policy is to reorganize into efficient districts where good business administration policies may be instituted. In still other districts small, expensive, inefficient schools are being operated. This is especially true of small high schools. Efficient school districts and efficient school centers within the district are essential to sound business administration.

The business affairs of a school system should not be studied atomistically. It is much easier to gain an integrated concept of business administration by taking a look at the flow of operations in the total educational enterprise and the interrelationships of all of those operations. For the purpose of business administration, the activities of the educational enterprise may be described as follows: (1) planning operations, (2) budget operations, (3) spending and receiving operations, (4) educational operations, (5) staffing and staff training operations, (6) service operations, (7) insuring operations, and (8) evaluating operations for all of the foregoing operations. The board of education, school personnel, citizens, and even pupils play their respective roles in these operations.

Planning operations involve the formulating of educational policies and programs, the forecasting of student population and building needs, the forecasting of revenue and expenditure needs, the planning and programming of innovations and many other matters.

Budget operations include the translation of the educational program adopted into a spending plan and the fiscal implementation of that plan.

Educational operations are the educational activities carried on at individual schools by principals, teachers, and their supervisory and consulting assistants.

Spending and receiving operations cover the procurement and management of revenues, the authorization of expenditures, purchasing and contracting, the payment of funds, the keeping of accounting records, reporting and auditing.

Staffing operations are concerned with the recruitment, employment, assignment, training, evaluation, promotion, and dismissal of personnel.

Service operations include general administration and supervision; the construction, operation, and maintenance of the school plant; the operation of a transportation system; the operation of school lunchrooms; the storage and distribution of supplies and equipment; the operation of warehouses; personnel accounting; property accounting; and pupil personnel services. Small systems may not provide all of these service operations, but large school systems may have more operations than those listed.

The *insuring operations* are the bonding of officials and all employees who handle funds, the insuring of school buildings and equipment, the securing of workmen's compensation insurance and liability insurance, the bonding of contractors, the protection of school funds in depositories, and the protection of employees by provision for retirement and/or social security.

The *evaluating operations* discussed in more detail in Chapter 20, involve the appraisal of educational policies and programs, budgeting procedures, accounting procedures, school plant and equipment specifications, purchasing procedures, transportation services, school plant operation and maintenance procedures, storage and distribution of supplies and equipment, school lunch operations, and many other matters. These operations cannot be evaluated effectively unless the effect of each operation on other operations is analyzed. No operation stands by itself. The efficient coordination of all these operations is a major task of the educational administrator.

In the remainder of this chapter, more extended discussions are presented of the operations of the school system with which business administration is directly involved.

The authors have given much emphasis in this book to the theoretical, philosophical, and legal bases of organization and administration. The managerial and operational "know-how" of administration is also of great importance. Theoretical and philosophical concepts are of but little value to the practicing educational administrator, unless he also knows modern managerial and operational procedures. Such managerial techniques and tools as budgeting, accounting, auditing, reporting, cost analysis, population projections, surveys, evaluations, data processing, purchasing, product testing, insuring, bonding, and many other techniques are well known to modern educational administrators. Some basic concepts and recent developments relating to these procedures are discussed in this chapter.

The PERT Management Technique

It might be assumed that all of the important management techniques had been developed many years ago by Taylor, Fayol, and their followers; however this assumption would be far from accurate. Operations research and the discovery of new uses of the digital computer are producing some new and promising management techniques. An example of this is PERT (Program Evaluation and Review Technique).

PERT was developed by the Navy's Project Office in order to program the development of the Polaris missile. Its use was credited with reducing the anticipated time of the production of this missile by almost three years. The technique has been most useful in programing nonrepetitive operations, such as the production of a missile, the construction of a school plant, or the programing of any major innovation. It is now being adopted by many business, industrial, and educational organizations. PERT is essentially a planning technique which was originally developed to control time in production, but it is also now being used to control costs. PERT time is described very briefly below.

The method of PERT is quite simple. In fact the elements of this technique have been used by successful administrators for many years. The steps are as follows:

First, initially, every significant event that must occur to realize the end objective is selected and defined. . . .
Second, the sequence and interdependency between events is established. This is done graphically by means of a flow chart, which in PERT jargon is called a network. . . .
Third step in the process is to put a time value upon each activity. PERT requires three such time estimates: (1) optimistic, (2) most likely, and (3) pessimistic. . . .
Fourth in the series of PERT steps, the three estimates are computed to find "expected" time for completing the activity. . . .
Fifth, the computer then totals "expected" times along every possible

path of the network to determine the "critical path"—the longest distance in time between beginning and end. . . .

In the sixth and final step, what derives from this series of computations is a report card in the form of standard printouts that "focus management attention on those areas where corrective action is most needed and can do the most good."[1]

Any shortening of the time for the completion of a project can be accomplished only by shortening the time required for the "critical path." This might be accomplished by such methods as overtime or shifting of materials and manpower from a path with "slack time" to the critical path.[2]

Although PERT was designed to control complex operations by means of digital computers, it can readily be used for less complex operations that do not require the use of computers. For example, it is now being used by many researchers to schedule and control research projects.

SCHOOL BUDGETING

A school budget is an educational plan with an estimate of the receipts and expenditures necessary to finance it for a definite period of time. School budgets are usually made for a period of one fiscal year, although budgetary needs are sometimes projected for some years into the future. The school fiscal year should include a complete scholastic year in order to simplify the estimating of expenditures. Furthermore, the school fiscal year should coincide with the tax levying and collecting year, in order that the flow of revenue may coincide with the flow of expenditures during the school year. The most commonly used fiscal year, and perhaps the best for boards of education, is the year beginning July 1 and ending June 30. A fiscal year beginning on January 1 is particularly unsuited to school operations, because fractions of two different operating years must be budgeted within one fiscal year.

Almost all school systems in the United States now operate on some type of budget. These budgets may vary all the way from simple lump sum estimates of receipts and expenditures listed on one sheet of paper to comprehensive documents of a hundred pages or more setting forth detailed estimates of receipts and expenditures with accompanying ma-

[1]Howard Simons, "PERT: How To Meet a Deadline," *Think*, May 1962, pp. 13—17. (Reprinted by permission from THINK Magazine, published by IBM, Copyright 1962 by International Business Machines Corporation.)

[2]See PERT Orientation and Training Center, *PERT Fundamentals*, Vol I, *Networking* 0–712–769 and Vol. II, *Scheduling and Planning* 0–712–770 (Washington, D.C., U.S. Government Printing Office).

terial fully interpreting the budget. The budgetary process may be nothing but ascertaining the revenue that will be available and allocating it in such a manner as to minimize complaints. On the other hand, the budgetary process may involve carefully studying educational needs, estimating the revenue necessary to meet educational needs, and planning the procurement of the necessary revenue to implement the educational program agreed upon. It is this latter type of budgetary process that has been found to be most effective in promoting the development of adequate educational programs.

The school budget is the instrument through which the people can determine both their educational and their financial policy. Therefore, effective school budgeting must include:

1. The preparation of the budget in such a manner as to provide an educational program that gives effect to educational policies previously determined;
2. The budget document, which may be defined as a systematic plan and statement that forecasts the expenditures and revenues of a school system during a stated period of time;
3. The presentation, consideration, and adoption of the budget;
4. The administration of the budget;
5. The appraisal of the budget.

Some of the procedures necessary for modern school budgeting are presented in the following paragraphs.

Educational Planning

As has been pointed out in Chapter 1, the purposes of education must be defined and agreed upon before an educational plan can be developed. But educational planning is much more than a pious statement of philosophy and purposes. Such statements as "we believe in a democratic philosophy of education," "we believe in educating the whole child," and "we believe in the child-centered school" do not constitute an educational plan. Definite plans for implementing the philosophy and purposes of the school system must be developed before action can be taken. Educational plans must present the quantity and quality of educational services being proposed. The statement of the proposed educational plan will include both a short-range plan for the scholastic year and a long-range plan reaching some years into the future. It will include information on such questions as the following:

1. Who should be educated? That is, will educational opportunities be limited to grades 1 to 12, or will the program include kindergartens, a junior college, and adult education opportunities?

2. What will be the probable enrollment in each age group or school program during the next five to ten years?
3. What additional sites, buildings, equipment, and personnel will be needed during the next five to ten years?
4. For how many days during the year will the school be kept open?
5. Should sufficient staff be employed to operate the schools during the summer months for enrichment and recreational purpose?
6. Should the school plants be planned to serve community purposes as well as the regularly organized school program?
7. What should be the pupil load per teacher?
8. What level of qualifications should be possessed by teachers?
9. What provisions should be made for exceptional children?
10. What provisions should be made for clinical and guidance services?
11. What provisions should be made for pupil transportation?
12. Should senior high schools be comprehensive high schools, or should vocational schools be provided?
13. Should special teachers of art, music, and physical education be provided for elementary schools, or should elementary rooms be self-contained?
14. What variety of educational programs should be provided in junior and senior high schools?
15. Should a school lunch program be provided, and what should be its characteristics?
16. What health services should be provided by the school system?
17. What special provisions should be made for the culturally different?

This is an incomplete list, but decisions must be made on matters of this kind before a budget incorporating the educational plan can be constructed. Taxpayers are much more reluctant to support a lump sum increase in the budget than an increase they understand. Increases should be analyzed in terms of the educational plan. For example, the public can evaluate a $200,000 increase for reducing the average class size from 32 to 30, but it has no basis for evaluating an unexplained $200,000 increase in the budget.

Preparing the Budget

Once the educational plan is agreed upon, estimates can be prepared indicating the probable costs of the plan. The word "costs" is used deliberately, because there are different costs for different levels of quality in many components of the educational program. Therefore, several alternative budgets and subbudgets should be prepared before the final budget is adopted. These alternative budgets will show the additional costs necessary to provide additional services or a higher quality of service. This whole process of developing the educational plan and the budget presents an ideal opportunity for utilizing the cooperative procedures described in Chapter 6. Representative citizen committees, classroom teachers, principals, supervisors, and other interested parties should be given adequate opportunity to share with the board and the superintendent the responsibility of developing the educational plan. Representative advisory groups should be given broad opportunities to study alternative educational plans and to present their recommendations to the board. This process results in communitywide participation in the educational planning and budget making. Only through the process of participation in the planning can there be genuine understanding of the budget.

Unfortunately, in the typical school system the superintendent and his staff, with perhaps a committee of the board, prepare the budget document. A notice that the board will have a public hearing on the budget on a certain date is published in the newspaper. Usually, no one attends the hearing with the exception of a few people interested in keeping the tax rate down and perhaps a few newspaper reporters hoping to get a story from attacks being made on the budget. The people who are genuinely interested in the school budget do not usually attend the public hearing, because it is a "cut-and-dried affair" and there is no genuine opportunity to participate. This common but primitive method of budget preparation is partly responsible for lack of adequate financial support of the schools in many districts.

Form of the Budget

The form of the formal part of the budget will vary in different states and in different districts, depending somewhat upon requirements of state law and the accounting system used by the district. Following, however, are two generalizations concerning the formal part of the budget that can be applied to practically any school budget.

1. The estimates of receipts and expenditures should be classified under the same revenue sources and account classifications as are used in the ledgers of receipts and disbursements for the accounting system. This is essential to proper budget control.
2. The budget data should include at least the expenditures for the previous fiscal year, the budget for the current year, the estimates of receipts and expenditures for the ensuing fiscal year, the assessed valuation, the tax rate required, and the schedule of maturing indebtedness.

As previously mentioned, the formal budget should incorporate a definite statement of the educational plan. Other interpretive material might include various types of unit cost analyses, data for comparable school systems, trends in receipts and expenditures adjusted for variations in the purchasing power of the dollar, and any other information that will help the board and the public to make intelligent decisions concerning the budget.

The superintendent and his staff should have the responsibility of preparing the formal part of the budget. However, many persons, including citizens' committees and teachers, may participate in preparing the supplementary material accompanying the budget.

Another form of budget with considerable merit is coming into use. It is called the performance budget.[3] The formal part of the budget as described above is too technical to be understood by many laymen. The performance budget is designed to tell laymen what is to be achieved rather than what is to be bought. It is actually not a revolutionary form of budget. The traditional budget shows only what is to be bought. The performance budget actually supplements the traditional budget by describing briefly after each item of expenditure what is to be achieved. Therefore, the performance budget is considerably longer than the traditional budget. However, the use of a performance budget does not eliminate the desirability of supplementing the budget document with a clear statement of the educational plan and other interpretative material. The performance budget gives extremely desirable information concerning what is achieved, but it presents a somewhat atomized statement of the educational plan. Probably the best type of budget form is the performance budget, supplemented by the different types of interpretative information described before.

Presentation and Adoption of the Budget

The budget should be formally presented to the board several weeks before it is adopted, and it should be approved prior to the beginning of the fiscal year for which the budget is made. It should not be inferred that the budget is "news" to the board when it is first presented. Board members should have been appropriately participating in the preparation of the budget throughout the year. For instance, the board should have been making decisions throughout the year on educational programs and policies that must be reflected in the budget. Therefore, the budget when it is presented should actually represent largely a summary of decisions that have already been made by the board after careful studies involving many people. Wide publicity should be given

[3]Henry H. Linn, ed., *School Business Administration* (New York: The Ronald Press Company, 1956), pp. 169–170.

to the budget during its preparation, and opportunity should be given for public hearings. But public hearings without a planned process for broad participation are almost worthless. Although mass means of communication should be used in publicizing the budget, little is accomplished by publishing only a formal statement of receipts and expenditures. Most of the publicity should center around the educational services and facilities being considered.

Administration of the Budget

There should be a centralized administration of the budget. No budget can be kept in balance if numerous persons make expenditures without preauthorization. The superintendent or his representative must have the responsibility for administering the budget.

If the budget is to have any meaning, it must be put in operation. A budget is not an effective instrument for implementing an educational plan if it is filed away and referred to only at long intervals. Programs must be organized; persons must be employed; supplies must be purchased; buildings must be constructed, equipped, maintained, and operated; and many types of services must be provided. These and many other things all cost money, and unless the budget serves as a real guide to spending, there will be so much overspending on some items that there will be no money left for others. The choice then is to fail to finance certain items in the budget or to incur a deficit. Either alternative prevents the full achievement of the educational plan. Therefore, the budget is the instrument used to keep all expenditures in balance, in order that the total educational plan is made a reality.

The detailed amounts budgeted for receipts and expenditures should be entered into the account books or machine records for receipts and expenditures. Most standard forms provide space for listing the budget amount for each budget appropriation. However, it should not be assumed that real budget controls are being exercised unless accounting is on an accrual basis. It should be obvious that cash accounting alone is insufficient to provide the information necessary for budget control. If one adds the expenditures to date for a particular expenditure account and subtracts the sum from the amount budgeted for that account, the difference does not represent the real balance available in that account, because it does not take into consideration the obligations against that account that have not yet been paid. Under accrual accounting (1) estimated revenues are counted as available when earned, even though the cash has not been received, but the estimates are adjusted periodically for gains or losses; (2) as soon as contracts or purchase orders are signed, the obligations so incurred are charged immediately to the amount affected as encumbrances, and when the corresponding bill is paid, the procedure is to credit the account with the original encumbrance and charge the final payment to it. Under accrual accounting, therefore, the unencumbered balance in an account is the difference between the amount budgeted and the sum of cash expenditures plus the encumbrances that have not been credited. In other words, the real balance in an expenditure account is the difference between the amount budgeted and the sum of cash expenditures plus obligations made against that account that have not yet been paid.

FINANCIAL ACCOUNTING

School financial accounting systems should furnish: "(1) an historical record of receipts and expenditures; (2) a basis for evaluating the faithfulness of stewardship, and; (3) a partial basis for both fiscal and educational management with respect to budget preparation, control, cost analysis and reporting."[4] Therefore, accounting is far more than bookkeeping. Very few school administrators are trained accountants. It is impossible in a book of this length to describe an adequate school accounting system. Even if such a system could be described here, state laws or regulations prevent the use of exactly the same system of accounting in all states. School systems vary greatly in size, and accounting needs differ. Furthermore, much published information is already available setting forth the details of school accounting. The U.S. Office of Education has published a number of handbooks on school accounting.[5] Thirty state departments of education publish manuals on school accounting. Handbooks and simple textbooks on bookkeeping applicable to school accounting are available from private publishers. For these reasons, the primary purpose of this section is to describe what should be accomplished by the accounting system.

Objectives of School Accounting

Budgeting, accounting, and reporting are physically separate operations, but from the standpoint of business management they must be so integrated as to result in a total structure that is internally consistent. For this reason the objectives of school accounting cannot be described in isolation from other operations. Following are some of the business

[4]John Guy Fowlkes and Abner L. Hansen, "Business Management–Accounting, Auditing and Reporting," in *Problems and Issues in Public School Finance,* ed. R. L. Johns and E. L. Morphet (New York: Bureau of Publications, Teachers College, Columbia University, 1952), Chap. 14.

[5]Paul L. Reason and Alpheus L. White, *Financial Accounting for State and Local School Systems,* U.S. Department of Health, Education and Welfare, Office of Education (Washington, D.C.: U.S. Government Printing Office, 1957).

management operations in which the accounting system plays a vital part.

1. A method must be provided for authorizing expenditures. The approved budget itself is a general authorization for spending money. But budget controls are necessary and preaudits of expenditures must be provided for. But preaudits of expenditures cannot be made unless cash and accrual accounting records are available.

2. In order for schools to operate, purchases must be made and contracts must be let. Purchases include a wide variety of supplies, equipment, services, materials, real estate, and other items. Contracts are made for personnel services, building construction and repairs, insurance, loans, and other transactions. Authorized procedures must be followed and forms developed for recording these transactions.

3. The board must pay for the obligations it has incurred. Therefore, the board must develop procedures by which it can ascertain what it owes. Invoices must be checked to see that the board has received the goods it purchased and that it is paying the price agreed upon. The length of time worked by employees must be verified and the amount owed employees under contract determined. Buildings under construction must be inspected and the proportionate part of the contract due at a particular time determined.

4. The payments made by the board must be recorded systematically, and the records must show at least to whom or to what agency or organization payment was made and for what purpose.

5. The board must have revenue if it is to pay its obligations, so revenue must be procured by local taxation, state and federal appropriations, or other sources. These receipts must be systematically recorded by source and by the fund or purpose for which they can be used. Special fund accounts must also be kept in order to meet the requirements of law and to discharge trust obligations. Receipts may be for current purposes, for debt service, for capital outlay, or for trust and agency purposes.

6. The board must make reports of its financial operations to the public. Therefore, account classifications of the budget, the accounting system, and the financial reports should be consistent.

7. Reports are made to the state and the U.S. Office of Education. Therefore, the accounting system must meet state requirements, and the information provided should be comparable with that provided by other school systems.

8. Business management policies need to be evaluated, and budgets must be prepared for succeeding years. Therefore, the accounting system must provide the information necessary for appropriate research. Cost analyses are of particular importance in evaluating certain policies. For that reason, the accounting system should lend itself to making the needed cost analyses.

This is not a complete list of what should be accomplished by the accounting system, but it can be used as a rough check on whether a board has a reasonably adequate system of financial accounting.

Financial Reports

Financial reports should be made to the board monthly and to the general public at least annually. The monthly financial report should be reconciled with the budget. The primary purpose of the monthly financial report is to provide the board with necessary evidence to evaluate whether proper budget controls are being implemented. Regular financial reports also serve as a stimulus to keep records up to date and to locate promptly any accounting errors. Boards of education commonly publish technical annual financial reports. Although this is usually necessary to meet the requirements of law, such reports are unintelligible to most laymen. The most valuable financial reports for laymen are reports that relate financing to the educational services provided. Progressive school systems periodically publish reports of this type.

Purchasing and Payment Procedures

Central purchasing should be provided for all budget funds except for necessary petty cash accounts. Competitive bids should be obtained on sizable purchases. These bids should be based on appropriate specifications, locally prepared or obtained from some reputable source. Teachers, principals, custodians, and others who use supplies and equipment should participate in preparing the specifications for the items in which they are respectively interested. Competitive bids usually save the board money and also improve public relations. The policy of quantity purchasing should be followed when possible, because better prices are obtained. Quantity purchasing requires advance planning and storage facilities, but both usually promote economy and efficiency.

The importance of the participation of teachers, principals, and supervisors in the preparation of specifications for instructional materials and equipment cannot be overemphasized. This is essential in order to provide assurance of the educational value of the items purchased. But performance tests should also be made of items purchased. Many items of equal educational value may vary greatly in durability and safety. Large school systems may find it desirable to establish their own performance-testing laboratories. Other school systems should avail themselves of the services of state, regional, or national testing bureaus or laboratories.

As mentioned previously, the business staff should continuously preaudit all financial transactions. But the board should have an independent external audit annually. It is essential that the audit be made by a competent person or persons not under the control of the board. Some states provide state auditors. In other states, the school system employs certified public accountants. State audits can be very valuable or of but limited value, depending upon the training of the auditors and the policies of the auditing department. Audits made by certified public accountants who are familiar with school accounting are quite valuable; others are limited in value.

The objectives of the audit program as stated in the proceedings of the Association of School Business Officials are as follows:

1. To safeguard money, property, and employees.
2. To determine the adequacy of the methods of internal check.
3. To maintain adherence to the established standards, policies, and procedures—financial, accounting, and operating.
4. To check condition and use of property and equipment, particularly from the standpoint of adequate return.
5. To maintain and coordinate internal auditing procedures with those of the public accountant.
6. To present accurate, complete, and unbiased statistics with respect to the operation of the educational system.[6]

Therefore, auditors should limit their activities to these objectives and avoid making recommendations in the area of educational policy.

OFFICE EQUIPMENT

The equipment needed in a business office is determined largely by the volume of transactions, and this in turn is determined largely by the size of the system and the complexity of its operations. Even small school systems need typewriters, adding machines, calculators, and duplicators including duplicating boards for posting certain types of records.

What types of machine accounting are useful? This depends upon

[6]Thor W. Bruce, "The Why and Where of Auditing," *Proceedings, Association of School Business Officials* (Kalamazoo, Mich.: Association of School Business Officials of U.S. and Canada, 1950), p. 236.

the uses that are made of the equipment purchased or rented. Casey has suggested that it is doubtful if a school district of 1500 to 2000 pupils should have any equipment more complicated than a listing machine.[7] Districts with a larger enrollment should consider the following principal types of machines: (1) nondescriptive accounting machine, (2) descriptive accounting machine, (3) data-processing equipment.

The most advanced equipment is data-processing equipment.[8] This type of equipment is designed to compute as well as to prepare financial records. This equipment can be used for many kinds of statistical services other than financial accounting.

What is the minimum size of a school district that can economically use data-processing equipment? This is difficult to determine because of the rapid advances being made in this field. Fortunately, this type of equipment can be installed on a cumulative basis. Also in many sections of the United States, computing center services are available for data processing. When such a center is available, the board need not purchase an expensive computer. This service makes it economically feasible for much smaller school systems to utilize this equipment than would be practicable without this service.

BUSINESS ADMINISTRATION SERVICES

The business administration services discussed in the following paragraphs are not always organized as a part of business administration. But these services are all closely related to business management. The efficiency of business administration is promoted if the business and financial operations described in this chapter are coordinated by one person. In medium- and large-size school systems this person usually bears the title of "assistant superintendent for business affairs." In fact, communications and services are usually improved if the central administrative office and the facilities described next are all located either on the same site or in close proximity to each other. A number of school systems have recently constructed all their central facilities on one large site centrally located in the district. It is usually very unsatisfactory to house the central office of the school system in the city hall or the county courthouse. This practice usually results in inadequate facilities and unnecessary involvement in partisan politics.

[7]Leo M. Casey, *School Business Administration* (New York: Center for Applied Research in Education, 1964), p. 44.
[8]See James W. Whitlock, *Automatic Data Processing in Education* (New York: The Macmillan Company, 1964).

Supply Management and Storage Facilities

When a board of education purchases supplies, equipment, and materials, it has simply converted money into physical things that are needed by the school system. Therefore, its responsibility for accounting does not cease. The goods purchased must be received, stored, delivered, and a control record system must be established.[9] These are the functions of supply management. The ultimate objective of supply management is to get supplies and equipment to the point of need at the time needed and in the required quantity without loss or damage. Quality service must also be rendered at a minimum cost of time and money. This requires skillful management indeed. Therefore, the person in charge of supply management, especially in medium- and large-size school systems, has a very important responsibility. He can either be of great assistance in implementing the educational plan or he can be a hindrance. He can either save the board money or he can waste money.

When something is ordered by the board, it must be received by some responsible person. That person must check the goods received against the bill of lading and the purchase order, and either attest to the accuracy of the shipment or give written notification to the business office of discrepancies in quantity, condition, or quality. Items purchased may be delivered by vendors to a warehouse, a school, a shop, or the central office. A copy of the purchase order should be sent to the point of delivery when purchases are made. When the deliveries have been checked, the purchase order with appropriate notations thereon, along with the invoice or other papers accompanying the shipment, should be sent to the business office. These papers constitute some of the vital original documents upon which financial accounting is based.

Central purchasing is essential to good business administration, because money is saved by quantity purchasing. Decentralized spot purchasing is wasteful in time and money. Quantity purchasing creates the need for storage space. When things are stored, the problem of getting them out of storage is immediately created. But the final objective is to get the supplies to the point needed, when needed, in the quantity needed, without loss or damage. Each school system planning its system of supply management must keep all these problems in mind. The size of the system will affect the magnitude of each problem, but not its nature.

School Plant Operation and Maintenance

School plant operation is concerned with the cleaning, heating, lighting, and other activities necessary to keep the plant open and in

[9] For an excellent discussion of supply management, see Henry H. Linn, ed., *School Business Administration* (New York: The Ronald Press Company, 1956), Chap. 10.

condition for daily use. School plant maintenance consists of the repair of buildings and the repair and replacement of equipment. They are separate but closely related operations. In school systems large enough to provide central services, school plant operation and maintenance are usually placed under the same person, bearing some such title as superintendent or supervisor of buildings and grounds.

SCHOOL PLANT OPERATION. Efficient plant operation is essential to the health, safety, and comfort of pupils and teachers. Furthermore, plant operations can either hinder or help the program of educational activities. School custodians have close relationships with pupils, and they can either be an asset or a liability for moral and ethical training. Modern school plants are expensive and contain complicated mechanical and electrical equipment. The operation of this equipment can either save money or waste money.

Obviously, it is poor educational and financial policy to turn the job of operating the physical facilities of the school over to an ignorant, untrained custodian of questionable character. Not so many years ago, it was the custom of some district boards to put the job of school custodian up for bids. The job went to the lowest bidder, and the custodian was frequently one of the least respected individuals in the community. This practice was never justified, and it is unthinkable today.

It is not the purpose of this section to describe detailed procedures for proper school plant operation but to present guides for administrative policies aimed at assuring adequate custodial services. Following are some guides for school custodial policies that should be considered by the administrator.

1. School custodians should be carefully selected. Consideration should be given to health, character, education, experience, and willingness to learn. The principal should recommend the custodian or custodians to the superintendent after consulting with the superintendent of buildings and grounds, if one is available.

2. A salary schedule should be provided for custodians giving due recognition to experience and quality of service. This schedule should be high enough to attract responsible and competent employees.

3. An in-service training program should be provided for school custodians. Only rarely are boards of education able to employ custodians who are already trained for the job. If a superintendent of buildings and grounds is available, he should direct this training program. If not, outside consulting help should be employed. Principals who are uninformed about school plant operation should participate in this or some other type of training program until they are able to give proper supervision to the custodians at their respective schools.

4. The job of school custodian should be defined and a work schedule developed. The superintendent of buildings and grounds should provide principals with consulting help for this task. Custodians should be trained to make simple repairs and adjustments in equipment but should not attempt complicated tasks. This will save time and money. Close coordination with the school plant maintenance department is essential, because the borderline between operation and maintenance is not always clear.

5. The custodian should be under the direct administration and supervision of the principal. If there are several custodians at a school, one should be appointed as head custodian. Direct orders to custodians should come through appropriate channels. Nothing is more frustrating to the custodian trying to complete his schedule of work than to be interrupted by a classroom teacher who suddenly orders the custodian to do something. Exceptions should be made in emergencies, of course, but the administrative principle that no employee should be required to take direct order from more than one person also applies to custodians.

6. Custodians should be employed for twelve months if possible. Many school systems put some custodians under the administration of the plant maintenance department during the summer months. This practice has much to commend it, because the maintenance staff usually needs to be expanded during the summer months and custodians need work.

7. A sufficient number of custodians should be employed to do a satisfactory job. It has been suggested that one custodian should be employed for every ten teachers, or one custodian for every 16,000 square feet of floor area to be cleaned. These are very rough ratios and cannot be equitably applied to individual school buildings. The labor required to clean and operate buildings varies with the condition and type of floor, the type of heating system used, the amount of ground maintenance required, the availability of labor-saving equipment, and other factors. Custodians can accomplish more work if given the proper equipment in any type of building, but some buildings are more adapted to labor-saving machinery than others.

8. When a local school faculty is considering policies affecting plant operation, custodians should participate in the faculty meeting. Custodians tend to have more interest in implementing policies that they help develop. Custodians should participate in such meetings as peers with the faculty. This is a rare practice, unfortunately.

9. Custodians should have the benefits of retirement, group insurance, sick leave, vacation leave, social security, and workmen's compensation.

These policies are based on the assumptions that the proper operation of the school plant is essential to a functioning educational program and that custodians are valued members of the school organization.

SCHOOL PLANT MAINTENANCE.   It has been estimated that 1.5 to 2 per cent of the replacement cost of a building must be spent annually for maintenance in order to keep it in good condition.[10] School buildings have an average life of approximately fifty years. If 2 per cent of the cost of a building is spent on it annually for fifty years for maintenance and repairs, the cost of repairing and maintaining the building over its life is as great as its original cost, assuming no change in the purchasing power of the dollar. If a building can be so constructed as to reduce maintenance cost to 1 per cent annually, half of the original cost of the building can be saved during its term of use. Therefore, the maintenance program starts with the construction and equipment of buildings. There is no economy in cheap, shoddy construction or flimsy equipment. Such construction requires a much higher percent expenditure for maintenance and repairs than the figures just cited, the plant will not have as long a life, and it is never as useful a tool as a properly constructed and equipped building. Industry and business have long recognized this as a sound principle, but some taxpayers seem to believe that somehow school plants are exempt from it.

Some large school systems have a school plant planning division as well as a school plant maintenance section. Other systems, usually not the largest, combine school plant planning with school plant maintenance. Whether these services are combined or separated in the organization, provisions should be made for close coordination of the two services.

The board of education must develop some type of plan for maintaining and repairing school plants. The alternatives are as follows: (1) outside contracting, (2) school employees, or (3) a combination of the two. Some of the most valid arguments for the board employing its own maintenance workers are as follows:

1. If the maintenance workers are school employees, the board can require a higher quality of service than it can obtain from many contractors.
2. Maintenance costs less because no profit is involved.
3. The time, cost, and trouble of advertising for bids and awarding contracts can be avoided.
4. School plant maintenance can be planned and scheduled more efficiently than by job contracting.

[10]Rufus A. Putnam, "A Year-Round Program of School Building Maintenance," *Proceedings, Association of School Business Officials,* (Kalamazoo, Mich.: Association of School Business Officials of U.S. and Canada, 1948), pp. 332–335.

Some of the most valid arguments for outside contracting are as follows:

1. Some types of maintenance and repair require heavy, expensive equipment that the board would use so infrequently as to make it uneconomical.
2. Some types of jobs call for specialized mechanics that the board cannot afford to employ full-time.
3. The peak load for school maintenance and repair is during the summer months, and the board cannot do the necessary work in the time allocated.

The evidence seems to indicate that the best policy is a combination of school maintenance employees and outside contracting. Very small systems have no alternative to outside contracting. Small systems frequently find it desirable to employ one or two handy repairmen. When school districts are of efficient size, a school plant maintenance department should be established. This department should be headed by a man who is administratively responsible to the assistant superintendent for business affairs.

School Transportation

School transportation continues to grow in importance. In 1941, 18 per cent of the pupils enrolled in the public schools were transported to school, and in 1966, approximately 33-1/3 per cent. In 1966, more than 16 million pupils were transported to school at a cost of some $680 million. It might have been assumed that the decline in farm population would have resulted in a reduction in the need for transportation. However, the increase in the suburban and rural nonfarm population has caused a much greater increase in the need for pupil transportation than the reduction caused by the decline in the farm population. It is anticipated that the increase in the need for pupil transportation will continue.

PURPOSES AND OBJECTIVES. The development of pupil transportation was necessary for the attainment of the American ideal that every child, regardless of where he lives or his physical handicaps, has the right to an adequate educational opportunity. Modern school systems now provide transportation for normal pupils who live beyond a reasonable walking distance from school, for physically handicapped pupils who live any distance from the school within its attendance area, for pupils who live on dangerous walking routes even if the walking distance is reasonable, and for educational trips for school classes. Therefore, school transportation should not be looked upon as a luxury any more than the school plant. It is an essential part of the total school program.

The use of school buses for educational trips is rapidly increasing.

The school bus is thus becoming an extension of the classroom. This is sound educational policy. Technically, the school bus is a part of the school plant. It is just as logical to use the school bus to facilitate the learning experiences of pupils as to use a library or a laboratory.

SCHOOL BOARD POLICIES.   The operation of the school transportation program involves numerous executive decisions. There is no area of school administration that requires a more definite and detailed statement of the board's policies than school transportation. If policies are not available to serve as a guide to executive decision making, too much of the school administrator's time will be spent on transportation problems, the program is likely to be wasteful, the service may not be adequate, and public relations may be damaged. The basic objectives of the board's transportation policies should be to provide safe, economical, and adequate transportation service to the pupils who need this service. Many factors contribute to such service. Some of these factors are discussed in the following paragraphs.

THE ROUTING AND SCHEDULING OF BUSES.   Basic to the organization of the transportation program is the determination of who should be furnished transportation services. That must be determined by board policy, subject to the limitations of state law. The board must determine (1) how far children must live from the school they attend in order to be entitled to transportation, (2) how far children must walk to the bus line before being entitled to special service on a spur route, and (3) what physically handicapped children are entitled to transportation. A reasonable walking distance to school varies among different states, primarily due to variations in the severity of the weather and in traffic hazards. Some boards have defined reasonable walking distance as one mile and other boards two miles. The average practice seems to be approximately one and one-half miles. Some boards set different distances for different age groups.

When the board has determined its policies with respect to what pupils are entitled to transportation, a spot map should be made of those pupils. The next step is to plan the transportation routes necessary to serve the pupils. Following are some factors to keep in mind when planning bus routes.

1. It is more economical to operate one large bus than two small buses over the same route.
2. Pupils should not be required to spend an excessive amount of time on the bus.
3. The cost of operating the bus and the time for the route are unnecessarily increased if more stops are made than are required to give reasonable service.

After the map of transportation routes is made, it is then possible to determine accurately the number and size of bus units needed. The transportation map should be made annually because of rapid shifts in pupil population to be transported.

PUBLIC OWNERSHIP VERSUS CONTRACT TRANSPORTATION. One of the most important policy decisions for the board to make is whether it should own and operate its own buses or contract for transportation services. Numerous studies have been made of this matter in a number of states. The advantages usually found for public ownership are as follows:

1. It is more economical because fleet operation is more efficient than individual operation, and profits are eliminated.
2. Better service is provided, because school employees are more responsive to supervision than private contractors.
3. Better equipment is provided, because private contractors frequently cannot finance proper equipment.
4. Better drivers can be selected, because the board is not restricted to the man who can buy a bus.
5. Routing and scheduling are more efficient, because the board owns the equipment and can control it.
6. The educational program can be carried out more effectively, because the board can use its own equipment for educational trips more readily than it can use contracted equipment.

About the only advantages of contracting are as follows:

1. The board knows at the beginning of the year exactly what its transportation costs are.
2. The administration has less managerial responsibilities.

The advantages of public ownership in most situations so overweigh its disadvantages that boards of education are rapidly changing to public ownership. At this writing, approximately two thirds of the school buses of the nation are publicly owned.

THE SCHOOL-BUS MAINTENANCE PROGRAM. If the board owns its own buses, a program for bus maintenance must be established. Attention has already been directed to the administrator's responsibility for routing and scheduling school buses and determining the services needed. The administrative and supervisory responsibilities for school transportation are so great that the superintendent needs a supervisor of school transportation if the board owns and operates twenty or more buses. In a small system the supervisor may work part-time as a mechanic. But with large fleets, he should spend his entire time in supervisory and administrative duties. These duties should include routing and scheduling of buses, supervision and in-service training of drivers and mechanics, dealing with the public on matters of transportation services, and many other transportation problems. If the school system is large enough to have an assistant superintendent for business affairs, the supervisor of school transportation should be directly responsible to him; if it does not have one, he should be directly responsible to the superintendent.

The supervisor needs a staff of mechanics and a school-bus garage in which they can work. The number of mechanics needed varies with the condition of the buses, the length of the routes, and the condition of the roads. One mechanic for every fifteen to eighteen buses is usually required for good service.

The soundest maintenance program is one that emphasizes preventive maintenance. Otherwise, all the district has is a repair program. The preventive maintenance program is based on regular, thorough, and systematic inspection to anticipate trouble and prevent it from occurring. Such a program minimizes road failures, promotes economy and safety, and provides better service. It is the job of the supervisor or his representative to make these inspections and to see that the necessary action is taken to correct deficiencies in equipment. It is also good business to employ good mechanics. Properly maintained school-bus bodies and chassis normally have a useful life of approximately ten years.

The School Food Service Program

The school food service program is now a major division of school operations. The National School Lunch Program alone cost more than $1,250,000,000 in cash and commodities in 1964–65. More than 17 million pupils in public and private schools, or 35 per cent of the total enrollment, were served food under the National School Lunch Program. Accurate data are not available for school lunch rooms not included in the National School Lunch Program. Approximately 34 million pupils were served milk under the Special Milk Program in 1964–65. Federal aid provided under the National School Lunch Act of 1946 and the School Milk Act of 1954 has greatly stimulated the school food service program.

Basic economic and social changes have created the need for the school lunch program. The most important of these changes are as follows:

1. The consolidation of schools and the transportation of children have increased the length of time that children are away from home, and also have prevented children from going home for lunch.
2. Millions of mothers are now working, and they are not at home to prepare food for their children during the noon period.
3. There is an increased public awareness of the importance of

good health and the contribution that proper nutrition makes to health.

4. There has been a change in the social thinking of the people. Formerly, it was generally assumed that each parent was responsible for providing the noon lunch for his own children and that school authorities had no responsibility. Compulsory attendance laws require parents to send their children to school. But schools are now organized and administered so that parents cannot discharge their normal responsibility for providing their children with a nutritious noon lunch. Therefore, the public now demands that school authorities assume at least a part of the responsibility for the food service program.

The school lunch operation is irrevocably an integral part of the school program. It is operated for pupils in a publicly owned building by school employees under the supervision of school administrators and supervisors subject to the control of the board of education. Furthermore, teachers commonly use school lunch experiences for valuable learning activities. The school principal has the important responsibility of organizing, supervising, and financing the school lunch program. He must operate it as a solvent enterprise without making a profit or incurring a loss. Many pupils, especially in communities with a low socioeconomic status, cannot pay for their lunches. He must somehow arrange for them to be fed. The school principal operating a lunch program in a poverty-stricken community is unfairly loaded with school-lunch financial burdens. Also, the labor cost is generally proportionately greater for lunches served in a small school than in a large school.

The teachers inevitably become involved in these problems. In elementary schools particularly, teachers frequently collect the money from pupils for their lunches. In high schools, pupils normally pay for their lunches at the principal's office or at the serving counter. In most states, the purchasing and accounting are done by individual schools. Consulting help may or may not be available from the central office. In many schools, therefore, too much of the principal's and even the teacher's time is spent in collecting and accounting for funds to operate an enterprise on a decentralized basis that is inherently inefficient and incapable of rendering the quantity and quality of service needed. Furthermore, the total cost per lunch served would be reduced by centralized financing, purchasing, and supervision, and by an increased volume of lunches served.

Following are some of the school-lunch operating policies that are generally recommended by authorities in this field:

1. The board of education, the superintendent, and school principals accept responsibility for the school lunch program as an important part of the total program.

2. The financing of the school lunch program is centralized. All receipts of school lunchrooms are sent to the central office and pooled with state and federal funds available for the lunch program. This pooling of resources prevents the penalization of small schools and schools compelled to carry a heavy free lunch load because of the socioeconomic level of the population. In practice, federal funds and surplus commodities are largely used to remove inequalities.

3. All purchasing except for some authorized perishables is done on a wholesale basis by the central office. All payments are made and all financial accounts are kept by the central office. Budgets are made for each lunchroom, and cost accounts are kept for each lunchroom, but all lunchrooms are financed as one program.

4. In systems of efficient size, a trained school food-service supervisor is employed. The supervisor works closely with the principal and school lunchroom managers. He plans menus in cooperation with lunchroom managers; carries on an in-service training program for lunchroom workers; works closely with the business office in purchasing, storing, and distributing food, equipment, and lunchroom supplies; keeps the lunchroom accounts; and, in general, coordinates all phases of the lunch program. He is a part of the business management office.

5. Lunchroom managers and their assistants are appointed by the superintendent upon the recommendation of the principal. They are administratively responsible to the principal.

6. Lunchroom facilities are functionally planned for food service operations. Those operations include receiving, storing, preparing, and serving food; cleaning utensils; disposing of garbage; and keeping control records. The capacity of storage facilities provided for lunchrooms is coordinated with the capacity of central storage facilities.

SAFEGUARDING SCHOOL FUNDS, PROPERTY, AND PERSONS

The administrator has the responsibility of developing a program for safeguarding school funds, property, and persons. A comprehensive program of this type has many facets. It includes (1) insurance and bonding, (2) elimination of fire hazards from school buildings, (3) elimination from school plants of hazards to life and limb, (4) protection of pupils from traffic hazards, (5) removal of temptations to steal by protection of cash for which school employees are responsible and by adequate accounting and stock control records, and (6) protection of the health of pupils and school employees. Other measures could be added to this list; however this section is concerned only with safeguarding funds, property, and persons by insuring and bonding procedures.

Safeguarding School Funds

School funds are kept on either time or demand deposit in a bank or banks selected by the board of education as its depository. In some states, the depository must be approved by a state agency. If the balance in a school fund will not be needed for six months or more, it should be placed on time deposit or invested in high-rated government securities, because demand deposits usually draw no interest. These securities are normally short-term securities, because the maturity date of the securities purchased should correspond closely with the time the board will need its money. If balances are invested in long-term securities, the board must market its securities before maturity. An unfavorable change in the bond market would cause the board to lose a part of the principal of the investment. Security of principal is much more important to the board than rate of interest when it invests public funds. Time deposits have greater flexibility than bonds. This is an advantage to the board, especially for small balances or balances for which it is difficult to predict accurately the time of need.

When school funds are on either time or demand deposit, those funds should be fully protected at all times from loss due to bank failure. The Federal Deposit Insurance Corporation protects deposits up to $10,000. However, this protection is of little value to boards of education for large school systems that require operating balances of several hundred thousand dollars or even of a million or more dollars. Small school systems can secure adequate protection from the F.D.I.C. by depositing funds in several banks and securing $10,000 of insurance for each deposit. This procedure is not practicable for a medium- or large-size school system because the protection would be far from sufficient. The standard procedure is to require the depository bank to place in escrow in another bank approved by the board collateral equal to the amount of funds on deposit. If the depository bank fails, as much of the collateral as is necessary to return the board's funds is sold. The board of education should approve as collateral only high-rating government securities.

A corporate depository bond can also be used to protect school funds on deposit, but it is more expensive. Therefore, it is not commonly used.

Property Insurance

Boards of education have invested large sums of money in school buildings and equipment. This property is subject to heavy damage from fire and in some areas from storms and earthquakes. Heavy property losses result in serious budget difficulties and even financial disaster, especially for small school systems. Therefore, good management requires that a board of education protect itself against such contingencies. The purpose of insurance is to protect a board from a risk that it cannot afford to bear. Most boards of education carry fire insurance on buildings and equipment, and many others carry windstorm and other types of protection in addition.

The insurance needs of a board of education vary widely. A small school system of limited resources with only one or a few buildings proportionately carries a much greater risk than a large school system with several hundred buildings located on widely separated sites. The loss of one building not protected by insurance in a small school system will cause a financial crisis, but the loss of a single building in a large system may have but a limited effect on financial operations.

Fire insurance is expensive. A number of large city school systems with widely scattered risks have solved the problem of the high cost of fire insurance by becoming self-insurers. This is usually done by the board establishing an insurance reserve from funds that would have been paid to private companies for insurance. A few states, particularly Alabama and South Carolina, have established state insurance plans for insuring school buildings. Experience with well-managed self-insurance plans protected by adequate legislation has shown that from 40 to 50 per cent can be saved in insurance costs. State insurance of school buildings or self-insurance by large school systems is practicable and it would save large sums of money, but this policy is bitterly fought by private insurance companies.

Following are some recommended procedures for obtaining maximum returns for the insurance dollar:

1. Procedures for accurately appraising the value of school buildings and contents should be developed in order to determine insurable value. This is necessary to determine the amount of insurance to carry and to appraise losses.

2. Coinsurance is the most economical plan of insurance. Except for large, low-risk fire-resistive buildings, 80 per cent or more coinsurance should be carried. If a blanket district policy is used, there is some advantage in 90 to 100 per cent coinsurance.

3. The most complete fire insurance coverage is obtained under the recently developed insurance form known as the Public and Institutional Property Plan. It is available only for public buildings such as schools. Under this plan, school buildings and contents can be insured for the replacement cost rather than depreciated value. Under this type of policy, buildings and contents are insured for an agreed-upon amount in lieu of coinsurance, but this amount cannot be less than 90 per cent of value which must be sworn to annually by the insured.

4. A blanket type of insurance policy is easier to administer than specific insurance on each building.
5. A five-year term policy saves money, and it can be so scheduled that one fifth of the premiums due for the five-year term may be paid each year. This simplifies budgeting.
6. Construct buildings that have a low fire risk and consequently carry low rates of insurance.
7. Inspect buildings regularly for fire hazards and eliminate, as far as practicable, any factors endangering pupils and employees or causing higher rates. After factors causing higher rates are eliminated, take the necessary steps to secure rate reductions.
8. Boiler insurance should be included in the insurance program. One of the major benefits of this type of insurance is the inspection service provided. This service is designed to prevent boiler explosions, thereby safeguarding both persons and property.[11]

Liability Insurance

The school board is not liable for the acts of its agents in the large majority of states. The courts generally hold that boards of education are not liable for negligence, unless the statutes of the state specifically make them liable. The immunity of governments has had a long history, but the trend of legislation and court decisions is to increase the liability of boards of education and other agencies of state and local governments.

Regardless of legal liability, every board has the moral responsibility of protecting the public, pupils, and even its own employees from the negligence of its agents. It is particularly important that persons be protected from personal injury and property damage caused by motor vehicles operated by the board.

The question of nonliability of boards of education has sometimes been raised by insurance companies when settling claims under a liability policy. This can be prevented by requiring the insurance company to include in the contract a waiver of the claim of nonliability of the board.

Boards of education should carry liability insurance of appropriate types to protect persons against bodily injuries and property damage caused by the negligence of agents of the board. If this is not done, the board of education has no legal authority in most states to reimburse persons who have suffered such injuries or damages.

Workmen's Compensation Insurance

Approximately half of the states require that the employees of boards of education be given the protection of workmen's compensation

[11]For a detailed discussion of school fire insurance, see Linn, *op. cit.*, pp. 312–329.

insurance. It is not equitable to deny that protection to the employees of a board of education when it is given to the employees of business and industry. This protection should become universal. Some districts even provide workmen's compensation for students. Medium- and large-size school systems can wisely be self-insurers for workmen's compensation. In small districts, insurance should be carried.

Surety Bonds

Boards of education are concerned primarily with three types of bonds as follows: (1) fidelity bonds to insure against dishonesty of employees, (2) public official bonds to insure against nonperformance or malperformance of duties by officials, and (3) contract bonds to insure against nonperformance of contracts.

Fidelity bonds should be required of all employees who handle money. Such bonds not only protect the board against loss of funds but also stimulate the person bonded to keep proper records and to follow authorized procedures. Blanket bonds to cover all employees are now coming into common use.

Public official bonds cover much more than fidelity bonds. Under such bonds, the surety company is required to make good any misuse or misappropriation of funds as well as any funds lost by the dishonesty of the official. Such bonds are required of superintendents, board members, treasurers, tax collectors, and similar officials.

Contract bonds include bid bonds, labor and material bonds, and faithful performance bonds. It is particularly important that bonds of this type be required of building contractors. All bonds should be obtained from reputable surety companies. Personal bonds should never be accepted. Ordinarily, the board of education pays the costs of the bonds it requires.

Retirement and Survivors' Benefits

Retirement systems are in effect a type of insurance. It is in this type of insurance that the benefits of governmental operation have been fully demonstrated. The evolution of the federal Social Security System and the growth of state and local retirement systems of all types have made it imperative that boards of education obtain retirement benefits for all full-time employees. If this policy is not adopted, the board of education cannot bid successfully in the competitive manpower market. A complete retirement plan contains adequate provision for each of the following: (1) pension upon retirement, (2) a disability allowance, (3) survivors' benefits when an employee dies prior to being eligible for retirement.

Retirement systems were started by local school systems long before the states entered into this field. But experience has shown that state retirement systems are generally financially stronger than local retirement systems. Therefore, practically all states have retirement systems for teachers. Not all states, however, have retirement plans available for other full-time employees.

Some states have combined the teachers' retirement plan with the federal Social Security System. Other states, Ohio and Florida for example, have expanded teacher retirement plans to include all the benefits of social security. There seems to be some advantage to this latter plan. Teachers can probably obtain benefits equal to or more liberal than those provided in the federal Social Security System at a lower cost to themselves through teachers' retirement systems than through Social Security. The provision in 1966 of Medicare without cost to persons who are not members of the federal Social Security System further increased this advantage.

SOME IMPORTANT PROBLEMS
AND ISSUES

The control of the school budget is a very live issue in a number of school districts. Who should be the immediate beneficiaries of school board spending is also an issue in some school districts. These two issues are presented in the following paragraphs.

Should the Local School Budget Be Approved by Some Agency Other than the School Board?

A board of education is fiscally independent when it is directly responsible to the people for its financial program and its educational policies. A board of education is fiscally dependent when its budget is subject to review, revisions, or approval by any noneducational agency or commission.

The principal arguments that have been advanced for fiscal independence of school boards are as follows:

1. Schools should be kept independent of partisan policies.
2. Education is a state function. An intermediary authority standing between the state and the local school board makes it impossible for the board to be in fact responsible to the state and the people.
3. Fiscal control of school boards by noneducational governmental agencies leads to *de facto* control of educational policies.
4. Control of school affairs by municipal or other noneducational local governmental agencies often leads to coercion in pro-

fessional and technical matters and in the management of expenditures.

5. Fiscal independence leads to greater stability and continuity in educational planning.

6. Fiscal dependence leads to competition for the local tax dollar, thereby intensifying controversies between local governmental agencies and school authorities.

7. Fiscal dependence complicates school administration.

8. Fiscal independence is the only sure way to protect school funds from diversion to nonschool purposes.

9. There is no evidence that fiscal dependence results in greater economy and efficiency.

10. The people should be able to express themselves on the important problem of education without having issues confused by a mixture with other governmental problems.

11. Separation of fiscal control from responsibility for educational results violates the basic administrative principle that authority and responsibility should go together.

12. It is desirable to keep educational control close to the people to preserve the elements of democratic government and to provide for the freedom essential for adaptability, adjustment, and invention.

The principal arguments that have been advanced for fiscal dependence of school boards are as follows:

1. There is a place for a unified and coordinated local financial structure. Intergovernmental relations are more complex and there is much duplication of effort and overlapping of functions when schools are independent of local government.

2. Determination of expenditures for all purposes should permit the weighing of the relative merits of each service. This recommends a single legislative authority.

3. Coordination of services in which the schools and local government are mutually interested is facilitated.

4. School services when delegated to local control and responsibility are in reality legitimate aspects of local government, the same way as police protection, public health, and similar services of general social significance.

The research on fiscal independence versus dependence affords little objective evidence to support either set of arguments. It is doubtful if this issue can ever be resolved by objective evidence, because it involves the determination of the relative importance of different social values. The determination of relative social values is a philosophical problem, and philosophical propositions do not readily lend themselves to statistical evaluation.

If one believes that centralization of the fiscal planning of all governmental services has greater social value than more direct determination of educational policy by the people, he will support fiscal dependence of boards of education. If one believes that the decentralized determination of educational policy is of greater social value than centralized fiscal management, he will support the fiscal independence of school districts.

Generally speaking, the states have imposed more rigorous statutory and constitutional tax limitations on boards of education than on city and county governments. What is the relationship between tax limitations on boards of education and fiscal independence?

Should Boards of Education Give Local Vendors Preferential Treatment?

Many boards of education are under considerable pressure to buy everything possible from local vendors, even at higher prices than would be paid to outside bidders. Some local contractors also bring pressure upon boards of education to award building contracts to local contractors, even though better bids can be secured from outside bidders. Local vendors and contractors advocating this policy argue that since they are local taxpayers they have a right to the board's business. This argument ignores the fact that schools are agencies of the state, and in most states, boards of education receive a large portion of their revenue from the state. To pay higher prices than are necessary in order to do business with local vendors and contractors is an unfair burden to the taxpayers of the community and the state and becomes something like a subsidy to local business interests.

Boards of education following sound business practices follow the policy of securing competitive bids on all items of any consequence purchased by the board. Bidding should be on the basis of specifications prepared by the professional staff of the board of education. The laws of most states require that building contracts be awarded to the lowest responsible bidder. However, sound practices with respect to many other types of important purchases are far from universal.

A few states have laws designed to give preference to local vendors. Under what circumstances, if any, should preference be given to local vendors?

Selected References

Allen, Clifford H., *School Insurance Administration*. New York: The Macmillan Company, 1965.

Association of School Business Officials of the United States and Canada,

Annual Volumes of Proceedings. Evanston, Ill.: The Association, 1957 to date.

Casey, Leo M., *School Business Administration.* New York: Center for Applied Research in Education, Inc., 1964.

Featherston, E. Glenn, and D. P. Culp, *Pupil Transportation: State and Local Programs.* New York: Harper & Row, Publishers, 1965.

Finchum, R. N., *Fire Insurance Economies Through Plant Management.* U.S. Department of Health, Education and Welfare, Office of Education. Washington, D.C.: U.S. Government Printing Office, 1965.

Hill, Frederick W., *The School Business Administrator.* Evanston, Ill.: Association of School Business Officials, 1960.

Johns, Roe L., and Edgar L. Morphet, *Financing the Public Schools.* Englewood Cliffs, N.J.: Prentice-Hall, Inc., 1960.

Knezevich, Stephen J., and John Guy Fowlkes, *Business Management of Local School Systems.* New York: Harper & Row, Publishers, 1960.

Reason, Paul L., and Alpheus L. White, *Financial Accounting for State and Local School Systems.* U.S. Department of Health, Education and Welfare, Office of Education. Washington, D.C.: U.S. Government Printing Office, 1957.

Roe, William H., *School Business Management.* New York: McGraw-Hill Book Company, 1961.

Salmon, Paul B., *Fire Insurance Principles and Practices,* Bulletin No. 18. Evanston, Ill.: Association of School Business Officials, 1958.

Whitlock, James W., *Automatic Data Processing in Education.* New York: The Macmillan Company, 1964.

19

Financing the Educational Program

More people than ever before recognize that the progress of civilization depends fundamentally on developing the human resources in all countries of the world. Basically, this development is determined by the extent, kind, and quality of education provided. An adequate program of education would require a tremendous increase in expenditures in most countries. However, the nations in which the masses barely produce enough to sustain life cannot at present afford to finance more than nominal improvements in education. Fortunately, some of the more prosperous nations have recognized this as a major problem of common concern and have provided some technical and financial assistance. However, there has been little agreement on purposes and procedures and, consequently, only limited progress has been made toward solving some of the most serious problems.[1]

Those who participate in developing plans for an adequate program of education and its financing must take into account the entire development program needed by a nation in order to ensure appropriate coordination and avoid severe shortages or surpluses in certain areas. The planners must provide for the wisest possible use of scarce funds

[1]See Barbara Ward, *The Rich Nations and the Poor Nations* (New York: W. W. Norton & Company, Inc., 1962), Chaps. 1, 5, and 6.

in a manner most compatible with the development objectives appropriate for the nation.[2]

Even many of the more prosperous nations that have made substantial progress with education have failed to face realistically some aspects of their own problems and thus continue to handicap their own development. In the United States, for example, the people in many of the less wealthy school districts and states cannot provide adequate educational opportunities; in other districts they can afford to do so, but often do not. Such problems as inequitable opportunities for Negroes and for children from culturally disadvantaged homes not only in slum areas of cities but also in some rural and suburban areas have only recently begun to be faced. There are still people in most communities, and a majority in some, who oppose further improvements in education that would increase costs. This situation is effectively summarized in the following statement:

> In most countries, the financial support of education, though greater than ever before, has failed to keep pace with the increased social demands upon education. It is perhaps not unfair to say that political leaders and the general public almost everywhere are somewhat schizophrenic on the subject of education. They have high praise for the virtues of education; they rely heavily upon it to help the new generation solve great problems to which the older generation has found no solutions; but when it comes to spending more money for education their deeds fail to match their words.[3]

THE POLITICS AND ECONOMICS OF FINANCIAL SUPPORT

Burkhead has observed that: "Education is one of the most thoroughly political enterprises in American life—or for that matter in the life of any society."[4] For some aspects, such as the selection of teachers and details of the curriculum, the basic decisions in most countries are made by educators. For other aspects, such as the amount and kind of financial support, the basic decisions are always made by the people or their representatives—or by political and economic leaders. Under favorable circumstances, these decisions may be influenced by the recommendations of educational leaders, but the most potent factors are likely

[2]William J. Platt, *Toward Strategies of Education* (Menlo Park, Calif.: Stanford Research Institute, Jan. 1961), p. 6; see also Theodore L. Reller and Edgar L. Morphet, eds., *Comparative Educational Administration* (Englewood Cliffs, N.J.: Prentice-Hall, Inc., 1962), pp. 12–13.

[3]Philip H. Coombs, "Educational Planning in the Light of Economic Requirements," in *Forecasting Manpower Needs for the Age of Science* (Washington, D.C.: Office for Scientific Personnel, Organization for European Economic Cooperation, Sept. 1960), p. 29.

[4]Jesse Burkhead, *Public School Finance, Economics and Politics* (Syracuse, N. Y.: Syracuse University Press, 1964), p. 93.

to be the demand for education and the importance attached to it by political and economic leaders.

Political Factors

In many countries the relationship between national politics and financial support for education is inherent in the structure that has been established. If the structure is highly centralized and education is definitely an instrument of national policy, the amount of support to be provided for education is clearly a political decision. In the underdeveloped countries, education tends to be both overvalued and undervalued. It tends to be overvalued because many people and some of the politicians have come to think of it as a panacea—as a new form of magic—that will work miracles. It tends to be undervalued because too often it is more strongly supported through vote-attracting speeches of politicians, by the establishment of some institution or program for prestige purposes, and by appointment of second-rate persons to strategic educational positions, than by an honest effort to develop a sound program and provide necessary financial support.[5]

In the United States, state appropriations for public schools and institutions of higher learning must be approved by a legislature that always includes some conservative members who are more concerned about "protecting the interests of the taxpayers" than about determining how much is required to assure adequate financial support for the educational program. Moreover, school boards have only the power to obtain and use local funds for schools that is granted them in the constitution and in laws approved by the legislature. All legislatures are subject to the influence of many kinds of pressure groups, some of which spend substantial sums of money in preparing reports, and on lobbies to convince legislators that any significant increase in expenditures for education "would be disastrous." Fortunately, there are always educational and other groups interested in convincing legislatures that adequate financial provisions for public education are essential. The net result has been substantial progress in some states and very conservative provisions in others.[6]

The decisions regarding financial support in local school systems are also in the political domain. The school board is elected by nonpartisan popular vote in most local school systems and is appointed, usually by politically elected officials, in others. Thus, while the schools are presumably removed from partisan political control, all basic policies

[5]Adam Curle, "The Goals of Education in Underdeveloped Countries," in *Challenge and Change in American Education*, ed. Seymour E. Harris *et al.* (Berkeley, Calif.: McCutchan Publishing Corp., 1965), Chap. 5.
[6]During recent years a number of economists and political scientists have become interested in the politics of education and have made some important and revealing studies. In addition to Burkhead, *op cit.*, see *Selected References* for Chap. 9.

are subject to political considerations. Either the school board or the people must approve any proposal. All expenditures except for some minor items must be authorized by the board that must first approve the budget. While the recommendations of the superintendent and his staff carry considerable weight in most school districts, the board must make the policy decisions, even on matters that have to be submitted to the voters.

Since rather substantial funds for education are now provided by the federal government, the role of politics in decisions made by the national Congress cannot be ignored. For many years, even though substantial numbers of people favored increased federal support, Congress failed to approve any proposals except for limited aspects of the program. The opposition of influential minorities has been an important factor in the rejection of all proposals for general federal aid. Funds have been made available only for special purposes, primarily because certain important problems have been recognized and a majority of the people have been able to agree that support for these aspects is important.

Economic Considerations

While decisions regarding the extent and kind of financial support for education will never be removed from the political realm, some recent developments may help to provide a more objective basis and a sounder rationale for these decisions. These include (1) an increasing recognition by economists that education has considerable economic value as shown by recent studies, (2) strong evidence from research studies that under appropriate conditions there is a relationship between cost and quality in education, and (3) the development through research of bases and procedures for apportioning funds that will make possible equality of educational opportunity.

Every nation has to make investments in things (roads, factories, power plants, and so on) and in people (education, health services, and so on). Economists have long accepted the fact that investments in things constitute tangible physical capital which is essential for further development. Only comparatively recently have economists begun to recognize that prudent investments in people create human capital which is necessary for progress. Unless a society can develop its human resources, it can develop little else. As noted by DeWitt, "Human resource development is the social process of the production, distribution, and utilization of the knowledge, the skills, and the capacities of all the people in a society."[7]

[7]Nicholas DeWitt, "Investment in Education and Economic Development," *Phi Delta Kappan*, 47, No. 4 (Dec. 1965), 193–196.

Schultz, a well-known economist from the University of Chicago, has noted that even though most people in this country think of schooling as being virtually free, most of the costs are actually borne by the students and their parents, especially in the case of mature students who might otherwise be employed. On the basis of careful studies, Schultz concluded that, even when all costs of education including earnings forgone are taken into consideration, "the rate or return may be as high or appreciably higher than that on investment generally."[8] Thus when the benefits come in the future, as they usually do in the case of education, schooling has the attributes of an investment that can affect either future consumption or future earnings, and is a major source of the human capital essential for the development of a nation. As the human capital is developed through education, the economic wants of the people change. One of the changes presumably would be an insistence on higher-quality provisions for and programs of education. Moreover, as the people and their representatives in state legislatures and Congress more clearly recognize that well-planned expenditures for quality education constitute an investment that pays substantial dividends and facilitates state and national progress, they should become more interested in increased investments that will provide further dividends. Thus, wise political decisions can also be viewed as wise economic decisions, and wise economic decisions in this area should be recognized as wise political decisions.

RELATIONS BETWEEN COST AND QUALITY IN EDUCATION

How much should it cost to educate the children of a particular state or local school system? This question has been raised in some form in every section of this country since schools were first organized. The answer is not easy, because many factors are involved. The greater the differences in points of view regarding the purposes and objectives of the schools and the kind and quality of education to be provided in any state or community, the sharper the conflicts are likely to be regarding financial support for schools. In many situations, therefore, it may be advantageous and perhaps necessary to seek greater agreement on de-

[8]Theodore W. Schultz, *The Economic Value of Education* (New York: Columbia University Press, 1963), p. 6; see also Edward F. Denison, *The Sources of Economic Growth in the United States and the Alternatives Before Us* (New York: Committee for Economic Development, Jan. 1962); Frederick Harbison and Charles A. Myers, *Education, Manpower and Economic Growth: Strategies of Human Resource Development* (New York: McGraw-Hill Book Company, 1964); Fritz Machlup, *The Production and Distribution of Knowledge in the United States* (Princeton, N.J.: Princeton University Press, 1962); John Vazey, *The Economics of Education* (London: Faber & Faber, Ltd., 1962).

sirable purposes and characteristics of the educational program as a basis for resolving the problem of financial support. However, adequate support is essential for good schools, and agreement must sooner or later be reached on sound financial policies as well as on the objectives of education.

Closely related to any discussion of costs and provisions for support of schools is the question as to whether or when increased funds mean better educational opportunities for the children. Certain aspects of this question are relatively easy to answer; others are difficult.

The general problem is complicated by factors such as the following: (1) districts and schools vary in size; (2) some districts and some schools are much more effectively organized and administered than others, and (3) some teachers do a much better job of teaching than others with similar training and experience. As pointed out in Chapter 10, the expense of providing for a reasonably adequate educational program is much greater in small schools and districts than in those that are adequate in size. Organization, administration, and teaching effectiveness may directly affect the quality of the educational program in larger as well as in smaller schools. It is necessary, therefore, to recognize that increased expenditures in some districts will not result in as much improvement in the educational program as in others, unless some of the background factors and conditions are improved.

There is considerable evidence indicating that, when conditions are favorable and all factors are reasonably equal, increased expenditures within reasonable limits do result in a better program of education.[9] However, many improvements cannot readily be measured by the use of comparatively simple devices. It is usually necessary to utilize a series of measures that will provide evidence regarding progress toward the attainment of objectives of education which are difficult to achieve, yet which are essential for a satisfactory program of education in a democracy.

After studying ten elementary school districts in California that were among the highest in expenditures relating to instruction for a four-year period and ten of comparable size that were among the lowest, Crandall reached some significant conclusions even on the basis of achievement test scores.[10] He administered standard achievement tests to all students in grades four through eight who had been in the district

[9]Paul R. Mort, "Cost-Quality Relationship in Education," in *Problems and Issues in Public School Finance* (New York: National Conference of Professors of Educational Administration, Bureau of Publications, Teachers College, Columbia University, 1952), Chap. 2; see also Committee on Tax Education and School Finance, National Education Association, *Does Better Education Cost More?* (Washington, D.C.: The Association, 1959).

[10]James Henry Crandall, "A Study of Academic Achievement and Expenditures for Instruction" (Ph.D. dissertation, University of Calif., Berkeley, 1961).

during the entire four years and analyzed the results by groupings on the basis of intelligence quotients: low, middle, and high. He found that higher expenditures were positively associated with higher academic achievement at every IQ interval in these grades. The effect seemed to be cumulative. The differences were significant with a high level of confidence except for the group having an IQ of over 130. The evidence provided by this study supports and reinforces information available from other kinds of measures.

Studies that use appropriate measures for determining progress in attaining significant educational objectives indicate clearly that increased expenditures almost always result in improvements in the educational program in schools in which the expenditure level is at or below the national average. There is considerable presumptive evidence that the educational program may be improved when the expenditures are increased, even in school systems with a fairly high level of costs.

A statement by a prominent British economist who studied the costs of education in the United Kingdom is pertinent: "Every teacher, every councillor, every parent must be aware that the grave inadequacies, past and present, of our educational provision can be ascribed in large part to inadequate expenditure."[11]

RESPONSIBILITY FOR FINANCIAL SUPPORT

The principle of state responsibility for the support of education means that the citizens of each state determine what legal and other provisions (except for those made by the federal government based on the interest of the people of the nation in education) are made for support of the public schools in the state. Thus, through the constitution they adopt, the people of each state may either limit severely the financial support for schools or challenge the legislature and the citizens of each local school system to provide adequate support. Subject to these constitutional provisions, the legislature of each state may likewise either impose rigid financial limitations and restrictions or may encourage reasonably adequate financial support for schools.

Legally, no local school system has any authority to provide revenues, or even to expend funds for schools, except as that authority is granted by the constitution or by the legislature.[12] Such authority has been granted, however, in some form in every state except Hawaii. Consequently, the people in each local school system or their board of education may either fail or refuse to provide sufficient funds and thus

---

[11]John Vazey, *Costs of Education* (London: George Allen & Unwin, 1958), p. 17.
[12]Newton Edwards, *The Courts and the Public Schools*, (Chicago: University of Chicago Press, 1955), Chap. 10.

handicap their own schools, or they may provide generously for the support of those schools. Thus, variations in support of education found in different parts of the country are explained in part by state and local attitudes and legal provisions, in part by the attitude of the federal government toward federal support for schools, and in part by variations in the ability of districts and other factors discussed later.

In reality, the plan of financial support found in most states is a partnership plan. The people in each local school system are required or authorized to provide certain funds from local sources, the state makes available on some basis funds from state sources, and the federal government may provide funds, in its discretion, from federal revenues. The total amount available in each district from all sources determines in large measure the kind and adequacy of educational opportunities that can be provided through its schools.

INEQUALITIES IN EDUCATIONAL OPPORTUNITY

If every district in each state had equal ability to support schools and if the states were equal in ability, the need for state or federal support of schools would be less urgent than under present conditions, except as a means of broadening the tax base and providing greater equity for taxpayers. However, there are significant variations in ability that create serious problems.

One way to obtain some indication of probable differences in educational opportunity is to examine expenditures for public elementary and secondary schools. A comprehensive ten-year analysis made on the basis of 1960 data showed that about 2 per cent of the children in the nation were attending schools in which the expenditure per equivalent classroom unit (for comparable items of current expense) was nearly four times the expenditure in schools in which 2 per cent of the children at the other extreme were enrolled. The median expenditure per classroom unit in New York was more than three times as great as that in Mississippi, the state with the lowest median expenditure.[13] There still are marked differences among the states in current expense per pupil in average daily attendance and on a classroom unit basis. In 1965–66, for example, the estimated range was from $318 in Mississippi to $869 in New York.[14] It is not likely that a state spending less than one half of the amount per pupil expended for public schools in another state is

[13]Forrest W. Harrison and Eugene P. McLoone, *Profiles in School Support; A Decennial Overview,* U.S. Office of Education, Miscellany No. 47 (Washington, D.C.: U.S. Government Printing Office, 1965), pp. 1–7.

[14]*Estimates of School Statistics, 1965–66* (Washington, D.C.: Research Division, National Education Association, Dec. 1965), Table 12, p. 34.

providing educational opportunities equal to those in the state with the higher expenditure. Although there are some differences in cost of living and in other factors affecting expenditures in the various parts of the country, such factors do not account for the marked differences in expenditures for schools.

Differences in expenditures *within* many states are even greater than those *among* the states. Some of the extremes, however, are brought about by high expenditures in small districts and do not necessarily reflect differences in educational opportunities resulting from variations in expenditures. When small districts are omitted, the differences in expenditures per pupil within states range from about 2-to-1 in a few states up to 3- or 4-to-1 in others. Obviously, there are wide variations in educational opportunity in many states. This means, in other words, that there are many children who do not yet have adequate educational opportunities. In fact, one of the most important responsibilities in many states would appear to be to devise and implement plans that would assure equality of educational opportunity for all children. One of the first steps would be to bring low-expenditure districts at least up to the state median.[15] Districts with meager resources have little opportunity for choice or meaningful decision making with reference to the educational program. Only when funds become reasonably adequate can local responsibility begin to flourish, largely because the range of choices and of meaningful decisions has been significantly increased.

Differences in expenditures among districts do not necessarily reflect variations in ability to support schools. They might and do, in some cases, come from differences in interest and willingness to provide funds for education. Nevertheless, the evidence shows that (1) there are marked variations in ability among states and among the districts in each state, and (2) in general, the states and districts with least ability have been making as great an effort to support schools as the more wealthy, or an even greater effort.

Various measures have been used in an attempt to determine the financial ability of each state to support schools. It seems probable that no one measure proposed is entirely satisfactory, yet the evidence shows clearly that the states do differ considerably in ability. Thus, New York has almost three times the personal income per child from five through seventeen years of age as that of Mississippi.[16]

Some of the measures used to determine the ability of districts in each state to support schools are briefly discussed later in the chapter.

---

[15]Harrison and McLoone, *op. cit.*, Chap. 2.

[16]*Rankings of the States* (Washington, D.C.: Research Division, National Education Association, Jan. 1966), Table 47.

The studies show that the range in ability varies from 8- or 10-to-1 in several of the large-district states to several hundred-to-one in some of the small-district states.[17]

FINANCE AND DISTRICT ORGANIZATION

As previously noted, the problem of developing sound programs for financing schools is much more complicated in states with a large number of small districts, or local school administrative units, than in states in which districts have been reorganized. Any state that has a large number of small districts will have islands of wealth and of poverty resulting from the wide range in the ability of local school systems to provide for the support of their schools. Reorganization of these districts into local school administrative units of more adequate size would reduce considerably the range in local ability, because some wealthy and some poor districts would be combined into larger units in the process. Through reorganization alone the range in ability of districts in several states has been reduced from more than 100-to-1, to 10- or 20-to-1.

By providing substantial state funds and apportioning them on the basis of need, a state can help to overcome some of the inequalities due to inefficient district organization. One danger in such a situation is that the state, in its attempt to assure adequate educational opportunities, may make available enough funds for unnecessary small districts to provide, with limited local effort, schools that are reasonably satisfactory from the point of view of the people in such districts. Under these conditions, they may be encouraged to continue small districts. The state would then find itself in the position of continuing to support an uneconomical and inefficient plan of organization.

As already pointed out, studies have shown that generally equivalent educational programs cost less per pupil as the size of schools and school districts approaches adequacy. In most cases, where many small districts are found, proper reorganization of such districts could result either in reduced expenditures for the same kind of program or in better educational returns for the same expenditures. Reorganization of districts in itself will not assure a better educational program, but it will make possible the development of good schools at a reasonable cost.[18]

---

[17]Roe L. Johns and Edgar L. Morphet, *Financing the Public Schools* (Englewood Cliffs, N.J.: Prentice-Hall, Inc., 1960), pp. 157–158.

[18]American Association of School Administrators, *School District Organization* (Washington, D.C.: The Association, 1958), Chap. 9; also, Johns and Morphet, *op. cit.,* pp. 146–150.

CONTROL OF SCHOOL FINANCE

The American people have been especially concerned about provisions for control of school finance, because they recognize that the agency that controls finance may also control the educational program. Three major problems in this area have received considerable attention: (1) What agencies, if any, of the state or local government other than the agency established for education should have control over school finance, and what controls should they exercise? (2) How much control should the state establish over fiscal affairs of local school systems? (3) What safeguards should be established that will help to assure the citizens of each local school system that the fiscal affairs pertaining to their schools are being properly handled? (See Chapter 18)

Kinds of Control

In most states, as noted in Chapter 10, either the board of education or the voters have the power to determine, within prescribed limits, the amount of school district funds needed and the manner in which those funds will be expended. However, the prescribed limits vary considerably among the states, and in some instances, among the various types of districts within a state. Many of the limitations are prescribed by the constitution or laws and thus are "visible." Others are much more subtle and may become apparent only when a decision has to be made. Examples of prescribed limitations include a maximum millage that may be levied on the assessed valuation with or without a vote of the people; authorization for the people to vote bonds only up to a certain per cent of the assessed valuation of the property (e.g., 2 per cent, in Indiana and Kentucky); a requirement that certain funds or a percentage of these funds be used only for a narrowly designated purpose, such as for salaries of classroom teachers or certain kinds of supplies; a provision that only property owners may vote in bond elections and that two thirds of these must vote favorably. Provisions of this type seem to be totally inconsistent with the concept of local responsibility and indicate that the legislature is not willing to trust the judgment of local school boards or people very far.

An impressive example of a more subtle type of control is provided by the myth accepted in many states that tax levies or bond issues must be based on the assessed valuation of property, and that this should represent only a small percentage of the market value. Moreover, this percentage often varies greatly among districts in the same state. When the legislature fixes a maximum millage that may be levied by school districts, and the local assessor decides that property is to be assessed at only 20 or 25 per cent of full value, he is denying access to potentially available funds and actually is determining the kind of educational program that can be provided in the district. Indirect or hidden controls of this type which have become part of the mores in many states should be clearly identified for what they are, and should not be tolerated by a people who believe in adequate educational opportunities for all. Fortunately, steps have been taken in a number of states to assure more equitable assessment practices and, in some states, assessment at full value. The Court of Appeals in Kentucky and the Supreme Court in Florida have recently ruled that all property in those states must be assessed at full value and that nothing less is equitable. Is there any defensible reason why this policy should not be adopted in all states?

In districts in which the law requires that the school budget be approved by some other local government agency (as in Maryland and North Carolina) or by a state agency (such as the educational budget officer in New Mexico) the possibility of external control is inherent in the law. Whether it becomes benign or ruthless may be determined by the personnel of the agency that has the responsibility for approval. In such situations, the board that is responsible for the educational program can only recommend the amount of funds needed and, therefore, in a fundamental sense, cannot be held responsible for the kind of program provided. In many instances, the two agencies work together in a reasonable harmony; in others, however, a forward-looking school board has had to learn that it must be conservative or wage a losing battle.

Many subtle controls are inherent in the value structure and aspirations of the people. If the people in a district are satisfied with a low-quality program, they may either elect conservative, "tax-conscious" members to serve on the board, or vote against proposals for realistic tax increases, or do both. As long as the people in any area are sharply divided about the "tasks" of the public schools,[19] or have low aspirations relating to education, they may not only be complacent about unrealistic financial limitations that are imposed but may supplement those by some controls of their own choosing.

Expenditure Determinants

James and his associates have listed three major clusters of variables that seem to determine educational expenditures: (1) wealth or ability to pay; (2) governmental arrangements and decision-making processes for permitting boards and citizens to express their preferences regarding proposed expenditures, and (3) the aspirations of the people, including their demands for educational services, which vary considerably from

[19]See Lawrence M. Downey, *The Task of Public Education* (Chicago: Midwest Administration Center, University of Chicago, 1960).

one district to another.[20] The limitations inherent in the first of these for poorer districts can be ameliorated or eliminated by the organization of adequate school districts and a realistic program of state support; those in the second can be reduced by removing inhibiting controls and increasing local responsibility; those in the third can be overcome only by better understanding of the value of education and the development of higher aspirations on the part of the people which, in some cases, can be enhanced by outside influences and incentives.

In some respects the ideas of state control and of local responsibility seem to be incompatible. Minimum standards that help to assure reasonably adequate educational opportunities through the state should not interfere with meaningful local responsibility. If, however, the people in any area are prevented from doing what must be done in order to have a satisfactory program of education, such a limitation not only interferes with but discourages proper exercise of local responsibility. Local school administrative units organized throughout the state on a scale large enough to function effectively and in a position to insist that they be permitted to exercise responsibility for which they are prepared should help to ensure that restrictive controls are kept to a minimum and local responsibility and fiscal initiative encouraged.

SOURCES OF REVENUE

Revenue receipts for public school purposes may be classified on bases such as (1) income from tax sources and from other sources, (2) income from local, state, and federal sources, and (3) income from property and nonproperty tax sources.

INCOME FROM TAXES AND OTHER SOURCES. Most revenues for public school purposes have been for many years derived from tax sources. Currently, only about 1 per cent of the total is derived from income from state permanent school funds and endowments, and some 3 per cent comes from county and local revenues from permanent funds and lands, gifts, fees, and other nontax sources. Thus, about 96 per cent of all revenues for support of public schools comes from tax sources, including federal and state appropriations, and only about 4 per cent from nontax sources.

INCOME FROM FEDERAL, STATE, AND LOCAL SOURCES. The percentage of receipts for public schools derived from federal sources has consistently been rather small. During the past 35 years it increased from about 1 per cent near the beginning of the period to 3.8 percent in 1964–65. However, following the passage of the 1965 Federal Education Act, it jumped

[20]H. Thomas James, J. Alan Thomas, and Harold J. Dyck, "Wealth, Education and Decision-Making in Education," Cooperative Research Project No. 1241 (Washington, D.C.: U.S. Office of Education, June 1963).

to about 8 per cent of the total. The percentage from state sources has increased from slightly less than 17 per cent in 1929–30 to nearly 40 per cent during the past fifteen years. The percentage from county and local sources has declined considerably. In 1929–30, receipts from these sources constituted 82.7 per cent of the total, and in 1964–65 only about 56.5.[21] Following the passage of the 1965 federal act relating to schools, the percentage declined to about 53 per cent, because of the substantial increase in the proportion of the total derived from federal sources.

State revenues for schools come chiefly from legislative appropriations and, in some states, from earmarked taxes. About 80 per cent of the funds provided by the states comes from appropriations from the general fund. All but a dozen states provide more that one half of their state funds for schools through appropriations from the general fund.

INCOME FROM PROPERTY AND FROM NONPROPERTY TAXES. The traditional major source of revenues for the support of schools in America has been the property tax. However, as the economy of the country has changed and as the nation has become industrialized, most states have tended to shift to other sources of revenue for a substantial portion of the total. As late as 1930, more than 80 per cent of all school revenues was derived from property tax sources. The shift has been such that only about 55 per cent has come from property taxes during recent years. There has been a further shift from state property taxes to county and local property taxes for schools. Only twelve states derive revenues for school purposes from state property taxes, and only about seven of these receive more than 1 per cent of the total from that source.

The percentage of total school revenues derived from property taxes varies greatly among the states. Eight states receive 75 per cent or more of their total school revenues from property taxes, while at the other extreme three states receive less than 20 per cent from that source.

While almost all state funds for schools are derived from sources other than the property tax, nearly all county and local school funds come from property tax sources. Although less than 0.2 per cent of state revenues for schools are derived from property taxes, approximately 98 per cent of all county and local school revenues come from that source. Other local governmental agencies derive only about 70 per cent of their local revenues from property tax sources.

FINANCING THE LOCAL SCHOOL PROGRAM

In comparatively few school districts are the schools supported entirely by funds derived from local sources. In the poorest districts,

[21]*Rankings of the States, 1966*, Tables 71–73, pp. 43–44.

complete local support for an adequate school program is impossible because of the limited resources available. In some of the wealthy districts, adequate local support could be provided on the basis of a reasonable tax effort. Actually, most districts receive funds for their schools from both local and state sources, and practically all now receive some federal funds.

In most states the constitution or laws enacted by the legislature require that separate levies be made for current operation and for retirement of bonded indebtedness. Some states authorize or require separate levies for other purposes such as a building fund, community services provided by the schools, or adult education. Revenues from the separate levies must usually be used for the purposes for which the levy has been made. Certain special levies, levies above those authorized to be made by the board, and, indirectly, levies for retirement of bonds, usually must be authorized by vote of the electors of the district in accordance with the controlling legal provisions found in the state.

About one third of the states have authorized the use of certain local sources of revenue other than the property tax for support of the schools. In all except a few large or wealthy districts, however, these sources are so limited that the revenues received from them represent only a negligible proportion of the total. In the mid-1960s they exceeded 3 per cent only in Delaware (4.1), Alaska (8.3), and Pennsylvania (18.2).

In developing a plan for financing its schools, a district must determine the amount of state funds to which it is entitled; note and observe fully any restrictions on the use of those funds; ascertain whether it is eligible to receive any federal funds, and if so, meet all requirements for obtaining and using them; determine what local funds are authorized; take the necessary legal steps to obtain those funds, and observe all legal requirements relating to their use. If the total amount thus available during any year is insufficient to finance the proposed school program, the board must obtain additional funds by vote of the local electors, endeavor to get the state appropriation increased, or reduce its proposed expenditure for the educational program or for certain aspects of the program.

STATE SCHOOL SUPPORT PROGRAMS

Every state provides some funds from state sources for public school purposes. The percentages vary considerably among the states. In 1965–66, four states (Iowa, Nebraska, New Hampshire, and South Dakota) provided from state sources less than 20 per cent of the total revenues for their public schools, while four others (Delaware, Louisiana,

New Mexico, and North Carolina) provided more than 65 per cent. Hawaii is the only state that operates and finances from state funds all of its public schools, but Alaska and Maine operate and finance schools in unorganized areas.

The kinds of appropriations for schools and the procedures used in distributing funds vary even more strikingly than the percentage of revenues provided by the state. Some 400 different funds or grants for schools are provided by the states, or an average of about 8 per state. The range is from 2 in two states to more than 12 in each of several others.

A surprisingly large proportion of the states distribute most funds as flat grants; that is, they provide the same amount per census child, per pupil, or per some similar unit, regardless of the wealth or economic status of a district. These funds help to relieve the burden on the local property tax and thus enable all districts to provide schools, but they assist the most wealthy districts as much as the poorest. More than half of all state funds are apportioned as flat grants.

Some states emphasize special-purpose appropriations and narrowly restrict the purpose for which these funds can be used by local school systems, while others provide general-purpose funds (grants) that can be used for any current school purpose at the discretion of the district. Studies have shown that while special-purpose funds may provide some stimulation, they tend to restrict local initiative and otherwise handicap districts in planning their own programs.[22] In spite of this evidence, some states still distribute more than 80 per cent of all state funds on this basis.

In some states the legislature appropriates fixed amounts for a biennium or other period of years, and, consequently, the amount per pupil is automatically reduced as the enrollment increases; in others, a designated amount is provided per pupil or per some other unit of need. Most states apportion all funds on the basis of objective formulas prescribed by law; a few use subjective measures that leave discretion to state officials. Some penalize all small school districts by distributing all or most funds on average daily attendance or some similar basis. Others make adjustments to ensure that reasonably adequate funds will be available for necessary small schools. A few provide special rewards for all small schools and districts. Some states attempt to determine what a reasonably adequate program should cost and to see that such a program

[22]See Lester N. Neulen, *State Aid for Educational Projects in the Public Schools* (New York: Teachers College, Columbia University, 1928); J. S. Wrightstone, *Stimulating of Educational Undertaking* (New York: Teachers College, Columbia University, 1933), Chap. 8; and Arvid J. Burke, *Proposed Changes in Financial Support for Rural Schools of New York State* (New York: Teachers College, Columbia University, 1936), p. 225.

is financed from state and local funds; a few others (for example, Nebraska and New Hampshire) do little more than make a gesture toward helping schools, presumably on the false assumption that if districts want to do so, they can finance good schools, regardless of their wealth or poverty.

In fact, there are so many different practices and variations of practices that all cannot be equally defensible. Sometimes both "good" and "bad" practices are found in the same state, and the bad may largely offset the beneficial effects of some of the good practices. Surely, no practice that tends to perpetuate existing conditions regardless of necessity, that provides financial rewards for inefficient practices, or that penalizes wholesome developments should be considered satisfactory. One of the great needs in many states is for a thorough and realistic reappraisal of the entire finance program, with a view to developing sound and equitable procedures. Difficulties, however, often arise from the fact that vested interest groups benefit from inequitable practices, and desirable improvements may be resisted, regardless of what the facts may show.[23]

THE FOUNDATION PROGRAM

The development of reasonably sound and fairly adequate foundation program plans by a number of states has constituted one of the most encouraging trends of the past four decades. In 1923, Strayer and Haig made a significant study in New York State,[24] that, supplemented by the studies of Mort[25] and others, provided the basis for modern concepts of foundation programs. As a result of these and subsequent studies, it is now possible to develop a reasonably sound and equitable program of financial support for the schools of every state. However, traditions and political factors have prevented the adoption of such a program in many states.

Characteristics of a Defensible Program

Any defensible plan for financing public schools should enable the people of a state, and of each adequately organized district in the state, to provide essential educational opportunities and adequate programs for all at a reasonable and equitable cost to the taxpayers. The

[23]Edgar L. Morphet and Erick L. Lindman, *Public School Finance Programs of the Forty-eight States,* U.S. Office of Education Circular No. 274 (Washington, D.C.: U.S. Government Printing Office, 1950), Chaps. 5 and 6.

[24]G. D. Strayer and R. M. Haig, *The Financing of Education in the State of New York* (New York: The Macmillan Company, 1923).

[25]Paul R. Mort, *State Support for Public Schools* (New York: Teachers College, Columbia University, 1926).

characteristics of such a plan have been worded in various ways by different authorities, but should include the following:

1. The plan of financial support for schools in each state should be designed to assure a foundation program providing essential, reasonably adequate, and well-rounded educational opportunities for all who should benefit from public education.

2. The foundation program should be supported by an equitable combination of funds from local, state, and, insofar as applicable, federal sources; it should constitute a bona fide partnership plan.

3. Each school district (or district and county) should be expected and required to make the same minimum local effort toward financing the foundation program.

4. The state should provide for each district on an objective basis, the difference between the funds available from the required uniform minimum tax effort and the cost of the foundation program.

5. The plan for financing the foundation program should assure reasonable equity for all taxpayers.

6. The educational and financial provisions for the foundation program should encourage sound and efficient organization, administration, and operation of local school districts and schools.

7. The foundation program plan should provide maximum opportunity and encouragement for the development and exercise of local leadership and responsibility in education.

8. The citizens of each local school system should be authorized and encouraged to provide and finance such educational opportunities beyond the foundation program as they desire.

9. The foundation program plan should be cooperatively developed by representative citizens who have a genuine interest in and concern about public education.

10. The program and procedures should emphasize continuous evaluation and sound long-range planning.[26]

Developing the Program

A basic step in any state is to analyze the existing state plan, using procedures such as those outlined later in this chapter. The purpose is to bring to light some of the strengths, weaknesses, and problems in connection with the present plan.

The first step in developing the foundation program itself is to determine the scope and quality of the educational program considered essential for all districts, and the level at which it should be supported.

[26]Adapted from Johns and Morphet, op. cit., pp. 268–270.

This can be done either by using average practice in the state or in some group of districts in the state, or by attempting to determine and get agreement on the services to be included in a desirable foundation program. It is now generally recognized that average practice may include both good and bad features and may not represent desirable practice. Furthermore, if average practice is used as the basis for the program, it may tend to perpetuate undesirable features.

A procedure that has been successfully used during the past few years in several states is for committees of educators and lay citizens to study the needs and to attempt to reach agreement on the major features of a desirable program of education. This procedure has the advantage of helping people throughout the state to understand the problems of the schools and the possibilities that may be attained through a good educational program. Experience has indicated that once people are agreed on what constitutes a satisfactory foundation program, or a variable level program that includes an incentive plan (see pp. 516–517), they are likely to insist that it be established and adequately financed.

Measuring Need

Many states have used crude measures of need in developing their finance programs. Every study of the subject has shown that such measures as the school census and even average daily attendance are inequitable.

The *weighted pupil plan,* if properly developed, provides a valid unit for measuring need for most aspects of the program. For example, if the cost for a pupil in an elementary school of three hundred or more is used as a basic measure or unit of need, the pupils in small elementary schools and in small and large high schools can be weighted in terms of costs or other related factors and be used to measure units of need in those schools.[27] However, there are three problems commonly encountered in connection with the use of this unit: (1) it is difficult for legislators and other laymen to understand the relationship of the weighted pupil to the school program in operation; (2) if existing costs are used in arriving at the weighting, there may be a tendency to freeze into the state program undesirable or inequitable practices regarding expenditures, and (3) it tends to center attention on costs rather than on the educational program.

The *adjusted classroom unit* has been used during more recent years by a number of states instead of the weighted pupil plan. A basic step is to determine the number of pupils per teacher (for example, 27) that will facilitate effective teaching in elementary and high schools

[27]Paul R. Mort and Walter C. Reusser, *Public School Finance* (New York: McGraw-Hill Book Company, 1951), pp. 491 ff.

other than the smallest schools. Fewer pupils per teacher are utilized for necessary small, isolated elementary and high schools. Such units can then be used in arriving at the number of teachers (teacher units) needed, except that special adjustments (in number of pupils per teacher) will need to be made for classes of exceptional and disadvantaged children and for vocational and adult education programs. Supplementary units are provided for administrative and professional facilitating services needed in the ratio of one such unit to every six to ten teacher units, depending on the kind and extent of such services considered essential in the state. The sum of the teacher units and the administration and facilitating service units for a district constitutes the number of *classroom units* to be included in the foundation program for professional personnel for the regular school year (traditionally, from nine to ten months).

Many school systems are now operating summer or extended programs, and an increasing proportion of the professional personnel is employed on a year-round basis. The classroom units used for such services can be converted by applying a ratio appropriate to the extended time served, or this ratio can be applied to the amount included for salaries for the personnel involved. The amount to be included in the foundation program for salaries of professional personnel is determined by multiplying the total number of units by an adequate fixed amount per unit or, preferably, by using a salary ratio or index plan with adjustments for training and experience groupings and for responsibilities.

To the amount included in the foundation program for professional salaries should be added an amount for all other current expense except transportation, determined by multiplying the number of classroom units (or the number of pupils in average daily membership or attendance) by an adequate amount per unit. To this should be added the separately calculated cost of transportation, to obtain the total cost of the foundation program. Some states also add an allowance per classroom unit for capital outlay in determining the total cost. Each district then receives from the state the difference between the amount derived from its required local levy and the total cost of the foundation program for the district.[28]

Determining Local Ability

When a foundation program is developed in any state, it becomes very important to use objective and equitable measures of local ability to finance the program. A few states use a combination of county and district taxes as a means of reducing inequalities within each county. If

[28]See Johns and Morphet, *op. cit.*, pp. 280–287, for detailed explanation of this procedure.

the measures used are inequitable, districts whose ability is overestimated receive less state funds than those to which they are entitled, and districts whose ability is underestimated receive more than their fair share of state funds.

Many states that developed foundation program plans some years ago required a uniform local tax levy based on the assessed value of property in the district (or county and district). However, in a number of states, assessment practices were not uniform; consequently, inequities were incorporated in the program. Several states still use the prescribed uniform levy, regardless of the assessment practice. A few states have made considerable progress toward establishing uniform assessment practices, but uniformity of assessment seems to be difficult to attain in most states.

Several states that have not been able to achieve uniformity of assessment practices have adopted one of two alternatives. Some have established a ratio plan that requires the state tax commission or some other appropriate body to make studies of ratios between assessed and actual value (or some designated percentage of actual value) of property in the various counties and to establish assessment ratios on the basis of those studies. These ratios are then used in determining local taxpaying ability and ascertaining the funds that should be provided locally to support the foundation program. When this plan is used, a county or city may determine its own assessment policies, but if the ratio is low in any district it must make a proportionately higher levy to provide the funds required for the foundation program than would otherwise be the case. The ratio plan should be equitable and should work satisfactorily if the assessment ratios are fairly determined. However, in practice, some difficulties have been encountered in determining fair and proper ratios.

Some states have not been able to establish either uniform assessment practices or the assessment ratio plan, nor have they been willing to use a fixed levy because of recognized variations in assessment practices. These states have developed an index of taxpaying ability that is designed to measure the ability of each local school system to provide the funds required to meet the local cost of the foundation program. In developing this index it is essential that statistical procedures be employed that utilize economic factors (sales tax receipts, amount of passenger automobile license tax paid, value of farm products, and number of gainfully employed workers for each county, or similar measures) to predict the relative proportion of the true value of property in each county, since most school districts can levy taxes only on property. The ratio between the county total of each of these items and the state total is then combined into an index of taxpaying ability that, when applied to the yield from a prescribed levy on the total assessed valuation of property in the state, will determine the proportion of the total that should be provided by each county. The proportion for each district can be determined on the basis of the ratio between the assessed valuation of property in the district and that in the county.[29] Equalized valuations, when valid and reliable, are preferred over the index of taxpaying ability as measures of local ability.

Implementing the Foundation Program

More than forty states have some type of foundation program plan. In many of these states, however, the program is very limited, and in others it utilizes some rough and inequitable measures. Some people have maintained that there should be two types of state grants: a flat grant in which all districts participate, and a small "weak district" foundation program fund for the poorer districts. Several states have plans of that type. One of the difficulties encountered in practice is that, since the wealthy districts are often the more politically powerful, flat grants tend to be increased as much as or more than foundation program funds, regardless of equity.

Ideally, districts that have sufficient resources to support the complete foundation program from the required local effort should not be entitled to any foundation program or flat-grant funds. However, it is usually not feasible and probably not desirable to deprive districts of state funds they have been receiving, unless serious inequities are involved. In the interest of attaining a common point of view and avoiding unwholesome competition, several states have developed one comprehensive foundation program plan which includes a provision that no properly organized district shall receive less than a designated amount per classroom unit from the state. Thus the conflict of interests inherent in two separate funds tends to be reduced, and the stage is set for increasing the foundation program sufficiently so that all districts will eventually participate.

A few large-district states have already developed a comprehensive foundation program plan sufficiently broad and inclusive so that all districts are legitimately entitled to participate in the program. Thus there is no division of interests, and any increase in the funds, once all districts participate, tends to benefit all proportionately.

Within the past few years, a few states (for example, California, Rhode Island, and Wisconsin) have developed a new type of "incentive plan" as a supplement to the foundation program and, at the same time,

[29]See *Index of Local Economic Ability in State School Finance Programs* (Washington, D.C.: National Education Association, 1953); also, *Problems and Issues in Public School Finance*, pp. 231 ff.

to ensure that the poorest districts (which can obtain only nominal funds from higher local levies) can be in a position to improve their programs. If the extra funds provided by the state for districts that make levies beyond the minimum required are made available roughly in inverse proportion to ability, the poorest districts can have available for each additional mill of local effort (probably within prescribed limits) approximately as much per classroom unit as the more wealthy districts. Evidence pointing to the desirability of adopting such a plan as a means of improving education in many districts is provided in a study by Johns, Kimbrough, and their associates.[30] In a study of all districts in Florida, Georgia, Kentucky, and Illinois, having a population of 20,000 or more, they found that districts that were making a low effort to support their schools eighteen years ago tended to continue as low-effort districts during the entire period. A properly developed incentive plan could become one means of helping these districts to improve their educational programs.

FINANCING CAPITAL OUTLAY

The problem of financing capital outlay, especially school buildings, has become acute in many areas as a result of increases in school population, accumulated unmet building needs, and the sharp rise in building costs.

LOCAL PROVISIONS. The traditional pattern for financing the construction of school buildings has been to assume that it is entirely a local responsibility. In most states, however, there is a legal as well as a practical limit to what districts can do. Local financing of school construction means that in most communities all or almost all the costs have to be paid from property taxes.

A few of the larger and more wealthy districts should be in a position to finance some of their construction on a pay-as-you-go basis. However, during the past few years, all but a few have had to resort to bond issues. Many of the more wealthy districts have ample resources to finance needed buildings through bond issues or through a combination of bond issues and pay-as-you-go provisions. However, the issuance of bonds by any district means that extra expenses are incurred.

No matter what limit is set on taxing or bonding capacity, there are some districts in every state that cannot provide the buildings they

[30]Roe L. Johns and Ralph B. Kimbrough, *Relationships Between Socioeconomic Factors, Educational Leadership Patterns, Elements of Community Power Structure, and Local School Fiscal Policy,* Cooperative Research Project No. 2842 (Gainesville, Fla.: University of Florida, 1967).

need under any realistic legal limitations. If the limitations were removed, some could not pay for the buildings without excessive effort.

STATE PROVISIONS. Although a few states have provided some assistance for school plant construction for some time, most did little or nothing until they were confronted with the emergencies that followed World War II. More than one half of the states now have some plan for state assistance in financing school capital outlay, but many of these are either so limited that they do not meet the needs or are only emergency provisions that expire in a short time unless they are extended. Many state emergency plans have not been very satisfactory. They usually require applications from needy districts, and approval in many instances is based partly on subjective factors. Because of the detailed requirements that must be met, participating districts in some states have been subjected to undesirable state controls.

Several states, notably Pennsylvania, Maine, Indiana, and Georgia, sought to solve the problem by establishing state building authorities under some appropriate title. Most of these encountered some difficulty in establishing such authorities and also learned that the problems are not solved by this device alone. When buildings are provided for poor districts under this plan, there must also be state aid to enable such districts to pay their rental charges without having to reduce their funds for current operation.

Several states have made substantial progress in the development of long-range plans with appropriate provisions to meet accumulated needs. In Florida, for example, to the value of the classroom unit included in the foundation program each year an amount is added that is designed to be sufficient to enable districts to replace all buildings over a period of fifty years. This replacement allotment is supplemented to provide for needed expansion on the basis of increases in attendance. Districts that desire to do so may borrow funds from a state bonding authority to meet their emergency needs, and are limited only to a percentage of the value of the classroom unit multiplied by the number of units times the number of years over which the loan is to be provided. Thus, districts are no longer limited to assessed valuation, and have an assured income for capital outlay that may be used to amortize loans or to provide new buildings as needed.

Although the criteria that should be observed in developing a sound plan of state aid for building construction have been generally agreed upon by authorities, they are followed in practice only by a few states. Undoubtedly, if this phase of the problem of financing education is to be solved satisfactorily, most states will have to develop more realistic plans in the next few years than they have done thus far.

programs, this is one of the most significant purposes. In many schools and communities, there is a tendency for people to wait for others, perhaps the board of education and administrators, to effect important improvements or advancements in the educational service. Skill in making appraisals is not readily available. It has to be developed through the process of carrying studies to completion. The development of the talents of staff and citizens through study of the educational system is extremely important because of its relationship to problems of implementation of improvements in the educational service. It is important also because of the contribution that it makes to the development of the people themselves—a goal fully in accord with the purposes of education in a democracy.

To TEST NEW APPROACHES TO PROBLEMS AND TO CONDUCT PILOT STUDIES IN THE CONSIDERATION OF WHICH ADVANCEMENTS CAN BE EFFECTED. As school systems become larger and society more complex, essential experimentation in "lighthouse" schools or school districts can no longer be assumed to occur inevitably. Decentralized school systems have facilitated variety and a real measure of adaptation in the approach to problems. But many children are in large school systems that are not highly decentralized. Further, there are many potent forces in our culture that seek conformity rather than experimentation. Despite the work done in the universities, it is too much to expect that they will carry on the needed research in the field of education. There would thus appear to be a pressing need for programs of action research through which steps toward educational advances can be taken.[1] These programs would be planned and carried through by individual schools and school systems with assistance, in some cases, of staff members of colleges, universities, and state departments of education. These programs generally involve appraisal in establishing base lines or starting points, in collecting data during the study, in analyzing data, and in formulating conclusions. Such programs will not only offer new precepts directly but will also make important contributions to the development of members of the staff. They should not be expected to offer important contributions unless resources in materials and staff time are provided.

TYPES OF APPRAISALS

The variety of types of appraisals is extremely large. Many appraisals may not be readily classified, since they involve components or procedures that are not commonly combined. Quite appropriately,

[1]Stephen Corey, *Action Research to Improve School Practices* (New York: Bureau of Publications, Teachers College, Columbia University, 1953).

appraisals are tailored to the purposes and needs of a given situation. Despite the difficulties that may be encountered in classifying studies, the following types are offered to give a better understanding of the range of characteristics of appraisals. A given study may well belong in several of these categories.

Geographical or Governmental Unit

Educational studies may pertain to the local school system, to the intermediate unit, to the state, or even to federal activities or relations. They may also deal with only one unit of a system such as a high school. For example, accreditation studies generally concern themselves with a single school.

Limited Area or General (Comprehensive)

Studies may be general or comprehensive, giving attention to many of the large number of services or areas found in a state or local school system. Such studies may result in an evaluation of such services as administration, pupil personnel services, textbooks, instructional services, school-community relations, staff, curriculum, student achievement, business services, or financial procedures and needs. On the other hand, the appraisal may be limited to a single one of these areas or services.

Continuous, Periodic, or Irregular

Some school systems have a planned, continuous program of evaluation. This may be done through a revolving program whereby each service may be carefully appraised once in each five-year period. Under this arrangement, some phase of the system is under study at all times. In other cases, provision is made for a periodic study of procedures and achievements. A comprehensive study at the end of each five- or six-year period, with studies of specific problems or areas at any time when the need appears, is a desirable arrangement. In the great majority of instances the studies carried on are irregular, initiated only when the need has grown extremely pressing. One result of this is that the studies are frequently carried through in too short a time, with the issues not clearly defined, with too little involvement, and with great difficulty in implementation because of the emotional overtones that have developed in the community.

Outside, Internal, or Cooperative

In this category reference is made to those who assume a major share of responsibility for the conduct of the study. Are they members of the local school staff, the high-school student body, or citizens of the community? Or are they outside experts who conduct the study and prepare and submit a report? A couple of decades ago, the outside expert had an experience background and an objectivity that was very difficult to find in local personnel. On the other hand, too frequently, he may have had an insufficient insight into the reality of the situation under study, and consequently, antagonisms developed toward the expert and his report. As a result, many surveys are said to have led to regrettably little change in practice.

In one sense the internal study is the extreme opposite of the outside study. The advantages of the outside study become the disadvantages of the internal and vice versa. With an emphasis upon change in practice, rather than upon the production of a report that recommends change, a turn has been witnessed in recent years toward studies carried on by the educational staff or citizens of the community. Many school systems, especially smaller ones, have a staff inadequate in numbers, experience, or competency to carry appraisal projects through in a satisfactory manner. Nearly all communities and school systems, however, have resources that can be utilized in studies and that will develop through such experience.

Thus, the cooperative study, in many situations, holds the largest promise. The cooperation of the local staff and citizens with the outside consultant can produce a team that has the advantages of the external and internal study and avoids the disadvantages of both of them. Although this view is believed to be basically sound, it should be noted that the cooperative study is not necessarily an easy road. To a very great degree, it must be developed in the light of the situation and resources at hand. It frequently requires considerable modification of attitude and understanding of role on the part of consultants, local staff, and citizens.

Status, Diagnostic, or Implemental

Studies may be classified as to purpose in one of these groups. In the status study the intent is to arrive merely at a valid description of the existing situation. Such a study is difficult if attention is given to how life is actually lived in the educational organization, rather than to the formal organization that has developed. At times, a status study is warranted because of questions that have been raised, or there may be a need for a clear base picture. In many instances, however, a study that is diagnostic is sought. It not only reveals the existing situation but probes into factors associated with the conditions found. In an increasing number of cases an implemental study is sought. Change is desired and direction of change is being sought. Although this is a highly desirable objective, it should be noted that at times there is the danger that change is sought without reasonable regard for research results and present status. This can result in indefensible change, in unsound action, and in lack of appreciation of the need for soundly planned and executed research efforts. Although this danger should be recognized, it is nevertheless true that the implemental type of study is the most defensible in many educational situations.

More than any other, the implemental study calls for the involvement of those within the community and the organization that is being studied, for implementation cannot be done by outside expert consultants. If it is done, it will be done by the staff of the organization and the citizens including the members of the board of education of the community. In the well-executed implemental study much of the needed change will be introduced during the course of the study. There is no justification for waiting until the study is completed to effect needed change. Implementation may be of different types. Some changes can be introduced by the staff itself. Other changes, which involve basic policy, may need to be approved by the controlling board before being introduced. The implemental study may be expected to take a longer time than the status study. It will also result in a different type of report. Its success will be judged on the basis of the change actually effected, rather than by the quality of the report produced.

CRITERIA FOR APPRAISAL

Any defensible appraisal should recognize and be in accord with certain criteria. Many of these have been developed in the field of measurement and evaluation. Generally, however, in education when measurement and evaluation are discussed, reference is made only to the instructional area and not to the many aspects of the educational system, all of which are related more or less directly to instruction. Attention here is centered upon the total program. Following are some criteria to guide the appraisal of the program.

EFFECTIVE APPRAISAL IS DEPENDENT UPON CLEARLY DEFINED EDUCATIONAL OBJECTIVES. The desirability of any type of classroom, of a personnel practice, of a given administrative organization, of curriculum materials, or of a school community communication program can only be appraised in terms of its contribution to the objectives of the educational enterprise. Appraisal in these terms may be difficult. However, attention must be focused in this manner, or practices may be accepted because of unsound assumptions regarding their value, because of tradition or because others employ them. To avoid the tendency of general educational objectives to become vague and to have little meaning in various specific situations, it is frequently desirable to establish objectives of each of the various educational services. These, of course, should be established in relation to the basic objectives. For example, a statement of purposes of the personnel program should reveal the relationship of the personnel program to the objectives of the educational system. Such specific statements of objectives are a foundation in light of which various personnel practices can be appraised more readily than if only the basic educational objectives are defined.

APPRAISAL MUST BE VALID.   This requires that the appraisal be what it purports to be. It implies consistency or reliability as well as soundness or truthfulness. Valid appraisal remains the most difficult aspect of the work. In an enterprise as vast and complex as the school system, many instruments may be used in such a manner or with such interpretation as to lack validity. To attain some measure of validity, a number of steps should be taken, among them the following: general and specific objectives should be clarified in order that they may be used as a guide in the development or selection of appraisal devices; insistence should be made that varied data be collected pertaining to the service being appraised; recognition of the difficulty of attaining a valid appraisal should be granted and methods sought to improve validity. This may involve defining the job or area of service being evaluated, a willingness to delay making judgments, a desire to seek additional evidence, and a recognition of the limitations of data and judgments made.

The difficulty of arriving at a valid appraisal may be so great as to cause many who are reasonably well informed to shy away from the responsibility. However, it must be recalled, as suggested earlier, that evaluation of some type will be made inevitably. Further, it is clear that more valid appraisals can be made by qualified people who are willing to work at the process. An appraisal is a process that must extend over a considerable period of time. By beginning with areas for which data are more readily available and for which instruments are developed, the competence of the evaluators can be improved. They can then push on into some of the more difficult aspects. In this process it is important to avoid regarding the appraisal of some one aspect of the program as a valid appraisal of the whole program. A valid appraisal of the extent to which certain skills and knowledges have been attained may furnish a quite inadequate basis for a valid appraisal of the school or school system.

BASES OR STANDARDS FOR THE APPRAISAL MUST BE ESTABLISHED.   An appraisal must be made with consideration of some base or standard. Such standards are important assists in the determination of the data to be collected and are essential to its analysis and interpretation. Perhaps the most desirable base is the actual result or effect of the operation. The actual behavior of youth after they have completed school —their achievements, attitudes, competencies—are thus extremely important aspects of an evaluation. This, however, involves a long period of time, for the status of a youth at the completion of school may not reveal his future development, which nevertheless will be related to his former educational experience. Regarding many aspects of the educational system it is, therefore, necessary to appraise on some other base.

Standards of one form or another are widely employed in appraisals. They may be statements of the achievement that is expected or believed to be desirable. In some instances they are expressed in terms of what are regarded as best practice. Thus there are standards regarding the manner in which the board of education should function, the education that teachers should have, the organization and functioning of the guidance program, the organization and functioning of the purchasing department, and the skills and knowledge that children on the average and under specified conditions may be expected to achieve by the end of a given number of years of schooling.

In making appraisals it is important to note that norms are not necessarily appropriate standards. In many situations, normative practice or attainment is neither to be expected nor desired. In too many instances, resort to norms is found in appraisals. The avoidance of the norm as a standard is desirable.

In many appraisals it will be possible to evaluate both in terms of results and in terms of standards. For example, standards regarding the organization of business services may be employed, and an appraisal may be made. These services may also be appraised in terms of their ability to provide the materials needed by teachers at the time they need them.

Many of the instruments of appraisal contain or have complementary statements of standards. This would be true, for example, of instruments for evaluating school plants, and of instruments for self-evaluation by teachers. This is also true of more comprehensive appraisal instruments such as the *Evaluative Criteria*[2] and *Evaluating the Elementary School—A Guide for Cooperative Study*.[3] In the case of achievement tests, norms are frequently furnished. They can be used as a base for the formulation of standards, along with other factors such as the social and economic background of the students and their educational, intelligence, and health histories.

[2]*Evaluative Criteria* (Washington: Cooperative Study of Secondary School Standards, 1960).

[3]*Evaluating the Elementary School—A Guide for Cooperative Study* (Atlanta: Southern Association of Colleges and Secondary Schools, 1951).

APPRAISAL MUST BE COMPREHENSIVE. This principle does not suggest that all aspects of a situation must be evaluated at one time. However, if limited phases of the program are studied, the limitations must be recognized in any conclusions drawn or results reported. Furthermore, in accord with this principle it is very important that appraisals be planned so that the various essential approaches are employed. It is important to avoid the all too common practice of gathering a few data—generally those that are most readily available—and then developing recommendations that might not be defensible if data concerning many other phases of the program had been collected and analyzed. The tendency to evaluate only with reference to limited aspects of the work is common within the classroom. It is also common in studies of school systems. For example, when an evaluation is made of administration, in many instances, attention is given only to administrative structure. Although structure is important, it is really only of great importance when seen in the light of administrative procedures and practices. But it is much more difficult to describe validly how an organization is administered. As a consequence, too often we are satisfied with a mere analysis of structure.

APPRAISAL MUST BE CONTINUOUS. At the beginning of this chapter we stated that appraisal is inevitable. In a sense, it is also inevitably continual. However, it is not necessarily carried forward continually in a carefully planned manner. Rather, it is customary to appraise only periodically—perhaps at the end of a year or of five years. Such periodical, more intensive appraisals may be very important. They can be fitted into a long-range, continual program. However, standing alone, they are not sufficient. This is true because evidence regarding many services needs to be gathered continually, and adjustments need to be made. The terminal evaluation is necessarily a somewhat limited one. For example, at the end of the period it is too late to gather data pertaining to some of the procedures employed. Only certain types of data remain to be examined. Furthermore, terminal evaluation lacks much of the opportunity for in-service development of people (staff and lay citizens) that is offered through a continual program. Finally, the problem of appraisal is so large and difficult that, only if it is carefully planned and continually carried on, at least in some aspects, is it likely to be sufficiently comprehensive to be valid.

APPRAISAL MUST BE COOPERATIVE. Cooperation marks various phases of the appraisal program; in fact, most aspects of the program need to be cooperatively planned and executed. Cooperation is essential to the collection of many types of necessary data, to their interpretation, and to the development of recommendations and their implementation.

Cooperation may be seen as involving the local administrative and teaching staff, as well as lay citizens. The development of the skills of cooperation may take considerable time on the part of leaders and of various parties. Unless the need of developing ability to work together in the evaluation process is recognized and plans for the development of this ability are made and carried through, a high quality of cooperation is not likely to be achieved. Early attempts may be characterized by defensiveness on the part of some and overaggressiveness on the part of a few. Competent leadership that insists upon planning the collection of essential data, avoiding the development or acceptance of generalizations before the data are collected, seeking additional data where the need for them is indicated, and recognizing the limitations of the data collected can result in the development of skills in cooperative appraisal that will be an extremely important force in the development of better educational opportunities.

APPRAISALS MUST BE INTEGRATED AND INTERPRETED INTO A PORTRAIT. Much appraisal is isolated and piecemeal. When it is referred to the larger purposes of the institution, it lacks significance. It is, therefore, essential that plans for appraisal include the bringing together of the various types of data. Many evaluations take on added validity when seen in terms of other data. Nearly all evaluations take on added meaning when they become a part of a larger whole. It is easy, for example, for a teacher to use intelligence test data improperly, if he has no other data than the test results. If he can see the intelligence test data with reference to the home and environmental background, the previous educational experiences, the personal history of the child, and other matters, he is much less likely to overvalue a single result such as a test score. Similarly, it is easy to "appraise" an administrator with only a few facts available, and many do not hesitate to do so. However, it is also clear that any reasonably sound appraisal must be based upon considerable data pertaining to the various situational factors that are interlocked with the administrative behavior. The case method of reporting a development or of studying administration has considerable merit because it requires an awareness of the whole picture, of the many facts in the situation as seen by different people who are involved.

GUIDELINES FOR CONDUCTING THE APPRAISAL OF A SCHOOL OR SCHOOL SYSTEM

With the criteria in mind, brief attention will be given to some guidelines that may prove useful in planning and conducting an appraisal. They should be regarded as suggestive only, and not all-inclusive. Obviously, they will need to be modified and developed to fit the needs of a given situation. They are believed, however, to have general applicability.

1. *The administrative staff should take the initiative in formulating policies and plans pertaining to the appraisal of services, schools, and the school system.* Failure of the administrator to lead in this manner, however, should not prevent other interested parties from seeking action along these lines.

2. *The board of education should consider and adopt policies pertaining to appraisal.* They may well cover such matters as the general and specific purposes; the role of staff and outside consultants; the release of staff members for participation; the provisions for the costs of such programs, and the methods of reporting results of appraisals.

3. *Involvement of staff and citizens should be sought.* Such involvement may be achieved gradually, as the various people participating develop skill in making a cooperative effort.

4. *Careful attention should be given to the nature of the involvement.* Certain people may provide valuable assistance in developing policies, as experts with reference to certain techniques such as public opinion polling, or as collectors of data. People who may render excellent service in one role as a participant may have much less interest in and much less ability to contribute in another situation. Involvement must be related to competency and interest.

5. *Provision must be made for leadership and coordination of the program.* This will necessitate the appointment of a planning committee. It will also require the appointment of someone as the executive secretary or director. If he is a member of the staff, which he generally should be, he should be released from other duties sufficiently to enable him to carry the work forward promptly and effectively.

6. *Provision must be made for the collection and analysis of data.* At times, members of a committee are expected to do far more routine data gathering than is reasonable. As a result the work does not get done or does not get done in reasonable time, and interest lags. As a consequence, the contribution that many people could make is not made. Some routine data collecting by members of a committee may be desirable, since this will give an understanding of the problem. It is indefensible to enmesh committee members who should be wrestling with policy matters in detailed data collecting and analysis.

7. *The desired role of the consultants should be made clear.* Are they to furnish leadership in planning the study, in developing techniques and procedures, in developing competencies of

participants, in formulating standards that will be employed in the study, in preparing the report? Or is it the view that they will write the report as they generally did in the non-participating type of study?

8. *Provision should be made for implementation of recommendations during the course of the study.* This is true whether policy changes are involved or only administrative procedures. Of course, recommendations that may be dependent upon other as yet incomplete phases of the appraisal should not be adopted.

9. *Provision should be made for reporting the plans and progress of the appraisal continually.* An appraisal frequently causes anxiety on the part of many people. This can only be overcome through a frank presentation of the purposes and plans. Generally, the cooperation of many people is involved in an appraisal. The necessary level of cooperation will not be secured in any manner other than through providing the opportunity for full and open discussion of what is planned. This will involve face-to-face meetings, as well as regular reports to staff and public. Again, it should be noted that this is not likely to be done unless responsibility is fixed upon some one individual or committee. Furthermore, adequate resources in terms of time and facilities must be provided.

10. *An adequate budget and other resources must be provided.* The budget should provide funds for secretarial services, production of materials, and the expenses and time of consultants. It should also provide for released time for such staff members as may be expected to carry a substantial responsibility. A policy statement, should be developed regarding staff members on released time who are participating in the program. Many members of the staff and the community will be involved in a manner that is not extremely burdensome. However, it should be recognized that a comprehensive appraisal cannot be expected to be done well by people already fully engaged in other responsibilities. There should be no hesitancy in establishing a budget that will make it possible to do the job well. It will almost certainly produce returns well in excess of the investment.

SOME IMPORTANT ISSUES

The remaining pages of this chapter will be devoted to a discussion of several of the more important issues pertaining to appraisal.

Are Board of Education Members Competent
To Appraise the School System?

Many board of education members recognize that the appraisal of the school system or of various aspects of it is their most difficult task. The policies that they establish and the decisions that they make are necessarily based upon appraisals. They are required to make decisions at times without adequate data as a base.

Given our administrative and organizational structure for schools, there is probably little to be gained in debating whether or not board members are competent. It is perhaps better to recognize that they vary in competence and that the variation is not wholly a matter of personal qualities. Rather, their competence is mainly related to the extent to which they have established policies that furnish them with needed standards and data when confronted with an issue. Probably the extent to which they have adopted such policies is largely dependent upon whether their administrators have helped them recognize the need for carefully planned appraisals.

The appraisal recommended here should involve self-evaluation as one aspect of it. For example, many boards of education could profit much by an appraisal of the manner in which the board functions. This would center attention upon such questions as: Does the board become too much involved in administrative detail? Does it have an agenda carefully prepared and supplemented by essential material? Is it prepared to receive questions and complaints and to act soundly with reference to them—recognizing the need to secure more data if that is essential? Has it adopted policy statements regarding important issues pertaining to the development and conduct of the instructional program? Are the meetings of the board well conducted, or are they interminable affairs that do not build public confidence? Answers to these questions could be found in part by the analysis of the minutes and policy statements of the board of education, or by the employment of a competent observer. However, in addition to these approaches, the board itself might well plan to review periodically its procedures and to develop more effective ones. Carrying on such study of board procedures would also assist the board in developing ability to establish policies for the general appraisal program.

Just as self-evaluation or participation by the board members in the evaluation process would contribute to improvement, so self-evaluation or participation by others who would be involved in or related to the service under consideration would also contribute. In this process, of course, attention must be given to the development of the competency of board members. This can be accomplished by the board through attendance at meetings of state board of education associations and of professional organizations, through reading, through visiting schools with definite purposes after some knowledge of the educational service has been developed, and through board of education meetings and materials prepared for use at them. Similar attention should be given to the development of competency among students, members of the professional staff, and lay citizens to participate in appraisals. Thus, in the case of the board of education member as in that of others involved, the question is largely not one of competency but rather of the development of competency. Such competency will of course be related to the respective roles to be played by various individuals and groups in the evaluation process. Some will remain on the policy level and recognize only the necessity of sound criteria and standards. Others would become highly competent in using and interpreting the results of difficult and complex techniques.

Conscientious and new board members will be concerned about their competence to make appraisals. What can each do to improve his competence? What can teachers and administrators do to assist them in this work?

Does the Local School System Have the Competencies
within It To Carry Through
the Essential Appraisals?

Developing adequate and valid appraisal programs for a school or school system is one of the most difficult responsibilities confronting the educational administrator. This difficulty is the result of a number of factors, such as the paucity of emphasis upon or realization of the importance of appraisal; the complexity of the aims and services requiring appraisal; the inadequacy of the professional preparation of the staff; the tendency for many to make appraisals with little regard to validity; the inadequacy of a staff or staff members with many other demands for their time; and the difficulty of being objective when intimately involved.

These complexities might cause the administrator and others to avoid appraisal or at least to restrict its scope. Under these circumstances, the administrator may "welcome" an appraisal by an outside group rather than undertake it with the assistance of the local staff. Clearly, he could hold that the talent has not been developed within the staff and, therefore, that competence to undertake the job does not exist.

Although the competency may not presently exist and the system may as yet be unwilling to devote the necessary resources in money and time to carry an appraisal through, this is not inevitably a sound long-range answer. The local school district that is large enough to have essential staff personnel to develop sound programs of education, can do much of the job of appraisal. It has people within it of sufficient basic talent, if that talent is developed.

The answer would thus appear to be that the adequate local system can carry forward a very large part of the appraisal program. It may need to undertake various aspects of the responsibility over a period while it is improving its ability to carry on evaluations. It may need the assistance of consultants from the state or intermediate unit departments of education, from colleges and universities, and from other local school systems. Gradually, however, it can develop its abilities and reduce the dependence upon consultants, or utilize them with reference to aspects of the problem for which it has not yet developed competency.

It is important that the desirability of accepting this approach be recognized. The teacher who teaches but does not evaluate is substantially limited as a teacher. The administrator who administers with little attention to appraisal may be producing results of which he is quite unaware. Sound administration demands reasonably adequate knowledge of the results. The school system that sees itself as an organization of some importance must engage in appraisals. The question is largely one of how best to develop the competency to make appraisals and how to provide for carrying them through. It involves not only having the talents but also time to exercise them.

What plan for developing the competencies of staff members should be recommended to the board of education? How can local staff members overcome the lack of sound perspective resulting from too close identification with the service being appraised?

Should Appraisal Be Carried on by an Agency Which Is Semiautonomous?

This issue has assumed larger importance because of increased concern regarding more adequate evaluation, the growth of external examinations, the close relation of appraisal to research and development, the recognition that a substantial part of the appraisal effort should be carried on by an agency which is staff- rather than line-oriented. It can be argued that a semiautonomous agency would be more likely to make appraisals regarding sensitive areas than a line organization unit. An administration may find it difficult to encourage research that involves approaches not officially approved. There is, therefore, the problem of building a new institutional form that will satisfy the needs of the organization (which may not always be recognized) but not be too largely a part of it.

Quite possibly such an agency should be one of the most important elements of an intermediate or metropolitan unit, if one to meet the needs of adequately sized local units were developed. This would enable the agency to have much greater resources than any one district would provide in terms of staff and technology. The development of such an agency would probably do much to meet in a more satisfactory manner the call for uniform external examinations or for external surveys and studies. Too little attention has been given to appraisal. The belief which teachers and citizens have that satisfactory results are not being achieved needs to be recognized and used as the base for the development of new approaches, new programs and more vigorous action and evaluation. Too frequently, the needed facts, whether they be the extent to which certain objectives are being achieved or the results of a public opinion poll, are not available. In spite of the difficulty of securing necessary data, steps to secure them can no longer be delayed. One of the more promising ways of meeting this need may indeed be the development of new units which are semiautonomous. It would appear that the Elementary and Secondary Education Act of 1965 may contain the seeds from which educational centers and applied research laboratories of the type envisioned here may secure much encouragement and assistance. Such a development could indeed have an enormous impact on the development of education in the United States.

What semiautonomous appraisal agencies exist in your state? How effective are they in contributing to the appraisal needs of local and intermediate units?

Should the Cooperative Study Be Generally Employed, Rather Than the Survey Conducted by Outside Experts?

There are certain circumstances in which it may be preferable to have a study conducted by outside experts. Among the conditions that may make this desirable are the need for results of the appraisal at a time that could not be met through a cooperative procedure; the breakdown of confidence in the ability of the local staff to participate; charges, conflict, and consequent emphasis upon investigation rather than study, which may make local participation undesirable or unacceptable; inadequate numbers or lack of competence of local staff.

In all other situations, the cooperative approach offers greater promise and has many advantages. Among the most important advantages are the resultant development of an understanding by the people in the local situation of how to carry through an appraisal, in itself an important educational achievement; the greater promise of effective implementation; the stronger results derived from combining the understanding of the local people and the special, objective competence of the expert consultants; and the lower costs.

Is the cooperative approach preferred in the case of studies of the state educational system as well as the local system? Will the community regard the results of the cooperative study as highly as the report of the outside experts?

What Should Be the Role of Consultants in the Appraisal Process?

Formerly, many "consultants" did the job and presented a report. Implementation was then up to the local professional staff and citizens. Generally, this is regarded as an undesirable use of the consultants. In fact, it suggests a role other than that of consultant.

Approaching the role of the consultant in a positive manner, we may quickly note the possibility of various roles.[4] The consultant in his various roles may possess experiences in procedures to be followed to establish a planning committee and develop guidelines by which the study will be conducted; in knowledge of research results and literature in the areas under study; in techniques that are available or may be developed to collect data; in procedures to be used to treat data and develop conclusions and recommendations; in procedures to implement studies.

In all these roles the consultant should be seen as an adviser, stimulator, and guide, rather than as the one who furnishes the answers. This relationship may be difficult to attain. The consultant himself may be impatient with the time that may be involved in working through the many problems that confront those who undertake an appraisal. The staff and citizens involved may be more in the habit of accepting answers than working independently or cooperatively. Therefore, at times they will probably be quite insistent that the consultant tell them what is best, what is the right answer. At times they may turn in the other direction and resist the recommendations of the consultant, believing that he wishes to make decisions for them.

Especially when there is tension within the community or school, the development of a sound consultant-participant relationship will be difficult. Then, some of the participants are greatly concerned about the role that they are seen to be playing and may take extreme positions to make "clear" where they stand. It is not suggested here that the consultant should not feel free to suggest, to offer illustrations, to stimulate. These things will generally be expected of him, and he has a responsibility for them. However, he must be careful not to permit his

[4]W. W. Savage, *Local School Systems and Their Consultants* (Chicago: Midwestern Administration Center, University of Chicago, 1955).

suggestions to become the answers without genuine study on the part of the participants. He must be aware of the resources of the group and its members, many of which may be latent, and he must constantly seek the development of these resources.

The consultant also must center attention upon the purposes and must be able to judge movement toward their attainment. Frequently, the production of a report may come to be the goal, even though this was originally not the primary purpose. The tangibility of an attractive report is appealing, in contrast with many of the less concrete results of appraisals. A report may be desirable, but it must not be confused with implementation or the attainment of the goals.

With more experience in appraisal, less defensiveness on the part of staff, and more ability to engage in self-evaluation, various individuals and groups will develop similar perceptions regarding the role of the consultant. This will be an important development insofar as appraisal programs are concerned, whether the consultant be from outside the system or a member of the local system with staff rather than line responsibilities.

Are consultants with necessary competencies available? If not, how can they be provided? Who should appraise the work done by the consultant? What procedures should be used to appraise his work?

Are Adequate Aids Available or Must Each System Develop Its Own?

One of the encouraging aspects of the appraisal situation is the large number of aids that are available. The wide variety of tests that relate to various areas of instruction and various abilities is well known. Comprehensive guides to appraisal such as the *Evaluative Criteria* may also be employed. In addition, criteria that can be used in evaluation may be located in much of the literature pertaining to the areas of service of the school system. Thus, there are criteria or guides that can be used to appraise the guidance services, business administration, the personnel program, and the library service. In some cases there are numerous scorecards or guides for appraisal available, such as those used in evaluating a school plant. In the study of public opinion, instruments that have been used can be located with little difficulty.

Despite the availability of material that may be used in whole or part, it will always be necessary for the state or local school system to devise its own program of appraisal. Some aspects of that appraisal may be greatly assisted through the use of existing instruments. But consideration regarding the best instrument available will always be required. Frequently, no instrument will be judged adequate or appropriate for the situation at hand. An existing instrument may need to be modified. Possibly a different approach would appear more promising.

Fortunately, the variety of approaches or techniques has increased in recent years. There is, therefore, less likelihood that dependence upon one technique will be satisfactory. Certain approaches may supply a picture of a situation as it is seen from one point of view. But there may well be other points of view that are essential if a more valid picture is to be gained.

The importance of identifying, selecting, or developing instruments and approaches for the specific situation or problem is also brought to mind when attention is turned to interpretation of results and implementation. In most of the rather complex situations that may be appraised in a school system, the use of an instrument without careful study could easily result in unsound conclusions.

This would be true even in the case of the evaluation of a relatively simple matter such as a school plant. The most important basic question to such an evaluation would be the educational philosophy, aims, and program. No evaluation instrument can supply the answers to this question. The results of the application of any housing evaluation form would have significance only in the light of the desired educational program.

The necessity of local responsibility for the development of the program would be even greater in the case of more complex problems. Suppose, for example, an appraisal of administrative behavior would be desirable. A scorecard could be used, but it probably would have little validity. It would probably strive for form more than substance. The question of who would use it would also be an important one. But if the problem were studied seriously various other techniques would need to be employed. A case might be prepared that would reveal the behavior of the administrator in developing a specific program or in handling a given issue. This case would need to picture his behavior as seen by a number of parties, such as the administrator himself, fellow administrators, teachers, students and their parents. Various records might also be reviewed to get a glimpse of administrative behavior. A teacher or fellow administrator might serve as a participant observer gathering data that could later be analyzed. Quite possibly it would be important to gather data regarding the conceptions of the role of the administrator held by a number of those associated with him. As these various data were brought together, assuming that criteria of desirable administrative behavior had been developed, it would be possible to carry through an appraisal. Such a program appears difficult because it would involve the use of techniques that are not now widely familiar. However, the adequate school district has staff members who, with consultant help, could develop the essential competencies to conduct such a program. This, of course, assumes that administrative behavior is recognized by the school system as a matter of genuine importance and that the staff members are of such maturity that they wish to grapple with problems of this difficulty.

Should each school develop an appraisal program in relation to its purposes? Is appraisal of the state program of education as essential as that of the local school system? What are the limitations of instruments and techniques developed by other school systems?

Is the Growing Emphasis upon National or Statewide Achievement Testing Desirable?

One of the results of the increased concern for quality education and high achievement has been the development of widespread external testing programs and the demand for uniform state testing programs. No one would deny desirability of gaining more adequate knowledge of our students as a basis for guidance, selection for certain kinds of further education opportunities, evaluation of experimental and regular educational programs, remedial work, and similar purposes.

However, there is reason for some concern because of the following: the number of tests sponsored in secondary schools which overlap and may be extremely time-consuming; the tendency for that which is tested to be regarded as more important than the untested; the ease with which testing and appraising are regarded as synonymous; the improper use or extremely limited use of results; the extreme belief by some in their validity, objectivity, and scientific quality; their impact on the study habits of students; the control which they exercise on the curriculum and instructional procedures.

It must be recognized that testing programs in many schools have been inadequate and the results have been inadequately used. Steps to correct these conditions should be taken. Provision should be made for making external tests a part of the program of evaluation to the extent which the results justify this action. Even statewide programs, if marked by flexibility and encouragement to local school systems to develop sound programs to meet their needs, may be desirable. However, the experiences of other societies which have seen their schools reduced to the pursuit of rigid, conforming, test-ridden programs of study should not be ignored. Rather as a result of their experiences and with a knowledge of the limitation of our program of testing and evaluation and of the hidden threats of some programs, it should be possible to develop programs of evaluation that will ensure far more adequate knowledge regarding students and competence in utilizing the results.

Describe and evaluate the external testing in a local school system. How does it relate to the appraisal program of the district? What have been its principal effects?

Are Accreditation Studies
a Desirable Type of Appraisal?

Accreditation studies are a type of appraisal that is essential if there are to be accreditation agencies. Accreditation must be based upon some evidence, and the rather comprehensive type of study that has become common in recent years is a great advance over the type of inspection by an individual that formerly was the basis of being accredited. The *Evaluative Criteria* developed by the Cooperative Study of Secondary School Standards in 1940 (revised in 1950 and 1960) was a guide to evaluation well above former aids of this type. It directed attention to the many aspects of the life of the school and recognized the need for considering the philosophy of the institution under study. It offered concise statements of what was judged to be good practice as a basis for the evaluation.

Since the appearance of the *Evaluative Criteria*, attempts at accreditation have increased. Forms have been developed for the evaluation of elementary schools, with the implication, in some instances at least, that they may also be rated. Somewhat similar instruments have been developed for the evaluation of junior colleges and for professional programs such as teacher education.

Perhaps no one questions the desirability of developing aids or forms of the type used in accreditation studies. What is questioned by many people is the method of use of these aids and the long-run influence that they may have.

A most worthwhile or desirable use of such appraisal guides is for purposes of self-evaluation. A staff, in cooperation with citizens and students, can well afford to engage periodically in a careful evaluation of the type made possible by the use of one of these guides. Such an evaluation will bring together many kinds of data and point out many problems that may otherwise be overlooked. It is a good procedure for a staff to employ in order to develop competence in recognizing and providing for the problems of the school. Such exhaustive evaluation can be carried out as a part of the appraisal for accreditation purposes. However, there is always the danger that the staff will quickly assemble quantities of data largely for the use of the visiting appraisal committee. The staff may be suspicious of the purpose of the visit and not really look at the needs of the school, but rather close ranks to meet the visiting committee. It may even refuse to accept self-evaluation as an essential for self-improvement. How self-evaluation can be made the major aspect of accreditation remains an issue.

The extent to which accreditation has come to be on a self-evaluative basis varies considerably at different school levels and in different parts of the country. In some areas this approach has been emphasized, in others the major emphasis appears to be on the work of the visiting evaluation committee, which may be rather rigid in its application of the appraisal guide.

Perhaps even more disturbing than the method of applying guides for accreditation purposes is the long-run effect of their use. Even if their immediate effect may be good because they bring shortcomings to attention and therefore stimulate action, their long-run effect may be unfortunate. This is true whether self-evaluation or evaluation by visitors is employed. For the mere use of such forms may tend to narrow the range of approaches to a problem. True, they help the poor school more nearly to approach the better. But do such forms really cause the better schools —those enjoying more favorable situational factors—to push ahead into new territory, or do they cause a type of complacence to develop? Isomorphism,[5] the tendency of institutions to grow more alike and narrower in range, is particularly dangerous in a society in which conformity is highly valued. It would appear necessary for our society to seek variety of practice rather than conformity in education.

In justice to those who have developed the present guides for accreditation, it should be noted that at least some of them have not been unaware of this problem. Consequently, they have sought evaluation in terms of the philosophy of the individual school and have avoided routine or formal reports of results. Despite their awareness of the problem, the question remains whether accreditation studies do not have the effect of reducing the range of efforts, and especially the range above the median. Quite possibly the question raised here is larger than that of accreditation. It surely relates also to the unfortunate use of standard tests in some schools and to the much too common tendency to accept norms as standards. Can we develop the needed educational provisions in a climate of conformity—a climate that may result in more uniformity of practice and less vigorous exercise of initiative than would necessarily result from the operation of a highly centralized government?

How can appraisals be conducted to avoid the dangers inherent in them? Can appraisals release initiative and encourage the acceptance of responsibility for narrowing the gap between the ideals and commitments of society and its practices? Can appraisals avoid the norm and facilitate the attainment of equality rather than identity of opportunity? How can appraisal avoid retarding the front runners?

[5]See treatment of this problem in David Riesman, *Constraint and Variety in American Education* (Lincoln: University of Nebraska Press, 1956).

Selected References

Brickell, Henry M., *Organizing New York State for Educational Change.* Albany: University of the State of New York, State Education Department, 1961.

College Testing: A Guide to Practices and Programs. Washington, D.C.: American Council on Education, 1959.

Cronback, Lee J., *Essentials of Psychological Testing.* New York: Harper & Row, Publishers, 1960.

Evaluating the Elementary School—A Guide for Cooperative Study. Atlanta: Southern Association of Colleges and Secondary Schools, 1951.

Evaluative Criteria. Washington, D.C.: National Study of Secondary School Evaluation, 1960.

Gardner, John W., *Excellence, Can We Be Equal and Excellent Too?* New York: Harper & Row, Publishers, 1961.

Hand, Harold C., *What People Think About Their Schools; Values and Methods of Public-Opinion Polling as Applied to School Systems.* Yonkers, N.Y.: World Book Company, 1948.

Hyman, Herbert, *Survey Design and Analysis—Principles, Cases and Procedures.* New York: Free Press of Glencoe, Inc., 1955.

Leeper, Robert R., ed., *Strategy for Curriculum Change.* Washington, D.C.: Association for Supervision and Curriculum Development, 1965.

Sumption, Merle R., *How to Conduct a Citizens School Survey.* Englewood Cliffs, N.J.: Prentice-Hall, Inc., 1952.

Testing, Testing, Testing. Washington, D.C.: American Association of School Administrators, Council of Chief State School Officers, National Association of Secondary School Principals, 1962.

Wrightstone, J. Wayne, Joseph Justman, and Irving Robbins, *Evaluation In Modern Education.* New York: American Book Company, 1956.

Index

Index

H

I

J